The Inside Story

1. The new Curtiss Model K 12 aeronautical motor.
2. A Curtiss J. N. in flight.
3. The Curtiss Flying Boat built for Rodman Wannamaker.
4. A Curtiss Mailplane.
5. The famous Curtiss J. N. 4D. on which over 98% of all American and Canadian pilots were trained.
6. The Curtiss O. X. motor regarded by experts as the best 90 H. P. aeronautical motor made.
7. The Curtiss Model L Triplane.

8. A Curtiss Triplane Flying Boat.
9. Another view of the Curtiss K, 12 motor—this motor is 25% lighter than any other 400 H. P. motor so far produced.
10. The familiar J. N. profile.
11. The Curtiss Engineering Corporation Plant at Garden City, L. I.
12. The fuselage assembly floor.
13. A recent commercial Curtiss tractor.
14. A Curtiss twin J. N.

15. A rear view of the Curtiss H. S. 2 flying boat.
16. A Curtiss triplane military tractor.
17. Three early Curtiss military tractors.
18. The gigantic navy N. C. 1 flying boat, built by the Curtiss Engineering Corp., recently flown with 51 persons aboard. The largest flying boat in the world.
19. A modern English type of military tractor.
20. A Curtiss Triplane Hydro.
21–22. Building flying boat hulls for the Navy.

CURTISS AEROPLANE & MOTOR CORPORATION

Factories and Flying Fields: Buffalo   Hammondsport, N. Y.   Newport News, Va.   Miami, Fla.

PENDULUM II

**The Story of America's Three Aviation Pioneers:
Wilbur Wright, Orville Wright, and
Glenn Curtiss, the "Henry Ford of Aviation"**

including

**How the Partnership of Alexander Graham Bell
and Glenn Hammond Curtiss led to the
Founding of the American Aviation Industry**

by

JACK CARPENTER

*"I am not one of those hyphenated Americans that
claims allegiance to two countries."*
Alexander Graham Bell

*"Saving time is the equivalent of increasing the duration
of life...time used in traveling from point to point is
largely wasted. This is where the airplane comes in."*
Glenn Hammond Curtiss

*"No truth is without some mixture of error, and no error
so false but that it possesses some elements of truth...
argument is merely a process of mutually picking the
beams and motes out of each other's eyes so both can
see more clearly...After I get hold of a truth I hate to
lose it again, and I like to sift all the truth out before
I give up an error."* **Wilbur Wright**

International Standard Book Number: 0-9600736-2-0
Library of Congress Catalog Card Number: 2003104111

Printed by Industrial Printing Group, Santa Ana, CA 92704.

Note: For a more complete picture of this era, see:
      www.GlennHCurtiss.com.
Front cover: Henry Ford visiting Glenn Curtiss,
      Hammondsport, NY, 1913.
Back cover: Glenn Curtiss and Alexander Graham Bell mourn the
      death of Tom Selfridge, their Aerial Experiment Associat-
      ion partner. Illustration by Daniel Witkoff.
Endpapers: Curtiss advertisement, *The Saturday Evening Post*,
      March 1, 1919; pp. 110 (front), 111 (back).

Profile: G.J. (Jack) Carpenter Jr., a Southern California native, since his youth has been interested in *"what actually happened"* (e.g., at Illinois College he had a private interview with Russia's Aleksandr Kerensky). An Eagle Scout, he was in Naval aviation training when World War II ended, and 19 when commissioned a Naval officer and BNS-degreed from Notre Dame. Then, though accepted at Harvard, he earned an MBA at Stanford. His career includes marketing, management, residential development in Southern California and New England, and antiques and fine art. Since 1974 he's written of early aviation history: author of PENDULUM, PENDULUM2, co-author of WALDO: Pioneer Aviator; creator of www.GlennHCurtiss.com.

*T*he pendulum swings, slowly –
from ignorance and misinformation – to truth and knowledge.

*D*edicated to the memory of the many aeronautical pioneers who, unfortunately, have been all but forgotten in the story known by so many Americans today.

A few are: Bernt Balchen, Tom Baldwin,
   Lincoln Beachey, Washington Chambers,
      Octave Chanute, Ted Ellyson,
         Eugene Ely, Charles Grey,
            Clement Keys, Charles Kirkham,
               Samuel Langley, Charles Manly,
                  Arthur Nutt, John Porte,
                     Augustus Post, Hugh Robinson,
                        Tom Selfridge, George Spratt,
                           Gustave Whitehead, Charles Willard,
                              Charles Witmer, Forrest Wysong...

...and to my brother, Win, the real flier in the family (Lt. USAAC, B-17 co-pilot, shot down, prisoner Stalag Luft 3), who I located at Bowman Field, Louisville, KY – and he and I flew home to Jacksonville, IL, in a BT-13 (No. 9582) on Sep2, 1945 (see pp. 489).

PREFACE

Three of mankind's greatest inventions occurred in the years beginning this story: the telephone, the automobile, and the airplane - with all engulfed in momentous patent battles. The victors of two, Alexander Graham Bell and Henry Ford, then played crucial roles in the third, the epic fight between the Wright brothers and Glenn Curtiss.

"History, we are told, is a kind of literature – a story under the obligation to be as true as the historian can make it" (Peter Gay, New York Public Library).

And if American aviation history was truly told, our children would know that *Glenn Hammond Curtiss* was the greatest person in it; that he was most responsible for founding America's preeminent aviation industry; that from 1911 to 1948 Curtiss companies 'led the world in aviation'; that he was *"The Henry Ford of Aviation."*

And they would know that *Alexander Graham Bell* was his partner *and* cofounder of our aviation industry; a major figure in the development of flight in America - who with Henry Ford helped Curtiss thwart the Wright brothers' monopoly of world aviation.

And they should also know that the late 19th century development of the lightweight internal combustion engine ushered in the age of the automobile *and* of the airplane (Scientific American 8Apr'11: *"The lack of a suitable motor had been the greatest obstacle in the way of air navigation"*). Many men in Europe and America - *including a young Henry Ford and younger Glenn Curtiss* - eagerly used these new engines to match their dreams.

Briton *Charles Grey* (1875-1953. Founder and editor, *The Aeroplane*, 1911-1939; editor, *Jane's All The World's Aircraft*, 1916-1941), arguably the world's most knowledgeable person on flight's early days, in 1953, shortly before his death wrote:

"Strange thing isn't it that the U.S.A. has never recognized Glenn Curtiss as by far the greatest man America has ever produced in Aviation? Think of the early Hammondsport products. Then the Jenny. Then the first flight onto & off a ship. Then the first flying boats. The big & little Americas...& their descendants, the F boats of Felixstowe, from which descend...trans-Atlantic boats...Then the N.C. boats, first across the Atlantic, & the string of Curtiss record-breakers, & Schneider winners. And the D-12 engines, from which the Rolls Falcon, & ultimately the Merlin are descended...So far as I know there is nobody in the World who has claim to have influenced aircraft design & production as he did, or had done. But the capitalists who bought the bogus Wright patents ganged up on Curtiss & 'slapped him down,' as they say in the States, & he was too proud to fight back on propaganda. He left his products to fight for him."

Much as I felt when completing *WALDO: Pioneer Aviator*; its first chapter dealing with his co-founding of Naval aviation, when I tagged him *'The Henry Ford of Aviation.'*

Curiosity then led me to write *PENDULUM: The Story of America's Three Aviation Pioneers, Wilbur Wright, Orville Wright, and Glenn Curtiss, the Henry Ford of Aviation*, uncovering what I then thought was basis for much of the extreme anti-Curtiss bias at the

Smithsonian: a long-hidden 1948 'Agreement' with Orville Wright's heirs which resulted in the return of the 1903 Flyer from its 20-year hiatus in Britain's National Museum.

But Curtiss's contemporaries should be noted: In TIME magazine's issue of 24Oct 1924 – its cover of "Glenn H. Curtiss" was this: *"Though his works were everywhere present, his name on every man's lip, the face and figure of Glenn Hammond Curtiss were not in evidence in Dayton. At least every other plane of those assembled bore a Curtiss motor. Not one plane but bore some evidence to the contributions he has made to mankind's knowledge of the air and his agility in it..."*

In 1973 Richard K. Smith wrote that Curtiss *"...was one of the world's great pioneers of aviation...but unlike the Wrights he was less a research man than a developer. Curtiss was a great* ad hoc *engineer whose genius was in his ability to improvise, synthesize, and simplify promising ideas and devices at hand, and to transform them into something immediately useful – and marketable. The Wright's manufacturing ventures were short-lived. Curtiss, however, had a tough Yankee talent for business and quickly moved from bicycles to motorcycles, engines, and aviation."*

And in 1979 Peter Bowers wrote: *"Following the dissolution of the AEA...Glenn Curtiss undertook the design and manufacturer of aeroplanes on his own at Hammondsport. In the period 1909-14...this remarkable man engaged in a fantastic amount of personal activity – designing, building and testing new models, making exhibition flights, instructing, forming new companies and establishing new flying fields, defending lawsuits, writing books and...articles, and conducting a brisk domestic and export trade, almost any one of which would have been a full-time job for an ordinary man."*

In 1981, Louis S. Casey, former Curator of Aircraft, National Air and Space Museum, Smithsonian Institution, wrote: *"In the field of aeronautics no name is better known, or has had greater influence, than the name of Glenn H. Curtiss. The name brings visions of a pioneer, a giant industrial complex, an era in aviation and many other things to many people. Curtiss is all of these and second only to the Wright brothers in the annals of aviation...From the birth of the airplane at the turn of the century...to the mid-century, the Curtiss name was synonymous with aircraft of quality and quantity..."*

And in 1991 Robert Gandt wrote: *"A cloud has surrounded Curtiss's name because of the insinuation, without basis in fact, that he pirated the Wright brothers' inventions. Many biographies of the Wrights...depict the brothers as heroes wronged by Curtiss and his AEA colleagues."*

As with many things, one learns from exploration. As such, I've learned that there's far more underlying the anti-Curtiss bias than simply an 'Agreement,' flawed though it may be; for almost a century, since 1906, when the Wrights allied with Wall Street's J. P. Morgan, there's been a subtle but pervasive bias (and an impressive power to deceive) against Curtiss (and, ironically, Bell), the Wright's only real competitor.

Writing *PENDULUM* convinced me that there was far more to Bell's story than had ever been told. Therefore, preparing for this, its 2nd edition, I added a biographical chapter on Bell and material on how his partnership with Curtiss led to the founding of the American aviation industry.

I then sent its preface to, among others, Bell's great-grandson, Gilbert Grosvenor, of the National Geographic Society (*"...the largest private nonprofit scientific and educational organization in the world"*), for comment. His reply (see pp. 442) is a most historically important letter, clearly revealing that Bell's story and, particularly, his relationship with Curtiss, had never been fully or honestly told.

With American *and* Canadian histories suffering from the bias, half-truths, lies and character assassination spread for nigh a century about Curtiss, hopefully one will understand that virtually all that's known of early aviation history - whether in books or, more commonly today, TV documentaries – has emanated from the Smithsonian National Air and Space Museum (NASM) and/or the National Geographic Society.

And, with the caveat that *history is truth*, what you are about to read may not be what you have been led to believe. Unlike beauty, history is not in the eyes of the beholder. It must be based upon fact, not fancy; upon *"What actually happened"* (*Leopold von Ranke*). *The record speaks for itself.* And it should not be the result of powerful constituencies demanding it affirm rather than inform. Furthermore, though the Chinese discovered history as knowledge, inspiration and insight for the future, it's wrong when revisionist historians take on the mantle of philosophers. *Wisdom may be the result of hindsight, history should never be.*

As to what's typically known of America's early aviation history - with so much based upon the Smithsonian (with its 180-degree shift *and* semi-secret <u>Agreement</u>, as you will see); or the narrow priorities of Wall Street; or by a incorrect story spread by the Grosvenors and the National Geographic Society - *bias has created it.*

Regardless of parentage, bastardized history is illegitimate history.

Thusly, as a lie – by whom and how often told - takes on the guise of truth, I have written this story by *viewing events in the context of their times* with *contemporary* accounts of the participants (typically italicized) *before* being massaged by others. Scan the bibliography as indication of my resolve for truth, and *consider the source* and its agenda.

In addition to 'setting the record straight,' my goal is to make an honest story known; bias casts a perfidious shadow when it involves the *molding of young minds.*

True, the Wright's work - *built upon the work of many before them* - solved the riddle of flight: three-dimension control - but their wing-warping was so flawed that it killed many - *if not the majority* - of its pilots.

"Of the first thirty-three fatal accidents, the twin-propellered Wright biplane accounted for almost a quarter. As a consequence of this unlucky record, the American machine came to be looked upon by many flyers as a 'killer.'"   Henry Serrano Villard

Though first to fly, *technology quickly passed them by* (only *one* American firm - but briefly - took out a Wright license).

Safe, effective control came *only* with Bell & Curtiss's ailerons.

Regardless, a clever patent attorney combined with an incredibly extensive pattern of bias have fabricated today's Wright mystique.

An explanation:

One of the more fascinating things I've experienced in writing is how one book leads to another: <u>WALDO: Pioneer Aviator</u> in 1988 followed by <u>PENDULUM</u> in 1992, which revealed the unknown role of Bell.

Everybody knows Alexander Graham Bell, few know of his role in aviation.

Virtually everything known of Bell comes from the Grosvenors, a family so blessed a century-past with his name, the largess of his success, and of the National Geographic Society, that they've taken on the trappings of royalty while deifying their quasi-Canadian heritage and, it would appear, all things Canadian. So much so that bias has warped the history known by most of us. This has made telling this story difficult, for I, like most Americans, have great reverence for it, the Smithsonian, and the Library of Congress.

It was Alexander Graham Bell (the man from whom their all came) who, in 1874, long before inventing the telephone, filed papers for American citizenship - and, upon becoming one, reveled in it, noting: "*I am not one of those hyphenated Americans who claim allegiance to two countries.*"

The National Geographic Society was co-founded in 1888 by Gardineer G. Hubbard, Bell's father-in-law. Its first employee was Bell's son-in-law, Gilbert H. Grosvenor, who joined it in 1899. Thereafter, *for over a century,* the Society's leadership, in nepotistic ascension, went from the father to the son to the grandson, today's Gilbert M. Grosvenor.

A reader of aeronautical history may become disquieted by the <u>*Geographic*</u>'s 1988 100th-year issue, page 376: "...*The Aerial Experiment Association...was formed in 1907 to build a flying machine of each member's design. In 1909 Douglas McCurdy's Silver Dart flew half a mile at 40 mph, the first airplane flight in Canada...*and on page 380...*Eventually Bell brought together a high-spirited group of other young men, including Glenn Curtiss, organized as the Aerial Experiment Association. The Wright brothers had by then risen above their own kite experiments to create a true airplane, and so the AEA built on that* (not true), *developing several successful machines...*"

Nothing is said about the AEA's work at Curtiss's Hammondsport, New York, base, *site of virtually all of its work and successes.* The *Silver Dart* was their *fourth* aircraft. Its *first* flight was at Hammondsport on 6Dec'08, *two months before* its Canadian flights of 23-24Feb'09 - and six months *after* The 4th of July, 1908, when Curtiss flew the *June Bug* for its historic "*First Official Flight in the Western Hemisphere.*"

Another example, an August, 1927, <u>*Geographic*</u> article (pp. 233): "*Selfridge later associated with the Wright Brothers and became one of America's pioneer aviators* (e.g., Selfridge was the *first* American military person to fly an aeroplane). *He was killed in line of duty at Arlington, Virginia...*" The *opposite* is true. Selfridge never '*associated*' with the Wrights. He was their competitor - and was killed as the US Army's observer/ passenger in a flight piloted by Orville Wright, the airplane's *first* fatality.

Finally, Gilbert M. Grosvenor's 7Jul1994 letter to the author is an extraordinary revelation of deceit and bias as he wrote: "*...The Silver Dart was purely Canadian: Douglas McCurdy designed, helped construct and flew it. Flights at HammondsPort are incidental; the first flight in the British empire in Baddeck is history. <u>You</u> choose to ignore the whole point of the* Silver Dart...*"

Thus he revealed that he and the National Geographic Society *have never told the true story of these events.*

A comprehension of what Curtiss wrought is in <u>*Jane's Encyclopaedia of Aviation*</u> (*to 1980*): Boeing produced approximately <u>*54*</u> aircraft models (e.g., in WW2 Boeing, Douglas and Lockheed built 12,731 B-17s); Curtiss/Curtiss-Wright <u>*62*</u> (e.g., almost 14,000 Curtiss P-40s were built; In 1948 Curtiss-Wright withdrew from military airplane competition, and in 1966 ceased aircraft production); Douglas/McDonnell Douglas <u>*49*</u> (e.g., 10,654 DC-3/C-47s were produced); Lockheed <u>*36*</u> (e.g., Lockheed built 9,923 P-38s); Martin/Martin Marietta <u>*24*</u> (e.g., Martin built over 5,000 B-26s); and Wright <u>*13*</u> (e.g., "*the final aircraft...*[of 1915]...*the Navy purchased a single example.*" Thereafter Wright was almost solely an engine manufacturer).

And it should be obligatory for any student of this era to read Peter M. Bower's monumental 635-page <u>Curtiss Aircraft 1907-1947</u> to appreciate the vast scope of aeronautical activity by Curtiss – surely surpassing that of *any* other organization in the world.

In World War II General Motors was America's largest defense contractor; Curtiss-Wright *second*; Ford third.

From 1908 to 1948 Curtiss was the proudest name in America's skies.

And then something happened. Glenn Curtiss became the hero America forgot.

Thus I wrote <u>*PENDULUM*</u>; *t*o repeat portions of its original preface:

Though the interplay between Curtiss, Bell and Ford in the Wright patent fight may be the focus of this story, increasingly it became the story of what had and is happening in the Smithsonian Institution's treatment of the lives of Curtiss and the Wrights. As the reader will discover, in the beginning the Smithsonian knew only one aeronautical hero, Samuel Pierpont Langley. Then came the Wrights, tending to take his credits away. Curtiss enters the scene, originally in partnership with Langley's close friend, Bell, diffusing many allegiances. Soon the historical community was divided between the Smithsonian, supporting the memory of Langley, and the Wrights - with Curtiss and Bell causing considerable anguish. The Smithsonian then solidified its support of Langley and, indirectly, of Curtiss. This caused Orville (Wilbur now dead) to take certain actions considered negative (*such as sending the 1903 Flyer to the British national museum*). This impasse existed for many years - until attitudes began to shift in the Smithsonian, leading finally in 1948 to the return of the Flyer for display in *our* national museum.

But since its return the historical fortunes of Curtiss have greatly eroded.

In 1969 Bernard Weisberger wrote in <u>*American Heritage*</u>: *"Curtiss was not just another manufacturer. He was to aviation what Ford was to the automobile: a founding father, a prophet, an evangel, a worker of miracles who. could assemble the cash and equipment to turn the spidery drawings of inventors (himself included) into finished hardware...he belonged to the generation of young Americans who seized the gasoline engine and raced exuberantly with it into the twentieth century...The list of his awards was a blue book of aviation's early sponsors: the Scientific American Trophy, the Courtlandt Field Bishop prize, the Gordon Bennett Cup, the Robert J. Collier Trophy, the W. E. Kelly Cup, the Grand Prix Passenger Prize, and the Langley Medal of the Smithsonian...He invented the flying boat...pioneered water landings and takeoffs, sold his seagoing flying machines to the Navy, and personally taught...sailors to fly...By 1914 he...created the Curtiss Motor...and...Aeroplane Company...(which) would build more than 200 kinds of aircraft, using sixty-seven of Curtiss' patents."*

And, in the finest *contemporary* assessment of the Wrights, in 1910 Victor Lougheed (half-brother of Allan and Malcolm Loughead, founders of today's aerospace titan, Lockheed Martin) wrote in his 514-page <u>*Vehicles of The Air*</u>: *"...the Wrights levied upon every possible source of information and, frankly commencing with Chanute's help and a modification of the Chanute biplane glider, which they regarded as the most advanced construction existent...entered upon a deliberate, unremitting, and enthusiastic prosecution of an at first thankless task, which for sturdy perseverance in the face of obstacles and sensible disregard of ignorant opinions, has few parallels in the history of invention. Having from the outset more faith in experimental than analytical methods, the Wrights set themselves first to the task of confirming or correcting the various formulas of their predecessors concerning wind pressures, the sustaining effects of different inclined sur-*

faces, etc. Progressing from these to the various possible methods of steering, and the maintaining of lateral and longitudinal balance, they tirelessly tested a constantly improving series of constructions by hundreds of kites and gliding experiments...Having thus secured an amount of practice that enabled them to make reasonable safe gliding flights of considerable length in calms and moderate winds, they next undertook the application of a motor, naturally turning to a automobile mechanism as the most promising source...This resulted, on December 17, 1903, in four flights in calm air (No, it was a virtual gale)...*On March 22, 1904, a United States patent was applied for on a wing-warping device, in combination with flat sustaining surfaces, indicating either a failure ...to appreciate fully the absolute importance of definitely and correctly curved surfaces, or else constituting a lack of 'full disclosure' demanded by patent law. The construction described in the patent specifications being obviously inoperative, these were repeatedly objected and rejected by the patent office examiners, and it was not until May 22, 1906, that the claims were allowed - even then on the basis of inoperative construction. Throughout 1904 the Wright experiments continued, surrounded by the utmost secrecy, but it was definitely attested by Chanute that during this year they increased the length of their longest flight to 1,377 feet. It was not until nearly the end of September, 1905, months after Montgomery's flights...and publication of his construction, and some time after his patent was applied for, that the Wrights commenced to be conspicuously successful - with parabolically-curved sustaining surfaces and a system of wing-warping closely resembling that of Montgomery's patent and not at all like that claimed in the Wright patent. Following these successes, which though well authenticated were kept out of the newspapers and well away from the general public, vigorous but quiet efforts were made during 1906 and 1907 to sell to European governments, not patent rights, but 'secrets' of construction. Little success resulting, because of the terms and conditions that were stipulated, and European aviators having by this time progressed to the point of making long flights, this policy was abandoned late in 1908, and the Wrights came out into the open with their machines - Orville Wright in the United States and Wilbur Wright in France - with the result that they were quickly able to establish new distance and duration records, which stood for nearly a year. At the present time* (1910), *however, the Wright machine does not hold a single distance, duration, speed, weight-carrying, cross-country, or altitude record in the world, and has borne out the numerous critics of its construction by being responsible for an undue proportion of the accidents that have occurred in the history of power-propelled heavier-than-air-machines."*

And Mitchell Wilson wrote: *"Alexander Graham Bell must have been a delightful man to know and an exasperating one to work with...The Wright brother's story is truly moving and tragic in a particular American way because the goals of their time confused them. They wanted to be considered as creative scientists - which they really were – but they also wanted to be rich men."*

If the question were asked: *"What would world aviation have been like in 1910 if there had been no Wright brothers?"* the answers might be:

1. *"Man would still be earth-bound"* by some.
2. *"The same as it actually was in 1910"* by better informed others.
3. *"About where it was in 19_15_"* by those knowing the *full* truth of the matter – for the Wrights inhibited flight far more than they accelerated its development.

Some conclusions:

The Wrights and Curtiss were innovators by nature, with strikingly similar parsonage upbringing, education and backgrounds.

Though wrongly assumed by Orville, the honor of being the *first* to fly was Wilbur's.

For all intents and purposes, in 1905 the Wrights stopped inventing, attempting then (emulating Bell's experience) to create a world-wide Air Trust *monopoly.*

The Wrights *first* (in writing) offered their invention to a foreign country (Britain) and made their *first* contract with a foreign country (France).

In August, 1909, when Orville was negotiating in Berlin, Curtiss was the sole American at the world's *first* air-meet, at Reims, France (he beat Bleriot to win).

And but a few months later (Oct'09), when Wilbur was teaching America's *first* military aviators, Orville was in Berlin giving the Kaiser's son his first flight.

Curtiss was awarded American F.A.I. Aviator *License No. 1*, the Wrights Nos. 4 & 5. In Europe Curtiss was *No. 2* (Bleriot No. 1), the Wrights Nos. 14 and 15.

Wrights were the sole beneficiaries of their success; most with Curtiss shared in his.

Chanute and Spratt, described by Orville as "*...our most intimate associates in those early years,*" along with most in aviation then, became their enemies.

In 1914, *8-of-14* of the Army's North Island *Wright*-trained pilots were killed.

A design disaster – *and too often a killer* – 1915 saw the last Wright aeroplane.

Bell and Curtiss were friends and partners – with *never* a mentor relationship.

Bell, Tom Baldwin, McCurdy, Post, Chambers, Ellyson, Hunsaker, Robinson, Towers, Manly, Richardson, Verville...were lifelong friends of Curtiss.

"*To reconstruct history according to its ifs, its might-have-beens, or should-not-have-beens, is an engaging intellectual pastime...*"   Robert Selph Henry

Note: In an effort to improve relevance and understanding of this turn-of-the-century period, money amounts are typically shown converted to approximately what they would be today. However, since there appears to be no uniform or accepted method to accomplish this, the author has used the most readily common denominator: hourly and/or daily semi-skilled labor wage rates to establish multipliers, e.g., In 1914 a manufacturing worker earned about 22 cents an hour, $11 per week, $550-575 per year (in 1896 *The New York Times* cost one cent, today 100 times as much; ca. 1935 a haircut, 20 cents; 2-egg breakfast, 10 cents). Today a worker earns $12 an hour or $480 a week, thus creating a conservative multiplier for 1914 of 45. This formula gave these text multipliers:

1890 - *80X*	1910 - *47X*	1930 - *25X*	*advent of World War II*
1895 - *65X*	1915 - *45X*	1935 - *30X*	*there has been steadily*
1900 - *55X*	1920 - *35X*	1940 - *25X*	*increasing inflation*
1905 - *50X*	1925 - *30X*	*...from the*	*continuing into today.*

On 16Jun94 Donald L. Kohn, Director, Division of Monetary Affairs, Board of Governors, Federal Reserve System, wrote the author: "*...I certainly agree with your point ...Your basic approach...is correct. In particular, using the ratios of price or wage indexes is the appropriate way to convert dollar amounts from one period into equivalent amounts in another period...*"

CONTENTS

Alexander Graham Bell's invention of the telephone is well known, but other aspects of his life are either unknown or, at best, quite murky, especially those of his fascination with flight and contributions towards the growth of American aviation. This chapter will primarily sketch Bell's better known life and may be repetitious, but will serve as a foundation for what follows.

Samuel Pierpont Langley spurs Bell's interest, leading to his experimenting with heavier-than-air flight. Wilbur and Orville Wright enter the scene, succeed in manned flight, and then attempt to dominate world aviation.

Curtiss's life is one which should be, but is not, known to most Americans. That historical curiosity caused the author to write Pendulum, *from which much of this chapter - and the balance of this story - is taken.*

Now, knowing the backgrounds of Bell and Curtiss and how they became acquainted, we enter the focus of this story: their partnership. And the events of the times necessarily include much of what others, particularly the Wright brothers, were then doing.

Triumph and tragedy mark a year that sees Curtiss and Bell, challenging the Wrights, succeed in flight; Baldwin's airship success; the aeroplane's first casualty; and honor and recognition for the Wrights in Europe and America.

The feud begins; Curtiss suffers Herring's manipulations; the Wrights, honored and feted, spend much time in Europe on business; Curtiss challenges for the rule of American air. The American money establishment spawns long-standing biases.

THE GREATEST ADVENTURE*

The story of the four Americans who invented the airplane:
Wilbur Wright, Orville Wright, Alexander Graham Bell and
Glenn Hammond Curtiss
(*When the risk, death, is compared with the reward, which was inestimable)

Imagine – if you will – that you are a certain young man around a hundred years ago. Tomorrow you're going to attempt to fly – in a strange, somewhat birdlike contraption of cloth, sticks and wire – with a sputtering motor turning a windmill-like blade that, hopefully, will propel you into the air...where, at a modest height, only fifteen feet or so, you risk crashing - being maimed or killed - but *if* you succeed, if only for a flight of a few hundred feet, you will have achieved man's dream of ages, *To Fly!*

Yours is not a story of Greek mythology; you are not Daedalus or his son, Icarus, who flew - and then died when the sun melted his wings of wax.

No, you're an American embracing the new wonders of the Industrial Revolution. You have dreamed the dreams – and now, with the limited knowledge fitfully gained by many others – and by your own studies (none were taught) – you're taking that latest marvel of man, the *internal combustion engine*, and using it to power your dream....

Of you there are four, three at first unknown...

But one is known to all, but not for this.

Alexander Graham Bell has harbored this dream to fly since the oldest of the others was but a small boy – but now he is too old to fly.

One of you, Wilbur Wright, is the first to dream this dream *when* that engine is available. And then, enlisting his brother Orville's help, on a cold, windy day in 1903, he becomes the *first* to capture that dream. .

But soon Bell, the foursome's first such dreamer, finds the man to *help* him achieve his dream: Glenn Hammond Curtiss, America's foremost maker of lightweight engines. At first without the dream, he soon catches the fever – and with an acute focus this brilliant, talented Yankee helps Bell realize his dream, now also his, as he begins to achieve a measure of success that, in time, will become *unequaled* in the annals of flight.

That is this story - one of dreams, passion, spirit...and the qualities and frailties of four very uncommon men, Wilbur Wright, Orville Wright, Alexander Graham Bell, and Glenn Hammond Curtiss - as they live *Man's Greatest Adventure, the invention and development of the airplane.*

Chapter **1** *Alexander Graham Bell: 1847-1890*

 *lexander*

Graham Bell's invention of the telephone is well known, but other aspects of his life are either unknown or, at best, murky, especially those of his fascination with flight and contributions towards the growth of American aviation. This chapter will primarily sketch Bell's better known life and may be repetitious, but will serve as a foundation for what follows.

In the beginning it was Scotland's theater that ingrained speech with the Bell name. *Alexander* Bell (3Mar1790-1865), Alexander *Graham* Bell's grandfather, originally a shoemaker, mastered elocution on the stage where he began performing as a comedian in his twenties. Also, he supplanted his theatrical duties as a prompter and became proficient in its rudimentary sign language. And, as an evolution from stagecraft, he undertook the teaching of speech and the correction of stammering, briefly prospering as an English master at St. Andrew's Grammar School.

Graham Bell's father, Alexander *Melville* Bell (1819-1905), following his parents' marital problems, moved with his father to London. There his father published The Practical Elocutionist, followed in 1836 by Stammering, and other Impediments of Speech, and, when approaching fifty and popular as a reader of Shakespeare, became renowned as London's *"celebrated Professor of Elocution."*

To recover his health, Melville Bell was shipped off to St. John, Newfoundland, where he had a brief interlude in *"commerce."* Upon his recovery he rejoined his father in speech therapy, and by his mid-twenties was carving out a modest niche for himself.

Chance then took him to Edinburgh, Scotland, where he was smitten by *Eliza Symonds* (1810-1897), a petite, bird-like lass of some means who, though musically inclined, was to suffer deafness with age.

Their romance and ensuing fifty-two-year marriage produced three sons: *Melville* James (1845-1870); *Alexander* (3Mar1847-2Aug 1922. Originally called "Aleck," in 1858, on his eleventh birthday, "Graham" was added to this middling-son's name), and *Edward* Charles (1848-1867).

When Aleck was born the electromagnetic telegraph, which so revolutionized communication, had yet to connect Edinburgh with London (though pioneered by *Joseph Henry* [1799-1878], the first secretary of the Smithsonian Institution, *Samuel F. B. Morse* [1791-1872] conceived it in 1832 and made it practical in 1837 with his single-needle *relay* system; U.S. patent No. 1,640 in 1840 [in England Charles Wheatstone and William Fothergill Cooke patented a five-needle system in June, 1837]. Its first trial was in 1843 between Washington and Baltimore.).

Melville Bell became noted as *a teacher of the deaf to talk* and for his unique system of *visible speech*. In 1849 his "A New Elucidation of The Principles of Speech and Elocution" was published in the first edition of <u>The Principles of Speech.</u>

"Visible speech was a concrete method of (symbols) enabling the dumb to teach themselves how to speak. To Alexander Melville Bell it was evident that deaf mutes were silent, not because they lacked the physical organ used in speaking, but because they could not hear. Their vocal cords were ready to respond when called upon but the clamor of tongues around them meant nothing. They existed, these poor souls, lost to the finer pleasures of living, in a soundless void. But by learning the symbols they could acquire the faculty of making the sounds designated; and from this, in time, would come the ability to speak. As the organ of speech was the same in all mouths (e.g., when the pupil closes his lips and passes his voice through his nose, the resulting sound is *m* - no matter the language), the symbols were universal. They meant the same to a Chinese child unable to ask for rice or a Bantu crone in an African kraal as to a deficient child in a sheltered English home."

Thomas Costain

George Bernard Shaw used "Visible Speech" in <u>Pygmalion</u>.

In 1872 Aleck delivered a paper to London's Philological Society: *"The System of 'Visible Speech' was invented by my father, Mr. A. Melville Bell, professor of vocal physiology; and it constitutes a new species of phonetic writing, based not upon sounds, but upon the actions of the vocal organs in producing them..."*

When 15 young Aleck's interest in invention was whetted when he and his father visited *Charles Wheatstone* (1802-1875), famed for his work in cryptography, the physiology of vision and the science of sound, including electrical apparatus (giving him priority claim for the telegraph, challenged by *Alexander Bain*'s punched-paper-tape printing telegraph and electric clock - though telegraphic innovation apparently began in 1753 with the Scotchman, *Charles Morrison*'s proposal for a 26-wire electrical telegraph).

But their main interest was Wheatstone's work on *Baron Wolfgang de Kempelen*'s device for imitating the human voice.

From earliest times man has sought to duplicate the actions of living things; the 18th century saw a zenith, a Golden Age in *"automata."* Several of the most fascinating, emerging from the genius of clock-makers, were *Achilles Langenbucher*'s automatic musical-playing instruments of 1610, and arguably the most gifted were created by *Jacques de Vaucanson* (1709-82). His amazing 1738, life-size, 12-tune flute player was followed by his masterpiece: a *canard* that waddled, fluttered its wings, swam as if in water, preened, drank water and ate and digested fish which it excreted...in a 'natural' way. Its weight-driven mechanism had more than a thousand moving parts (more complicated than Patek Philippe's *Grande Sonnerie*) concealed inside the duck and in its base.

In 1769 von Kempelen built *"The Turk,"* famous as an unbeatable chess player (a deceptive automata with movements by a cleverly hidden human). Other well-known makers of robots were the Swiss father-son, *Pierre* (1721-90) and *Henri-Louis* (1752-91) *Jaquet-Droz.* Pierre's masterpiece was a *'scrivener'* who dipped his pen in an inkwell and wrote a limited number of words. For Paris' 1783 exhibition their *'draughtsman' "carefully executed several drawings, of which he first sketches the essential features and then adds the shading. Finally he retouches and corrects his work; to do this, he raises his hand from time to time, so as to get a better view of what he is doing. The various movements of the eyes and hands faithfully imitate nature. "* It was so perfect that the elder Droz was tried for sorcery. Fortunately an enlightening age saw him acquitted.

As wondrous as these machines were, they couldn't talk - until von Kempelen built his *"speaking machine"* with its childish voice - and explained its mystery in his: The Mechanism of Human Speech. Melville and Aleck saw his amazing machine when a copy was brought to London.

Challenged by their father, Aleck and *"Melly"* (Melville) worked to duplicate von Kempelen's machine with at-hand materials and equipment: a lamb's larynx (provided by a butcher after their first attempt tortuously ended a cat's life); a tin tube for a throat (actuated by lung power); gutta-percha (the 'first' plastic, made from tree sap - today seen in antique daguerreotype cases) for forming a partial skull containing jaw, teeth, pharynx and nasal cavity, and soft-rubber lips and cheeks. There was a lever-actuated soft-rubber palate stuffed with cotton, and an ingenious, articulated, six-section rubber-covered tongue which uncannily reproduced lifelike motions.

To demonstrate their masterpiece, Melly blew through the tin tube as Aleck manipulated the levers to produce *"Mama! Mama!"* so realistically that a neighbor asked: *"what can the matter be with the baby?"*

This taught Aleck how human beings achieved speech: not simple, but understandable.

Seeking a fuller understanding, Aleck continued his studies and in 1865 discovered that bottles of varying capacity and/or neck size produced different sounds when blown into. Next, he expanded these experiments with tuning forks ("pitch-forks"), arguably his first step towards the invention of the telephone.

In March, 1866, as a six-foot, quite handsome young man turning 19 and taking account of his future, he wrote *Alexander Ellis*, London's phonetician and developer of a "universal alphabet," about his theory of vowel tones learned from tuning fork experiments.

Ellis' reply: *"...I find you are exactly repeating* (Hermann von) *Helmholtz's experiments for determining the musical tones of the vowels...*(with electromagnets Helmholtz kept several tuning forks in continuous vibration, finding he could adjust the loudness of each to synthesize vowel sounds)... *I should be very glad if you could repeat these very interesting experiments."*

His investigations went forward with new enthusiasm.

After completing studies at the University of Edinburgh and London's University College (1868-70), Aleck briefly worked with his father.

Then, to regain his health (both brothers had died of tuberculosis, the age's great killer), in 1870, when 23, he emigrated to Canada with his parents and settled in Brantford, Ontario (45 miles west of Buffalo, New York).

Melville Bell never returned to England, continuing to lecture on Visible Speech in Canada and the United States, while on a nearby farm Aleck recovered - briefly working near Montreal transcribing the language of the *Mohawks* into a Visible Speech phonetic alphabet.

In 1871, due to his father's previous commitments, Aleck took a proffered position to teach at the Boston School for Deaf Mutes, later known as the Horace Mann School (*photo, next, Bell is top center, right*). He also lectured at Boston University and soon began his own school of vocal physiology.

Boston School for Deaf Mutes, 1871:

Boston, then America's center (*"The Hub"*) for higher education, scientific studies and the industrial revolution sweeping the country, was "the Boston of Mr. Longfellow, Mr. Emerson, and Mrs. Julia Ward Howe; and the elegant young gentleman from London's intellectual circles was made to feel very much at home. In appearance he was the personification of the romantic fictional hero of the day - tall, slender, very pale, with dark expressive eyes, subject to infernos of feeling, both of gaiety and despair."

Mitchell Wilson

Thus was his heritage steeped in speech.

While this is the story of Bell and Curtiss, it's also the story of aviation in America involving others. Therefore, to give the reader an interplay of "what actually happened" (*Leopold von Ranke*), the author has selected information as it chronologically happened.

16Apr1867: *Wilbur Wright* born on a farm near Millville, Indiana, the third son of *Milton* (1828-1917, of English ancestry) and *Susan* Catharine Wright (1831-1889, daughter of German-born Johann Gottlieb Koerner).

19Aug'71: *Orville Wright* (1871-1948) born, in Dayton, Ohio.

Their father, Milton, a strict, God-fearing man, in 1868 was made editor of the official organ of the United Brethren Church, and elected a bishop in 1876. In 1902 he became embroiled in an internal church financial and factional problem on which he was assisted by Wilbur and Orville. They thus acquired their legal knowledge - and ready propensity to use the courts to assert their position.

After their mother's death (probably the source of their mechanical aptitude), the brothers became close to *Katharine* (1874-1929), their helpmate and perceptive younger sister. It's said: "without her loyal cooperation, both sympathetically and financially, it is doubtful if Wilbur and Orville would have been successful at all."

"*The Bishop's Boys,*" though completing the required studies, never received high school diplomas. Regardless, they were avid readers, curious, inventive, and (especially Wilbur) outwardly of a serious demeanor.

Wilbur, 22:

Wilbur was the tallest, about five-ten, and slimmest at 140 pounds. Orville, about 135 pounds and five-seven, was but slightly taller than Katharine. (See photos, pages 251, 277)

Wilbur Wright (3Apr'12): "*From the time we were little children my brother Orville and myself lived together, played together, worked together and, in fact, thought together. We usually owned all of our toys in common, talked over our thoughts and aspirations so that nearly everything that was done in our lives has been the result of conversations, suggestions and discussions between us.*"

But their letters reveal Wilbur, *truly with the spark of genius*, as the leader and originator of most of their work.

In March, 1909, Bishop Wright wrote Katharine: "*...It does not make much difference about you, but Wilbur ought to keep out of all balloon rides. Success seems to hang on him...*" while after Wilbur's death Orville lived as if in his shadow, as if Wilbur was in the next room.

In life they were inseparable; bachelors with neither apparently ever close to marriage. During experimenting at Huffman Prairie they rode the interurban trolley, often accompanied by *Charles Edward Taylor* (1867-1956), their machinist-associate, who observed their reactions to females: "*If an older woman sat down beside them, before you knew it they would be talking...If a young woman sat next to him* (Wilbur) *he would begin to fidget and pretty soon he would get up and go stand on the platform until it was time to leave the car...I think the boys were mentally flying all the time and simply didn't think about girls.*"

Science appeared to be their sole obsession.

Wilbur and Orville on the rear porch of their home at 7 Hawthorne Street, Dayton, in June, 1909, at the height of their fame:

In 1948 Charles Taylor recalled:
"Both boys had tempers... They would shout at one another something terrible. I don't think they really got mad, but they sure got awfully hot."

"The unique bond of intellectual collaboration was not based on similarity of temperament, but rather on contrast. They were complementary to each other.

"Apart from their passionate interest in the same thing, almost the only characteristic they had in common was gray-blue eyes. Orville resembled his mother, and was meticulous over his clothes. Wilbur was more like his father, and perfunctory about his appearance. The extraordinary collaboration between the two brothers, unparalleled in the history of science, seemed to some extent to be a repetition in the realm of intellectual understanding of the deep affection that had united their father and mother...They formed a family group of exceptional understanding...Their affections were deeply engaged among themselves. They had an extraordinary cohesion, which continued through all the great affairs in which they were subsequently involved."

J.G. Crowther

Continuing work begun in 1865 while a student, Bell experimented on a multiple telegraph (sending several messages at the same time over a single wire). This work evolved into his study of transmitting speech by electrical waves.

"Bell knew that if a musical note were sounded near several...tuning forks, only the fork tuned to that...note would start vibrating. He reasoned that if he were to send over a wire an electric current vibrating with the frequency of a...note, an electromagnetic tuning fork tuned to that note would respond. If he were to send several such...over the same wire at the same time, and there were several electromagnetic tuning forks connected...

the currents would sort themselves...each fork vibrating with its own frequency. Bell's plan...could send as many messages simultaneously as there were notes in the musical scale." *Mitchell Wilson*

Bell, envisioning commercialization of the multiple telegraph, interested several Bostonians into backing him. One, railroad magnate, banker and heir to one of America's oldest fortunes, *Gardiner Greene Hubbard* (1822-1897), *photo, right*, was keenly interested in telegraphy,. He was chairman of the Clarke School for the Deaf (and in 1888 co-founded the National Geographic Society and was its first president). He became acquainted with Bell because of his deaf daughter, *Mabel*, ten years Bell's junior.

Mabel Hubbard met 26-year-old Bell when brought to him by her companion and tutor, *Mary True*. Mary told Mabel: *"May, all the world - the world that stammars or is deaf - is talking about this man! He's a Scot who came to Boston from Canada a year or two ago with his 'Visible Speech' his father invented. He draws the symbols on the blackboard, and by following them anyone can produce any sound in the world! Oh, don't look skeptical. I was, but he convinced me. And I have seen the two little deaf boys whom he taught to speak. And he has the marvelous faculty of making even children comprehend what he wants of them!"* Helen Waite

Bell's contemporary, *Thomas Alva Edison* (1847-1931) was also working on telegraphic invention (born less than a month before Bell, on 11Feb'47 in Milan, Ohio, he married in 1871, six years before Bell, and in 1865 as a *first-class* telegrapher was earning $100 to $125 a month, a princely sum, well over $10,000 today).

Furthermore, while also in Boston, in 1869 he and *Sam Ropes* devised a telegraphic printer, the second of Edison's 1,093 American patents. And moving to New Jersey in 1871, he invented a stock printer (sold for $40,000, about *$3-1/2 million* today), and working with *Charles Batchelor* (who, in 1884, introduced *Nikola Tesla* to Edison and America) and *John Kruesi*, invented the important quadruplex telegraph in 1874 and the "electromotograph" in 1875.

However, as Edison's success grew a darker side emerged - that of a media-savvy egomaniac who was quick to take credit for work done by an increasing list of disgruntled collaborators. One was Frank Sprague, whose name Edison removed from his electric railway as Sprague complained that he was doing *"everything possible to wipe out the name Sprague and to give Mr. Edison the reputation properly belonging to other men's work."*

In addition to Edison and Bell epitomizing what *Thomas Kuhn* (1922-1996) theorized: that scientific innovation is "a series of peaceful interludes punctuated by intellect-

Edison in his late twenties, when he was launching his first inventions.

ually violent revolutions...(in which)...one conceptual world view is replaced by another," there were remarkable similarities in their lives, e.g., Edison became deaf and Bell married a deaf woman.

Also, the Charles Williams, Jr. Electrical Shop, 109 Court Street, Boston - "the fulcrum of electrical experimentation in America" – was pivotal in both their lives: Edison made the working model for his first invention, his 1868 vote recorder, there (designed to speed up votes in Congress, something it didn't want). And both focused on commingling concepts, particularly the telegraph and phonograph. Though Bell continued his dedication to the deaf, with the exception of his passion for flight, success tempered his resolve for further invention – while Edison, with his life-long interest in technology and innovation, was always ready for another roll of the inventor's dice.

"During the spring of 1874, while experimenting with a stylus and chemically impregnated paper for automatic reception, he and Batchelor had observed a fascinating phenomenon: when the paper was wrapped around a cylinder, and both the cylinder and the stylus were connected to a battery, friction increased or decreased according to the strength of the current. The stylus dragged against the chemical paper when there was no current, but slid over it when electricity was applied...The truly remarkable powers of Edison's mind, which multiplied devices from a single idea like a dividing amoeba and then compartmentalized the creations and endeavors, were now being tested to the limit. Still in his middle twenties, he was a one-man conglomerate, spanning the entire field of telegraphic development."

Robert Conot

The Youth's Companion, 24Oct'89:

Increasingly at the Hubbard's Cambridge home, Bell became ever closer with Mabel. She recalled: *"Our lessons continued irregu-*

EDISON'S BEGINNING IN BOSTON.

Thomas Edison had been in several Western telegraph offices, where he was looked upon as an expert, and was at length ordered to Boston to fill a vacancy. The weather was warm, and he donned linen clothes and a broad-brimmed hat. Before he reached Boston the weather turned cold and stormy, but just as he was, linen duster and all, he reported at the telegraph office.

He walked into the superintendent's room and said, "Here I am."

The superintendent looked the young fellow over with a critical eye, and asked, "Who are you?"

"Tom Edison," was the reply.

"Who's Tom Edison?"

The young operator explained that he had been ordered to report for duty, and the superintendent told him to sit down in the operating-room. His advent there created considerable amusement, and the operators guyed him not a little. Edison sat quietly, making no outward sign of disturbance. An hour or more passed, and then a New York sender, noted for his swiftness, signalled the office. There was no one to receive his message, the operators all being otherwise engaged.

"Let the new fellow take him," said the superintendent.

Young Edison sat down at the instrument, and for four hours and a half wrote out messages in a clear, round hand, stuck a date and number on them, and threw them on the floor for the office-boy to pick up. The time he took in numbering and dating were the only moments he was not writing out transmitted words.

Faster and faster ticked the instrument, and faster and faster moved Edison's fingers, till the rapidity with which the messages came tumbling out attracted the attention of other operators, who, when their work was done, gathered around to witness the spectacle. At the close of four hours and a half, and of the New York business, there flashed from New York the salutation

"Hello!"

"Hello yourself!" ticked back Edison.

"Who are you?" sounded the instrument.

"Tom Edison," was ticked back.

"Tom Edison, I'm glad to know you," came over the wires. "You are the only man that could ever take me at my fastest, and the first man that ever sat at the other end of my wire for over two hours and a half. I congratulate the office in getting you there."

The young man in the limp duster and slouch hat had won his first laurels in the Boston office. He was never guyed after that first day.

9

larly, but they were no longer confined to articulation, indeed they never had been. Alec used to give me information of the most miscellaneous kind and we often got into political discussions."

Bell also wanted to show vocal sounds visually. He was particularly interested in manometric flame, a French concept that used gas flame and a set of mirrors to visually represent sounds, and began experimenting at the Massachusetts Eye and Ear Infirmary with vibrating membranes which actuated a stylus on a rotating drum.

Thus he continued the work of *Philipp Reis*, a young German musician who, in 1861: "...designed an instrument *(which, from the Greek, he called a 'telephone')* which reproduced musical sounds: a membrane, against which a lever rested, vibrated under the pressure of acoustic waves and thus moved the lever, interrupting an electrical current. The current, circulating in an electromagnet, caused a wooden box placed elsewhere to vibrate." *Eco & Zorzoli*

In 1874 Bell applied for American citizenship, which was granted in 1882. There-after, with patriotic pride, he revered in being *an American citizen*, standing strongly for the basic precepts of what being one is all about, e.g., Years later, when a hotel in Sydney, Nova Scotia, turned away *Charles Thompson* (a negro who served the Bells for 35 years) and his wife, he raised a furious fuss, writing Mabel:

"I anticipate a stirring time, and the matter may even become a National issue. I think the people here...are so fully aroused that it is unnecessary for me to do anything further...This is a Canadian affair...I can help materially, however, by being interviewed in the United States...I better write to the American consul in Sydney..."

And in 1894, in the midst of a great depression, Mabel wrote Elsie: *"Papa rather sympathizes with...Coxey's Army, namely to force the Government to give them work... I think Papa...holds that as Government is of the people by the people and for the people, it is bound to provide for its starving members...*
Papa thinks there is something wrong in a system which feeds and gives criminals work, but refuses it to honest labor. Papa (sees) the Government as the original instrument of the people..."

Early on, needing assistance constructing his electrical apparatus at the Williams shop, Bell met *Tom Watson, a young journeyman electrician* (1854-1934, *photo, right*).

Soon, finding that both lived in Salem, they began walking nearby beaches together, and one day Bell startled Watson, saying:

"You know...someday we will be building machines which will be capable of flying the air like...gulls...at a far greater speed."

Shortly, Bell coupled the concept of transmitting speech vibration into electrical impulse, telling Watson:

"...that it would be possible to transmit sounds of any sort if we could only occasion a variation in the intensity of an electric current exactly like that occurring in the density of the air while a given sound is made."

In the spring of 1875, hoping to patent his multiple telegraph (theoretically far superior to Edison's quadruplex), Bell went to Washington (his work and travel co-funded by Hubbard and leather manufacturer *Thomas Sanders* [1840-1911], fathers of deaf children - and both to participate, one-third each, in Bell's inventions. Also, in exchange for teaching 5-year-old George Sanders, Bell received room and board at Sanders' mother's home in Salem, where he also experimented - and she was his sometime-mother-in-need.)

In Washington he soon became discouraged by the patent bureaucracy, and met with the Smithsonian's aging *Joseph Henry* (whose experimenting in electricity was so pivotal). Henry listened to his impassioned description of his work and, intrigued by voice-activated transmission, viewed Bell's apparatus the next day, counseling: *"Under no circumstances should you think of giving up."*

Wise counsel, altering Bell's life and prompting his life-long assistance to others. Years later he would explain that he was *"repaying an old debt."*

"The fundamental element in telephonic transmission consists of an iron diaphragm ...close to a magnet on which is wound a conductor wire; in the first transmitter constructed in this way the voice made the diaphragm vibrate and stimulated currents in the conductor which reached the receiver...on similar lines; variable currents made the receiving diaphragm vibrate by...attraction, and it was...able to reproduce the sounds. In 1873 Bell began...construction of an artificial ear consisting of a diaphragm of iron which vibrated when placed near a magnet surrounded by a metal wire in which current was induced...he succeeded in converting acoustic vibrations into alternating current. He was however still thinking...of visualizing sounds...it was... two years before he saw how to use his discovery properly."   *Eco & Zorzoli*

On 4May'75, Bell wrote Gardiner Hubbard: *"I have read somewhere that the resistance offered by a wire...is affected by the tension of the wire. If this is so, a continuous current of electricity passed through a vibrating wire should meet with a varying resistance, and hence a pulsatory action should be induced in the current...*(relative) *in amplitude, as well as in rate of movement, to the vibrations of the string...*(Hence) *the timbre of a sound* (an essential to speech) *could be transmitted...*(and) *the strength of the current can be increased ad libitum without destroying the relative intensities of the vibrations..."*

This recognition of *variable resistance* legally established Bell's *priority of invention of the telephone* (telephone: "sound over a long distance").

His mind racing with ideas, he soon needed Watson full-time as his assistant.

"As it was, they had a sufficient number of inventions to keep them desperately busy. Besides the multiple telegraph, Aleck *(soon simply "Alec")* was contriving an 'autograph telegraph' *(Hubbard's pet project)* that would send telegrams in a person's handwriting *(an early Fax. In 1840 Scottish clock-maker Alexander Bain proposed his Syphon*

Recorder, a picture transmitter and receiver on a pendulum apparatus; then, in 1843/46 his "electric printing" using punched paper tape was the first fax. *Arguably the first 20th-century demonstration of facsimile technology was at an MIT alumni dinner in New York on 11Jun1927. The author owned the original of one of that evening's messages: signed by and from Charles Lindbergh, just returned to Washington D. C. from France)*, and try-ing to perfect the invention closest to his heart, the 'machine to hear for deaf children.'

This would be his 'phonautograph,' or 'sound writer.' *(Evolving from the 1874 Brant-ford experiments using a dead man's ear. Bell's curiosity as to why the membrane-ear drum's vibrations actuated ear bones led to his thinking: Could an electrically actuated membrane produce sound waves in air?)* They had something of the sort at the Massa-chusetts Institute of Technology *('Boston Tech' until it moved across the Charles River to Cambridge in 1916)*, and Aleck took his already-full schedule apart to spend hours study-ing and experimenting with it. He found that when a person talked or sang into the mouthpiece the vibrations of his voice made a tracing on a sheet of glass covered with lamp-black. Also one of the professors at the Institute let him borrow something called a 'manometric capsule,' and Aleck demonstrated it to the intrigued Thomas Watson."

Helen Waite

In a 24May'75 letter to his parents Bell wrote: *"I think that the transmission of the human voice is much more nearly at hand than I had supposed..."*

Whether it was Edison unknowingly emulating Bell or the other way around, it ap-pears that each, engrossed in their wide-ranging work, found night best for creative think-ing. Thus became legend Edison's naps and his sleeping beside his work - and Bell's working until three in the morning, then a walk under the stars, and a sleep so deep that often near-heroic efforts were needed to awaken him before mid-day. These habits are not unusual for creative work: typically the time for thought and inspiration is not during the hectic day, but during a long walk alone in a quiet place; or while contemplating at day's end; or after the children have been put to bed.

And often with invention there is a meeting of persistence with chance: on the 2nd of June, 1875, in the Williams's attic, with Bell in one room and Watson another, Watson was idly plucking the transmitting clock-spring reed. A very surprised Bell heard it as a *continuous* sound rather than of the usual pulses. Immediately he realized that they'd dis-covered what they were seeking: the *accidentally plucked* reed was inducing its own vi-brations into the electromagnet behind it.

"At that moment the telephone was born."

"This was the difference between the telephone and every other telegraphic device that had preceded it. Telegraphy transmitted sharply defined pulses of current, each pulse having the same intensity, even though the current pulse for a dash was longer than for a dot. A telephone required a continuous current whose intensity could vary exactly as the sound waves in the air."

Mitchell Wilson

As if Bell didn't have hands full with invention and teaching, romance stirred his breast. His love for Mabel was such that he wrote Mrs. Hubbard, confessing being in *"deep trouble...I have discovered that my interest in my dear pupil...has ripened into a far deeper feeling...I have learned to love her...I promise beforehand to abide by your decision..."* Mabel was seventeen, too young for marriage

Thus ensued a fascinating interplay of letters between a love-struck Bell and a yet-to-be-smitten Mabel - and her very hesitant parents. Finally, sensing advantage, Bell wrote the Hubbards: *"I feel myself still hampered by promises that I should not have made...I must be free to do whatever I think right and best - quite irrespective of your wishes - or those of other people...When I am sure of her affection I wish to be engaged to her. When I am in a position to offer a home I wish to marry her - whether it is two years or two months!...If you do not like my conduct in the matter... you can deny me the house - and I can wait."*

Mrs. Hubbard replied: *"I give you back your promise, entirely, unreservedly. I believe your love to my Mabel to be unselfish and noble. I trust you perfectly. If you can win her love I shall feel happy in my darling's happiness."*

On the next day, 26Aug'75, described by Bell as *"the happiest day of my life..."* they became engaged, and in his courtship journal he wrote: *"...shall not record any more here. I feel that I have at last got to the end of all my troubles - and whatever happens I may now safely write: FINIS!"*

In September, emotionally and physically drained by the whirl of events, he went to Brantford to rest and smooth a strained relationship with his father. There, and some say, desperately short of funds (and embarrassed from asking his future father-in-law for money), he made an ill-conceived contract with *George Brown*, editor of the <u>Toronto Globe</u> and a leading Canadian MP, granting him a *half* interest in a British patent-to-be for $300 (not an idle sum, approximately $30,000 today), an arrangement that would greatly bedevil him. Regardless, returning to Boston he had the beginnings of his patent specification written, and by the end of October essentially completed.

"As the last weeks of the old year ebbed away and 1876 dawned - the year of incredible happenings for Alex Bell - he was back in his old treadmill of teaching the deaf, accepting pupils with defective speech, training teachers in the use of Visible Speech - and working every spare minute far into the night on his telephone...He has left his comfortable and pleasant quarters at Mrs. Sanders.' He was frankly afraid that uninvited people would invade the...attic and steal and copy his instruments and apparatus, so he had moved into two rooms in an attic at 5 Exeter Place, Boston, and he and Tom Watson fitted up a laboratory there. The place became so much like home to Tom that he...took another of the attic rooms in Exeter Place." *Helen Waite*

25Nov'75: At the Hubbard's for Thanksgiving - and Mabel's 18th birthday - they became engaged as she told him that she loved him better than anyone but her mother.

Melville Bell then wrote Mabel, expressing his *"great satisfaction"* and adding a father's assessment: *"Alec is a good fellow and, I have no doubt, will make an excellent husband. He is hot-headed but warm-hearted – sentimental, dreamy, and self-absorbed, but sincere and unselfish. He is ambitious, to a fault, and is apt to let enthusiasm run away with judgment...With love you will have no difficulty in harmonizing...I have told you all the faults I know...and this catalogue is wonderfully short."*

But when Hubbard learned of Bell's agreement with George Brown he immediately intervened. However a British patent must *precede* one filed elsewhere, and though some murkiness exists as to the events and timing, early in February, 1876, Hubbard learned that Brown, in spite of the agreement, did not intend to register the patent in London.

Therefore, without consulting Bell - "*He may be a great inventor, but he's an obdurate Scotchman*" - on the *morning* of *14Feb'76* he had his Washington attorneys file Bell's application for the telephone patent.

That *same* afternoon William Baldwin, attorney for Chicago's *Elisha Gray* (1835-1901 – who, in 1872, formed the Western Electric Manufacturing Co.), filed his *caveat* (a notice of intention to take out a patent) for "*an electric speaking machine.*"

In this "age of invention" one might think that much of what occurred happened in some sort of vacuum. Far from it! Each aspiring inventor (and his attorneys) appeared to be fully aware of a counterpart's activities. It was more like a game of chess, often augmented by powerful interests, rather than of one inventor unknowingly putting something over on another. As to the actions of the parties, there are differing perspectives:

In one, Gray never put plans to paper until after a month in Washington, much of that spent at the Patent Office - where Bell's notarized specifications were admired by "*some people in the Patent Office.*"

In the other, "Bell had submitted no models. His experiments with electroharmonic telegraph were elementary compared to Gray's and Edison's. His description of the apparatus he intended to use was crude - it had not, if fact, any practical value for transmitting speech..."
                                                                                              Robert Conot

In his caveat Gray wrote: "*I claim as my invention the art of transmitting vocal sounds or conversations telegraphically through an electric circuit.*" Portions of his claims appeared spurious, some unworkable, others non-proven. While Gray's candid nature makes malfeasance unlikely, one should not assume him unaffected by Bell's being about to patent. Whatever caused him to synthesize his concepts at that precise moment is conjecture, *it was not mere chance,* though Bell wrote his parents "*Such a coincidence has hardly happened before.*"

Also, things did not always go smoothly. For instance, with one of Bell's submittals a maze of conflicting claims issued from the Patent Office: On 16Feb'76, patent examiner Zenas Fisk Wilber ("an alcoholic, chronically in need of money...easily corruptible," acquainted with Edison, in an office "structured to invite perjury, bribery, mis-dating, and other trickery:" *Robert Conot*) gave Hubbard's attorneys notice that Bell's *harmonic multiple telegraph* application of 25Feb'75 was in interference with Gray's application of 23Feb'75, and also with that of the Dane, *Paul la Cour*'s of 2Mar'75.

This required that priority of conception be determined by costly hearings susceptible to Wilber's indebtedness to Major Bailey of Pollok and Bailey, Hubbard's and Bell's attorneys. And Bell learned that: "*...another whose name was withheld but I have discovered it to be Mr. Edison of New York, who has evidently been employed by the Western Union Telegraph Company to try to defeat Gray and myself.*"

William Baldwin, Gray's attorney, wrote Samuel White, Gray's sponsor, about Bell: "(he) *has been very much annoyed by spies set upon him, probably by Western Union and...thinks they are trying to play him and Gray off against each other...*(Baldwin found Bell) *intelligent, gentlemanly, and well-disposed."*

Edison, retained by Western Union's president, William Orton, and supplied with Reis's work, in spite of increasing deafness worked on harmonic telegraphy but failed in making a speaking telephone - though his carbon transmitter would make Bell's telephone *practical.*

This was a stressful time for Bell. On 29Feb'76 he wrote his father: *"If I succeed in securing that Patent without interference from the others the whole thing is mine - and I am sure of fame, fortune, and success if I can only persevere in perfecting my apparatus."*

And there was an exchange between Bell and Mabel which, in conclusion, he wrote: *"...Procrastination is indeed my besetting sin. Help me, Mabel, to conquer it. I will not disguise from you dear what a blow this misfortune has been to me - for I had looked to this new patent to avoid all conflict with Gray - & to place the control of the new system of Telegraphy entirely in my own hands. I feel it more deeply than anything that has ever happened to me - except one thing! and you know what that is....Just received a kind note from your father. If any telegram comes for me today please send it to the University tomorrow morning."*

The next month, on March 10th, Bell and Watson, in separate rooms, were testing a newly designed transmitter when Bell, by Watson's later account, spilled battery acid on his trousers and cried out: *"Mr. Watson, come here. I want you!"* Watson bounded through the door, shouting *"I can hear the words!"* These staid, Victorian-era men expressed great exuberance!

Bell's version differs slightly, possibly because he considered the spill inconsequential or, more likely, inappropriate. In his laboratory notes, 12Mar'76:

"I then shouted into M (mouthpiece) *the following sentence: 'Mr. Watson - come here - I want to see you.' To my delight he came and declared that he had heard and understood what I had said. I asked him to repeat the words. He answered 'You said - 'Mr. Watson - come here - I want to see you.' We then changed places and I listened to S* (the reed receiver) *while Mr. Watson read a few passages from a book into the mouthpiece M. It was certainly the case that articulate sounds proceeded from S. The effect was loud but indistinct and muffled. If I had read beforehand the passage given by Mr. Watson I should have recognized every word. As it was I could not make out the sense - but an occasional word here and there was quite distinct. I made out 'to' and 'out' and 'further;' and finally the sentence 'Mr. Bell do you understand what I say? Do - you - un - der - stand - what - I - say' came quite clearly and intelligibly. No sound was audible when armature S was removed."*

On 10Mar'76 Bell wrote his father: *"...to announce a great failure* (George Brown's inaction) *and a great success...This is a great day...I feel that I have...struck the solution of a great problem - and the day is coming when telegraph wires will be laid on to houses just like water or gas - and friends converse with each other without leaving home* (see 25Mar'78)"

Regardless of how it happened, *they had succeeded.*

Bell's home-use telephone prediction is an example of his amazing prescience, an uncanny insight, repeated time and again, to foresee the unimagined results of innovative technology.

The telephone patent was approved on Bell's 29th birthday, 3Mar'76. Gray did not contest it, writing him on 5Mar'77: "...*Of course you have had no means of knowing what I had done in this matter of transmitting vocal sounds. When, however, you see the specification, you will see that the fundamental principles are contained therein. I do not, however, claim even the credit of inventing it, as I do not believe a mere description of an idea that has never been <u>reduced to practice</u> - in the <u>strict sense</u> of that phrase - should be dignified with the name invention...*"

On 7Mar'76 <u>Patent No. 174,465</u> was issued. *The prize was won!*

Gardiner Hubbard, with his fine analytical mind, was getting involved in Bell's work, volunteering questions on several technical problems. And, while impatient awaiting the multiple telegraph, he was dismayed at several of Bell's habits, at least once enlisting Melville Bell to get a suggestion made: in mid-April Melville wrote his son: "...*Stick to the autograph till you bring it into practical use...* (until then) *I would suspend all other experiments.*" A few days later Hubbard wrote: "*If you would take Mr. Williams' man* (Watson) *as I proposed and work with him or let him work steady on one thing until you had perfected it you would soon make it a success...While you are flying from one thing to another you may accidentally accomplish something but you probably will never perfect anything...If you could make one good invention in the telegraph you would secure an annual income as much as the Professorship and then you could settle that on your wife and teach Visible Speech and experiment in telegraphy with an easy...conscience.*"

He even got Mabel to write that she wouldn't marry him until he'd completed the automatic telegraph. Bell responded that she "...*almost broke my heart...I want to marry you, darling, because I love you...and I wish to feel that you would marry me for the same reason*"...adding that he had no intention of giving up on the telegraph but that she made him wish that he'd never heard of it.

And Hubbard knew his future son-in-law, as when he interceded regarding a proffered professorship: "...*If you were tied up to rules and hours it would be very irksome and hard...You are not like other men and you must therefore make allowances for your peculiarities...If you could work as other men do you would accomplish much more...But you must overcome these habits by your own will, and not by rules imposed by a college.*"

In 1876, to celebrate the 100th anniversary of the United States, a massive "*United States International Exposition*" was held in Philadelphia (a miniature is in the Smithsonian). Hubbard, as chairman of the Massachusetts exhibit, wanted Bell there; the official catalogue listed: "*A. Graham Bell: Telegraphic & Telephonic Apparatus and Visible Speech.*" However, due to teaching commitments Bell thought it impossible - but Hubbard's insistence and Mabel's maneuvering soon saw him packed and on the train.

Though a reluctant attendee, he was fortunate being at his exhibit (part of "*Group XXV...instruments of precision, research, experiment, and illustration, including telegraphy and music* among *the principal American exhibitors...Atlantic and Pacific Telegraph...Edison's American Automatic Telegraph; Western Union Telegraph...*") in Machinery Hall, "*1402 feet in length and 360 feet in width,*" the world's largest building, at just the right moment, as noted below.

Illustrated History of the Centennial Exposition:

"*It has been the duty of the Centennial Commission to examine, appreciate, and confirm in legal form...the recommendations of the judges for awards...by 250 gentlemen...in twenty-eight groups.*"

Though not listed, Bell was awarded a medal "*of bronze, round in shape, four inches in diameter...chaste in appearance...largest of the kind ever struck in the United States... about twelve thousand were presented...exhibitors...*"

The exposition was open for six months...*"number of days open: 159; Paid admissions: 8,004,325; Free admissions: 1,785,067; Total admissions: 9,789,392* (one-in-four of the then-40 million Americans)*; Grand total of receipts: $3,813,749.75*"

Its 50-cent admission was quite a sum when a journeyman's wage then was much less than $2 a day.

As with other curious events in this tale (the stuck reed and spilled acid, whatever), there was another accidental but pivotal event:

The exposition was closed on Sunday, June 25th, as the judges were going from exhibit to exhibit. But it was so beastly hot they'd decided the exhibit just before Bell's would be their last. Then one of their group, *Dom Pedro II (1825-91),* the emperor of Brazil, spied Bell, whom he'd met earlier, on

May 10th when visiting the Boston School for the Deaf and had watched him teach Visible Speech. In spite of the heat he insisted they witness Bell's demonstration.

Then Dom Pedro, 500 feet away, exclaiming *"I hear! I Hear!"* heard "*To be or not to be...*" Absolutely fascinated, the judges then spent over three hours testing, listening and examining Bell's "*far speaker.*"

England's judge, Irish-born *William Thomson* (1824-1907. In 1852 he described the heat pump, and in 1892 was made Lord Kelvin) stated:

"*Young man, you have achieved one of the marvels of the ages. I predict that this invention of yours definitely is <u>to be!</u>...this is the most wonderful thing I have seen in America!*"

Later this momentous day Gray visited Bell at his hotel, as Bell noted: "*We have explained...all matters in dispute and...decided...it may be advantageous to...unite our* (multiple telegraph) *interests...to control...Western Union...if those associated with us can be brought to...understanding...*(or there would be lawsuits) *and the...result will be that the Western Union can...buy up whatever part they choose...*"

Bell later wrote that Gray: "*satisfied me that he was an honorable man...independent inventor...my suspicions unfounded.*" Thus reinvigorated, he set up "*telephony*" demonstrations between Hubbard's house and barn, one that amazed and enthralled the fortunate few permitted to speak or listen.

And he expressed his thoughts on fame and fortune, writing Mabel: "*...the real reward of labour...is <u>success</u>...a medal far more valuable than any made of gold...a medal that you may wear around your heart - and...will wear as long as history itself!*"

In 1879 he added: "*...I can't bear to hear that even my friends should think that I stumbled upon an invention and that there is no more good in me.*"

25Mar'78: Bell, to the organizers of the New England Electric Telephone Co: "*At the present time we have a perfect network of gas pipes and water pipes throughout our large cities. We have main pipes laid under the streets communicating with side pipes with the various dwellings, enabling the members to draw their supplies of gas and water from a common source. In a similar manner it is conceivable that cables of telephone wires could be laid underground, or suspended overhead, communicating by branch wires with private dwellings, counting houses, shops, manufactories, etc., uniting them through a main cable with a central office where the wire could be connected as desired, establishing direct communication between any two places in the city. Such a plan as this, though impractical at the present moment, will, I firmly believe, be the outcome of the introduction of the telephone to the public...I believe in the future wires will unite the head offices of telephone companies in different cities, and a man in one part of the country may communicate by word of mouth with another in a distant city.*"

As to further invention, Bell spent a great deal of time with the "*photophone.*" In 1878 he had said "*If you insert selenium in the telephone battery and throw light upon it you change its resistance and vary the strength of the current you have sent to the telephone, so that you can hear a shadow.*" In 1879, assisted by *Charles Sumner Tainter* (1854-1940, also from Williams' shop, who, in 1885, developed the "*Dictaphone*"), he began its development.

Succeeding in the same week of February, 1880, as his daughter, Marian, was born, he exulted: "*Two babies in one week!...Both strong, vigorous, healthy young things, and both destined I trust to grow into something great...*"

"Bell's photophone made sound waves vibrate a beam of reflected sunlight. The receiver changed the varying light intensity back into sound. Bell found that selenium's electrical resistance changed the different light intensities, and equipped his radiophone receiver with the first true 'photoelectric' cells."   *Mitchell Wilson*

Though the photophone's promise was never realized, it did have some interesting offshoots: the "*intermittent-beam sounder*" in 1880 and, in 1881, the "*spectraphone*" for exploration of the infrared spectrum.

In 1896, considering it "*...the greatest invention I have ever made; greater than the telephone,*" Bell spoke on what he now called "*Radiophony*" to students at Illinois College (Founded by Yale men in 1829 in Jacksonville, Illinois; the oldest college west of the Alleghenies. 'If Lincoln had attended college he'd have gone there;' as did three-time Democrat presidential-aspirant William Jennings Bryan. It continued to attract notable speakers, one, Russia's *Aleksandr Kerensky*, with whom the author, then a freshman, had a private interview on 28Mar1944).

While vacationing at his parent's home - and apparently in response to Mabel's counsel to "*...Try the line between Brantford and Paris, and do your utmost to induce some one to take up your foreign patents and allow you to go on working...*" he attempted a long-distance call: Setting up in the telegraph offices in Brantford and in Paris, eight miles distant, he clearly heard his father's words "*To be or not to be...*" Now he knew that "*...undulatory current can be used upon telegraph lines.*" Another test, Brantford to five-mile-distant Mount Pleasant, was also successful - but the Canadian authorities and newspapers were unimpressed.

"...while the neighbors had plenty of fun listening and taking turns talking and singing into the queer contraption, they went away laughing at the *'cracked notion of Crazy Bell.' 'Yes, sir,'* one of them commented years later, *'when I was a kid we thought he was a regular nut.'*"   *Helen Waite*

The author, who's written extensively of aviation history, is reminded of a similar reaction to the Wright's first flight; and, in 1909/10, the Canadian military, deeming the aeroplane impractical for military purposes, stilled Canada's aviation development (by the *Canadian Aerodrome Company*, in which Graham and Mabel Bell were principals).

Back in Boston, at Hubbard's insistence Bell retained Watson full-time at $3 a day (a most handsome wage) plus *a tenth-interest in invention*, thus joining Bell, Hubbard and Sanders in their "*Patent Association.*" They were an exceptional team to make the telephone, now with transmitter and receiver, into something more than a gadget. In Watson's words: "*Mr. Bell decided his baby had grown big enough to go outside and prattle over a real telegraph line instead of gurgling between two rooms.*"

The Walworth Mfg. Co. permitted their after-hour hooking instruments to the telegraph line between its Boston office and its Cambridge factory, two miles away. Getting excellent communication, hookups followed between Boston and 16-mile-distant Salem, and finally Boston and New York City, over 200 miles distant away.

28Nov'76: The Boston *Post* about "Electric Telephony:" "*The application of this discovery promises to completely revolutionize the business of transmitting messages by electricity between distant points...Professor Bell is continually improving his invention, and he doubts not that he will ultimately be able to chat pleasantly with friends in Europe while sitting comfortably in his Boston home...*"

Prescient as Bell was, it is doubtful that even he could have imagined the lengths to which communication had expanded a century later: on 8May'94, the author watched President Clinton on CNN-TV answering viewer's questions from around the world.

This is about when Mabel began making an impact on Bell's life and fortune. While he was nigh hopeless in business, Mabel had her father's quick mind and acumen for it. Thus, with the invention proven, she helped him, now introduced as *Alexander Graham Bell*, and Watson embark upon a series of "telephonic lectures."

12Feb'77: The first, in Lyceum Hall at Salem's Essex Institute (one of America's premier museums) was free. An entranced, standing-room-only audience witnessed conversation and song between Watson, in Boston, and Bell and others in the hall, and The Boston *Globe: "SENT BY TELEPHONE. The First Newspaper Dispatch Sent by a Human Voice Over the Wires."*

Noting the packed house, Bell reasoned lectures could be moneymakers. The next, 23Feb'77, saw five hundred 50-cent (about $25 today) tickets sold; thereafter he charged a flat $200 per lecture.

The Providence *Star* wrote: *"Salem Witchcraft...*(Bell), *a tall, well-formed gentleman in graceful evening suit, with jet-black hair, side-whiskers and moustache, light complexion, forehead high and slightly retreating, nose aggressive and black eyes that could look through a water commissioner...*(his) *scientifically beautiful utterance* (was) *of itself a pleasure worth going far for..."*

"Alec would take...telephones and go to Salem, Providence or New York – wherever he seemed...welcomed (e.g., 25Apr'77: "*...to a less-than-capacity audience in Huntington Hall,*" Lowell, MA); advertise a lecture, place a number of receivers in strategic locations in an auditorium - much like loudspeakers of today - connect the telephone to the wires of some obliging telegraph company, and proceed to lecture, interspersing conversations with Mr. Watson in Boston. The Watson part in the demonstration would begin with '*Good evening, how do you do?*' Then Tom would sing a few songs he knew...'*My singing was always a hit...the telephone obscured its defects and gave it a mystic quality. I always encored!'"*   *Helen Waite*

The first lecture's income was $149. Then, with $85 which should have paid his over-due rent, Bell had a sterling telephone made for his fiancee's charm bracelet; she later described as *"perhaps the most historically interesting thing I have."*

By year-end Bell and Watson perfected the second phase of their invention, making it into a workable instrument. Bell completed its specifications on 13Jan'77 and on the 15th filed for a patent. On 30Jan'77 Patent No. 186,787 was issued for a telephonic "box" with a transmitter *and* receiver, including a metallic diaphragm-armature and a permanent magnet with coil having a "quick-acting" compound "U" form.

But problems were brewing. The enterprise was so cash poor that late in 1876 Hubbard offered their telephone patent to Western Union for $100,000 (about $10 million today). It was declined, most likely in hopes for Edison's success improving Bell's patent.

Note: Edison commented: "*Everybody steals in commerce and industry, I've stolen a lot myself. But I know how to steal.*" With the arcane rules of the Patent Office he made the *improving* of another's invention – and thus gaining certain of their patent rights - into a questionable art form.

"In fact Edison was said to have a knack for picking up other inventors' ideas and rushing them to the Patent Office. With Tesla it was to be just the opposite. Ideas chased each other through his mind faster than he could nail them down. Once he understood exactly how an invention worked [in his mind], he tended to lose interest, for there were always exciting new challenges just over the horizon." *Margaret Cheney*

13Jan'77: Joseph Henry missed the demonstration at the Centennial Exposition and Bell thus made one for him at the Smithsonian. In appreciation, Henry then wrote of "*...the value and astonishing character of Mr. Bell's discovery and invention.*"

17May'77: A demonstration in New York city noted among its attendees the presidents of Columbia University, New York University, and the Stevens Institute; William Orton of Western Union and Thomas Eckert of Atlantic & Pacific Telegraph; a British group studying American telegraphy; several scientists; and Cyrus Field, the Atlantic cable's promoter.

Also, Bell's group made their first advertisement: "*The proprietors...are now prepared to furnish Telephones for the transmission of articulate speech through instruments not more than twenty miles apart...Conversation can easily be carried on after slight practice...a few trials the ear becomes accustomed to the peculiar sound...*"

But, regardless of the high-and-mighty paying heed to young Mr. Bell and his telephone, he was facing financial ruin. Nearing a physical breakdown, he anguished: "*I've had enough of the telephone. I'm through with the damn thing. I'm going back to teaching as soon as I get a job.*"

25Jun'77: But fate quixotically smiled - as he wrote Sarah Fuller, director, the Boston School for Deaf-Mutes - when William Reynolds, a Providence businessman: "*...tempted me to negotiate with him for the sale of part interest in my English patent on the telephone and has kept me backwards and forwards between Boston and Providence for the last...ten days arranging matters - but at last the matter has been settled, and I have sold him a portion of my patent for five thousand dollars cash* (around $400,000 today)*...I shall leave Boston on the eleventh of July with my wife! We shall spend the summer and autumn abroad, returning in October. The wedding is to be very quiet and very few people...asked but I must have my dear friend Miss Fuller.*"

9Jul'77: Bell, Hubbard and Sanders formed the *Bell Telephone Company* as a "*voluntary association*" with 5,000 shares apportioned thirty percent each, plus Watson's ten percent. Also, Bell formed the *Bell Trust* with virtually all his patents, past and future, and European telephone rights, in favor of his eventual children, with Hubbard as trustee. Alex and Mabel were to receive its income up to $3,000 per year (over a quarter-million-dollars today) with any excess added to its goal of $200,000 (about $20 million today).

11Jul'77: Emboldened with Reynold's cash, Mabel and Alex were married at the Hubbard's Brattle Street home in Cambridge. The groom gave his bride "*an exquisite cross of eleven round pearls, the prettiest he could find in Boston*" plus 1,497 of his 1,507 shares in the telephone company.

To begin their honeymoon they visited Niagara Falls and Brantford, and then returned to Boston during the great railroad strikes and riots in the summer of 1877. In Montreal, Mabel wrote: "*...we were so doubtful about our chances of reaching Boston undisturbed that Alex bought a revolver and ammunition enough to kill a hundred men...I think he was...disappointed not to have a chance to show it off.*"

They then sailed on the S.S. *Anchoria* to Scotland (where she suffered a surfeit of fish and oatmeal), and her pregnancy prompted renting a house in London's South Kensington (four stories, large grounds, 17 furnished rooms - including one for each servant - for 225 pounds annually, about $40,000 today). And Bell began putting on weight, his 165-pound wedding-weight gradually increasing to a hefty 250 pounds.

The telephone enterprise was experiencing growth: Charles Williams, Jr's shop (to evolve into the massive Western Electric Co.), struggling to make instruments, saw its output rise to over twenty-five units a day. In July, Boston had over 200 customers and 600 in another month. Also, new licensees were established in New England, Pennsylvania, New York, Ohio, Indiana, South Carolina, Georgia and Florida - with many pending, including San Francisco, Chicago, Pittsburgh, Baltimore and Washington DC.

21Feb'78: The New Haven District Telephone Co. issued the first telephone directory: fifty phones for its forty-seven subscribers, eleven residential.

On 23Sep'77 Mabel wrote: "*Alec...went out for a long walk this morning and saw some sea gulls flying and since then has been full of flying machines* (at a time of much such experimentation in England and France)."

A week later: "*What a man my husband is! I am perfectly bewildered at the number and size of the ideas with which his head is crammed...Flying machines to which telephones and torpedoes are to be attached occupy the first place just now from observations of sea gulls...Every now and then he comes out with 'the flying machine has quite changed its shape in a quarter of an hour' or 'the sigarshape is dismissed to the limbo of useless things...*"

To demonstrate his telephone, Bell used the telegraph lines between such diverse points as England to Jersey, Dover to Calais, and Dublin to Holyhead. These climaxed on 14Jan'78 with a demonstration for Queen Victoria (Mabel denied audience) which she described as "*most extraordinary.*"

After overcoming a brief patent challenge, Reynold's new *Telephone Company, Limited*, began England's first commercial telephone usage. However its auspicious beginnings flagged under Reynold's management. Combined with Edison's patent variations, it all came to a head in mid-1879, when Hubbard, as trustee, reorganized. Soon he brought $50,000 home to the trust, and in a year's time the revitalized company was worth over $100,000 (about $10 million today).

8May'78: *Elsie May Bell* (1878-1963), their first child, was born in London. She had normal hearing (Mabel's deafness had been caused by scarlet fever).

Bell felt a compulsion to create. In September, 1878, he wrote Mabel: "*Make me work, there's a good little girl - at anything, it doesn't matter what, only make me work, so that I may be accomplishing something.*"

Though speculative, apparently he was committed to scientific innovation and the teaching of the deaf. Fame was secondary, great wealth also: *the challenge was the improving of man's existence.*

Sanders *(left)*, the group's best businessman, was having difficulty keeping their growing company solvent. In February, 1878, the *New England Telephone Co.* had been formed and contributed "*...the first money...I can ascertain that has been advanced by any one in any part of the world to forward your invention...*"

Accordingly, in March he wrote Bell: "*I have exhausted my means and stretched my credit to its utmost, having received no aid from Mr. Hubbard...from the first...*" and later, contrary to Hubbard's wishes, adding his views for the incorporation of the company: "*...It is the worst policy imaginable to refuse to part with such a portion of our interest as to make what we have left valuable..*" Fortunate in deed were they in having Hubbard's legal mind, Sander's business pragmatism and Bell's neutrality for, in July, events forced Hubbard's hand and the company was reorganized as a corporation able to sell stock.

In March, 1878, the company was sued by Western Union's *American Speaking Telephone Co.*, established to "*supply superior telephones by the original inventors, Thomas A. Edison* (his carbon-button transmitter *was* better), *Elisha Gray, and* (Tuft's College's) *Professor A. (Amos) E. Dolbear.*" In cross suit, the Bell Company sought an injunction against *Peter Dowd*, the nominal defendant, agent for Western Union's *Gold and Stock Company*, prohibiting its renting of Edison/Gray-type telephone equipment.

On 14Apr'77, thirteen days before Edison's carbon transmitter application, German immigrant *Emile Berliner (*1851-1929) filed a caveat for a variable-pressure transmitter. Frustrated in his own attempts, Watson got the company to hire Berliner, thus acquiring his caveat and other inventions – which included the flat disc record ("*plates*").

Bell then filed an interference preventing the issuance of Edison's patent.

The legal struggle was lengthy - with Bell in 1878 acquiring Francis Blake's variable resistance carbon transmitter, and using Berliner-Blake principles until 1892, when it little mattered. The final settlement awarded Bell Edison's telephone rights

Note: *Scientific American*, 5Jul'15: "*To Berliner and Edison belongs the credit of having made the telephone a commercial invention.*"

Concurrently, by 20Sep'76, Dolbear claimed conceiving a modification of Bell's apparatus incorporating a sheet-iron diaphragm in lieu of a membrane, and a straight-bar

Dolbear's friend, Percival Richards, took these concepts to Hubbard, who told him that Bell had already investigated them and wasn't interested, and Richards told Dolbear on 6Jan'77.

On 15Jan'77 Bell applied for a patent incorporating a metal diaphragm and permanent magnet; granted on 30Jan'77 as No. 186,787.

On 20Mar'77, Dolbear wrote Bell: "...*I think that a mutual acquaintance informed him as to what I was doing and before I could get working order he, by the aid of a skilled electrician and working nights and Sundays, completed his and got it patented instanter, so I suppose that I shall lose both the honor and the profit of the invention.*"

Dolbear may have hastened Bell's patent application but there is ample evidence that Bell, having conceived virtually identical improvements, did not pirate his ideas. Regardless, Dolbear was a nuisance - eventually teaming up with Western Union in a lawsuit.

In November, 1878, the young Bell family, hoping to sidestep business problems, returned from England by way of Canada. However, Watson was at the dock, urging his immediate return to Boston to assist in the defense in the patent wars.

Mitchell Wilson,
   The Evolution of The Telephone:

And what a thunderstorm it was:

"This second lawsuit - or series of lawsuits...(was) the largest patent litigation in history...longest, and...most bitterly contested. Bell was...faced not only with financial ruin but...personal disgrace. The...chorus of his rivals...

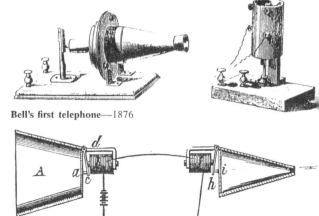

Bell's first telephone—1876

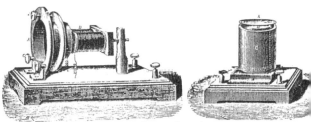

Bell's first telephone, 1876—a schematic diagram

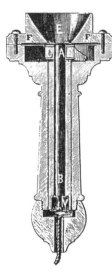

Bell's second telephone: transmitter and receiver

Commercial form of Bell's telephone

incited a universal and unreasonable hatred against Bell. *'This man is a perjurer, a fraud, and a thief!'* No less than six hundred claims...against Bell's *'infringement of other people's rights.'*

"It was...an amazing example of the parasitic human desire to eat at another('s) table...to poison their host...(It) dragged on for years; thousands upon thousands of pages of testimony...several...lawsuits were carried to the Supreme Court...in every case the decision was in favor of...Bell." *Thomas & Thomas*

During this period Bell wrote Mabel: *"The more fame a man gets for an invention, the more does he become a target...if my ideas are worth patenting, let others do it... endure...worry, the anxiety...expense...the feverish, anxious life* (is making me) *irritable, peevish...disgusted with life..."* and further: *"Don't be so distressed about the article in the* Times, *I am...troubled too...because you are...Let the press quarrel over the inventor of the telephone...Why should it matter...who invented...so long as the world gets the benefit of it? Why should it matter...what the world says...so long as I have obtained...which I laboured and have got you my sweet...darling wife?...why should it matter...you and... little Elsie so long as the pecuniary benefits...are not taken from us - and so long as you are conscious of my uprightness and integrity?...priority will...be settled by the Patent Office...Truth and Justice will triumph in the end...Let others vindicate my claims...but keep me out of the strife...I am sick...and...done with it altogether, excepting as a plaything to amuse...*(my further work) *let it be from the love of science..."*

Umberto Eco and *G.B. Zorzoli* provide a European perspective:

"*Antonio Meucci*, born in Florence in 1808, fled from Italy after the insurrections of 1833...he was a stage mechanic in Havana...in his spare time went in for electrotherapy to relieve...rheumatic pains. During...his experiments he placed a copper strip in a patient's mouth while holding another holding close to his own ear...to identify the affected part while passing a (electric battery) current...through the two points...feeling the current the patient screamed and it seemed to Meucci...in the next room, that he heard the noise through the strip in his ear. Although...only imagination, it was...important since it gave Meucci the idea that words could be transmitted by...electricity...Meucci pursued his researches. First he used a cardboard cone to receive the sounds better, then he tried to insert an animal membrane to increase the vibrations...and finally he replaced the copper strip with a conductor wire wound round a...bar of soft iron. It would be wrong...to refer to this as a telephone as the essential element was still missing and was...introduced by Meucci in 1854 (when) he substituted a metal diaphragm for the membrane and constructed the first telephone microphone and receiver. The metal diaphragm was essential because vibrations near the iron bar caused a variation in the magnetic field which generated the sound currents. In 1856 Meucci set up the first telephone line in history, between the candle factory which he owned on Staten Island and his sick wife's bedroom. Meucci's telephone was more or less complete and quite efficient...he had already foreseen a telegraphic-type of call sign and a way to supply the speaking circuit through a battery... *(10Apr1989, The New York Times noted a commemoration that in 1871 Meucci filed a caveat with the Patent Office for an invention that transmitted speech by electricity but lack of money prevented him from securing a patent)*...During this period, in order to experiment with his telephone over a long distance. Meucci got in touch with the president of the New York District Telegraph Co., who promised to try it...The test never took place but the designs which Meucci had sent in were never returned...Graham Bell, the company's advisor, presented his request for a patent very shortly after, and in view of the similarity between the two systems suspicion was aroused that he had profited by Meucci's designs. The controversy lasted some time and in 1883 there was a court case won by Bell. The truth is that, as with many other inventions, the technological situation was ripe and similar ideas occurred simultaneously to several gifted men. Reis's 'telephone' was constructed in 1861 and when Alexander Graham Bell applied for a patent on 14th February 1876, a Chicago electrician, Elisha Gray, lodged another application less than two hours later. Gray's telephone was almost identical with Bell's and in some ways better...a court case established Bell's claim. When production of telephones began...the Patent Office was besieged by at least thirteen applications from...inventors who claimed to be the first...Edison among them. Meucci, for lack of money, was forced to remain outside the controversy, from which Bell emerged victorious."

Unheralded and unknown, Meucci died in 1889.

The European patent situation was murky and contentious: After the British patent question was settled, Germany's appeared lost; a local representative saved Austria; and in France it was salvaged by Hubbard's legalistic maneuvering. In Scandinavia, Norway's Jens Hopstock took out patents in Bell's name and was initially rewarded. But error and apparent duplicity soon led Hubbard to have Reynold's organization take over there, also.

"As for other foreign rights not included in the trust, Bell like...Napoleon, parceled out nations as gifts to sundry relatives. Australia, for example, went to Symonds cousins. His father got three-fourths of the Canadian rights and Charles Williams the remainder, in return for supplying a thousand telephones. Mrs. Hubbard was later given Bell's rights in Scandinavia, then sold them to Mabel for twenty thousand dollars in cash. Italy was saved when a wealthy Boston friend, one of the Sears family, volunteered to pay the patent expenses as a gift; Bell insisted, however, on regarding the money as a business loan. Then he gave Italy to his brother Melly's widow Carrie, now the wife of a Brantford farmer named George Ballachey. Assorted nations went to Uncle David, Bell cousins, and others..."

Robert Bruce

10Nov'79: After many years of legal skirmishing, the trial finally concluded with Western Union receiving twenty percent of the Bell Company's stock while relinquishing its telephone business and patents thereto (the "great *Dowd* battle" was settled in 1881).

It had been a time that revealed Bell's prodigious *"capacity for long-sustained mental effort"* (A similar description to Bishop Wright's of Wilbur when, in 1912, he was in a patent fight with Curtiss and, *in effect*, Bell: "*Wilbur began his examination on the testimony in the Curtiss case. The amount of his intellectuality, in describing their invention, was marvelous. It must have greatly wearied him*").

James Storrow (of Boston's Charles River-hugging Storrow Drive), Bell's attorney, wrote him: "*You know how much I like to work with you because you are quick to catch an idea - but the real excellence of your deposition and its naturalness lies in the fact that*

27

in telling your own history you are telling the story of the man who invented and who knew that he had invented the electric speaking telephone."

Among many incidents during the litigation, one was unusually wry: Early in Gray's cross examination, when his 5Mar'77 letter to Bell was introduced, he said: *"I'll swear to it, and you can swear at it!"*

But, as Britisher William Preece observed in 1878, peace was not to be: *"When once ...a new thing is shown to be true, a host of detractors delight in proving that it is not true. The inventor is shown to be a plagiarist or a purloiner or something worse... Professor Bell will have to go through all this..."*

"This time it was a charge of 'collusion and bribery' entered against him by the Attorney General of the United States (*Augustus Garland, former Senator from Arkansas*). Instigated by Pan-Electric Company, this charge represented Bell as having contrived with the Patent Office...to give him a claim to patents he had stolen from other inventors. And thus the Government of the United States, as plaintiff, was indicting Bell for *'having perpetrated the most gigantic fraud of the century.'*

"A most gigantic fraud it was; but Bell was not the perpetrator. In the congressional investigation that followed - amid a deluge of journalistic garbage heaped upon Bell without the slightest shred of evidence - it was established that not only was Bell innocent of the charge but that the Attorney General was personally interested in the Pan-Electric Company to the extent of a million-dollar investment....

"The case was becoming too 'hot' for the Attorney General and the Pan-Pacific Company - especially since the backers of this company were already under injunction for infringement of the Bell patents. The case against Bell was dropped - and from then on he was allowed to live in peace."   *Thomas & Thomas*

James Storrow, again Bell's counsel for these government charges (which began in 1888), was further witness of his mind and memory when, at one point in this complex case, Bell's fury was abated by his publishing a 19-page pamphlet refuting Garland's claims.

The trial concluded in 1892. Bell's direct and cross-examination filled 445 pages of a Bell Company's 1908 account. The end of all litigation - comprising over six hundred cases, big and small, fascinating in concept, fraud and legalistic bombast - came after eighteen wearying years. Trial records filled 149 volumes. The verdicts were absolute:

Alexander Graham Bell conceived, made practical and patented the telephone.

Regardless, Dolbear and Gray - continuing their careers, in Dolbear's case, invention and teaching at Tufts, for Gray oft-times illustrious and profitable invention - did not cease venting their frustrations.

In 1901 Bell wrote: *"Ever since the commencement of litigation in telephone matters, I have been obliged to keep silence - my counsel always advising me that the <u>Courts</u> would look after my reputation and sustain my rights - which they have always done. This* *was pretty hard to do at first, and I can remember how I used to writhe - in silence - under the unscrupulous attacks which were made upon me. But as years went by I became callous and indifferent as to what people thought or said about me or the telephone...For some time past I have felt that the articles which have appeared in the public press demanded some reply, but I did not care to undertake it myself, and my old defenders have all passed away...I had almost reached the conclusion that the time had come for me to speak out in my own behalf, when the sudden death of Elisha Gray caused me to change my mind...I had a very high respect for Elisha Gray, and have always had the feeling that he and I would have become warm friends had it not been for the intermeddling of lawyers and the exigencies of lawsuits...Whatever Mr. Gray may have thought of me, I have always had the kindest feelings towards him; and it therefore seemed inopportune that I should say anything in conflict with his claims...when we are all mourning his loss."*

From its beginnings The Bell Trust suffered because of misunderstandings between Bell and his father-in-law, but in 1880 the air cleared and under Hubbard's able trusteeship grew; by 1887 it had almost reached its $200,000 goal, and by Hubbard's death in 1897 was $260,000 (approximately $15 million today).

While patent disputes subsided, other problems developed. In 1879 the Bell Co., its debt burdensome, merged with the New England Telephone Co. to form the National Bell Telephone Co.; soon Bell, Sanders and Hubbard were relegated to but serving on its five man executive committee.

Watson, young and wealthy, left invention for a life of travel, self-education, and business. In 1901 he founded one of America's biggest shipbuilders, the Fore River Ship and Engine Co. But earlier, on 8Jul'77, when dismantling their old laboratory, he'd had the foresight to save a precious memento:

"This wire connected Room No. 13 with Room No. 1, at 5 Exeter Place, and is the wire that was used in all the experiments, by which the telephone was developed, from the fall of 1875 to the summer of 1877, at which latter time the telephone had been perfected for practical use. T. A. WATSON"

15Feb'80: The Bell's second child was born, in Washington. Christened *Marian* (1880-1962), after Mabel's younger sister, she was always known as *"Daisy."*

From 1880-on Bell tended to dismiss business matters while reaching a sometimes difficult contentment with life and family, now including two daughters (the deaths of two sons in premature childbirth greatly scarred their parent's lives). Years later he commented: *"I am not a business man and must confess that financial dealings are distractful to me and not at all in my line."*

Bell and Mabel, who in March, 1879, owned 1106 of National Bell's 7,250 shares, about 15 percent then selling for about $65 a share, had little idea of just how profitable the company would become. Mabel thought that an income of $15,000 a year, enough for a *"fine house and a carriage,"* about right. Alec thought otherwise, that $5,000 (approximately $450,000 today) was ample. In 1880 Bell wrote his father that his Americansources income alone totaled $24,000 (about $2-1/4 million today): "*We should be able to live on that.*"

However, Mabel, apparently believing that the stock price would never be so high again, pleaded: "*Enclosed please find a bank power of attorney to sell seven hundred of my shares at sixty-five dollars each immediately. Mama says Papa and Mr. Morgan* (John Pierpont Morgan, 1837-1913, Wall Street's all-powerful head of money and monopoly, e.g., In 1902, challenged by 'Trustbuster' Theodore Roosevelt, he told the President: "*Have your man* [the Attorney General] *talk it over with my man* [his attorney]." That Morgan somehow equaled or out-ranked the president incensed Roosevelt) *both think this the time to sell, that later on I won't be able to get so much money, so...sell out immediately, please, please, please, please, please, PLEASE, PLEASE, PLEASE. Are you sufficiently impressed by the importance ...now? If you love me do do something right away the moment you get this...*"

Within seven months they'd sold most of their stock; average price of $250-a-share. By November, after the announcement of the Bell Company's agreement with Western Union, it sold for $1,000. In 1881 they sold a third of their remaining stock and, in spite of all the corporate evolutions between 1877 and 1879 - from the Bell Co. to the Bell Telephone Co., then the New England Telephone Co. and finally to the National Bell Telephone Co. - in 1883 their investments were worth around a million dollars (over $90 million today) yielding an annual income of over $35,000 (about $3.5 million today).

Regardless, they spent more, causing Hubbard's 1893 comment of Bell's not being "*as considerate in regard to your expenditures as you were ten or twelve years ago...*"

"For some years telephones were so expensive that only the rich could afford them... in the 1880s it cost about $10 to have a phone installed - which in those days was as much as a servant earned in a whole year!" *Richard Tames*

In 1882 the Bells moved into "*one of the largest and probably the most costly of... *(Washington's) *new houses...perfectly built and elegant in every appointment*" at 1500 Rhode Island Avenue, an entire block on Scott Circle. Its cost, including remodeling and finish, was well over $125,000 (approximately $10 million today).

In 1889 a reporter visited Bell in his third-floor office-study: "*...Books are everywhere. An easy lounge lies in front of the fire, and a globe stands in one corner. At a common flat walnut desk, sitting on an office chair cushioned with green leather, Mr. Bell works. The desk is covered with books and papers ...A porcelain hand with letters pasted on it lies at one side, and this, I am told, is an invention for teaching deaf children to converse with each other by touching certain spots on the hand, which represents letters...Bell had...the dark complexion of a Spaniard. His face is full and regular, and his forehead very high and whiter than the rest of his face. His hair is thick, and its color is that of oiled ebony. His face is covered with a full, black beard, which curls and twists, and his eyes are a soft, velvety black. He dresses usually in business clothing, and he is democratic in his manners...*"

Soon after the reporter's visit the house was sold - for $95,000 - to *Levi Morton*, the new vice-president under President Benjamin Harrison.

After renting a couple years on 19th Street, they built a three-story, red brick and stone home at 1331 Connecticut Avenue, across the street from the Hubbard's and next door to banker-cousin Charles Bell's new residence. They remained there for the rest of their lives (razed in 1930; today it's an office building) except during Washington's hot summers, when they'd escape to cooler northern climes, usually New England.

However, in 1885, venturing further they discovered the charms of Nova Scotia; quaint Baddeck village and especially its nearby headlands and inlets. And its many Scot-named inhabitants reminded him of the lochs of his youth.

They returned in1886 and purchased fifty acres on Redhead Point, overlooking a lovely ocean inlet called Bras d'Or Lakes. Over the next seven years they purchased the surrounding land, even a cottage on Baddeck's side of the bay.

In 1889 Bell renamed his expanding property *"Beinn Bhreagh,"* Gaelic for Beautiful Mountain, and in 1892, from a Boston architect's plans, they built their summer home for $22,000 (well over $1.5 million today).

When completed in 1893, *"The Bell Palace at Baddeck...Said To Be The Finest Mansion in Eastern Canada,"* was a massive Victorian *"French chateau"* with eleven fireplaces and rooms enough for twenty-six people, plus servants. Over the years they added guest and employee cottages, a laboratory, warehouse, wharves, boathouses, stables, dairy, farm, orchards, and gardens. By 1907 there were twelve miles of roads serving Bell's baronial village.

31

"The Bell Palace at Baddeck...":

Elsie May, Mabel, Marian (Daisy) and Alec Bell in December, 1885:

Typically, the family lived in Washington in winter, heading to Cape Breton in the spring.

In 1895 Beinn Bhreagh's expenses were $10,000 (well over a half-million today), for which Mabel explained to her father:

"I am not at all troubled about our financial condition, it is much better than it was this time last year, and our income is large enough for any reasonable family.. It is only that we always spend before we get our money...I can't see why we shouldn't have a good time with our money while...young enough to enjoy it."

In 1896, considering her income "*moderate,*" Mabel wrote her mother: "*I do try to be careful, yet there is eight hundred* (about $50,000 today) *owing on the vase for Momma's golden wedding...I will not hire a carriage and pair as I intended, but must get a trap* (front seat divided to allow access to rear seat; rear seat-back foldable) *because the carryall* (a light, covered 4-person carriage) *Perrin drives is really not respectful...*"

At the same time Bell wrote Hubbard: "*I highly approve of your plan of reinvesting the income of the Trust as far as possible, it is the only way in which we can save anything...*" However, in *1900* Mabel calculated their income as *$37,615.63* (well over $1-1/2 million today) and expenditures as *$45,415.53* (over $2 million today), and in *1913* the <u>Mentor</u> magazine wrote: "*His income is said to be more than $1,000,000 a year*" (over $45 million today).

Earlier Gardiner Hubbard lamented to his wife: "*Eighteen months ago I knew not where to beg or borrow one hundred dollars...It does seem as though the good time might really come at last. I wished several times last night that we were ten years younger and might have that much more time to enjoy it...*"

And Watson's sagacity is notable: "Tom Watson...saw clearly how valuable was the contribution of each (*Bell, Hubbard, and Sanders*) and they...recognized the value of Watson's intelligence, youthful energy, and unmatched telephonic experience...for keeping the...quality of the company's instruments and...competence of its agents...ahead of the competition at the crucial time of first public impressions...And when in February 1879 Hubbard reluctantly but inevitably surrendered the absolute voting majority given him by his and Mabel's...stock, and with it his dictatorial authority, he left Theodore Vail (*recruited from the Railway Mail Service*), prototype of the new class of professional corporate managers, in masterful charge of operations. Bell's luck was in the box and driving four-in-hand."
                                                                    Robert Bruce

Soon Vail's genius had Western Union's Western Electric taking over Williams' beleaguered shop and led to the motto: "*One Policy, One System, Universal Service.*"

In 1890 Mark Twain wrote a Christmas piece for the New York *World*: "*It is my heart-warm and world-embracing Christmas hope and aspiration that all of us - the high, the low, the rich, the poor, the admired, the despised, the loved, the hated, the civilized, the savage - may eventually be gathered together in a heaven of everlasting rest and peace and bliss - except the inventor of the telephone.*"

In good humor, Gardiner Hubbard complained. Twain responded: "*To the father-in-law of the Telephone*"...explaining that the Hartford telephone system was "*The very worst on the face of the whole earth...And if you try to curse through the telephone, they shut you off. It is this ostentatious holiness that gravels me. Every day I go there to practice and always I get shut off...For your sake I wish I could think of some way to save him, but there doesn't appear to be any. Do you think he would like me to pray for him? I could do so under an assumed name, & might have some influence...Meantime, good wishes and a Merry Christmas to you, Sir!*"

As the end of the century approached, Bell found himself increasingly absorbed with things other than telephones. One of his last was in October, 1892, when he was the central figure at the historic opening of the New York-Chicago telephone line:

In addition to their life in Washington and Baddeck, the family, in the grand style of the day, traveled the world: Europe in 1880, 1881-82, 1888, 1891-92, 1895, 1901 (Alec stayed home), 1907, 1909, and 1920; Mexico in 1895, Japan in 1898, and most of the Orient in 1910 - with Bell quietly relishing the adulation so often showered upon him.

However, regardless of his being such a famous and popular figure, he was a very private person, as he wrote to Mabel in 1883: "*I have made a great many acquaintances but very few friends.*"

Several have attempted to discern or explain facets of Bell's hidden self. Mabel, the one that should him best, in 1895 complained: "*Your deaf mute business is hardly human to you. You are very tender and gentle to the deaf children, but their interest in you lies in their being deaf, not in their humanity, at least only in part.*" And earlier, in 1876, he'd told Mabel: "*I often feel like hiding myself away in a corner out of sight...Whenever I try to say anything I stop all conversation. If there is anything of value in what I say people leave all the talking for me to do - and I don't like it at all.*"

Although within the realms of Washington considered a private person, in Baddeck Bell's nature changed markedly. *Grace*, Mabel's sister, noted that he "*is quite a different person here from what he is in Washington. Here he is the life and soul of the party...*" with Mabel's comment: "*Nothing is done without him. He is forever on the go. At night when all are sleeping he paddles about...When a high wind is blowing or the boat is to be moved he is up, no matter how early the hour, directing, arranging everything...*"

And, with a keen sense of humor, he was adept with a pun or joke, though at times its gist may have been was lost on the responder; one, Uncle David Bell's son, *Charles*, in 1880 when briefly his secretary. Later Charles courted Mabel's sister, *Roberta*, and, like Alec, was rebuffed by her father because of having no means of supporting a wife. But love persevered, they married, and Charles Bell became a successful Washington banker. Roberta died in 1885 and in 1887 he married Grace, the Hubbard's other daughter.

With the most famous Bell in Washington, the family congregated there. In 1881 Melville and Eliza moved to nearby Georgetown, sharing a home with the Symonds girls, Eliza's three unmarried nieces. And Melville's brother, David, and his wife moved next door, with Aileen, their daughter, keeping house.

But fame - and genetics - has its price. In 1890 Alec wrote Mabel: "*I feel more and more as I grow older the tendency to retire into myself and be alone with my thoughts. I can see that same tendency in my father and Uncle in an exaggerated degree - and suppose there is something in the blood. My children have it too, but in lesser degree – because they are younger I suppose. You alone are free of it - and you my dear constitute the chief link between myself and the world outside.*"

And time and again there's Mabel's wifely wisdom. In 1888 she wrote: "*Accept all invitations to dinner you get and meet all the great men you can - I want to hear all about them. I always feel as if you were my second self and all of the gorgeous people you meet I meet too, and enjoy far more than if I really met them. Never mind a little dyspepsia. We'll go home to Cape Breton and live on bread and milk the rest of the summer.*"

And in 1895 she wrote from Paris: "*I cannot bear to think of you living all alone, shut in yourself, holding no communication with your neighbors...<u>Please please</u> don't go back to such a life...Please try to come out of your hermit cell...I want you to succeed in your experiments, but not to lose all human interest in the process...*"

Helen Keller, Anne Sullivan and Bell, July, 1894:

In 1887 an Alabama newspaper editor, having almost given up hope of finding a teacher, brought his deaf and blind daughter to see Bell. As he tried to communicate with the six-year-old girl, though complete words never exchanged, feelings were.

Eighteen years later *Helen Keller* described that experience as "*the door through which I should pass from darkness to light.*"

Though Bell's work with her was significant, it's not of this story. However, *Anne Sullivan*, Helen's extraordinary companion and tutor, wrote of him:

"*Gifted with a voice that itself suggested genius, he spoke the English language with a purity and charm which have never been surpassed by anyone I have heard speak. I listened to every word, fascinated...I never felt at ease with anyone until I met him. I was extremely conscious of my crudeness*

35

...Dr. Bell had a happy way of making people feel pleased with themselves. He had a remarkable faculty of bringing out the best that was in them. After a conversation with him I felt released, important, communicative. All the pent-up resentment within me went out ...I learned more from him than from anyone else. He imparted knowledge with a beautiful courtesy that made one proud to sit at his feet and learn. He answered every question in the cool, clear light of reason...(with) *no trace of animus against individuals, nations, or classes. If he wished to criticize and he often did, he began by pointing out some-thing good I had done in another direction..."*

But his focus upon his work, friends, *and* this young lady caused problems. His daughters were maturing into lovely young ladies and he was not paying attention.

Earlier, in 1885, Mabel had written him: "*Your children need you, their characters are unfolding and they are a puzzle to me. All our lives we may regret that you are too absorbed in irregular night work – tending where? - to give them the care I cannot. I believe in God. Perhaps the reason our boy was taken from us so early was that we have not done our duty by the children we have...Why was our wealth given to us if not to give* you *time to make up to* your *children what they lose from their mother's loss..."*

In 1895, Elsie, in an oblique reference to Helen Keller, said to her mother: "*Mamma, do you know I don't think Papa quite appreciates us. He thinks I can't do anything but swim and that is because he taught me himself.*"

And later that summer, after Mabel got Alec to join them in France, she wrote: "*At home he always has something* (now including genetics and sheep breeding) *in which he is absorbed, but away, with nothing to do but be attentive to his wife and children he devotes himself absolutely to that, and they enjoy it.*"

And his night-working habits were always cause for comment. Early in their marriage Mabel wrote: "*...Our worst quarrels have always been about that. No, the front rank belongs to that all important one of getting up in the morning, but this follows close behind.*" With no solution in sight, in 1904 he resolved: "*For years past, I have formed the habit of retiring at 4 A.M. and I have come to the conclusion that it would be best for us all around if I could substitute early morning work for late night work.*"

It didn't work. And getting him up often took Herculean effort. Elsie recalled him as: "*...the soundest sleeper I have ever known...He was so hard to awaken that he often stayed up all night in order to be up on time for an early morning engagement. His eyes were very sensitive to light and he used to wind a heavy bath towel around his head to keep out the light.*"

Another facet of his personality, noted in 1885: "*I have found by experience that I can only deal with one thing at a time. My mind concentrates itself on a subject that happens to occupy it and then all things else in the Universe - including father, mother, wife, children,* life itself, *become...of secondary importance...*"

Mabel added: "*The thing he was working on was always the biggest and most important thing to him for the time being...he could not be moved.*"

Even though, since 1880, he'd been a member of Washington's prestigious *Cosmos Club* - its membership composed primarily of the scientific establishment - he preferred one-on-one discussion. In 1906 Mabel cautioned her daughter: "*Just let him talk and don't have other people maintaining private conversations at the same time. He likes what he calls 'general conversation' when each one at the table listens to one speaker and is listened to in turn. Even two people talking privately and softly together bothers him."*

There's a history here: With Washington attracting some of the nation's most distinguished individuals, including those of scientific achievement, as early as 1879 Gardiner Hubbard introduced his son-in-law to the joys of stimulating discourse among intellectual peers. By the mid-80s, Bell, playing the piano and accompanied by cello and violin, was hosting Monday evening musicals. At first more social than cerebral, by the mid-90s they'd evolved into his noted *Wednesday Evenings*.

He was most careful in planning and orchestrating these. One guest would usually give a short talk on his specialty, followed by a discussion and then wide-ranging conversations in which Bell, with his usual aloofness, usually listened rather than participated.

Among the nineteen guests in April, 1896: William McGee, G. Brown Goode, Edward Morse, naturalist Alpheus Hyatt, William Brewer, Samuel Scudder, engineering's William Sellers, medicine's John Shaw Billings and George Sternberg, Senator Francis Cockrell of Missouri, Postmaster General William Wilson, and one of Bell's few intimates, John Wesley Powell, the one-armed explorer of the Grand Canyon and director-emeritus of the U.S. Geological and Geographical Survey. And, possibly to add sparks, paleontology foes Othneil Marsh and Edward Cope.

And he was an omnivorous reader, e.g., in 1892 he told Mabel that after an evening reading Jules Verne he continued: *"...my usual reading, Johnson's Encyclopaedia. Find this makes splendid reading matter for night. Articles not too long - constant change in the subjects of thought - always learning something I have not known before – provocative of thought - constant variety."*

In 1907, about when our story begins to coalesce, Mabel wrote her husband: *"You have lived too much by yourself. You've talked about nature and solitude and all that, but you haven't been in a crowd at all and that's what you need."*

In 1880, honoring Bell's invention of the telephone, France awarded him its *Volta Prize* (established by Napoleon to honor Italian physicist *Alessandro Volta*, 1745-1827, who, in 1775, described his *electrofore perpetuo* [electrophorus] for producing and storing a charge of static electricity, leading to modern electrical condensers).

In 1881, planning to mainly experiment with things electrical and with assistants Chichester Bell, his English cousin and a competent chemist, and Sumner Tainter, Bell used the 50,000 franc prize, $10,000 (well over three-quarters of a million today) to fund the *Volta Laboratory*, with this preamble: *"We fully decided...to devote our time to something that would pay...so that I might have a self supporting laboratory..."* and, as he explained years later, we *"...agreed that none of us should claim as his own, ideas that had not been reduced to writing. We were all provided with scribbling-books and our claims to invention were to stand or fall by our written notes. The result of this process is seen in the fact that my name does not appear in any of the patents covering the Graphophone (a simple reversal of Edison's "phonograph"). I was the most delinquent in the matter of written notes, and my work which was largely that of directing and guiding the various lines of experiments did not come out in any patentable form."*

Their first project was the *spectraphone*, an offshoot of the *photophone*, which, just before his death, Bell declared: *"...as the greatest invention I have ever made; greater than the telephone.*" Though he now termed it *Radiophony*, it was never proven useful for much beyond six or seven hundred feet - and Marconi's development of Tesla's invention of radio (Patent No. 645,576 of 1897) doomed it.

But their work took a turn when, on 2Jul'81, President James Garfield was shot and Bell, with his *induction balance* apparatus, tried to locate the imbedded bullet. Though his concepts were valid, a series of mishaps - including a steel-sprung bed - spelled failure for Bell and an unrelated death for Garfield (if they'd let the bullet be, like with many similar Civil War wounds, he may have survived).

This led him to a *telephonic needle probe* for locating bullets. Interestingly, this precursor of X-ray (discovered by Wilhelm Roentgen in 1895) was usurped from an uncomplaining Bell by John Girdner (who even claimed its invention) and was used in the Sino-Japanese War, the Boer War and World War I until supplanted by X-ray.

Also, the death in 1881 of Edward, Bell's second son, because of respiratory failure after premature childbirth led to his manually-powered *vacuum jacket* (an early variation of polio's half-century-later mechanically-powered *iron lung*).

Their Volta Laboratory's work rivaled Edison's Laboratory. Sumner Tainter:

"*We made many experiments with etching records and also with electroplating or building up of the record; with various arrangements for bringing in some auxiliary power to work the cutting style; with various methods of reproducing the sound without contact with the record (magnets, air-jets, and radiant energy were used for this purpose – antedating laser). Differently shaped cutting styles and those not adapted to cutting were tried. Much time was devoted to electrotyping, moulding and making copies of records. Records were made by means of photography, and by sensitive jets of liquids. We experimented with stearine* (the solid portion of a fat), *stearine and wax, stearine and paraffin, wax and oil. We tried many forms of reproducers making records of music by direct transfer of the vibration of the sound board. We made records by jets of semi-fluid substances* (including maple syrup) *deposited on the recording surface, also records on narrow strips of paper coated with wax-like composition* (tape recordings); *records on wax-coated paper, disks and tubes, with many forms of machines for using wax-coated disks and cylinders, with many forms of recorders and reproducers for wax-coated cylinders and with various forms of speaking and hearing tubes.*"

By 1884 Chester Bell and Tainter had several concepts for which patents were applied in 1885 and 1886. On Chester's specialty, telephone transmitters using jets, he received four patents, while Tainter received two for phonographic devices. But a problem arose when the most important innovation, Tainter's idea, the incising specification, was issued as Patent No. 341,214 in *both* their names. Tainter was not mollified upon learning that the attorney's wanted: "*the Bell name hitched on to a patent, for it improved the outlook from the business man's standpoint. The justice of the matter did not trouble them.*" In 1888 Bell cleared the air by giving Tainter "*exclusive credit...for the instrument in its present condition.*"

Negotiations were initiated to merge Volta and Edison, but Edison's tough bargaining and focus on lighting doomed it – while reinvigorating him with the phonograph and his desire to out-invent the Volta group - whom, alluding to their copying his phonograph, he referred to as a "*bunch of pirates.*" As things turned out, *whom* the brigands were is conjecture, for Edison used Tainter's *floating stylus incising* instead of indenting the wax cylinder in his phonograph.

In 1886, Chester and Charles Bell led the group's evolution into the Volta Graphophone Co., which reemerged as American Graphophone Co. with Bell, Tainter, and the Bell brothers major stockholders. Its profits provided a comfortable existence (in 1890 Bell sold his quarter-share for $100,000, over $6-million today).

Sumner Tainter continued his remarkable phonographic work, and, in 1905, retired to San Diego (where Waldo Waterman first flew in 1909; and, in 1911, Glenn Curtiss achieved so much of his pivotal aeronautical work), while Chester Bell returned to Oxford, England, "experimenting in a small way" until his death in 1924.

Though Bell's interest in invention may have waned, his interest in science and technology did not: to the end of his life he sought "to achieve something great."

In 1889, apparently under Mabel's urging, he and two new assistants, William Ellis and Baddeck's Arthur McCurdy, set up a laboratory in a stable behind Bell's father's Georgetown home; described by a reporter in 1895: "*...passing through a workshop containing benches and machinery,* (we) *came into a large room walled with shelves and filled with models and instruments of all kinds...Filling up nearly the whole floor was what at first sight seemed a model of a new threshing machine* (at a time when most Americans still lived a farming life and harvesting innovations were rife)...*It was a typesetting machine for the instruction of the deaf* (Ottmar Mergenthaler's linotype machine revolutionized printing but a decade earlier)...*by which words could be put upon a blackboard and the letters distributed again. On the shelves in the walls at the left were...fifty models of telephones...among them the first one Mr. Bell ever made...Beyond this were scores of cylinders used in experiments up-on the graphophone, little bottles of selenium ...many scientific instruments, inventions illustrating new and yet unexplained theories as to the property of matter, originated by Mr. Bell...*"

They worked on producing phonograph records, making prints from photographs; sonic sounding; an automatic telephone switchboard; the photophone, now called radiophone (see above); the vacuum jacket; the induction balance; lifeboat water-making devices; wired brain-to-brain thought transference; a fast, revolving-hull boat; and "*seeing by electricity*" using selenium, and, later, Roentgen rays and florescent screens. None, however, ever developed to caveats or patents.

Though Edison's life is not our focus, it would be remiss to not include its summary:

"A natural tendency is to measure Bell against Edison. The two men were born within a few days of each other; they were both famous for inventive concepts astonishing in their combination of simplicity, originality, and social impact; and they even leapfrogged each other in their inventive work. Bell, like Edison, retained fertility of technological imagination well into later life. But unlike Edison, Bell did not show it to the public. He recorded his ideas in his private notebooks and moved on without devoting himself to cultivation and harvest, whereas Edison never ceased to push his...ideas through development and patenting to commercial use."
Robert Bruce

"The Edison system of lighting was beautifully conceived down to the very details and as thoroughly worked out as if it had been tested for decades...Neither sockets, switches, fuses, lampholders, nor any of the other accessories necessary to complete the installations were wanting; and the generating of the current, the regulation, the wiring with distribution boxes, house connections, meters, etc., all showed signs of astonishing skill and incomparable genius."
Emil Rathenau, Paris, 1881

Edison, seated, and phonograph co-inventor Charles Batchelor, right, and Uriah Painter, Washington, 1878:

Edison's Laboratory, Menlo Park, 1880:

The Youth's Companion, 22Jun'05:

A MUSICAL CLUB
Listening to a Vocal or Instrumental Masterpiece or New Opera.

THE EDISON PHONOGRAPH enables Schools, Clubs or Families to hear the choicest music performed by the best artists, at their own school, meeting-room or home. For instance, a faithful reproduction of the performances of the 23d Regt. Band will be a guide to other bands how to render the music, or a vocal gem will be sung by the voice of a famous artist, selections from Shakespeare and the best authors or poets may be obtained as recited by eminent actors or readers.

In a word the musical and literary world will give its treasures to owners of the Phonograph at the smallest cost.

Full information sent Free on application.

THE NORTH AMERICAN PHONOGRAPH CO.,

30 Park Place, NEW YORK.   Ledger Building, PHILADELPHIA.
17 West Swan Street, BUFFALO.   Masonic Temple Building, CHICAGO.

The Youth's Companion, 23Nov'93:

"Edison's inventions are like the building blocks of an obelisk rising out of the history of the world. No other man has ever been responsible for striking the spring of so much wealth, nor had such influence on the lives of so many people...today's telephone speaker..The microphone...radio vacuum tube...alkaline battery...stored electricity... motion-picture studio...phonograph...kineto-scope...electric light and power...He was a scientific primitive with talent enough to push ahead, but not the education or sophistication to know that he was, presumably, attempting the impossible. He was the epitome of the practical inventor..."

Robert Conot

Make Money

WITH AN

Edison Phonograph

Any boy can do it. Amusement halls in big cities charge you 1c. to 5c. to hear each Edison Record. You can give Phonograph concerts to friends and neighbors and charge 5c. to 10c. admission—$1 to $2 per concert profit.

Everybody enjoys the Edison Phonograph-- big folks as well as little. There's always fun where there's a Phonograph. It soon pays for itself.

If you lack the money, ask your parents to buy one for you. Then pay them back from the concert profits.

The improved Edison Phonograph is the most perfect type of sound reproducer. It costs no more than inferior imitations, yet being constructed on the only correct scientific and mechanical principles, is far superior to all others. Edison Gold Moulded Records are highest in quality, yet lowest in price of any good records. *Every genuine Edison Phonograph* and *Edison Gold Moulded Record* bears the inventor's Trade Mark signature, thus:

TRADE MARK

Thomas A. Edison

Edison Phonographs cost from $10 up; Records, 35c. each. Write us for free list of Records and new booklet, "Home Entertainments With the Edison Phonograph," which tells how any boy or girl can conduct a Phonograph concert and make money.

Phonographs sold by dealers everywhere.

National Phonograph Co.

13 LAKESIDE AVE., ORANGE, N. J.

The Youth's Companion,
12Oct'05:

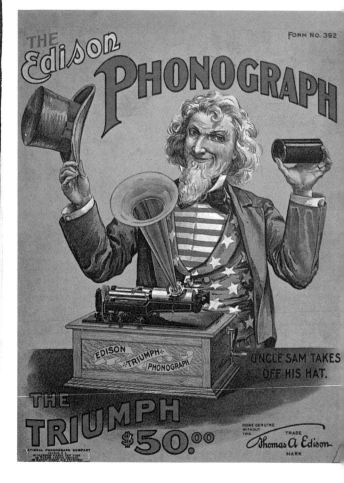

Chapter **2**   **Bell and The Beginnings of Flight: 1891-1906**

S *amuel*

Pierpont Langley spurs Bell's interest, leading to his experimenting with heavier-than-air flight. Wilbur and Orville Wright enter the scene, succeed in manned flight, and then attempt to dominate world aviation.

In the spring of 1891 Bell's inventive juices were stirred anew by thoughts of heavier-than-air flight.

Living in Washington, he became acquainted wih *Samuel Pierpont Langley* (1834-1906), since 1887 the third Secretary of the Smithsonian Institution.

Langley's earlier career had centered around physics and astronomy. In 1878 he invented the bolometer, which measured solar radiation to a millionth-degree.

But for many years he had been fascinated by flight - which began when director of the Allegheny Observatory and continued at the Smithsonian with studies of the lift and drag of moving plane surfaces.

The results, published in *Experiments in Aerodynamics* in 1890 and in 1891 in the *Smithsonian Contributions to Knowledge,* concluded that heavier-than-air flight was surely attainable.

Well aware of her husband's interest, in April, 1891, Mabel wrote him in Baddeck:

"I wish you were here only to attend the National Academy meeting and to hear the discussion on Professor Langley's flying machines. Of course the papers treat him more respectfully than they would anyone else, still they cannot resist a sly joke now and again..."

By late May, his interest whetted, Bell had begun testing the lift of propellers.

And in June, in spite of the warm weather, he returned to Washington because of *"flying machines,"* there being nothing more fascinating or challenging to him and Langley.

PROF. SAMUEL P. LANGLEY, THIRD SECRETARY OF THE INSTITUTION.

Professor Langley was born at Roxbury, Mass., in 1834. In his earlier life he was a civil engineer and architect. In 1865 he became an assistant to the director of Harvard Observatory; a few months later he was appointed a professor of mathematics at the United States Naval Academy and in 1867 accepted an invitation to the chair of astronomy in the Western University of Pennsylvania at Pittsburgh. The Observatory is at Allegheny City, and here Professor Langley has accomplished work which has won for him great distinction among astronomers and physicists. Professor Langley has been connected with several astronomical expeditions to observe solar eclipses. He was in charge of the Signal-service expedition to Mount Whitney, Col., in 1881. He has received degrees and honors from institutions of learning all over the world. He has been President of the American Association for the Advancement of Science and is a member of the Council of the National Academy of Sciences.

VISITOR'S GUIDE to The Smithsonian Institution, ca.1889-90, author's collection:

15Jun'91: An excited Bell wrote: *"...they flew for me today. I shall have to make experiments on my own account in Cape Breton. Can't keep out of it. It will be UP with us someday!"*

From then on, but not to dominate his activities or change his comfortably paced lifestyle, flight was foremost in his mind. From 1892 to 1897 he experimented at Baddeck, initially with helicopters, one even with steam-tipped rotors.

In 1893 in McClure's Magazine he's quoted: *"The more I experiment the more convinced I become that flying machines are practical...I have not the shadow of a doubt that the problem of aerial navigation will be solved within ten years. That means an entire revolution in the world's methods of transportation and of making war. I am able to speak with more authority on this subject from the fact of being actively associated with Professor Langley...in his researches and experiments..."*

And McClure's comment: *"Professor Bell has the happy faculty of expressing great ideas in simple words...He is as enthusiastic as a schoolboy thinking of the kite he will make as big as a barn door. His black eyes flash, and they seem all the blacker contrasted with his white hair; the words tumble out quickly, and those who have the good fortune to listen are carried away with the magnetism of this great inventor."*

In 1894 Mabel wrote her mother: *"Alec is simply gone over flying machines and his papers on signs, and there is very little good to be got out of him..."*

And in 1895, while in Mexico's mountains, he observed: *"...Soaring buzzard's wings turned up at tip...surface air almost calm...moved in spiral...horizontal velocity not less than 30 feet per second..."*

Bell was aware of such as *Alphonse Penaud*'s rubber band-powered, inherently stable, flying models of 1871 (Penaud, a young French genius, patented an amphibious airplane with retractable wheels in 1876, but with no suitable engine it was never tried. In 1880, when 29, he committed suicide), and his experiments covered a wide spectrum: gunpowder rockets for propulsion, pinwheel helicopter rotors, spring-powered models, monoplanes...naturally with many attendant mishaps.

Beginning in late 1894 and continuing through 1897, he concentrated on wings, propeller blades and whirling devices similar to Langley's.

But at times Langley's maddening exactitude tempered his ambitions, prompting Mabel's writing from Paris: *"...if Mr. Langley has changed your ideas, why then I can't see why you should not come over..."*

but a month later, getting to the crux of our story, she wrote: *"...I do so want your name associated with successful experiments in flying machines. I don't like to think of your stopping them unnecessarily..."*

Early in 1896 Bell is quoted in the *Cincinnati Enquirer:* *"I am at present engaged in trying to solve the problem of aerial navigation...I believe that it will be possible in a very few years for a person to take his dinner in New York at 7 or 8 o'clock in the evening and eat his breakfast in either Ireland or England the following morning..."*

9May'96: But all was tranquil between Bell and Langley when, on the Potomac River near Quantico, Virginia, Bell was the sole witness for the first trials of Langley's *"aerodrome"* (mis-coined by Langley from a Greek combination he thought meant *"air runner"*): a steam-powered, 16-foot model flying machine.

Camera-in-hand, Bell was mid-river in a rowboat, Langley, nervous on a pier, as the aerodrome was catapult-launched from a houseboat.

Bell took *"instantaneous photographs"* as Langley's craft became the *first* heavier-than-air machine to achieve *sustained* flight.

He wrote about this in Nature on 28May'96, and more extensively in McClure's Magazine, June, 1897 (author's collection): *"The 'Flying machine' By Professor S. P. Langley...With illustrations...from photographs by A. Graham Bell."*

This 15-page article describes Langley's work and first flights, with Bell's account:

"Through the courtesy of Dr. S. P. Langley, Secretary of the Smithsonian Institution, I have had on various occasions, the privilege of witnessing his experiments with aerodromes, and especially the remarkable success attained by him in experiments made upon the Potomac River on Wednesday, May 6, which led me to urge him to make public some of these results.

"I had the pleasure of witnessing the successful flight of some of these aerodromes more than a year ago, but Dr. Langley's reluctance to make the results public at that time prevented me from asking him, as I have done since, to let me give an account...

"On the date...two ascensions were made by the aerodrome, or so called 'flying machine,' which I will not describe here...than to say that it appeared to me to be built almost entirely of metal, and driven by a steam engine which I have understood was carrying fuel and...water... for a very brief period, and...was of extraordinary lightness.

"The absolute weight of the aerodrome, including that of the engine and all appurtenances, was...about 25 pounds, and the distance from tip to tip of the supporting surface was... about 12 or 14 feet. The...propulsion was by aerial screw propellers...there was no gas or other aid for lifting it in the air except its own internal energy.

"...the aerodrome, at a given signal, started from a platform about 20 feet above the water, and rose at first directly in the face of the wind, moving at all times with remarkable steadiness, and subsequently swinging around in large curves of, perhaps, a hundred yards in diameter...ascending until its steam was exhausted, when, at a lapse of about a minute and a half, and at a height...between 80 and 100 feet in the air, the wheels ceased turning, and the machine, deprived of the aid of its propellers, to my surprise did not fall, but settled down so softly and gently that it touched the water without the least shock, and was in fact immediately ready for another trial.

"In the second trial...it repeated in nearly every respect the actions of the first, except that the direction...was different. It ascended again in the face of the wind, afterwards moving steadily and continually in large curves...with a rising motion and a lateral advance. Its motion was, in fact, so steady, that I think a glass of water on its surface would have remained unspilled (yet another example of Bell's remarkable prescience). *When the steam gave out...it repeated for a second time the experience of the first trial ...and settled gently and easily down. What height it reached at this trial I cannot say, as I was not so favorably placed as in the first; but I had occasion to notice that this time its course took it over a wooded promontory, and I was relieved of some apprehension in seeing that it was already so high as to pass the tree tops by 20 or 30 feet. It reached the water 1 minute and 31 seconds from the time it started, at a measured distance of over 900 feet from the point where it rose.*

"This...was by no means the length of its flight. I estimated from the diameter of the curve...from the number of turns of the propellers, as given by the automatic counter, after due allowance for slip...that the actual length of flight on each occasion was slightly over 3,000 feet. It is...safe to say that each exceeded half an English mile.

"From the time and distance it will be noticed that the velocity was between 20 and 25 miles per hour, in a course which was taking it constantly 'up hill.'...I have seen a far higher velocity attained by the same aerodrome when its course was horizontal.

"I have no desire to enter into detail further than I have done, but I cannot but add that it seems to me that no one who was present...could have failed to recognize that the practicability of mechanical flight has been demonstrated."

ALEXANDER GRAHAM BELL
Inventor of the Telephone, Explaining the Tetrahedral Principle on Which His New Air Craft is Built

In the New York *World* Bell later wrote: *"The problem of the flying machine has been solved. Those who read this article are reading of a fulfillment of a world-old dream...fifteen years ago a man who had the temerity to deliver a serious lecture on the prospects of navigating the air would have ruined his professional reputation by the indiscretion. Now the much-derided 'cranks' are having their innings..."*

But research and investigation is, by its very nature, fraught with disappointment and dead-ends. As such, it's not clear just how Bell got into tetrahedral kites but it probably evolved from his interest in tetrahedral structures.

In a 1903 *Geographic* article he wrote that the tetrahedral cell *"is applicable to any kind of structure whatever in which it is desirable to combine the qualities of strength and lightness. Just as we can build houses of all kinds of bricks, so we can build structures of all sorts out of tetrahedral frames, and the structures so formed as to possess the same qualities of strength and lightness which are characteristic of the individual cells. I have already built a* [sheep] *house..."* (long before Buckminster Fuller's Geodesic Domes of the 1950s).

Urged on by Mabel, Bell applied for and in 1904 received Patent No. 770,626 (his first since 1886) for *"...a structure...essentially of skeleton tetrahedal elements...with... adjacent elements...directly connected at...their corners..."* (How many of today's campers assembling their lightweight tents know this?)

Aware of Hargrave's success with box kites, Bell now considered tetrahedral kites. In 1898 (when the Wrights were also thinking about flight) he wrote Mabel: *"...the importance of kite flying as a step to...flying machine grows upon me."*

Also, in a 1903 <u>Geographic</u> article, he wrote that, since 1899 *"I have been ...at work upon experiments relating to kites. Why, I do not know, excepting perhaps because of the intimate connection of the subject with the flying-machine problem."*

While the Wrights considered kites a *step* in the process, Bell got side-tracked into considering his as the solution. In 1907 one of his last tetrahedral kites, pulled by a steamboat, lifted a man 170 feet in the air. Immense, it was made of 3,000 V-shaped cells - and was exceptionally stable.

Positioning a kite on the "Ugly Duckling," Bell, right, 9Aug'07:

1892 - The 'bicycle craze' sweeping America in the early 1890s prompted the Wright brother's interest in cycling and Orville's purchase of a *safety* bike (see later), soon leading them from a small, innovative job-printing business into bicycle sales and repair.

In the spring of 1893, in a shop on West Third Street in Dayton, they formed the *Wright Cycle Co.* to manufacture their *"Van Cleve"* $65, *St. Clair"* $40, and, in 1896, the $27 (over $1,500 today) *"Wright Special."*

1891: And their interest in aeronautics was initiated with articles in Century Magazine by Sir Hiram Maxim and Langley - and was furthered watching a ballooning exhibit at Chicago's 1893 Columbian Exposition & World Fair.

9Aug'96: *Otto Lilienthal* (1848-1896), the German *"father of gliding flights"* ("Birdflight as the Basis of Aviation: A Contribution Towards a System of Avation Compiled from the Results of Numerous Experiments by O. and G. Lilienthal," published in 1889, Berlin) who said: *"To fly is everything,"* killed in the crash of his bird-like hang glider.

He died still believing that the secret of flight lay not only in curved wings but in their flapping - that a powered ornithopter was the way to manned flight.

It is said his final words were: *"Sacrifices must be made."*

Orville Wright: *"In 1896 we read...of the experiments of Otto Lilienthal, who was making some gliding flights from the top of a small hill in Germany. His death a few months later while making a glide...increased our interest in the subject, and we began looking for books pertaining to flight."*

1896-97: Chicago's *Octave Chanute* (1832-1910), most respected of late-19th Century American engineers. Among his many credits, the presidency, the American Society of Civil Engineers. Born in Paris to a family steeped in intellectual and academic traditions, he came to America in 1838. With railroads sweeping the country – and talented in mathematics - at 17 he apprenticed to a rail survey crew, embarking upon mechanical engineering. By 1860 he was chief engineer, supervising track-laying for several railroads, followed by triumphs in designing the Kansas City Bridge, first over the Missouri River, and Pennsylvania's Kinzua Bridge - and the Chicago Stockyards complex.

Since about 1875 he'd collected information on flight in America and Europe, and in 1891, after retiring from active engineering, wrote his first of 27 aviation-related articles in Railroad and Engineering Journal, followed in 1894 by Progress in Flying Machines (complementing James Means Aeronautic Annuals of 1895, '96 and '97). Thus he became the *"encyclopaedist of aeronautics."*

In 1897, this 65 year old man with a young mind set down ten problems basic in solving heavier-than-air flight. Item Seven: *"Maintenance of the Equilibrium"* (control), more important than all the others combined. In 1896, while perfecting the Pratt-trussed biplane glider, Chanute's assistants *Herring, Avery, Butusov* and *Ricketts* made over a thousand flights on Lake Michigan's dunes near Miller, Indiana *(below)*. The *Chanute-Herring Glider*, miscalled the "Chanute Glider," evolved into the "*Popular Mechanics* Glider" following its description in its Apr'09 issue (but was *first* shown in the Mar'09 issue of Fly magazine).

Popular Mechanics, Apr'09 (right):

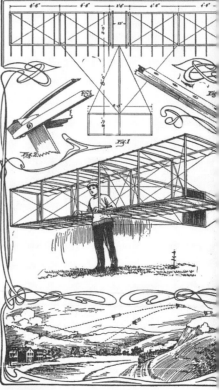

<u>Aviation</u>, 7Nov'27: *"From two dusty packing cases in the attic of a Chicago museum four of the world's most precious model airplanes have recently been discovered. They were the property of Octave Chanute, often called "the Father of American aviation', and were used by him in his study of the theory of flight as well as his practical experiments in attempting to establish the principle of equilibrium for heavier-than-air machines...His (1896) summer's work convinced him that biplane type of glider most nearly satisfied the requirements for securing 'automatic stability at all off angles of flight and conditions of wind,' which was the problem he had set himself to solve..."*

Georgia-born Augustus Moore Herring (1867-1926), called an *"amusing cuss"* by Wilbur, was destined to be one of the most enigmatic figures in aviation history, part charlatan, part real, one rarely knowing which. In 1888, due to an incomplete thesis, he failed to graduate in mechanical engineering from Hoboken's Stevens Institute. By 1894 he'd flown a Lilienthal-type glider equipped with a novel spring-controlled movable tail, and in 1895, just prior to Langley's first flights, briefly worked for him. He left Chanute after a disagreement about powering the glider, Chanute thinking it premature because of unsolved problems of balance and control.

From Chanute's diary: 31Aug'96: *"...Herring cut down 3-winged machine to two surfaces...Took a number of leaps, the longest 97 ft., and found machine stable and well able to support weight in a 15-mile northerly wind..."* 4Sep'96: *"...Got out Herring machine in forenoon. Took 10 or 12 beautiful glides..."* 13Sep'96: *"...Mr. Manley of the Record came out to make sketches. Met at hill by Mr. Herring who told him his story of a disagreement with O.C. (Chanute) for publication. Took the photo from the plate holder and another photo of the ground over which he had glided and got them developed...Then he packed in with his effects and took away next morning."*

In 1897, Herring continued experiments, and, with Matthias Arnot's backing, added propellers and a small, 2-cylinder compressed-air motor. It also had a (first) landing gear of two wide-spaced wheels *(photo, left)*.

On *11Oct '98,* Herring claimed to have made *the first powered flights* of 50 and 72-feet.

Earlier, in 1896, he'd applied for a patent on a biplane with a wheeled chassis, horizontal and vertical rudder with flexible controls, a special wing curvature – but with no trace of ailerons.

Though the Patent Office found nearly twenty fresh claims, in 1898 it refused his application, stating: *"...no power driven aeroplane has yet been raised into the air with the aeronaut or kept its course wholly detached from the earth for such considerable time as to constitute proof of mechanical usefulness."*

However, British historian Philip Jarrett writes: *"American historians have stated that Herring's attempts to patent his powered triplane were unsuccessful. This is not entirely true. In fact, although his application to the US Patent Office was rejected in January 1898 because the machine had not demonstrated 'proof of practical usefulness,' it was accepted by the British Patent Office. The patent, now taken out jointly by Chanute and Herring, was communicated to...Thomas Moy and was filed in Moy's name. It was applied for on June 25, 1897, and accepted on July 25, 1898, as No. 15,221 of 1897...The patent was also accepted in France..."*

During this period Chanute and Britain's *Percy Pilcher* (1867-1899) began a correspondence. On 29Nov'97 Chanute wrote Pilcher, who received it on 8Dec'97 (remarkably fast mail service): *"I have been hoping to see in the prints* (newspapers) *some accounts of your aeronautical experiments...I hope that you have continued your work, and have had abundant success, both in gliding and with a motor. I am still disinclined to apply the latter, as I wish to work out thoroughly the question of automatic stability...before taking any chances of accident with an engine...*

"Mr. Herring and I resumed our experiments with our former machine last September...I enclose...some photos...illustrating...flights They now number well up to 1,000 without the slightest accident, and I begin to think that we have pretty well eliminated all the hidden defects Still the man has to move occasionally to preserve his balance on this machine, and my idea is that he should not move at all, except to steer. That the wind itself should readjust the apparatus as often as the equilibrium is compromised, so as to leave the man free to run the motor, and to direct the course. I shall be very glad to hear from you and to exchange views..."

23Jan'98: Pilcher to Chanute: *"It was a great pleasure to receive your letter of November 29th...I am very much interested in your work with regard to automatic stability ...I should have been very sceptical about your high machines, I mean stable machines with the supporting surfaces so far above the man - I cannot help attributing the easiness of handling of my last wing...to the surface being...very low down...*

"I intend to make a machine something like one of your multiple sail ones, but without any automatic arrangements - I am anxious to see how I get on with it -

"From the tone you have taken...I imagine you to be much more desirous of having the general problem of flight solved, than that you should have all the honour...

"...I have an oil (gasoline) *engine on hand, but which is not yet quite finished, which I hope to put in a machine in the Summer..."*

10Feb'98, Chanute (in San Diego - for his wife's health) to Pilcher: *"...I am greatly pleased with the impression which you have derived from my writings. You are quite right: I am much more desirous of having the general problem of flight solved, than that I shall have all the honour...You are very welcome to make and use one of my multiple wing machines, and I hope that you will hit upon improvements to it which shall be all your own...*

"I regret that I cannot extend to you the same license to reproduce a 'two-surface' machine. This has a regulator designed by Mr. Herring, who believes that money is to be made out of it, and who has left me to work on his own account. He has all my good wishes, but I fear he is working towards an accident..."

3Jun'98, Chanute to Pilcher: *"...Mr. Herring has nearly completed a new 'two-surfaced' machine, to which he has applied screw propellers, driven by a compressed air engine. It will probably be tested within a month. I shall be very glad to learn of your own progress this summer, and to keep you advised as to what we do here..."*

Then ensued brief notes, Pilcher's of 24Jun'98, Chanute's of 5Aug'98 and 8Jan'99 – until, in Sep'99 Pilcher's latest flying machine neared completion: a triplane to be powered by an air-cooled *"light oil engine"* with two finned, cast bronze, opposing cylinders, steel-forged pistons, and an enclosed crankcase weighing all-told around 40 pounds.

"Historians have often stated that the triplane was the outcome of...Hargrave's... kites. This claim, however, was made in complete ignorance of the influential link between Pilcher and Chanute and the strong evidence it provides of the inspirational influence of the Chanute multiplane and biplane gliders..."   *Philip Jarrett*

On a rainy Saturday, 30Sep'99, Pilcher demonstrated his craft - gliding only - the engine was giving problems, and on the third glide *"'Mr. Pilcher rose very well,' traveling some 150 yards and reaching a height...between 30 and 60 feet. Suddenly 'a snap was heard,' the Hawk's tail 'was seen to collapse,' and the glider somersaulted forward, its wings folding upward...the Hawk 'came down heavily...with a crash that could be heard hundreds of yards,' and with Pilcher underneath the wreckage..."*

Percey Pilcher died on 2Oct1899.

1897-98: The Wright brothers begin to focus on heavier-than-air flight.

30May'99: Wilbur Wright to the Smithsonian: *"...I believe that simple flight at least is possible to man and that the experiments and investigations of a large number of independent workers will result in the accumulation of information and knowledge and skill which will finally lead to accomplished flight..*

"...I am about to begin a systematic study of the subject in preparation for practical work to which I expect to devote what time I can spare from my regular business. I wish to obtain such papers as the Smithsonian Institution has published on this subject, and if possible a list of other works in print in the English language...I am an enthusiast, but not a crank in the sense that I have some pet theories as to the proper construction of a flying machine. I wish to avail myself of all that is already known and then if possible add my mite to help on the future worker who will attain final success..." (Interestingly, his letter is first person with no mention of Orville.)

The Smithsonian sent a wealth of material, including articles and pamphlets by Chanute, Langley, Means, Louis-Pierre Mouillard and Lilienthal, which were received by Wilbur on 2Jun'99 (remarkably fast, both bureaucratic *and* postal service).

Jul-Aug'99: Idly twisting an empty bicycle innertube carton, Wilbur discovers his/ their concept of flexing or warping wings.

They then construct a Chanute-type 5-foot biplane kite with cord-operated wing warping to control lateral balance, successfully testing it on Dayton's Seminary Hill.

13May1900: Then, seeking assistance, Wilbur writes Chanute: *"...For some years I have been afflicted with the belief that flight is possible to man...I have been trying to arrange my affairs in such a way that I can devote my entire time for a few months to experiment in this field...I believe no financial profit will accrue to the inventor of the first flying machine, and that only those that are willing to give as well as to receive suggestions can hope to link their names with the honor of its discovery. The problem is too great for one man alone and unaided to solve in secret."*

Thus began a long and, until much later, close relationship with then 68-year-old Chanute, who ranked with Lilienthal and Langley *"in having brought heavier-than-air flight to the brink of reality."*

In May, 1899, Bell wrote Mabel that...*"The Laboratory Annex was so filled by the big kite that there was no room for experiment...Just fancy a kite 14 feet 7 inches long by 10-1/2 feet wide and 5 feet 2 inches high! A monster - a jumbo - a 'full-fledged white ele-phant'...I am no longer young* (at 52) *and the experiments on which I have been engaged for years should be completed sufficiently for publication, so that younger men can take up the thread of research...Don't take me...away from my work until it is finished - or I am!"* (an insightful prelude of Bell's hopes for "younger men").

As always, Mabel was there with love and support. In 1901 she wrote: *"I do so appreciate all the wonderful, unfailing, uncomplaining patience that you have shown in all your work and the quiet, persistent courage with which you have gone after one failure after another. How many there have been, how often an experiment from which you hoped great things has proved contrary. How very, very few and far apart have been your successes. And yet nothing has been able to shake your faith, to stop you in your work. I think it is wonderful and I do admire and love you more as the years go by. But oh how I wish that you may have success at last."*

"As to Bell's contributions to aviation up to this point, it can be argued that he helped keep Langley at it; and that Langley's example, his writings, and the literature supplied and recommended on request by his Smithsonian Institution helped in turn to set the Wright brothers going. The history of flight, like all history, is a web so complex and finespun that no strand can safely be called redundant."   *Robert Bruce*

September 3, 1900: Wilbur writes his father: *"It is my belief that flight is possible and while I am taking up the investigation for pleasure rather than profit, I think there is a slight possibility of achieving fame and fortune from it..."*

13Sep1900: Wilbur, soon followed by Orville, arrive and set up their first camp in the bleak, wind-torn landscape near *Kitty Hawk*, North Carolina. Their shop was left in charge of *Charles Taylor*, their trustworthy assistant who built their first engines and has been called *"the unsung hero"* of man's conquest of the skies .

Orville to Katharine: *"The economics of this place were so nicely balanced before our arrival that everybody here could live yet nothing be wasted. Our presence brought disaster to the whole arrangement. We, having more money than the natives, have been able to buy up the whole egg product of the town and about all the canned goods in the store. I fear some of them will have to suffer as a result."*

23Sep1900: Wilbur to his father: *"...I have my machine nearly finished. It is not to have a motor and is not expected to fly in any true sense of the word. My idea is merely to experiment and practice with a view of solving the problem of equilibrium..*

"I have not taken up the problem with the expectation of financial profit..."

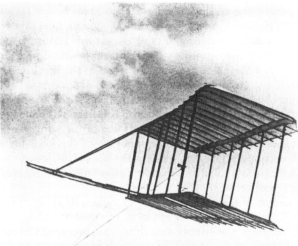

They began *"scientific kite flying"* with their 16-1/2' wingspan, 52-lb. biplane *Glider No. 1,* at Kill Devil hill (*"Big Hill"*), a 100-foot dune 4 miles south of Kitty Hawk (three hours round-trip afoot, an hour when they got a bike).

Things went well: *"...control of the machine proved even better than we had dared to expect, responding quickly to the slightest motion of the rudder..."* until 14Oct when a gust of wind smashed it.

Wilbur summarized the experiments: *"Everything seemed to us to confirm the correctness of our original opinions: (1) that practice is the key to the secret of flying; (2) that it is practical to assume the horizontal position; (3) that a smaller surface set at a negative angle in front of the main bearing surfaces, or wings, will largely counteract the effect of the fore and aft travel of the center of pressure: (4) that steering up and down can be attained with a rudder, without moving the position of the operator's body; (5) that twisting the wings so as to present their ends to the wind at different angles is a more prompt and efficient way of maintaining lateral equilibrium than shifting the body of the operator."*

26Nov1900: Wilbur writes Chanute: *"...It is not our intention to make a close secret of our machine, but at the same time, inasmuch as we have not yet had opportunity to test the fullest possibilities of our methods, we wish to be the first to give them such test We will gladly give you for your own information anything you may wish to know, but for the present would not wish any publication in detail of the methods of operation or construction of the machine..."*

1901: Wilbur: *"...if you are looking for perfect safety, you will do well to sit on a fence; but if you really wish to learn you must mount a machine and become acquainted with its tricks by actual trial..."*

They construct *Glider No. 2,* designed to carry a man. It had wings of 22-foot span and 7-foot chord. After determining the correct wing curvature, they hooked up the wing warping, controlling it with cables linked to the pilot's *movable hip cradle,* interestingly, a similar concept to the, later, A,E.A. *shoulder yoke control.* (Note: Normally, balance is controlled by a sitting or hanging pilot shifting his weight, e.g: 'hang-glider.')

4Jul'01: Wilbur writes Chanute about a proposed visit by his researcher-associates: *"...We would be pleased if our labors should be of similar benefit to others. We of course would not wish our ideas and methods appropriated bodily, but if our work suggests ideas to others which they can work out on a different line and reach better results than we do, we will try hard not to feel jealous or that we have been robbed in any way. On the other hand we do not expect to appropriate the ideas of others in any unfair way, but it would be strange indeed if we should be long in the company of other investigators without receiving suggest-ions which we could work out in such a way as to further our work..."*

10Jul'01: Returning to Kitty Hawk, they erect a building for their larger glider, but flying was not very successful and they do not learn as much as hoped.

They had visitors, Chanute, and his associates, *Edward C. Huffaker* of Tennessee, whom they later termed *"disagreeable,"* finding both his work and personal cleanliness wanting, and *George Alexander Spratt* (1870-1934) of Philadelphia, whom they liked very much - and hordes of mosquitoes.

The weather was disagreeable, too… *"we saw it a waste of time to attempt to do anything at this season of the year.."*

On 17Aug they closed camp and later Wilbur wrote *"...we were quite discouraged. We doubted that we would ever resume our experiments."*

18Sep'01: From Wilbur's paper *"Some Aeronautical Experiments:" "The difficulties which obstruct the pathway to success in flying machine construction are of three general classes: (1)...construction of the sustaining wings. (2)...generation...of ...power...to drive the machine...(3) Those relating to balancing and steering the machine...Men already know how to construct wing or aeroplanes...Men also know how to build engines and screws of sufficient lightness...This inability to balance and steer still confronts students of the flying problem...When this one feature has been worked out the age of flying machines will have arrived.."*

"...the summer's observation taught them...

"1. Published lift characteristics for curved surfaces were definitely in error.

"2. Over-all efficiency depended upon L/D rather than lift alone.

"3. The relative position of the upper and lower wings decreased the theoretical total lift of the individual surfaces...they noticed biplane effect.

"4. The customary method of expressing the air force acting on a wing in terms of a pressure normal to the chord line had led them into a misconception of the net lift and drag components..."   *M.P. Baker*

Wilbur in the 1901 glider, soaring almost motionless:

Chanute, Orville, Huffaker, and Wilbur, standing:

27Oct'01: Chanute writes Wilbur: *"...The view which you take, that the time spent in aeronautical investigations is a dead financial loss, is eminently sagacious and wise. I feel that way myself...the only method by which I have avoided neglecting my business has been to take up aeronautics intermittently..."*

During the winter, realizing the correct testing procedure was to move air *against* the object, they construct a wind tunnel. Made of wood, it was 16-in. square and 8-feet long. A 2-cylinder, 2-hp gasoline engine, originally built for shop power, drove an emery-wheel shaft with a homemade metal fan at one end while the object to be measured, shaped from old hacksaw blades and scrap, was suspended by wires in the other end. (Note: "Frank H. Wenham is generally credited with designing and operating the first wind tunnel, in 1871. A fan driven by a steam engine, propelled air down a 12-ft. tube to the model. The wind tunnel's great capacity for controlled, systematic testing quickly made whirling arm devices obsolete." NASA.)

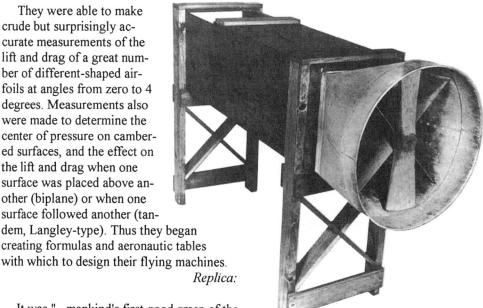

They were able to make crude but surprisingly accurate measurements of the lift and drag of a great number of different-shaped airfoils at angles from zero to 4 degrees. Measurements also were made to determine the center of pressure on cambered surfaces, and the effect on the lift and drag when one surface was placed above another (biplane) or when one surface followed another (tandem, Langley-type). Thus they began creating formulas and aeronautic tables with which to design their flying machines.

Replica:

It was "...mankind's first good grasp of the complex theoretical formulas required to predict the lifting power and behavior of different types of wings, and a clear idea of which wing designs would work and which were useless." *Sherwood Harris*

The Wrights drew the following conclusions:
1. Increasing aspect ratio does not increase maximum lift but does lower the attack angle at which maximum lift occurs.
2. Curvature gives greater lift to a surface and a steadier rate of increase.
3. The camber ratio of a curved surface has a more marked effect on drag.
4. By having the maximum camber point forward, lift is increased at the smaller angles.

They observed the inefficiency of biplane effect, the effects of the taper and cut-outs in the wing form, and noted the stall point, though not defining it as such.

This latter item, stalling, was to cause their aeroplanes considerable grief.

18Nov'01: Chanute to Wilbur: *"...It is perfectly marvelous to me how quickly you get results with your testing machine; the checks on Langley's curve having been sent almost by return mail. You are evidently better equipped to test the endless variety of curved surfaces than anybody has ever been."*

22Nov'01: Wilbur to Chanute: *"...Our measuring experiments so far have been merely preliminary...We should be very glad indeed to have the profiles of bird wings which you have measured. It is like Spratt says: 'Whatever the birds have is all right, and cannot be greatly improved.'*
"I can see that there are reasons why Mr. Langley should possibly be disinclined to republish Lilienthal, yet it is more properly the work of an institution than a private individual as there is no hope that the sales of the book would repay the cost of publication...Possibly it is unfair to Mr. Langley to suspect that some chapters were not included in the translation because they seemed to trespass on...that he may have deemed his own, but their omission seems...strange..."

27Nov'01: Chanute was, quite literally, the 'clearinghouse' of aeronautical information, evidenced by his letter to Wilbur:

"I have your letter of 22d & 24th, and first will give you the news.
"I have a letter from Mr. Langley, saying...
"I have a letter from Marvin (Charles F. Marvin, chief of the Weather Bureau)...
"I have a letter from Berthenson of St. Petersburg...
"I have a letter from Major Moedebeck (German, author of the *Pocket Book* and chronicler of Lilienthal's notes)...*says he wrote Lilienthal's brother in Berlin...*
"I am amused with your apology for writing long letters, as I find them always too brief."
(...plus the correspondence with Percy Pilcher, noted earlier).

23Dec'01: Wilbur to Chanute: *"...As to your suggestion in regard to Mr. Carnegie, of course nothing would give me greater pleasure than to devote my entire time to scientific investigations; and a salary of ten or twenty thousand a year* ($450,000 to $900,000 today) *would be no insuperable objection, but I think it possible that Andrew is too hard-headed a Scotchman to become interested in such a visionary pursuit as flying...I do not think it would be wise for me to accept help in carrying our present investigations further, unless it was with the intention of cutting loose from business entirely and taking up a different line of lifework..."*

4Jan'02: <u>Scientific American</u>: *"Of late years the efforts of experimentalists in the field of aeronautics have been directed rather to the airship than to the aeroplane. Indeed, the whole history of this fascinating science has been marked by a pendulum-like swing between the aeroplane and the navigable balloon. Maxim, Lillienthal* (sic) *and Langley are not heard from so much as De la Vauix and Santos Dumont..."*

9Jan'02: America's first aeronautical club, *The Aero Club of New England*, was founded in Boston, its activities limited to ballooning.

1Jan'02: Chanute to Wilbur: *"....I learn confidentially....that the Directors of the Exposition at St. Louis are even now discussing a project for making the research of aerial navigation a prominent feature of that show, which they also talk of postponing till 1904. The plan suggested...to offer a number of prizes, the first of $50,000* (approximately $2-1/2 million today), *for the best performance of various classes of aerial apparatus..."*

13Jan'02: Chanute to Wilbur: *"I received your recent letter before leaving Chicago, and came via St. Louis on request of the World's Fair people. They propose to appropriate $200,000 in promotion of aerial navigation. One main prize of $100,000, under terms and conditions which are to be formulated, $50,000 in minor prizes and in aid of inventors...and $50,000 in general expenses...Would you be inclined to compete?"*

19Jan'02: Wilbur to Chanute: *"...Your letter from St. Louis of course interested us very much...Whether we shall compete will depend much on the conditions under which the prizes are offered. I have little of the gambling instinct, and unless there is reasonable hope of getting at least the amount expended in competing I would enter only after very careful consideration. Mathematically it would be foolish to spend two or three thousand dollars competing for a hundred thousand dollar prize* (approximately $5 million today) *if the chance of winning be only one in a hundred..."*

7Feb'02: Wilbur to Chanute: *"...The matter of lateral stability and steering is one of exceeding complexity, but I now have hopes that we have a solution. The fore-and-aft stability will not give us serious trouble again, I think. Skill will be required but the capacity of control will be adequate for any emergency short of a whirlwind. The great trouble will be to obtain proper skill.*
"The newspapers are full of accounts of flying machines which have been building in cellars, garrets, stables and other secret places, each of which will undoubtedly carry off the hundred thousand dollars at St. Louis. They all have the problem 'completely solved,' but usually there is some insignificant detail yet to be decided, such as whether to use steam, electricity or a water motor to drive it. Mule power might give greater <u>ascensional force if properly applied</u>, but I fear would be too dangerous unless the mule wore pneumatic shoes. Some of these reports would disgust one if they were not so irresistibly ludicrous..."

13Feb'02: Chanute to Wilbur: *"...I have a letter from Capt. (Ferdinand) Ferber (1862-1909), of Nice, France, who has made some glides himself on a Lilienthal machine. He says that he is in a state of admiration of your performances and wishes me to convey his felicitations.*

"I have also heard from Means, from (Godfrey L.) *Cabot, from T. P. Ferguson, from Banet-Rivet, from C.E. Myers and from C. Edwards to the same effect. They seem to have recognized my handwriting on the envelope.."*

14Feb'02: Wilbur to George Spratt: *"....I am sorry that Mr. Langley has not adopted Mr. Chanute's suggestion to help you in your experiments with an appropriation. I sometimes think that Mr. L. is a little bit jealous of Mr. Chanute and takes pleasure in slighting him in such a way as this...*

19Feb'02: Wilbur to Chanute: *"...The <u>Moedebeck</u> article...interested me greatly. The paragraphs on Pilcher, Chanute, Herring and Hargrave are models of succinct clear statement. I especially like the way in which you bring out the principles they worked upon and what their experiments indicated or discovered. The section on our...work is certainly not undercolored. The question is rather whether our work is sufficiently important to justify so favorable a notice..."*

23Mar'02: Wilbur to Chanute: *"....I think that the St. Louis Exposition authorities will have to increase the amount of...prizes, as I have already been offered so many shares of the prize by various persons who have a cinch on it, that the sum of my shares would amount to more than the total prize. Consequently, the St. Louis men must put up more money or take advantage of the bankrupt law..."*

31Mar'02: Chanute to Wilbur: *"...I have been asked...to be in St. Louis about April 13th to meet* (Alberto) *Santos-Dumont (1873-1932) and to discuss with others the conditions which should be laid down for the aerial contests..."*

Note: Santos-Dumont's airship No. 2 of 1898 was the *first* to use an internal combustion engine; a *DeDion-Bouton* modified into a 78-pound 2-cylinder of 2.5 hp.

3May'02: <u>Scientific American:</u> *"Commenting...upon the present prospects of successful aerial navigation...the great difficulty in constructing a practical balloon airship was the great surface presented by the balloon to the wind, and the impossibility of producing a light motor of sufficient power to hold the airship against any but the most moderate winds...also...the inherent difficulty of the aeroplane was its lack of what might be called static stability, and the difficulty of controlling the machine in making landings. The strong point in the one type is the weak point in the other. The airship can float and possesses stability, but its bulk and weight are fatal to speed and control. The aeroplane has no capacity for flotation and soaring except when in motion, and in its present stage of development it is a contrivance full of the greatest risk to life and limb. On the other hand, it is by far the lighter type of the two, and if the problem of control can only be solved, the questions of securing high speed and a wide radius of action, are merely a question of the production of a motor of great power for a given weight..."*

27May'02: Chanute to Wilbur: *"...Last evening I had a call from Mr. Herring, who is out of a job and is urgent to be employed to rebuild the multiple-wing and the two-surfaced machines, in order to test them in comparison with your own...what would you prefer, i.e., to rebuild them yourself or have Herring do it? There would be some advantage in having him rebuild the multiple wing..."*

30May'02: Chanute to Wilbur: *"...I suggest you take out a patent or caveat on those principles of your machines as are important, not that money is to be made by it, but to save unpleasant disputes as to priority..."*

17Jul'02: Wilbur to Chanute: *"...That church matter has taken on a phase which may possibly delay our departure for Kitty Hawk till about the 20th or 25th of August, I hope no longer than that..."*

Note: *"That church matter"* is tangential to the Wright's story. In Kelly's <u>Miracle at Kitty Hawk</u> it is explained: *"It had become known in the inner councils of the United Brethren Church that a layman connected with the church publishing business had mishandled some funds. Bishop Wright, tolerant as he was, could not condone dishonesty and wanted to see the man removed, if not prosecuted. But one faction sought to whitewash the case, to hush up any possible scandal, and started a fight to oust the Bishop from office.* (The "phase" noted above).
"Wilbur went to work on the account books and found proof of dishonesty. Then he wrote a blistering tract, setting forth the facts and the Bishop's determined view on them. He made a study of the legal aspects of the case. The whole Wright family became as much concerned over the church issue as they were about the flying experiments. Bishop Wright was never deposed, but the fight went on for a long time."

For almost three years.

28May'05: Wilbur to Chanute: *"...I returned a few days ago from a week's trip to Michigan to attend the General Conference of the church in which my father is a bishop. It was the decisive battle in the contest of which you have heretofore heard us speak. We won a complete victory; turned every one of the rascals out of office, and put friends of my father in their places..."*

But the Bishop did retire, *immediately*.

1902: After extensive redesign, much based on their wind-tunnel testing of airfoil sections, the Wrights design *Glider No. 3* with wings of a less camber ratio of 1/25, spanning 32-feet with a 5-foot chord.

20Aug'02: Katharine Wright to her father: *"...Will is thin and nervous and so is Orv. They will be all right when they get down in the sand where the salt breezes blow...They think that life at Kitty Hawk cures all ills...The flying machine is in process of making now. Will spins the sewing machine around by the hour while Orv squats around marking the places to sew....I'll be lonesome enough by this time next week and wish that I could have some of their racket around..."*

29Aug'02: The Wrights return to Kitty Hawk, and by September 2nd complete the assembly of their new glider. During the next two months they would make almost 1,000 glides, several of over 200 yards.

"The air was in fact conquered then. Only an engine and propellers were needed to make the glider an airplane."
                                                                        John McMahon

Wilbur in the 1902 glider:

5Sep'02: Wilbur to Chanute: *"...As to the choice of a man to experiment your machines we wish to get the one whom you think most available. In a former letter I expressed a preference for Mr. Avery because several things I had heard about Mr. Herring's relations with Mr. Langley* (in 1895 problems and hostility had arisen when Herring had been employed by Langley at the Smithsonian) *and yourself seemed to me to indicate that he might be of a somewhat jealous disposition, and possibly inclined to claim for himself rather more credit than those with whom he might be working would be willing to allow..."*

16Sep'02: Orville's diary: *"At 8:30 saw buzzards soaring over sand hills* (much as Bell had observed in Mexico). *Conditions seemed to be such that they were not able*

16Sep'02: Orville's diary: *"At 8:30 saw buzzards soaring over sand hills* (much as Bell had observed in Mexico). *Conditions seemed to be such that they were not able to soar over plains but took to hills where they had considerable trouble in gaining altitudes of more than 50 to 75 feet above top of large hill. We watched them with field glasses at a distance of 1,200 ft. Angle of birds above horizon was from 4-1/2 degrees to 5-1/2 degrees...We could see the under side of wings all time when facing us, we being directly in line of wind from them, and the upper side slightly when they soared from us...A buzzard trying to soar on small hill with slope of 7-degrees 10-minutes was barely able to sustain itself..."*

16Sep'02: Wilbur to Spratt: *"...The main thing though is a new machine. We have the two surfaces completed and the uprights in place, but the rudder is not yet quite done. It is 32' X 5' spreading an area of 305 sq. ft. altogether. The curvature is about 1 in 25. We had it out making some tests of its efficiency today and are very much pleased with the results of our measurements..."*

As testing progressed, the glider changed from having a double fixed tail-vane to a single fixed vane to, in turn, a single movable ship-like rudder and finally, as noted below, into interconnected control between rudder and wing warping.

Herring accompanied Chanute to Kitty Hawk, arriving on 5Oct. He experimented with the glider built for Chanute (Chanute partially - and incorrectly - blamed its poor showing on Herring), while assisting the Wrights in their investigations.

Older brother Lorin Wright and George Spratt, both welcome, had arrived separately earlier, and accommodations, primitive at best, became cramped.

2Oct'02: Wilbur: *"...Our new machine is a very great improvement over anything we had built before and over anything any one has built. We have beaten all records for flatness of glides...We are being very careful and will avoid accident of serious nature if possible...Everything is so much more satisfactory that we now believe that the flying problem is really nearing its solution."*

3Oct'02: Orville's diary (paraphrased): *"In telling Wilbur at breakfast about the idea that had come to me in the night (to convert the vertical tail from a fixed vane to a rudder that could be moved - to recover lateral balance or to make a turn – toward the low wing, thus compensating for the increased drag imparted to the high wing by its greater angle of attack), I first caught the eye of my brother Lorin to alert him that something important was about to be said and to warn him particularly to note Wilbur's reaction. Knowing Wilbur's unconscious habit of sometimes pushing his prerogatives as older brother and of assuming priority for himself in the conception of any new ideas, I fully expected my suggestion to be brushed aside with an 'Oh, yes, I was already considering that.' Instead, Wilbur listened attentively and remained silent for a minute or two. Then without hesitation, he not only accepted the change but startled me by proposing further bold modification of interconnecting the rudder wires with those of the wing warping so that by a single movement the operator could effect both controls."*

Within a few hours, with remarkable synergism, the brothers distilled and completed the essential elements of their control system.

6Oct'02: Orville's diary: *"We completed the change in the vertic. tail...which is now operated in conjunction with the wing tips, turning toward the wing with the smaller angle of incidence so as to give it more resistance, and thus allow the wing with the larger angle to rise more quickly."*

17Oct'02: Langley to Chanute: *"I should very much like to get some description of the extraordinary results which you told me were recently obtained by the Wright brothers. I have today a letter from Mr. Herring, who was in the city, speaking of some ideas which he would like to submit on the possibility of carrying larger weights for the power, depending chiefly on surfaces of the requisite arrangement, form and curvature. I understand that he has spent the last few weeks with you, and I have inferred that he might have been with you at these Wright trials, and have those in mind in what he writes. I have not, however, felt able to take him again into the Smithsonian service..."*

20Oct'02: Katharine to Bishop Wright: *"Lorin came home last Wednesday afternoon...The boys are having splendid success...Mr. Chanute and Mr. Herring were still there when Lorin left. They were all busy setting up Mr. Chanute's machine that was made in* (San Diego) *California. Herring's machine, made for Mr. Chanute, was a total failure. It would not fly at all."*

3Nov'02: Wilbur comments: *"Into the last ten days of practice we crowded more glides than in all of the weeks preceding. In two days we made about two hundred and fifty, all of which were made in winds ranging from nine to sixteen and three quarters meters per second* (37mph). *The duration of these glides ranged from seven to sixteen seconds. This practice enabled us to very greatly increase our skill in the management of the machine. We increased our record for distance to 622-1/2 ft., for time to 26 sec..."*

After completing about eleven hundred flights they closed the camp; the knowledge learned formed the basis for their patent applications.

21Oct'02: Chanute to Langley: *"...I have lately gotten out of conceit with Mr. Herring, and I fear that he is a bungler. He came to me in July, said that he was out of employment and urged that I let him rebuild gliding machines 'to beat Mr. Wright...' I consented to building new wings for the multiple-wing machine, but could give it no attention as the work was done at St. Joseph, Mich. Herring adopted new forms of wings and reduced the total weight from 33-1/2 lbs. to 27 lbs., but when the machine was tried by him in N. Carolina it proved a failure, and he said that he did not know what was the matter."*

23Oct'02: Langley to Chanute: *"...I had...already made up my mind about the gentleman in question* (Herring)...*I telegraphed* (the Wrights) *and wrote to them at Kitty Hawk, but have no answer, and suppose their experiments are over..."*

The Wrights replied to Langley that they had broken camp and ended their experiments. In another letter to Chanute they commented that Langley made *"no mention of his experiments on the Potomac."*

3Dec'02: Wright Cycle Co. to Daimler, and approximately twenty other automobile/engine manufacturers: *"...possibility of obtaining a gasoline engine which would develop 8 to 9 brake H.P., would weigh no more than 180 lbs. Or an average of 20 lbs. per H.P., and would be free from vibration.."*

None were found.

Note: In 1885, Germany's *Gottlieb Daimler* and *William Maybach* built the *first* gasoline-powered land vehicle, their "*Einspur*," a two-wheeled motorcycle.

7Dec'02: Langley to Chanute: *"...I should be very glad to hear more of what the Wright brothers have done, and especially of their means of control, which you think better than the Penaud. I should be very glad to have either of them visit Washington at my expense, to get some of their ideas on this subject, if they are willing to communicate them."*

9Dec'02: Chanute to Wilbur: *"...This brings me the enclosed letter* (above) *which seems to me cheeky...I think you had better patent your improvements..."*

29Dec'02: Wilbur to Spratt: *"...We have recently done a little experimenting with screws* (propellers) *and are trying to get a clear understanding of just how they work and why. It is a very perplexing problem indeed.*
"We are thinking of building a machine next year with 500 sq. ft. surface, about 40 ft. X 6 ft. 6 inches...If all goes well the next step will be to apply a motor..."

4Apr'03: Chanute to Wilbur: *"Your experiments are attracting a good deal of attention in Paris. I have had to give several talks, and to promise to write something for publication.* L'Aerophile *wants your picture and that of your brother Orville to publish with the article I have agreed to prepare. You are therefore...to go to the photographer and be 'took,' and send me two copies of each at Chicago...You might as well get the photographer to print at my expense a lot of pictures...There is a run on them; I have given out most of those I had with me.*
"It seems very queer that having ignored all of this series of gliding experiments for several years, the French should now be over-enthusiastic about them. The Germans and the English have taken more notice..."

20Apr'03: Wilbur to Spratt: *"...Regarding the matters on which you have asked my advice I must confess that I am at a loss just what to say. If you were to ask me to give advice on the best method of turning handsprings or some other trivial matter I would gladly give bushels of it, but regarding a matter which might affect the whole course of a man's life, I almost fear to give any, lest injury might result from it, instead of good, as intended. I can suffer the consequences of my own mistakes with some composure, but I would hate awfully to see some other person suffering from an error of judgment of mine. Nevertheless, I have a great desire to see you succeed, and if you feel free to communicate the matters you have in mind, I will promise to do what I can to help you either with advice or with assistance in obtaining help to carry forward the work, provided of course that the matters communicated are in my judgment meritorious..."*

27Apr'03: Wilbur to Spratt: *"...It was not my intention to advocate dishonesty in argument nor a bad spirit in a controversy. No truth is without some mixture of error, and no error so false but that it possesses some elements of truth. If a man is in too big a hurry to give up an error he is liable to give up some truth with it, and in accepting the arguments of the other man he is sure to get some error with it. Honest argument is merely a process of mutually picking the beams and motes out of each other's eyes so both can see more clearly. Men become wise just as they become rich, more by what they save than by what they receive. After I get hold of a truth I hate to lose it again, and I like to sift all the truth out before I give up an error."*

1903: The new *Flyer,* their first *'flying machine,'* is constructed based upon their research and computations. It is quite large, wings spanning 40 feet 4 inches by a 6-1/2 foot chord.

Later, on 15Nov'03, Orville writes: *"...Mr. Chanute says that no one before has ever tried to build a machine on such close margins as we have done to our calculations. He said that he nevertheless had more hope of our machine going than any of the others. He seems to think we are pursued by a blind fate from which we are unable to escape...He doesn't seem to think our machines are so much superior as the manner in which we handle them. We are of just the reverse opinion."*

The Wrights needed a motor to power their machine. Finding none (note 3Dec-'02), they designed and, assisted by Charles Taylor, build their own. It was a straight-forward, dependable design modeled *after* the *Pope-Toledo* automobile engine (at a time of few automobiles); 4-cylinders, 4-inch bore and stroke, aluminum block and crankcase with cast iron cylinder sleeves, pressure liquid cooling and an overhead camshaft. There was no carburetor, the metered fuel was injected directly into the intake manifold, and fired by a magneto *'make and break'* ignition. Complete with accessories it weighed 170 pounds and, warmed up, developed approximately 12 horsepower at 1,200 rpm with the primitive kerosene-byproduct fuel then available (It makes an interesting comparison with Curtiss's 1903 engines, page 114).

The original 1903 Wright motor:

To start, the exhaust valves were relieved so that, under no compression, the pistons ran freely, permitting the propellers to be set spinning. Then the valves were tripped, causing compression and the resultant starting of the engine. The only engine control was a lever with a wide range of ignition-timing settings; retarding the spark slowed the engine, advancing speeded it up.

And the motor had to power a propeller, little understood then. Finding scant help in marine applications, with the novel assumption that a propeller in air would act differently than one in water, after testing many designs in their wind tunnel they used their aeronautical airfoil calculations to design a propeller so that its forward surface developed thrust much in the same way as a wing produced lift. It had a remarkable *66-percent efficiency.*

They then discover that a single propeller's gyroscopic effect made turning difficult, and decided upon two counter-rotating propellers balancing each other. This arrangement of one propeller behind each wing became the hall-mark of all but the last Wright designs.

It was a major factor in costing them the lead in aviation.

17Jul'03: Chanute to Wilbur: *"...How is the vertical tail operated? I fear that it will not do to strike out the clause altogether, and you did not desire that the warping of the wings should be mentioned at all.*

"...Have you seen that...Langley is about to test his man-carrying machine?"

22Jul'03: Wilbur to Chanute: *"...Prof. Langley seems to be having rather more than his fair share of trouble...with pestiferous reporters and windstorms. But as the mosquitoes are reported to be very bad along the banks where the reporters are encamped he has some consolation...I presume that you are to be one of the guests of honor at the launching festivities. Our invitation has not yet arrived."*

24Jul'03: Wilbur to Chanute: *"...The vertical tail is operated by wires leading to the wires which connect with the wing tips. Thus the movement of the wing tips operates the rudder. This statement is not for publication, but merely to correct the misapprehension in your own mind. As the laws of France and Germany provide that patents will be held invalid if the matter claimed has been publicly printed we prefer to exercise reasonable caution about the details of our machine until the question of patents is settled. I only see three methods of dealing with this matter: (1) Tell the truth. (2) Tell nothing specific. (3) Tell something not true. I really can not advise either the first or the third course..."*

27Jul'03: Chanute to Wilbur: *"...I was puzzled by the way you put things in your former letters. You were sarcastic and I did not catch the idea that you feared that the description might forestall a patent. Now that I know it, I take pleasure in suppressing the passage altogether. I believe however that it would have proved quite harmless as the construction is ancient and well known..."*

12Sep'03: Chanute to Wilbur: *"...I am really sorry for Langley. He has had more than his share of mishaps, and the pesky reporters are giving him a reputation of a bungler..."*

25Sep'03: The Wrights return to Kitty Hawk to find that fierce winds have damaged their building. Repairing it, they also construct a second, larger hangar building. Then, while getting their *"flying machine"* ready, they practice gliding in the 1902 glider and both Chanute and his protege, Spratt, pay visits.

1Oct'03: Wilbur to Chanute: *"....We made about 75 glides, nearly all of more than 20 second's duration. The longest was 30-2/5 seconds which beats our former records. We did some practicing at soaring and found it easier than we expected. Once we succeeded in remaining almost in one spot for 26-2/5 seconds and finally landed fifty feet from the starting point..."*

Interestingly, in January, 1907, Curtiss on his *"monster motorcycle"* would cover a mile in *exactly* the same time, 26-2/5 seconds.

7Oct'03: Langley's *"great aerodrome,"* 55 feet long, 48 feet wide with a 1,040 s.f. wing area, equipped with *Charles Matthews Manly*'s (1876-1927; pp 475) brilliant 52-hp engine (*"Father of all Radial Airplane Engines"*) and with 125 lb. Manly as pilot, attempts flight. It was reported: *"The immense airship sped rapidly along its 70-foot track, was carried by its own momentum for a hundred yards and then fell gradually into the Potomac River, whence it emerged a total wreck..."*

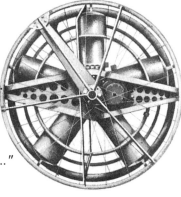

Next page, <u>Scientific American</u>, *17Oct'03, from photographs "courtesy of the* <u>Washington Star</u>,*"*
                    (author's collection):   *Manly's engine:*

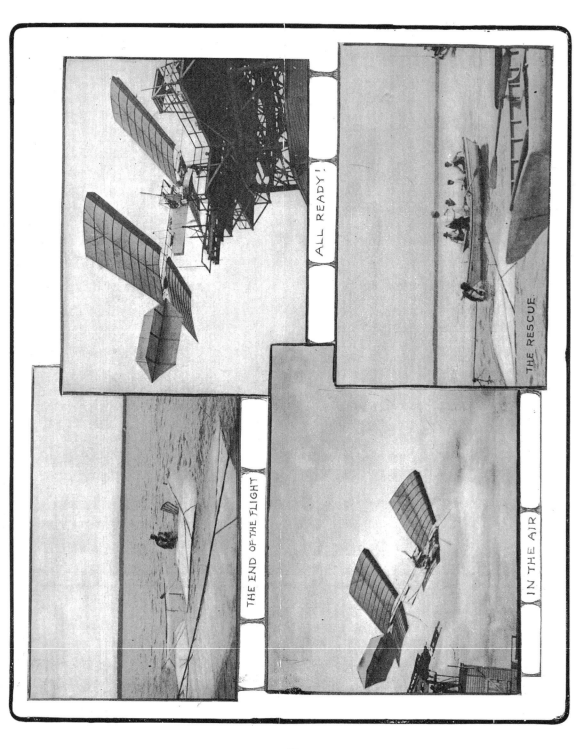

ALL READY!

THE RESCUE

THE END OF THE FLIGHT

IN THE AIR

16Oct'03: Wilbur to Chanute: *"...I see that Langley has had his fling, and failed. It seems to be our turn to throw* (dice) *now...I wonder what our luck will be..."*

2Dec'03: Wilbur to Spratt: *"...Mr. Chanute had been gone nearly two weeks before your letter reached us...He was with us just a week but the weather was so bad that we did little but sit around the stove and talk. We have not tried to glide the big machine yet, and probably shall not this year, as favorable days are very scarce... We hung it on its wing tips some days ago and loaded the front set of trussing to more than six times its regular strain in the air. We also hung it by the tips and ran the engine and screws, with a man on board. The strength...seems 'O.K.'..."*

28Oct'03: From its 1902 Annual Report, the Smithsonian reprints Wilbur's 1901 lecture, "Some Aeronautical Experiments," as *Smithsonian Publication* 1380.

Langley's Second Attempt:

8Dec'03: Langley makes a second attempt at flying his Aerodrome. Another failure, almost identical to the attempt of two month's earlier.

The Washington Post: *"There was a roaring, grinding noise - and the Langley airship tumbled over the edge of the houseboat and disappeared into the river sixteen feet below. It simply slid into the water like a handful of mortar."*

The press, frustrated and annoyed by Langley's secrecy, greets this with a further storm of derision, prompting the public to become so apathetic and skeptical of heavier-than-air flight that when there is real news of success it leaves them unmoved (see 10Jan'10, *Los Angeles Times).*

"Langley's powered models flew over the Potomac with 'inherent stability,' for long flights. This may be the 'breakthrough' that Lanchester and Penaud foretold with flying toys. Also, Langley had the most advanced light powerplant designed and built for him by his young engineer, Charles Manly. Manly's engine (*an evolution of Stephen M. Balzer's pioneering radial engine*) could have made Langley's machine fly, if successfully launched. Langley was no engineer and was off base in expecting an inherently stable airplane to be steered like a boat. The Wrights invented control about three axes. Planes have been flown with horizontal and vertical rudders only, but are no good in rough air, or for landing on a windy day."

> *Jerome Clarke Hunsaker (1886-1984. Aeroresearch pioneer; head, Aeronautical Engineering, MIT, 1933-1952, whom the author met in 1974)*

Orville figured that up to this time it'd cost them less than $1,000 (about $50,000 today) for everything associated with their flying experiments, including transportation between Dayton and Kitty Hawk. In contrast, the total cost of Langley's endeavors exceeded $73,000 (about $3-3/4 million today).

13Dec'03: The Wrights never broke the Sabbath by working, a promise made to their father when they were very young. On this Sunday (apparently planning ahead) they read and bone-up on German (their mother's native tongue) and French.

Orville's diary, Monday, December 14, 1903: "...*We tossed up coin to decide who should make first trial, and Will won... Will started machine...I snapped watch as machine passed end of track. (It had raised from track six or eight feet from the end.) The machine turned up in front and rose to a height of about 15 feet from ground at a point somewhere in neighborhood of 60 feet from the end of track. After thus losing most of its headway it gradually sank to ground turned up at an angle of probably 20 degree incidence...Time of flight from end of track was 3-1/2 sec. for a distance of 105 ft. Angle of descent for the 105 feet was 4 degrees 55'. Speed of wind was between 4 and 8 miles.*"

Wilbur to his father and sister, December 14, 1903: "...*However the real trouble was an error in judgment, in turning up too suddenly after leaving the track, and as the machine had barely speed enough for support already, this slowed it down so much that before I could correct the error, the machine began to come down, though turned up at a big angle...*"

Wilbur to his father, telegram, December 15, 1903: "*Misjudgment at start reduced flight one hundred twelve power and control ample rudder only injured success assured keep quiet.*"

Orville's diary, Thursday, December 17, 1903: "...*wind between 20 and 25 miles ...I got on the machine at 10:35 for the first* (second) *trial...On slipping the rope the machine started off increasing in speed to probably 7 or 8 miles. The machine lifted from the truck just as it was entering on the fourth rail. Mr. Daniels took a picture just as it left the tracks. I found the control of the front rudder* (elevator) *quite difficult on account of its being balanced too near the center and thus had a tendency to turn itself when started so that the rudder was turned too far on one side and then too far on the other. As a result the machine would rise suddenly to about 10 ft. and then as sudden-*

2nd Trial, 10:35 AM, 17Dec03: A *"jump,"* see page 100.

Note 'belt-high' altitude, and extreme 'up,' stall-inducing position of elevators:

ly, on turning the rudder, dart for the ground. A sudden dart when out about 100 feet from the end of the tracks ended the flight. Time about 12 seconds (not known exactly as watch was not properly stopped)...."

"After repairs, at 20 min. after 11 o'clock Will made the second (third) *trial. The course was about like mine, up and down but a little longer over the ground though about the same in time. Dist. not measured but about 175 ft...."*

"At about 20 minutes till 12 o'clock I made the third (fourth) *trial. When out about the same distance as Will's, I met with a strong gust from the left which raised the left wing and sidled the machine off to the right in a lively manner. I immediately turned the rudder* (elevator) *to bring the machine down and then worked the end control...it had raised to a height of 12 to 14 feet...."*

"At just 12 o'clock Will started on the fourth (fifth) *and last trip. The machine started off with its ups and downs as it had before, but by the time he had gone over three or four hundred feet he had it under much better control, and was traveling on a fairly even course...till it reached a small hummock about 800 feet from the starting ways, when it began its pitching again and suddenly darted to the ground...The distance over the ground was 852 feet in 59 seconds."*

This 5th trial is <u>the first true flight of an aeroplane</u>. (See: Wilbur-Chanute letter, 2Nov06 defining the difference between a "jump" and true flight of *"over 300 feet."*)

28Dec'03: Wilbur to Chanute: *"...The controlling mechanisms operated more powerfully than in our old machine so that we nearly always turned the rudders more than was really necessary and thus kept up a somewhat undulating course especially in the first flights. Under the prevailing conditions we did not feel it safe to rise far above the ground...Consequently we were frequently at the point of touching the ground and once scratched it deeply but rose again and continued the flight. Those who understand the real significance of the conditions under which we worked will be rather surprised at the length than the shortness of...flights made with an unfamiliar machine after less than one minute's practice...*

"One of the most gratifying features of the trials was the fact that all of our calculations were shown to have worked out with absolute exactness..."

A <u>Western Union</u> telegraph was received in Dayton: *"Bishop M Wright   Success four flights thursday morning all against twenty one mile wind   started from Level with engine power alone average speed through air thirty one miles longest 57 seconds inform Press home Christmas. Orevelle Wright 525P"*

"The machine that flew that day was primitive. The Wright brothers themselves clung to outmoded ideas of design. Before long the brothers and their concepts of flying machines were also outmoded. Others arose and, spurred on by the success of the two brothers, added fresh ideas and new dreams. Everything about flight that originated with the Wright brothers has been improved or discarded entirely...They achieved their goal, but only after years of labor and frustration. The Wrights succeeded where others had failed because of their tenacity *and* their methodical approach to the problems of flight. To have had one attribute without the other would have been insufficient."   *Rubenstein & Goldman*

Their father said: *"Wilbur is 36, Orville 32, and they are as inseparable as twins. For several years they have read up on aeronautics as a physician would read his books, and they have studied, discussed, and experimented together. Natural workmen, they have invented, constructed, and operated their gliders, and finally their 'Wright Flyer,' jointly, all at their personal expense. About equal credit is due each."*

The brother's announcement is ignored or inaccurately reported by most of the press. However, both before and after their flight they described their experiences; e.g., in 1901 Wilbur explained their wing-warping to the Western Society of Engineers, elaborating further on it in June, 1904, as did Chanute in Paris that same year, statements that would later be considered "prior disclosure" in a patent sense.

26Dec'03: Herring to the Wrights: In this astonishing letter, Herring claimed to have independently solved the problem of powered flight, and suggests a joint company to market the *Wright Flyer* - *"the basis being a 2/3 interest for you two and a 1/3 interest for me."* He also asserted (correctly, it appears) that he, not Chanute, was the *"true originator"* of the biplane glider. Also, that he had been offered a substantial sum for his *"rights"* to interference suits against them (see 8Jan'04).

27Dec'03: Chanute to Wilbur: *"...The American Association for the Advancement of Science holds its winter meet in St. Louis, Dec. 28th to Jan. 2d. I have been asked for a paper on aerial navigation, and have made it very general...It is fitting that you should be the first to give the Association the first scientific account of your per-formances. Will you do so?..."*

28Dec'03: Wilbur to Chanute (Telegram): *"We are giving no pictures nor descriptions of machine or methods at present."*

Jan'04: Wright Brothers to <u>Associated Press</u>, clarifying and explaining the December flights: *"...From the beginning we have employed entirely new principles of control; and as all the experiments have been conducted at our own expense without assistance from any individual or institution, we do not feel ready at present to give out any pictures or detailed description of the machine."*

It would appear that their attitude, e.g., *"I have not taken up the problem with the expectation of financial profit..."* (23Sep'00) changed markedly following their return home after 17Dec'03. The family closed ranks, and thereafter the brothers sought ever-higher fame and wealth, vexing Chanute, their *only* non-partisan confident.

8Jan'04: Wilbur to Chanute: *"...A few days ago we gave to the press a correction (of an erroneous report), of which I send you a copy herewith. Nothing more will be given out, as we prefer to keep the story to ourselves till we are ready to make a full statement later in the year.*

"A copy is also enclosed of a letter received a few days ago from Mr. Herring (26Dec'03). This time he surprised us. Before he left camp in 1902 we foresaw and predicted the object of his visit to Washington, we also felt certain that he was making a frenzied attempt to mount a motor on a copy of our 1902 glider (see 17Apr '10) and thus anticipate us, even before you told us of it last fall. But that he should have the effrontery to write us such a letter, after his other schemes of rascality had failed, was really a little more than we expected. We shall make no answer at all..."

14Jan'04: Chanute to Wilbur: *"...(referring to the Wright's 5Jan'04 statement) 'All the experiments have been conducted at our own expense, without assistance from <u>any</u> individual or institution.' - Please write me just what you had in your mind concerning myself when you framed that sentence that way."*

18Jan'04: Wilbur to Chanute: *"...The use of the word 'any,' which you under-scored, grew out of the fact that we found from articles...a somewhat general impression that our Kitty Hawk experiments had not been carried out on our own expense, &c. We thought it might save embarrassment to correct this promptly...*

"We are at work building three machines with which we shall probably give exhibitions at several different places during the coming season. We may decide to enter one at St. Louis, and have written for copy of the revised rules & regulations...we may decide to make a try for it..."

20Jan'04: Chanute to Wilbur: *"...I was somewhat puzzled by your telegram at St. Louis. You talked while I was in camp of giving your performance, if successful, all the publicity possible, and you knew that I would not divulge the construction of your machine as I have never disclosed more than you...have published. Your telegram indicated a change of policy which you can more fully impart when I see you..."*

1Mar'04: Wilbur to Chanute: *"...Orville and I went down to St. Louis last month and took a look at the aeronautical grounds and surrounding country...we found things even less favorable than we anticipated. I do not know that there would be serious danger to life, but much of the ground over which the course must be laid is such as to make serious damage to the machine, in case of a forced landing, almost inevitable. It would probably be necessary to win the prize in three trials, or not at all. As there are no consolation prizes for flying machines ...we would have to win the grand prize or get nothing. It is a tough proposition...If we enter, it will be for the purpose of winning, not for the purpose of seeing how close we can come to it..."* (a wisdom in common with Curtiss: *"...if you are beaten before you start, why take the chance?"*)

Earlier, in the summer of 1902, Santos-Dumont visited St. Louis, commenting: *"...I at once saw that the splendid open spaces of the exposition grounds offered the best of race-courses. The prevailing idea...was to set a long course of many hundreds of miles - say from St. Louis to Chicago. This, I pointed out, would be unpractical, if only for the reason that the exposition public would desire to see the flights from start to finish. I suggested that three great towers or flag-staffs be erected...at the corners of an equal-sided triangle. The comparatively short course around them – between ten and twenty miles - would afford a decisive test of dirigibility, no matter in what way the wind might blow..."*

3Mar'04: Chanute to Wilbur: *"...I hope you will succeed so well when you resume experiment that you will see your way to entering for the grand prize. You are mistaken however as there being no 'consolation' prizes for flying machines. There are three of them if you can contrive to go slow enough..."*

14Mar'04: Wilbur to Chanute: *"...We are hard at work getting ready for spring. The new machine will be the same size as the old one but will weigh a little more, 800 lbs. probably. By gearing the engine to run a little faster we will not only carry the additional weight but will have enough surplus to increase the speed to about 40 miles an hour."*

This 1904 aeroplane was the development step between the *1903 Flyer* and 1905's *Flyer No. 3*, the *"practical flyer."*

19Mar'04: Chanute to Wilbur: *"...Mr. Santos-Dumont has visited St. Louis, has had the rules slightly modified, and will enter the race. I figure that with his 60 to 70 H.P., he can obtain a speed of 28 to 32 miles per hour.*

"I had a letter from Mr. Herring a month ago, stating that if I have any information on the subject of flying machines he would like to get hold of such matter for his paper, Gas Power *('for those who make, sell, or use gas or gasoline engines,' one of Herring's several projects). I am ashamed (almost) to say that I have not answered him..."*

29Mar'04: Wilbur to Chanute: *"...with everything working perfectly (Santos-Dumont) ought to be able to make the St. Louis course at an average speed of 18-3/4 miles...The changes in the rules do not affect us one way or the other but we approve of them because we would like to see someone knock down that prize.*

"Have you noticed in Moedebeck's *German paper that Herring is setting up a claim to be an independent discoverer of gliding simultaneously with Lilienthal, and the pioneer in everything that has or will yet be discovered in flying? He is an amusing 'cuss.'*

Note: Herring claimed invention of the forward adjustable rudder, offering as proof an 1894 copyrighted photograph, with the implication that the Wrights used it without acknowledgment. However, it was *not* part of the Wright patent.

> *"We are about ready to commence setting up our new machine. We have arranged for an experimental station about 8 miles east of Dayton and so will not go to Kitty Hawk this spring..."*

10Apr'04: Wilbur to Chanute: *"...Our patents have been filed already in England, France, Belgium, Germany, Austria and Italy, and probably Russia..."*

14Apr'04: Wilbur to Chanute: *"...Mr. Herring would seem to have a cinch on the St. Louis prize for flying models, if he can substantiate his claims published in the* Boston Journal..."

15May'04: Wilbur to Chanute: *"...It seems to be a case of going away from home to hear the news...Prof. Langley...announces that a Russian captain has made successful flights with an aerodrome..; while from Europe comes mysterious news of great things in America. Do you think that Mr. Herring has been working Mr. (Patrick Y.) Alexander, and possibly 'pulled his leg'?*

> *"Flyer No. 2 is approaching completion; another day ought to see it finished..."*

Similar to *Flyer No. 1*, it is heavier, stronger, with a more powerful 17-hp motor.

23May'04: The Wrights are ready for trials, in a 100-acre meadow at *"Huffman's farm at Simm's Station,"* eight miles east of Dayton near the *"electric road"* (interurban trolley). The press (*no* cameras) are among the guests invited to witness their *"attempt to fly,"* but there was *"too little wind."*

25May'04: A rainy day combined with, again, little wind, prevented flying.

26May'04: With some of the press still hanging on, determined to see if they could fly, they finally succeed, barely. It was rainy with little wind, and an engine *"not working right"* gave poor results. And the *Flyer* suffered damage. Reports differ whether the attempt covered 25 or 60 feet; it wasn't enough to erase many doubts. The press, harkening to *"Langley's folley,"* were typically unconvinced.

Orville and Wilbur and Flyer No. 2:

5Jun'04: Wilbur to Chanute: *"...We have made repairs in our machine and expect to be ready for trials on Thursday of this week. After a few flights we will know better what we will wish to do about entering at St. Louis...*

"The fact that we are experimenting at Dayton is now public, but so far we have not been disturbed by visitors. The newspapers are friendly and not disposed to arouse prying curiosity in the community."

21Jun'04: Wilbur to Chanute: *"...While we are getting ready the favorable opportunities slip away, and we are usually up against a rainstorm, a dead calm, or a wind blowing at right angles to the track. Today we had our first decent chance, but as the margin was very small, we were not skillful enough to really get started. The first two flights were for a distance of a little more than a hundred feet and the third two hundred and twenty-five feet...Orville almost got away, but after about 200 ft. he allowed the machine to turn up a little too much and it stalled it...*

"We have about concluded to enter the St. Louis contest but are reluctant to do this...until we are certain of being ready...We have one machine finished, another approaching completion, and a third well started...the parts are interchangeable..."

25Jun'04: Chanute to Wilbur: *"...upon return from St. Louis, where I spent a couple of days with the Exposition officials and Mr. Santos-Dumont.*

"The jury is to consist of the General Commissioner for Brazil, the Gen'l. Commissioner for England, & myself.

"...There have been some 90 applications, of which 5 have paid their entrance fees, but none of them seem to me to stand any show against Santos-Dumont..."

1Jul'04: Wilbur to Chanute: *"...The injury inflicted upon the Dumont airship is a rather strange affair. I think I will suspend judgment...and await developments..."*

After its arrival in St. Louis, Santos-Dumont's airship was mysteriously vandalized with long slashes cut in its envelope, causing him to withdraw from the competition. There was considerable speculation that *"it was done by a secret personal enemy of his."* Captain Tom Baldwin? See later.

28Aug'04: Wilbur to Chanute: *"...Since the first of August we have made twenty-five starts with the No. 2 Flyer. The longest flights were 1,432 ft., 1,304 ft., 1,296 ft. and 1,260 ft. These are about as long as we can readily make on our present grounds without circling...We think the machine when in full flight will maintain an average relative speed of at least 45 miles an hour. This is rather more than we care for at present...Our starting apparatus (a 20-foot tower with a 1,600 pound drop-weight) is approaching completion and then we will be ready to start in calms and practice circling."*

They first used it on September 7th.

In 1912 Wilbur recalled an enigma of the 1904 flights: *"...usually the machine responded promptly when we applied the control for restoring lateral balance (coming out of a turn) but on a few occasions the machine did not respond promptly, and the machine came to the ground in a somewhat tilted position. The cause of the difficulty proved to be very obscure, and the season closed without any solution of the puzzle."*

20Sep'04: Launching their *Flyer* with a new *"derrick-catapult,"* the Wrights complete their *first full-circle flight,* a circumference of 4,080 feet in 2 minutes 15-2/5 seconds, witnessed and described by Amos I. Root, editor of <u>Gleanings in Bee Culture</u>, 1Jan'05: *"Dear friends, I have a wonderful story to tell you - a story that, in some respects, out-rivals the Arabian Nights fables...God in his great mercy has permitted me to be, at least somewhat, instrumental in ushering in and introducing to the great wide world an invention that may outrank electric cars, the automobiles, and all other methods of travel...*

"It was my privilege, on the 20th day of September, 1904, to see the first successful trip of an airship, without a balloon to sustain it, that the world has ever made, that is, to turn the corners and come back to the starting point...there was not another machine equal to such a task...on the face of the earth..."

5Oct'04: Wilbur to Chanute: *"...Up to the present we have been very fortunate in our relations with newspaper reporters, but intelligence of what we are doing is gradually spreading through the neighborhood and we are fearful that we will soon have to discontinue experiment...In fact, it is a question whether we are not ready to begin considering what we will do with our baby now that we have it."*

15Nov'04: Wilbur to Chanute: *"...The American (patent) office has again rejected our claims but in so doing has suggested that the objections might be removed by slight changes in the wording...so it seems probable that we will get all that we have claimed.*

Note: The Wright's patent attorney, *Harold A. Toulmin* of Dayton, reasoning: *"Although men have been experimenting since 67 A.D., the Wright brothers discovered the secret whereby aeroplanes, or sustaining surfaces, could be steered and controlled through the air,"* helped them file claims that were extraordinarily broad, so much so that every other flying machine would infringe on it and give them a monopoly position of enormous value.

Furthermore, it was the brothers intent to implement their monopoly position in much the *same* manner so successful for Bell and his telephone patent (Marconi also tried copying Bell when, initially, he insisted upon leasing, not selling, his wireless telegraph/radio equipment and prohibiting its use with anyone else's):

"We wish it to be understood...that our invention is not limited to this particular construction, since any construction whereby the angular relations of the lateral margins of the aeroplane may be varied in opposite directions with respect to the normal planes of said aeroplanes comes within the scope of our invention."

"...On the 9th we went out to celebrate Roosevelt's election by a long flight and went around four times in 5 min. 4 sec..."

Note: During 1904 at Huffman Prairie the Wrights logged 105 starts and a total flying time of approximately 50 minutes.

26Dec'04: Chanute to Wilbur: *"...I have been thinking it not unlikely that you...be called upon to go to Japan. It could well afford to give you and your brother $100,000 for a few month's work in reconnoitering. Santos-Dumont would preferably be called upon by Russia, as that country follows the French lead..."*

Note: Regarding the reference to the Russo-Japanese War, in The Wright Papers editor McFarland characterizes the Wright's reaction to Chanute as *"preposterous."* However, if that were the case it certainly changed by the fall of 1905 when the brothers were aggressively soliciting military business both in Europe and America, e.g., Wilbur's prescient letter to Ferber, 4Nov'05: *"...With Russia and Austria-Hungary in their present troubled condition and the German Emperor in a truculent mood, a spark may produce an explosion at any minute. No government dare...risk of waiting to develop practical flying machines..."*

Collier's, 23Jan'04: *"A FLYING MACHINE THAT ACTUALLY FLIES, The Brothers Wright succeed where Langley failed, in driving an airship that is not a balloon. To sail three miles through the air at a speed of eight miles an hour against a breeze blowing twenty-one miles an hour is a most notable achievement in flying-machine experiments. Three years ago two brothers named Wright, of Dayton, Ohio, went down among the sandhills of the North Carolina coast. They were expert mechanics, and brought their own tools and machinery. They had studied the experiments of flying-machine inventors here and abroad. They were going to put their study and ingenuity to practical use. They tried the 'multiple wing' machine... then...turned to the gliding machine invented by Octave Chanute, and modified it to their purpose. Their first machine carried one of them three hundred and sixty feet, and another year a new apparatus sailed an eighth of a mile. Last year they made changes, and added a gasoline engine and propellers, with the final successful test late in December as a result...The machine, in which the operator lies at full length, is in some ways like a box kite with a rudder instead of a tail...they designed and built their propelling apparatus. One propeller, revolving horizontally, is placed underneath the centre of the machine's body. The other is like the screw of a steamship, whirling vertically at the rear. The gasoline engine...operates at will either or both of the propellers. The one beneath helps to hold up the machine; the one at the rear drives it in the direction toward which the operator points it...When the machine was sixty feet above the ground, the rear propeller began to do its work, sending the 'flyer' forward against the wind. Wilbur Wright was able to steer his craft as he pleased, with the aid of the horizontal steering gear...and after going three miles brought the machine gently to the ground without difficulty of mishap..."* Interesting reporting!

And among the many things going on in the Bell's lives, in 1888 Gardiner Hubbard co-founded the National Geographic Society, serving as its first president. In his introductory address he said: *"I am not a scientific man, nor can I lay claim to any special knowledge that would entitle me to be called a 'Geographer.'...Since my election I have been trying to learn...something of the history of science...In the fourteenth or fifteenth century, the mariner's compass was introduced...and then it became possible to venture far out of sight of land. Columbus boldly set sail...The present century forms a new era in the progress of geography - the era of organized research...America refuses to be left in the rear...In that other vast territory of the earth, the atmosphere that surrounds it, America has laid the foundations of a Geography of the Air...When we embark on the great ocean of discovery, the horizon of the unknown advances with us and surrounds us...The more we know, the greater we find is our ignorance. Because we know so little we have formed this society for the increase and diffusion of Geographical knowledge."* (Expatriate-Englishman [Italy] James Smithson, ca. 1754-1829, bequeathed "his whole fortune '*to the United States of America to found at Washington, under the name of the* <u>Smithsonian Institution</u>*, an establishment for the increase and diffusion of knowledge among men.'"*)

Growth languished under Hubbard for its <u>National Geographic Magazine</u> and its mainly Washingtonian society. Thus when he died Bell was thrust into its presidency.

Immediately things began to change. One of the society's first speakers was Amerst College Professor *Edwin Grosvenor*, author of a lavishly illustrated two volumes on Constantinople. He had twin sons, *Edwin* and *Gilbert* Hovey (1875-1966) who, in 1897, became acquainted with the Bells.

Romance ensued between Gilbert and Elsie - and in 1899, when Bell needed assistance managing the society, he convinced Gilbert to leave teaching and become its first full-time employee. Grosvenors have headed it since – for over a century.

To invigorate the society and its magazine, over his signature Bell wrote leading magazine and newspaper publishers extolling the <u>Geographic</u> magazine as a source of *"...reliable and timely items relating to all geographic topics that may be occupying the public mind..."* while counseling young Grosvenor: *"We must have today in the United States at least thirty millions of persons under the age of twenty-one...It should be possible to make the magazine...of so much value to the schools that it would be used as a sort of text book of current geography...and that the society must publish 'popular books on geographic subjects...THE WORLD AND ALL THAT IS IN IT is our theme...'"*

He urged that the society be made national and abandon its local nature by eliminating its dual class of active and corresponding members. Also he wanted nomination-for-membership forms in each issue, a practice proven highly effective. The January, 1905, issue, with its great number of photographic pages (plus Bell's approval of bare-breasted native women as *'geographic truth'*) saw the magazine's emergence as a mass-market periodical. One of Gilbert's most interesting accomplishments: *"By selling membership in the society instead of subscriptions, and making the magazine a free service to members he was able to secure tax exempt status as a nonprofit educational institution."*

Elsie and Gilbert were married in London in October, 1900. Their first child, *Melville* Bell, was born on 27Nov'01 in the Bell's Washington home. He was followed in 1903 by *Gertrude* Hubbard; *Mabel* Harlakenden in 1905; *Lilian* Waters in 1907; *Alexander* Graham Bell (1909-15 - born in Beinn Bhreagh, his Washington christening attended by President William Howard Taft, first cousin of his father's mother); *Elsie* Alexandra Carolyn in 1911 and *Gloria* Victoria in 1918.

While arranging lectures for the society, Gilbert met *David Fairchild* (1869-1954), a young government botanist. This led to his being their dinner guest in November, 1904, and meeting Marian (*Daisy*) Bell, which led to their marriage in April, 1905. The newlyweds lived with the Bells until their home, on forty acres of Maryland woodland, was completed a year later. On 17Aug'06 Alexander Graham Bell (*Sandy*) Fairchild was born, soon followed by two sisters.

Among the wonders of the 20th century was the automobile, and, as with most new things, Bell became an enthusiastic *"automobilist."* In July, 1905, he noted: *"We are in the 20th century & no mistake for after dinner, Mr. Hubbard took Mabel and myself for a little drive of about 40 miles (!) in his automobile..."*

Two months later Mabel wrote: *"...Papa seems to have thrown every other thought aside for the moment and gone in for automobiling as he goes in for everything he does, with his whole soul. Our machine is a Rambler...so far it has gone splendidly without accident, or stoppage of any kind. We came over fifty-three miles today from Gloucester."* This 5-passenger, 18-hp, 3-speed car had a two horizontal-opposed cylinder water-cooled engine (its cost would be about $60,000 today).

10Jan'05: Wilbur to Col. *John E. Capper*, R.E. (supt. of the Royal Aircraft Factory, Farnborough, and commander of Britain's *first* blimp-airship), following up on his visit to and meeting with the Wrights in Oct'04: *"...There is no question, but that the government in possession of such a machine as we can furnish, and the scientific and practical knowledge and instruction that we are in a position to impart, could secure a lead of several years over governments which waited to buy perfected machines before making a start in this line..."*

This was the *first* Wright offering of their invention.

18Jan'05: Wright brothers to Congressman Robert Nevin (as with Col. Capper, they'd met and spoken earlier, on 3Jan'05, but had *not* written him until this letter): *"The series of aeronautical experiments upon which we have been engaged for the past five years has ended in the production of a flying-machine of the type fitted for practical use. It not only flies through the air at high speed, but also lands without being wrecked...*

"The numerous flights...have made it quite certain that flying has been brought to a point where it can be made of great practical use in various ways, one of which is that of scouting and carrying messages in time of war. If the latter features are of interest to our own government, we shall be pleased to take up the matter either on a basis of providing machines...or of furnishing all the scientific and practical information...together with a license to use our patents; thus putting the government in a position to operate on its own account..."

Nevin brought the matter to the War Department's Board of Ordnance and Fortification, whose Maj. Gen. G. S. Gillespie responded on 24Jan'04: *"...It appears from the letter of Messrs. Wilbur and Orville Wright that their machine has not yet been brought to the stage of practical operation, but as soon as it shall have been perfected, this Board would be pleased to receive further representations from them in regard to it."*

Furthermore, until a patent was granted the government reasoned that it did not want to get involved, regardless of the fact that they considered the Wright's $100,000 price (almost $5 million today) unreasonable. The brothers were chagrined by this unexpected response.

1Mar'05: Wrights to British War Office: They offer to furnish a machine capable of carrying two men and flying for fifty miles without refueling. No payment would be required until a series of flights had been completed, and if none exceeded 10 miles, the contract would be void. Otherwise, 500 pounds-per-mile would be paid for the longest flight; e.g., if the flight were ten miles, the cost would be 5,000 pounds (about $2 million today), if fifty miles, 50,000 pounds (approx. $12 million).
13May'05: The British advise the Wrights that these sums greatly exceeded their expectations.

2Mar'05: Wilbur to Chanute: *"...I have secured and measured a crow...I have no measurement of its regular speed but think it...twenty-five miles an hour...I am far from believing that it expends less power, in proportion to weight and speed, than is readily attainable in a dynamic flying machine of large size..."*

10Mar'05: *Ernest Archdeacon* (Paris) to the Wrights: Archdeacon, a financier and expatriate Irish lawyer to become known as *"the father of French flying,"* expressed incredulity of the Wright's flights while none-the-less stating that if America was indeed ahead in flying machines, the French were *"surely first in lightweight motors* (e.g., *DeDion-Bouton* and Leon Levavasseur's *Antoinette*)." He closed with a challenge to the Wrights to *"come to give us lessons in France."*

11Mar'05: Wilbur to Chanute: *"...The German patent office has now held our application on the ground that the principle of twisting the wings is disclosed already... We had been congratulating ourselves that this had been overlooked by them. We fear that it may interfere with our being granted a broad claim on twisting the wings. It will...require careful handling to get around the objection..."*

29Apr'05: *"For on this day there ascended from the college grounds at Santa Clara (California), in the presence of thousands of spectators, an ordinary heated air balloon - to which was attached, not a parachute, but a 45-pound glider designed by Professor (John J.) Montgomery and mounted by an intrepid parachute jumper, Daniel Maloney ...At a height of about 4000 feet the aeroplane was cut loose from the balloon and commenced to glide, under the most absolute control imaginable, to the ground. In the course of the descent the most extraordinary and complex maneuvers were accomplished - spiral and*

and circling turns being executed with an ease and grace almost beyond description, level travel accomplished with the wind and against it, figure-eight evolutions performed without difficulty, and hair-raising dives were terminated by abrupt checking of the movement by changing the angles of the wing surfaces. At times the speed, as estimated by eye witnesses, was over sixty-eight miles per hour, and yet after a flight of approximately eight miles in twenty minutes the machine was brought to rest upon a previously designated spot, three-quarters of a mile from where the balloon had been released, so lightly that the aviator was not even jarred, despite the fact that he was compelled to land on his feet.."
Victor Lougheed

In 1909 Victor Lougheed wrote that <u>Scientific American</u>, 20May'05, *"declared that 'An aeroplane has been constructed that in all circumstances will retain its equilibrium and is subject in its gliding flight to the control and guidance of an operator.' Octave Chanute characterized the flight as 'the most daring feat ever attempted,' and Alexander Graham Bell had no hesitation in asserting that 'all subsequent attempts in aviation must begin with the Montgomery's machine.'"* He futher wrote: *"It is a fact of quite inescapable significance that recent (1909) activity and present successes in aeronautics do date most definitely from the public flights of the Montgomery machine in 1905...Subsequent to publication and circulation of these accounts* (<u>Scientific American</u>, 20May'05 and another in <u>Motor</u>, Jun'05) *there promptly followed the experiments with motor-propelled machines by Ferber in France in 1905; the fairly successful glides by Archdeacon, and of Bleriot and the Voisins* (brothers Gabriel and Charles), *over the Seine in June and July, 1905; the remarkable sustained flights of the Wrights over Huffman Prairie, Ohio, between September 26 and October 5, 1905, and the flights of Santos-Dumont...in August and September, 1906..."* Concluding that *"...it was Montgomery's successes that gave definite and recorded beginning to the now fast advancing period of man's mastery over the most elusive medium in which he aspires to travel...that of the bird...fruitlessly envied and copied, and copied and envied by earth-bound man from the fables of antiquity until March and April, 1905."*

23May'05: Chanute to Wilbur: *"...I enclose a letter...indicating that the Germans doubt your achievements, as do the French. I have been much amused by your remarks as to the latter ('...The last sentence of Capt. Ferber's letter is a broad hint that in France the Americans are not to be believed upon their mere word. We regard all such intimations with great amusement and satisfaction...') and think you have sized them up about right..."*

23May'05: The Wrights assemble *Flyer No. 3* at *"Simms."* It is similar to the 1904 machine but with the horsepower raised to 20. The total weight, man included, was approximately 870 pounds. For the first time they have a machine that can rise to a considerable height.

Beginning on June 23rd, they make over 160 flights during the 1905 season at Huffman Prairie. The Flyer, controlled by lying prone on the lower wing, used skids (no wheels until 1910) and because of the rough ground was catapult-launched by their *"peculiar 'derrick-and-weight' method"* off a rail.

They became quite proficient at flying; e.g., on their forty-sixth flight Wilbur was *airborne for over thirty-eight minutes* for about thirty rounds of the field and covered approximately twenty-four miles.

Wilbur commented: *"...During all the flights we had made up to this time we had kept close to the ground, in order that, in case we met any new and mysterious phenomenon, we could make a safe landing. With only one life to spend we do not consider it advisable to attempt to explore mysteries at such great height from the ground that a fall would put an end to our investigations and leave the mystery unsolved."*

And they *"deliberately unlinked the 'irrevocable' connection between warping and rudder movement,"* their final assertion of *constant pilot control.*

Orville stated: *"...The controls of the 1905 machine were operated in a slightly different manner from those of the 1903 machine. The vertical rear rudder was not connected up, so as to automatically operate in conjunction with the wing warping, but instead was coupled up to a lever* ("the split-handle lever"), *so that it could be operated either independently of the warping or in conjunction therewith. It was operated in this manner in a few flights in 1904, but not in many..."*

Also, they discover that the 1904 turning enigma, actually a 'stalled condition,' was correctable by slanting the nose slightly downward (only partially solving a problem to prove deadly to so many Wright aviators).

30May'05: Chanute to Wilbur: *"...I am very glad indeed to know that you stand ready to furnish a practical flying machine for use in war...*

"As an American I greatly regret that our government has apparently decided to allow foreign governments to take the lead in utilizing your invention..."

1Jun'05: Wilbur to Chanute: *"...We would be ashamed of ourselves if we had offered our machine to a foreign government without giving our own country a chance at it, but our consciences are clear...*

"It is no pleasant thought to us that any foreign country should take from America any share of the glory of having conquered the flying problem...We have taken pains to see that 'Opportunity' gave a good clear knock on the War Department door. It has for years been our business practice to sell to those who wished to buy, instead of trying to force goods upon people who did not want them..."

18Jun'05: Wilbur to Chanute: *"...We have no intention of forgetting that we are Americans, and do not expect to make arrangements which would probably result in harm to our native country. The exact date of meeting the British representative is not fixed but will probably be within a month..."*

16Jul'05: Wilbur to Chanute: *"...We have made nearly ten trials with the 1905 machine but have accomplished nothing notable as yet, the longest flight being only 750 ft. We have made several changes in the operating handles and have had some trouble...acquiring familiarity with them. We are sure they will be a good thing when we have learned the combination properly, but they have cost us several rather unlucky breakages, aggravating several weeks of delay."*

6Aug1905: Wilbur to Chanute: *"...The tragic death of poor Maloney* (killed at Santa Clara, 18Jul1905) *seemed the more terrible to me because I knew it was coming and tried in vain to think of some way to save him. I knew a direct warning would tend to precipitate rather than prevent a catastrophe. The Montgomery pamphlet showed an entire misapprehension of the real facts...and it seemed to me something awful that poor Maloney should cut loose high in the air* (from a balloon piloted by Charles K. Hamilton) *and lightly cause the machine to dart and describe circles without knowing that there were critical points beyond which it would be absolutely impossible for him to right the machine..."*

Note: *Daniel Maloney*, as earlier noted, was described as having held the crowd *"spellbound with amazing and complex maneuvers....Startling turns, spirals, figure eights, hair-raising dives and other difficult evolutions were performed with ease and grace..."*

9Aug1905: Chanute to Wilbur: *"...I have a letter from Spratt, who is greatly pleased of some recent experiments, and who says that his form of construction is the solution of the problem of stability. His account of his theory is somewhat perplexing by rea-son of his misapplication of words and terms..."*

Note: In 1944 Waldo Waterman was presented with, apparently, a similar theory by Spratt's son. The *"Spratt Wing"* caused comment, problems for Waldo (who didn't think much of it); the expenditure of quite a sum of ConVair's money, and in the end was judged unfeasible. See WALDO: Pioneer Aviator, pp. 411-413.

However, on 12Aug1993, *George G. Spratt* wrote the author: *"...Although my father lived till 1934 a bout with rheumatic fever left his heart so damaged that he was unable to do much active work after the early 1920's. In the late 20's I started to study better ways to stabilize and control an aeroplane than the elevator, rudder, aileron system then in use. During the early 30's I spent many hours flying a test bed in the form of a roadable aircraft studying the various wing axes and airfoils - see EAA film* Aviation Oddities. *About 1935 Vincent Bendix took an interest in the project and an experimental single place aircraft was built at his plant in South Bend. About this time I learned that this type of development was better carried out from the water than an airport so worked from my ketch in the Chesapeake till the war. Near the close of the war Consolidated Vultee decided to get in on the expected boom in private flying by having a roadable aircraft ready. To this end they brought Waldo with his Dunne type Studebaker roadable* (apparently considering the concept of a 'flying automobile' viable and Waldo, first to successfully build and fly one coast-to-coast, the expert) *and me with my Controlwing flying boat to their Stout Research Division in Dearborn. After considerable study management decided on the Controlwing, naming Waldo chief engineer on the construction of the prototype to be built at the Stout Research Division. In March* (1945) *Model 103 was taken to Elizabeth City for flight testing. Control and stability were good but the aircraft was impossibly heavy for the tests we needed to make. Waldo was no longer with Convair. The decision was made to take the aircraft to the Nashville Division. Here, with fewer engineers, it was largely rebuilt, bringing the weight within reason. After considerable flying at Nashville the project was moved to San Diego and flying continued until Odlum and his Atlas Corporation took over. They had no interest in private aviation and one day I returned to the plant to find that the aircraft had been cut up and consigned to the scrap pile. So then back to the Chesapeake and a series of flying boats.*

Sincerely, *George*

<u>Pendulum</u> *is excellent!"*

In the fall of 1905, at one of Bell's Wednesday Evening dinners attended by David Fairchild, Simon Newcomb, Samuel Langley and Octave Chanute, Chanute was asked: *"What evidence have we, Professor Chanute, that the Wright's have flown?"*

"I have seen them do it," he replied in words that left a *"tremendous impression"* on those present.

From the end of September and into early October the Wrights were attaining spectacular successes, capped on October 5th by the best flight of the year: Wilbur was aloft for 39 minutes and 23 seconds for a distance of 24.2 miles, during which he averaged 38 miles an hour and circled the field 29 times.

This one flight covered more distance and time than the total of all the previous flights of 1903 and 1904.

6Oct'05: At another Wednesday Evening dinner, Bell rose to dramatically announce: *"I hold in my hand a telegram telling me that the Wrights have been in the air for thirty minutes. <u>Thirty minutes,</u> gentlemen!"*

Flyer No.3 was the world's first *practical* aeroplane. It's most notable features:
1. Flight range increased to 24 miles.
2. Endurance increased to over 38 minutes.
3. Catapult used for launching.
4. Rudder operated independently. It was concurrent with, but not attributable to, this change that they learned to avoid turning stalls by careful use of the elevator instead of attempting correction only with the rudder.

"With the 1905 machine, they were able to bank, turn, fly in circles and in figure eights. For a brief period in history, the brothers...were at the very pinnacle in aviation development. They were doing routinely what was impossible anywhere else in the world."
Rubenstein & Goldman

9Oct'05: Wright Brothers to Secretary of War: *"Some months ago we made an informal offer to furnish to the War Department practical flying machines suitable for scouting purposes. The matter was referred to the Board of Ordnance and Fortification, which seems to have given it scant consideration. We do not wish to take this invention abroad, unless we find it necessary to do so, and therefore write again, renewing the offer.*

"We are prepared to furnish a machine on contract, to be accepted only after trial...to carry an operator and supplies...sufficient for a flight of one hundred miles; the price...according to a sliding scale based on performance...of at least twenty-five miles at a speed of not less than thirty miles an hour.

"We are also willing to...build machines carrying more than one man."

9Oct'05: Wilbur to Ferdinand Ferber: *"...It is our present intention to first offer it* (the Flyer) *to the governments for war purposes, and if you think your government would be interested, we would be glad to communicate with it."*

1905: *Gabriel Voisin* (1880-1973), *Ernest Archdeacon* and *Louis Bleriot* (1872-1936) found the world's *first* airplane factory in Billancourt, near Paris.

18Oct'05: The *Aero Club of America* is founded. In December, planning a January, 1906, exhibition (in conjunction with the Automobile Club of America) it obtained exhibit acceptances from Bell, Langley, General Adolphus W. Greely of the Signal Corps, Charles Marvin of the Weather Bureau, and Allen of Patents, among others. Member *Albert F. Zahm,* of Catholic University, requested that the Wrights send photographs, models and whatever, and that they act as *"champions...to uphold the honor of our country"* by making a public flight.

In reply to Zahm (22Dec'05) Wilbur states: *"...It will give us great pleasure to furnish the Aero Club a collection of photographs, for their show next month.*

"We have never made models and consequently can furnish nothing...The (Kitty Hawk) *machines...we did not try to preserve them...*(what of today's relic?)

"...our exhibit this time must be confined to gliding pictures..."

19Oct'05: Wilbur to Chanute: *"...We are not anticipating an immediate visit from the Britishers...and do not expect anything until we write or stir them up...*

"...On the 26th we passed the ten mile mark for the first time...On Oct. 3rd. a larger gasoline can was used and the record raised...On the 5th of October made a flight of 38,956 meters (24.21 miles) *in 38 min. and 3 sec. Gasoline exhausted. We had neglected to fill the can full before starting.*

"Some friends whom we unwisely permitted to witness some of the flights could not keep silent, and on the evening of the 5th the <u>Daily News</u> *had an article reporting that we were making sensational flights everyday...Consequently we are doing nothing at present..."*

19Oct'05: Wrights to U.S. War Department: *"...We cannot well fix a price, nor a time for delivery, till we have your idea of the qualifications necessary to such a machine. We ought also to know whether you would wish to reserve a monopoly on the use of the invention, or whether you would permit us to accept orders for similar machines from other governments, and give public exhibitions, etc..."*

24Oct'05: The U.S. War Department took this action: *"It is recommended that the Messrs. Wright be informed that the Board does not care to formulate any requirements for the performance of a flying machine or take any further action on the subject until a machine is produced which by actual operation is shown to be able to produce horizontal flight and to carry an operator."*

4Nov'05: Wilbur to Ferber: *"...For when it becomes known that France is in possession of a practical flying machine other countries must at once avail themselves of our scientific discoveries and practical experience. With Russia and Austria-Hungary in their present troubled condition and the German Emperor in a truculent mood, a spark may produce an explosion at any minute. No government dare take the risk of waiting to develop practical flying machines independently. To be even one year behind other governments might result in losses compared with which the modest amount we shall ask for our invention would be insignificant...*

"Under the present circumstances we would consent to reduce our price to the French government to one million francs..."

The proposal was to supply an initial machine for a *"modest"* $200,000 (about $12 million today), which, as with the British, seemed quite high to the French...

"...and the brother's almost paranoid secretiveness about their invention made them exasperating to deal with. Even after the patents...were granted...they refused to reveal details of their machine, much less the machine itself, to prospective buyers in advance of a firm agreement."   *The First Aviators*

8Nov'05: Wilbur to Chanute: *"...Saturday was an ideal day for record breaking but we were too disgusted to care to make use of it. Yesterday we went out and dismantled the machine...we have no thought now of further experiments at our present grounds.*

"Regarding...Capt. Ferber...We have written him...and assured him that we regard it an advantage rather than a disadvantage...since the possession of a practical flying machine by the French makes it imperative for other European governments to come to us at once..."

28Nov'05: Wrights to British War Office: *"...we are not willing to show the machine to the representatives of any government in advance of an agreement as to terms of sale."*

28Nov'05: Wilbur makes inquiries to the French ambassador preliminary to a formal proposal to France, which they now consider their best prospect.

4Dec'05: Wilbur to Chanute: *"...We are investigating a report which Mr. Manly made of our experiments...but we are not certain whether he was here himself... Do you know any means of finding out whether he was wearing a moustache about the 1st of October?...It is evident that the news was obtained by some underhand method...*

"...we are unwilling to show the machine to the attache' of any government without some assurance that a sale will follow a demonstration that the machine can

really fly as we claim. We think it a poor time to bargain as to terms after the goods have been partly delivered..."

6Dec'05: Chanute to Wilbur: *"...I think that you will readily establish that it is not a gold brick you have to sell, and that there will be a good deal of hesitancy about the price.*

"...Mr. Manly is about 5 ft. 6 in. tall, youthful...and with a brown moustache.

"Would you like to have your matters privately presented to the President or to some member of Congress, so as to lead for a request for past correspondence?"

8Dec'05: Wilbur to Chanute: *"...We think it too soon to think of organizing a company until we know whether there is a prospect of selling the invention as a strict secret...*

"Word just received from our attorneys is to the effect that all of our claims will be allowed in U. S. patent...

"...we are inclined to think that the best course regarding the correspondence with the American War Department is complete suppression. We do not think there would be any advantage in bringing the matter to the attention of the President, or Sec. of War, unless they were previously fully convinced of the practicability of the machine and the desirability of securing it for the government. No such condition exists at present. Neither can we see any advantage in letting it become generally known that we have been turned down by our own government. It will be a hindrance to successful negotiations with any other government. We have not informed a single person outside of our own family, except yourself. We think it best to maintain secrecy as to the progress of all negotiations with governments."

9Dec'05: Chanute to Wilbur: *"...I think you are quite right in deferring an organization till you see how your pending negotiations will come out, and in awaiting conviction on the part of the President. He may blame you hereafter, however, for not calling his attention to your recent achievements.*

"...I believe that the 'man in this (New York) *city' alluded to was either Herring or Manly, as both of them seem to have given points and information to the writer of the article..."*

13Dec'05: Wilbur to Chanute: *"...I am afraid my opinion* (about his disclosure of negotiations) *of Capt. Ferber would not look well in writing...*

"Several weeks ago we concluded that too much time was being wasted by England and France in coming to close quarters, so we decided to apply a mild outside pressure. At the same time we released you, we wrote to Diensbach (German), *Besancon* (French), *and Alexander* (English), *as well as Col. Capper* (English), *giving a detailed statement of our later experiments* (below). *The desired effect seems to have been produced in France, at least...They* (English) *have no doubt learned from the Paris papers that our hint was not a mere 'bluff,' but we have no word from London as yet..."*

Col. J.E. Capper: *"I wish to invite very special attention to the wonderful advance made in aviation by the brothers Wright. I have every confidence in their uprightness, and in the correctness of their statements. It is a fact that they have flown and operated personally a flying machine for a distance of over three miles, at a speed of 35 mph."*

14Dec'05: Chanute to Wilbur: *"...I believe that your...papers would now greatly appreciate your permission to publish some accounts of your performances...*

"I think the President should also have copies of the papers.

"I think you are wise in allowing some publicity to occur. I do not see how it can injure your pending negotiations."

21Dec'05: Chanute to Wilbur: *"...I had a call from Mr. Herring this morning, who said that he was hunting up exhibits for the Aero Club of America, to be displayed in New York, Jan. 13th to 29th. He made the assertion that you had written to somebody that your screws were 8 feet in diameter and that your motor was placed on the bed of your machine. He added that the motor had 4 cylinders of 4-inch bore, and that the total weight was 950 pounds, some 70 pounds of this being iron bars which were shifted during flight..."*

22Dec'05: Wilbur to Zahm regarding Aero Club exhibit: *"...When (we) began experimenting in 1900 it was purely for the pleasure of it. We did not expect to get back a cent of the money we spent. Consequently we agreed with each other that it should under no circumstances be permitted to infringe upon our time and money needed for our business...*

"...after several seasons we found ourselves standing at a fork in the road. On one hand we could continue playing with the problem of flying...On the other hand we believed that if we would take the risk of devoting our entire time and financial resources we would conquer the difficulties in the path to success...We finally decided to make the attempt...as a strict business proposition until such time as we had recouped ourselves...We shall endeavor to secure our pay in such a way as will permit the world in general to receive the benefit of the invention within a reasonably short time, with the least possible restriction on progress."

27Dec'05: Wilbur to Chanute: *"...The idea of selling to a single government as a strict secret has some advantages but we are very much disinclined to assume the moral responsibility of choosing the proper one when we have no means of knowing how it will use the invention...it is very repugnant to think of hiding an invention of such intense human interest until it becomes stale and useless.*

"We are fully as much surprised as you were to learn that our offer to Ferber covered sales to individuals as well as his government, but they have some strange ways in France and we did not wish to be caught napping. A letter just received from Ferber states that the 'friend' is M. Fordyce (scouting for Paris' leading newspaper and an indirect agent of the French Government)..."

28Dec'05: Bishop Wright's diary: *"...a Frenchman by the name of Arnold Fordyce came to investigate and drive a trade for a flying machine..."*

30Dec'05: *"...In the afternoon, Wilbur and Orville sign up a contract with Mr. Arnold Fordyce, of Paris, to furnish a flyer, &c., for one million francs."*

Wilbur wrote: *"Our 1905 improvements have given such results as to justify the assertion that flying has been transferred from the realm of scientific problems to that of useful arts."*

Contract in hand - after logging 50 flights and a total time aloft of 3 hours and 40 minutes in 1905 - they stopped flying to protect their secrets while searching for additional business in Europe. *They would not fly again until 1908.*

It is an irony of history that the man whose success they most wanted to emulate, Alexander Graham Bell, was to become their most formidable competitor.

"Stung by the press, angered by their own government's rejection, convinced that almost everyone with whom they came in contact was out to exploit their work and to cheat them, the brothers, in effect, went underground. Flight was their secret, and they were going to guard it to the utmost..." *Harry Combs*

"The Wright brothers had gone into utter hibernation, as far as practical flight was concerned, between October 1905 and May 1908. They had applied for a patent for their machines that was slow in being granted. In the meantime they tried to influence, in respective order, the Governments of the United States, Great Britain and France, into purchasing the rights on their aeroplanes. They offered a package deal in the sense that negotiations should be all or nothing - the takeover of the rights on the trusted testimony of the brothers without detailed prior examination of the machines - since they feared rejection of the offer after adequate commercial spying on their exclusive features. All these negotiations at first were unsuccessful...This impasse was broken in 1908 when satisfactory business arrangements were made with both the United States and the French..." *Allen Andrews*

1Jan'06: Bishop Wright's diary: "...*Wilbur & Orville get letters from England, France, and Austria...*"

2Jan'06: Wilbur to Chanute: "...*We have made an agreement by which the secret formulas are communicated, not to the syndicate, but to the government direct. We give a license to manufacture only for government use. The syndicate cannot exploit the invention commercially...They are to post a forfeit of 25,000 francs by Febr. 5th, and deposit one million francs* (approximately $10 million today) *in a New York bank by April 5th, of which sum 750,000 frs. is to become ours absolutely as soon as we have delivered a machine to them, after a trial flight of 50 kilometers...The balance is...ours absolutely after...three months...*

"We agree to furnish no machine or instruction to any other nation or individual until...three months from...delivery. We reserve all rights to sell to other governments after that time...

"We have just received a letter from...Vienna, who, having seen that we are offering the invention to the French for 1 million francs, write to inquire whether they cannot become the purchasers...If the idea of acquiring the machine in different countries...should spread, we may be able to secure all the renumeration we care for, and establish free trade in flying machines within a year or two. Nothing would suit us better, but we shall not begin counting our chickens until we are sure of them..."

7Jan'06: Chanute to Wilbur: *"...I am delighted to learn that you have sold a flying machine to the French...and this without onerous restrictions as to sales to other nations.*

"This may not make for peace as much as an exclusive sale to one nation, for now they will all have a machine, and I fancy that the French have acted so promptly because they expect early war, but it will make you world famous and eventually millionaires..."

10Jan'06: Wilbur to Chanute: *"...If the French deal goes through all right, we will have no difficulty in securing all the money we need without exploiting the invention commercially or assuming any business responsibilities. It will leave us entirely free to pursue a number of scientific studies...*

"Do you expect to attend the N.Y. Aero Club show next week?"

11Jan'06: Wilbur to Chanute: *"...Do you know of a small island anywhere, a half mile wide and a mile or two long, which is reasonably level & smooth and free from trees? We are looking for a place where we can at least partly control the activity of spies."*

12Jan'06: Chanute to Wilbur: *"...I think the vicinity of Tampa is too much infested with tourists & fishermen...*

"I believe the surest way of finding an adequate place would be to hire a launch, either at Tampa or at Key West, and to coast along like tourists..."

In 1891 *Henry B. Plant* (1819-99) Florida's principal West Coast developer, competing with *Henry M. Flagler*'s (1830-1913) magnificent, 1888, $2 million, Ponce de Leon Hotel in St. Augustine, constructed an even more resplendent hotel, the Moorish-revival, 511-room Tampa Bay Hotel, costing almost $3 million (about $225 million today).

Flagler, like Curtiss a native of western New York, of Hopewell near Hammondsport, was cofounder with *John D. Rockefeller* of the Standard Oil Company. And was Florida's preeminent East Coast developer, a role that Curtiss would pursue a quarter-century later.

Likely, Chanute had been Plant's guest - one of the many "tourists" paying $3 a day for the finest in food, rest and culture - when a New York apartment cost $1.50 a week. Flagler's hotel is now Flagler College; Plant's the impressive centerpiece of the University of Tampa.

Jan'06: At the Aero Club of America's *first* exhibit, held in conjunction with New York's Automobile Show, Curtiss's exhibit featured his new lightweight airship motors; the modified four-cycle, two-cylinder, 5-horsepower V-motor used in the *California Arrow*, and two-cylinder, 10-horsepower, and three-cylinder, 15-horse-power motors of similar construction.

Aero Club member Bell was there with his exhibit of tetrahedral kites, and was searching for a lightweight motor to power them. His exhibit - crowned with a sign: *"THE OIONOS, A Soaring Kite Adapted to Gliding Flight When Freed From its Cord."*

After considerable time spent with tetrahedral kite experiments, late in 1904 Bell discarded Hargrave's designs in favor of a single multicell airfoil with a horizontal tail, later adding a pendulum flight governor. In flight it resembled a large bird, hence *Oionos*, Greek for bird of omen.

Mabel and Alec Bell:

This was when Bell and Curtiss met, with Bell noting in his diary: *"A 15 horsepower motor can be obtained from the Curtis Motor Cycle Company – weighing 125 lbs - (double cylinder) and can probably be considerably lightened. Safe to say 150 lbs for motor fittings, oil, etc. at outside figures."*

In April *"Curtiss No. 1"* arrived in Nova Scotia.

13Jan'06: <u>Scientific American:</u> *"...Unfortunately the Wright brothers are hardly disposed to publish any substantiation or to make public experiments, for reasons best known to themselves. If such sensational and tremendously important experiments are being conducted in a not very remote part of the country, on a subject in which almost everybody feels the most profound interest, is it possible to believe that the enterprising American reporter, who, it is well known, comes down the chimney when the door is locked...would not have ascertained all about them and published them long ago? Why particularly...should the Wrights desire to sell their invention to the French government for a 'million' francs? Surely their own is the first to which they would be likely to apply. We certainly want more light on the subject."*

30Jan'06: Wright Brothers to Arnold Fordyce: *"...After careful consideration...we are ready to enter into a contract to furnish a flyer such as you proposed - to carry two men, to start from the level, and to rise during the flight to a height of 300 meters.*

"...We are therefore compelled to make the date of delivery of a two-man flyer May 1st, 1907 (earlier if possible), and the price two million francs (over $16 million today).

"...If we are released from the exclusive option clause, so that we can sell our present design of flyer to others at once, we are willing to make the proposed changes...at a small additional cost - 1,200,000 francs (about $10 million today).

"The last proposition of your telegram, to postpone the date of the first deposit, we cannot consider for an instant. You were scarcely aboard your ship before new developments brought us to the realization that we had committed a grave error in granting a five weeks' exclusive option without a bonus. We will never again sacrifice opportunities by giving exclusive options without immediate and adequate deposits..."

31Jan'06: Wilbur to Chanute: *"...You are at perfect liberty to inform correspondents that the French contract is not exclusive. Three months after the machine is delivered we are free to begin deliveries to any other country.*

"A letter...describing the Aero Club show says: 'One wall of the exhibition room had been preserved for flying machine pictures divided under these heads: Lilienthal - Herring - Wright Bros. - Langley - Maxim - Pilcher, from left to right, in the same order.'

"I was under the impression that I learned somewhere that you had conducted some experiments about 1896 or 1897. Possibly my memory is at fault."

3Feb'06: Chanute to Wilbur: *"...Are the French to send their operators to be instructed by you in this country? You might be at a disadvantage if you had to go abroad before receiving your money.*

"I am very much amused to learn how Herring arranged the exhibits. I sent the Aero Club all told 15 models."

Feb'06: The British War Office notifies the Wrights that the terms of their proposal are unacceptable.

Early Feb'06, Bell in *The New York World: "The impossible* (has happened) *in aerial navigation and I am proud of the fact that America leads the world...To the Wright brothers, of Ohio, belongs the credit."*

27Feb'06: Derided by the failures of his "buzzard," a haunted Samuel Perpont Langley is felled by two heart attacks, dying in Aiken, South Carolina.

At his funeral Bell, his most stalwart friend, says: *"His flying machine never had an opportunity of being fairly tried,* (but) *the man and his works will permanently endure."*

This may be a good place to comment on Bell's thoughts on religion. Mabel, with whom he occasionally attended Presbyterian or Episcopalian services, said: *"...he never denied God."* Nor did he espouse God or any particular religion. However, in 1901, after reading a Unitarian treatise, he wrote Mabel: *"I have always considered myself an Agnostic but I have now discovered that I am a Unitarian Agnostic."*

2Mar'06: Wilbur to Chanute, commenting on Langley's death: *"...No doubt disappointment shortened his life. It is really pathetic that he should have missed the honor he cared for above all others, merely because he could not launch his machine successfully* (Wilbur, like others, was unaware that the Aerodrome's shortcomings far exceeded launching problems). *If he could only have started it, the chances are that it would have flown sufficiently to have secured to him the name he coveted, even though a complete wreck attended the landing...The fact that the great scientist, Prof. Langley, believed in flying machines was one thing that encouraged us to begin studies..."*

7Feb'06: Wilbur to Chanute: *"...The French war office has taken over the contract and has deposited the forfeit of 25,000 francs with J. P. Morgan & Co. in New York. We are to receive 3/4 of a million francs immediately after the trial flight, and before instruction is given to operators. All is to be done in America if we so elect. We will insist on payment in advance if we go abroad..."*

14Feb'06: Chanute to Wilbur: *"...I think the developments you mention in Germany are not 'strange.' They are mean. The Kaiser had probably made up his mind to a war with France. The taking over of your machine by the latter causes him to pause, as he may not know that the sale is not exclusive.*

"Perhaps information to the Kaiser... (of) the facts might change his attitude..."

18Mar'06: Chanute to Wilbur: *"...I am very glad...to learn that your German patent is allowed. I enclosed a little clipping stating that the Germans were about to undertake the construction of war balloons and aeroplanes. It is not impossible that Mr. Herring may offer his services towards building the latter, so I think I will write to Major Moedebeck...that your sale to the French is not exclusive..."*

1Apr'06: Wilbur to Chanute: *"I telegraphed to you this morning asking you to be present at the final conference with representatives of the French Government...The real object of their coming was to secure an extension of the exclusive feature of the contract...we must either give way, or give an extension of time...We have assumed great liberty in presuming to request you to make a special trip to Dayton on our account but trust that you will not be offended..."*

2Apr'06: Bishop Wright's diary: *"Mr. O. Chanute, Chi., came. His visit with the four Frenchmen in Wright brothers' office. He, W.V.R. Berry, & Arnold Fordyce, sup with us..."*

7Apr'06: Chanute to Wilbur: *"...I regret that your deal with the French was not closed, as delays may bring about complications, but I believe that it will go through all right. I think I would have agreed to the going up to the 300 meters* (approximately 1,000 feet) *after the other conditions had been complied with and terminated acceptance.*

"...Having occasion to write Major Baden-Powell (British)...: *'The Wrights are building another machine. It is my impression that their arrangement with the French is not yet fully closed, the Government having brought forward some additional requirements which the Wrights deem unreasonable. You know, I presume, that in no case is an exclusive right to be given'..."*

19Apr'06: Chanute to Wilbur: *"I had a telegram...from Mr. Alexander: 'Will arrive Dayton Friday morning. Must leave ten same evening for Washington.'*

"As I had an engagement for that day I had to telegraph my regrets...

"...I hope...this will result in placing your machine in the hands of the British..."

28Apr'06: Wilbur to Chanute: *"Mr. Alexander spent a day with us and then started home by way of Washington and New York...I think he was asked to get information...by the government...*

"...Of course we have no thought of commercial exploitation even if the French deal falls through. Our position is constantly becoming stronger in other countries and we will soon find a sale somewhere. The French will buy eventually and probably under less favorable conditions than obtain today...

"...We had written to the German war office several weeks ago, as also to Italy, Russia, Austria, and Japan.

"The U. S. patent has been granted on the gliding machine..."

The French negotiations dragged on, largely because the end of the Moroccan in-surrection lessened their desire to try aeroplanes as war machines.

8May'06: Wright Cycle Co. to War Office, London: *"...We are now offering to the various governments our complete invention...*

"No government has been offered or granted a permanent monopoly of the fruits of our labors...

"...we would be very glad to discuss the whole subject...with His Majesty's Gov-ernment."

21May'06: The Wright brothers write President Theodore Roosevelt of their plans for a trip East and request an interview. The president's secretary, *William Loeb, Jr.,* replied that they could pay their respects to the President any day at noon except Tuesday and Friday. They canceled their plans.

22May'06: The Wright patent is granted embodying these words: *"...it is possible to move the forward corner of the lateral edges of the aeroplane* (wing) *on one side of the machine either above or below the normal planes of the aeroplane, a reverse movement of the forward corners of the lateral margins on the other side of the ma-chine occurring simultaneously."*

And, as wing warping induced a turning, it was necessary to interrelate the verti-cal rudder for control:

"...the construction is such that the rudder will always be so turned as to present its resisting-surface on that side of the machine on which the lateral margins of the aeroplane present the least angle of resistance."

4Jul'06: Wilbur to Chanute: *"...We no longer consider it necessary to preserve strict secrecy regarding the American and French negotiations...We think it best however to say nothing for publication. The British and other negotiations remain confiden-tial..."*

25Jul'06: Wilbur to Chanute: *"...(Major Moedebeck) no doubt correctly voices the expectation of the German officials that by refusing to buy they can compel us to make our machine public. I think they will be disappointed when they find out how the matter works out.*

"...Possibly the French also hope that we will turn our attention to commercial exploitation, thus making the machine public...

"We have given notice to (J.P.) Morgan's, to Fordyce, and to the Frenchmen in Washington, and unless the forfeit is turned over we will enter suit...My own idea is to stand pat and wait for something to happen which will bull the market. 'All things come to him who waits.' Excellent opportunities have been abundant in the past three years. I see no reason why similar chances should not occur within the next three..."

The forfeit, approximately $5,000 (about $225,000 today), was paid in October, the *first* money earned by them since they gave up their bicycle business.

31Jul'06: Wright Cycle Co. to British Military Attache: *"...For a sum of one hundred thousand dollars* (about $4-1/2 million today) *we offer to furnish a flyer, train a British operator in the use of it, and grant full rights to manufacture flyers...*

"For one hundred thousand dollars additional we offer to impart confidentially our scientific knowledge and discoveries...

"If the complete invention be purchased we would agree that neither instructions nor machines should be delivered by us to any other government (the United States excepted) for a period of six months..."

22Aug'06: Chanute to Wilbur: *"...I left with Mr. Cabot* (Boston) *my collection of clippings about you, and copies of extracts from letters concerning your negotiations with our government, so that the rights of the question will be made known to the proper parties should you be criticized for dealing with a foreign government in advance of your own..."*

8Aug'06: Col. Edward Gleichen, the British military attache in Washington, following a visit to Dayton, wrote: ...(the Wright brothers) are *"intelligent looking, not 'cranks,' apparently honest - their venerable father being bishop of some hazy denomination - and with little or none of the usual braggadocio of the Yankee inventor...being modest, even shy, but with a firm determination to take not a penny less than the prices quoted in their latest offer."*

4Sep'06: Wilbur to Chanute: *"...The only knowledge we have of Mr. Herring going to Germany is based on the interview...in the* Paris N.Y. Herald *last May...*

"Captain Baldwin is at the fair in Dayton this week, but the wind has been too strong for him to attempt a flight...Mr. Curtiss, who is building the motor for Prof. Bell's experiments this fall, called to see us..."

13Sep'06: In Paris, Alberto Santos-Dumont was acclaimed *"first to fly"* (challenging the 42-meter flight of 12Sep'06 by Denmark's J.C.H. Ellehammer) after a 60-meter flight in his 50-hp Antoinette-powered, tail-first, box-kite *"14 bis Aeromobile"* (originally to be launched from his *No. 14* airship).

24Sep'06: Walter Berry to Wrights: This letter indicated that the French broke off negotiations because they considered the limited period of their monopoly not worth a million francs, and that Berry hoped the Wrights would cut their price and reopen discussions through Fournier.

7Oct'06: Chanute to Wilbur: *"Upon my return from...British Columbia I find here the enclosed letters from Mr. Cabot and Mr. Renard, who both seem to think...you will have difficulty in selling your machines at the price asked. I think myself that it is very high, but an emergency may enable you to obtain it..."*

10Oct'06: Wilbur to Chanute: *"...Our friends do not seem to exactly understand our position in the matter of supposed delay...We merely refuse to let our hand be forced...There is no such thing in the world as absolute value for anything...If it were indeed true that others would be flying within a year or two, there would be reason in selling at any price but we are convinced that no one will be able to develop a practical flyer within five years. This opinion is based upon cold calculation. It takes into consideration practical and scientific difficulties whose existence is unknown to all but ourselves...We do not believe there is one chance in a hundred that anyone will have a machine of the least practical usefulness within five years..."*

15Oct'06: Chanute to Wilbur: *"...The value of an invention is whatever it costs to reproduce it, and I am by no means sure that persistent experimenting by others, now that they know one success has been achieved, may not produce a practical flyer within five years.*

"The important factor is that light motors have been developed (e.g., Curtiss)*...but are you not too cocksure that yours is the only secret worth knowing and that others may not hit upon a solution in less than 'many times five years'? It took you much less than that and there are a few (very few) other able inventors in the world. The danger therefore is that others may achieve success..."*

28Oct'06: Wilbur to Chanute: *"...I am not certain that your method of estimating probabilities is a sound one. Do you not insist too strongly upon the single point of mental ability. To me it seems that a thousand other factors, each rather insignificant in itself, in the aggregate influence the event ten times more than mere mental ability or inventiveness...The one thing that impresses me as remarkable is the shortness of the time within which our work was done. It was due to peculiar combinations of circumstances which might never occur again...We look upon the present question in an entirely impersonal way. It is not chiefly a question of relative ability, but of mathematical probabilities...Is it not wise to let the results of the season's experiments in Europe and elsewhere demonstrate that a really practical flyer is not the work of months but of years, in the meanwhile so improve the capabilities of our own machine as to greatly increase its value and lead over others?...We are also carefully considering the best methods of advancing sales..."*

1Nov'06: Chanute to Wilbur: *"I have your letter of Oct. 28th and do not agree with your way of thinking.*

"I presume you have seen...that Santos-Dumont made a short flight on Sep. 13th...I fancy that he is now very nearly where you were in 1904...

"I suppose you can do no better than to wait the result, for the outcome will depend not only upon the 'mental ability,' which you misunderstood me as constituting the sole cause, but upon mechanical instinct and that conjunction of circumstances which is sometimes called luck.

"Be this as it may, I suppose that you realize that (Robert) *Esnault-Pelterie* (1881-1957), (Ferdinand) *Ferber,* (Louis) *Bleriot* & (Gabriel) *Voisin. Barlatier & Blanc, Vuia, Cornu, Cody, and a German syndicate are also experimenting with dynamic flying machines. Some of them may develop something...I do not believe that it would be wise to be very stiff as to terms should a good offer come from the British War Office..."*

2Nov'06: Wilbur to Chanute: *"...You say 'I fancy he is now very nearly where you were in 1904'...I cannot resist making a forecast* (of Santos-Dumont's flight) *before the details arrive.*

"From our knowledge...we estimate that it is possible to jump about 250 ft., with a machine that has not made the first steps toward controllability...

"You have possibly forgotten that we stayed in the air 59 seconds in a wind of twenty miles' velocity in the year preceding 1904...

"...When someone goes over three hundred feet and lands safely in a wind of seven or eight miles it will then be important for us to do something. So far we see no indication that it will be done for several years yet. There is all the difference in the world between jumping and flying. We have never considered light motors the important point in solving the flying problem..."

They were correct, Santos-Dumont's first flight was a 198-foot jump, but on November 12th, with a more powerful Antoinette motor and Esnault-Pelterie's interplane ailerons (possibly based upon *Matthew Piers Watt Boulton*'s British patent of 1868), he flew 726 feet, winning the Aero Club Prize.

17Nov'06: <u>Scientific American</u>: *"Santos-Dumont made a brilliant performance at Paris on the 23rd of October with his new aeroplane. He succeeded in making a flight of some 200 feet, keeping at a distance of ten feet above the ground all the while, and thus winning the $600 Archdeacon cup...Such a flight with a motor-driven aeroplane has never before been publicly made... The eight-cylinder* (steam-cooled) *Antoinette motor weighs but 170 pounds and gives 50 horsepower..."*

Santos Dumont in the Basket of His Aeroplane "14-bis."
Note the control lever and wheel for the box rudder in front. The 50-horse-power motor is just back of the basket.

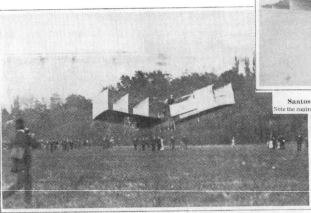

The Aeroplane Making Its First Successful Free Flight With Its Owner in Control.
The machine flew about 200 feet at an elevation of 10 feet from the ground.

8Nov1906: Wilbur to Chanute: *"...The cause of the difference in estimating the time required for producing a practical flyer is apparently deep-seated. The difference in estimating time results from radically different conceptions of what the flying problem really is, and from different views as to what it was that enabled us to succeed. The nature of the problem seems to us to absolutely forbid a quick solution..."*

11Nov'06: Chanute to Wilbur: *"...I do not understand what you have in mind in saying that 'The nature of the flying problem seems to us to absolutely forbid a quick solution.' For if it involves discovering a secret, it is possible that other researchers may stumble upon it."*

18Nov'06: Wilbur to Chanute: *"...It is the complexity of the flying problem that makes it so difficult. It is not to be solved by stumbling upon a secret, but by the patient accumulation of information upon a hundred different points, some of which an investigator would naturally think it unnecessary to go into deeply. That is why we think a quick solution impossible.*

"The newspapers contain reports of further experiments by Santos-Dumont, including a flight of two hundred meters...It is the first real indication of progress that has been displayed in France in five years...Whether M. Santos will find the motor an aid or encumbrance in his attack upon the real problems of flight only the future can tell. Much might be said on both sides..."

28Nov'06: Chanute to Wilbur: *"...I still differ with you as to the possibility of your being caught up with if you rest upon your oars. It is practice, practice...which tells and the other fellows are getting it. I did not believe that there was a secret, but your previous letter squinted that way, and I wanted to bring you out."*

30Nov'06: Bishop Wright's diary: *"....There is much in the papers about the Wright brothers. They have fame, but not wealth, yet. Both these things, aspired after by so many, are vain."*

1Dec'06: Wilbur to Chanute: *"...We are sorry to miss seeing you, as it seems that the favorable conditions we have been waiting for six months have now arrived and we have some opportunities we would be glad to talk over with you, the best from a financial standpoint that we have had. There is nothing definite yet, but we are to meet the people interested in New York next week..."*

1-8Dec'06: At New York's combined Aero and Automobile Show at Grand Central Palace there were more discussions between Curtiss and Bell, concluding with Bell's ordering his second Curtiss 4-cylinder motor (Curtiss was then making three of the new air-cooled V-8 engines, two for airship customers; one for himself. Of note, in 1907 Edward R. Hewitt made America's first automotive V-8, and in 1914 Cadillac first offered a production water-cooled V-8).

The Wrights and Chanute, accompanied by *Augustus Post* (1873-), co-founder/secretary of the Aero Club of America, attended the Aero Club Show.

6Dec'06: While in New York the Wrights meet with *Frank R. Cordley* of Flint and Company, initiating discussions about international sales representation.

15Dec'06; <u>Scientific American</u> editorial, <u>the Wright's *first* recognition</u>: *"In all the history of invention, there is probably no parallel to the unostentatious manner in which the Wright brothers of Dayton, Ohio, ushered into the world their epoch-making invention of the first successful aeroplane flying-machine..."*

20Dec'06: Wilbur to Chanute: *"...we went to Washington, where we met Prof. Zahm, Dr. Bell, Prof. Marvin, Prof. Moore, and several of the Smithsonian men. Dr. Bell and Prof. Zahm were especially kind...*
    "Flint & Co. now offer us $500,000 (approximately $25 million today) *for our rights outside the United States. We reserve the latter...Their idea seems to be to depend on getting possession of the market by being first in the field rather than depending on patents alone or secrecy alone...What do you think of it?...The price and terms are satisfactory and we would accept if we felt sure of their character."*

Note: "Charles R. (Ranlett) Flint, a wealthy, free-wheeling industrialist, had already earned the title Father of Trusts, and was perhaps the international private arms middleman." *John E. Walsh.*
    And in <u>Fortune,</u> Mar'30: *"...*The innumerable corporations he (Flint) has put together include American Chicle, International Business Machine (In 1914 *Thomas J. Watson,* searching for a new challenge after being forced out of his mentor, *John Henry Patterson*'s National Cash Register Co., associated with the "Trust King" by taking over management of Flint's Computing-Tabulating-Recording Company, the predecessor of *IBM.),* and United States Rubber. His greatest feat: organizing the Republic of Brazil and within six weeks providing it with a navy"
    There was this interesting view of Flint in <u>Woman's Home Companion,</u> Sep'03: *"Mr. Charles R. Flint's instructions to his yacht-builder were terse and to the point. When the man came prepared with plans and specifications, Mr. Flint waved them aside. 'I want the fastest boat afloat,' he said. 'I do not care how you build it or what it will cost. Build for me a craft that will break the speed record.' When the Arrow was delivered to Mr. Flint a number of months later, the magnate took her out for a trial trip over a measured-mile course...Her owner stood aft, watch in hand. In affairs of commerce he was always cool and collected. His deals were executed with the* sangfroid *of a Napoleon. Now he was transformed...he clapped his hands in an ecstasy of triumph. 'Forty-five miles per hour!' he cried. 'That beats the record!'"*
    Flint was the American counterpart of *Zacharias Basilejos Zaharoff* (1850-1936), international financier and munitions manufacturer who "always remained far behind the scenes and was commonly termed the 'Mystery Man of Europe.'" Also in <u>Fortune</u>: "He began life a poor Greek...he is ending it the richest man in Europe...He was the greatest armament salesman the world has ever known; for fifty years his job was to foment wars and supply armies. Always, despite his tremendous wealth, his myriad of activities, he has remained an unknown, almost unreal figure..."

22Dec'06: Chanute to Wilbur: *"...I have known Mr. Flint for 25 years...I understood that he is a very rich merchant who has had extensive dealings with the South American republics and with European war departments.*

"The terms and price which he offers you seem much better than I thought possible but there remains the moral question of what precautions should be taken if the invention passes into the hands of a single nation.

"That government, I believe, would be Russia...Its purchase may mean a new war against Japan and much bloodshed..."

28Dec'06: Chanute to Wilbur: *"I have been thinking over your pending negotiations and have not been able to solve any better precautions than those which you mentioned, e.g., 'to have the privilege of going for prizes' (this will make a market for machines) and 'to publish anything you choose after a limited time' (this may avoid any undue advantage taken by one purchaser over another); but I would not make that time more than one or two years, and I should want the money paid before entering any military service.*

"...There is some truth in (Ferber's) *argument that it is better to sell many machines at a moderate price than a few at a very high price...this seems to be Mr. Flint's idea also..."*

ca. 1907 - Charles Thompson chauffeuring John McCurdy, front, Casey Baldwin and Bell, rear, in the 1905 Rambler at Beinn Bhreagh:

Chapter *3* **Glenn Hammond Curtiss   1878-1906**

*C*urtiss's

life is one which should be, but is not, known to most Americans.
That historical curiosity caused the author to write Pendulum, *from*
which much of this chapter - and the balance of this story - is taken.

21May'78: *Glenn Hammond Curtiss* was born in the Methodist parsonage on Orchard Street in Hammondsport, a lovely lakefront village at the south end of Keuka Lake, most southwesterly of New York's Finger Lakes (beside the hamlet of Pleasant Valley, where, in 1860, Charles Champlin founded the American wine industry). He was the son of Frank Curtiss (harness-maker son of minister Claudius G. Curtiss and Ruth Bramble Curtiss, a school teacher before her marriage) and Lua Andrews Curtiss (whose father was grocer-druggist Henry Andrews - and whose mother was a niece of artist-telegraph inventor Samuel F. B. Morse).

The home of his youth was one "of warmth, music, prayers, big dinners with many guests, and a tolerance of individual and collective foibles. Money was always tight. When Glenn...was still an infant, the two generations of Curtisses pooled their resources and bought a big white house with green shutters on the heights of Hammondsport known as Castle Hill."   *George C. Wilson*

When Glenn was almost six and his sister Rutha not quite two, both their father and grandfather died. Thereafter the often lonely boy grew into a self-reliant young man *"handy at fixing things"* fascinated with mechanics and electricity. An avid reader of Popular Mechanics, he *"would think half an hour to do fifteen minutes' work."*

1892: At fourteen, Curtiss, excelling in math but dismal in spelling, completed the eighth grade, the extent of his formal education. He then joined his mother in Rochester (he had been mainly raised by his grandmother Curtiss, with whom he was very close, while his mother remarried and moved to Rochester for special training for Rutha, his deaf younger sister).

He worked at the Eastman Dry Plate and Film Co. (only four years after *George Eastman*'s [1854-1932] 1888 introduction of the *Kodak* No.1, a photographic revolution, the first hand-held camera designed to use roll film), earning $3.50 to $4 for a 10-hour-day, six-day-week (about seven cents-an-hour) stenciling film. Characteristically, he devised a better way of doing his job, increasing production almost tenfold, which led to his transfer to the new camera manufactory. And he was learning photography.

Curtiss ca. 1910:

He was a child of the turn-of-the-century's transportation revolution; *"His appetite for speed has always been insatiable."* and soon his *"ingenuity, mechanical skill, persistence, enterprise, daring"* was making him a name...*"his bicycle was the speediest, his sled coasted farthest, his motorcycle a wonder of the day, his skate-sail unique, his birds'-egg collection largest and rarest of his comrades..."*

When he was ten the *"safety"* bicycle exploded upon America, creating a decade-long craze of unimagined proportions. America's watch and jewelry business plummeted, book sales also while piano manufacturing halved.

For the first time in history man had a safe means of rapid transportation dependent solely upon his own energy and skill.

Note: In 1876 Harry J. Lawson developed the chain-driven *"safety"* bicycle with two equal-size wheels, like today's. Briton John Kemp Starley's 1885 *"Rover Safety"* was perfected by the Humber firm, and then with Scot-Irish John Boyd Dunlop's (1840-1921) 1888 pneumatic tire invention, which soon saw the dangerous high-wheelers replaced.

By 1896 there were over 400 bicycle manufacturers in the United States.

Curtiss's dream was to own a *"wheel."* But bicycles were prohibitively expensive - a *Columbia* (America's oldest manufacturer, founded in 1877 by Alexander Pope, filed for bankruptcy in 1991) cost $100 (well over $3,000 today), the second line *Hartford* $80, $60 and $50 for the cheapest - *almost three month's wages.*

By carefully saving his earnings he purchased his first bike and became a telegraph delivery boy – soon not giving a second thought to peddling the unpaved 70 miles between Rochester and Hammondsport to visit his grandmother, where shortly he returned to live and begin a newspaper route.

And he took to bicycle racing. Riding his yellow Stearns Racer, he became the bicycle speed champion of New York's lower lakes region. *"He had tremendous endurance. He was never a quitter. He would do anything that was fair to win."* His belief was: *"What is the need of racing unless you think you are going to win? And if you are beaten before you start, why take a chance?"*

Note: In the 1890's bicycle racing rivaled baseball as America's national sport. With world-class cyclists like Arthur A. Zimmerman and Marshall "Major" Taylor, the black American, it drew huge crowds of as many as 30,000 fans.

Curtiss, assisted by "Tank" Waters, two of the "Hammondsport Boys," 1896:

"Curtiss was always eager for speed, to get from one place to another in the quickest time with the least amount of effort. He was obsessed with the idea of traveling fast," the same challenge that has propelled man from afoot into the space age, reaching for ever *less time between two points,* on land, water, in air, space...or computer.

7Mar'98: Glenn Curtiss, 19, married *Lena Pearl Neff* (1880-1949), a sawmill superintendent's daughter. With this new responsibility he took employment at Saylor's photography studio in Hammondsport, while still bicycle racing.

1900: Described as having a clever mechanical bent with an inventor's curiosity, persistence and a good business head, he is given the opportunity to open his own bicycle shop by his racing sponsor, pharmacist Jim Smellie.

Like *Henry Ford* (1864-1947) a *"child of rural Populism,"* he resembled Ford in other ways – he had a wary eye on *"big business,"* and in the pursuit of his own interests, whether sport or business, he demonstrated a sharp focus and a high degree of opportunism.

"His idea was, first, to find out just how to do it, and then do it. Then he would find out how fast a certain task could be performed, and get through with it at top speed. The surplus time he devoted to tinkering with something new."

When full grown he was tall and slim, best described in a 1910 Fresno, California, account: *"Curtiss is a tall man over six feet, but slender and clean cut. He is said to weigh in at less than 150 pounds, machine side* (naked). *His face is one that would attract immediate attention anywhere - deep-set eyes, with a thoughtful expression; the freshness of youth, mingled with a suggestion of determination and intrepid hardihood. He is composed...his much talked of modesty is a reality. There is not the least suggestion of forwardness, nor even of professional briskness and volubility usually associated with persons whose names fill the daily news columns. Then one remembers that Curtiss is before all else a student, an inventor, a master of one of the great modern sciences, and one quits looking for the cast of a showman."*

A Frenchman's description of Curtiss and the Wrights:

"These men might be brothers as far as resemblances go. They are all retiring, conservative, sharp-featured, blue-eyed and ambidextrous. They all have bird faces. Look at them as they stand watching the clouds and you will see it. They resemble each other in their manner of speech, their movements and their build."

A thick moustache made Curtiss appear older than twenty-two when *G.H. Curtiss, Dealer in Harness and Horse Furnishings, Also Bicycles and Sundries* opened for business in a 12-foot storefront on Pulteney Street on Hammondsport's town square (still with its delightful Victorian-era bandstand).

One day a customer gave a dollar bill for a 25-cent purchase. The total change in the cash drawer, Curtiss's pockets, and in those of his two-man staff, 30-cents.

1902: He expanded his business, acquiring Smellie's agency for *Stearn, Columbia, Cleveland, National* and *Racycle* bicycles.

Curtiss and his store on Hammondsport's town square:

In order to race faster, in 1901, by trial-and-error he fabricated his first motor castings, mail-ordered (*"...per cut no. 5 in your catalogue. Money order enclosed"*) from Buffalo's E.R. Thomas Company, manufacturer of the *Auto-Bi*, *"reputedly the first practical motorcycle in America."*

His engine was a crude one-cylinder (2-by-2-1/2-inch) air-cooled affair, which he had finished in Frank Neff's machine shop (Neff, his wife's uncle, invented the wire hood for capping champagne bottles).

With little known about carburetors, he fabricated a tomato can fitted with gauze screens, and for the *make-and-break ignition* used the loan of Dr. Philias Alden's electric shock treatment spark coil. The drive wheel was driven by a friction-roller V-belt pulley, which he found worked best (and there was pedal power when all else failed).

Trying out his new motor-bicycle, dubbed the *Happy Hooligan* (after a popular comic-strip character), proved a terrifying ride.

Note: Motorcycle manufacturing was just beginning. Rivaling Thomas's claim, some believe that in 1900 Charles Metz's Waltham Mfg. Co. made America's first practical motorcycle. Worldwide, in only two or three decades there'd be some 300 manufacturers: British makers would offer nigh 600 models; and by 1936 Germans produced over 150,000, nearly half the world's output.

Curtiss then bought the largest engine casting he could find, and, with Neff again helping machine and finish it, made a second motor-bicycle. No thing of beauty, it was fearsome in its bulk and power: It *"exploded only occasionally, but when it did it almost tore itself loose from the frame."*

Prudently, to test it he went out of town and up a steep hill.

But still seeking maximum horsepower with minimum weight, he designed his first engine (similar to the 1889 French *DeDion-Bouton* engine, *"the first internal combustion engine for...aircraft,"* with which Cleveland's Peerless Mfg. Co. pioneered its three-wheeled *"motorette"* tricycle) and then had John Kirkham, at his small foundry at Taggart's, halfway up the valley to Bath, do its casting and machining.

15Mar1902: Curtiss opens a branch store in Bath and, discovering the profit potentials of manufacturing, had his own *Hercules*-brand bicycles made in nearby Addison.

May'02: He opened a second store in Corning. Soon he had two of Hammondsport's first telephones, and received its first *"special delivery registered letter."*

He was 24 years old - overseeing a growing business, and what he termed his *"industrial incubator"* for developing new ideas. And old Hammondsport friends would always call him *"Glenn,"* newer acquaintances usually *"G.H."*

In 1896 brothers *Charles and Frank Duryea* built 13 two-passenger runabouts in Springfield, Massachusetts..."the first time that an automobile company was organized and produced more than one car from a single design," [*Richard P. Scharchburg*] thus *beginning America's automotive industry.*

1893 Duryea

In Germany, *Karl Benz* patented his single-cylinder *Motorwagen* in 1886; the Duryeas made their first runabout in 1893; and Henry Ford *(right)*, when working for Detroit's Edison Illuminating Co., built his first engine and *"quadricycle"* in 1896, just five years before Curtiss's first engine.

30May'02: On Labor Day in Brooklyn, competing against the best American and foreign makes, Curtiss places well in the New York Motor Cycle Club's races. Thus introduced to the vast American market, orders for powerful, lightweight *Hercules* motorcycles soon forced the abandonment of his father's old harness supply business.

The *G.H. Curtiss Manufacturing Co.* was founded, underwritten by a small group of local men, including $1,000 from J. Seymour Hubbs and $500 each from brothers Victor and Lynn Masson, Henry Miller, banker Aaron G. Pratt, professor Plough and George H. Keeler (all to be well-remembered later).

Orient Buckboard
PRICE $375

Patented March 10, 1903
4 H.P. Speed 30 Miles per Hour
The Cheapest Automobile in the World
Write for Catalogue
WALTHAM MFG. CO., Waltham, Mass.

Dec'02 - Curtiss, Hammondsport's first automobile owner (a steam model traded for a *Hercules* motorbicycle), became, like many men of that age (Bell included), an *"automobilist."*

He acquired agencies for *Orient Motor Buckboard, Thayer-Miller,* and the just-introduced *Ford* – and from 1903-on attended the New York auto show exhibiting *Hercules* motors, and a *"motor bicycle,"* $200 and *"motor tandem,"* $250 (about $10,000 and $12,000, respectively today).

30May'03 - Memorial Day - before 6,000 at the *National Cycling Association* meet at the Empire City Racetrack in Yonkers, Curtiss on his *Hercules* sped over 60-mph to beat the rival Hendee-built *Indian* racers. He also won the New York Motor Cycle Club gold medal in open hill climbing – and became nationally famous as the *first* American Motorcycle Champion, winning victories on his motorcycles, powerful and lighter than the *Indians, Auto-Bi*s and others.

A crowd-pleaser, he was exciting to watch, not 'devil-may-care' but calculating his chances and withdrawing if the odds were too great. But when the opportunity presented itself, he'd handily out-smart and out-race the opposition.

Curtiss and his single-cylinder Hercules:

Barney Oldfield, the 999, and Henry Ford:

In 1901 Ford, like Curtiss, raced his 2-cylinder, 26-hp race-car 10 miles at 69.2-mph. Then, backed by Tom Cooper, he built two monster, innovative 4-*vertical* cylinder cars, *"Arrow" and "999"* (named after the famous locomotive that pulled the Empire State Express 112.5-mph in 1896). In the *Arrow* he raced 92-mph, and in July, 1902, ex-cyclist *Barney Oldfield* ran the *999* on Grosse Point's oval mile in 55-1/2 seconds.

The parallels between the careers of Ford and Curtiss are striking - in their timing, their passion for racing, their patent fights, and their eventual positions in their respective industries - with Curtiss becoming *"The Henry Ford of Aviation."*

But, first-and-foremost, they were engine men - devoted to manufacturing economical state-of--art engines - for automobiles, motorcycles, and, eventually, aircraft.

Keith Seward's description of Ford could also be of Curtiss: *"All the attributes ...daring, ambition, mechanical genius, inexhaustible energy and a capacity for undivided attention...capped...by a will of iron."* However, Ford's basic simplicity and engineering genius veiled a hunger for power and oft-dangerous societal ignorance.

16Jun'03: The *Ford Motor Company* is incorporated, capitalized at $100,000 ($5 million today) with $28,000 in cash. Ford held 25-1/2% of the stock.

Very successful, by 1Oct'03 Ford's sales exceeded *$142,000*. In 1903 its *Model A* cost a *"modest"* $850, $200 more than an *Oldsmobile*, $100 more than *Cadillac's Runabout* - a *"rich man's plaything"* when a semi-skilled worker earned *$1.50 per day.*

Insight into Ford's early history is Stan Grayson's article on the Dodge Brothers in Automobile Quarterly, 1979: *"Like most early automobiles, the first Fords were, in reality, assembled vehicles and the Dodges were responsible for the heart of the machine. Their $162,500 contract called for the production and delivery of 650 engines, transmissions and axles to which Ford would add a frame, wheels, tires and wooden body – built by the C.R. Wilson Carriage Company – in his modest Mack Avenue facility. By spring 1903, Dodge Brothers was employing 150 men and nearly the entire shop was devoted to Ford production. Components were transferred on horse-drawn wagons to Ford where they were tested and installed...Even after Ford formed his Ford Manufacturing Company in 1905 – to reduce somewhat his dependence on the Dodges and to make his own engines for the Model N – John Dodge was named a vice-president. Dodge Brothers continued to build engines for the Ford Model B and Model K and continued to share in Ford's growing profits..."*

Finding *Hercules* trademarked by a California firm, in 1904 Curtiss began using a fancy Spencerian *"Curtiss"* (a variation of Platt Rogers Spencer's prized penmanship – first used by Frank Robinson for *Coca Cola*'s famous trademark); by 1905 it was on all Curtiss products.

Ford's similar Spencerian logo *"was used on some of the 1904 Model C cars, where it appeared as an element of the Ford Motor Company name on a brass plate forming part of the starting handle aperture"* (Henry Ford Museum).

IN PRESENTING our line of Hercules Motor Cycles and Motors we wish to impress the fact that our product is of the highest possible grade throughout. We have spared no time or money to perfect the machines, which are manufactured of the best obtainable materials and in a most accurate and workmanlike manner. *All parts are built to guage and are interchangeable.* Each motor develops the power at which it is rated, and is thoroughly tested before leaving the factory.

We have substituted *Roller Bearings* in place of the ball bearings, the feature of our last year's motors and to which we attribute much of their success. Although ball bearings possess many good features and are very durable, roller bearings possess the same good features and are still more durable and will practically *never wear out.*

5 H. P. Double Cylinder Motor

Price with spark timing device, spark plugs, exhaust valve lifters and intake valve throttle for controlling speed

$150.00

Weight 60 pounds (12 pounds per H. P.)
Width of crank case 4 inches, over all 6 inches.
Height—16 inches.
Bore of Cylinders—3 inches.
Stroke 3 inches.
Speed—300 to 3500 revolutions per minute.

This motor is fitted with our new roller bearings and is built with the same care and accuracy as our single cylinder motor.

The connecting rods are attached to the same wrist pin and the motor receives an impulse from each cylinder alternately at each revolution. This motor is designed for racing machines or for cycles where great power or speed is desired, but can be used very successfully on automobiles.

This motor is perfectly balanced and presents the same advantages for motor cycles that the multi-cylinders do for the automobile, namely: Smoothness of running and a great range of speed on a direct drive.

We will equip either single or tandem with this motor at an extra cost of - - - - - $75.00

The complete machine is marked with the same care in construction and finish, and each detail is worked out to a nicety. The design and construction of the frame, the position of the motor, etc., is correct from every point of view, and is being copied by other manufacturers. Our machines are thoroughly practical and reliable, easy riding, easy to control, and at the same time powerful and speedy. They are free from objectionable features such as vibration, noise, extreme width and bulkiness, and while the machine is what may be called heavily built there is no unnecessary weight. The machines are built with large gasoline and lubricating oil capacity, which we have found by experience, a very desirable feature.

Hercules Motor Work

for 1903

Elegant in Design and Finish, Speedy and Reliable

Hercules Motors

Powerful,
Durable,
Light and
Compact

G. H. Curtiss Manufacturing Company . . .

Hammondsport,
New York, U. S. A.

28Jan'04: *"Curtiss made the highest grade motorcycle engine in America."* Designing a new 2-cylinder, 5-hp motorcycle, he took it to the Florida Speed Carnival where, competing with the best from America and Europe, he raced it 67.36 mph on Ormond Beach's 10-mile straight-a-way to set a *seven-year world record* (North of Daytona Beach, Ormond raceway opened in March, 1902, and was the world's fastest speedway until 250-mph speeds moved events to Utah's Bonneville salt flats in the mid-1930s).

The author on Ormond Beach:

Jun'04: "Captain" *Thomas Sackett Baldwin* (1854/58-1923) "is best known...for his work with dirigibles...An acrobat, tightrope walker, inventor, balloonist, parachute jumper...he designed, built and flew the first...successful dirigible balloon in the United States. He had been to Europe and seen the dirigibles of Santos-Dumont and Zeppelin. In the early months of 1904, he returned to California to see if he could improve on their designs and...challenge the foreign-born designers. As usual the problem of a motor was one not easily solved. Baldwin was acutely aware of the problem of weight and also of power required to meet wind resistance. One day he saw a Curtiss motorcycle...got in touch with Curtiss and this led to a friendly association that was to last for years. In a sense Baldwin was responsible for interesting Curtiss in aviation."   *Kenneth M. Johnson*

Baldwin was an early associate of California's glider pioneer-showman, *John J. Montgomery* (1858-1911). In 1887, over San Francisco's Golden Gate Park, he made America's *first* parachute jump. Though widely heralded in Europe, some (e.g., Wilbur) regarded him as more showman than scientist (though Orville thought him a friend). He first used a Curtiss motor to power his 52-foot *"California Arrow."* No thing of beauty, it was America's first successful dirigible "airship" when it completed a full-circle flight over San Francisco Bay on 4Aug'04, the *"exceedingly light"* Curtiss motor largely credited for its success.

25Oct'04: The *California Arrow,* the only dirigible to fly successfully, was the rage at St. Louis's *Louisana Purchase Exposition.* Piloted by Roy Knabenshue (in deference to Baldwin's girth), it capped its *"astonishing"* performance with a flight of 3-1/2 miles to a height of 2,000 feet and a perfect return to its start. This huge fair covered 1,400 acres with every conceivable exhibit and attraction, including 100 automobiles, one *"driven from New York under its own power."* During its 7-month run over 20 million (of an 80 million American population) were to *"Meet me in St. Looie, Looie, Meet me at the fair!"*

23Nov'04: Baldwin visits Hammondsport. *"I'm Curtiss,"* Curtiss said, wiping his oil-grimed hands. Baldwin stayed several days as Curtiss's house-guest, the first of many visits, as he and Curtiss reached agreeement on providing motors for Baldwin's airships, the next *"rubber cow"* being the *City of Portland.*

Hammondsport was becoming *"The Cradle of Aviation."*

In 1905, at Oregon's *Lewis & Clark Exposition,* the *City of Portland* was manned by 17-year-old beginner-pilot *Lincoln Beachey* (1887-1915), and Curtiss was awarded the fair's "Highest Award" gold medal for its "huge" 7-hp motor. *"Soon all dirigible balloons operating in this country were driven by Curtiss motors."*

The growing business saw a 20'x60' "shop" (factory) built beside Curtiss's home, a second in 1905 and a third in 1906. By 1907 Glenn Curtiss had grown from a diffident youth to a somewhat taciturn, hard-headed young Yankee manufacturing *over 500* motorcycles a year.

Note: Milwaukee's William Harley and Arthur Davidson's new company sold one *Harley-Davidson* motorcycle in 1903, two in 1904, and eight in 1905 - but by 1910, *after* Curtiss's move to aeroplanes, over 3,000. In 1912 Hendee's *Indian* (built in Springfield, Massachusetts, since 1901), was the largest seller, but by 1920 Harley-Davidson had become the world's largest manufacturer.

19Oct'05: Growing demand for motorcycles required enlarged facilities, and the incorporation of the *G.H. Curtiss Manufacturing Co., Inc.,* with directors Lynn Masson, Aaron Pratt, Monroe M. Wheeler and G. Ray Hall. Curtiss, 27, was president of a corporation with capital stock of $40,000 (about $2 million today) employing over 30 men, but even with a night shift, unable to keep up with the orders.

Henry Ford was 33 when he built his <u>first</u> *"dream car,"* his 500-pound, 2-cylinder "quadricycle."

"But in the first decade of motorcycling, the young man from Hammondsport, New York, was the brightest flame in the industry." Tod Rafferty, <u>Classic American Motorcycles</u>.

In 1904 Curtiss constructed his 3-wheeled *"Wind Wagon"* for testing Baldwin's propellers. Two years later, near Paris, *Ferdinand Ferber* made a similar vehicle.

Baldwin, Curtiss and the Wind Wagon:

A glimpse of Curtiss's hands-on approach occurred when he interrupted a conversation to rush into the shop to fashion a just-conceived idea, the *twist-handle throttle,* common on all motorcycles today.

A 1905 Sunday outing, Mr. & Mrs. Leonard "Tank" Waters, left, and Lena and Glenn Curtiss, right. Note throttle connection to right handle on the tandems:

22Nov'05: *The Ford Manufacturing Company* is incorporated with capital stock of $100,000 (about $5 million today) with forty-one year old Henry Ford to receive a salary of $300 per month; raised tenfold, to $3,000 per month, in December 1907.

Jan'06: At the Aero Club of America's first exhibit, held in conjunction with New York's Automobile Show, Curtiss's exhibit featured his new lightweight airship motors; the modified 4-cycle, 2-cylinder, 5-horsepower V motor used in the *California Arrow,* and 2-cylinder 10-horsepower, and 3-cylinder 15-horsepower motors of similar construction.

Apr'06: Baldwin (and his competitors) needed more power and Curtiss developed a radical new engine with two banks of 2 cylinders, each installed in a *"V"* shape. Baldwin used this powerful 18-hp V4 engine on his new, much-larger *"City of Los Angeles."* This was about the time of San Francisco's earthquake and fire (18-20Apr'06) which destroyed Baldwin's facilities there. He relocated to Hammondsport, beginning his long association with Curtiss (together they built 13 airships).

Hammondsport, already a major motorcycle center, now, with the country's most prominent aeronaut (combined with the Wright's secrecy), became *America's aeronautics center*; and nearby Watkins Glen on Senaca Lake was an ideal airship haven.

Curtiss's work with Baldwin led to propeller experiments, about which little was known. As noted, in 1904 he'd made the wind wagon for testing propellers, but its "fearful racket" scaring man and beast soon saw it converted to a *"windboat"* (introduced to the Everglades by Curtiss in the early 1920's), and an *"icecycle"* on Keuka Lake in winter (like Waldo Waterman's *"Hydroglider"* on Big Bear Lake in 1925-26).

16May'06: Curtiss sold a Thayer-Miller automobile, manufactured in Columbus, Ohio, and planned to accompany its new owner when taking delivery. Having read of the Wright's flying machine activities nearby, he thought this an excellent opportunity to promote his motors, and wrote them:

"DearSirs:- We have read of your success with the Aeroplane and thinking we might be of service to you in getting out a light and powerful motor with which to carry on your work we take the liberty of writing you on the subject. We have built a large number of motors for aerial purposes. We have sold motors to Stevens, Knabenshue, Tomlinson and others: while Capt. Baldwin has used ours exclusively for the last two years, as you doubtless know has made some twenty-three success return flights at Portland, Ore...We recently shipped to Dr. Bell's Nova Scotia Laboratory a motor designed for Aeroplane work...Yours truly, G.H. Curtiss Mfg. Co. per G.H. Curtiss."

There was no reply. "...Yet strangely there was a link, a connection that was soon to bring Curtiss into that small coterie of birdmen which Langley had created. The 'Riddle of Destiny,' as Charles Lamb wrote, 'brings together surprising personalities, usually through obscure channels.' Curtiss came in contact with the Wrights through the dirigible. At first Curtiss was not interested in any form of flying. Dirigibles and balloons were mere fantasies...the Wright brothers' success at Kitty Hawk was only hearsay...Langley was unknown, and so, too, was his assistant...Herring. Yet all of these were to come together through the action of one man, Thomas Baldwin..."   *Owen Lieberg*

In Sep'06, Curtiss accompanied Baldwin to the Dayton Fair, which, on the 6th, the Wrights also attended and assisted in corralling Baldwin's runaway *City of Los Angeles* airship. Thus introduced, a meeting followed with discussions on aeronautics and motors, but mainly focused on propellers, a subject of keen interest to all. They didn't see the Wright's *Flyer*, but were shown in-flight photographs of it.

Years later (28Feb1914) Baldwin recalled in <u>The New York Times</u>: *"I sometimes suggested to Curtiss that he was asking too many questions, but he kept right on. The Wrights had the frankness of schoolboys in it all and had a rare confidence in us. I am sure Curtiss at that time never thought of taking up flying."*

4Sep1906: Wilbur to Chanute: *"...The only knowledge we have of Mr. Herring going to Germany is based on the interview...in the Paris N.Y. <u>Herald</u> last May...Captain Baldwin is at the fair in Dayton this week, but the wind has been too strong for him to attempt a flight...Mr. Curtiss, who is building the motor for Prof. Bell's experiments this fall, called to see us..."*

This Dayton meeting later assumed sinister overtones for the Wrights; they claimed that Curtiss' rapid progress in aviation was due, at least in part, to information that he had then learned.

Returning to their airship, Baldwin and Curtiss tried a Wright suggestion to cut *"out some of the inner surface of the blades on the big propellers, so as to reduce the resistance and allow it to speed up, and it showed a remarkable improvement."*

Curtiss noted this in his 22Sep'06 letter to the Wrights, adding: *"...We are getting well started on the 8-cylinder motor for* (Charles Oliver) *Jones. It certainly looks good on the drawings. Will let you know how it pans out as to power etc..."*

This is apparently the first mention of Curtiss's development of the air-cooled V-8 motor, to become his standard aircraft-type engine.

In 1906 Henry Ford, now with 51% of the stock, controlled Ford. In 1907, developing his revolutionary *Model T* (his first *left*-hand-drive car), he discovered it far easier to conceive a cheap car than to make one: light construction and low-quality materials only resulted in a car that would soon shake itself to pieces. It had to be easy to make, tough enough to take the road's pounding, simple to operate and cheap to repair and maintain.

With his absolute company control, Ford solved the design and manufacturing problems, which included the slicing the top off the engine, thus making the *first modern engine* with a single cylinder block and a separate, bolt-down cylinder-head. Then, the introduction of vanadium steel completed the job; allowing him to achieve the lightness with durability that became the hallmark of the Model T, which Ford introduced in 1908 for $825 (about $30,000 today).

By 1909, when America had over 475 car manufacturers, Ford's sales exceeded $9 million with profits of over $3 million.

1-8Dec1906: At New York's combined Aero and Automobile Show, at the Grand Central Palace, there were more discussions between Curtiss and Bell, concluding with an order for a 4-cylinder motor, Bell's second Curtiss motor.

The Wright brothers, with Chanute, also attended - accompanied by *Augustus Post* (1873-), co-founder and secretary of the Aero Club of America.

About this time Henry ("*Henny*") Kleckler was hired as Curtiss's foreman. Soon, as his trusted "right arm," he assumed the factory's day-to-day responsibilities. Later he recalled those times as *"the best years of my life..."* Glenn was *"one of the finest men I ever worked for or with."*

Typically, Curtiss made friends slowly; once made, they were lifelong.

First page of the 1907 Curtiss catalog showing the factory and its most powerful, top-of-the-line, 2-cylinder tandem motorcycle:

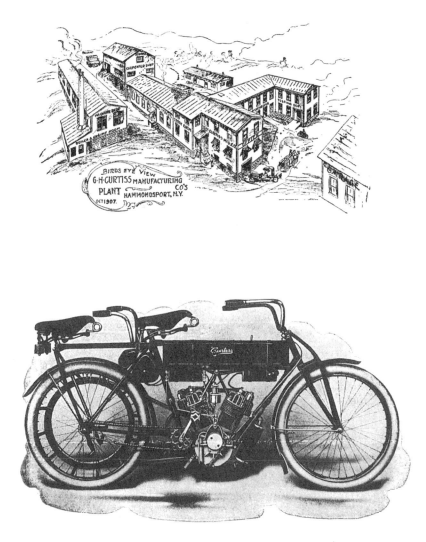

24Jan'07: Building an oversize frame to accommodate his new 40-hp, V8 motor, Curtiss created a behemoth of a motorcycle (it was to motorcycles what Henry Ford's huge 80-mph *"999"* was to automobiles) and, naturally, wanting to see how fast it would go, with Baldwin and his old racing partner, Tank Waters, he attended Florida's Speed Carnival at Ormond Beach. First, with a single-cylinder machine he did the mile in 1:02, following with a 2-cylinder in 46.4 seconds, *both new world's records.*

Then, in a leather jacket, special leather helmet and a belt to keep him from being blown off, with everything ready, on the new V8 machine he took a 2-mile running start on the 10-mile course. He sped down the sand...*"and could see nothing but a streak of gray beach in front, a blur of hills* (low bluff) *on one side, and the white ribbon of foaming surf on the other."* Air pressure flattened him to the frame...he had no thought but to hang on.

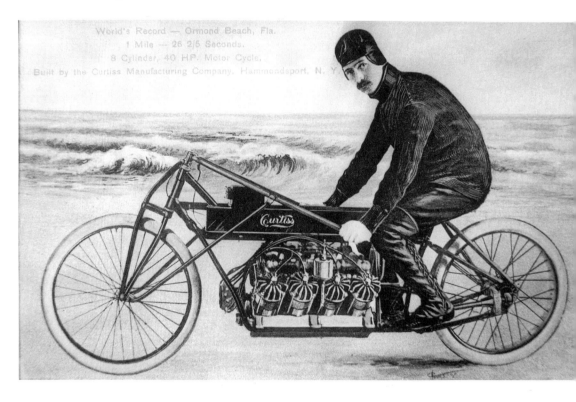

He was clocked traveling a mile in 26-2/5 seconds, an incredible *136-mph,* eclipsing Fred Marriott's 1906 record of 127.66-mph in a streamlined Stanley Steamer.

Headlines read: *"The Fastest Mile," "The fastest man in the world,"* and *"Bullets are the only rivals of Glenn H. Curtiss of Hammondsport"* as he said: *"It satisfied my speed-craving"* - and that engine was *"our first aeronautical motor."*

Never ridden again (the terrific strain on the transmission left it barely together), that motorcycle is in the Smithsonian. It wasn't until 1930 that a *2-wheel* vehicle went faster.

THE 200-HORSE-POWER BENZ RACER IN WHICH OLDFIELD MADE 128.89 MILES AN HOUR. A
NEW WORLD'S RECORD.

2Apr'10 <u>Scientific American</u>: Barney Oldfield raced this car 128.89-mph. But no one traveled faster than Curtiss until 23Apr'11, when Bob Burman covered the flying mile in 25.4 seconds - 141-mph - in Benz's 200-hp "*Blitzen*" (Lightning) racer.

The author beside this same car in Stuttgart's Mercedes-Benz Museum:

Chapter **4** *The Partnership 1907*

N. ow,

knowing the backgrounds of Bell and Curtiss and how they became acquainted, we enter the focus of this story: their partnership. And the events of the times necessarily include much of what others, particularly the Wright brothers, were doing.

En route to Florida, and in response to Bell's invitation made at the Auto Show, Curtiss stopped for a visit at his Washington home. Bell, warmly greeting him, was soon describing his kite research and plans for the new, more powerful motor. And an empathy, a bond, began to form between him and Mabel because of his ability to communicate with her, as with his own deaf sister, Rutha.

ALEXANDER GRAHAM BELL'S SUBURBAN RESIDENCE AT WASHINGTON, D. C.

28Jan'07: Wilbur to Chanute: *"We returned from New York Saturday after a conference with Mr. Flint. The original proposition was that they purchase outright the foreign rights, but Mr. Flint found some of his foreign associates opposed to this and we on our part found that we would necessarily grant things that we were indisposed to give up. They next proposed to become selling agents for foreign countries with the condition that we receive everything until $500,000 had been reached and that beyond that we receive half. We did not like the idea of giving them full control of the selling department without some guarantee of results. They next proposed that if we would consent to give a private exhibition before the Czar of Russia they would guarantee to pay us $50,000 whether any business followed or not; and that, of any business, we should receive 90% and they 10% up to $500,000 and an equal division thereafter. They to pay all expenses of the exhibition. We have this offer now under consideration...We also discussed...a proposition according to which we retain full control of the terms and places of selling and they work under our directions so far as we choose to give any. We to be entirely free to handle the American business...In this case they to receive 20% of foreign profits up to $500,000 and 40% thereafter. They to forfeit agency if the business amounts to less than $200,000 ($10 million today) in six months, if we desire...We are more favorably disposed toward this plan ...as we retain full control...and merely utilize their services and assistance.*

"Mr. Flint has become very much interested in the matter...He will attend to...Russia himself. In Germany and Austria he expects to operate through the Mauser gun people...His French associates were very lukewarm. In England he would expect to cooperate with a large gun company...

"At first we were indisposed to consider any agency proposition, but in thinking it over we see some advantages over attempting to handle the foreign business entirely alone...The fact that we had the support of such influential people would make the government less disposed to ignore us, with the intention of stealing our invention later..."

30Jan'07: Chanute to Wilbur: *"...I believe that the first proposition, e.g., $50,000 and expenses...and 90% of sales up to $500,000, with an equal division after that, will yield you the greater reward, particularly as I do not see how you can retain 'full control of the terms and places of selling' unless you go along with your agent ...the agent must have some latitude to effect sales.*

"It seems probable that the first sale will be to Russia, and...I send you my correspondence with Berthenson...of the aeronautical department at St. Petersburg...he said that he would advise his people. He seems to have done so.

"I also enclose Mr. Flint's letter to me. Please return these various documents when you have got through with them."

8Feb'07: Wilbur to Orville: *"We have tried to sound the German Government through (Isidor) Loewe on a proposition to furnish 50 machines at $500,000 ($25 million today), one fourth payable at demonstration. The Russian business is called off till we learn the attitude of Germany...In the German business, Flints, Loewe, and Berg take 1/3 each of commission...This offer is good only for a contract for 50 machines ($10,000 each, over $500,000 today)...Would you be willing if necessary to* *furnish 12 machines for $200,000* ($16,666 each, almost $800,000 today), *with initial payment of... $100,000?...*

"*...I told them (Flints) that we were not willing to consider any proposition that called for less than $100,000* (over $5 million today) *on demonstration and delivery of first machine...*"

23Feb'07, Israel Ludlow, <u>Collier's</u> *magazine: "...we can 'point with pride,' as the politicians say, to the fact that the most successful attempts to fly have been made by two young Americans, Wilbur and Orville Wright of Dayton, Ohio. These young inventors run a bicycle machine-shop on the outskirts of the town. Newspaper reporters, special correspondents, and Sherlock Holmes photographers hover about... more or less continuously, but the Wrights go on serenely and...have kept the descriptions of their machine and pictures of it from the public...They have taken out no patents, and, except for some dealings with war departments, have shown no desire to put it on the market. It is generally believed...that they have constructed an aeroplane which has flown, on several occasions, at the rate of forty miles an hour for...nearly an hour. Nothing equal to this has been done either here or abroad...*

"*There have been many surmises as to...their secrecy, but there appears to be no doubt that they have done what they claimed...The inventors...have stated that if individuals with...knowledge of aeronautics saw their invention they could duplicate it, and the reward which should rightly be theirs would go to others...*

"*Dr. Alexander Graham Bell, the inventor of the telephone, has been greatly interested of late years in aerial navigation, and has made many experiments with his tetrahedral kites...*

"*Many expedients have been adopted to raise aeroplanes from the ground, that their equilibrium in flight might be tested. Professor Montgomery of California carried his aeroplanes one or two thousand feet up in the air by a hot-air balloon and then cut loose. Chanute of Chicago jumped from the top of the sand-hills, and others, like Dr. Bell, flew their inventions as kites...*

"*When the goal of aerial locomotion has been gained a change in civilization and human customs will take place greater than that brought about by the locomotive and the steamboat. A new world, the sky, will be opened; a new point of view will be given the painter and the poet, and there will be an awakening to a broader and closer international fellowship.*"

13Apr'07: Orville to *Reginald A. Fessenden* (1866-1932, who, on 24Dec'06, added "*a range of sound*" to *Guglielmo Marconi's* [1874-1937] 1895 "*wireless telegraphy*" radio invention): "*...The trouble has not been in the getting of patents but in deciding whether patents would be of much value to us after we have them. We have always thought that our best market would be with the governments, and it has been a very serious question with us as to whether patents would give us adequate protection against governments - especially foreign governments. We have a patent on our early gliding machine, but have not applied for protection on any of our work of the past five years. We have generally been informed that secrets were worth more to governments than patented articles. For that reason we have taken out no patents since we found...practical use in our invention...*"

2May'07: Chanute to Wilbur: *"...I do believe that events are coming your way.*

"If I were not afraid of interfering with your plans and wishes I might easily stir up the U. S. War Dept. I was called on a few days ago by a newspaper reporter who said that the American people will mob you if you sell your invention abroad and it is used against the United States..."

16May'07: Bishop Wright's diary: *"...Wilbur got a telegram from Flint, and at 10:00 P.M. started for New York to take ship for London. He goes to talk with agents in London, Paris, and Berlin (with all expenses to be paid by Flint)."*

16May'07: Wilbur to Orville: *"...write Toulmin...& request him to give the two patents promptest possible attention. Go over all the claims in the old patent and wherever desirable see that corresponding claims go into the new ones. I think it probably desirable...not to specify in all the claims that the twistable surfaces are the 'wings,' or supporting surfaces, but merely call them 'horizontal surfaces.'*

"In the U.S. correspondence be careful not to give them any chance to put us in a bad light as very unreasonable, &c...

"Don't let the magneto matter go till the last minute. Apple may not have them.."

16May'07: Wilbur to Chanute: *"We received a telegram from Flint yesterday...requesting that one of us sail for Europe Saturday, so I grabbed a few things and started the same evening...*

"Before leaving home we received a communication from the U.S. Board of Ordnance & Fortification notifying us that the Board had under consideration several propositions for the construction and testing of flying machines...we will give the matter serious attention.

"It is reported by Dr. Bell that the Langley machine is to be tried again..."

Note: After reading a brief item on the Wright machine in <u>Scientific American</u>, President Theodore Roosevelt sent it to Secretary of War Taft to *"Investigate."* Taft sent it to the Board of Ordnance: *"Investigate."* Upon inquiry the Wrights remained steadfast at $100,000 ($5 million today), a sum which the Board did not have available.

25May'07: Wilbur to Orville: *"We reached the coast of Ireland about the middle of yesterday afternoon...We reached...London at 12:30...Mr. Berg met me and took me to Morley's Hotel opposite the Nelson Monument in Trafalger Square...Berg is fully convinced that there is little hope of doing business with England or the French Government in the near future...it is almost hopeless to steer it through in time of peace.*

Note: Flint's *Hart O. Berg* (1865-1941), a graduate engineer head-quartered in Paris, was one of America's earliest international arms salesmen (and manufacturer) of machine guns, automatic pistols, electric automobiles, Simon Lake's submarines - and Wright aeroplanes.

"In Germany Loewe is afraid to do anything toward bringing it to the personal attention of the Emperor...From all accounts every official near the Emperor is in constant terror of losing his standing...I am sure we can do nothing in Germany without Berg and Loewe, and I consider it useless to try in England just now...Berg is anxious that I should go over to Paris Monday and talk with Deutsch (Henri Deutsch de la Meurthe)*...He thinks our chances of doing business with the French Government would be much better if we had a few men like Deutsch at the head of the business...*

"...It is not our intention for the present to let it be known that I am in Europe, except to a very few."

4Jun'07: Chanute to Orville: *"...I think Wilbur's views will be modified by his journey ...the Europeans are catching up with you more rapidly than I had believed. Of course they will meet many mishaps and breakages, but they are learning from each failure, especially as the various aviators are present at each other's trials, and are educating each other..."*

8Jun'07: Orville to Chanute: *"...I do not feel uneasy that any of those that we read about...are pursuing us very closely...It would not appear...that their progress is as rapid as ours was.*

"...Of course there is always a possibility that some unheard-of investigator may come into the light with a machine far in advance of any machine of the known inventors, but we have always considered this a remote possibility..."

Spring'07: Considering Curtiss *"the greatest motor expert in the country"* and impressed with his daring, Bell visits Hammondsport. There his strong persuasions, including a fee of $25 per day (about $1,500 today) plus travel expenses, finally succeeded in getting Curtiss (who thought believers in flying machines *"a bit unbalanced"*) to visit Baddeck to instruct on the operation of the new, sometimes rough-running motor (four carburetors solved the problem).

But Bell had something more in mind: With three young *"partners"* lined up, he was evolving a plan *"to get into the air"* (phrased in his "Home Notes," 19Jul'07). In addition to U.S. Army Lt. *Thomas Etholen Selfridge* were recent Toronto University engineering graduates *John (Jack) Alexander Douglas* (preferred by Scotsman Bell) *McCurdy* (1886-1961) and *Frederick Walker "Casey" Baldwin* (1885-1948).

McCurdy was the second son of Arthur McCurdy, for many years Bell's private secretary. After his mother's early death the Bells had wanted to adopt him. Later, ending an eventful aviation career, much of it with Curtiss, he was named Nova Scotia's Lt.-Governor in 1947.

In 1906 Mabel asked McCurdy to bring home a friend from college for the summer recess. He suggested Casey Baldwin. Mabel answered: *"He is exactly the kind of fellow from your description that I want associated with Mr. Bell."* Casey, so tagged because of his prowess at baseball - *"Casey at the bat"* - was the son of Canadian Premier Robert Baldwin. Following his visit he became, for all intents and purposes, *"the son the Bells never had."* (their lost sons would have been about his age) and a life-long Baddeck resident.

"The fifth member of the group was Glenn H. Curtiss, whom Bell had met at a New York motor show. Curtiss, though a very young man, had already achieved much fame as a manufacturer of motorcycle engines, and he was employing eighty-five men at his factory in Hammondsport, NY. Bell knew that such a man would be invaluable to the newborn association. Motor experts of any kind were few and far between in those days, but Curtiss's particular kind of engine, one which was light, compact and simple, was precisely the kind of power plant which heavier-than-air flight demanded." *H.Gordon Green*

1907 - Curtiss, kneeling behind motorcycle, and Hammondsport employees:

9Jun'07: Orville to Wilbur: *"...In case a company is to be formed, we should have at least one half of the stock in order that freeze-out games could not be worked on us...An order for $200,000 (about $9 million today) worth of machines would still leave us in full control of the business. If a company is considered I do not think it best to suggest selling the secrets...*

"The wing twisting with the hand levers is a great improvement over the old system...

"I have the drawings for the automatic control almost done...

"I would give three cents to see you in your dress suit and plug hat!"

10Jun'07: Wilbur (Paris) to Orville (cablegram): *"...Deutsch is apparently in earnest. Would you be disposed to consider proposition by which we get $200,000 cash (over $10 million today) and half the stock for Europe cash on demonstration? 50 Kilometers? I recommend."*

10Jun;07: Orville to Wilbur (cablegram): *"...O.K. if price named is without commission. Keep a stiff upper lip. U.S. desires more information."*

11Jun'07: Wilbur (Paris) to Orville: *"We had a talk with Fordyce yesterday morning and found him in an almost rambunctious mood. The people back of him...are too much interested in the personal and political end of the game to suit us...(Letellier) would not be near as valuable as Deutsch, who is the 'Standard Oil' king of Europe ...The idea I have arranged to submit is for the formation of a company with international ownership, in which Deutsch, Loewe, will be the principal French and German representatives, and in which we will aim to get English, Italian, & possibly other stockholders. The stock is to be 3,500,000 frs. of which 3,000,000 frs. ($30 million today) represents our invention and 500,000 frs. cash working capital...So we really would get 1,500,000 frs. in cash and share of cash, and also half the stock...Along with Flints we would control the majority of stock...*

"With such a company our stock will be of great value if the business has such future as can reasonably be expected..."

20Jun'07: Orville to Chanute: *"...I am of the opinion that our delay in coming out with our machine has placed us in a better instead of a worse condition...The late telegrams from Wilbur seem to indicate that there is a very good prospect of doing business, and at a better price than any of our former deals...Telegrams received (from Wilbur)...indicate that an offer has been made to us of about $250,000 cash, and a half interest in a company with a $250,000 cash capital above the sum paid to us...the offer amounts to $375,000 (over $17 million today) for a half interest...*

"You may feel free to write to any of the papers you wish. We simply desire that no description be given of our machine itself....We think it a...good plan to keep them guessing until we are ready to come out into the public with it."

2Jul'07: Wilbur's diary: *"Rec'd cable from Orville refusing consent to proposition to French Government. Do not understand why he objects...*

"...Berg and Fordyce saw Humbert, who reported that the trouble was that the war office feared we were...humbugging them, and would never make a trial.."

2Jul'07: Wilbur to Orville: *"I received your cable turning down the French Government deal this morning. At noon the Government also turned it down, so I am turned down on both sides, after both sides had, as I thought, indicated their approval quite definitely. I am absolutely in the dark as to the reasons.*

"I confess that I am a little hurt that you should refuse to take this job yourself and then turn (down) my recommendations after I supposed you had given your assent to every important point in the proposition submitted. I have cabled to you for instructions, so that an offer can be made to Germany.

"I have had no letter from you since...June 11th...though I have asked for word both by letter and by cable."

28Jun'07: Curtiss, in his work and travels with Baldwin, had yet to leave the ground. Now, testing the latest *California Arrow*, he gave it a try: *"He shot into the air to the height of several hundred feet and then proceeded to do a little speeding. Sailing about leisurely after he had demonstrated perfect control of the ship was too tame for this holder of many world's records, and so he registered 20 miles per hour in this wonderful invention of Captain Baldwin's, something unprecedented. He alighted where he started, enthusiastic over the sensation of airship sailing."*

6Jul'07" Wilbur's diary: *"...Received cable from Orville suggesting my return home, but Berg thinks it better to have him come over here...I think any new agreement with Flints should be made with all parties present, but believe Orville had better come over here so that he may be thoroughly familiar with situation and ready to close any government or company deals if opportunity should arise. The year must not be allowed to slip away without doing something..."*

7Jul'07: Wilbur Memorandum: *"...When I left home Orville gave two instructions: (1) Do not jump into formation of company at once. (2) In no event accept less than $200,000* (over $10 million today) *net cash for half interest.*

"Immediately on my arrival the formation of company with Deutsch as sponsor was raised...(Orville's) *answer gave the desired permission.*

"After talk with Deutsch...I saw that we could get a company organized with $700,000 stock, of which $350,000 stock (over $15 million today) *would be assigned to Wrights, and $250,000 cash* ($12-1/2 million today) *cash to W's, the remaining $100,000...as working capital...more than fulfilled Orville's requirement. (Especially as Canada, Australia, Mexico, South America, Japan, and others were retained by us.) But as it was impossible to do business...without agreeing to 300 meters height, I sent cable #3* (to Orville)...*The answer was not very satisfactory...In any event, I could have purchased enough stock out of my own share in the $200,000 cash to make good Orville's demands, if he was not satisfied with what I had done. I could not stop to argue with him by cable with such a situation facing me. The other part of the* (Orville's) *answer was a troublesome one. It amounted to an indirect refusal to go 300 meters in France, and destroyed all hope of doing business of any kind in Paris. I considered this a bad mistake...I put to him in cable #4...whether I should refuse 300 meters in Europe...His answer was exasperating because he made a time condition and left me to guess how much time I should specify...Luckily an intimation was received...that our proposition was not accepted, so I was saved the mortification of having to refuse to stand by an offer I...made, with Orville's supposed approval.*

"As Orville had said 'Do nothing without I consent,' I could only cable for...limits of what I could offer Germany....I could do nothing without information as to nature of his objections. So I sent cable #7. His answers...do not give one word of information on the one thing I need to know, viz: What is the matter with the offer to France, that he finds it so unacceptable after accepting the individual points? Under the circumstances I feel that the only wise plan is to act on his instructions 'You act as you think best,' as the French business must be settled within...48 hours, and I feel sure he would approve my offer if he were here and understood the situation, and the consequences of hedging at this time."

11Jul'07: Orville to Wilbur: *"...You complain that I turned your proposition to the French Minister of War down after having led you to think it was satisfactory. I do not understand how you can say that...You surely remember that I have been decidedly opposed, since our experience of last year, of offering either to sell any exclusive time or secrets...I was not in favor of taking up the business in France anyway, until we had seen what Flints could do in new fields. I did not care to have them come in after we had made some prospects there...*

"I am so completely disgusted with them that I would like to sever our connection ...We employed them in order that we wouldn't have to be bothered with the business ...But they have been so tricky that it keeps us busy watching them.

"...I have had only one letter a week from you (these very short) in the last month or more. I have practically no information of what is going on. When you cable, you

never explain anything so that I can answer with any certainty that we are talking about the same thing.

"...You have not answered a single question I have asked in my cables. I did not answer your first cable the other day asking whether you should withdraw the French proposition, for...I did not understand what you were talking about..."

11Jul'07: Chanute to Wilbur: *"...I am somewhat chagrined by the enclosed clipping which states that you are not making much headway in your efforts to sell your flying machine to the French government, after failing in Germany. I hope this is not true, yet if it results in your selling to England, as I have always desired, I shall be pleased...Have you changed your opinion that you will not be caught up with for five years, now that you have seen what other aviators are doing?"*

14Jul'07: Orville to Chanute: *"...Our European negotiations have developed some very interesting situations in the past few weeks...M. Deutsch withdrew and the road to an early contract appeared clear, when suddenly the negotiations were brought to a sudden stop by certain parties...demanding that we raise the price several hundred thousand francs in order to furnish them an opportunity for graft.*

"Wilbur told them we would not consider such a proposition...and (we would) *offer it directly to the Minister of War...The bandits withdrew.*

"I received a cable last night from Wilbur asking me to ship goods and to come to Paris at once, as they are ready to close.

"I will probably leave within the next five or ten days.

"The terms of the contract are more favorable to us than those of a year ago, excepting that we are now required to make the flights in France...(p.s.) Please consider this confidential."

Mid-Jul'07: Journeying to Cape Breton (as had Langley for several summers before him) to attend to the recalcitrant motor, Curtiss arrived at Beinn Bhreagh to be greeted by the Bells, Selfridge, Baldwin and McCurdy. Initially, being the only one of the group not from a well-to-do family or university educated, he was distanced somewhat, but his well-known exploits coupled with his quiet demeanor soon overcame any initial constraints as a fellowship began developing.

19Jul'07: Bell notes: *"...experiments...point to an early conclusion of the problem of powered flight...Now it appears to me that in the above personnel* (Curtiss, Selfridge, Baldwin and McCurdy) *we have an ideal combination for pursuing aerial researches..."* providing each man with an opportunity of *"making a name and reputation for himself as a promoter of aviation or mechanical flight...and the honor and glory that will attach to those who succeed."*

Mabel Bell proposes an *"association"* funded with her $20,000 contribution (from the sale of inherited real estate, about $1million today), and if necessary an additional $10,000 from her husband that *"ought to suffice to put our first machine successfully in the air."* Bell defines his role: *"My special function, I think, is the coordination of the whole - the appreciation of the importance of the steps of progress - and the encouragement of efforts in what seem to me to be advancing directions."*

15Jul'07 - Curtiss with Bell's "Curtiss No. 2." It was then installed in a boat with an innovative tetrahedral-shaped hull for propeller testing:

Top: Curtiss testing a propeller:
18Jul'07 - Bottom: Curtiss with Gertrude Hubbard Grosvenor, grandaughter of
"Gampie" Bell, hovering, right:

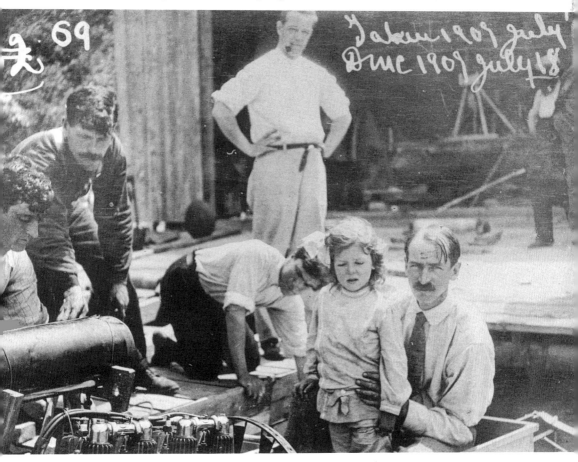

Curtiss (thirty and earning *over $3/4 million a year in today's dollars)* was quietly en-
joying this new, most stimulating environment. And increasingly intrigued by the many
experiments, he finally yielded to Bell's strong entreaties and agreed to return in September to join the group – though remaining very much 'his own man.'

17Jul'07: Wilbur to Katharine: *"...When I first came over, Berg & Cordley thought
that they were businessmen and I was merely a sort of exhibit. But their eyes have
gradually opened, and now they realize that I see into situations deeper than they do,
that my judgment is...sound, and that I intend to run them rather than have them run
me..."*

20Jul'07: Wilbur to Bishop Wright: *"...When the telegram came from Flints asking
that one of us go to Europe at once, I saw instantly what was involved, and asked
Orville to go. I did this for two reasons: (1) Because I wished the job of putting the
final touches to the engines, and preparing the machine for shipment. I am more
careful than he is, at least I think so. (2) Because it was evident that the man who
went to Europe would have to act largely on his own judgment without much con-
sultation by letter or cable. I felt that I was more willing to accept the consequences
of any error of judgment on his part than to have him blaming me if I went. I never
for a minute was so foolish as to suppose that the final decision should be made by
the man at home who, from the nature of the case, would necessarily be less competent to form a sound judgment than the man at the seat of action. When Orville insisted that I should come, I told him that I must be free to settle matters to the best of
my judgment as they arose, as it would be impossible to wait for letters to pass back
and forth or to explain things clearly by cable. Opportunities must be seized as they
pass, or they are gone beyond recovery.*

*"On my way to New York I wrote to him urging him to employ help and get the
machine ready so he could follow me promptly. Instead of tending to his work, and
letting me attend to mine, he seemed to have felt no responsibility as to his own
work, but the whole responsibility as to mine...When he cabled me about U.S. propositions, I answered 'Full power has been given to you'...On the other hand I never
expected to depend on him to settle European questions till he came over. It would
be the height of folly to depend on the judgment of one who could not know the exact
situation at the moment a decision was necessary.*

*"...His complaint about not being able to find things is due to no fault of mine. I
wanted to attend to that end of the job myself, but he happened to be in one of his peculiar spells just then, and I soon saw that he was set on finishing the machine himself. So far as his letters indicate, he spent his time on things of no use in the present
situation, and left the necessary things undone.*

*"Well, I will stop complaining. I suppose he has been so worried that he has not
been really himself. But it would have been much better if he had attended energet-
ically to his department, and avoided interference in mine...*

*"...(p.s.) Flints were quite right in keeping silent. If they had attempted to com-
municate or negotiate directly with Orville, there would have been a fuss here immediately."*

28Jul'07: Wilbur's diary, Paris: *"Orville arrived at 7:A.M...very much tired out and went to bed for a few hours...We lunched at the Alcazar and spent most of the afternoon...sitting in the park along the Champs Elysees."*

1Aug'07: Wilbur's diary, Paris: *"Signed new agreement with Flints..."*

1Aug'07: The War Department establishes an Aeronautica Division under Brig. Gen. James Allen, Chief Signal Officer: Capt. Charles De F. Chandler, Corp. Edward Ward and Pvt.1c. Joseph Barrett.

5Aug'07: Wilbur's diary, Berlin: *"...Berg went to see Herr Loewe* (Mauser gun co.) *at 10....We went together to see him about 5 o'clock....Loewe stated to Berg that there was much antagonism to us on account of the Ferber reproduction of our letter containing reference to the Emperor* (4Nov'05), *and said that he was told that the military department would not be disposed to do anything even if we should be able to do all we had claimed."*

7Aug'07: Wilbur's diary, Berlin: *"Went...to see Gen. von Lynckner...he was disposed to do business if a satisfactory basis could be arrived at, but that no such sum as 1,000,000 was available and the basis would be quite different from French proposition...*

"...went to Loewe's office and talked over proposed offer...Price, 100,000 marks for first machine; 50,000 M. for training. Royalty of 30,000 each on first 10 machines; 20,000 each on next ten; 15,000 on next 20; 10,000 on next 100, and 5,000 beyond that for period of patents...Telegram to O.W."

8Aug'07: Orville's diary, Paris: *"Telegraphed Will...: 'Not think it advisable to submit proposition to German war dept. while offer to French war dept. is pending in present condition'..."*

9Aug'07: Wilbur to Orville (Telegram), Berlin: *"Have you received my letter of Aug. 8th? I wish...your opinion of Germany terms. Very important take advantage of Loewe's presence Berlin...Should begin action...without delay unless France sure. You talk with Cordley and wire us."*

16Aug'07: Wilbur's diary, Berlin: *"Rec'd from O.W. copy of form of proposition proposed by technical dept. of F(rench) war office. Seeing that it was apparently in bad faith, I decided to return at once to Paris and change the basis of negotiations or withdraw."*

17Aug'07: Wilbur to Orville (Telegram), Berlin: *"I recommend offers to German war department flights similar to offers to France when are able to. At price 25,000 and 10,000 training will receive royalty of 7,000 each* (on first) *ten machines, then 5,000 each next ten, then 3,000 until 40, then 2,000 each. No exclusive...Minister of War guarantees fair play."*

17Aug to 16Sep'07: Wilbur's diary, Paris: *"On return to Paris drew up a new form of proposition similar in principle to the proposed German offer, but Fordyce for some reason was much opposed to presenting it and made all sorts of ridiculous objections to the form of it, saying it was not good French, &c., &c. We finally concluded that the French were not in proper spirit to receive such a proposition and finally on Aug. 24 sent a letter to the Minister of War, by Fordyce, withdrawing all offers. Mr. Berg went to Marienbad and Mr. Cordley to Berlin, while Orville & I stayed in Paris, waiting for Mr. Loewe to return to Berlin from his vacation. I finally went to Berlin, Sept. 16th. On September 5th Mr. Fordyce showed us a letter from Comm* (andant) *Targe acknowledging receipt of our letter withdrawing all offers."*

2Sep'07: Wilbur (Paris) to Chanute: *"...I spent two weeks in Berlin early last month and found a much readier spirit to negotiate than expected. Capt. von Kehler, who is manager of the Emperor's motor airship society, had shown himself exceptionally friendly and interested in advancing negotiations with his government. It was thought best, however, to withdraw our offers to France before starting here. We had a pledge from the Minister of War, Gen. von Einem, that if we would come to Germany we would receive fair treatment. As we found a very different spirit cropping out in the French negotiations, we finally decided to withdraw here and try countries we could trust further."*

14Sep'07: Chanute to Wilbur: *"...I am surprised that you have not closed a contract with the French. I felt confident that the strife which has broken out at Casablanca would incline them to pay almost any price...*

"...I hope that you will succeed in effecting a sale, although it does not seem to me that if Germany purchases on those terms it will not make for peace.

"I suppose that the French papers say much more and pitch into you savagely, but I see few of them. I note...that L'Automobile...*gives a description and criticism of your apparatus and pronounces it useless for practical war purposes...*

"...I shall be glad to learn from you whether something can be informally said as to your views concerning an arrangement with the U.S. government."

25Sep'07: Wilbur's diary, Berlin: *"Wrote O.W...advising him to be ready to leave Paris on short notice if the Stewart* (owner of Barnum-Bailey Buffalo Bill shows) *business proved serious. Cordley received a cable from F*(lint) *& Co. suggesting that they join with Stewart in an offer to us of $50,000 cash down and 33 percent of profits to half million and 18 percent beyond to $1,000,000* ($50-million today) *for our world business..."*

2Oct'07: Wilbur's diary, Berlin: *"Word from Cordley that O.W. was in London. Telegraphed to have him come to Berlin at once....I think Berg was somewhat actuated by jealousy, but my reason was a desire to have a full talk with Orville as soon as possible. Had a conference with Loewe who advised prepare a proposition here soon as possible, and to avoid show business for the present."*

30Sep'07: The *Aerial Experiment Association* (A.E.A.) is organized at Beinn Bhreagh, with a compact formalized the next day before the American Counsel-General in Halifax, as follows:

"WHEREAS, the undersigned, Alexander Graham Bell, of Washington, D.C., U.S.A., has for many years been carrying on experiments regarding aerial locomotion at his summer laboratory at Beinn Bhreagh, near Baddeck, N.S. Canada, and has reached the stage where he believes that a practical aerodrome can be built on the tetrahedral principal, driven by an engine and carrying a man, and had felt the advisability of securing expert assistance in pursuing the experiments to their logical conclusion, he has called to his aid Mr. G.H. Curtiss, of Hammondsport, N.Y., an expert in motor construction, Mr. F.W. Baldwin and Mr. J.A.D. McCurdy, of the Toronto Engineers, and Lieutenant T. Selfridge, of the 5th Field Artillery, U.S.A., military expert in aerodromics, and

"WHEREAS, the above named gentlemen have all of them given considerable attention to the subject of aerial locomotion, and have independent ideas of their own which they wish to develop experimentally, and

"WHEREAS, it has been thought advisable that the undersigned should work together as an association in which all could have equal interest, the above named gentlemen giving the benefit of their assistance in carrying out the ideas of said Alexander Graham Bell, the said Alexander Graham Bell giving his assistance to these gentlemen in carrying out their independent ideas relating to aerial locomotion, and all working together, individually and cojointly in pursuance of their common aim to 'get a man in the air' by the construction of a practical aerodrome driven by its own motive power and carrying a man."

Curtiss, McCurdy, Bell, Baldwin and Selfridge:

With the object *"to build a practical aeroplane which will carry a man and be driven through the air by its own power,"* the Aerial Experiment Association was philosophically committed (by Selfridge) *"...to walk in the footprints of those who had gone before, and then advance beyond."*

Bell was named Chairman; Curtiss, Executive Officer and Director of Experiments at $5,000 per year *"for taking temporary leave of his factory to come to Baddeck"* but upon his insistence, half-pay when absent; Selfridge, Secretary (as an Army officer he declines a salary); Baldwin, Chief Engineer, and McCurdy, Treasurer, both at $1,000 per year (about $50,000 today).

They adopted a program to build five *"aerodromes"* (from Langley's incorrect combination of Greek words meaning *"air runner,"* a term used interchangeably with *"aeroplane"* into 1911), one for each member of this *"happy, enthusiastic coterie."* Other than Bell's tetrahedral craft, there was to be a pooling of ideas, but giving each member the final say on *"his"* machine. As things worked out, the four younger member's machines were of a similar, unique, biplane configuration, each an improvement of the former.

Tom Selfridge was born on 2Feb'82 in Mt. Clemens, Michigan. Shortly after graduating from West Point he was assigned to the First Field Artillery in San Francisco, where he distinguished himself during the earthquake. Then, assigned to the Army's new Aeronautical Division, he undertook the study of aeronautics, soon becoming one of the best informed on what little was known of aeronautics. Desiring practical experience, he sought a meeting with Bell, and on 3Aug'07 Bell's friendship with President Theodore Roosevelt saw him detailed as the Army's observer in Baddeck. This led to his joining the AEA, where he was described: *"Liked by everyone. Quiet, serious, responsible, and determined, he was yet full of quiet fun."*

Coincidentally, Tom Baldwin and his airship then performed in Halifax, and the two Baldwins, young "Casey" and the "Captain," met (their names, long associated with Curtiss, were to greatly confuse the press) and Bell was *"delighted"* to witness manned flight for the first time.

22Oct'07: Wilbur (Berlin) to Katharine: *"...Our negotiations here are not brought to the point of settlement yet...We doubt whether an agreement will be reached before we have really made some demonstrations somewhere, and stirred up some excitement.*

"Orville left for Paris this noon. He has a letter from Lieut. (Frank S.) Lahm (1846-1931. 1906 winner of the James Gordon Bennett balloon race from Paris to England), *who wishes to know whether it is too late for the United States to get a deal with us...*(Orville) *will go on to England...Meanwhile we will develop the German situation further. We believe we can do better here, with Orville in Paris or London.*

"...One of the German papers had a cartoon on us a few weeks ago...The Gebruder Wright are represented as bargaining over the sale of a 'cat in a bag.' Orville is at one end bargaining with France while I am working Russia at the other end. France has a wheelbarrow full of money and is down on its knees begging us to accept it. The pile is marked 3,900,000 francs. Orville with a pipe in his mouth leans

indifferently against the bag containing the wonderful machine, and with a bare glance at the 3,900,000 frs. holds up four fingers to indicate 4,000,000 frs. (about $35 million today) *is our bottom price. At the other end I am almost equally indifferent, though Russia is represented as pulling its last rouble out of its pocketbook.*

"As soon as France scrapes up another 100,000 frs. we will sell out and come home."

30Oct'07: Wright Brothers to U. S. War Department: *"...Our course in asking from governments large sums for the first machine has been based upon an impression that governments often appropriate inventions useful in warfare, and tell the inventor to prosecute a claim under the law. But, since the inventor, who has claims to prosecute before he has realized any money from his invention, must transfer the principal interest in his invention to capitalists in order to raise the money to prosecute the claims, he does not derive much profit...even after judgment in his favor has been obtained. If we obtain assurances that we shall receive fair treatment ...we...will make every reasonable concession...to provide a basis of agreement...*

"Our European business will demand our presence...next spring, but...Nothing would give us greater pleasure than to furnish the first machine to it (U.S.)..."

6Nov'07: Wilbur's summary of conversations with Flint's Berg: *"...Re agencies, we don't want you to feel that there is any obligation on our part to give you agencies independent of this agency. We want you to consider this your agency on making the twenty percent. We want you to look at it in this light: immediately you have outside interests, your interests become entirely different from ours, which we don't want. My idea is this: I don't want to build up a big business. I want to get some money out of it. I want the business built up so as to get the greatest amount of money with as little work. Sell few machines at a big profit, so that we can close out - if we could get the business into such shape as to get government sales on royalties.*

"...Our motto is not 'lots of machines,' but 'most money'..."

1Dec'07: Chanute to Wilbur (just returned from Europe): *"....The newspapers have stated that you have been in Berlin, in St. Petersburg...London, as well as...Paris, but with no intimation that you have closed any...negotiations. I hope you have, for the French seem to make greater progress than you anticipated and may detract from the value of your invention..."*

9Dec'07: Wilbur to Chanute (a lengthy summary of the European negotiations): *"...(regarding the negotiations with Deutsch, French, and Loewe, German) We expected to secure large subscribers in England, Italy, and possibly Austria, for most of the remaining two fifths. It was not the intention to have many small stockholders. With such men in it the company would have been strong enough to command the respect of any government or person disposed to pirate our inventions, and it my belief that the profits of the business would have amounted to several million dollars* (times 50 for today's dollars) *within a half dozen years.*

"...There seemed to be no active (German) opposition anywhere, but as they were under no apprehension of being beaten by the French they finally decided to reject our proposition...We...thought it best to wait till the opening of a new season...

We did not like to disclose our machine at the tail end of the year and give imitators all winter to manufacture copies of it. We do not wish to get into lawsuits before we get the business properly organized and started...We do not fear any serious competition until after we show our machine..."

1-10Dec'07: The New York Aero Club Show.

13Dec'07: Orville returns from Europe.

15Dec'07: Chanute to Wilbur: *"...I regret that you have not made more positive sales. It looks to me as if the government officials are keeping you dangling in the expectation that some of your competitors will discover the secret and they can get your invention cheaper. The newspapers meanwhile represent that Esnault-Pelterie and (Henri) Farman (1874-1958) are making great progress, so that it may take less than the five years you estimated for one of them to catch up with you...My feeling would be to sell, even though you do not get your original price, which I always thought too high.*
*"...(P.S.) I have taken the liberty of having...*Geographic Magazine *sent....you..."*

Note: In the Smithsonian Treasury of Science contributing author *M. P. Baker* wrote (from The Smithsonian Report for 1950): "The years 1906 and 1907 were devoted *(by the Wrights)* to intense developing and testing of an airplane that would be of practical value to the United States Army..."
Contrasting that incorrect statement with *"what actually happened"* - as detailed above - and more particularly with Wilbur's *own* words at the start of this period, *13Dec'05*, provides an acute insight for Americans as to the correct Wright story.

23Dec'07: The Army Signal Corps issued specifications for a military flying machine: *"...capable of carrying two men and sufficient fuel supplies for a flight of 125 miles, with a speed of at least 40 miles an hour..."* Bids were to be opened 1Feb'08.
From the day the bid advertisement appeared the Signal Corps became the butt of much journalistic abuse, e.g., The New York Globe, brushing aside the claims of the Wrights as an unconfirmed rumor, commented: *"...A machine such as described in the Signal Corps specifications would record the solution of all the difficulties in the way of the heavier-than-air airship, and, in fact, finally give mankind almost complete control of the air as it now has of the land and water...Nothing in any way approaching such a machine has ever been constructed..."*

The American Magazine of Aeronautics, Jan'08, used even stronger language: *"There is not a known flying machine in the world which could fulfill these specifications at the present moment...Perhaps the Signal Corps has been too much influenced by the 'hot air' of theorizers, in which aeronautics unfortunately abounds."*

But European activity is impressive. <u>Scientific American</u>, 18Jan'08:

"NEW EUROPEAN AEROPLANES AND AIRSHIPS. Aeronautical experimentation abroad still continues actively, and every day, almost, sees the production of some new airship or aeroplane, or new trials of those already constructed.

"The latest of these aeroplanes is that of two Parisian aeronauts, Messrs. Gastambide and Mangin. This machine...was constructed in three week's time...is of the monoplane type, consisting of two wings attached to a central longitudinal body, the wings being set at a dihedral angle...The wings are readily detached from the body part of the machine. They are attached to aluminum girders which are sufficiently strong to sustain without injury the weight of a man standing upon them. They are braced by means of steel ribbons instead of steel wires, as the former do not offer so much resistance to the air. The aeroplane is mounted upon three pneumatic-tired wheels, the two forward wheels being pivoted so that they can be turned in order to steer the machine when it is running along on the ground...All the wheels are carried on spring-supported forks, which reduce the shock when the machine alights. The 50 horse-power, 8-cylinder, V (steam-cooled Antoinette) motor is placed at the forward end of the body, and carries a two-bladed propeller upon its crankshaft...The machine has a vertical rudder at the rear, but no horizontal rudder is provided, as the inventors found from their experiments with a model that the setting of the planes (wings) *at a suitable angle upon the body is sufficient. They expect to control the height of the aeroplane when in flight by varying the speed of the motor...The inventors expect to attain a speed of about 33 miles an hour with their machine.*

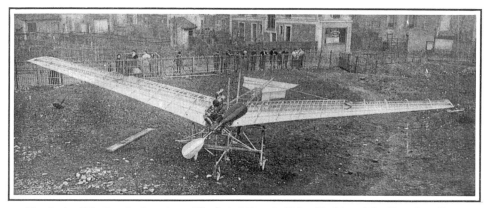

The Gastambide-Mangin Aeroplane—The Latest French Flying Machine of the Monoplane Type.
Spread of wings, 32.8 feet ; diameter and pitch of propeller, 6¼ x 4¼ feet ; engine, 8-cylinder V motor of 50 horse-power.

"Two other of our photographs show the appearance of the latest Bleriot (No.6) *aeroplane before and after its mishap due to the breaking of the wings while in flight as a result of the failure of one or more of the guy wires. As can be readily seen....M. Bleriot* (a manufacturer of automobile head lamps) *has modified the Langley type machine which he first used successfully last summer, until it is now practically a monoplane, since the rear pair of planes have deteriorated into a horizontal rudder formed of two planes - one on each side of the body - which can be separately set at different angles to allow of making a turn. There is also a vertical rudder placed between these two planes...*

The Bleriot No. 6 Aeroplane As It Looked Before Its Accident.

This aeroplane is a modified Langley-type machine the rear planes of which have been shortened and made to form a horizontal rudder.
Spread of wings, 36 feet; supporting surface, 269 square feet; weight, 935 pounds.

"On November 16th, during its first test, the new aeroplane made a short flight at a speed estimated to be about 90 kilometers an hour (56-mph)...*On December 6th, in a splendid flight of 400 to 500 meters* (1,300 to 1,600 feet), *it made a complete circle. It was on the 18th of December that the accident happened...The machine struck the ground head first and turned completely over, and that M. Bleriot was not killed or seriously injured, seems quite marvelous. This accident has shown that constructors of aeroplanes should pay more attention to the strength of the parts.*

The Bleriot Aeroplane After Its Accident in Which the Wings Broke While the Machine Was in Flight.

The photograph shows the machine upside down viewed from the rear and gives a good idea of the length of the rear planes as compared with those in front.

"Another of our photographs shows the new Antoinette aeroplane (shown with talented artist *Leon Levavasseur,* designer of its engine and co-designer of the aeroplane) *which has recently been constructed after the designs of Capt. Ferber...The 100-horsepower, 16-cylinder, V motor is to be placed in the framework between the wings, and the aeronaut will sit just back of it..."*

The New Antoinette Aeroplane, Showing Its Large Size in Comparison With a Man.

This aeroplane, which was built after Capt. Ferber's design, is the largest flying machine thus far constructed in France. It will have a 100-horse-power engine and the total weight of the machine and operator will be over 1,000 pounds.

30Dec'07 - On AEA letterhead, Curtiss writes the Wrights, offering them one of his latest engines: *"...we have been making considerable progress in engine construction. We are now turning out in addition to the 15, 20, 30 and 40 H.P. air cooled engines, a 4-cylinder vertical 5X5 water cooled and an 8-cylinder V 5X5 water cooled which we rate at 50 and 100 H.P. respectively.* (The first indication that he is making water-cooled engines)...

"We would be glad to furnish you with one of these gratis...

"The writer has been getting rather deeply mixed in Aeronautics and Hammondsport is getting to be quite a headquarters for this class of work...

"I understand from Gen. (James) *Allen* (Chief of the Army Signal Corps)...*that the department are anxious to know more about your machine and will take steps which may lead to your giving a demonstration...*

"I should like very much to have you come to Hammondsport at any time you can find it convenient, not only that we may talk engine, but we would feel honored to make you our guests as long as you would care to stay."

17Jan'08: Wilbur's restrained reply, neither accepting the engine or invitation, and not mentioning the A.E.A., concluded: *"....We remember your visit to Dayton with pleasure. The experience we had together in helping Captain Baldwin back to the fair grounds was one not soon to be forgotten."*

1Jan'08: Wilbur to Chanute: *"...I note from several remarks...that you evidently view the present situation in aviation circles with much different eyes from what we do. I must confess that I still hold to my prediction that an independent solution of the flying problem would require at least five years...I have confidence that our prediction will still stand solid after the scythe of time has reaped several fresh crops of French predictions..."*

145

*Aerial Experiment Association partners, Curtiss, Baldwin, Bell, Selfridge and McCurdy,
October, 1907:*

Chapter **5** *The Most Momentous Year   1908*

T
riumph

and tragedy mark a year that sees Curtiss and Bell, challenging the
Wrights, succeed in flight; Baldwin's airship success; the aeroplane's
first casualty; and honor and recognition for the Wrights in Europe
and America.

Jan'08: The start of the new year finds Curtiss discussing gliders with the Aero Club's
Augustus Post when a telegram arrives from Bell: *"Start building. The boys will be down*
next week."

Soon the younger AEA members (*"Bell's boys"*), shortly followed by Alec and
Mabel Bell, gather in Hammondsport, all Curtiss's guests at *"the house on the hill."*

Their first project was *The Hammondsport Glider..."a gliding machine modeled after*
the machines that have been successfully used in America and France," using plans supplied to Bell by Chanute. It had a rigid box-frame, a design which avoided problems with
the Wright's patented wing warping - which they considered structurally unsound and potentially dangerous (the same as reasoned in 1904 by engineer-trained Robert Esnault-
Pelterie). And with considerable help from Captain Baldwin, expert at light framework
and fabric construction, the glider was completed by the end of January and all except
Bell took turns learning to fly it.

Curtiss flying the glider, his first heavier-than-air experience:

Bell commented about their need to learn as much as possible about aeronautics, including *"what little was known or surmised of the machine of the Wright brothers, who were then working in secret and allowed very little information to leak out."*

Bell was very critical of the Wright's secrecy and thus promoted the fullest possible publicity, inviting all to watch the A.E.A.'s experiments. There was also the belief, expressed by Selfridge, that Herring and not the Wrights had been the first to fly (note earlier).

15Jan'08: Selfridge, the AEA's 'chief investigator,' wrote the Wrights: *"...asking your advice...connected with gliding experiments, which we started here last Monday. Will you kindly tell me what results you obtained on the travel of the center of pressure both on aerocurve and aeroplanes?"*

18Jan'08: Wilbur replies to Selfridge: *"...The travel of the center of pressure on aeroplanes is from the center at 90 degrees toward the front edge as the angle becomes smaller..."*

13Jan'08: Henri Farman, in a Voisin machine, won the 50,000 franc (over $500,000 today) *Deutsch Archdeacon Prize* for a flight of one kilometer; 500 meters, turn, and return to the starting point.

20Jun'08, Scientific American:

MM. Henri Farman and Earnest Archdeacon in the Former's Aeroplane.

Farman's French Aeroplane--First to Make Long Flight

Popular
Mechanics,
13Jan'08:

16Jan'08: Wrights to <u>Scientific American</u>'s Stanley Beach: *"...We do not think that what Farman has done will have any...effect on the price of practical flying machines. He has used only those things which are very old, and ...not protected by patents....Mr. Farman has not yet found any solution of these problems, much less one free from infringement."*

16Jan'08: Wilbur to Chanute: *"Of course it is not possible to know just how the financial end of our flyer will come out...It would have been a great advantage if we could have organized our company before beginning business, but we will still do very well unless we are much mistaken. The governments will each spend many times $200,000 ($10 million today) on flying machines within the next fifteen years (patent time left), and we think we will have patents, knowledge, and business associations sufficient to insure a good share of it coming our way. Yet we may be mistaken....On my way home...I stopped a day at Washington and went back a week later to meet the Board of Ordnance. I was not very favorably impressed with the attitude of Gen. Allen, and while the Board was courteous I did not feel like 'hustling' for an order very hard. When I first learned that the Board was advertising for bids I doubted its good faith, but am now inclined to think I did them an injustice in suspecting such a thing..."*

FRENCH AERONAUT WINS $10,000 PRIZE

Henry Farman, the French aeronaut, who for the past few months has been startling France with his wonderful flights in an aeroplane, won the Deutsche-Archdeacon prize of $10,000 in January by making a circular kilometer, which is a little more than a circular half-mile, without his machine touching the ground.

With a preliminary run of 100 yd. over the ground the aeroplane rose to a height of 15 ft., then with outstretched wings it sailed away across the fields at a height of from 25 to 35 ft. at a speed of 24 miles an hour. It reached the outer mark, described a graceful circle, and went sailing home on an even keel. It is estimated that with the curve described by Farman the aeroplane covered a distance of nearly a mile. The motor used has 8 cylinders and developed 50 hp. It weighed 176 lb.

Count Henri de la Vaulx, Farman's most feared competitor for the prize, met with serious accidents in his first trials, which placed him out of the contest. One of the wings of his aeroplane bent at the shoulder and the great birdlike machine shot to earth at a tremendous speed, seriously injuring its owner and completely wrecking itself.

27Jan'08: Wilbur to Chanute: *"...your views do not in all respects coincide with our own. You think a serious accident in the French camp would benefit us. We do not think so...If Farman should be killed by a fall, it would injure us to the extent of thousands of dollars, we believe.*

"...We have never seen any indication of a new solution of the problem of lateral stability. Of course if the dihedral angle furnishes a satisfactory solution of this problem we have not...and never had, the basis on which to found a company...

"...You are quite mistaken as to the matter of shifting of weight in our machines. We do not shift weight. We combine right and left wings of variable inclination with means of preventing movement about a vertical axis..."

27Jan'08: Wrights to General James Allen: *"We herewith enclose a ($25,000) bid for furnishing the Signal Corps with a heavier-than-air flying machine with a certified check for two thousand five hundred dollars ($2,500)...We enclose a photograph of our machine of 1905, which was similar to the one we now propose to furnish. We would request that this, as well as the drawings, be kept confidential..."*

8Feb'08: The Wrights, low on funds, lowered their price from $100,000 to $25,000 (still quite a sum, over $1 million today) and were awarded a contract for a two-man flying machine - as was Herring for his $20,000 proposal - subject to trials. Twenty-two bidders responded.

Apparently always the schemer, Herring had planned to obtain a War Department contract by virtue of his lower price, and then sublet it to the Wrights for a liberal commission (see 20May'08). The brothers *"refused to help him in that matter."*

That was the likely reason for Herring's later attempt to make *"technical delivery"* of his machine (see 12Oct'08): in a large case, containing a dismantled engine and an odd assortment of wooden spars and metal fittings, avowing them to be parts of an aeroplane nearing completion

20Feb'08: Chanute to Wilbur: *"...I regret to find that our views still differ as to the eventual business outcome of your procedures.*

"I note...that you have been awarded a contract to furnish a flying machine to our government for $25,000...I hope that you will have as great a financial success as the mechanical success which I expect you to attain..."

24Feb'08: Tom Baldwin's low bid of $6,740 won a contract to supply the Army Signal Corps with its *first* powered airship, a large 96-foot two-man dirigible. Its Selfridge-designed propeller was to be powered with Curtiss's *first* water-cooled motor, a 24-hp, aluminum-jacketed, 4-cylinder engine capable of running continuously for over two hours. This was the *first* engine to use such a cooling system *and* to be covered with the new lightweight metal. Curtiss planned to tend it during the trials, scheduled for August.

Scientific American, *18.Jan'08:*

Motors

for airships and other purposes where light and powerful engines are required.
1 to 40 H. P. Air Cooled.
50 & 100 H. P. Water Cooled.
Adopted by War Department. Send for catalogue B.
G. H. CURTISS MANUFACTURING CO.
Hammondsport, N. Y.

Curtiss and Baldwin:

8Mar'08: Wilbur to Chanute: *"...I am sending you...a spare copy of our first patent. The later patents have not been issued. They cover broadly the idea of using horizontal surfaces adjustable about a transverse axis as to face forward at different angles on right and left sides, in combination with means of correcting the resulting disturbance of balance about the vertical axis by the use of rudders, vanes, or resistances in front, behind, or on the wing tips....We also have the flexible rudder capable of being curved simultaneously with its adjustment to different angles above or below the horizontal. We do not believe it will be found easy to construct machines comparing in quality with ours without palpable infringement of our claims. In flying only the best possible machines will be used. After the first machines it is the intention to bring the price to...where governments will use scores of them..."*

15Mar'08: Wilbur went to New York to discuss the French contract with Flint & Co., and on the 16th wrote Orville: *"...Berg says the company is expected to prosecute infringements. We would have to defend any suits directly against ourselves to annul the patents. We might find it advisable to help prosecute infringers. The expense of such litigation in France is much less than in America and cannot be protracted forever as at home..."*

12-17Mar'08: The A.E.A. Drome Number 1, Selfridge's *"Red Wing"* (wing fabric color), a design resulting from endless nightly discussions by four young men, none of which had ever seen an aeroplane before. The result, unlike any other, a biplane with bow-shaped wings (both cathedral and dihedral angles), powered with a Curtiss 40-hp (probably nearer 25-hp) 8-cylinder, air-cooled motor (virtually identical to the one used for the record ride at Ormond Beach a year earlier).

12Mar'08 - With the ice starting to break up, it was boated up the lake and unloaded:

12Mar'08: With Selfridge temporarily ordered to Washington, *Red Wing* was *"operated"* by Casey Baldwin (the *first* Canadian to fly) on its maiden 319-foot flight over the ice of Keuka Lake.

"It sped over the ice like a scared rabbit for two or three hundred feet," Curtiss wrote, *"and then, much to our joy, it jumped into the air...It had taken just seven weeks to build a machine and get it ready for the trial; ...it had taken just 20 seconds to smash it"* on its final flight on 17Mar'08, from which Casey Baldwin emerged unscathed.

It was reported as *"the first public flight of an aeroplane in the United States,"* a claim contested by the Wrights because of their 1904 and 1905 flights near Dayton's interurban trolley line, which, though they *"did not advertise"* they timed for when the trolley was *not* scheduled to pass.

17Mar '08, Red Wing, final flight:

17Mar'08, Curtiss in Red Wing:

16Apr'08, <u>The Youth's Companion</u>:

THE AEROPLANE "RED WING."

Contracts have been awarded by the War Department for three flying-machines heavier than air. If the machines do not fly they will not be accepted; but the contractors—Wright Brothers of Dayton, Ohio, A. M. Herring of New York, and J. F. Scott of Chicago—are confident that they will succeed. The Wright Brothers recently announced that they had sailed in the air for fifteen miles or more at the rate of thirty miles an hour. Their flights have been made in comparative private, or in the presence of only trustworthy persons who would not disclose the secret of construction. A new competitor for the honors of the sky made its first flight in public near Hammondsport, New York, in March. The aeroplane *Red Wing*, having three hundred and eighty-five feet of sustaining surface, propelled by a forty-five horse-power motor, after running on the ice of Lake Keuka for four hundred feet, rose in the air, sailed three hundred and nineteen feet and came down again. Alexander Graham Bell, who has been experimenting with tetrahedral kites, is one of those interested in the development of this aeroplane. The design for it was made by Lieutenant Selfridge of the army. All the lighter-than-air flying-machines yet made have been aeroplanes, and as an English authority on the subject says, are "more properly skimming dishes than air-ships."

❦ ❦

Red Wing, Lake Keuka, March, 1908:

18Mar'08: Anxious to participate, Herring arrives in Hammondsport.

23Mar'08: Bishop Wright's diary: *"...the Wright brothers get word that* (Lazare) *Weiller accepts their terms for French rights"...for 500,000 francs* (about $5 million today) *upon the successful demonstration and delivery of the first machine, plus fifty percent of the founder's shares in the new company, La Compagnie Generale de Navigation Aerienne* (the French Wright company), *and 20,000 francs for each of four follow-up machines..."*

8Apr'08: Wilbur to Chanute: *"I am on my way to Kitty Hawk to get a camp in shape for a little practice before undertaking the...trials at Washington and in France...*

"We would have preferred to let the arrangement of European sales rest till after the U.S. business had been finished, but...we thought, on the whole, it would be safer to accept it. It includes both government and commercial rights for France & its colonies. The contract also provides for the sale of four additional machines beyond that used in the demonstrations; we are to have an extra 20,000 frs. each on these machines, 80,000 frs. in all (apprx. $850,000 today). *About half will be profit..."*

13Apr'08: Chanute to Wilbur: *"...I congratulate you upon your French arrangment..I see in* L'Aerophile *that you have bought 7 French motors of 40 H.P. each, and I hope that they will give you full satisfaction...*

"(p.s.) Will keep confidential your French arrangement unless you desire me to make it known."

Contract in hand – *after abandoning their camp for over four years* – they return to Kitty Hawk to hone their piloting skills to meet the French performance requirements. A new building is erected, and the 1905 machine is modified for both a pilot and a passenger, *sitting upright*, with the controls changed accordingly.

Kitty Hawk as it was on their return, 1908. Note abandoned 1902 Glider:

As to the pilot's position, it was not easy to lie flat with your head raised to see forward:

"I used to think," Orville recalled in 1917, *"the back of my neck would break if I endured one more turn of the field."*

8May'08: Wilbur's diary: *"...We were ready for the first flight about seven o'clock ... We made nine flights in the morning...in the afternoon...Mr. Salley, the newspaperman, came over...and interrupted experiments, but after his departure W. W. made a flight of about 2,230 ft. in 59 1/2 sec..."*

9May08: Wilbur's diary: *"...telegram from Berg saying Weiller refused to postpone our French business. Unless we can secure a little time, it will be necessary for one of us to start to Europe within a few days..."*

14May'08: Wilbur's diary: *"...Orville and Chas.* (Charles Furnas, their Dayton assistant) *tried a flight together and after one false start sailed away nicely. They passed around the West Hill, came north alongside the Little Hill by the sound, and back by way of starting point...*

The *first flight of an aeroplane with a passenger* - demonstrating that the new machine would meet the Army's two-passenger requirements.

But Kitty Hawk's May weather was getting the best of them. *"After dinner I tried alone...and was continuing the course followed on the first round when the machine suddenly darted into the ground when going with the wind at a velocity of about 85 kilometers an hour. The front framing and upper surface were wrecked...I was thrown violently forward and landed against the top surface...I received a slight cut across the bridge of my nose, several bruises on my left hand, right forearm, and both shoulders. The next day I felt a little stiff all over...We tore the machine apart ...and the three of us dragged it back to camp, a distance of about a mile and a quarter. The heat was almost unbearable...We went to bed completely fagged out..."*

16May'08: Bishop Wright's diary: *"...Weiller had consented to postponement of Wrights' coming to France...In evening* (Katharine) *expresses Wilbur's trunk to New York. Telegram from Wilbur, at 10 P.M. Starts to France Wedn(esday)."*

19May'08: Wilbur to Katharine: *"I reached N.Y. this morning...and went to the hotel where I found my trunk and hatbox...I do sometimes wish though that you had raised the lid of my hat box, which was not locked, and put some of my hats in it before sending it on...*

"...Good-bye to Sterchens for a few months (the pet name for Katharine, short, in German, for "little sister")*..."*

13 Jun '08: <u>Scientific American</u>:

———— ◆◇◆◆ ————

OUR AEROPLANE TESTS AT KITTY HAWK.

BY ORVILLE AND WILBUR WRIGHT.

The spring of 1908 found us with contracts on hand, the conditions of which required performance not entirely met by our flights in 1905. The best flight of that year, on October 5, covered a distance of a little over 24 miles, at a speed of 38 miles an hour, with only one person on board. The contracts call for a machine with a speed of 40 miles an hour, and capable of carrying two men and fuel supplies sufficient for a flight of 125 miles. Our recent experiments were undertaken with a view of testing our flyer in these particulars, and to enable us to become familiar with the use of the controlling levers as arranged in our latest machines.

After tedious delays in repairing our old camp at Kill Devil Hills, near Kitty Hawk, N. C., we were ready for experiments early in May. We used the same machine with which we made flights near Dayton, Ohio, in 1905; but several modifications were instituted to allow the operator to assume a sitting position, and to provide a seat for a passenger. These changes necessitated an entirely new arrangement of the controlling levers. Two of them were given motions so different from those used in 1905 that their operation had to be completely relearned.

We preferred to make the first flights, with the new arrangement of controlling levers, in calm air; but our few weeks' stay had convinced us that in the spring time we could not expect any practice at that place in winds of less than 8 to 10 miles an hour, and that the greater part of our experiments must be made in winds of 15 to 20 miles.

The engine used in 1905 was replaced by a motor of a later model, one of which was exhibited at the New York Aero Club show in 1906. The cylinders are four in number, water cooled, of 4¼-inch bore and 4-inch stroke. An erroneous statement, that the motor was of French manufacture, has appeared in some papers. This is, no doubt, due to the fact that we are having duplicates of this motor built by a well-known Paris firm, for use in European countries.

The longer flights this year were measured by a Richard anemometer attached to the machine in the same manner as in 1905. Except in the first few flights, made over regular courses, it was found impracticable to secure accurate measurements in any other way. These records show the distances traveled through the air. The measurements of the velocity of the wind were made at a height of six feet from the ground at the starting point, and were usually taken during the time the machine was in flight.

The first flight was made on the 6th of May, in a wind varying from 8 to 12 miles an hour. After covering a distance of 1,008 feet measured over the ground, the operator brought the machine down to avoid passing over a patch of ground covered with ragged stumps of trees.

In the morning of May 8 several short flights were made in winds of 9 to 18 miles an hour. In the afternoon the machine flew 956 feet in 31 seconds, against a wind of a little over 20 miles an hour; and later, a distance of 2,186 feet in 59½ seconds, against a wind of 16 miles. These distances were measured over the ground.

On May 11 the Richard anemometer was attached to the machine. From this time on the flights were not over definite courses, and the distances traveled were measured by this instrument. Three flights were made on this day in winds varying from 6 to 9 miles. The distances were: 0.78 mile, 1.80 miles, and 1.55 miles.

On May 13 four flights were made. The anemometer on the machine registered a distance of 0.60 mile in the first; 1.85 miles in the second; no distance measurement in the third—time, 2 minutes and 40 seconds; and 2.40 miles in the fourth. The velocity of the wind was 16 to 18 miles an hour.

On May 14 Mr. C. W. Furnas, of Dayton, Ohio, who was assisting in the experiments, was taken as a passenger. In the first trial, a turn was not commenced soon enough, and to avoid a sand hill, toward which the start was made, the power was shut off. The second flight, with passenger on board, was in a wind of 18 to 19 miles an hour. The anemometer recorded a distance traveled through the air of a little over 4 kilometers (2.50 miles) in 3 minutes and 40 seconds.

The last flight was made with operator only on board. After a flight of 7 minutes and 29 seconds, while busied in making a turn, the operator inadvertently moved the fore-and-aft controlling lever. The machine plunged into the ground, while traveling with the wind, at a speed of approximately 55 miles an hour. The anemometer showed a distance of a little over 8 kilometers (5 miles).

The frame supporting the front rudder was broken; the central section of the upper main bearing surface was broken and torn; but beyond this, the main surfaces and rudders received but slight damage. The motor, radiators, and machinery came through uninjured. Repairs could have been made in a week's time, but the time allowed for these experiments having elapsed, we were compelled to close experiments for the present.

These flights were witnessed by the men of the Kill Devil life-saving station, to whom we were indebted for much assistance, by a number of newspaper men, and by some other persons who were hunting and fishing in the vicinity.

The machine showed a speed of nearly 41 miles an hour with two men on board, and a little over 44 miles with one man. The control was very satisfactory in winds of 15 to 20 miles an hour, and there was no distinguishable difference in control when traveling with, against, or across the wind.

———— ◆◇◆◆ ————

20May'08: Wilbur (New York) to Orville: *"...You will see...that our French business is not in very good shape. As near as I can make out Deutsch has drawn out again. It is evident that we will have a hard pull...but I think things will go better with someone to steady Berg...*

"I stopped a few moments at the Century *office...it is my opinion as firmly as ever that we need to have our true story told in an authentic way at once and let it be known that we consider ourselves fully protected by patents. One of the clippings ...intimates that Selfridge is infringing our patent on wing twisting. It is important to get the main features originated by us identified in the public mind with our machines before they are described in connection with some other machine. A statement of our original features ought to be published and not left covered up in the patent office. I strongly advise that you get a stenographer and dictate an article...have Kate assist in getting it in shape if you are too busy.*

Note: It appears that the publishing of patents was not then done, explaining much of the contemporary ignorance by Bell - and others - of the Wright patent.

"...keep me informed as to what you decide to do in the American business..."

20May'08: Wilbur to Orville: *"....Herring called up by telephone* (apparently a somewhat unique event) *twice today but I was inaccessible. He is said to be working some on a machine, but it is my opinion he will never go to Washington..."*

29May'08: Wilbur's diary: *"Sailed from N.Y. (21May)...reached Paris, about 10 o'clock."*

The A.E.A.'s next aerodrome, Casey Baldwin's *"White Wing,"* was designed to provide *"lateral stability"* using Bell's idea for *"moveable surfaces at the extremities of the wing piece."* Also, Bell added *"...it might be worth while considering whether the protruding ends might not be made moveable and be controlled by the instinctive balancing movements of the body of the operator...what we want to do is reef one wing and extend the other"* (note nautical terms).

This was the A.E.A.'s first use of *ailerons.* It caused problems with the Wrights and their less efficient wing-warping, which, while providing a measure of lateral control altered the drag of the wings and produced a tendency for the aeroplane to skid. Also, warping altered wing bracing and lessened the wing's strength and rigidity. It's doubtful that Bell was aware that the aileron, called *"elevon,"* was used by Robert Esnault-Pelterie in '04, by Santos-Dumont in '06, and by Bleriot in '07.

Curtiss, later: *"If the Wrights had thought of it they would have incorporated it in their patent."*

On March 8, 1908, at Fairfax City, Virginia, *William W. Christmas* (1866-1960) flew his sophisticated aileron-equipped biplane, clouding further the issue of ailerons. In 1914 he received a patent for his *"recessed aileron"* which, in 1923, the United States government purchased for $100,000 ($3 million today).

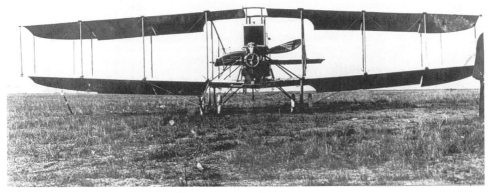

Christmas aeroplane, 1912:

In 1908 Esnault-Pelterie built an exceedingly modern-looking *"REP"* aircraft - a rotary-engine powered monoplane with canard winglets, 4-blade tractor propeller, tricycle landing gear, and a streamlined enclosed body. The revolutionary, lightweight air-cooled *"Gnome"* rotary engine was invented in 1907 by France's *Louis and Laurent Seguin*, who introduced their 7-cylinder 50-hp Gnome *"Omega"* in 1909.

18-23May'08: A.E.A. Drome No. 2, *"White Wing,"* with individually-controlled *"wing tips"* (ailerons) and the first American use of wheels, in a tricycle (second, again, to the French), replacing *Red Wing*'s skids. Also, its controls were better placed and the porosity of the wing's cotton fabric was reduced by varnishing (first use of *"wing doping"*).

18May'08: Its first flight, at Harry Champlin's Stony Brook Farm race track in Pleasant Valley (first aerodrome flight seen by Bell), had Baldwin *'driving'* for 279-feet:

Post, Bell and Selfridge studying White Wing:

Bell, with his remarkable prescience, was prompted to write: *"I have no doubt but that in the future, heavier-than-air machines of great size, and of a different construction from anything yet conceived of, will be driven over the earth's surface at enormous velocity, hundreds of miles an hour, by new methods of propulsion...Think of the enormous energy locked up in high explosives! What if we could control that energy and utilize it in projectile flight!*

"We may conclude that neither our Army or Navy could defend the United States from attack through the air. This requires the addition of a third armed force system of military defence, a National Air Force quite distinct from the Army and the Navy, capable of co-operation with both and also of acting independently of either. This might well be made a distinct department of the government, on the model of the Army and Navy Departments, and should be provided with a special college upon the model of those at West Point and Annapolis."

160

Tom Selfridge, first American military person to fly an aeroplane, in White Wing:

19May'08: An officer of the United States Army flew an aerodrome for the *first* time when Lt. Selfridge *"soared as gracefully as a bird"* in *White Wing,* his second flight covering 240-feet. Mrs. Bell was thrilled to see these flights while Bell was impressed with the realization that ample power and control were at hand, and that only the skill of the operator determined longer flights.

They "were obliged to develop with home talents the arts of brazing, welding, enameling, wood treatment, cloth filling, wire fastenings, turnbuckles, etc., and, most important at the time, to invent a new method of lateral balance. Some of the wood was cut and seasoned on the hills near Hammondsport. For bamboo to be used in the outriggers they had to send to Japan. Supply houses for such material were nonexistent and every detail of the machines had to be planned, engineered and manufactured." *Lyman Seely*

21May'08: On his 30th birthday, Curtiss, his prowess at motorcycle racing accelerating his transition to flying, made his first aerodrome flight in a slightly-modified *White Wing.* It had a steerable nose wheel and a tail wheel. After his flight of 1017-feet in two jumps, the longest yet, he commented: *"I felt very much elated,"*...and we are finding it easy to take off, but *"it was most difficult to get back to earth without smashing something."*

In that evening's discussion he told Bell: *"Although I have given the subject of aviation much thought, it wasn't until I flew White Wing today that my ideas of how to operate a heavier-than-air flying machine are really tangible enough to be of service to another...The art of flying, even though but the short distance of a thousand feet, gives a person something to work from, and his ideas follow on a more practical course."*

On the second throw-of-the-dice the young AEA members were achieving fantastic results. Not only were they flying, they had apparently solved the critical lateral control problem with their *"wing tips."*

Two days later McCurdy, already proven accident-prone riding a motorcycle (Curtiss said: *"McCurdy used to give us daily demonstrations of how to fall off a motorcycle scientifically."* Photos show him on crutches), took his first and last flight in *White Wing*, crashing after an erratic 183 yards but spared further injury when he was *"deposited gently"* on the ground.

Curtiss's competitive instincts were aroused by <u>Scientific American's</u> announcement of an impressive trophy (a costly 32" sterling work-of-art) to be awarded for heavier-than-air flight under the auspices of the Aero Club of America. There were to be three annual contests, progressively more difficult, the first a flight of at least one kilometer (3281 feet). With this in mind, he co-designed and helped build the next drome - while assisting in Baldwin's preparations for his Army airship trials.

Curtiss experimenting with propellers and wing surfaces in a new wind-wagon:

2Jun08: Wright Brothers to General James Allen: *"...We will make all possible haste in the preparations for the delivery of the machine and hope to be able to make the trials before the first of September."*

3Jun'08: Wilbur (Paris) to Orville: *"I am a little surprised that I have no letter from you yet...*

"I found our affairs here about like Peter Cartwright (a Methodist circuit-rider) *reported religion to be on one of his circuits - 'looking upward' - in other words, flat*

on its back...I have told Berg that he had made a mistake in getting us mixed up in this foreign business at this time...We would have been as well or better off without a contract.

"...Our position is improving rapidly as it always does when one of us is here to meet people and infuse a little confidence in them...Everyone is getting more & more interested and enthusiasm will follow...I hope you have an application for American patent on our front rudder already under way...

"...I am looking for a place where we can practice, train operators, &c., instead of a ground merely for a demonstration..."

25May-2Jun'08: Henri Farman exhibition:

3Jun'08: Orville to Wilbur: *"On my way back from Kitty Hawk I stopped at Washington...I took a pretty good look over the grounds at Fort Myer* (Virginia), *and the country in some distance around...about as tough ground to fly over as one could well expect...*

"I found the ground...much smaller than you had reported...not nearly so large as the field at Simms, but much smoother...Lieut. Lahm has charge of the aeronautical division at Fort Myer...They are very anxious to have us begin the trials. I do not see any indication that they are making any preparation for Herring's trials.

"...Our mail has increased about ten-fold...All the steel, aluminum, and metal works of the country are now wanting us to try their products. Dozens of inventors are offering us their inventions at rock-bottom prices.

"I am sending an account of what we did to the <u>Sci. American</u> (see below) <u>Aeronautics</u>, *Aero Club of America,* <u>Aerophile</u>, *and* <u>Mitteilungen</u>..."

7Jun'08: Orville to Wilbur: *"...I see by one of the papers that the Bell outfit is offering Red Wings for sale at $5,000 each. They have got some nerve."*

8Jun'08: Wilbur's diary: *"Berg and I went down to Le Mans...to inspect some grounds...We will probably locate here..."*

9Jun'08: Wilbur (Paris) to Katharine: *"...I have no word from Orville since leaving Kitty Hawk. Does he intend to be partners any more? It is ridiculous to leave me without information of his doings and intentions..."*

11Jun'08: Wilbur's diary: *"M. Bleriot called in this morning at Berg's office while I was there, and offered us the use of his shop in Neuilly...At noon I saw Mr. Rolls* (see 30Jul'10)*...He wished to get one of our machines. I told him I would have to consult Orville as to date of delivery and price..."*

15Jun'08: Orville to Wilbur: *"...It looks to me like we will get a very good patent.*

"...Knabenshue called up by telephone...He is talking of coming down to talk over the exhibition business. He says everyone now wants flying machines.

"...Chanute had an article in the Independent *last week criticizing our business methods, and saying that we have always demanded an exorbitant price.*

"I have a letter from Newton, of the N.Y. Herald*...He saw Herring's machine. He says it is a little thing with a pocket edition of a motor.*

"...I am now planning to set the machine together before shipping to Fort Myer. I think it will be policy to try to make the flights in the early part of August. The winds will probably be lighter...and the sooner the trials the more lenient the Department will be, it's my opinion..."

17Jun'08: Wilbur (Le Mans) to Orville: *"I opened the boxes yesterday and have been puzzled ever since to know how you could have wasted two whole days packing them. I am sure that with a scoop shovel I could have put things in within two or three minutes and made fully as good a job of it. I never saw such evidences of idiocy in my life. Did you tell Charley* (Taylor) *not to separate anything lest it should get lonesome? Ten or a dozen ribs were broken...One surface was so bad that I took it completely down...The radiators are badly smashed; the seat is broken; the magneto has the oil cap broken off, the coils badly torn up, and I suspect the axle is bent a little; the tubes of the screw* (propeller) *support are mashed and bent. The only thing I ever saw resembling the interiors of the boxes is the rattler at a foundry...To be brief, things must be packed at least ten times as well as they were...*

"...We have been delayed because we have been unable as yet to get anything to replace (lost bolts)*. It is going to take much longer for me to get ready than it should have done if things had been in better shape."*

20Jun'08: Wilbur to Orville: *"...Farman said he tried putting auxiliary surfaces on the wing tips, but found they were not sufficient. He would like to get one of our machines as soon as we have them to sell. Keep this mum for the present..."*

28Jun'08: Orville to Wilbur: *"...Curtiss et al. are using our patents, I understand, and are now offering machines for sale at $5,000 each, according to the* Scientific American*. They have got good cheek!..."*

5Jul'08: Wilbur to Orville: *"...I have seen the statement you sent to* Aerophile (3Jun'08)*. It is very good but should have said that in some of the flights two men were carried. I have been taking some pains to have the chief points of our patents* *well published so as to let the general public become accustomed to linking these ideas with us before others attempt to steal them...*

"...you have never sent me a copy of your letters to British war dept. I ought to see them. I have asked you to tell me the date when British business must be worked to hold patent, but you seem to never notice requests or instructions..."

9Jul'08: Wilbur to Orville: *"...If you had permitted me to have an anticipation of the state in which you had shipped things over here, it would have saved three week's time probably. I would have made preparation to build a machine instead of trying to get along with no assistance and no tools. If you have any conscience, it ought to be pretty sore...I will not attempt to catalog my troubles, both because I have not time and paper enough, and...you are probably having troubles enough of your own..."*

21Jun-10Jul'08: A.E.A. Drome Number 3, Curtiss's *"June Bug."* The honor of naming it almost went to Mrs. Malinda Bennitt, who had provided young Curtiss rent-free space for his first bicycle shop, but her hesitation prompted Bell's naming it.

"Curtiss seems to have realized that an aeroplane, like a bicycle or a ship, needed forward speed...to make it easily controllable so he used less wing surface and greater speed; a characteristic...with his machine for years to come." *Lyman Seely*

He designed the *June Bug* to reduce wind resistance, and powered it with a more powerful, 40-hp air-cooled V8 motor. Also, it was the first to use the shoulder yoke aileron control system suggested by Bell's *"instinctive balancing"* idea.

21Jun'08: June Bug - note Alex and Mabel Bell to right:

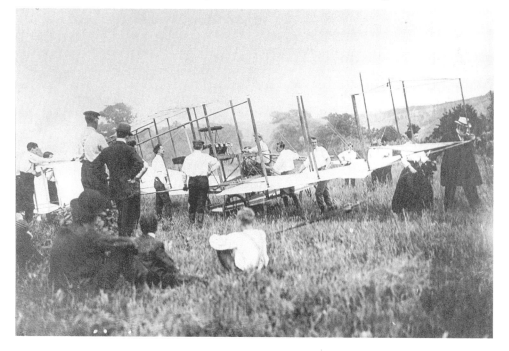

Baldwin, Selfridge, Curtiss, Bell, McCurdy and Post:

21Jun'08: Curtiss flew *June Bug*, wings varnished (yellow), for flights of 456, 417 and 1,266 feet.

Curtiss and the June Bug flying past the still-standing Stony Brook Farm barn:

And he performed the *first side-slip:* Desperately trying to avoid landing on a vineyard's menacing stakes, he turned the wheel. The machine answered its rudder as he successfully made a flat, side-ward turn to a safe landing.

On June 25th he flew 2,175 feet and, just before dusk, an astonishing 3,420 feet, prompting a wire to Bell: *"...telegraphed and telephoned secretary Aero Club of America that we are now ready to try for the <u>Scientific American Cup</u>. Hurrah. Selfridge."*

Augustus Post *(left)*, the Aero Club's secretary, immediately advised Charles Munn, <u>Scientific American</u>'s publisher, of this challenge. Taken off-guard, he'd been trying since June 4th to get the Wrights to try for the trophy, and immediately wrote Orville (25Jun'08) of the A.E.A.'s challenge, offering to put them off if they would compete. However, since the rules stipulated a takeoff from level ground, the Wrights would have to use wheels, which they never had.

30Jun'08: Orville to Charles Munn: *"...I have not been able to think of any way of changing our machine so it could compete for the <u>Scientific American</u> trophy within the next month or two. All of our machines have been designed for starting from a track...*

"Personally, I think the flying machines of the future will start from tracks, or from special apparatus (catapult?). *The system of pneumatic wheels, now used in Europe, has not proved satisfactory...Of course wheels can be applied to our machine as well as to others...At the first opportunity we will fit up one machine to start without a track."*

Munn and Post, out of time (and patience) with the Wrights, accepted the A.E.A.'s challenge, commenting that *"of all the efforts being put into the development of flying machines in America, none has been more systematic and thorough than that of the members of Dr. Alexander Graham Bell's Aerial Experiment Association."*

It would take place on Independence Day, *The Fourth of July, 1908,* in Hammondsport.

And was attended by an Aero Club delegation of twenty-two prominent New Yorkers including Alan Hawley and Post, submarine inventor-Simon Lake, Karl Dienstbach, representing the Imperial German Goverment, George Gary of the New York Society of Engineers, <u>American Journal of Aeronautics'</u> editor Ernest Jones, Walter Kimball of the Aeronautical Society of New York, <u>Scientific American's</u> Stanley Beach, David Fairchild (Bell's son-in-law), and the ubiquitous Augustus Herring (at first a loud, negative voice). Also, many newspapermen to witness the *first publicly-advertised flight in America.*

4Jul'08: The Aero Club's Charles Manly (a Cornell-educated mechanical engineer; Langley's assistant 1898-1905) measured the course as periods of rain dampened hope for a flight: Curtiss would not fly *"until the wind was just right."* Finally at 7 pm, the sky clearing, *June Bug,* wings gleaming from a new coat of varnish, was rolled out of the tent and Curtiss (note shoulder-yoke for lean-reactive aileron control) attempted the challenge.

Something wasn't right; it was too difficult to control. Curtiss landed, and after a brief discussion with Selfridge, the angle of incidence of the tail section was changed slightly and the front control rewired. At 7:30 pm a second attempt was made – and Curtiss and *June Bug* flew into history as the Associated Press clicked the news around the world.

"In one minute and 40 seconds Mr. Curtiss had ridden witch fashion astride a motor-driven broomstick (an age-old image of 'manned' flight), *as it were, 80 feet more than a mile through the air and used up in the flight less than a quart of gasoline."*

THE ORIGINAL AVIATOR
—Briggs in Chicago *Tribune.*

David Fairchild's description of the (first) flight:
"Suddenly the group of people around the machine scattered into the fields. Curtiss climbed into the seat in front of the yellow wings, the assistant turned over the narrow wooden propeller, there was a sharp loud whirr and a cloud of dust and smoke as the blades of the propeller churned in the air...The men holding the gigantic bird let go. It started down the track on its rubber-tired wheels going faster and faster. Then, before we realized what it was doing, it glided upward into the air and bore down upon us at the rate of 30 miles an hour. Nearer and nearer it came like a gigantic ochre-colored condor carrying its prey. Soon the thin, strong features of the man, his bare outstretched arms with hands on the steering wheel, his legs on the bar in front, riveted our attention. Hemmed in by bars and wires, with a 40-horse-power engine exploding behind him leaving a trail of smoke and with a whirling propeller cutting the air 1200 times a minute, he sailed with 40 feet of outstretched wings 20 feet above our heads."

Curtiss won the first leg of the <u>*Scientific American Trophy*</u> with this, the *"First Official Flight in the Western Hemisphere."*

Earlier, upon Marian (Bell) and David Fairchild's arrival in town, *"Curtiss suggested that we go and see the* June Bug*, which had been taken to the field where she was to be flown. Curtiss got out his automobile and we were given the seats of honor, while fourteen other men and boys climbed onto it too. Glenn drove to the canvas tent which housed the flying machine...I photographed the machine from every possible angle, and even took a picture of Marian in the driver's seat with her hands on the wheel..."*

Note: Primarily due to the Wright's extreme paranoia over secrecy, at this time, other than those that witnessed the *June Bug* flight and a few in Hammondsport, few Americans - *probably less than 50* - had seen an airplane fly. However, today, accustomed as we are to instant communication, most think that virtually everyone in late December, 1903 and early 1904 were aware of the Wright's success. *Not so!* One can search, as I did, countless contemporary publications and *find nary a mention, and not one for several years.* Much of the world – more so in the United States – were ignorant of airplane flight - <u>until this pivotal 1908 event</u> – which focused upon, *also,* what the Wright's had (supposedly) accomplished. If you recall, virtually the only published article about the Wright's success had been in an obscure bee-keeping journal. And this explains why, in 1910, when Curtiss flew in Los Angeles - *almost seven years after the Wright's flight - most southern Californians were ignorant and skeptical of it.* The author's curiosity about this historical conundrum led to his writing <u>Pendulum</u> – and to this manuscript.

David Fairchild continues: *"...Marian took up a position in the potato patch with Douglas McCurdy, and Mrs. Curtiss and I stood not far from them...I had determined to secure a picture of the first flight. Suddenly we heard the roar of the propeller...there came towards us this strange, white, flying apparition, with the long, slender form of Curtiss out in front...With his hair streaming in the wind, he flew almost over us...I felt Mrs. Curtiss grip my arms as she cried out in alarm, 'Why does he fly so high?'"*

The next day's celebrations saw an embarrassed Curtiss carried on the shoulders of Selfridge, Baldwin and McCurdy. News wires made him nationally famous, more so because the Wrights had not yet publicly flown - and the *June Bug*'s flight had erased many doubts that man could fly.

Telegraphed, Bell's reactions were euphoric and decisive. He wired: *"Hurrah for Curtiss! Hurrah for June Bug! Hurrah for the Aerial Association!"*...and to Curtiss: *"Accept our heartiest congratulations upon your magnificent success."*

Curtiss was 30, the *same* age as Bell when he achieved his success.

Bell wired his attorneys to immediately determine *June Bug's* patentable features: They found several, including the wing tips (ailerons); shoulder yoke aileron control; tricycle landing gear; and the combination steering of front ground wheel and rudder.

But the "secret of June Bug's success, more than any other single factor was the air-cooled, V-8 lightweight Curtiss engine with 40-hp." *Flight*

"A skeptical press was at last beginning to realize that the secrecy of the Wrights was not helping the public's faith in their claims to fly and that Glenn Curtiss had done more in one afternoon than the two brothers had done in the five years since they flew above the sand dunes at Kitty Hawk." *Owen Lieberg*

10Jul'08: Experiments continued, and after his eighteenth *June Bug* flight an exultant Curtiss wired Bell: "*made complete turn* (circle)."

13Jul'08: Curtiss to Bell: "*...the following is an enumeration of the difference between Aerodromes No. 2* (White Wing) *& No. 3* (June Bug):

"*In No. 3 the wing tips were so set that when not in use, they were in a neutral angle while those in No. 2 when not working as controls were parallel to the surfaces. The gearing of the wing tips was simplified by the new arrangement of wiring necessitated by the operator's seat being moved farther to the front.*

"*The main weights are separated by a greater distance in No. 3 than in No. 2. The engine was set five inches farther back and the man two feet farther to the front. The front control was also moved farther out and the front edge of it now 10 feet 10 1/8 inches in front of the front edge of the main planes thus making the machine 27 1/2 feet long. Five square feet have been added to the area of the front control, its total spread being now 13 feet 10 inches as compared with 11 feet 8 inches of No. 2. The nose is now wedge shaped instead of pointed and has been left uncovered.*

"*The running gear consists of three wheels as before, but the wheels base has been extended two feet. It has also been greatly strengthened by two large wooden members running fore and aft which are to be used as skids in case the wheels break....*

"*The wings have been made so that they can be easily removed from the engine bed section and their surfaces have been varnished with a mixture of gasoline, yellow ochre, paraffin and turpentine in order to make them air-tight. The yellow ochre was used for photographic purposes. The working surfaces of the machine have been reduced from 408 to 370 square feet. Switch and spark controls have been placed on the front steering wheel.*

"*The lower plane has been greatly strengthened by eight guy wires fastening it to the hubs of the wheels and bottom of the skids.*

"*The engine section has been made up of lighter material, the struts being only 3/4 of an inch thick at their widest part and 2 1/4 inches long instead of one inch thick at their widest part and 4 inches long as was used in No. 2. Additional guy wires have been added to this section and it is now more rigid than before.*

"*The propeller has been cut down from 6 feet 2 inches to 5 feet 11 inches, and is now turning up to about 1200 rpm. instead of 1050.*

A. G. BELL, F. W. BALDWIN, J. A. D. McCURDY, G. H. CURTISS & T. E. SELFRIDGE.

E. A. SELFRIDGE, ADMINISTRATOR OF T. E. SELFRIDGE, DEC'D.

FLYING MACHINE.

APPLICATION FILED APR. 8, 1909.

1,011,106.

Patented Dec. 5, 1911.

5 SHEETS—SHEET 1.

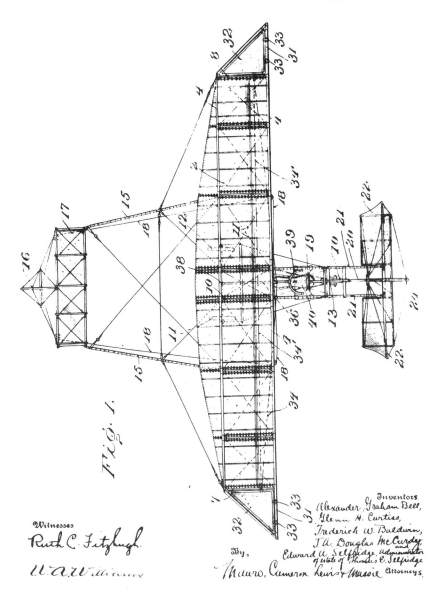

FIG. 1.

Witnesses

Ruth C. Fitzhugh.

W. A. Williams

Inventors

Alexander Graham Bell,
Glenn H. Curtiss,
Frederick W. Baldwin,
J. A. Douglas McCurdy,
and
Edward A. Selfridge, administrator
of estate of Thomas E. Selfridge

By,

Mauro, Cameron, Lewis & Massie Attorneys.

A. G. BELL, F. W. BALDWIN, J. A. D. McCURDY, G. H. CURTISS & T. E. SELFRIDGE.
E. A. SELFRIDGE. ADMINISTRATOR OF T. E. SELFRIDGE. DEC'D.
FLYING MACHINE.
APPLICATION FILED APR. 8, 1909

1,011,106.

Patented Dec. 5, 1911.
5 SHEETS—SHEET 5

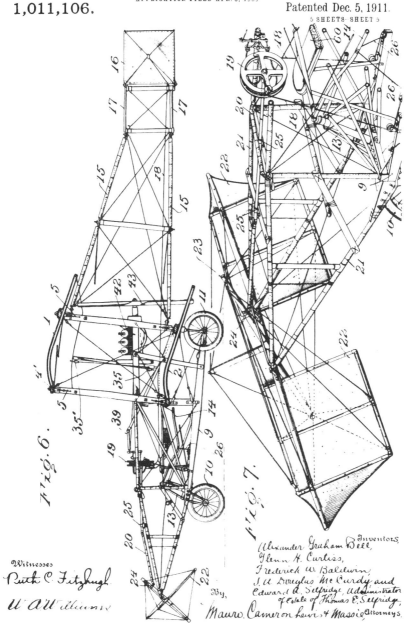

Witnesses
Ruth C. Fitzhugh
U. A. Williams

Inventors,
Alexander Graham Bell,
Glenn H. Curtiss,
Frederick W. Baldwin,
J. A. Douglas McCurdy, and
Edward A. Selfridge, Administrator
of Estate of Thomas E. Selfridge,
By,
Mauro, Cameron, Lewis & Massie, Attorneys.

"The tail has been made spar-shaped from side to side so as to conform to the general shape of the main surface. The vertical surfaces of the tail have been removed and the area of the vertical rudder increased from 27 inches to 36 inches square...

"It has been decided to do away with the screw sockets of the vertical posts and to cut turnbuckles on each socket. We are also to use balloon rubber silk for the surfaces. These last changes have not yet been made however. The distance between the center of gravity of the operator and the center of gravity of the engine is...six feet..."

10Jul'08: Wilbur to Chanute: *"...I have been at Le Mans for some three weeks setting up one of our machines* (in Leon Bollee's automobile factory), *but my mischance and insufficient carefulness I scalded my side and left arm pretty badly. Fortunately the injuries have healed without any complications and I will be all right in a day or two more. It will probably be near the end of the month before I am ready to begin practice, as the machine was less completely finished when shipped than I supposed it to be and I have no real assistant..."*

10Jul'08: Wilbur to Orville: *"...It might be well to write...Curtiss that we have a patent covering broadly the combination with wings to right and left of the center of a...machine which can be adjusted to different angles of incidence, of vertical surfaces adjustable to correct inequalities in the horizontal resistance of the differently adjusted wings.*

"Say that we do not believe that flyers can be made practical without using this combination, and inquire whether he would like to take a license to operate under our patent for exhibition purposes. I would not offer...manufacturing rights."

19Jul'08: Orville to Wilbur: *"...I notice that Chanute has written an article for* Mitteilungen, *in which he again criticizes our business methods, says we have spent two years in fruitless negotiations because we have asked a ridiculously high price, but that now we have gone to the other extreme in making a price to our own government. He predicts that Herring will fail, but that we will succeed, unless we meet with an accident. I think I will write him...He seems to be endeavoring to make our business more difficult...*

"...I had been thinking of writing Curtiss. I also intended to call the attention of the Scientific American *to the fact that the Curtiss* (no mention of Bell or the A.E.A) *machine was a poor copy of ours; that we had furnished them the information as to how our older machines were constructed, and that they had followed this...very closely, but...failed to mention the fact in any of their writings."*

"...the Wright brothers were more certain than ever that the Aerial Experiment Association had profited from the information contained in their letter to Selfridge. How else could the association have progressed from gliding to a flight of a kilometer and a half in six months? *Grover Loening.....*wrote many years later that both brothers were adamant in claiming that they had released priceless data on wing surfaces in their letter to Selfridge of January 18, 1908. But the only data on wing surfaces in that letter concerned the travel of the center of pressure, and no one has ever shown that the Aerial Experiment Association put that information to use in any practical way."

Fred Howard

20Jul'08: Orville to Curtiss (still no reference to the A.E.A. or Bell): *"I learn from the* <u>Scientific American</u> *that your June Bug has moveable surfaces at the tips of the wings, adjustable to different angles on the right and left sides for maintaining the lateral balance. In our letter to Lieutenant Selfridge of January 18th, replying to his of the 15th, in which he asked for information on the construction of flyers, we referred him to several publications containing descriptions of the structural features of our machines, and to our U. S. Patent No. 821,393. We did not intend, of course, to give permission to use the patented features of our machine for exhibitions or in a commercial way.*

"This patent broadly covers the combination of sustaining surfaces to the right and left of the center of a flying machine adjustable to different angles, with vertical surfaces adjustable to correct inequalities in the horizontal resistances of the differently adjusted wings. Claim 14 of our patent...specifically covers the combination which we are informed you are using. We believe it will be very difficult to develop a successful machine without the use of some of the features covered in this patent.

"The commercial part of our business is taking so much of our time that we have not been able to undertake public exhibitions. If it is your desire to enter the exhibition business, we would be glad to take up the matter of a license to operate under our patents for that purpose.

"Please give Capt. Baldwin...best wishes for...success in the...government tests."

Curtiss immediately forwarded the letter to Bell, who replied: *"It is obvious that we may expect to be brought into a lawsuit with the Wright brothers, if we make any public exhibitions of our apparatus for gain without an arrangement with them. I do not know...the circumstances that led to the adoption of the moveable wing tips as I was in Washington at that time; but if, as I have reason to believe, their adoption was due to a suggestion of mine that moveable wing tips should be used, contained in a letter to Mr. (Casey) Baldwin, I may say that this suggestion was made without any knowledge upon my part of anything the Wright brothers may have done. They had kept the details of construction of their machines secret; and I was ignorant of anything contained in their patent. I have no copy of their patent here, and do not...know whether their claim covers our wing tips... The matter should be enquired into by Mssrs. Auro, Cameron, Lewis and Massie, and reported upon by them. They are more competent than we are to determine this point."*

29Jul'08: Orville to Wilbur: *"...I have a reply from Curtiss saying he is not intending entering the exhibition business as has been reported by the papers, and that the matter of patents has been referred to the secretary of the Aero. Experiment Assn...A Mr. Todd...with* <u>World's Work</u>*...says Curtiss complains of his machine as being very sensitive to the slightest winds, and that it tends to follow a sinuous course. I told him I thought that was due to the arching of the surfaces: e.g, the large dihedral angle of the lower one. He explained a great deal of the details of their machine, and spoke of several features which he thought especially ingenious, such as a cradle for the back, which operated the wing tips. They explained to him how the operator instinctively moved toward the high side, and that this movement of the body turned* *the tip on that side to a less angle. I showed him one patent which contained all the special features to which he referred.*

"...Baldwin did not have his machine together before shipping to Ft. Myer...Todd says our machine is ever so much stronger than the June Bug. He saw them test the engine and propeller for Baldwin's machine at Hammondsport. The propeller broke - one blade flew off - and the engine and shaft was considerably injured before the engine could be stopped.

"...I am looking for news every day that you have made a flight. I do not think much of the plan of moving the wing-tip and rudder lever as you wrote...Either one in itself would be all right, but to work the proper combination would be much more confusing than the system we used in the South. I have decided to use that system at Washington...

"...Farman was expected to arrive at New York today. If you don't hurry he will do his flying here before you get started in France."

In early August, after carefully reviewing the differences between the Wright and A.E.A. machines, and the report made by his lawyers, Bell wrote Curtiss: *"...The wings of the Wright machine are flexible; ours are rigid. To correct tipping, the Wrights warp both wings; this increases the drag on one side and reduces it on the other making the machine turn. The Wright patent provides for co-joint* (simultaneous) *use of the rudder to correct this turning tendency. In our Hammondsport machine the moveable tips are not part of the supporting surface, so they can be turned at a negative angle. In operation the rear of one is raised and the rear of the other lowered at precisely the same angle to the line of advance. No turning effect is produced and the use of the rudder is not necessary.*

"I am decidedly of the opinion, and Mr. Cameron concurs, that our invention is not covered by the Wright brother's patent. If we can only grasp and express the essential features, I am inclined to think we may obtain an independent patent of value which will not be subordinate to the Wright brother's patent in any respect."

In effect, Bell pointed out that by warping each wing in a different way the Wright's created a difference between the drags of the wings which required corrective rudder action, whereas the A.E.A.'s *"wing tips"* avoided this complication. Later, on 5Dec'11, this position was buttressed when Patent No. 1,011,106 for a *"Flying Machine,"* including ailerons, was granted to all the members of the AEA.

Note: In 1913 Bell was granted another patent, No. 1,050,601, for an unique *"vertical balancing rudder which, when the machine is in a normal horizontal position, lies approximately in the medial vertical fore and aft plane of the machine...when the balance is disturbed, the rudder is turned* (by shoulder yoke)*...(its) resistance...operating to restore the balance..."* Briefly tried (see pp. 279), it was not proven better than ailerons.

The Wright's position, especially on ailerons, was to become bitterly contested - both in the United States and in Europe. Over a half-century later it still seemed *"incomprehensible selfishness"* to Britisher *Allen Andrews,* echoing many sentiments.

28Jul'08: Orville to Lt. Lahm: *"We expect to make shipment of the flying machine to Fort Myer next week. We understand that the tent...is now occupied by Mr. Baldwin. We can set our machine together in the balloon shed..."*

8Aug'08: The Bishop's diary: *"...Wilbur is reported to have made a successful flight...at Le Mans, France this afternoon..."*

Only a small crowd was at Hunaudieres race track to see Wilbur's first European attempt at flight, excitedly engulfing him upon his success.

But by the next day's flying (the Wrights never flew on Sunday), Monday the 10th, the crowd was over 4,000.

5Aug'08: Wilbur to Orville: *"Last Saturday I took the machine out for the first time and made a couple of circles. On Monday I made two short flights...the first...a complete 3/4 of a circle with a diameter of only 31 yards...and landed with wings level...In the second flight I made an 'eight' and landed at the starting point. The newspapers and the French aviators nearly went wild with excitement. Bleriot & Delagrange were so excited they could hardly speak ...You would have almost died of laughter if you could have seen them...You never saw anything like the complete reversal of position that took place after two or three little flights of less than two minutes each.*

"Deutsch telegraphed to inquire whether he could have the 100,000 frs. stock and definitely took it. The English Mercedes-Daimler Co. have written to know whether they can have England on same terms as published Weiller contract. They would also like to arrange the German business, I presume through the German Daimler Co. I have asked them to send a man to talk over matters.

"...On Thursday I made a blunder in landing and broke three spars and all but one or two ribs in the left wings and three spar ends of the central section and one skid runner. It was a pretty bad smashup...It did not shake me up a particle.

"I have not yet learned to operate the handles without blunders, but I can easily make turns of three hundred feet diameter. On the other hand I find the winds...tremendously gusty. I have not dared anything above 5 or 6 miles an hour yet...We have

obtained the use of the Camp d'Auvours a few miles east of Le Mans and have put up a new shed...

"In your flights at Washington I think you should be careful to begin practice in calms and keep well above the ground...I think the system I am using will be all right when I become familiar with it..."

In the control system used by Wilbur, the wing-warping and the rudder were operated by the "stick" while the elevator was operated by a separate lever.

The two-seat *Wright-A Flyer* had a wingspan of 41-feet and was powered by a 4-cylinder, 30-hp motor driving twin propellers 420-rpm for a speed of 40-mph.

Wilbur in the Flyer:

16Aug'08: Orville to Wilbur: *"We were greatly rejoiced last evening to learn that you have succeeded in your first flight in making a complete circle. The effect of this will be good, in view of the fact that Farman is unable to do anything but straight flights at Brighton Beach...Herring has asked for, and has been granted, an extens-- ion of time! Baldwin seems to be having trouble too...I am going to take some of the old aeronautical papers along with me to Washington to show some of the news- papermen there where the ideas used in European and American machine came from ...give me your opinion of the claims that cover Curtiss' machine, ie, one using sep- arate pieces on the ends of the wings that can be adjusted. Claim 14 was intended to cover this point. It uses the term 'portions'..what do you think of organizing a com- pany here? I believe that now will be the time, before too many begin infringing our patents..."*

Long skeptical of reports about the Wright's flying, the Europeans were shocked, in- credulous at these flights, accustomed as they were to their own limited flying.

9Aug'08: The French newspaper, <u>Le Figaro</u>, described the event: *"It is not the first time that a man has risen from the earth in a machine heavier than air, but yester- day's achievement reestablishes the historical truth and repairs an injustice. Hitherto the honor of the first flight had been attributed to M. Santos-Dumont, whose merits remain what they have always been...Now the first flight of the Wright Brothers took place in 1903. They were renewed and perfected during the four succeeding years, and, although guaranteed by a witness whose competency ought to have been suf- ficient authority for the statement, namely Mr. Octave Chanute, the Chicago pro- fessor who is an expert in aviation, nothing but incredulity reined in Europe, and even in America. The Messrs Wright were called humbug and regarded as 'bluffers,' the more so as they followed up their experiments with negotiations for the sale at high prices in the old and the new world of the patents of their machine. In 1905, pourparlers were begun by France for the purchase of the Wright aeroplane. They resulted, in 1906, in an option to MM. Fordyce, Henri Letellier and Desouches, who suddenly felt doubts and ceded their options to the American Government. Thereup- on the French Government intervened and, on the urgent advice of Captain Ferber, decided to act. M. Etienne, then Minister of War, sent a mission to the United States. He offered the Wright Brothers 600,000 francs for their machine on condition that they should previously execute a flight of 50 kilometers at an altitude of 300 meters.*

"This condition put an end to the negotiations. But in April, 1908, M. Lazare Weiller, the well-known manufacturer, entered into pourparlers with the Wright brothers and signed a contract...for 500,000 francs...if the aeroplane...with two persons on board, accomplished a flight of 50 kilometers. Yesterday's trial showed that the Wright aeroplane will fulfill the stipulated condition...it had on board...the burden...of the second person in the form of a heavy sack."

Witnessing the flight, *Louis Bleriot* commented: *"I consider that, for us in France and elsewhere, a new era in mechanical flight has begun. I am not sufficiently calm after the event thoroughly to express my opinions. My view can but be described in the words - It is marvelous...The machine at present shows its superiority over our aeroplanes, but have patience! In a little while, Mr. Wright will be equalled and even surpassed."*

The European press lionized Wilbur. In a dozen languages his every action and utterance was reported. A song, *"Il Vole,"* written in his honor, was sung whenever he made an appearance, and tens of thousands of postcards showing him and his *"clipper of the clouds"* were printed.

The American reaction was considerably different:

"It's Only a Toy"—New York Journal

The strong interest of Europeans in solving the mysteries of flight - as contrasted by the apathy in America - was the fundamental reason why the aeroplane developed so much more rapidly there than in its birthplace, the United States.

But it wasn't long until Europeans "...realised, the Wrights had shot their bolt as significant and indeed unique aerial pioneers. Increasingly the Europeans became aeronauts, adapting the machine and training the man to achieve a more complete fusion of the two finite members in this potentially infinite symbiosis."   *Allen Andrews*

The development styles of the Wrights and Curtiss, in spite of possessing "Yankee ingenuity" in abundance, differed greatly. Navy Captain *Washington Irving Chambers,* who worked closely with them, described Curtiss as: *"always ready to make experiments and as progressive as the Wrights were conservative."*

The Wrights were sound thinkers, tenacious, systematic and patient. And being unmarried free of distracting family responsibilities; they would spend endless hours methodically experimenting using the emerging art of aeronautical engineering. And they carefully photographed everything - *the photo of their second trial a classic.*

Called a *"mechanical wizard,"* Curtiss was all business, whether in the factory or on the flying field. Speaking little, he attacked a problem with logic, cut-and-try methods and at-hand materials - and he photographed all of his activities. But he differed in one significant attribute from the Wrights: normally a mild man, when racing Curtiss was a ferocious competitor that *"hated to be beaten."*

Aug'08: Curtiss motorcycles won *all* events in F.A.M. National Endurance Contest.

19Aug'08: Bishop Wright's diary: *"...Orville started to Washington City, this evening...Both he and Wilbur peril their lives; perhaps Orville most by the unsuitableness of the grounds at Ft. Myer."*

His concerns were real. "No more daring feat could be imagined than taking these flickering moths cross-country. General George Squier...required (Orville) to fly ten miles (from Ft. Myer) around Arlington cemetery (to Shuter Hill, across a heavily wooded valley) and back because *'it was the most difficult thing we could think of'.*"

Carl Solberg

18Aug'08: Baldwin and Curtiss demonstrate the American military's *first* airship, *Signal Corps One,* at Ft. Myer.

"Curtiss always remembered those two hours over the fields and forests of Virginia. From his position at the front...it often seemed as though the air pressure would force the nose of the limp, hydrogen-filled bag into the propeller with disastrous results. When the propeller threatened to hit the bag, Curtiss would throttle back on the motor. Baldwin, at the rear, was likewise cognizant of the danger, but failed to comprehend that Curtiss was aware of it but in control. In his excitement he exhausted his extensive vocabulary. Curtiss could hear nothing, he said, due to the noise of the engine. However, upon landing they discovered that Baldwin's plain and fancy cussing had been clearly discernible to those on the ground."

William Reed Gordon

Besieged by reporters for comments, Curtiss said: *"Lay it all to Baldwin's great knowledge of airship construction and his skill at handling such craft,"* while Baldwin said: *"What could I have done without Curtiss? He can make anything and do anything!"*

Photograph by the Pictorial News Co., N. Y.
GLENN H. CURTISS ADJUSTING THE PROPELLER-BLADE OF THE
BALDWIN DIRIGIBLE.

Photograph by the Pictorial News Co., N. Y.
CAPTAIN THOMAS S. BALDWIN.

Baldwin also contracted to teach Lahm, Selfridge and Benjamin D. Foulois to fly *Signal Corps 1*. It then went to the Army Balloon School at Fort Omaha, Nebraska.

Its Curtiss 4-cylinder, 25-hp water-cooled engine was *America's first military aircraft engine*. Driving a 22-foot tubular-steel shaft mounted to a Selfridge-designed wood pro-peller, SC-1 achieved a speed of 19.61-mph.

"It was the motor – the first four-cylinder water-cooled type made by Glenn Curtiss - that was the key to the future of aviation, for it broke the power barrier that allowed man to overcome the obstacles of gravity and the inherent disadvantages of lighter-than-air vehicles..."
C.V. Glines, Jr.

Selfridge and Bell at Baldwin's Ft. Myer trials:

5,6Aug'08: Selfridge and McCurdy witnessed Henri Farman's Brighton Beach flights and McCurdy commented: *"Farman's attempts were very disappointing indeed. The first day he flew 140 yards at an elevation of 3 feet and a rate of 20 miles an hour. He made two such flights and then wheeled the machine back to the tent. The next day there were 3,000 persons in attendance, and it was too windy..."*

The A.E.A.'s younger members were clamoring to exhibit *June Bug* - and to contest it with Farman and *"make some money for the association,"* which Bell was quick to quench, saying: *"...so long as we are an Experiment Association carrying on experiments, not for gain but...to promote the art of aviation in America, there can be no possible ground for legal action...But the moment we begin to make money, look out for trouble."*

Farman's tour ended a failure, and he returned to France.

29Aug'08: Curtiss flys *June Bug* over 2 miles.

23Aug'08: Orville (Washington) to Wilbur: *"I arrived here Thursday evening, and found that our materials had just arrived....Chas. Taylor & Chas. Furnas are here with me...The Baldwin machine has been out each evening. They gave it a speed of 19.61 miles in the speed test. There is now a controversy as to whether he is entitled to 20 miles or only 19...Baldwin thinks they have been very strict with him. I am not looking for much trouble, if I can get the practice which I expect... Everyone seems very friendly and the newspapermen are kindly disposed...Herring announces that he is not going to ship his machine by express but is going to fly it here from New York. The Signal Corps does not hesitate to express its scepticism. Herring was granted an additional 30 days."*

25Aug'08: Wilbur (France) to Orville: *"The excitement aroused by the short flights I have made is almost beyond comprehension. The French have simply become wild. Instead of doubting that we could do anything they are ready to believe that we can do anything. So the present situation is almost as troublesome as the former one...I advise you most earnestly to stick to calms till you are sure of yourself. Don't go out even for all the officers of the government unless you would go equally if they were absent. Do not let yourself be forced into doing anything before you are ready. Be very cautious and proceed slowly in attempting flights in the middle of the day when wind gusts are frequent...That English crowd, Daimler Mercedes, is ready to make a contract similar to the Weiller contract but at a higher price...I am waiting to make further investigations, and consider other offers..."*

25Aug'08: Chanute to Wilbur: *"I have been much gratified in reading...of your success and triumphs in France...it is pleasant to learn...admiration has succeeded distrust...hope...no...accident or incident will retard your final success..."*

David Fairchild wrote: *"I saw Orville one morning at the Cosmos Club talking to Professor Chanute, and asked him why Wilbur and he had kept their flights secret from the public for nearly five years. Chanute spoke up: 'I think that you made a mistake, Orville,' he said. In reply, Orville called attention to the French contracts ...Chanute waved his hand and said: 'What do they amount to? A few hundred thousand dollars. Before you convinced the public that you really flew, other inventors* (Santos-Dumont, Farman, Delagrange, Curtiss) *have made public flights.'"*

3Sep'08: Orville in an *A-Flyer* makes his *first* flight at Ft. Myer.

Signal Corps Log: *"...Distance covered: Went around drill grounds once and a half... Time in flight: 1' 11"... Remarks: Right-hand side of front skid broken in two places and skid in one place. Main brace broken at front rudder brace and on front skid; short brace also broken..."*

Orville and Post, Ft. Myer, 5Sep'08:

6Sep'08: Orville to Wilbur: *"...Curtiss was here Thursday and Friday. They have not been able to make the motor on the dirigible run more than a minute or two without missing about half its explosions. Ours runs without a miss. Selfridge has been trying to find out how we do it!..."*

Curtiss accompanied Selfridge to Fort Myer, staying for the first two days of trials. He wrote Bell: *"The first flight of the 3rd was rather short as Mr. Wright said he was unaccustomed to the machine, and the levers seemed awkward for him. He made a wrong move and headed for the tent, which necessitated immediate landing. In this landing, with the machine tilted...one runner struck first causing the machine to swing around sideways and broke the runner off.*

"The next day he did better...and made as fine a landing on its skids as you would make on wheels. The Wright machine, as you know, is launched on a monorail by means of a weight in a derrick-like tower. But this catapulting device includes the tower, and a big weight drops to operate the pulleys and rope to give the machine its·initial velocity after the engine has been started. The system, however, doesn't seem to be very well liked

by the Army people here. I believe that all who have seen our machine and the Wright prefer our method of starting on wheels to skids. I think in a few years all machines will be using wheels and skids will be a thing of the past.

"I had some talk with Mr. Wright and nothing was said about his patents on adjustable surfaces. He has nothing startling about his machine and no secrets."

On 9Sep'08 David Fairchild accompanied Curtiss to the trials; first seeing a Wright he commented: "*Having seen the* June Bug *run along the ground on wheels...I was not as impressed with the Wright machine...(Curtiss) also criticised this feature...As Curtiss and I returned from Ft. Myer in the street car, he said to me, as though the idea had just come to him: 'I believe that I could fly the* June Bug *up-side down – could turn over in it,' and I remember telling him that he was crazy, the idea seemed utterly fantastic.*"

9Sep'08: Orville makes two long flights, one of 57 minutes, the second of over an hour-and-two-minutes (world's *first* flight over an hour). Also this day, for the first time in public, Orville took up a passenger, Lt. Frank P. Lahm, for a flight of six minutes and 24 seconds.

11Sep'08: Bell to Orville (telegram): "*On behalf of the Aerial Experiment Association allow me to congratulate you upon your magnificent success. An hour in the air makes a historical occasion.*" But there is no front-page story.

6Sep'08: Wilbur to Orville: "*The weather has been some thing fierce for several weeks...Yesterday morning I made a flight of 19 min. 48 sec. I estimate the distance over the ground at 19 kilometers...a little over 37 miles an hour...*

"In the second flight yesterday I made the same mistake as at Hunaudieres and with a similar result...I am about ready to discard...fore-and-aft movement of the right hand as dangerous...Berg has gone to Vienna to see Deutsch, the big banker of that city...I may spend part of the winter in Italy. There is a $10,000 prize offered by the King of Italy which I may go after..."

13Sep'08: Wilbur (Le Mans) to Katharine: "*'You ought to seen it! You ought to seen it! Great big sing!' I refer to the excitement roused by Orville's dandy flights. However, I suppose you have seen some of it in America too. When I made my first flight over here the sudden change from unbelief to belief roused a furor of excitement I had not expected to see renewed, but the news from America seems to have been sufficient to repeat the stir...Well, it was fine news all right and lifted a load off of my mind. I have been making short flights almost every day this week as the weather has been much better...The new system of levers was rather difficult to learn to operate and I made many blunders, only two of which damaged the machine however...I think now that I will have no further trouble, and that I will have an exactness of control such as we have never had before...*"

13Sep'08: Orville to Wilbur: "*I suppose you have had...reports of the flights I have been making this week...*

"*The Navy department seems much interested. Lieut.* (wireless telegraphy pioneer George C.) *Sweet, who was detailed by the Navy department to witness and report on our flights, is very enthusiastic. He says he believes that every war vessel will soon be equipped with machines. They will want machines to carry two men, fly for*

George C.) *Sweet, who was detailed by the Navy department to witness and report on our flights, is very enthusiastic. He says he believes that every war vessel will soon be equipped with machines. They will want machines to carry two men, fly for four hours, and carry floats so that they will not sink in case the engine stops...Every one here is very enthusiastic, and they all think the machine is going to be of great importance in warfare..."* (Note: On 2Dec1908 Lt. Sweet wrote "The Sweet Report," the *first* memorandum recommending aviation for the U.S. Navy.)

17Sep'08: Bishop Wright's diary: *"...Orville injured. Orville's disaster at 5; Selfridge's death."*

Because of Selfridge being ordered to demonstrate the army's new dirigible at the Missouri State Fair, Bell and others urged Lt. Sweet, whose turn it was, to yield it to him. Thus Selfridge became the passenger - but only after Major George Owen Squier, Acting Chief Signal Officer, overruled Orville's objections because of his A.E.A. membership. Selfridge then flew as Orville's official observer, the somber looks on their faces revealing the strain of their relationship. There was trouble at 75-feet altitude, the flyer, in an uncontrolled dive, fell to the ground *"with a sickening thud."*

The crash scene. Major Squier (in straw hat) approaches, left:

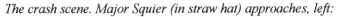

An eyewitness reported: *"I happened to be among the first to come to the scene of the disaster and I found the aeroplane crumpled up and the passengers lying motionless amongst the splintered framework. Lieutenant Selfridge, in particular, was bleeding profusely from the head, and when removed both he and Mr. Wright were still unconscious."*

Orville broke his thighbone and several ribs, and survived following seven week's hospitalization.

Tom Selfridge dies, *the aeroplane's first casualty.*

Mrs. Bell writes *"her boys:"* *"I can't get over Tom's being taken. I can't realize it; it doesn't seem possible. Isn't it heartbreaking?...*
"I am sorry for you in this breaking of your beautiful association. But it was beautiful and the memory of it will endure - Bell, Curtiss, Baldwin, Selfridge and McCurdy. It was indeed a 'brilliant coterie,' as one newpaper said..."

19Sep'08: Bell, Baldwin and McCurdy were honorary pall-bearers at Selfridge's funeral, held with full military honors in Arlington Cemetery. Curtiss, delayed, joined them the next day when they met at Bell's Connecticut Avenue home.

Members of the Aerial Experiment Association

The Aero Club of America formed a committee, headed by Frank Lahm, with Bell and Curtiss, to erect a memorial honoring Selfridge in Arlington Cemetery.

Jerome Fanciulli, a young Associated Press Congressional reporter (to become associated with Curtiss), witnessed the crash, and years later told *Harry Combs: "When he crashed I was one of the first to reach the plane. There never was a correct story of what happened. The newspapermen wrote that a propeller broke, but there was no truth to that. There wasn't anything to it except that Lt. Tom Selfridge was very heavy. He was the heaviest passenger Orville had taken up. When Orville made his turn, never having had that experience with so heavy a passenger before, the air-*

plane started sliding down. And of course Orville didn't know, but if he had put his plane into a nose dive he would have come out of it all right...

(However, photos show Selfridge a man of *average* build, shorter than Bell and close to Wilbur, about 5' 9" and 140 pounds - about 10 pounds heavier than Orville and *not* the 175 pounds noted by Fred Howard or intimated by Fanciulli.)

"(Orville had not stalled)....*No, he slid sideways. He side-slipped and struck the ground with his wing - and cart-wheeled. It happened because he had extra weight and was making a sharp turn with very little power. And he might not have had enough height even to dive out of it. I'd say he was about a hundred and fifty feet, perhaps.*"

Note: In a letter on 6Jun'09 from Wilbur to Chanute, (also see 14Nov'08): "*...After-looking over the Ft. Myer machine we have decided that the trouble came in the following manner. One blade of the right propeller developed a longitudinal crack... Orville...stopped the engine and attempted to turn...so as to land...but found the tail inoperative. He therefore twisted the wings...The maneuver succeeded very well and the machine had faced back toward the derrick and descended a third or more of the distance to the ground without any indication of serious trouble. He next moved the lever to straighten the wing tips so as to go straight ahead, but the machine instantly turned down in front and made almost straight for the ground...He pulled the front rudder to the limit, but for a time the response was very slow. Toward the end something seemed to change and the machine began to right but it was too late. The ground was struck at a very steep angle and with terrific speed. The splitting of the propeller was the occasion of the accident; the uncontrollability of the tail the cause.*
"*Now that we have located the trouble we are certain that its recurrence can be avoided...I am glad it was no carelessness of Orville that brought about the catastrophe...It is the first time we have ever had any indication of trouble with our propellers...*"
However, in 1936 Jack McCurdy told David Fairchild *"that many pilots classed this crash as a 'tail spin,' believing that the wire broke after the spin started."*

20Sep'08: Wilbur to Katharine: *"I received the news of the awful accident...just as I was finishing preparations for...the Michelin & Comm. d'Aviation prizes. The death of poor Selfridge was a greater shock to me than Orville's injuries, severe as the latter were. I felt sure 'Bubbo' would pull through all right, but the other is irremediable...I cannot help thinking over and over again 'If I had been there, it would not have happened.' The worry over leaving Orville alone to undertake those trials was one of the chief things in almost breaking me down a few weeks ago and as soon as I heard reassuring news from America I was well again...Tell 'Bubbo' that his flights have revolutionized the world's beliefs regarding the practicability of flight...I am sure that as soon as Orville is well on the way to recover you will enjoy yourself immensely at Washington...I am glad you are there to keep your eagle eye on pretty young ladies. I would fear the worst if he were left unguarded. Be careful yourself also..."*

Major Squier commented: *"...but no one who saw the flights of the last four days at Ft. Myer could doubt for an instant that the problem of aerial navigation was solved. If Mr. Wright could never again enter an aeroplane, his work last week at Ft. Myer will have secured him a lasting place in history as the man who showed the world that mechanical flight was an assured success. No one seems to realize at this close range what a revolution the flights portend. The problem is solved, and it only remains to work out the details."* (In 1934, when a retired General, Squier founded Muzak, the oldest purveyor of *"business music."*)

21Sep'08: Wilbur flew for over an hour-and-a-half, and carried his first passenger.

But his relations with the French press are strained because of an agreement he'd naïvely made with a New York magazine. It caused him to be constantly fighting *"unauthorized"* photographers, scuffling with them both at Les Hunaudieres, and, in 1909, at Fort Myer.

24Sep'08: Katharine to Wilbur: *"...Major Squier said that I could sign for you...for an extension. Mr. Chanute* (who apparently witnessed the accident) *will help me make out the form..."*

26Sep'08: Wright Brothers to Signal Corps: *"In order to give Mr. Orville Wright time to recover from his late severe injuries, we beg...to request an extension of time to make the official tests..."*

28Sep'08: Wilbur to Orville: *"I have been making flights almost every day...*
"...If I swipe the 5,000-franc prize of the Commission of Aviation I will try to send some home."

Wilbur took personages for rides. One, Major B.F.S. Baden-Powell, brother of the founder of Boy Scouts, detailed the experience for the Dec'08 <u>Aeronautics</u>: *"Having clambered in among various rods and wires one struggles into the little seat arranged on the front edge of the lower plane, and places one's feet on a small bar in front. A string is found crossing just in front of one's chest, and Mr. Wright gives directions that this must not be touched. It is a simple contrivance for cutting off the ignition and stopping the engine. In event of any accident the body will probably be thrown forward, and pressing against the string, immediately stops the engine...All being ready, coats are buttoned, and caps pulled down to prevent being blown off...*
"The driver bends down and releases the catch which holds the anchoring wire. The machine if off! It bounds forward and travels rapidly along the rail. The fore-planes are meanwhile pressed down to prevent the machine lifting prematurely, but when about half the length of the rail has been traversed, the lever is pulled back, the planes come into operation, and the whole machine rises almost imperceptibly off the track. The ascent must be very gradual. When the machine leaves the track it glides so close to the ground that one often doubts if it is really started in the air, but then it gradually mounts...

"So steady and regular is the motion that it appears exactly as if it were progressing along an invisible elevated track. Only just now and again, as a swirl of wind catches it, does it make a slight undulation like a boat rising to a big wave. Mr. Wright, with both hands grasping the levers, watches every move, but his movements are so slight as to be almost imperceptible. Having soon reached the end of the ground, the machine is guided around in a large semi-circle, gracefully leaning over as it turns...All the time the engine is buzzing so loudly and the propellers humming so that after a trip one is almost deaf."

29Sep'08: Chanute to Katharine: *"I...believe that the account that reached you was greatly exaggerated. I met Sergeant Downey after I left you and spoke to him about the occurrence.*

"He says that Dr. Bell went in the shed after almost everything was packed up, but there was no cover on the aeroplane box. That a dispute arose about the width of the wing and Dr. Bell said, 'Well, I have a tape in my pocket and we will measure it.' That this was the only measurement taken is what I gathered, but you had better see Sgt. Downey when opportunity serves and get an understanding of what occurred."

Apparently Bell's A.E.A. involvement made anything he did suspect to the Wrights.

7Oct'08: Chanute to Wilbur: *"When I left Orville...he was pronounced quite out of danger...and although he was still weak...he had recovered his pluck and mental poise; the old genial smile had come back.*

"...I congratulate you heartily upon the magnificent success which you have achieved in France, upon the recognition which is now accorded you, and upon the prospect that you will reap a fortune from your labors...I hope that you will occasionally find time to give me news of yourself..."

7Oct'08: Bishop Wright's diary: *"...Wilbur took Mrs. Hart Berg in an aeroplane flight, the first woman that ever had a flight* (left)." (But Leon Delagrange took Madame Pelterie aloft on 8Jul'08).

Signal Corps Log, Fort Myer: *"October 12, 1908 - Mr. A.M. Herring and Mr. B. Clegg arrived. Aeroplane arrived, and started to put aeroplane together."*

"October 13, 1908 – Explained parts of machine to Board at 4 P.M. until 7 P.M. and packed machine for shipment and left at 10:30 P.M."

Clegg, left, and Herring:

The Herring *"flying machine"* was delivered, and carried away, in two small cases. Lt. Lahm considered its partially assembled engine *"a beautifully built 5-cylinder air-cooled radial."*

William Inglis, after interviewing Herring, commented: *"His gaze meets yours with the utmost frankness, and yet it is impossible to escape the belief that the intelligence back of those eyes is busy with something else even while the man gives candid answers to every question."*

Another insight is by Jerome Fanciulli: *"He was a very clever fellow, a faker. He had it written all over him. I went to New York when he was trying to get a Signal Corps contract. I went with some members of the Aero Club of America and several others. We visited his shop (where, apparently, the only income was from making toy aeroplanes). He had a beautiful shop, beautiful propellers, and all that sort of thing. But as young as I was then, I immediately sized him up as a faker. I reported my opinion to General Allen of the Signal Corps."* Harry Combs

18Oct'08: Wilbur to Orville: *"It seems very difficult to find any chance to write letters...*

"You have probably learned that we convoked the scientific commission for the official trial a week ago...took M. Painleve, vice pres. of the commission...for a trip of an hour and ten minutes...This finished the official trials...Yesterday the Prime Minister Clemenceau...were to have been here, but the motor had another of its spells so we notified them...not to come.

"...I had intended to come home as soon as I could train my men, but the <u>Daily Mail</u> *has offered a prize of $2,500 for a flight across the Channel, and has offered to privately give me $7,500 extra, $10,000 ($500,000 today) in all, if I will go for the prize and win it. The latter is confidential...Another prize of $10,000 will soon be announced...at Nice, or Monaco...I am personally inclined to chuck the prize business and get home as soon as possible. What do you think?...*

"...Herr Loewe was...here. He offered $25,000 and 1/4 interest in the business for our German interests. I merely smiled. We had better wait a little longer...

"I have the patent business started (upon which the French company was based). *Thierry has taken 5,000 francs stock in the company. Weiller keeps 150,000 francs, Deutsch takes 100,000 frs., and Bernheim, chief constructor to the French navy takes 100,000 frs. The remaining subscriptions are for smaller amounts. We will probably*

take 250,000 frs. The total is to be 700,000 frs. ($7 million today). If we get an order from the government...the stock will be worth at least 50 frs. above par..."

5Nov'08: Wilbur speaks to the Aero-Club de France, including more than two hundred distinguished guests: *"For myself and my brother I thank you for the honor you are doing us and for the cordial reception you have tendered us this evening.*

"...But it is not...necessary to look too far into the future; we see enough already to be certain that it will be magnificent. Only let us hurry and open the roads..."

13Nov'08: Wilbur to Orville: *"...Arnold F(ordyce) write me that he has a customer who will offer us 750,000 francs for our English business, but I am desirous of knowing who it is and whether he is a bona fide customer or merely a speculator desirous of getting a contract with the intention of reselling."*

14Nov'08: Orville to Wilbur: *"It is two weeks today since I left the hospital at Fort Myer, yet I am just beginning to get about the house on crutches...*

"...We had made three rounds of the ground...On the fourth round, everything seemingly working much better and smoother than in any former flight, I started on a larger circuit with less abrupt turns. It was on the very first slow turn that the trouble began...I heard (or felt) a light tapping in the rear...I decided to shut off the power and descend as soon as the machine could be faced in a direction where a landing could be made...two big thumps, which gave the machine a terrible shaking, showed that something had broken...I then discovered that the machine would not respond to the steering and lateral balancing levers, which produced a most peculiar feeling of helplessness. Yet I continued to push the levers, when the machine sudden turn to the left (the right wing rising high in the air) till it faced directly up the field. I reversed the levers to stop the turning and to bring the wings on a level. Quick as a flash, the machine turned down in front and started straight for the ground...Selfridge up to this time had not uttered a word...But when the machine turned headfirst for the ground, he exclaimed 'Oh! Oh!' in an almost inaudible voice.

Note: In 1903 Wilbur wrote: *"...One day my brother noticed in several glides a peculiar tapping as if some part of the machine were loose and flapping...Some weeks later, while I was making a glide, the same peculiar tapping began again in the midst of a wind gust...the machine suddenly...dropped a distance of nearly ten feet and in a twinkling of an eye was flat on the ground."*
Today it's known that this was a stall, the "tapping" or buffeting a symptom of an impending stall.

"I pulled the rudder lever to its limit, but there was no response...I then looked at the rudder and saw that it was bent to its limit downward...The first 50 ft. of that plunge seemed like a half minute, though I can hardly believe that it was over one second at most...Suddenly just before reaching the ground, probably 25 feet, something changed - the machine began to right itself rapidly. A few feet more, and we would have landed safely...

"I do not like the idea of you attempting a Channel flight when I am not present. I don't have much faith in your motor running. You seem to have more trouble with the engine than I do...

"The Signal Corps people are very enthusiastic...this is just the beginning of business with us...says the U.S. is going to be our best customer. The Navy Department also is much interested...

"...The check for 50,000 francs ($500,000 today) was received from Mr. Berg several days ago. I will deposit most of it in the Building Association...

"...At what price is the French company expecting to sell machines? We will have to regulate our price in America somewhat according to the European prices. Shall I sell any machines here to private individuals? I see that the N.Y. Aero Club is talking of buying one. What price shall I quote here?

"I have an awful accumulation of work on hand. I have over five hundred letters that remain unanswered..."

14Nov'08: Wilbur to Orville: *"I very strongly suggest that you and Kate, and Pop too if he will, should come over to Europe immediately. It is important to get machines ready for the spring business and the spring and winter races...There is more to be done than I can do...I believe it would be the best thing you could do."*

22Nov'08: Chanute to Paul Renard, a French aeronautics activist: *"I received...your kind letter...asking what, in the Wright brother's aeroplane, comes from me and what has been added by themselves.*

"As in almost all inventions, the later aviators have profited...from the prior labors of their predecessors. Wenham had proposed the biplane glider; I had added to it a reinforced (Pratt truss) *frame and had published my designs...when Wilbur Wright wrote me in May 1900...that he wanted to experiment, without financial motive, explaining to me a method of experimentation from which I dissuaded him, and asking me where he might find a favorable location...*

"...After having made some gliding experiments at Kitty Hawk in October 1900, Wilbur...wrote me a long account thereof, and invited me to come to see him. I was present at a part of his experiments of 1901, 1902, 1903, 1904, and 1905...we became intimate. In eight years we have exchanged perhaps 200 letters...

"I cannot indicate to you how much I was able to be useful to the Wrights...Ideas are absorbed unconsciously, and the important thing is to choose the good ones. However, I think I can tell you what the principal improvements are which they have added to the machines of their predecessors.

"As I already said, I had improved the two-surface glider...and had demonstrated ...that there was little danger of accident. The Wrights placed the vertical control device in front...They placed themselves prone on the machine...They added the warping of the wings, an idea which I believe was quite personal to them, although Mouillard...patented it...in the United States on May 18, 1897...

"But the Wrights' most important merits lie in their application of a motor to the glider. They made a study of lifting surfaces...They designed a propeller with a performanc superior...They thought out a very effective transmission, and designed a sturdy and reliable motor. All this, built with their own hands and put into operation by themselves, at their own risk and peril."

10Dec'08: Orville to Wilbur (Le Mans): *"Merry Christmas!...We have all been hoping that you would be home for Christmas but we have now given that idea up.*

"Unless plans are changed Sterchens (Katharine) *and I expect to start about the first of January...*

"We will ship tomorrow that parts for five machines...Some of the members of the N.Y. Aero Club have been raising some money to buy a flyer. What price shall I ask?...

"...Our application for patent on the front rudder was allowed...I believe my having met some of the patent office people at Washinton will help us some in getting patents through."

28Dec'08: Wilbur to Aero Club of Sarthe: *"I enclose herewith 50 francs, being my entry for the Coupe Michelin, for which I desire to make trial on Friday, 31 December 1908, at the Camp d'Auvours."*

28Nov'08: The *Loon,* A.E.A. Drome No. 3A. Curtiss's first try at a seaplane. He and McCurdy, who worked well together, fitted the *June Bug* with pontoons - but all attempts to fly were unsuccessful. It was difficult enough getting the under-powered *June Bug* off the land, and the extra effort to un-stick the *Loon* from the water was too much. Finally, on 2Jan'09, Bell was sent this message: *"Gave vaudeville performance tonight by moonlight with Loon. First hydro test successful, second aerodrome test fairly successful, third submarine test most successful of all. Experiments ended. Curtiss and McCurdy."*

6Dec'08 (Hammondsport), 23,24Feb'09 (Baddeck): A.E.A. Drome No. 4, An improved evolution from the *June Bug,* McCurdy's *"Silver Dart"* was the most sophisticated of their machines - and the first to use Curtiss's new water-cooled V8-cylinder 50-hp engine, *mounted low* with a chain drive.

30Nov'08: A.E.A. *Bulletin* No. 21: *"...It was our original intention to carry two persons in the Silver Dart, one sitting directly behind the other; hence a seat was designed for the purpose and made adjustable so that it could be slipped forward and backward readily in balancing up the machine. The second man would sit directly over the theoretical center of pressure at our traveling speed, so that the carrying of the passenger or leaving him behind would not affect the balance. The tips* (ailerons) *are controlled by a device which does not interfere with the man sitting behind the operator, and the device is also adjustable with the seat..."*

Three views of Silver Dart's passenger arrangement:
McCurdy,
    Curtiss,
        and Curtiss sitting behind pilot McCurdy follow:

23Feb'09: McCurdy flying Silver Dart at Baddeck, Canada's first aeroplane flight and the "First Flight in The British Empire":

31Dec'08: Wilbur flew 77 miles nonstop in two-hours-and-twenty-minutes to win the coveted *Michelin Trophy* with its 20,000 franc prize ($250,000 today).

This was the zenith of the Wright's greatest year (Wilbur at Camp d' Auvours):

Chapter  *1909*

T_{he}

feud begins; Curtiss suffers Herring's manipulations; the Wrights, honored and feted, spend much time in Europe on business; Curtiss challenges for the rule of American air - and the American money establishment spawns long-standing biases.

1Jan1909: Wilbur (Le Mans) to his father: "*I suppose...Orville will have started for France, and possibly Kate with him...*" (she was her brother's "social manager").

"*We have arranged that Orville and Kate shall have free accommodations at the best hotel at Pau, which is one of the great winter resorts of France....The* (flying) *grounds* (Pont-Long) *are about 8 miles from Pau...it will be a...good place.*

"*It is probable that from Pau we will go to Rome for a month before returning to America. The Aeronautical Society of Rome offers us $10,000 ($1/2 million today) for a machine and training of an operator. The government is interested...and will probably order some machines.*

"*Yesterday...I made another try for the Michelin Prize...After landing I...took M. Barthou, the Minister of Public Works, for a ride. He informed me...the government ...decided to confer the Legion of Honor upon both Orville and myself...*"

Early in January, 1909, Bell wrote Curtiss: "*Time passes rapidly, and the day assigned for the dissolution of the Association will be upon us almost before we know it. So much work has been done by other people...having the general features of our...aerodromes...that it is extremely doubtful whether patents of any great value can be obtained to represent our work at Hammondsport. We are liable to come into contact with numerous patents; and should any patents we obtained turn out to be subordinate to other patents already granted, the owners of these patents, not being affiliated with the Association would be liable to make trouble.*

"When the Association finally dissolves the only way in which the members can obtain any substantial reward for their labors will be by the manufacture and sale of aerodromes embodying features produced by the Association. This means either that the Association must be converted into a manufacturing corporation, or that the Association will sell out its rights to some manufacturing company...Now no company will give the Association anything for its inventions unless they are patented, or at least patentable...it should, therefore, be the special object of the Association during the remaining months ...to...not simply...'get into the air'...but to get into the air by means of a patentable nature...

"...I would, therefore, urge that we...bend all our efforts to the development of practical improvements of a patentable nature...to enable us, or some of us, to endow the Association and extend a helping hand to others who may be seeking to advance the art of Aviation by experimental methods."

21Jan'09: Curtiss, in New York <u>Herald:</u> *"It is true that the Aerial Experiment Association will probably disband in March because we have accomplished what we intended to do."*

22Jan'09: Approached by Ernest Jones and Wilbur Kimball, Curtiss signs a contract with the Aeronautic Society of New York to build an aeroplane for $5,000 ($250,000 today); agreeing to deliver in May a machine that would be *"in many ways different from the aerodromes of the Aerial Experiment Association,"* and to hold the Society immune from costs or problems that might arise from possible patent infringement. In turn, the Society agreed to keep the contract secret until Curtiss was no longer affiliated with the A.E.A.

But, as secrets do, it leaked out - and to Bell's query Curtiss replied that if the A.E.A. went into manufacturing, the order would go to it, if not, then his company.

29Jan'09: This led to a meeting at Beinn Bhreagh - and, by February 19th, apparently an agreement on forming the American Aerodrome Company in Hammondsport with a nominal capital of $100,000 ($5 million today). The A.E.A. was to transfer its property and inventions in exchange for stock; Mabel to receive one percent of A.E.A. shares for each $1,000 she'd contributed; and the balance divided equally between the members.

At this same time Courtlandt Field Bishop *(left)*, president of the New York Aero Club of America, had joined with Herring and Tom Baldwin urging Curtiss to form a new, independent, aeroplane company – showing him, among other things, news clippings of French, Belgium, and German syndicates clamoring to lure Herring to Europe with offers of over $100,000 (over $5 million today) for the rights to manufacture his "patented" machine.

And, there was an exchange of telegrams between Curtiss and Herring: *"Best possible backing, small company first, way clear to million, better come here now. Herring."*

"Proposition agreeable. Curtiss."

"Can close $90,000 basis, 50 stock, $25,000 cash, $15,000 purchase money mortgage, will cash mortgage, salary $5,000, we control company, I keep foreign patent, give interest to you, help work men, wire if accepted. Herring."

"Both messages received, I should have 50 cash as per letter, how about 30 cash, 20 good mortgage, 40 stock, if this is agreeable, will come first of week. Curtiss."

"Accept on basis your telegram, can you persuade Dr. Bell one of our incorporators? All others big names, big future. Herring."

Curtiss replied: *"I do not think Mr. Bell would consider making any connection with this company as he has a plan for a big organization, and I think best not to mention this at present; however, if I should come with you I think the other scheme would be given up"*

...and, later: *"I don't know the value of your patents, but I assume they are fundamental and strong."*

Committed, Curtiss returned to Hammondsport to attend to, among other things, this venture. There's speculation as to what he divulged while in Baddeck, but, because of Bell's ethical standards and that they continued a warm relationship, it's probable that Curtiss made his plans marginally known. Substance for this is a telegram he sent McCurdy after returning to Hammondsport: *"Bishop agrees for* (<u>Scientific American</u>) *cup trial...made Herring proposition which he verbally accepted, took order for aeroplane from aviation society* (Aeronautic Society of New York)."

"Alexander Graham Bell must have been a delightful man to know and an exasperating man to work with. I have the feeling that I know him intimately, and every time I think of him I find myself smiling, the way one does about an old friend."   *Mitchell Wilson*

Long before they met, Bell knew that Curtiss was a very successful businessman. He then learned he was – resolutely - his own man. Raised virtually fatherless, with the strong guidance of his grandmother, Curtiss had earned his independence the hard way. On the other hand, Bell had never had the challenge of raising a son – while Mabel was a constant, peripheral presence – and typically aware of but *one side* of the events.

As such, Curtiss was reluctant in joining Bell, and, after becoming an A.E.A. member often chaffed under his unilateral, father-like leadership.

Curtiss respected Bell, and was his friend, but never felt beholden to him.

3Feb'09: Wilbur makes the first flight at Pau - continuing into late March training three French fliers: Comte Charles de Lambert, Paul Tissandier, and Capt. Lucas-Girardville. He made fifty flights, forty as pilot and ten with a student. There were important visitors, including many of royalty: England's King Edward VII, Dowager Queen Margherita of Italy, and Spain's King Alfonso.

19Feb'09: The *Herring-Curtiss Aeroplane Co.* incorporated with Herring as president; Curtiss, vice-president and general manager. Curtiss pledged his existing business; Herring to assign his Army contract, patents of undetermined value on automatic gyroscopic stability devices, and other aeronautical devices. The capital of $360,000 ($18 million today) was subscribed by Allan Hawley, Cooper Hewitt, and several other "*big-city financiers*," with an interest held by Bishop (in addition to his Aero Club presidency, he was brother-in-law of Herbert Parsons, a "*prominent Republican Congressman...and a personal friend of Theodore Roosevelt*").

It is America's *first* aircraft manufacturer at a time when other modes of transportation were catching the public's eye:

<u>Scientific American</u>, *15May'09:*

The evolution of Curtiss's association with Herring is of interest. During the *June Bug's* <u>Scientific American</u> event, Herring's voice was the strongest protesting the judge's rulings. Hence it was quite unexpected when, with a totally changed demeanor, he showed up in Hammondsport while the *Silver Dart* was under construction. Most friendly, he assisted McCurdy and Curtiss (Casey Baldwin was in Baddeck) with many suggestions.

A tall, handsome, imposing man, Herring was, at 41, several years senior to the younger A.E.A. members – and ten years Curtiss's senior. Combined with his well-known experience with Langley and Chanute (the public side, anyway) - and that many believed he'd successfully flown in 1898 - made him a man to be listened to.

Also, he charmed Captain Baldwin and Cortlandt Bishop, two of Curtiss's closest associates, to the limitless potentials of a new aeronautical company - "*way clear to million*" (when a million *was* a million) - with plans for Baldwin to head balloon and airship production, Curtiss aeroplane manufacturing - and all funded with Bishop's cash.

Baldwin and Herring hit it off well, both being about the same age and with similar "snake-oil-salesman" tendencies.

And the shy, studious Bishop, heir to considerable wealth, was an easy mark.

During this time Curtiss and Herring became well acquainted, spending many evenings together as Herring stressed his favorite subject, the potentials in this new field of aviation: "*The time is now, before the Wright brothers create an air trust.*"

Increasingly intrigued by the financial prospects of aviation, a chord was struck with Curtiss - and after Herring left in October, he thought about his future:

Rarely had opportunity been so clear; always before his career had been the result of circumstance. Now, for the first time, was the opportunity to frame his own future.

Based upon his Herring talks and his observations, he began to think that money could be made. Weighing everything, including - according to *both* Herring's and Bell's lawyers - that the Wright's patents were not inviolate *and* that Herring had patents necessary to build aeroplanes without problems, a window of opportunity appeared:

Why not exploit aviation before the Wrights had their way?

Also, Herring, with Bishop's support, intimated that other millionaire members of the Aero Club would invest in the new company (they didn't), helping convince him that Herring's proposition was better than Bell's.

Thus beguiled, Curtiss was adroitly maneuvered into associating with a manipulative and clever flimflam man, certainly not the first - nor last - in American business.

However, after pledging his business (with over 100 employees, a weekly payroll over $2,000, and a 1908 net profit of $120,000 - *about $6 million today*), it became painfully clear that, among other things, Herring's "patents" were but worthless applications (though England had accepted them in 1898) - and even the Army revoked his contract in late September.

At this time Curtiss was America's preeminent motorcycle manufacturer.

While planning to foresake motorcycles for aeroplanes, Curtiss was being challenged by Hendee's *Indian*, and, sometime later, *Harley-Davidson*, for American motorcycle leadership, and thusly covered part of his bet.

To retain his position on the forefront of the motorcycle industry (and manufacturing over *1000* motorcycles, almost double the year before), he planned to supply 500 engines and parts to the *Marvel Motorcycle Co.*, a new firm headed by longtime friend C. L. "Tank" Waters - which he helped organize and finance ("Capital Stock $50,000")...and located virtually next door.

Marvel Motorcycle Company

MANUFACTURERS OF THE

ᴇᴀʙ "MARVEL" UNION CODE	MARVEL MOTORCYCLE	INCORPOR. —◂ CAPITAL $50
VATERS, ᴄʀᴇᴛᴀʀʏ ᴀɴᴅ ᴍᴀɴᴀɢᴇʀ	HAMMONDSPORT, N. Y.	

Regardless, the short-lived (little over a year) Herring relationship was to prove costly.

23Feb'09: McCurdy, in the Silver Dart, makes the *first flight in Canada* - and the *first flight by a British subject in the British Empire*.

29Mar'09: McCurdy's final A.E.A. flight, a full circle of three-and-a-half miles at fifty feet.

He made approximately 200 flights, over 1,000 miles, before this most sophisticated A.E.A. machine crashed on 4Aug'09 (just after 2Aug'09, when Casey Baldwin became the *first* passenger in the British Empire).

The flights the Silver Dart – and the Canadian members of the A.E.A.- are memorialized in Canada:

22,24Feb'09: The A.E.A. experiments with Drome No.5, Bell's powered tetrahedral *Cygnet II*. Too cumbersome, to Bell's great disappointment it did not fly.

McCurdy the 'pilot,' others are clustered around its rear-mounted engine and propeller:

Orville, left, Katharine and Wilbur at Pau:

5Mar'09: Orville (Pau) to brother Lorin, their business manager: "...*We expect to finish up here in a week or two, when we will proceed to Rome. I may in the meantime go to Paris to show how to set machines together. It will probably be May before we are ready to start home. We have made a contract for some demonstrations* (for a "*substantial fee*" from <u>Berliner Lokal-Anzeiger</u> newspaper) *at Berlin before the end of September, which will bring us back here again as soon as we are through in America...*"

3Mar'09: An announcement is made at the New York Aero Club of the new *Herring-Curtiss Aeroplane Company,* Cortlandt Bishop stating: "...*We have lost the Wright brothers* (rumor had it they planned to manufacture in Europe) *and we do not intend to let the foreigners take everyone else of prominence in developing aerial flight. If Congress will offer no incentive to inventors to remain in their own country, the next best thing is to keep them here by private enterprise...*"

Casey Baldwin commented in the A.E.A. <u>Bulletin:</u> "...*That level-headed American business men should back Mr. Herring has created quite a furore in aeronautical circles. It probably means that Mr. Herring has some more convincing arguments than he has ever made public, or - is it really the Curtiss Company with Mr. Herring's patents to flourish in the eyes of bewildered capitalists? So far as we know, the Herring patents are only talking points at present...*"

6Mar'09: Bell wires Curtiss: "*Please write fully concerning your arrangement with Herring and how it affects your relations with the A.E.A.*"

Curtiss replied: "...*Mr. Herring showed me a great deal, and I would not be at all surprised if his patents, backed by a strong company, would pretty well control the use of the gyroscope in obtaining automatic equilibrium. This seems to be about the only road to success in securing automatic stability in an aeroplane...*(Prescient thinking. Curtiss would help Elmer Sperry perfect this in 1913).

"*I am planning to go to Washington to see Mr. Charles Bell* (trustee of the A.E.A., Bell's cousin, and president of Washington's American Security and Trust Company) *as soon as I am sure of the outcome with the Herring proposition. There is no reason why the Aerodrome Company should not be formed if the Herring deal goes through, unless the members of the Association would care to come into the Herring combination. This would please Mr. Herring, I am sure...Mr. Herring was intending to write to you about the matter.*"

31Mar'09: The AEA, having met its objective "*to get into the air,*" is disbanded. For Bell it had been "*a band of comrades on a great adventure...as if having four brilliant sons to share his life and work. Now it was over.*"

Bell turned over to Curtiss all of Hammondsport's A.E.A. assets, including the *June Bug,* and favorably sold him its American patents. Also, Curtiss was left free to operate in the United States without competition from Casey Baldwin or John McCurdy (who soon went to work for Curtiss), with a similar stipulation that he couldn't compete with the other members in Canada.

When Daisy Fairchild, Bell's daughter, visited Hammondsport to pick up several items for her father, she met Herring, and wrote: "...*Mr. Herring was especially* (cunningly?) *enthusiastic over tetrahedral construction which he believes is going to be a great feature in flying machines. He has promised to call you over the long distance telephone to discuss it. It will be interesting to hear your opinions about him. Mr. Curtiss says he's an authority on all kinds of aeroplanes, but all others without exception (the ones I talked to) were uncertain as to whether he is a genius or a fool.*"

Bell later said that Curtiss was moving into "*pretty fast company*" and that he hoped he could hold his own.

Note: In the protracted patent litigation between Curtiss and the Wrights, Curtiss chose to not rest his defense on A.E.A. patents, sparing Bell from direct involvement in the bitter struggle.

June 1909: The *Canadian Aerodrome Company* is formed in Baddeck by Bell, Baldwin, William Bedwin (who joined the A.E.A. after Selfridge's death), and McCurdy, with, again, Mabel's financial backing. After building five aircraft it was disbanded when the Canadian Army, deeming the aeroplane impractical for military purposes, ceased its support.

Scientific American, *19Mar'10:*

Messrs. McCurdy and Baldwin flying in their " Baddeck No. 2 " biplane.

This is the first aeroplane to be equipped with a six-cylinder automobile motor. It has made many successful flights in Canada.

A contemporary perspective, Fly *magazine, Jun'09 (next):*

16   *F L Y*   *June, 1909*

ALEXANDER GRAHAM BELL

By FELIX J. KOCH, A.B.

ANYONE who goes to Baddeck, a secluded little hamlet of the Bras d'Or county, Nova Scotia, the home of Dr. Alexander Graham Bell, expecting to see the great inventor without meeting with many difficulties, will be sadly disappointed.

To begin with, one must make his appointment by telephone through the secretary and telephone service to the home of the inventor of the telephone to the home of the inventor of the telephone is probably the poorest in the whole world to-day. Then again, Mr. Bell is one of the men who sleeps by day and works by night very largely, and as a result one makes the appointment for late in the afternoon.

The secretary in our case failed to be specific and the drivers of the local liveries are insistent. They have good reasons to be exact with Mr. Bell, for Bell's place is one of the attractions of the countryside and it would be a great loss to the touristry were it closed against inspection. Whenever a driver takes a visitor too close within the bounds, therefore, Bell sounds a warning and it is one that is heeded at once.

When, however, we finally reached the great inventor, he was at his best. He was walking from his laboratory to his home, a fine old man; snowy white beard; snowy white head; a suit of tweed that went deep down into his riding boots and on either arm a stripling, a discipline of his in his magic arts. We followed him into the parlor of his sumptuous summer home, called Beinn Bhreagh, and waited while he donned a smoking jacket of velvet and slippers, then he talked.

"Yes, I am engaged now heart and soul in studying aerial navigation by means of kites," he said. "I took to this primarily because I was in need of outdoor exercise. At first I went into the experiment for amusement's sake, pure and simple, then when I found the great practical possibilities of aerial flight, I took to it seriously. I learned that the great handicap to kite navigation has been that as one increases the size of a given model the weight increases not in proportion, but as the cube of the dimensions. At the same time the supporting surface is increased only by the square of the dimensions. In consequence when one increases the size beyond a certain point, it will no longer uphold the object. There is, therefore, tremendous difficulty in getting a size which will lift men and the engines necessary to propel it.

"I feel, however, that I have derived the method of increasing the size of the structure indefinitely without increasing the weight, and so can now build a kite to any size and yet have it fly quite as readily as would a smaller one.

"For fifteen years I have been pondering upon this subject and what was originally simply a matter of amusement to me begun for the pleasure and outdoor life it afforded, is now occupying the greater part of my attention. In fact, I am now working seriously upon a flying machine for the kite has practically evolved into a flying machine."

Mr. Bell's largest kite to-day is one of 1,300 cells and has been christened "The Frost King." Each of these cells has a capacity of twenty-five centimeters. The shape of the kite is novel, though cellular kites as such are not new, being originated by Hargrave, in Australia, over two years ago.

The kite has long been used practically at Blue Hill, and in the weather station at Wash-

ington, Congress having made the appropriation for the bureau to continue experiments with it at Mt. Weather.

It has been found, however, that one could not always raise the kites when he wishes, owing to contrary winds, then too a curious phenomena served as a barrier. In flying kites a thin wire is used and occasionally in the upper air this would be struck by lightning and completely eaten up, while the kite disappeared as if by magic and after this happened several times, the feature was discontinued.

Kites were also used for observing the upper strata of the air over the ocean since there one could get at weather conditions at great elevations. This is still done very extensively on the Caribbean Sea.

Last year, in July, there was a meeting in Europe of the International Meteorological Congress which made observations at heights of one mile elevation. In Europe for this purpose they use balloons made to explode in the air and so attract attention as it comes down, the Meteorological instrument being returned to the bureau by the finder.

In the United States, however, kites are used. To Bell, therefore, came the idea that to his kite he would add a propeller, in which case it would need a great structure to carry the added weights. It was found that if a kite would carry a man, engines, etc., in a ten-mile breeze, one only needed an engine pulling it at the rate of ten miles an hour to accomplish this. Professor Bell, has been directing his efforts to these motive power experiments carried on at Baddeck, at which place he employs from three to twenty men as his experiments require.

During the last ten years, Mr. Bell has published nothing regarding the subject, but has recorded his discoveries in notebooks. From time to time he has been tempted to revise and promulgate these for the benefit of the

public, but up to the present time has not done so.

For the past twenty-five years it seems he has not been directly connected with the telephone, in fact as soon as the scientific work in connection with it ceased he withdrew.

Alexander Graham Bell has also been identified with the graphophone and the story of the discovery of this instrument is rather interesting:

"My name is not generally associated with the graphophone," he says, "since it was developed by three men associated together, who agreed that whatever discovery was made should not be claimed by any single one of them.

"The organization was known as the Volta Laboratory Association. Edison was the inventor of the first form of phonograph, and so the public credited him with originating the graphophone as well.

"After Edison invented his phonograph, however, he devoted his time principally to the electric light neglecting the phonograph altogether, and so for a great many years it remained little more than a scientific toy.

"In 1880 the French government decreed me the Volta prize of 50,000 francs. This prize was originally founded by Napoleon in honor of the visit of Volta to Paris, and is granted by a standing committee of the French academy who make recommendations to the Government who appropriates the money to the individual. I was the third recipient.

"I invested this money in the Volta Laboratory Association, which constituted of Dr. Chichester Bell, of London, England (a cousin), demonstrator of organic chemistry in the University College and Sumner Tainter, of Washington, a maker of optical instruments, and myself. All three are still alive.

"It was understood at the time of our association that each of us was to work upon the graphophone merely as a hobby, and finally all three worked together conjointly to develop the same into an article of commercial value, the result being a graphophone produced in this laboratory.

"At first we took to developing the art of engraving sound records instead of Edison's system of indenting, by which they displaced the tin foil, but did not remove it from the record made and so did not achieve great results.

"The Volta experimental laboratory only existed as long as the capital lasted, then a company was organized and each of the three of the Volta Association were given shares. The three men went back to their several works leaving a graphophone company in charge and this company put the invention in operation and as soon as the commercial value was established, I dropped out of it.

"At the present time all my attention is given to the study of the principles of aerial flight, which is perhaps the most interesting subject that man can consider."

The Wright Brothers, with Their Father, Listening
to the Sounding of Their Praises.

<u>Scientific American, *15May'09:*</u>

RETURN OF THE WRIGHT BROTHERS.

The sudden rise of the Wright brothers from the obscurity of the struggling inventor to international fame and no small measure of wealth has in it a strong dash of the romantic. The exploits of these two Americans during the past eight months have placed our country far in the van of other nations in the art of flight with heavier-than-air machines. Starting with the first public exhibitions in France and America, which were made simultaneously by Wilbur and Orville Wright, respectively, last September, the career of the former of the two brothers especially has been practically a continuous ovation. First at Le Mans, where on December 31st he made an unparalleled flight of nearly 100 miles in 2 hours and 20 minutes; later at Pau and Rome, where he taught several pupils how to operate the aeroplane in a dozen 15-minute lessons each, Wilbur Wright has been lauded in the highest terms, and has been the recipient of distinguished attentions from the most prominent rulers of European countries. Orville Wright, since his accident at Fort Myer, has not made any flights; but he is, we understand, to resume the carrying out of the very difficult government contract next month. This involves a 10-mile cross-country flight across a deep valley, which is something the like of which has never been accomplished even by Wilbur Wright during all the 3,000 miles he has flown abroad, although he has at times risen more than 350 feet in height tests over smooth ground. In cross-country flying, however, both Farman and Bleriot so far hold the records.

The idea of selling aeroplanes to governments, which these two inventors had in mind when they went abroad, seems to have succeeded almost beyond expectations. Italy, Germany, Russia, and England have either purchased or negotiated for aeroplanes, while in France the selling of the patent rights to a syndicate has made possible the rapid introduction of the machine.

After completing the contract with our own government, which will be done next month at Fort Myer, the inventors intend to make further experiments looking toward the perfecting of an automatically stable aeroplane.

19Apr'09: Bishop Wright's diary: "...*Moving pictures of Wilbur's flights were shown at theater...*(the *first* moving pictures taken from an aeroplane - by a Universal cameraman with a Bioscope camera that Wilbur took up at Centocelle, Italy). *The Wright's European Triumph has been complete. They have been honored by royalty and feted, as far as they would permit. Seldom have Americans been received with such acclaim in Europe...*"

13May'09: Bishop Wright's diary: "*Flags, Chinese lanterns, and electric lights are being arranged. Eleven carriages met the Wright brothers and Katharine at the depot...and a four-horse carriage pulls them home, where thousands meet them around our house. Over 10,000 came at night.*"

17May'09: Wilbur to Chanute: "...*We are busy at work on the machine we will use at Ft. Myer. The old one was so badly broken up that we will make all but the motor and transmission new...*

"*On the way home we stopped a couple days in London...we have taken orders for about a half dozen machines which are being constructed for us by Short Brothers. We have had opportunities to close out our English business but have preferred to hold on to it for the present. We sold in France and Germany, and will probably close a contract for Italy very soon. After sailing we learned that Lt. Calderara at Rome had met with an accident...I left him with greater misgivings than my other pupils, because he was a cigarette fiend, and was being very badly spoiled by the attention and flattery he was receiving..."*

19May'09: Chanute to Wilbur: *"...I have, of course, rejoiced over your triumphs in Europe and was particularly gratified with the sensible and modest way in which you accepted your honors, both abroad and since your return to this country. It encourages the hope that you will still speak to me when you become millionaires..."*

29May'09: The *Golden Flier,* or "Gold Bug" (Herring-Curtiss-1) built for the Aeronautic Society of New York for $5,000 (about $250,000 today).

16   *F L Y*

THE CURTISS BIPLANE

Built for the Aeronautic Society of New York. On July 17th, at Mineola, L. I., Glenn H. Curtiss covered 29 miles in 52 min.

Description of the Curtiss Biplane
By GLENN H. CURTISS

THE surfaces of this machine are superimposed and separated by posts four and one-half feet long. The width of each surface is twenty-nine feet, and the depth four and one-half, making a total lifting area of about 260 square feet. The total weight, including operator, is 550 pounds. This machine is the smallest biplane yet built. The fabric of the surfaces is a rubber-covered silk stretched to the tightness of a drum head over laminated ribs. Nearly the entire frame work is of Oregon spruce. A few pieces of bamboo and some tubing are used for braces. The running gear consists of three twenty-inch pneumatic tire wheels, the front wheel being fitted with a brake to bring the machine more quickly to a standstill after alighting. The fore and aft control is effected by a movable pair of planes two feet deep and six feet wide placed ten feet ahead of the main surfaces. A single surface tail of the same dimensions is ten feet behind the main sur-

face. Lateral stability secured with the use of movable surfaces at either extremity of the main planes.

The operator's seat is well up between the surfaces in the center panel. Behind him is the radiator and then the engine, to which a six-foot propeller is directly attached. This engine is of a new design, four cylinder vertical with four and three-quarters bore and four-inch stroke. It develops twenty-five horse power at 1300 revolutions per minute, which is the most power for the piston area yet secured in gasoline engines. The cylinders are copper jacketed, having valves in the head. Lubricating is by force feed pump mounted on the cam shaft and the oil forced through the hollow shaft to the bearings. The water pump is also a part of the engine and mounted on the cam shaft. Ignition is by Bowch magneto driven by enclosed gears. The engine complete with pumps and magneto weighs 100 pounds.

This bamboo-framed machine differed in several ways from the earlier A.E.A. machines; e.g., instead of movable winglets it had *"balancing planes"* (ailerons) midway between the outer sections of the now-parallel, single-surface wings; a steering wheel controlling the rudder: pushing it forward or back operated the elevators; and what became known as the *"Curtiss shoulder yoke"* controlled the balancing planes by the pilot's instinctive tendency to lean. Curtiss's description appeared in <u>Fly</u>, *Aug'09, above (Note: As to the Bosch ad, Robert Bosch was the author's great uncle, removed):*

Beginning June 26th, Curtiss trained with it for the upcoming Reims meet.

10Jul'09: He wrote the Wrights: *"I wish to express my admiration for the fine exhibition of flying I witnessed at Ft. Myer...I got in a couple of small flights for the Society at Morris Park last Saturday...We have seized the opportunity to secure some trials on Long Island where there are better grounds...*

"In regard to patent matters, I want to suggest that if you contemplate any action that the matter be taken up privately between us to save if possible annoyance and publicity of law suits and trial."

16Jul'09: Curtiss wired Bell: *"First long flight this morning, 15 miles."*

AERONAUTICS.

RIVAL OF WRIGHTS.

Glenn H. Curtiss on Long Flight.

Twenty-five Hundred People Witness Great Aeroplane Trial.

Breaks Year's American Records and Wins Aero Club Trophy.

Is in Air Nearly Fifty-three Minutes Over Course at High Speed.

[BY DIRECT WIRE TO THE TIMES.]

NEW YORK, July 17.—[Exclusive Dispatch.] By making a circular flight over the Hempstead Plains, near Minola, L. I., lasting 52 minutes and 40 seconds, Glenn H. Curtiss early this morning again broke the year's American records for aëroplane trials, and came within 22 minutes of equaling Orville Wright's record, made at Washington last year.

Prior to this flight, Curtiss made one complete circle around the mile and a half course, and landed, winning thereby the prize of $250, which had been offered by Cortlandt Field Bishop, president of the Aëro Club of America, for a kilometer flight in a new machine.

Curtiss's big flight was made in competition for the Scientific American trophy, which at the end of three years goes to the contestant who has made the best progressive record.

Curtiss had notified the Contest Committee of the Aëro Club of America that he wished to make a record for the trophy, and an extraordinary flight was anticipated. Consequently, many enthusiasts gathered in Minola the night before. The various hotels were so crowded that several persons were obliged to spend the night on porch chairs.

Curtiss began his second flight in the presence of about 2500 people shortly after 5 o'clock. He had his machine under perfect control at all times.

It is estimated that he traveled about thirty miles and drove the apparatus at a speed of about thirty to thirty-five miles an hour. His height while he was soaring varied from fifteen to forty feet.

As soon as he landed, the machine was surrounded by a crowd of enthusiasts, who wished to carry Curtiss on their shoulders, but rubbing the particles of dust from his eyes, he broke away, and smiling, said that he wanted his breakfast.

"I came down," said Mr. Curtiss, "because my gasoline supply was running low and the wind was getting rather uneven. I will continue my trials until Monday. I may try a cross-country flight between Minola, Westbury and Garden City. I also expect to take up H. J. Wehman in order to instruct him in the handling of the machine."

Dr. Alexander Graham Bell is the theoretical man who devised the Curtiss bi-plane. Curtiss is the practical genius who put into concrete form Dr. Bell's ideas by building the present machine.

<u>Los Angeles Times</u>, *18Jul'09 (note last paragraph):*

Bell immediately replied: *"Heartiest congratulations from all. Hope this means the <u>Scientific American Trophy</u> for you..."*

17Jul1909: After moving to his selection of the Society's new aviation field, the Washington Avenue Field (beside Hempstead Plains, a vast meadow adjoining Mineola Fair Grounds) in Garden City, Long Island, he flew the Flier non-stop 24.7 miles at 35-mph for 52 minutes 30 seconds, winning for the *second* time the *Scientific American Trophy*.

This Long Island location, with airfields known as Hazelhurst, Curtiss, Roosevelt and Mitchel Fields, became historic.

The Aeronautical Society then formed the Aeronautical Exhibition Co., but on 16Aug'09, before they'd done much exhibiting, the Wrights obtained a restraining order and demanded restitution for any financial losses because of exhibitions already held.

25Aug'09: The Herring-Curtiss Co. was similarly served; its counsel, Monroe Wheeler, stated: "*These suits will be defended, and it will be the policy of the defense to disprove all claims of infringement by showing that many of the infringements alleged were fully covered by patents taken out by Mr. Herring and his associates in the Herring-Curtiss Company before the Wrights applied for patents...*"

The Scientific American Trophy won by Glenn H. Curtiss.

The *Golden Flier's* sale was the *first* of an airplane in the United States. *Charles F. Willard* proceeded to exhibit it around the country, and eventually with Curtiss at the *first American Air Meet* at Dominguez Field (southwest of Los Angeles) in January, 1910.

16Jun1909: Chanute to Wilbur: "*I thank you warmly for...giving me an account of the causes...that led to the accident to Orville and to Selfridge...This is the first complete statement which I have received, as I would not let Orville talk about it when he was in the hospital...*

"*You must be now pretty well satiated with glory. The harvesting of prizes, the receiving of unstinted praise, the reception of numerous medals, are now about to be capped by the acclaim of your fellow townsmen...I hope that when the present shouting is over you will continue to achieve further success and to receive ample rewards of all kinds...*"

3Jun1909: *The Youth's Companion:* "*It is said that the last order given by ex-President Roosevelt was for the striking at the Philadelphia Mint, of the 'honor medals' of solid gold which the Aero Club...is to present to the Wright brothers...*"

11Jun'09: Arriving home from Europe, the Wrights are awarded the medal by President Taft: "*...perhaps I do this at a delayed hour.*"

17,18Jun'09: Large Dayton reception for the Wrights (see pp. 208):

28Jun'09: Bishop Wright's diary: "*We arrived in Washington...Orville met us and took us to the Raleigh House, where we took rooms in the 8th story...The Senate adjourned & Congressmen came to witness a flight...*"

Author's collection:

```
           Washington, D. C.,
           January 18, 1909.
```

```
     The Preliminary Committee of the

Aero Club of Washington  invites  you

to attend a meeting of the Organizing

Committee, in the office of the Chief

Signal Officer of the Army, Room 436,

War Department, on  Saturday, January

23, at half past four o'clock.
```

[signature]
Chairman Committee

```
              WAR DEPARTMENT,
   Office of the Chief Signal Officer,
              Washington.
```

```
     The inclosed card is sent in care 

should  desire to witness the trials of 

aeroplanes to be held by the United  Sta

Signal Corps on the drill ground, Fort M

Virginia.  The exact dates for the offic

trials cannot be definitely stated at  t

time,  but  when  decided  they  will be 

nounced as promptly as possible through 

public press.
```

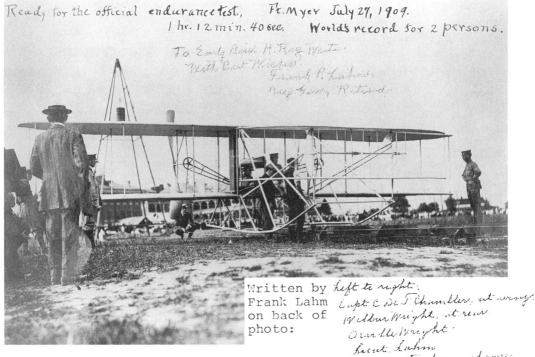

*Ready for the official endurance test, Ft. Myer July 27, 1909.
1 hr. 12 min. 40 sec. World's record for 2 persons.*

*To Early Bird H. Ray Waite.
With Best Wishes.
Frank P. Lahm,
Brig. Genrl. Retired.*

Written by
Frank Lahm
on back of
photo:

*Left to right:
Capt. C De F Chandler, at wing.
Wilbur Wright, at rear
Orville Wright.
Lieut. Lahm
Charley Taylor, mechanic
Lieut. F. F. Humphreys*

Inscribed on front: *"To Early Bird H. Ray Waite. With Best Wishes. Frank P. Lahm, Brig. Genrl. Retired;"* on the reverse *"Left to right: Capt. C. De F. Chandler, at wing; Wilbur Wright, at rear; Orville Wright; Lieut. Lahm; Charley Taylor, mechanic; Lieut. F. F. Humphreys."*

25Jul'09: Louis Bleriot (1872-1936) flies the English Channel.

In France - the only country with almost a dozen different aeroplane engines and the most advanced flying machines - in addition to Bleriot there were many pioneering aviators: Henri Farman (1874-1958), Leon Delagrange (1873-1910), Hubert Latham (1883-1912), Charles and Gabriel Voisin...all following Santos-Dumont who, in 1909 introduced his

Demoiselle, a popular, small monoplane with a tiny Darracq engine.

The *"Infuriated Grasshopper," right"* could only be flown by aviators like 110 lb. Alberto Santos-Dumont.

But he soon gave up flying and re turned to Brazil. In 1932, blaming himself for the destructive roles of the airplane in WW1 and a Sao Paulo revolution, at 59 he committed suicide.

Today Brazilians revere him as the
"Father of Aviation."
He is also remembered with *Cartier*
jeweler's famed *Santos "Tank"* watch
(from the British Tommies' WW1 term
for their first tracked armored vehicles,
the initials for which were "W.C.").

27Jul'09: *1910* <u>Aviator's Year Book</u>,
London: *"Orville Wright covered with a
passenger 45 miles in 1 hr. 12 mins. 40
secs. before President Taft at Fort Myer."*

Alberto Santos-Dumont:

Lt. Foulois and Orville Wright:

30Jul1909: Bishop Wright's diary: *"....We had telegram from Katharine at 7:00 an-nouncing that Orville* (with observer-passenger 125-pound Lt. Benjamin Foulois) *had flown ten miles (officially) in 14 minutes and 42 seconds. Home Sunday at 9:00. Lorin estimates that deducting the turn will give his average speed 43 miles..."*

Orville completes the Ft. Myer trials before as many as 10,000 spectators. The brothers then sell *"Miss Columbia"* to the Army in their *first* aeroplane sale. The $30,000 payment (approximately $1-1/2 million today) included a $5,000 bonus for flying 42.6-mph, exceeding the 40-mph requirement.

Fly, Jul'09: *"Prof. Alexander Graham Bell is taking a much-needed rest 'from reporters and flying machines,' is motoring in the south of England."*

9Aug1909: New York Herald: Article about Curtiss's selection by the Aero Club for the International Aviation Meet to be held at Reims, France, August 22-29, 1909.

10Aug'09: Orville (New York) to Wilbur: *"I am enclosing a clipping from N.Y. Herald. I think best plan is to start suit against Curtiss, Aeronautic Society, etc., at once. This will call attention of public to fact that the machine is an infringement of ours. Mr. Cordley favors starting suits in Europe at once and prosecuting them vigorously. It may be a good idea to resign (or withdraw) our names as honorary members of the Aeronautic Society if suit is brought against it.*

"If suit is brought before the races are run at Reims, the effect will be better than after...Cordley wants to cable Flint to get affairs in shape to begin suit in France simultaneously, or immediately upon my arrival..."

18Aug'09: The Wrights bring suit against the Aeronautic Society, the Herring-Cur-tiss Co., and Curtiss, personally, for alleged patent infringement, stating that they were *"the true, original, first and joint inventors of new and useful improvements in flying machines"* and had created an invention of *"great value."*

Note: One should know that the Wright brothers were allied with, arguably, *the* two most formidable names in the American financial establishment: J. Pierpont Morgan and Charles R. Flint – which helped embellish their names and negate that of Glenn Curtiss with a bias continuing, apparently, even to today.

21Aug'09: Wilbur to Orville (France): *"At the beginning of last week I went East and met Mr. Toulmin at Washington for the purpose of starting suit against the Curtiss crowd. Tuesday I went on to New York and got information as to incorporation, &c. As Hammondsport is in a different district from New York it was necessary to bring two suits, one against the Aeronautic Society and one against Curtiss and Herring-Curtiss Co. The suits were filed before the week closed..."*

26Aug'09: Chanute to Ernest Jones (of *Aeronautics*): "...*I think the Wrights have made a blunder by bringing suit at this time. Not only will this antagonize very many persons but it may disclose some prior patents which will invalidate their more important claims...*"

1Sep'09: Chanute to Jones: "...*I believe that aviators should commend the Wrights for bringing the suit so as to establish the limits to which other inventors may go, and Mr. Curtiss should welcome it as likely to assist in the sale of his stock and his machines, if decided in his favor...*"

Note: Chanute continued to state that he had disclosed to the Wrights the element of wing-warping, as in Mouillard's 1897 patent. However, with Orville's statement of their having had no desire to use such features, and Judge Learned Hand's legal interpretation, it was disallowed. Careful study leaves one with conflicting viewpoints which do not adequately solve the enigma.

It is far more a matter of bias and opinion than anything like a hard, factual assertion.

"Wing warping was certainly the first idea for lateral control. It was used by Clement Ader in 1890. R. Marchal...made a study...in the 1960s and quoted Ader's claims in his application to the Bureau de la Propriete Industrielle in August 1890. These claims include a clear indication of wing warping...and one can only assume that it was translator trouble that prevented this from being more widely known."

Frank Howard and Bill Gunston

The Wrights initiated actions in Europe and the United States, stating: "....*So long as there is any money to be made by the use of the products of our brain, we propose to have it ourselves...*"

Though usually ignoring amateurs or 'inventors,' they mercilessly attacked those who built machines for profit...their profit.

"*Curtiss did not defy the law. We all defied a judge who refused to follow the law and introduced his own law. Where there is a law, judges must follow it. Judges cannot legislate...the judgment against Curtiss by Judge Hazel was very unpopular and no one stopped flying.*"

Charles Willard

"The nation's press seemed evenly divided on the Curtiss-Wright issue...Eastern and Southern newspapers were in the Wright camp...those in the Midwest and Far West sided with Curtiss against the giant 'Wall Street Air-Trust.' Several injustices were done to Curtiss in some press reports of Judge Hazel's decision...The court...far from suggesting that Curtiss had copied the Wrights, stated that when an already broad claim is liberally construed an infringement is established..."

Over Land and Sea

"The real fight was with Glenn Curtiss, since much personal feeling was involved. The first injunction against Curtiss (*3Jan'10*) was revoked, then quickly reimposed. A series of court battles followed, with the verdict finally granted in the Wright's favor."

Flight

15Sep'09: *The Association of Licensed Automobile Manufacturers:* "*a group of Wall Street investors*" hoping to profit from a monopoly based upon *George Baldwin Selden*'s automobile patent, sued Henry Ford for infringement.

In Rochester, New York in 1878 Selden (1846-1922), assisted by William Gomm, built a primitive 3-cylinder compression engine, and in 1879 applied for a patent for a "*...safe, simple, and cheap road locomotive, light in weight, easy to control, and possessed of sufficient power to overcome any ordinary inclination.*" Then on 5Nov'95, having never built an automobile, he received patent No. 549,160, the "*first one on record anywhere of a combination of an internal combustion engine with a carriage*" and legal claim to being the automobile's inventor. Later, when aware of his invention, the above association was formed to monopolize this industry. It advertised (1904): "*These manufacturers are pioneers in this industry and have commercialized the gasolene vehicle by many years of development and at great cost. They are the owners of upwards of four hundred United States patents, covering many of the most important improvements and details of manufacture. Both the basic Selden patent and all other patents owned as aforsaid will be enforced against infringers. No other manufacturers or importers than the above (therein listed) are authorized to make or sell gasolene automobiles and any person MAKING, SELLING or USING such machines made or sold by any unlicensed manufacturer will be liable to prosecution for infringement.*"

Earlier in 1909 Judge Charles M. Hough had upheld Selden's claim that it combined previously known elements into a new "*harmonious whole capable of results never before achieved.*"

Henry Ford, reportedly asking Edison's advice - and told to fight the monopoly and emboldened by the support of John Wanamaker, his New York distributor, retorted: "*There will be no let up in the legal fight...*(the Selden patent was a) *freak among alleged inventions...worthless as a patent and worthless as a device.*" (In 1895 Edison had pointed out that the internal combustion engine had a distinct advantage over electricity for motor vehicles unless a new and more economical storage battery could be discovered.)

"In the end the courts decided the Selden patent was valid, but that the Ford motor car was sufficiently outside its scope, as was every other automobile being manufactured in this country at the time - thirty-three years after the original conception...the American patent law is very explicit on the point, and there is no doubt that the Selden patent, when filed in 1879, was a highly original and ingenious conception."   *Mitchell Wilson*

19Aug'09: Orville and Katharine (taking leave for the last time from teaching Latin and modern languages at Dayton's Steele High School) arrive in Berlin to be "*received as personages of the first rank and offered the* (Hotel Esplanade's) *Imperial Suite*" for "*Some pride is taken in the fact that the grandfather of the Wrights was a German.*" They stay into October, setting up the German Wright company (the Reims air meet greatly accelerated Germany's entry into aviation).

Crowds as large as 200,000 came to Tempelhof Field to see Orville fly as he "*breaks records over Berlin, instructs the first German pilots, is presented to the Kaiser and Kaiserin and gives the German Crown Prince his first airplane flight*" - and meets General von Moltke, Chief of the General Staff.

1909

*Katharine and Orville, en route
to Europe:*

*Crown Prince Friedrich Wilhelm, center, watching Orville
(Farman aeroplane, rear):*

Orville, Crown Prince Friedrich Wilhelm (Great grandson of Queen Victoria, cousin of both Russia's Czar and England's King [who helped his father, the Kaiser, to exile in Holland after World War I], to be a supporter of Hitler), and Flint's Hart Berg:

22-29Aug'09: *International Aviation Meet, "The Great Reims Air Week"* is held in France's champagne region. This, the *world's first air meet*, was primarily Ernest Archdeacon's doing. It was very elaborate: Prizes of 200,000 francs (about $2 million today) grandstands for over fifty-thousand spectators, a restaurant seating six thousand, individual hangars with each aviator's name in large letters - all beside an oblong, 10 kilometer (6.2 mile) race course.

Thirty-two contestants, mainly French, one Englishman - and *one very lone* American were there to compete in altitude, speed and distance flights - testing their machine's endurance - and their skill and daring. They would fly a total of over 45 hours to win $37,000 in prizes (about $2 million today).

Earlier, the Aero Club's Bishop (and Curtiss's business associate) was in Europe, attempting to get the Wrights to represent America at this meeting. But they were heavily involved with Germany (above) and declined.

Bishop then insisted that Curtiss enter. However he was very reluctant, partly due to a growing unease with Herring, but finally relented - resulting in a press report: "...*the indomitable Glenn Curtiss petitioned the Aero Club of America to name him its representative in the speed race.*"

Curtiss's *Reims Racer* was a special high-speed design, similar to a *Golden Flier* but shaved of every ounce of weight. It was powered with a water-cooled 50-hp (probably nearer 35-hp) V8 motor, so new that it had only been bench-tested prior to shipment. And it had a larger, seven-foot propeller. And its 30-foot wingspan made it the smallest biplane at Reims (only Bleriot's monoplane was smaller).

Britain's Claude Grahame-White (1879-1959) commented: "*One of the most noticeable things about Mr. Curtiss was his American coolness. He and his mechanics did just what was necessary and no more...*"

GRANDE SEMAINE D'AVIATION DE CHAMPAGNE (Journée du 22 Août)
L'américain Curtiss et son biplan

"Another plane (in addition to the Antoinette) that seemed easier to control was the Curtiss biplane. It had extraordinary speed, and Curtiss appeared to fly relaxed and with confidence, unlike many of the others who had to give any movement intense attention."

Owen Lieberg

Always prepared to take a risk, Curtiss gambled with the success of the plane's design and workmanship, and had first flown it only a few days before the meeting was officially opened...but, as the sole American contestant, he said: "*I have only one aeroplane and one motor. If I smash either of these, it will be all over for America's chances in the* <u>*International Cup Race*</u>*.*"

Curtiss at Reims. The soon-shaven goatee covers a wound from a Baddeck ice-boat mishap:

Curtiss: "*After my preliminary flight, when I broke the course record, I realized that the flying conditions were now perfect for the pilot. The sun was shining, there was no wind, not even a breeze. Yet the sun's heat was creating turbulent conditions in what had been called the back stretch...The previous day the backstretch of the course had given some trouble to fliers and in the early afternoon had been dangerous. More than one had crashed,*

though without injury to anyone. It had to be flown with great care. It could not be avoided."

"*I knew it could get worse, so we hurriedly refilled the gasoline tank, gave the machine a final checking, and spun the propeller. Being far back from the takeoff line, I got the machine quickly off the ground and climbed as high as I could before passing the judges' stand below me. With the nose of the machine pointing down sufficiently to gain more speed, I headed for the far end of the field. The throttle was wide open, it was my only chance. I banked steeply as I turned toward the 'rough' part of the course.*

"*The air was wild. It seemed to be tearing at the wings. It pitched and rolled, but my speed gave me that little extra stability I needed. Seconds later I was through it, but I made up my mind to avoid it on the next lap. Banking sharply at the turns, there was nothing else now but to keep the throttle fully open and head for the final turn. It was all or nothing.*"

Coupe d'Aviation Gordon-Bennett:

Completing the course in an amazing 15-1/2 minutes, he landed - but had to wait until Bleriot had his turn.

There was a hush after Bleriot finished, then an announcement:

Curtiss had beaten him by 5.6 seconds.

Pandemonium broke loose! In the euphoria, Curtiss, sitting beside *James Gordon Bennett* in Bishop's car, was engulfed by excited, boisterous Americans and many dismayed Europeans.

Newsreel footage shows a broadly-smiling young man at probably the supreme moment of his life.

Praise was heaped upon him by proud Americans: Ambassador Henry White, Mrs. Theodore Roosevelt, her daughter Ethel and sons Quentin and Arthur, American Naval Attache F. L. Chapin, his brother, Roy D. Chapin (later of Detroit's Hudson Motor fame), Cortlandt Bishop, Boston's James Means...and mechanician-helpers, Tod (Slim) Shriver and Ward Fisher.

Ambassador White: "*I came to see you win, and you have done it*" as he congratulated Curtiss in the name of the people of the United States – and the <u>Herald</u> headlined him as "*The Champion Aviator of the World - fastest man of the earth and skies.*"

Curtiss, racing at the "*tremendous velocity*" of 47-mph, beat Bleriot by the narrowest of margins (Bleriot's monoplane, with a new, powerful 80-hp V8 engine, was destroyed the next day in a near-fatal crash) to win the most coveted speed prize: "*Coupe Internationale d'Aviation*" or *Gordon Bennett cup*, a handsome silver trophy crowned with a *Wright Flyer*, the "*Blue Ribbon of The Air.*" (Given by James Gordon Bennett, 1841-1918, the "*pampered, thoroughly unbalanced...cruel, sexist, racist, degenerate, alcoholic*" publisher of the <u>New York and Paris Herald</u> - who'd sent *Henry Stanley*, arguably the world's most intrepid explorer, to find Doctor David Livingstone.)

And there were ceremonies: notable, the dinner given by Ambassador White at the Embassy in Paris. Curtiss *almost* didn't go. Pulitzer's aviation-minded <u>New York World</u> wrote: "*Curtiss fears ceremony more than he fears the most perilous flight. He was not intending to go to the dinner, but when he had been solemnly promised that no one would call upon him to speak, he came.*" Later he said: "*I could eat off the gold plates all right. But when they wanted me to stand up and make a speech, I was lost. If only they would let a fellow talk sitting down it might not be so bad.*" His winnings totaled 38,000 francs, approximately $8,000 (about $350,000 today).

AMERICAN FLIES OFF WITH GRAND PRIZE.

Glenn H. Curtiss in a Wonderful Flight in Which He Smashes the World's Record For Speed Wins International Cup of Aviation.

BETHANY AVIATION FIELDS, RHEIMS, Aug. 28.—The international cup of aviation, known also as the James Gordon Bennet trophy, was won today by Glen H. Curtiss, American aviator, in the fastest aërial journey of twenty kilometers (12.42 miles,) ever accomplished by man.

His time—15m. 50 3-5s.—was only 5 3-5 seconds faster than that made by Bleriot over the same course. The other two French pilots, Latham and Lefebvre, finished respectively in 17m. 32s. and 20m. 47 3-5s. Cockburn, an Englishman, ran into a haystack as he was maneuvering for the start, and did not cross the line. There were no other starters.

The race lay between Bleriot and Curtiss, with Latham as a possible outsider. Lefebvre on previous performances apparently had no chance. Fortune favored the American. An accident two days ago to Bleriot's powerful and fast machine, with which he held the lap record, met a serious handicap, and he had no opportunity to try out the repaired machine.

Curtiss stole a march on his rivals by getting away early. Finding conditions favorable at 10 o'clock in the morning, he decided to take no chances in the fickle weather, and after a trial trip, in which he made the circuit of the course in 7m. 55 1-5s., lowering the world's record nine seconds, he started immediately on his attempt to win the cup.

MASTER OF MACHINE.

He handled his machine in masterly style. The first round, measuring 6.21 miles, was made in 7m. 57 2-5s., and the second round was covered in 7m. 53 1-5s., a world's record. This remarkable showing on the part of the American created consternation in the Bleriot camp.

Lefebvre, in a Wright biplane, but without hope of winning, flew over the course, but his time was five minutes slower than that of Curtiss.

Excitement grew steadily as 5 o'clock approached. Bleriot's and Latham's machines were run out. A few minutes later they crossed the line in quick succession. Bleriot went by the tribunes at a terrific pace and finished the round in almost the identical time of Curtiss' fast lap, covering the ten kilometers in 7m. and 53 3-5s., but his speed seemed appreciably to decrease on the last round and before he reached the final turn, the stopwatches showed that he had lost.

The French crowds were greatly disappointed at the failure of their countrymen, but largely because of the popularity of the Wrights, in France and the general French recognition of the wonderful stimulus Americans have given to the science of aviation, no foreign victory could have been so popular as that of an American.

RUN UP STARS AND STRIPES.

The judges immediately ran up the American flag and the bands played the "Star Spangled Banner." There was great rejoicing among the American spectators.

Ambassador Henry White, accompanied by Mrs. Theodore Roosevelt, Miss Ethel Roosevelt, Quentin and Archie, arrived in time to witness the flights by Bleriot and Latham.

When the American flag went up Curtiss, who had refused to accept congratulations until it was officially announced that Bleriot's time was slower than his, was escorted, or rather, dragged, from the shed to the Ambassador's box by several hundred enthusiastic Americans. Mr. White's first words were:

"I came to see you win and you have done it."

The Ambassador congratulated Curtiss in the name of the government and the people of the United States, and then presented Mrs. Roosevelt and the other members of a large party, who added their congratulations. The entire party then visited Curtiss in the shed, where the hero of the hour got into the seat and explained how the machine was controlled. Later the party witnessed the starts of Bleriot, Lefebvre, LeGrande and Bunau-Varilla.

They saw Bleriot just at dark clip 5 2-5 second off Curtiss's fastest round

GLENN CURTISS

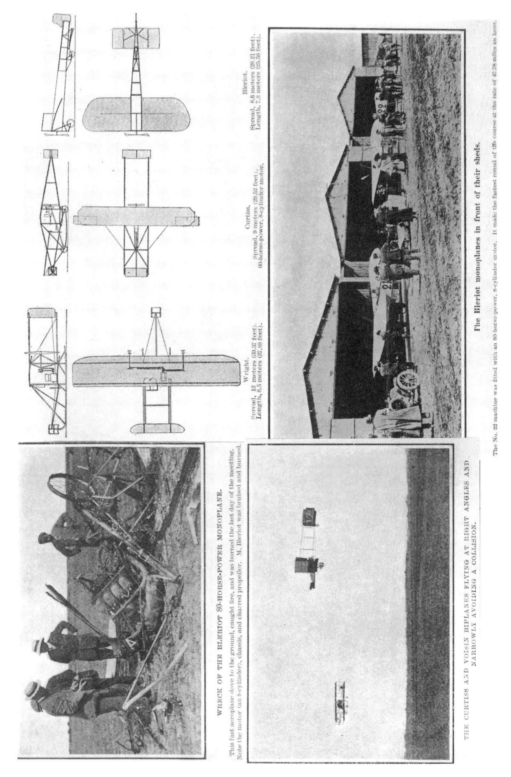

Wright.

Spread, 12 meters (39.37 feet).
Length, 8.5 meters (27.88 feet).

Curtiss.

Spread, 9 meters (29.52 feet).
60-horse-power, 8-cylinder motor.

Bleriot.

Spread, 8.6 meters (28.21 feet).
Length, 7.8 meters (25.58 feet).

The Bleriot monoplanes in front of their sheds.

The No. 22 machine was fitted with an 80-horse-power, 8-cylinder motor. It made the fastest round of the course at the rate of 47.28 miles an hour.

WRECK OF THE BLERIOT 80-HORSE-POWER MONOPLANE.

This fast aeroplane dove to the ground, caught fire, and was burned the last day of the meeting. Note the motor (an 8-cylinder), chassis, and charred propeller. M. Bleriot was bruised and burned.

THE CURTISS AND VOISIN BIPLANES FLYING AT RIGHT ANGLES AND NARROWLY AVOIDING A COLLISION.

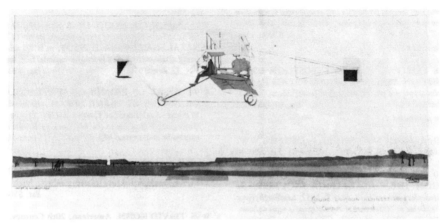

Gamy print "Coupe Gordon Bennett 1909 - Curtiss le gagnant," author's collection:

Commander F.L. Chapin, U. S. Naval Attache at Paris, reporting his observations of Reims: that *"...the aeroplane would have a present usefulness in naval warfare and that the limits of the field will be extended in the near future"*...and further noting that the day would come when aeroplanes operated from naval vessels both by a *launching device* (catapult) and by a *deckhouse floor* (flight deck).

"The impetus giving to flying by the Reims meet was incalculable, second only to Bleriot's Channel flight. The seemingly insignificant records were incredible at the time, and the reliability demonstrated by most of the machines dispelled many of the public's fears and misconceptions about flight. Fortunately, too, there were no fatalities to mar this good impression. Thereafter aviation's fortunes soared. Those pioneer pilots, Bleriot, Farman and Curtiss, also pioneered the aviation industry. Bleriot's plant produced civil and military aircraft until 1935; Farman, with his brothers, manufactured planes which had considerable influence on design; and Curtiss became a leader in American aircraft production."
Flight

"It was a pity that Orville Wright did not attend the Reims meeting, even as a spectator. He would have seen competitive aircraft, always useful to a designer, but he felt he could further his company's activities in Europe by staying in Germany that week."
Owen Lieberg

Bleriot thought wing-warping *"public property,"* using it until confronted by the Wright's patent. Discarding it, he became vocal in criticizing them for *"monopolizing an idea."*

It was during the Reims Meet that Curtiss and Bishop, prompted by the Wright suit, first compared notes on Herring, with both dumbfounded to learn that neither had checked his patent claims. And nor had Monroe Wheeler, to whom the incorporation had been entrusted. Bishop wrote Wheeler about a discussion he'd had with the Wrights: *"They told me certain things* (about Herring) *which, if true, put matters in a very bad light, both on moral and legal grounds, and if the facts are as they state them I shall regret having anything to do with the aeroplane...business."*

CURTISS GETS MORE PRIZES.

American Aeroplanist Wins at Italian Meet.

Princess Asks Permission to Fly With Him.

Rougier Praises Competitor for Generosity.

[ASSOCIATED PRESS NIGHT REPORT.]

BRESCIA, Sept. 12.—Glenn H. Curtiss, the American aviator who won the international cup at Rheims, added further honors to his brilliant record by capturing the grand prize in the aviation meet here today. Curtiss made his flight yesterday, covering 50 kilometers (31.05 miles,) or five times around the course, in 49m. 24s. His share of the $10,000 prize is $6000.

Rougier, the French aviator, also competed for the grand prize, making a flight of 50 kilometers in 1h. 10m. 18s., winning second money.

Curtiss also won the prize for quick starting, his time being 8 1-5s. Le Blanc was second in this contest, 9 3-5s.

Princess Letitia, step-mother of the Duke of Abruzzi, was present and received all the foreign aviators. She warmly congratulated Mr. Curtiss. She asked him in English:

"Would you take me with you?"

"I should be delighted if my machine were fitted for carrying passengers," replied Mr. Curtiss.

After several test flights had been made by the different aviators, Rougier started his attempt for the grand prize. He made the first lap in 13m. 50s. and the second in 19m. 42s., which included a stop to replenish the tank. The third lap he covered in 12m. 12s.; the fourth, 12m. 25s., and the fifth 12m. 9s.

Bleriot made several brilliant flights but did not compete for the grand prize, after which Curtiss entered for the altitude prize. He ascended to a height of 61 meters (about 165 feet,) thereby gaining second prize, while the first prize was awarded Rougier, who danced around with delight, saying:

"Curtiss is a true gentleman. He might have gone higher than I, but he promised to leave me the first prize and he has kept his promise. This is real American chivalry."

Lieut. Calderera was the winner of the passenger-carrying event, for which a prize of $600 was offered. He made four rounds of the course with Lieut. Severa. He also captured the national speed prize, the distance being one lap. Curtiss added to his winnings by taking one of the daily speed contests, as well as one of the daily height contests.

Also, Bishop was wary of the Wright's claims, to which Curtiss stated: "*I told him I thought our device was outside the claims of the Wright patents, and that the Wrights were not entitled to a monopoly of flying, and that I thought we had...a good chance of winning the suit. Mr. Bishop told me he didn't want to get into a fight, and I told him that I was on good friendly terms with the Wrights and had talked with them on various occasions, recognizing their great achievements in being the first to fly, and recognizing their patents, as I understood them. But I still contended that our neutral ailerons* (balancing planes) *were outside their claims and we should continue to use them, and if they brought suit ...we had a fair chance to win.*"

Sep'09: Royal Aero Club of Italy Meet, Brescia: Following a harrowing automobile drive with Bishop across the Alps (still very challenging, as the author discovered), Curtiss and the *Reims Racer* won the Grand Prize and Altitude Prizes, and Italian hearts even more so than he had in France.

In winning the Passenger Prize he carried *Gabriele d'Annunzio* (1863-1938), one of literature's most flamboyant personalities, who exclaimed: "*Until now I have never really lived! Life on earth is a creeping, crawling business. It is in the air that one feels the glory of being a man and conquering the elements. There is the exquisite smoothness of motion and the joy of gliding through space. It is wonderful! Can I not express it in poetry? I might try.*"

After learning to fly, in World War I d'Annunzio became one of Italy's aces, and his speeches were instrumental in bringing Italy into the war on the Allied side.

He led a life of romantic scandal and great adventure - renowned "as Italy's leading artist, a consummate stylist who combined the poetic grandeur of Dante and the classical writers with contemporary trends of naturalism, symbolism, and decadence."

Famous Aviators, 1909: a bald Wilbur; Curtiss, center; Mme. Raymonde de la Roche...:

Upon returning to Hammondsport - to a hero's welcome - Curtiss was prevailed to speak: *"Ladies and gentlemen, I'm back from France. Had a very nice time. Had a whole lot of luck and a little success. As you know, I had just had a common school education and I didn't learn any words big enough to show you my appreciation of my welcome home."*

Things began to unravel between him and Herring, prompted by the discussions with Bishop and Wheeler and aggravated by Herring's complaints that Curtiss was putting too little of his exhibition and prize earnings into the company.

    Also Henry Kleckler, Curtiss's trusted foreman, clashed repeatedly with Herring's fault-finding and meddling.

    As to prize earnings, Curtiss thought that since he was the one taking the risks he deserved the rewards.

    And he was having difficulty in seeing just what Herring was contributing, ending one discussion: *"What the hell have you done for the company?"*

En route home on S.S. La Savoie:

He wrote Bishop: "(Herring) *has always been a failure. He has fooled Mr. Chanute, Hiram Maxim, Professor Langley, and the U. S. government, and has deceived you and me. We cannot afford to take chances with him again...Out of consideration for the other stockholders I have about decided to make Herring a proposition to buy or sell."*

This led to some classic shenanigans:

Suspecting the existence of Herring's patents, the Herring-Curtiss Co. brought an action resulting in a State Supreme Court injunction to force Herring to turn them over. When the papers were served at the December 18th director's meeting, both Herring and his lawyer, J. John Hassett, excused themselves and disappeared. Then, apparently, they hired young Rumsey Wheeler (unaware he was the Judge's son) to drive to the Hammondsport Hotel and pick up a stranger (Hassett). After carrying out his instruction to proceed to the west side of the lake, "*a large man*" (Herring) popped out of the bushes. At this point, suspecting foul play, Rumsey dropped both, forcing them to trudge afoot the eight dusty miles to Bath to catch a train to complete their "*sensational getaway.*"

"He was surrounded by fanatics, fakers, get-rich-quick promoters and stunt performers, ballyhoo artists and come-on men. Practically all the mob were looking for something and none of them with anything to give; small wonder if at times he found it difficult to separate the occasional grains of wheat from so many bushels of chaff. But Curtiss was so preoccupied with the things he wanted to do he really paid but slight attention to what others were doing either to him or for him."   *Lyman Seely*

25Sep'09: *Hudson-Fulton Celebration:* While Curtiss was in Europe, Herring contracted (for $5,000) with Wanamaker's New York and Philadelphia department stores to display the Reims Racer immediately upon its return.

Therefore he had only a new untried, underpowered 25-hp *Hudson-Fulton Machine.*

Poor weather and too soft a landing area held him to only a single short, hardly-seen early morning flight, after which he left for St. Louis.

He wrote: "*...I could not remain in New York any longer, as I had accepted an engagement...to fly at St. Louis. I was obliged...much to my chagrin, and the disappointment of the crowds, to leave the city without making a flight up the river, although I did make a short flight over Governor's Island.*

"*Mr. Wilbur Wright, however, remained in New York, and during the following week made a magnificent flight up the river from Governor's Island to Grant's Tomb and return, a distance of about twenty miles. This gave the large part of New York's millions their first glimpse of an aeroplane in flight.*

LATEST PHOTOGRAPHS OF MASTER AVIATORS

WILBUR WRIGHT AND CANOE ATTACHMENT

GLENN CURTISS

COPYRIGHT 1909 BY GEO. G. BAIN

WILBUR WRIGHT GOVERNOR'S ISLAND

CROWD AROUND CURTISS'S SHED GOVERNOR'S ISLAND

CURTISS MACHINE

COPYRIGHT 1909 BY GEOG. BAIN

WRIGHT'S FLIGHT AROUND STATUE OF LIBERTY

Wilbur Wright's achievements in connection with the Hudson-Fulton celebration in New York included a flight from Governor's island Sept. 30 around the statue of Liberty in six minutes and thirty seconds, in which he attained a speed of fifty miles an hour.

In his flight yesterday up the Hudson river to Grant's tomb and return to Governor's island, a distance of twenty miles covered in a little more than half an hour, valuable experience was gained regarding urban air currents as affected by peculiar architectural conditions and heat and gases ascending from industrial plants and steam craft in motion.

4Oct'09: Wilbur flying to Grant's Tomb. Note canoe:

With Orville in Germany, honors went to Wilbur, flying on 29Sep from Governor's Island and around the Statue of Liberty, giving New Yorkers their *first* view of an aeroplane in flight.

On 4Oct. he flew to Grant's Tomb for $15,000 ($700,000 today). And just prior to Curtiss's return from Europe answered a reporter about the lawsuit:

"It is as friendly as any lawsuit may be, but it is of course for the purpose of preventing Mr. Curtiss from manufacturing machines which harm our patented features... Our principal claim rests on the control of the machine, and as that is the fundamental factor of all aeroplanes we are, of course, bound to defend it."

BACK TO EARTH.

WRIGHTS WILL MAKE NO MORE EXHIBITION FLIGHTS.

Will Spend Most of Their Time Hereafter in Business of Manufacturing Aeroplanes at Dayton, Announces Wilbur—Brothers Have no Desire to Be Regarded as Showmen—Better Motor Needed.

[ASSOCIATED PRESS NIGHT REPORT.]

NEW YORK, Oct. 5.—Unless some change of heart shall alter a decision announced today by Wilbur Wright, the spectacular flight made here yesterday by the Dayton aviator is the last which he or his brother, Orville, will make in public.

"Hereafter," said Mr. Wright, "we shall devote all our efforts to the commercial exploitation of our machines and only fly as a matter of experiment to test the value of whatever changes we decide to make in their construction."

Mr. Wright added that neither he nor his brother wished to be looked upon as showmen, and that all offers to fly for exhibition purposes would be rejected.

"The flight of yesterday," said he, "was more than an exhibition. It was more like the taking up of a challenge or the making of a record to stand as a milestone in the history of aërial navigation."

Wright left for Washington tonight to continue the instruction of army officers in aëroplaning. He expects to pass two or three weeks in teaching Lieuts. Lahm and Fowlers and other officers.

After that he will go to Dayton and arrange for the manufacture of his aëroplanes on an extensive scale.

"We have received many orders," he says, "but have fixed no time for delivery as yet. We are making a serious study of the aëroplane. Every time we go into the air, we make a study of some part of the mechanism, or some peculiar weather condition, with a view to improving our machine. We could not do that as hired attractions.

"I regard this New York flight of yesterday as a different proposition. My brother and myself regard our experiments as being in the same class with Fulton's experiments. We are working with an art that is still in its infancy. So I wanted to take part in this celebration, and thus pay my respects to the man who had the nerve to build the first steamboat.

"The accident yesterday taught me a lesson—that until motors are perfect, we shall have no perfect aëroplanes. The science of flying now depends upon the motor. My aëroplane seems perfect, but my motors are not. I hope the day will come when we shall have a perfect motor."

(Curtiss, continued from pp. 231) *"At St. Louis we gave a very successful meet. There were flights by Captain Baldwin, Lincoln Beachey, and Roy Knabenshue, in their dirigible balloons, and myself in my aeroplane. The weather conditions were favourable, and St. Louis turned out enthusiastic throngs..."*

22Sep'09: Captain *Ferdinand Ferber* (1878-1909) killed:

Captain Ferber Is Crushed to Death Beneath Motor of His Machine While Making Flight at Boulogne, France

[BY ASSOCIATED PRESS LEASED WIRE]
BOULOGNE, France, Sept. 22.—Captain Ferber, an officer of the French army, was killed near here this morning, while testing an aeroplane. While in the air the machine turned over and dashed to the ground, crushing the aviator to death beneath the motor.

Captain Ferber took part in the recent aviation contests at Rheims, where he flew in the race for the international cup, and gave an exhibition flight.

Captain Ferber had been detailed for several years to investigate aeronautics in the interest of the French army. He was at one time in charge of the extensive government reservation at Belleville, near Paris, where the army conducted a series of experiments in aviation.

7Sep'09: *Eugene Lefebvre* killed in a *Wright-A Flyer:*

ANOTHER MARTYR OF THE AIR

M. Lefebvre, who lost his life the other day while maneuvering in a biplane, was among the brilliant pupils of the Wrights. His circlings and wheelings won him third place in the speed contest and he was fourth in the contest for the Gordon-Bennett trophy.

11Oct'09 St. Louis: *"Theodore Roosevelt made an aeroplane flight today, and said it was the finest experience he ever had...Arch Hoxsey, a Wright aviator...said...(he)...made a good fellow voyager. Col. Roosevelt gripped the rail good and hard and looked straight ahead...instead of being afraid, he was having such a good time...Hoxsey was afraid he would fall out..."* (a very real possibility; no seat belts then)

Following St. Louis, Curtiss went to an exhibition at Chicago, spending the evenings of 12, 13 Oct. with Chanute discussing the Wright's suit. When he left he was firmly convinced in the strength of his legal position, and heartened to have him as an ally.

AEROPLANE FLIGHTS IN ST. LOUIS

Exhibitions of Machines Heavier Than Air Is Principal Feature of Today's Celebration of Missouri City's Centennial

GLENN H. CURTISS MAKES EARLY MORNING TESTS

Unofficial Estimates of Aero Club Give Honors of Balloon Races Started Monday to St. Louis III and the New York

[BY ASSOCIATED PRESS LEASED WIRE]
ST. LOUIS, Oct. 7.—Thousands of spectators thronged the National amphitheater, near Art Hill, in Forest park today, to see the first aeroplane flights west of Dayton, O.

But the first flight had already been made long before the crowd reached the park, Glenn H. Curtiss having stolen a march on the Centennial officials, newspaper men and his fellow aviators, by making two short test flights shortly after daybreak.

Not a dozen persons saw these trials, which lasted but a few minutes each. Curtiss drove a bi-plane of the same type which he used at Rheims, except that it carried an engine of 25-horsepower, as against one of 50-horsepower in the foreign contests.

Spurred by his rival's success, Francois Osemont, who is handling a Farman machine, was busy this morning testing his engine.

When Curtiss took his machine from its tent this morning the mist was still undispelled. After skimming the ground for 100 yards, he rose to a height of 40 feet, skirted a few trees, and made a perfect descent, after going about 1000 yards in 45 seconds. He made the run back under similar circumstances, landing near his tent without a jar.

CURTISS FLIES AT ST. LOUIS.

Engine Stops on Third Flight With Slight Damage.

Frenchman Fails to Get Off the Ground.

Three Dirigibles Also Make Short Journeys.

[ASSOCIATED PRESS NIGHT REPORT.]
ST. LOUIS, Oct. 7.—Glenn H. Curtiss, who won international honors in aviation at Rheims, France, made three aëroplane flights here today. One was more than a quarter of a mile and the shortest of the three was about 220 yards.

Curtiss's last performance of the day was cut short by his engine failing when he was about twenty-five feet from the ground. The machine glided to an irregular landing place and a rubber guy snapped. The aviator said the machine would be ready for service tomorrow. Curtiss used a bi-plane with a twenty-five-horse-power motor.

Curtiss wrote Bell: "*I spent two evenings in Chicago with Dr. Chanute, and from what he says the Wrights have little prospect of winning.*"

Oct'09: The U.S. Army establishes its *first* airfield at College Park, Maryland. Their new Wright Flyer is put into service with Wilbur teaching Signal Corps officers Frank Lahm and Frederick Humphreys to fly.

ARMY WRIGHT MACHINE IN FRONT OF A COLLEGE PARK HANGAR.

They learned "*by the seat of their pants*" - aided by Wilbur's instructions and demonstrations. The Flyer had no instruments, only a strip of cloth hanging from the landing skid in front of the pilot. When it blew straight, the pilot could relax; when it was at an angle, he knew he was off balance. With Wilbur, the cloth, and their aptitude, both men soloed after less than half-a-day's instruction.

2Oct'09: *Aviator's Year Book*, 1910: "*Orville Wright at Berlin took up the Crown Prince as a passenger. Afterwards he took his machine up to an altitude of 1,500 feet.*"

WRIGHT SOARS WITH PUPILS.

---•---

Lieuts. Lahm and Humphrey Handle Flyer.

---•---

Each Takes Three Flights With Instructor.

---•---

More Difficult Maneuvers Will Be Taught.

[ASSOCIATED PRESS NIGHT REPORT.]

COLLEGE PARK (Md.) Oct. 18.—In six flights at the government aviation school, under the direction of Instructor Wilbur Wright, Lieuts. Lahm and Humphrey demonstrated their ability to handle the government aëroplanes, purchased from the Wright brothers last summer by the Signal Corps. Each officer accompanied Mr. Wright on three flights.

Before the sun had risen the aëroplane was rolled from its shed and in what was virtually a dead calm, Mr. Wright and Lieut. Humphrey made a flight of more than eleven minutes duration.

The second flight, with Lieut. Lahm in the pupil's seat, was the longest made at the Signal Corps aërodrome, lasting for eighteen minutes and thirty-seven seconds.

In both flights Mr. Wright permitted the lieutenant to operate the machine unaided.

The third flight was made in a slight breeze, Lieut. Humphrey again accompanying Mr. Wright. The machine was in the air for more than ten minutes. Mr. Wright, accompanied by Lieut. Lahm then flew for eleven minutes and thirty-four seconds. While the machine was encircling the field it was pitched, and tossed by a ten-mile wind.

In the evening Mr. Wright was accompanied on the first flight by Lieut. Humphrey, who handled the machine unaided through most of the devious course.

On the last flight, Mr. Wright had Lieut. Lahm with him for more than eight minutes. As the machine sped around, Mr. Wright relinquished control of the craft to his pupil.

While flying about with Lieut. Lahm, and Mr. Wright, the aëroplane came abreast of a swiftly moving express train. So close was the machine of the air to its rival on the earth, that it appeared to be right above it.

The disturbance of the air created by the speed of the train seemed to affect the aëroplane, which swept down dangerously close to the earth. As the wind caught it, and aided it onward, it seemed to gain upon the train.

Longer flights and more difficult maneuvers are now to be attempted by the aviation class at the government aërodrome.

Lieut. Benjamin Foulois, who made the famous Alexandria cross-country run with Orville Wright, returned to-day from Nancy, France, where he had been as the representative of the United States army at the aëronautical congress. He will report at College Park tomorrow and it is probable that he will be added to the list of students of aviation.

1909: *Grover Cleveland Loening* (1888-1976), studying for his master's degree at Columbia University, is permitted to concentrate on aeronautics.

In June, 1910, he is awarded the *first* such American degree – and the beginning of his aeronautical career.

Like his mentor, Orville, a small man, he would become known as a knowledgeable, opinionated and starchy egocentric (the author met him in 1974).

In 1913 he was working for Orville, and later described flying in a Wright as "*like sitting on the top of an inverted pendulum ready to fall off on either side any moment.*"

14Oct'09: Chanute to Emerson Newell (Curtiss's lawyer):

"I have your letter of 8th, and saw Mr. G.H. Curtiss last night relative thereto.

"I understand from you that you want to find 'some prior art which will show that the warping of the planes themselves was old.' The bare idea of warping and twisting the wings is old, but there are several ways of accomplishing it...it will be for experts to determine what are equivalent devices. I do not remember any balancing devices such as Mr. Curtiss used. I dare say, however, that they are quite old."

A contemporary advertisement:

Oct'09: Late in October the New York state court ruled that Herring must turn over his alleged patents, and he finally complied. Upon examination they turned out to be patent applications dating back to 1895, none of which had ever been allowed in the United States. Regardless, Cortlandt Bishop, siding with Herring, broke with Curtiss; believing him wrong to go into exhibitions and not carrying out his corporate responsibilities (in 1914 they resolved their differences during the Wanamaker and Curtiss/Aero Club Trans-Atlantic flight project).

The Herring-Curtiss Co. was forced to file for involuntary bankruptcy.

Curtiss to Aero Magazine: *"The newspapers, as usual, have things somewhat mixed. Our business is in the hands of a receiver, but is not shut down. Our trouble is due to our connection with Mr. Herring, who organized the company, but did not put up any money or goods. He, however, acquired a controlling interest, and threatened to assume control of the business...In view of this, no money could be raised to carry on the business, and, together with the undesirable publicity from the injunctions, we were unable to meet our bills, and were forced into the hands of a receiver."*

Charles G. Grey, 1916: *"However, the quick French mind soon saw where the Wrights scored in their design, and by the middle of 1909 the Wright was already a back number. And, curiously enough, despite American ingenuity and engineering resources, American aeroplanes have never regained that brief lead they held for a few months in 1908..."*

30Oct1909: Bell to Curtiss (telegram): "*Wish you would come here for conference with Charles Bell before I return Baddeck. Want to go at once but would wait a day or two for you. Come right to my house and shake a paw for auld land syne.*"

2Nov'09: Bell's diary: "*Mr. Curtiss arrived here yesterday morning...After lunch had conference with Charles J. Bell on way to government testing grounds. Saw college grounds* (College Park, Maryland, where Wilbur was training the two officers) *and Wright machine. Met Wilbur Wright and several officers of Signal Service. Wright has large horizontal tail on machine and two solid looking wheels. Doubt whether wheels are* (illegible) *up, but did not care to examine the machine too curiously. Curtiss left by 3 P.M. train for New York to attend meeting of Aero Club.*"

The talk with Charles Bell was, likely, about the A.E.A.'s patent application, potential royalties of its use between Curtiss and the Canadian Aerodrome Company, and its bearing upon the Wright's infringement suits.

22Nov1909: The *Wright Company,* initially backed by Wall Street's J.P. Morgan (much as Bell, Edison, and <u>The New York Times</u> had been earlier, the Wrights ally with Morgan's infamous *'Money Trust'* and the *'Wall Street Establishment'*) and U.S. Steel's Elbert Gary (who dropped out), is incorporated - with offices at 527 Fifth Avenue, N.Y., and manufacturing in Dayton. It had a capital stock of $1 million and a paid-in value of $200,000, with the Wrights, joining an impressive roster of *"Robber Barons"* (see next) to receive $100,000 in cash (almost $5 million today), one-third of the stock and 10 percent royalty on each machine.

25Nov'09: Bishop Wright's diary: "*...I find that Wilbur and Orville have sold their United States rights to August Belmont, Howard Gould, Cornelius Vanderbilt, Edward J. Berwind, Russell Alger, T.P. Shonts, Morton F. Plant* (see 12Jan'06)*, Andrew Freedman, Robt. J. Collier & Allan A. Ryan. $100,000.*"

6Dec'09: Wilbur to Chanute: "*We are all home again after a rather strenuous summer and autumn. Orville and my sister had a splendid time in Germany...I finished the work at Washington...Since then we have been working very hard on the organization of our business and the preparation of our case in the suit against Curtiss & Herring...We have closed out our American business to the Wright Company, of which the stockholders are...Vanderbilt, Collier, Belmont...Ryan, Gould...We have received a very satisfactory cash payment, forty percent of the stock, and are to receive a royalty on every machine...will devote most of our time to experimental work...*"

Frank Russell (related to board member Russell Alger), was the new Dayton factory manager - to whom Orville brought an accumulation of mail, saying: "*I don't know what to do with this. Maybe they should be opened. But of course if you open a letter, there's always the danger that you may decide to answer it, and then you're apt to find yourself involved in a long correspondence.*"

One of the first acts of the new company was to hire two former newspapermen to be a buffer between the Wright brothers and the press; ensure full coverage on the patents issue; and see that they were quoted on all important aeronautical happenings - a far cry from their earlier press relations.

12Dec'09: Bishop Wright's diary: "...*Wilbur went to New York to see a photograph of Curtiss machine contradicting his affidavit. Thus the lawyers abuse Curtiss.*"

14Dec'09: Bishop Wright's diary: "...*Wright vs. Herring-Curtiss...came in U.S. Court...lawyer for Herring maintained there was no infringement. Claimed their fame rested on...skill as 'aeroplane chauffeurs.'*"

27Dec'09: Mabel, in their *Home Notes:* "*Alex much excited over new idea. I have persuaded him to dictate letter as follows to Baldwin and McCurdy. "Boys!-an Idea! Why not get Curtiss to come to Canada and manufacture engines for the Aerodrome Company? Why not take him into the company? He's sold the Hammondsport business to the Herring people - he has received the money for it and shares in the Herring company. He has now quarreled with Herring and has brought a lawsuit against him. If he resigns...there, there would be nothing to prevent him from coming to Canada. In event of war between Great Britain and Germany, while it would be quite true that American engines and aerodromes could not be imported into Canada, the war would not prevent Canadian aerodromes from being imported into the United States. The Canadian Aerodrome Company might supply...both for the British Empire and for the United States.*

"*Why should not the company replace the old A.E.A.? be organized by the Trustee in Canada and the old associates come together again in a commercial company? We should manufacture the whole thing, engines and all. A.G.B.*"

A nostalgic idea that never bore fruit.

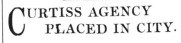

Dec'09: Los Angeles gets its first aeroplane dealer:

Note: Jane's Fighting Aircraft of World War I, 1919: "*The Canadian Curtiss Aeroplane Co., Ltd., Toronto, was the first Canadian firm to manufacture aircraft. It was working on large contracts for the British Navy and Army, and has produced landgoing aeroplanes and seaplanes (flying-boat type), with two or more engines apiece.*"

INNOVATION.

CURTISS AGENCY PLACED IN CITY.

FAMOUS BIPLANE SOON TO BE DEMONSTRATED HERE.

National Automobile Company Will Represent Eastern Distributors in California—Deliveries of Aeroplanes Promised After January 1—One Order Already Placed.

The first aëroplane agency definitely announced for the Pacific Coast has been obtained by the National Auto Company, which is to represent Wyckoff, Church & Partridge, general sales distributors of the Herring-Curtiss aëroplanes. L. H. Johnson is sales manager of the local agency.

The National Automobile Company has already placed an order for a Curtiss demonstrator. Deliveries can be made after January 1. Johnson asserted yesterday he had received one

order for a Curtiss flier, the purchaser being a local enthusiast who refused to give his name.

A. P. Warner, the Beloit auto accessory manufacturer, who was one of the first purchasers of the Curtiss biplane, made fifteen flights in two days shortly after receiving his machine. The instructions for operating, which are sent with each machine, are so complete, and the operation of the biplane is so simple the manufacturers do not send a demonstrator. Warner may bring his machine to this city and compete in the coming aviation contests.

The method of control is exceedingly simple. The movable balancing planes between the two main surfaces are operated through a specially designed device, which corrects the horizontal balance, as the body is moved from left to right, according to the manner in which the machine tips during the flight.

The fabric covering the planes is of rubberized silk balloon cloth. The frame work is constructed of Oregon spruce and bamboo with laminated ribs which are steamed and bent to a parabolic curve and are made of four-ply material. When the machine stands on the level floor the height from the floor to the top of the upper plane is seven feet.

Chapter **7** *1910*

L *itigation*

    grows; enmity by the Wrights and their partisans escalates against Curtiss. Curtiss flys from Albany to New York City. The public clamors to see aeroplanes fly; the exhibition business takes off. Flight records are set at the first American Air Meet. Curtiss demonstrates flight from a ship. Death Stalks the Skies.

3Jan'10: Bishop Wright's diary: "*News that the Wright brothers were granted an injunction against Herring Company, & Curtiss.*"

Judge John R. Hazel ruled that the Herring-Curtiss Co. was restrained from the manufacture and sale of aeroplanes infringing on patents "*for improvements in a flying machine granted May 22, 1906, to Orville and Wilbur Wright and subsequently assigned to the Wright Company.*"

8Jan'10: With his Scotch-Yankee fighting spirit thoroughly aroused (believing balancing-planes/ailerons an *improvement* and thus his to use, an inventor's tactic that Edison made an art form), Curtiss obtains a $10,000 bond, holding off Judge Hazel's injunction.

3Jan'10: <u>Los Angeles Herald</u> (next page):

CURTISS LOSES; WILL FLY HERE

INJUNCTION WILL NOT PREVENT FLIGHT

Wright Brothers Win Point in Aviation Case, but Decision Does Not Affect Los Angeles Meet

[Special to The Herald.]

BUFFALO, N. Y., Jan. 3.—Judge Basel in the United States court today granted the preliminary injunction asked for by the Wright brothers against the Herring-Curtiss company and Glenn H. Curtiss, restraining them from manufacturing and selling aeroplanes.

Arguments as to wether the injunction should be made permanent will be made before Judge Basel February 1. Until that time the Herring-Curtiss company may build airships by putting up a bond covering any damage which might be done the Wright brothers or which might be assessed against the company for alleged infringement of the Wright patent.

The injunction does not in any way prevent Glenn Curtiss or any of his aviators who will appear in Los Angeles from flying the Curtiss type of machine. The particular point involved is a technical one relating to curvature of the planes of the machine.

"Judge Basel's decision granting the Wright brothers's a temporary injunction will not prevent Mr. Curtiss and his aviators from flying in Los Angeles," said Jerome S. Fanciulli, personal manager of Gleen H. Curtiss, yesterday, after his arrival at the Van Nuys hotel, direct from New York. "As I understand the injunction, it is more a victory for us than for the Wright brothers. They asked for an injunction of such sweeping nature that it was absolutely unjust in all its phases. I believe Judge Basel wants to investigate the science of aviation and the patents and devices of aeroplanes most thoroughly before he renders any decision at all, which will affect permanently our company. We believe we are right and we think the Wright brothers claim too much credit for alleged inventions. It will require the United States supreme court to decide this question and it will take many months to fight it out.

Will Fly Here

"Mr. Curtiss will fly here and he will continue to build aeroplanes. All we have to do is put up a bond to protect the Wright brothers. I do not consider the injunction as being very important, for I feel sure the supreme court will give us our rights and settle the question for all time in our favor.

"Mr. Curtiss will leave New York shortly for Los Angeles. He will make numerous flights here, not for exhibition purposes, but for the prizes offered, in order to forward the sport of aviation. We will have four and possibly five machines here and we hope to carry off some of the big prizes.

"I have wired Charles K. Hamilton, one of our aviators now in Kansas City, to come here. Mr. Hamilton will break records, for he is one of the best aviators and one of the most fearless in the world today. He holds some long-distance and endurance records now, and will try to beat even those he has established.

Record for Daring

"Recently Mr. Hamilton flew in two snowstorms and went up in a forty-mile wind. This is the record for daring. The highest wind in which flights have ever been made before was fifteen miles, and that was considered most wonderful and extremely daring.

"At Lake Contrary, St. Joseph, Mo., Mr. Hamilton broke the record for speed. In a descent from a height of 500 feet, which, by the way, is a record for the United States, he made two and a quarter miles in one minute and thirty-five seconds. That is the fastest time ever made by an aeroplane.

"Los Angeles is the ideal place of the entire world for holding aviation meetings. The air currents for thirty years as studied and reported upon by the United States weather bureau prove this statement. The average velocity of the wind in and near Los Angeles is three miles an hour. This makes it ideal for flying at all seasons of the year. The climate is fine and the people enthusiastic. This makes it fine for the aviators. I look for the time when a permanent aviation field will be established in Los Angeles and when the kings of the air will meet here every little while.

Predicts Success

"I was more than surprised when I arrived here and found out how much had been done toward the success of the aviation meeting. Los Angeles is to be congratulated upon its initiative. New York would give a great deal to be able to hold a meeting at this season of the year.

"I believe some new records will be established in Los Angeles. All the aviators and balloonists coming here are bent on making records, for they feel they must demonstrate to the world that aviation is not a wild dream in order to preserve their own reputations. I know that Clifford Harmon, owner of the $5000 balloon New York, is anxious to make some aeroplane flights here. He has been studying the management and operation of biplanes for some time, and will probably go up in one of our machines.

"Mr. Curtiss no longer makes flights for exhibition merely. He has employed Mr. Hamilton for that purpose. He will make flights in order to forward the sport and for scientific purposes, but he will not make flights for any other purpose.

"It may have been forgotten by the public, but Mr. Curtiss made the fastest mile ever known. At Ormond Beach, on his eight-cylinder, forty-horsepower motorcycle, he rode a mile in 26 and 2-5 seconds. No railroad train ever went as fast as that.

"Mr. Curtiss will enter as many contests as there are during the Los Angeles meeting. He is now out after prizes. We had expected to have him try for the Michelin trophy here, but could not get a proper machine built in time."

Mr. Fanciulli is a former newspaper man, for several years having been stationed in the United States house of representatives for the Associated Press.

17Jan'10: Chanute interview in the New York <u>World</u>:

"DR. CHANUTE DENIES WRIGHT FLYING CLAIM

"Declares Brothers Were Not First by Many Years to Discover Balance Principle

"HAS TOLD THEM THEY ARE WASTING TIME IN SUITS

"'Father of Aeronautics' says the Strongest Point Attacked Is Protected by Patents"

"I admire the Wrights. I feel friendly toward them for the marvels they have achieved; but you can easily gauge how I feel concerning their attitude at present by the remark I made to Wilbur Wright recently. I told him I was sorry to see they were suing other ex-

241

perimenters and abstaining from entering the contests and competitions in which other men are brilliantly winning laurels. I told him that in my opinion they are wasting valuable time over law-suits which they ought to concentrate in their work. Personally, I do not think that the courts will hold that the principle underlying the warping tips can be patented. They may win on the application of their particular mechanism.

"The fundamental principle underlying the warping of the tips for the purposes of balance was understood even before the suggestion contained in d'Esterno's pamphlet fifty years ago. In modern time the warping tips were actually used in flight by Pierre Mouillard, a French engineer...protected by a patent granted him by the United States...

"The Wrights, I am told, are making their strongest attack upon the point that they warp the tips in connection with the turning of their rudder. Even this is covered by a patent...There is no question that the fundamental principle underlying was well known before the Wrights incorporated it in their machine."

20Jan'10: Wilbur to Chanute: *"The New York World has published several articles in the past few months in which you are represented as saying that our claim to have been the first to maintain lateral balance by adjusting the wing tips to different angles of incidence cannot be maintained, as this idea was well known in the art when we began our experiments. As this opinion is quite different from that which you expressed in 1901 when you became acquainted with our methods, I do not know whether it is mere newspaper talk or whether it really represents your present views...If however there is anything in print which might invalidate our legal rights, it will be to our advantage to know it before spending too much on lawyers, and any assistance you may be able to give us...will be much appreciated, even though it may show that legally our labors of...years to provide a system of lateral control were of no benefit to the world and a mere waste of time, as the world already possessed the system without us..."*

Wilbur to Zahm: *"The objections to our legal claims are technical, being based on old publications which did not lead to any result, and which are now of use only as a means of depriving us of legal rights to an invention which we independently conceived, worked into shape, and presented to the world at a time when effort in that line was considered a foolish waste of time and money. At present there seems to be a general tendency to concede our moral right to the invention, but to deny that we have any right to expect any monetary pay."*

10-20Jan'10: *First American International Aviation Meet*, Los Angeles, at Dominguez Field (in open country, southwest of the city). Promoted by air-minded actor Dick Ferris with *"Trolley King"* Henry Huntington's backing, this meet drew *"birdmen"* from the United States: Curtiss with the V8 Reims and two 4-cylinder machines, one for Frank Johnson, his California agent (pp. 239), and one for Clifford Harmon; Willard had the Aeronautic Society Curtiss; and Hamilton another Curtiss. *Louis Paulhan* (1886-1963), France's *"Napoleon of The Air,"* had two Bleriot and two Farman aeroplanes; and there were Didier Masson and Edward Miscarol, plus airships piloted by Knabenshue and Beachey - and an attendance of over *175,000* (when LA's population was barely 75,000).

Note: Didier Masson stayed in America, and was *first* to drop bombs *for real*, in the Mexian Revolution in 1913, and in 1916 was one of the *first* members of the Lafayette Escadrille.

As with Reims, Dominguez was largely ignored by the Wrights, though they attempted to stop Paulhan (see 30Jan '10) from appearing (the meet's star, he won $20,000, about $900,000 today).

Orville commented: *"Aside from Curtiss, Paulhan is probably the most skillful aviator in the world, and really more daring than his American rival."*

And young Waldo Waterman was there, an *"aviator"* without an aeroplane, who badgered a meeting with Curtiss and then worshipfully worked for him (no wages) during the meet.

Waldo's photo: Willard, Hamilton and Curtiss:

10Jan'10: <u>Los Angeles Times</u>:

"GLENN CURTISS FLIES OVER AVIATION PARK
"The first flight of an aeroplane west of the Great Plains was made by Glenn H. Curtiss...yesterday afternoon...It marked an epoch in the affairs of the West, for a flight had never before been made on the coast and native sons were skeptical of its accomplishment until they actually set eyes on the performance."

"A clean-cut, slender, sober-faced country boy with a modest, well-trimmed moustache, Curtiss appeared more like a scientist or college professor than a daring aeronaut...a

deliberate performer...who shunned spectacular feats...deaf to a grandstand or a cheering
mob...'sensational as...leaving home in his
auto for the office.'"   *J. Wesley Neal*

Curtiss won his share of prizes, and never
allowed his flyers to be reckless. Though
appearing reserved, he was always ready for
a joke; strict, but quiet and companionable.

After the meet the Reims Racer was sold
to Hamilton (who in 1905 had balloon-lofted
Montgomery's glider carrying the doomed
Maloney - and later that year piloted Lud-
low's *"Air-ship No.4"* glider towed over
New York's North River).
 He was then "first to fly (an airplane)" in
San Diego, and into Mexico – but in March
demolished it in Seattle.

"A great success...Dominguez...established
in Southern California an interest in the infant
science of aviation which was...to bring about
a concentration there of America's aircraft industry."   *Flight*

Curtiss hired Jerome S. Fanciulli, who'd considered him "*rather naive and...needed someone to manage his affairs, especially...public
relations,*" to run the *Curtiss Exhibition Co.*
 Fanciulli had enjoyed a good relationship
with the Wrights, and upon his
return east Curtiss suggested
he stop in Dayton and see
"*whether the Wrights would be
friendly to him*"...and that he'd
like very much "*to either form
a combination with them, or,
if they wouldn't consider that,
to get someone to make an
arrangement with them whereby the patent litigation should
be avoided.*"
 But Fanciulli never went:
"*The Wrights were very bitter*"
and refused to see him.

DIES IN RED-LIGHT RESORT.

GLENN CURTISS FLIES
OVER AVIATION PARK.

*Famous Sky Pilot Drives His Bi-
plane Nearly a Mile at Greatest
Height of Sixty Feet—Spectators
Satisfied of Success.*

Curtiss Biplane Flying at Aviation Camp.

READY TO START.

EXHIBITION FLIGHTS
TODAY'S PROGRAMME.

Mr. and Mrs. Glenn Curtiss posing at Dominguez:
"Old Oregon Trail 1852-1910" Monument Expedition, Paulhan in the air:

23. Ezra Meeker at Aviation Meet,
Los Angeles, 1910.

Curtiss flying before the crowds:
Frank Johnson, "the first native Californian to own and fly an aeroplane," Curtiss:

Scientific American, 19Feb'10:

Paulhan has expressed a willingness to fly in the vicinity of New York if Curtiss or some other interested person will have that injunction dissolved which now hangs over the heads of aviators using warpable planes or hinged wing tips. His brilliant success in California leads one to hope that his desire may be gratified in the interests of a sport of which the United States in general and the East in particular knows lamentably little. If Paulhan really gives an exhibition in these parts he will do much to stimulate New York's interest in aviation. The Hudson-Fulton flights were after all a fiasco, and yet they roused New York to an intense pitch of excitement. Paulhan ought to do better.

The first week of February the suit of the Wright brothers against Paulhan for an injunction restraining him from giving exhibitions in his Farman biplane was tried before Judge Hand in the United States Circuit Court in New York city. Judge Hand manifested great interest in the case, and his decision is awaited with interest. It is uncertain whether he will grant a preliminary injunction, as Judge Hazel did at Buffalo last December. In defending the attack of the Wrights upon the Bleriot monoplane, Mr. E. R. Newell asserted that Prof. S. S. Montgomery's patent, which antedates the Wright patent, covers the same system of plane warping as the Wrights themselves claim, and he further says that the machine as built to-day does not correspond with the patent. A full report of the Wright-Curtiss case and the text of Judge Hazel's decision appears in the current SUPPLEMENT.

Subsequent to the Los Angeles aviation meeting, M. Paulhan made excellent exhibition flights at San Francisco, Denver, and New Orleans. At San Francisco, on January 24th, he made several flights in a strong wind, the last and highest of which, of 12 minutes duration, was made after sunset. Two days later he rose to a height of 1,300 feet in a flight of 31 minutes' duration. On February 1st, at Denver, he was mobbed by a crowd of 30,000 people eager to see him fly. After three preliminary attempts, he finally left the ground and made two circuits of the course at Overland Park. The next day he made a 15-mile cross-country flight in a driving snow-storm. In starting, he ran his Farman biplane through snow three inches deep, and when he alighted, the planes and struts of the machine were in many places covered with snow, while Paulhan himself was suffering from the bitter cold. Previous to this long flight, he made a preliminary flight of 8 miles. On February 4th, after circling the Park successfully a dozen times, Paulhan twice was unsuccessful in starting in the distance at his disposal. The first time one of the wheels of his machine struck the fence and was knocked off, while the second time the machine crashed into the fence and was demolished. Paulhan was unhurt, but several spectators were injured.

As soon as he had finished flying at Los Angeles, Charles K. Hamilton went to San Diego, where he made a number of daring flights with his Curtiss biplane. On January 23d, after starting from the vast plain near the Hotel Del Coronado, Hamilton twice flew out over the ocean so far that he disappeared from view for ten minutes. When he re-appeared he came from a different direction. In the first flight he covered about 10 miles, and in the second one 15. The wind was blowing at times as high as 20 miles an hour. After circling upward to a height of about 800 feet, Hamilton stopped his motor and made a wonderful long straight glide to earth. This is probably a record performance, certainly the longest glide ever made in America. A week later, at Bakersfield, Cal., he made two excellent flights under difficult conditions. Starting from a half-mile track, he flew about the town and out over the desert and adjoining oil fields, finally landing successfully at the starting point. His mastery of the biplane seemed complete.

25Jan'10: Charles K. Hamilton flew a Curtiss from the Coronado Polo Grounds and made an emergency landing on North Island, the first airplane landing there.

23Jan'10: Chanute to Wilbur: "*...I did tell you in 1901 that the mechanism by which your surfaces were warped was original with yourselves...but it does not follow that it covers the general principle of warping or twisting wings...this being ancient...*

"*...I think I called your attention to* (Mouillard's) *method of twisting the rear of the wings. If the courts will decide...that you were the first to conceive the twisting of* the wings, so much the better for you, but my judgment is that you will be restricted to the particular method by which you do it. Therefore it was that I told you in New York that you were making a mistake by abstaining from prizewinning contests while public curiosity is...so keen, and by bringing suit to prevent others from doing so. This is...my opinion and I am afraid, my friend, that your usually sound judgment has been warped by the desire for great wealth.

"If, as I infer in your letter, my opinions form a grievance in your mind, I am sorry, but this brings me to say that I also have a little grievance against you.

"In your speech at the Boston dinner, January 12th, you began by saying that I 'turned up' at your shop in Dayton in 1901 and that you then invited me to your camp. This conveyed the impression that I thrust myself upon you at that time and it omitted to state that you were the first to write me, in 1900, asking for information...This, coming subsequently to some somewhat disparaging remarks concerning the helpfulness I may have been to you, attributed to you by a number of French papers...has grated upon me ever since...I hope that, in future, you will not give out the impression that I was first to seek your acquaintance, or pay me left-handed compliments, such as saying that 'sometimes an experienced person's advice was of great value to younger men'..."

29Jan'10: Wilbur to Chanute: "....Until confirmed by you, the interview in the New York _World_ of January 17 seemed incredible. We had never had the slightest ground for suspecting that when you repeatedly spoke to us in 1901 of the originality of our methods, you referred only to our methods of driving tacks, fastening wires, etc., and not the novelty of our general systems. Neither in 1901, nor in the five years following, did you in any way intimate to us that our general system of lateral control had long been part of the art, and, strangely enough, neither your books, addresses or articles, nor the writings of Lilienthal, Langley, Maxim, Hargrave, etc., made any mention whatever of the existence of such a system. Therefore it came to us with somewhat of a shock when you calmly announced that this system was already a feature of the art well known, and that you meant only the mechanical details when you referred to its novelty. If the idea was really old in the art, it is somewhat remarkable that a system so important that individual ownership of it is considered to threaten strangulation of the art was not considered worth mentioning then, nor embodied in any machine built prior to ours.

"The patent of Mouillard...does not even mention the control of the lateral balance...Unless something as yet unknown to anybody is brought to light...our warped judgment will probably continue to be confirmed by other judges as it was by Judge Hazel at Buffalo.

"As to inordinate desire for wealth, you are the only person acquainted with us who has ever made such an accusation. We believe that the...risks which we took, and the value of the service to the world, justified sufficient compensation to enable us to live modestly with enough surplus income to permit the devotion of our future time to scientific experimenting instead of business...We honestly think that our work of 1900-1906 has been and will be of value to the world, and that the world owes us something as inventors, regardless of whether we personally make Roman holidays for accident-loving crowds.

"You mention as a grievance that French papers....attributed to me some disparaging remarks concerning your helpfulness to us...But we also have had grievances extending as far back as 1902, and on one occasion several years ago we complained to you that an impression was being spread...that we were mere pupils and dependants of yours. You indignantly denied that you were responsible for it. When I went to France I found everywhere an impression that we had taken up aeronautical studies at your special instigation; that we obtained our first experience on one of your machines; that we were pupils of yours and put into material form a knowledge furnished by you; that you provided the funds; in short, that you furnished the science and money while we contributed a little mechanical skill, and that when success had been achieved you magnanimously stepped aside and permitted us to enjoy the rewards...

"...We have had too much real appreciation of your real helpfulness to us to wish to deny it...I cannot understand your objection to what I said at the Boston dinner...I certainly never had a thought of intimating either that you had or had not been the first to seek an acquaintance between us....I confess that I have found it most difficult to formulate a precise statement of what you contributed to our success. We on our part have been much hurt by your apparent backwardness in correcting mistaken impressions, but we have assumed that you too have found it difficult to substitute for the erroneous reports a really satisfactory precise statement of the truth. If such a statement could be prepared it would relieve a situation very painful to you and to us.

"...If anything can be done to straighten matters out to the satisfaction of both you and us, we are not only willing, but anxious to do...We have no wish to quarrel with a man toward whom we ought to preserve a feeling of gratitude..."

Coincidentally, Langley wrote: *"It has taken me, indeed, but a few years to pass through the period when an observer hears that his alleged observation was a mistake; the period when he is told that if it were true it would be useless; and the period when he is told that it is undoubtedly true, but that it has always been known."*

25Jan'10: Chanute to Spratt: *"...That which you saw may have been...an interview in the N.Y. Woodland of Jan. 17th concerning which Wilbur Wright took me to task, thus giving me an opportunity to partly free my mind concerning the mistakes which I believe he is making. He has greatly changed his attitude within the past three years..."*

2Feb'10: Chanute to Spratt: *"...He wrote me an angry letter...I answered reiterating the opinion and giving the basis on pages 97 and 106 of my book, as well as the Mouillard patent, and now have a violent letter from him in which he disputes my opinion, brings up various grievances and quite loses his temper. I will answer him in a few days, but the prospects are that we will have a row. I am reluctant to engage in this, but I think I am entitled to some consideration for such aid as I may have furnished."*

29Jan'10: Wilbur to Albert Zahm: *"...It seems to be conceded that we made the system of control, which we patented, a part of the art, and that all who are using it obtained it from us. The objections to our legal claims are technical, being based on old publications which did not lead to any result, and which are now of use only as a means of depriving us of legal rights to an invention which we independently conceived, worked into shape, and presented to the service of the world at a time when effort in that line was considered a foolish waste of time and money...there seems to be a general tendency to concede our moral right to the invention, but to deny that we have any right to expect any monetary pay..."*

30Jan'10: Bishop Wright's diary: *"Wilbur started to New York at 2:00 to attend the Paulhan trial, Tuesday."* (See Appendix, Jun'10)

Feb'10: The Smithsonian awards the *Langley Medal* to the Wrights.

On the 10th instant Wilbur and Orville Wright were presented with the Langley medals of the Smithsonian Institution by Chief Justice Fuller at Washington. Dr. Alexander Graham Bell and Senator Henry Cabot Lodge made brief addresses. Wilbur Wright announced that as soon as he and his brother get their American company under way, they expect to devote their time to research work in aviation. The two gold medals were designed by J. C. Champlain, a member of the French Academy, the reverse being from the seal of the institution, which was designed by St. Gaudens.

Secretary Walcott, Wilbur, Bell and Orville after presentation of the Langley Medal:

Chanute, the chairman of the committee of award, *did not attend this presentation* while Bell, a Smithsonian Regent and also a committee member, did.

On 27Jan'10 Chanute wrote Bell about the selection of the Wrights: *"...but the resolution says 'specially meritorious investigations,' and this seems to imply the presentation of a paper to make those investigations known to the world."*

He also wrote James Means: *"...as you probably know, Wright brothers are keeping their investigations secret and hope to make money out of the knowledge."*

Side-stepping his largely hidden agenda, on 4Feb'10 Bell replied that he perceived no distinction between 'investigations' and 'achievements' - and thus supported them.

Bell & Curtiss; 1910

28Apr'10, *The Youth's Companion:*

Langley's Aerodrome. — Dr. Alexander Graham Bell recently paid a high tribute to the work of the late Prof. S. P. Langley in laying the foundations on which the recent successes in aeronautics have been based. Langley stood almost alone among men of science in his faith that mechanical flight was practicable. The Wrights have said that his belief, combined with his standing in the world of science, was one of the influences which led to their early experimentation. Doctor Bell regards Langley's aerodrome as a good flying-machine, but it never had an opportunity to show what it could do because it was not successfully launched. Then public ridicule was heaped upon its designer, and he was discouraged.

1910-11: The Bells, accompanied by Casey Baldwin and Kathleen, his wife of two years, tour around-the-world. On return, Casey became Beinn Bhreagh's permanent manager at $2,500 a year ($120,000 today) plus a rent-free house - and thereafter lived an idyllic life, sailing and assisting Bell in his projects.

PAULHAN SERVED.

COUNSEL TO ARGUE CASE.

[BY DIRECT WIRE TO THE TIMES.]

NEW YORK, Jan. 4.—[Exclusive Dispatch.] Louis Paulhan, the noted French aviator has been served with an order to show cause on January 14 before the United States Circuit Court, why he should not be stopped from using the Farman and Bleriot aëroplanes. The order to show cause was issued at the instance of Williamson and Smith, lawyers, acting for the Wright brothers. Although the Frenchman was served he and his wife have left for Los Angeles.

On January 14 the lawyer must argue the question to show that his client has a legal right to the use of these machines. The fact that he left for Los Angeles does not interfere with the case, for it will not be necessary for him to be present expect by counsel.

Should the Wrights win their case on the final argument before the United States Court it means that the aviator would have to go back to France. The Farman and Bleriot machines are the only ones he uses and he would be left without anything that he might fly in.

This is the second time the Wrights have appeared in court, for earlier yesterday an action against Paulhan for infringement of patent was begun and the papers issued. If it is proved in this first case that the Wright patents are valid and that the defendant has been infringing on them, he will be compelled to reimburse the inventors for all profit made.

FRENCHMEN INCENSED.

DEFY THE INJUNCTION.

[ASSOCIATED PRESS NIGHT REPORT.]

PARIS, Jan. 4.—French aëroplanists believe the action of the Wright company is seeking an injunction against Louis Paulhan, who was served with papers on his arrival in New York, yesterday, is likely to deter foreigners from entering the international cup in the United States, this year, as the Wrights claim that practically every foreign machine, except the Voisin, infringes on their patents.

Henry Farman, whose machine Paulhan uses, said today:

"Although we do not employ the warping wing principle or any infringement of the Wright's patents, we anticipated some such action as the Wrights have taken. Before Paulhan left here, therefore, it was arranged that if any effort were made to get an injunction, the side planes used to modify the resistance of the air, should be removed, leaving the machine free from the objections which the Wrights have raised.

"Regardless of the justice of the Wrights' claim of infringement, however, we consider their action unsportsmanlike, as the machines were not sent to America to sell. At this stage of aëroplaning their action is distinctly harmful and certainly will tend to deter foreign aëroplanists from going to the United States."

COURT REFUSES TO ENJOIN PAULHAN.

[BY DIRECT WIRE TO THE TIMES.]

NEW YORK, Feb. 3.—[Exclusive Dispatch.] Judge Hand in the United States Circuit Court today declined to issue an order restraining Louis Paulhan, the French aviator, from making flights in Farman and Bleriot machines, b cause of alleged infringement of the Wright's patents.

He said that from the evidence produced he was inclined to favor the plaintiffs. The case hinges on the point of whether a flying machine rudder acts like a ship's rudder or whether it must be used in conjunction with the warping surfaces. Wilbur Wright proved his own best witness, showing the court how the airship rudder acts.

The court refused to order the defendants to give a bond covering any profits that might accrue to them pending final decision as to the merits of the Wright's patents.

Lieut. Lahm, who was instructed by Wilbur Wright in the use of the government aëroplane, made an affidavit for the opposing counsel as to the operation of the rudder but later asked to have it returned to make some changes.

Mr. Shearn refused to return the paper and Lieut. Lahm provided the plaintiffs with an affidavit of explanation. In his first statement he had opposed the Wright's version of the operation.

29Feb'10: Judge Hand grants a temporary injunction against Paulhan..."*security $25,000 for a month*" (quite a sum! Well over $1 million today).

252

Scientific American, 19Mar'10:

PAULHAN'S FLIGHT NEAR NEW YORK.

AVIATOR LOUIS PAULHAN succeeded last week in getting the bond which he is required to put up in case he flies reduced to $6,000 for one week, and on Friday, March 11th, he made two exhibition flights at the race track near Jamaica, L. I., before some 300 invited guests. Wilbur Wright and his lawyers were interested spectators, as it was thought that M. Paulhan would attempt to fly with his vertical rudder tied, or else without using the stabilizing flaps or ailerons. There was an 8 to 10-mile breeze blowing, and by starting against the wind Paulhan left the ground after a run of about 75 feet. He rose rapidly, and in the course of the two circuits of the track, made in 2:44, he reached a height of 75 to 100 feet. The biplane flew well and was not affected appreciably by the wind. Despite the sharp turns the machine did not tip very much in making them. It appeared to rock and pitch slightly, but was always under perfect control. The descent was made rapidly and at an angle of about 20 degrees. M. Paulhan made two more circuits in 2 minutes and 38 seconds.

Restrained from flying in the United States, Paulhan returns to France, commenting: *"I am most happy to be safe in France. I have finally escaped the nightmare of the past few weeks"*....branding the Wrights *"veritable birds of prey,"* and that Wilbur, arriving with lawyers at his Jamaica hangar, barely acknowledged his handshake and *"hurled himself on my machines."*

Note: In 1911 Paulhan became Curtiss's *first* foreign agent: *"...exclusive agent in France for the Curtiss aeroplane. Paulhan has purchased a Curtiss passenger-carrying hydro-aeroplane with dual control, which is to be delivered to him in Paris about January 15th, 1912."*

Thus began Curtiss's international business.

6Mar'10: New York *World:*

"FLY NO MORE IF
YOU DO NOT HIRE
WRIGHT'S WINGS"

"There seems to be much indignation in France about the attitude of Wilbur and Orville Wright over their patents. Some of the adverse opinion is real, some manufactured. On the other hand there is much public sentiment in the Wright's favor. This is voiced in La Liberte, an evening newspaper, which says: 'The Wrights ask only for royalty which certainly is due them. They have a perfect right to protect their patents. Sympathy should go out to them as inventors and pioneers, not as mere chauffeurs or mechanicians who learn to pilot aeroplanes.'"

This patent matter implodes and explodes throughout our story. One of the most balanced viewpoints is by *Fred Howard:* "Adjudicating the Wright basic patent, however, turned out to be a good deal more complicated than equating wing-warping with the use of ailerons. Judge Hazel's decision of January 3, 1910, had opened a Pandora's box of questions. What Wilbur and Orville had discovered in 1902 and patented in 1906 was the basic principle of flight - the only efficient way to control an airplane in flight...

"But is such a universal system, amounting almost to a basic physical principle, patentable? The U. S. Patent Office examiners thought so. Other men sincerely disagreed. A speculative approach to the problem is sometimes suggested: If the Wrights had invented the wheel, would they have been entitled to patent their invention? Or..If the Wrights had invented the wheel but had patented instead the axle, without which the wheel could not be set in useful motion over the ground, would they have been entitled to collect royalties from every man who used the wheel to his profit during the duration of their patent?

"...There never would be any legally satisfying answer to the question, but the battle in the courts would go on for seven long years, gathering size and momentum like a large snowball rolled down a snowy hillside, leaving exposed in its wake a dark and depressing collection of twigs, dead leaves, pebbles, and other detritus - or, in the case of Wright v. Curtiss, a sordid trail of hatred, invective, and lies that muddy the pages of aeronautical history to this day."

24Mar'10: The Wrights establish flight training at Montgomery, Alabama (now Maxwell Air Force Base). Its $250 ($11,000 today) cost included 5 minutes flying for each day of the ten-day course, plus service and maintenance instruction.

Their first student is Walter Brookins (1888-1953); a young Dayton man they'd known since he was four. Others were Arthur L. Welsh (1875-1912) of Washington, DC, and Arch Hoxsey (1884-1910) of Pasadena, CA. Other schools were at Augusta, GA. and Belmont Park, NY.

Welsh, Spencer C. Crane, Orville, Brookins, James Davis and Arch Hoxsey:

Wright pilots were either "*right-hand*" or "*left-hand.*" Those trained by the brothers sat on the right and learned to manipulate the wing-warping rudder lever (*split-handle lever*), located between the seats, with their left hand. They were "*left-hand pilots.*" When a left-hand pilot trained another, the student sat in the left seat and learned to use the lever with his right hand, a "*right-hand pilot.*"

Orville, a right-hand pilot, once flew as a left-hand pilot, sitting in the right seat manipulating the split-handle stick with his left hand: "*That was the wildest flight of my life...I never again attempted to pilot using the left-hand controls.*"

Thus confirming *Charles Grey's* assessment on the Wright's "*system of controls that could only be operated by jugglers...*(which) *killed most of its pilots...*"

6Apr1910: The Herring-Curtiss Co. was declared bankrupt. On 2Dec'10 the bankruptcy de-cree was issued; its causes: *1.* Over capitalization and lack of working capital. *2.* The Wright suit and its publicity, and necessity to guarantee purchasers against damages. *3.* The action by Herring charging fraud and embezzlement (unfounded by the court), with its publicity. *4.* Delay and inability to complete the Model G motors because of the litigation. *5.* The impossibility of borrowing money.

Note: In 1918 Herring resurrected the corporate shell, sued "*Glenn Curtiss and others*" for $5 million, charging the bankruptcy contrived to ruin him. In 1923 the courts ruled against him. He appealed, but died on July 17, 1926; Curtiss was *still* embroiled in this litigation at the time of his death (there is speculation that it was a factor in his death).

17Apr'10: The Boston <u>Post</u>: "...three successful aeroplane flights by A.M. Herring of New York and W. Starling Burgess of Marblehead at the Plum Island aviation field...this morning created a record...when the big machine started on each...of its three flights...20 miles an hour over the marshes...by its own power...the Herring-Burgess aeroplane...was the first machine in the world to leave...on skids...The crowd (including Norman Prince of Lafayette Escadrille fame) went wild..." *Scientific American, 19Mar, 1910 (photo):*

The Herring Biplane, showing novel stabilizing fins.

The Flying Lesson

Burgess Company and Curtis
Licensees under the Wright Patents

FLYING SCHOOL

Instructors: HARRY N. ATWOOD and W. STARLING BURGESS, both Wright graduates.

Lessons given on the Wright system, exclusively in the air.

Distance flown in first nine school days:

By instructors . . . . . . 683 miles
By pupils. . . . . 532 "

School opened May 30, 1911, at the Harvard Aviation Field, Squantum, Mass.

ADDRESS:

BURGESS COMPANY AND CURTIS
MARBLEHEAD, MASS.

Photo by *Boston Journal.*

Harry N. Atwood instructing a pupil in a Burgess-Wright Biplane before starting with passenger on the 137 mile Boston to New Hampshire flight, June 19, 1911.

While still with Herring-Curtiss, Herring secretly became involved with the *Burgess Company and Curtis, Inc.* of Marblehead, Massachusetts, founded by Starling Burgess and Greeley H. Curtis, telling them of his plans to make Herring-Burgess part of Herring-Curtiss...that "*he shortly expected to obtain for himself entire control of the Herring-Curtiss Co.*"

Herring's biplane, pusher-powered with a 25-hp Curtiss motor and a 4-blade propeller, had a rudder, forward elevator, and six or eight Voisin-like triangular shark fins on the top wing, designed to not infringe upon the Wright's patent. Also, lateral balance was by the hanging "aviator" swinging his body from side to side.

It was soon wrecked and Burgess-Curtis bought up Herring's contract ending a brief, ill-starred relationship.

In the fall of 1910 Burgess-Curtis became the _only_ American licensee under the Wright patents, letting it lapse two years later, on 31Dec'12

In 1916, as The Burgess Company, it was acquired by the wartime Curtiss organization. At war's end, in 1919, its factory mysteriously burned.

28Apr'10: Wilbur to Chanute: "*I have no answer to my last letter and fear that the frankness with which delicate subjects were treated may have blinded you to the real spirit and purpose of the letter. I had noted in the past few years a cooling of the intimate friendship which so long existed between us...My brother and I do not form many intimate friendships, and do not lightly give them up...We prize too highly the friendship which meant so much to us in the years of our early struggles to willingly see it worn away by uncorrected misunderstandings...If you will read the letter carefully I think you will see that the spirit is that of true friendship...*"

14May'10: Chanute to Wilbur: "*I am in bad health and threatened with nervous exhaustion...and am now to sail for Europe on the 17th...*"

"Your letter of April 28th was gratifying, for I own that I felt very much hurt by your letter of January 28th, which I thought both unduly angry and unfair as well as unjust.

"I have never given out the impression, either in writing or speech, that you had taken up aeronautics at my instance or were, as you put it, pupils of mine...

[Note: This paragraph contradicts an article in *L'Aerophile*, never seen by Wilbur, reporting on a talk Chanute gave to the French Aero Club on 2Apr'03. In detailing the work of the Wrights, he described their system of lateral control, which was, in effect, prior disclosure which should have nullified their German patent. Chanute closed by saying: "*...I have no other merit than that of taking up the experiments of Lilienthal...and of perfecting them as best I could, until others, more fortunate, take up my work in turn and carry it little by little to the perfect result. Progress in the sciences, and above all in aeronautics, is made, in fact, by successive stages...*"]

"The difference in opinion between us, i.e., whether the warping of the wings was in the nature of a discovery by yourselves, or had already been proposed and experimented by others, will have to be passed upon by others, but I have always said that you are entitled to immense credit for devising apparatus by which it has been reduced to successful practice.

"I hope, upon my return from Europe, that we will be able to resume our former relations."

"...But Chanute could see what the Wrights could not. They had taught the world to fly, but in so doing they had not simply invented a device, they had realised an ancient dream. Having unleashed it on the world, they could not then control it. Man would fly without paying the Wrights ten per cent." *Ivan Rendall*

May'10: The D-II *Canoe Machine*: another attempt by Curtiss to fly from water. In 1916, with a more powerful engine, he had limited success with canoes.

29May'10: Bishop Wright's diary: "...*Glenn Curtiss is reported to have flown from New York to Albany and back. An hour's rest on the way; 54 miles an hour.*"

A year earlier, in February, 1909, *Joseph Pulitzer* (1847-1911), publisher of <u>The St. Louis Dispatch</u> and New York's <u>World</u>, was the first American newspaper to emulate England's <u>Daily Mail</u> by offering a prize for long-distance flights, e.g., Bleriot's <u>Mail</u>-inspired channel flight.

It lay dormant until, on 23May'10, Curtiss wrote the sponsors: "*I have today sent my official notification to the Aero Club of America, announcing my intention to try for the <u>World</u>'s $10,000 prize for a flight between New York and Albany, and making an official entry for that prize...*

"*For over a year I have made exhaustive experiments with the object of perfecting a machine which would start from and alight on the water. It was my intention to give such a machine its first practical test by attempting to fly from Albany to New York over the*

Hudson River, with the hope of obtaining the <u>World</u>*'s most commendable Hudson-Fulton prize.*

"While my experiments have proved very successful, they have not been completed. It is my belief that the incentive offered by the <u>World</u> *to aviators and experimenters has been responsible for considerable activity similar to that in my own case.*

"If I should be successful in winning your prize, I would have only one regret; that there would be no further inducement for other aviators to make the same flight."

29May'10: With a machine christened the *Albany-to-NewYork-Flier* (an improved Golden Flier) or *Albany Flier*, or, as Curtiss preferred, the *Hudson Flier*, he won the prize (over $450,000 today) *and the* <u>Scientific American Trophy</u> for the third and *permanent* time by making a spectacular, 2-hour and 50-minute flight following the Hudson River 142 miles from Albany to New York City (not quite as Bishop Wright understood), stopping en route at Gill's Farm, Barnegat, near Poughkeepsie and at Inwood/Spuyten Duyvil (Note: The ability to take-off unaided was a major factor in this flight's success; see 292).

In preparation, he devised a crude flotation system: two pontoons lashed to the landing gear just above the wheels with a slanted planing board between to keep the aeroplane from nosing over. When testing he made the *first* water landing - in the shallows of Keuka Lake. The Flier's engine was a water-cooled 50 hp Curtiss V8.

Curtiss, ready to make the Albany-New York flight (note inner-tube life-preserver):

1910

The *World*: "*At times Mr. Curtiss's machine sped sixty miles an hour. All records in aviation were broken by this flight. Records for speed, for distance, and for both combined, went down before the steady wings of the Curtiss Aeroplane...*"

Approaching Storm King Mountain's 1340 foot crest, he climbed to 2000 feet. Just past, the aeroplane abruptly lurched forward and sidewise, losing 100 feet of altitude in a moment and nearly tumbling him out.

Watchers on the ground were frantic with excitement. Some shouted "*Go it, old boy!....She's bucking like a three-year-old.*"

Pushing the forward control, he managed to regain a semblance of control and continued on.

He said "*it was the worst plunge I ever got in an aeroplane...My heart was in my mouth. I thought it was all over...*" Later he recalled Storm King as "*the place I first learned that air went up and down as well as sideways.*"

Fiercely competing with the *World*, the Sunday flight was paced by *The New York Times*'s special train, and by the time of his noon arrival every New Yorker was straining to see him.

30May'10: *The New York Times*: "*Glenn H. Curtiss, in his aeroplane, flew down the Hudson Valley yesterday morning...The flying machine, floating above the New Jersey cliffs and the tall buildings of Manhattan, passed Forty-second Street at 11:51 o'clock and after encircling Liberty Island landed on Governor's Island at the stroke of 12.*

"*...Yesterday's flight was seen by excited crowds all along the line, and it was a most inspiring sight. Man has*

259

now conquered the air. As Orville Wright has said, aeroplaning is as yet only a sport, though the utility of the new machine in warfare is no longer doubted...But this much having been accomplished, the development of the airship practically and commercially and the growth of its usefulness as a carrier are only matters of time. For the present, however, the flight of Curtiss is the uppermost topic in aeronautics. It was a splendid feat, successfully accomplished with wonderful courage and skill, and it seems to make human flying more a reality than hitherto it has been."

31May'10: At a banquet at the Astor Hotel, Curtiss said: "*I carefully planned everything about the flight in advance except the possibility of making a speech.*"

As to the offensive capabilities of airpower, Curtiss told General Walter Howe: "*My aeroplane could have carried 300 to 500 pounds of excess weight composed of an air gun and picric bombs. I could have scattered destruction all along...between Albany and New York City.*" (he demonstrated this at Coronado in 1912)

This, the *"The Flight That Made Aviation In America,"* marked the birth of practical aviation in the United States. It was the *first* river flight, the *first* city-to-city flight, and the longest flight in American history. Curtiss was acclaimed *"King of The Air."*

"On the way to Times Square, Curtiss called at City Hall to deliver a letter of greeting from the mayor of Albany to the mayor of New York. It was a historic act. Dated May 29, 1910, that letter inaugurated the United States Air Mail Service."   *Owen Lieberg*

29May'10: President William H. Taft to the <u>World</u>: "*It seems that the wonders of aviation will never cease. I hesitate to say that the performance of Mr. Curtiss makes an epoch, because tomorrow we may hear that some man has flown from New York to St. Louis.*"

TO CURTISS BIG PRIZE.

Ten Thousand Goes to Aviator.

Sky Pilot Flies from Albany to New York City in Two and Half Hours.

Trip Along Over the Hudson Witnessed by Thousands, Who Wildly Cheer.

But One Landing Made in Journey of Hundred and Thirty-seven Miles.

[ASSOCIATED PRESS NIGHT REPORT.]

WASHINGTON, May 29.—[Exclusive Dispatch.] The President authorizes the following:

"I am intensely interested in what Mr. Curtiss has done. It seems that the wonders of aviation will never cease. I would hesitate to say that the performance of Mr. Curtiss is epoch-making, because tomorrow we may hear that some man has flown from New York to St. Louis.

"Mr. Wright told me at the time the ten-mile flight from Ft. Myer was made that the chief difficulty was in flying over unknown territory. Mr. Curtiss seems to have surmounted this and I am glad he has. His flight will live long in our memories as having been the greatest.

[Signed]

"WILLIAM H. TAFT."

NEW YORK, May 29.—Glenn H. Curtiss flew from Albany to New York City in an aëroplane today, winning the $10,000 prize offered by the New York World.

He covered the distance, 137 miles, in 2h. 32m. and came to earth as calmly and as lightly as a pigeon.

His average speed for the distance—54.06 miles an hour—surpasses any other record made by aëroplanes in long-distance flights, and, in its entirety, his feat perhaps eclipses anything man has accomplished in a heavier-than-air machine.

The start was made from Albany at 7:03 this morning under weather conditions as nearly perfect as the most fastidious aviator could demand.

One hour and twenty-three minutes later he had made his stopping place near Poughkeepsie, where there was an hour's intermission. Resuming his flight at 9:26, he sped southward and landed within the boundary of Manhattan Island at 10:35.

Only 100 yards north of the point on which his craft settled stretched Spuytenduyvil Creek, separating Manhattan Island and the mainland. Had he failed to cross this, his flight could have been in vain, but, as he swept over it, the prize was his. Thence to Governor's Island, his task was but the concluding lap of a race already won.

FLIGHTS COMPARED.

Paulhan's flight from London to Manchester—186 miles—exceeded the Curtiss feat of today in distance, but not in speed and danger. The Frenchman's average was 44.3 miles an hour, and below him lay English meadow land. Curtiss followed the winding course of the historic Hudson, with jutting headlands, wooded slopes and treacherous palisades. He swung high over the great bridge at Poughkeepsie, dipped at times within fifty feet of the river's broad surface and jockeyed like a falcon at the turns.

Only once did his craft show signs of rebellion. This was off Storm King, near West Point, when, at a height of nearly 1000 feet, a treacherous gust struck his planes. The machine dropped forty feet and tilted perilously, but Curtiss kept his head and by adroit manipulation restored the equilibrium of the machine.

Curtiss was up before dawn today, hesitant despite favorable weather conditions. But with eyes and brain cleared of the cobwebs of sleep, he went with his mechanics and a handful of spectators to Van Rensselaer Island, in the Hudson, three miles south of Albany, where he was to start.

Waiting at the river brink was a special train for Mrs. Curtiss and her party. From the train they could not see the actual start, but those on the island witnessed a remarkable scene.

NO PRELIMINARIES.

Curtiss arose from the ground like a rocket. There were no preliminary maneuvers; there was no trial flight. The aëroplane ran hurriedly over the surface of the island and darted straight for its goal, turning once for a moment to the west, so that Curtiss might comply with the terms of the competition under which he was flying and technically cross the Albany city line.

When the aëroplane reached a height estimated at 500 feet, it seemed for a moment to hold that level and then to rise higher. Curtiss was flying at a height which he had never attempted before. In seven minutes, he had been lost to view.

When the aëroplane was wheeled from beneath its canvas covering, shortly before 7 a.m., the sky was perfectly clear and what little wind was stirring blew from the north—a direction favorable to Curtiss—at four miles an hour.

With the signal that Curtiss was off, the special train of five cars and a locomotive gathered impetus and sought to follow. But so quickly had he flown that for twenty-one miles the locomotive, though running nearly a mile a minute, was unable to catch up.

At 7:26 a.m., however, the train came abreast of the aëroplane, and thence to New York City those on board kept the aviator in sight, but as he did not have to reckon with curves, track switches and reduced speed through towns, the man above kept a substantial lead.

FLIES HIGH.

Swiftly, town and countryside reeled by. Catskill was passed at 7:41, with the aëroplane a thousand feet above the Hudson.

At 8:05 Curtiss was still flying high and veering well toward the west bank of the river.

At 8:06, sixty-three minutes after the start, he soared past Rhinecliff ferry, fifty-four miles from Albany. Here there is a bend in the river, and Curtiss turned again to the west, passing overland to shorten his course.

Staatsburg marked the sixtieth mile point, and he had covered this distance in sixty-nine minutes.

With Staatsburg behind, the giant bridge spanning the Hudson at Poughkeepsie loomed ahead. The bridge itself is 212 feet high, but Curtiss topped it by 300 feet.

Then he turned westward and with the precision of a bird settled softly in the field three miles south of Poughkeepsie, at 8:26. He had flown the 74 miles from Albany in 83 minutes.

Though the landing place, known as Gill Meadow, had previously been selected, Curtiss was not expected this morning because of last week's postponements, and there was no gasoline or oil awaiting him. But, fortunately, two automobile tourists happened by and were eager to supply him.

His tanks had been filled with ten gallons of gasoline before he left Albany. Examinations showed three gallons remained, enough to have carried him to West Point. Curtiss was taking no chances and refilled his tank.

POUGHKEEPSIE CHEERS.

Fire alarm bells were rung as the aviator neared Poughkeepsie, but his progress was so rapid that few people had a chance to see him pass. On the Gill meadows a little group sighted him coming and sent up a cheer.

Coming down gracefully, his machine struck a grassy knoll, trundled along for thirty or forty feet, then came to a stop.

The special train, meanwhile, brought Mrs. Curtiss, who rushed from the car and hurried to her husband's side. She greeted him jubilantly, while the crowd cheered again.

With tanks refilled and with every wire and screw tested, Curtiss took his seat for the final dash to New York.

In a moment more the craft was again over the Hudson, and Curtiss turned his course south and was lost to view.

Exactly one hour was consumed at Poughkeepsie, for he arrived at 8:26, and departed at 9:26.

Curtiss passed the military academy at West Point at 10:02. Officers and cadets alike sent up a cheer after the aviator.

At Storm King the most sensational incident of the trip occurred. Curtiss was flying high at this point—1000 feet, he estimates—when a shifty wind caused the machine to drop and tilt. Never once losing control, he continued southward, passing in turn Peekskill, Ossinning and Dobb's Ferry.

Yonkers was passed at 10:30, at a height of 300 or 400 feet. Here Curtiss got his first glimpse of the Metropolitan tower. It loomed far ahead like a giant needle, and Curtiss knew he was nearing the upper limits of New York City.

NEARING GOAL.

Out of the haze that lay in the bend of the river at Yonkers he shot into the view of thousands who were awaiting his coming along the upper reaches of Riverside Drive and on roofs of big apartment houses in Washington Heights. A mere speck at first, the little aëroplane looked like a full flyer with wings on the gale. The motor was chugging steadily and sending the craft along at fifty miles an hour.

Rounding the big jutting nose of Alpine, on the Jersey shore, opposite Yonkers, Curtiss drove his machine across the river toward the east side of the stream and hugged the New York shore.

The crowds along the shore cheered and waved hats and handkerchiefs and the sharp, shrill screeches of the whistles of small pleasure craft joined with the more sonorous ones of the large craft in a hearty welcome.

On past Riverdale, flying straight as an arrow, came the aëroplane. It was abreast New York City and a few miles from the upper end of Manhattan Island.

Barring accident, it now seemed Curtiss must win the $10,000 prize; but suddenly, when he had reached a point midway between Spuytenduvil Creek, which separates Manhattan Island from the Bronx and Washington Point, the speed of the machine slackened perceptibly and it dropped until it seemed that it would touch the water. Then it came about prettily, pointing upward, and headed up the river. The spectators were nonplussed. Many of them believed that the machinery had gone wrong and that Curtiss had lost his race.

But Curtiss waved his hand assuringly. While passing Spuytenduvil he had seen, half a mile inland, a broad expanse of greensward, the upper end of Manhattan Island. To win the prize it was necessary only to land in Manhattan proper, and here was the chance without risk of further flight to Governor's Island or the Battery, thirteen miles away.

END OF TRIP.

Therefore, when he again came abreast of the mouth of the creek after his puzzling turn backward, Curtiss threw his steering wheel about sharply, glided above a railroad drawbridge and floated lazily inland, with the propellor barely turning. He maneuvered carefully, then alighted without mishap on the stretch of green which had caught his eye.

He had flown from Albany to Manhattan in two hours and 32 minutes, and the $10,000 was his.

Jumping lightly from his machine, the aviator inspected his motor, and, finding everything intact, sought a telephone and informed The World that he had arrived and claimed the prize.

Although he had won, weather and conditions were so propitious and he was feeling so gratified at success that Curtiss decided to give the city another view of his machine, and at 11.37 a.m. he shot away again for Governor's Island. It was during this part of his trip that he received the merriest greeting. He came down the river at an elevation of 200 feet.

NEWS SPREADS RAPIDLY.

News of his coming spread rapidly throughout the city. In police courts, magistrates heard and quickly disposed of cases, and hundreds rushed to the water front and tops of buildings became black with humanity. The greatest jam was at the Battery.

Down the river and up the bay he sailed as lightly and steadily as a swallow. Nearing Governor's Island, he began to descend, while cheers floated up from those who watched his approach. He landed easily on a stretch of the new made land within forty yards of the shed in which the aëroplanes were housed during the recent aviation meet.

Dismounting from his craft, soldiers volunteered to push it into the shed, while Curtiss received congratulations from Gen. Howe, commander of the Department of the East, and other officers. Refreshments were served in Corbin Hall, and Curtiss briefly related his experiences.

Mrs. Curtiss, who had arrived in New York on a special train, joined her husband as Curtiss was preparing to take the ferry for New York. He kissed her while the crowd cheered.

GETS BIG CHECK.

Half an hour later, Curtiss was in the World office, where a check for $10,000 was handed him.

The terms of the competition prescribed the flight must be the full distance from New York to Albany. It was optional to start from either end and Curtiss would have preferred to have started from New York, but if there is a worse aërodrome than Manhattan Island, spiked with skyscrapers and the water front the harbor clustered with shipping and crosscut by deflecting wind, he would like to have it shown.

Aëronauts and aviators tonight were unanimous that Curtiss had performed the most wonderful feat in the air the world has ever seen.

Curtiss was dressed for the trip in wading boots and sweater. His aëroplane carried pontoons, or floats, to prevent it sinking in case of a fall into the river. The pontoons are his own invention. A fifty horse power motor of his own make propels the craft, which, with the aviator in its seat, weighs 1000 pounds.

Curtiss is not a talkative man and his secretary explained the details of the trip. Curtiss merely smiled and nodded approval, now and then adding a few descriptive phrases first hand.

In winning the World prize today, Curtiss incidentally captured the Scientific American cup for the longest flight in America for a heavier-than-air machine. He had previously won two legs on the trophy and today's performance makes it his.

Curtiss is 32 years old, and was born at Hammondsport, N. Y.

CURTISS LANDING AT GOVERNOR'S ISLAND — WINNING THE WORLD'S $10.000 PRIZE MAY 29, 1910.

Curtiss completed this historic flight less than a year after his triumph at Reims:

Pulitzer's New York *World* and St. Louis *Post-Dispatch* promptly offered a prize of *$30,000* for a flight between those two cities in 100 consecutive hours.

Not be outdone, The New York Times and Chicago *Evening Post* offered a prize of *$25,000* for a flight in one week's time from Chicago to New York (handsome prizes indeed, well over a *million* dollars each today).

30May'10: *The New York Times* used a record *six* pages to tell the story, and on the 31st it quoted Curtiss: "*Some day soon aeroplanes will start from the decks of battleships and from the water, and I am not sure but what they could be launched from a battleship going at top speed even now. I also believe that a dozen aeroplanes, very similar to the machines of today, could annihilate a fleet of battleships of one thousand times their value, not to mention the havoc which might be wrought to a fortress or seaport city near which a ship could launch these flying machines...*"

30Jun'10: In a Hammondsport demonstration Curtiss pioneered aerial bombing for the Army, Navy and New York *World*. Although results did not impress the military, he later stated in *Aeronautics*: "*...that in order to accurately drop bombs in actual warfare, one man would have to be carried for the purpose of dropping the bombs, since it was impossible for the pilot to make accurate calculations of angle and speed.*"

And in 1921 General *William* (Billy) *Lendrum Mitchell* (1879-1936) got the War Department to tow the captured submarine *U-117*, the German light cruiser *Frankfort* and the "unsinkable" battleship, *Ostfriesland,* 100 miles off the Virginia Capes. Then Air Service Martin bombers sank the U-boat in 16 minutes; 14 bombs sank the *Frankfort* in 30 minutes; and seven 2,000-pound bombs sank the *Ostfriesland* in 21-1/2 minutes.

And in 1924, after touring the Pacific and seeing first-hand Japan's military establishment - *and possibly remembering a (today) long-forgotten 1915 incident, as reported in the* Los Angeles Times, *18 & 19April, 1915: "All signs for a permanent base for Mikado's Navy* (an ideal opportunity to secure a strategic military site with the Panama Canal just opened and Mexico convulsed in revolution)...*the water already mined, the Japanese naval forces which have occupied Turtle Bay, Lower California* (the best anchorage between Cabo San Lucas and San Diego), *400 miles below San Diego, seems to be preparing to stay..."* and the next day: "...*dispatches were received from Washington ...indicating that the fleet of Japanese war vessels...and the 4,000 soldiers...in Turtle Bay had abruptly quitted those waters before the arrival of the United States cruiser New Orleans..."* - he perceived its war-like, expansionist intentions.

Seventeen years before Pearl Harbor (and 31 years *after* Curtiss's prediction) - Mitchell predicted virtually everything except the date: *attacking planes from carriers at 7:30 AM* ...and the following attack on Manila's Clark Field within 2 hours!

13-18Jun'10: The Wrights exhibition team, managed by Roy Knabenshue, had its first flying exhibition at the Indianapolis Speedway. The team included Brookins, Ralph Johnstone (1886-1910), Frank Coffyn, Arch Hoxsey, Clifford Harmon and Phil Parmalee. Hoxsey and Johnstone,*"The Star Dust Twins"* or *"The Heavenly Twins,"* became the team's most popular flyers.

Also, this event marked Lincoln Beachey's first attempt at exhibition flying; a bit of a disaster when he couldn't get airborne and wrecked his Bleriot-like monoplane.

2Jun'10: *Charles Stewart Rolls* (1877-1910, of Rolls-Royce) crosses the Channel non-stop and round-trip in a Wright.

13Jun'10: Charles K. Hamilton (1881-1914), Curtiss's *first* exhibition aviator, made America's longest flight: 149 miles, New York-Philadelphia and return, in 3-hours 27-minutes, win-

Captain C. S. Rolls Directing Final Preparations for His Flight

ning the $10,000 prize of *The New York Times* and Philadelphia *Public Ledger*.

Red-haired with large ears, "*the diminutive Yale aeroplanist*" usually had the smell of alcohol about him. Earlier he'd been a daring parachutist with one special stunt: cutting loose from a balloon and opening and discarding another and another chute until he reached the ground with his *fifth* one.

GREAT TRIUMPH.

REMARKABLE AIR TRIP IS MADE BY HAMILTON.

Flies from New York to Philadelphia and Return—Delivers Letters Exchanged by Mayors and Governors. Breaks Cross-Country Records.

[ASSOCIATED PRESS NIGHT REPORT.]

NEW YORK, June 13.—Charles K. Hamilton rose in his aëroplane from Governor's Island this morning and sped without a break, eighty-eight miles to Philadelphia, in a remarkable cross-country flight, under the auspices of the New York Times and the Philadelphia Public Ledger. He made the trip in one hour and fifty-one minutes, leaving Governor's Island at 7:35, and landing at Philadelphia at 9:26.

Arriving at Aviation Field, he delivered letters from Gov. Hughes and Mayor Gaynor to Gov. Stuart and Mayor Reyburn, accepted messages of congratulations from them to bear in

Jersey swamp was the second mishap of the kind during the day, but a call to Governor's Island brought a new propeller with a new set of spark plugs and the aviator was able to finish within twelve hours, although twenty-four hours were allowed in the terms of his contract.

FIRST FAST AERIAL MAIL.

Carrying, as he did, letters between the two cities, Hamilton created the first fast mail by the air route to Philadelphia and return and demonstrated that an aëroplane can deliver mail from one city to another with the punctuality of government service.

8Mar'10, Cairo: Frenchwoman *Baroness Raymonde de la Roche* became the *first* licensed woman aviator. On 22Oct'09 she was the *first* woman to fly - in a Voisin at Chalons, France. She was killed at Reims on 8Jul'10.

15Jun'10: New York *Evening Mail*: "*The United States Circuit Court of Appeals today has dissolved the injunction...restraining the Herring-Curtiss Company from manufacturing aeroplanes on the ground that they were infringing the patents of the Wrights.*

"The decision is greeted by aviation experts throughout the world as a severe blow to the group of financiers who are supporting the Wright's attempt to form a so-called 'Air Trust.' The Wrights intend to carry the case to the Court of Highest Instance."

During the summer of 1910 Rochester's *Blanche Stuart Scott* (1886-1970), just famous for being the *first* woman to drive cross-country New York-San Francisco in a Willys Overland, finally persuaded Curtiss to teach her to fly.

Soloing on 2Sep'10 made her *America's first aviatrix.*

Then, joining the Curtiss Exhibition Team at the Chicago Meet, she said: *"I do not intend to get myself killed by foolish stunts."*

She became known as *"The Tomboy of the Air."*

In 1916 she retired from stunt flying and test piloting.

30Jul'10: *Scientific American*: *"Some details of Capt. Rolls' death are reported in newspapers...Rising to a height of about 100 feet, he turned and started to descend against the wind in one of those downward swoops which have made the flights of Paulhan, Brookins and Hamilton so successful. In such a maneuver the front elevators are called upon to sustain a pressure which may well be greater than that for which they are designed. In Roll's case it is said that the strain proved too much and that the (elevator) snapped from its supports. This theory of death is plausible, although it seems to us that the Wright machine in America, at least, is so staunchly constructed that such an accident is remote..."*

1Jul'10: Wilbur to *Scientific American*: *"The Scientific American of June 25th contains an editorial which says: 'Curtiss was using hinged wing tips in his earlier machines, with which he made public flights antedating the open flights of the Wrights.'*

Before his death Rolls, center, rode between Horace Short and Orville, with Wilbur in the back seat of a Rolls-Royce:

Cartoon by John T. McCutcheon, in the Chicago Tribune, on the Death of Capt. C. S. Rolls, the English Aviator

"The use of the catch expression 'open flights' is calculated to give to the general reader an entirely false impression regarding the real facts. The general construction of the Wright machines, and the method of control which has now become so widely copied, was well known to aviators in general and to Mr. Curtiss in particular long before he began building aeroplane....The American patent was published in 1906. The <u>Scientific American</u> of April 7th, 1906, published numerous pictures of Wright machines, and after mentioning the horizontal front rudder, says 'There may also be other patentable improvements for maintaining the traverse stability, such as a method of twisting the planes slightly at either end.' In 1907 Dr. Bell organized the Aerial Experiment Association, with Lieut. Selfridge as secretary, and Mr. Curtiss as chief of construction. Lieut. Selfridge wrote...asking for

information regarding the construction of gliders...At first only the general form of the Wright machine was copied...by Curtiss, but soon the adjustable tips began to appear, their necessity having become apparent. Judge Hazel was aware of these facts...In conclusion it should be stated that the expression 'open flights'...is misleading...in 1904 and 1905 we were flying...in a field alongside the main wagon road and electric trolley line from Dayton to Springfield, and hundreds of travelers and inhabitants saw the machine in flight. Anyone who wished could look. We merely did not advertise the flights in the newspapers." Note: Due to the Wrights careful timing of flights to coincide with the trolley's absence, *"hundreds"* may be misleading.

1910: In the Smithsonian's *Annual Report* there was a statement – incorrectly attributed to Wilbur - about Langley which was out-of-context and apparently to mislead; and a second, seemingly evasive, as to the Wright's offer to restore and present the *1903 Flyer* to the institution. These and subsequent actions tended to keep the Wrights (Orville after Wilbur's death) wary of relations with the institution.

11Jul1910, Atlantic City: Curtiss won a $5,000 prize as he *"set an American record for a fifty-mile flight in an aeroplane this afternoon by covering a half hundred measured miles in five-mile laps along the beach in 1h. 14m. 59s..."*

The next day it was reported that: *"Curtiss Proves Efficacy of Aeroplane in Warfare...tossed oranges and mimic bombs within three feet of the decks of the yacht...used in place of a battleship, during a sham battle...experts agreed that the experiments showed that a fleet of aeroplanes armed with bombs could wreck any warship before guns could be trained on them...Curtiss...dropped oranges...making...every shot a 'hit'..."*

12Aug'10: The Willard-Curtiss *Banshee Express*, an evolution of the Golden Flier with the 50-hp V8 engine. It was the *first* American usage of trailing edge ailerons (four, one for each wing), operating up and down, instead of Curtiss's usual mid-wing planes.

19Aug'10: Following a successful Pittsburgh exhibition, Curtiss organized an *"International Aviation Contest"* at the *"old Sheepshead Bay racetrack,"* Brooklyn. Curtiss's team of James C. "Bud" Mars, *"The Curtiss Daredevil,"* Willard, Eugene Ely, Jack McCurdy and Curtiss, were all in the air at the same time, then quite a feat.

There was a special exhibition: "With Lt. Jacob E. Fickel clutching the rifle...the plane took off. After gaining an altitude of three hundred feet, it circled the target...in the center-field of the race track. Four times, Fickel aimed and squeezed the trigger. Two of the four shots were bulls-eyes; the other two, near misses. The audience was thrilled. Perhaps there were some in the grandstand, too, who sensed the beginning of things to come."
Aaron Norman

Arch. Hoxsey, the Pasadena Beau Brummel of Aviators, at the Wheel of His Wright Biplane and in Flight at Asbury Park, N. Y.

PASADENAN CUTS HIS INITIALS WITH AIRSHIP

ASBURY PARK, N. J., Aug. 20.—The citizens of Asbury Park awoke this morning to find that while they slept two of the Wright aviators had accomplished a record feat of aeroplaning, having made long midnight flights by the light of the moon, the first night flights on record.

With a few friends and a score of summer colonists as spectators, Arch Hoxsey and Ralph Johnstone took out the new Wright machine for spins of about fifteen minutes each.

Johnstone went up first, and his flight was comparatively tame. Then Hoxsey started out for a moonlight skylark. He cut figure eights, roller coasted, darted upward in a spurt of 500 feet toward the moon and waved to the people down below from a height of 100 feet. When he tired of that he cut grapvines and what looked to be his initials.

Hoxsey a Pasadenan

Archie Hoxsey, star aviator of the Wright Brothers' camp, who in the wee hours of yesterday morning set the world thrilling in a wonderful moonlight flight at Asbury Park, N. J., is a Pasadena boy, and a former chauffeur for Charles Gates, son of John W. Gates, the multimillionaire. His wonderful flight has more than ever determined his friends here to bring him to California to fly and yesterday a shower of messages were sent the aviator congratulating him on his performance and urging him to come to Southern California to fly during the coming winter.

During the past ten days at Asbury Park, Hoxsey has arisen from the position of an obscure chauffeur to the position of one of the greatest aviators in the world. On several occasions he has risen in a Wright machine to a height of over 2000 feet and glided down, thrilling the entire crowd at the park by his daring. He has on occasion written his name in the air with his craft and showed his perfect control at all times.

11 Aug'10:
Leslie's Weekly,
typical of several
such meets:

Both Johnstone and Hoxsey made night flights at Asbury Park on August 19th. It was curious to see their Wright biplane, patterned for brief seconds against the brightness of a full moon, or flitting mysteriously in the mellow light across the Milky Way. Hoxsey claimed to have reached a height of 3,458 feet, but since night estimates are difficult to make accurately his claim must be taken with some reservation.

Those of the thousands who journeyed down to the old Sheepshead Bay racetrack on August 20th to see the opening of the air carnival and departed before the close missed the best thing at the meet. Four aeroplanes went whizzing and whirring all about the course at the same time just before 7 o'clock, and the spectators were lost in wonderment. The machines in the air were guided by Curtiss, Ely, Mars, and McCurdy.

To James McCurdy belongs the distinction of having first communicated by wireless from an aeroplane with a land station. On August 27th he sent the following message: Over Barren lsland, 6:54 P. M.

H. M. Horton: Another chapter in aerial achievement is recorded in the sending of this wireless message from an aeroplane in flight.   McCurdy.

Horton was the wireless operator on the roof of the Sheepshead Bay race-track grand stand. Horton had rigged up an ingenious sending apparatus, which was affixed to the steering wheel of an aeroplane. The energy was derived from a vest-pocket battery. The aerial was fifty feet of wire held straight by a lead weight, the whole trailing after the machine.

10Sep'10, *Scientific American (above):*

At the recent aviation meet held in Asbury Park last week the first public test was made of the new Wright biplane built for gusty weather. The machine is very similar to the standard type, practically the only change being in the fact that the horizontal rudder in front is left off. In the place of this, the warpable tail surface serves to control the motion up and down. The advantage of this arrangement is that there is nothing in the fore part of the machine to be caught by sudden puffs of wind. As heretofore constructed, wind striking the front horizontal rudder acted with a powerful leverage on the machine, due to the distance of the rudder in advance of the main planes. No such effect is experienced with the horizontal rudder at the rear of the apparatus. The air that passes through the machine is so cut up by the propellers that there is no opportunity for a sudden puff of wind to reach the rudders at the rear. The forward small vertical planes have been preserved in the new machine and are mounted in the framework of the skids. As the entire work of controlling the aeroplane vertically falls upon the rear horizontal plane, the latter is allowed a greater upward or downward curvature than heretofore. In next week's issue of the SCIENTIFIC AMERICAN a photograph and complete description of this machine will be published.

27Aug'10, *Scientific American*:

20Aug'10, *Scientific American:* "*Twelve months ago aviators were congratulating themselves that such rapid progress was being made in the art of flying with, relatively, so few disasters. During the past few weeks...however, there has been a deplorable increase in...accidents, a large proportion of which has been fatal...The beginner should remember that such a veteran as Capt. Baldwin spent many days of experiment in running his machine over the ground and becoming familiar with it before making an attempt at...flight.*"

The Wright Brothers   The Wrong Brothers

"*AERONAUTICS - The opening day of the meet at Asbury Park - August 10th - was marred by an accident to Walter Brookins* (Wright)*...not seriously injured, his chief disfigurement being that sustained by most aviators sooner or later...a broken nose...On the same day upon which Brookins was injured, a German aviator named Heim fell from a height of over 200 feet...using a Wright biplane...gravely injured...doubt as to whether he will recover.*"

In the same article are references of a French Antoinette crash, with no injuries, and of another Frenchman, apparently unscathed after wrecking his machine while in a cross-country series of flights that: "*demonstrated the practiability of the aeroplane as a rapid means of transportation. No doubt, within a couple of months, we shall have a similar demonstration in America.*"

There were an inordinate number of accidents:

Scientific American, 30Jul'10: "*An aviator named Ehrmann, while making a cross country flight in Spain, was struck by lightning. The machine fell blazing to the ground. The inventor escaped uninjured...At Mineola, L.I., recently Joseph Stevenson was nearly killed in a biplane built by Brauner of the Curtiss type. Although there was some evidence that the machine was wrecked because of instability, the chances are that the accident was largely due to the aviator's lack of skill...Some details of Capt. Roll's death are reported...It seems that Rolls was taking part in a competition for a prize of $1,250 for the nearest landing to a mark...*

" *Scientific American*, 10Sep'10: "*M. Legagneux was seriously hurt at Harve on August 27th while competing for a total distance prize. His machine struck a post, fell to the ground, and buried him under it...A Dutch aeronaut, Van Masdyk, while attempting a cross-country flight near Arnheim, Netherlands, on August 27th, came to a violent end. The motor of the aeroplane suddenly stopped, and the machine fell to the ground...*"

Scientific American, 5Nov'10: "*Lieut. Saglietti fell with a military biplane with which he was maneuvering on October 22nd, and was instantly killed...On Wednesday, October 26th, Fernand Blanchard lost his life in falling in a monoplane at Issy-les-Monlineaux, near Paris, after a successful flight from Bourges...Capt. Madiot, a military aviator, fell 240 feet on October 23rd in a Breguet biplane near Douai and was killed. The cause of the accident is unknown...On October 19th, Moisant wrecked the Bleriot monoplane which he brought to this country to compete in the events at Belmont Park. He made three laps of the Belmont field, when the machine plunged down head first, a mass of wreckage. Moisant crawled out uninjured. Moisant explained that he was trying to open his oil valve, and in so doing, lost control...Fred G. Eells, who has been doing some flying among the Hammondsport hills...in getting away over the rough ground...broke a controller wire, and dropped into a wheat field...collided with a fence post and wrecked his machine; fortunately, he was uninjured...To the list of fatalities must be added the names of two German aviators: At Muelhausen, Plochmann fell from a height of 150 feet, and died a few hours later in the hospital. He was flying in a biplane, and the cause of the accident is unknown. The second accident occurred at Welle, a short distance from Metz. Haas, the victim, was flying a German Wright biplane. The motor suddenly stopped, and he dropped from a height of 500 feet.*"

Sep'10: The *Curtiss Exhibition Company* was incorporated "*for the purpose of giving flight exhibitions,*" with Jerome S. Fanciulli as general manager (to resign in November 1912, at the end of the epic exhibition period, following a money disagreement).

Fanciulli said that in three years the exhibition company made over $1 million (around $50 million today), though Curtiss thought it nearer $400,000 ($19 million), *earnings which funded Curtiss's heavy court bonds and legal costs of the patent fight with the Wrights.*

The basis on which pilots leased (for a percentage of net proceeds) aeroplanes was determined by their proficiency. As Curtiss explained: "*The better class of aviators, and those who were less likely to have smash-ups, received a better percentage of receipts.*" Earnings ranged from a beginner's take of 25-percent, to 50-percent or better.

Initial Curtiss aviators were McCurdy, Ely, Hugh Robinson, James Ward, Lincoln Beachey and Charles Witmer.

In August, 1911, at Winona Lake, Indiana, shortly before he stopped exhibition flying, Curtiss took famed evangelist *Billy Sunday* for his first aeroplane ride; and baptism in aviation:

31Aug'10: *Scientific American,* 10Sep'10: "*Glenn H. Curtiss, on August 31st, flew from Euclid Beach, near Cleveland, to Cedar Point* (today the world's largest amusement park), *a distance of 70 miles without stopping...The flight is comparable with Curtiss' Hudson River achievement...Curtiss flew back on September 1st in the teeth of a high wind, making the distance in 1 hour and 42 minutes, and outstripping express train and homing pigeons.*"

Curtiss commented about this flight: "*It was a battle with the air every mile of the way from Cedar Point. At one point, particularly, off the cliffs just before reaching Cleveland, I thought my trip had ended. I was flying 500 feet high and suddenly dropped a sheer 100 feet. Instinctively I shut my engine partly off. Then I righted my aeroplane and the flight continued. This mishap, which came very near being fatal, was caused by a whirl of wind going the same way I was. If I run into other flights like this, I may stop flying."*

3-13Sep'10: *Harvard-Boston Meet, "The Greatest Aviation Meet in America."* Prizes of almost $100,000 (about $5 million today) attracted aviators from England: Grahame-White, Alliot Verdon-Roe and Thomas Sopwith; the United States: Curtiss, Willard, Clifford Harmon and Augustus Post – and for the Wrights: Starling Burgess with his Burgess-Wright, Johnstone, Brookins and Earle Ovington.

Post arriving with his crated Curtiss aeroplane.

At this time aeroplanes were crated and shipped by rail; thus the term *"crate"* for an aeroplane.

SEPTEMBER 8, 1910

PRICE FIVE CENTS

THE YOUTH'S COMPANION

NEW ENGLAND EDITION

CLIFFORD B. HARMON FLYING IN A FARMAN BIPLANE

CHARLES F. WILLARD, a Curtiss Operator

GLENN H. CURTISS

RALPH JOHNSTONE, a Wright Operator

The Harvard—Boston Aviation Meet
Atlantic, Mass., September 3–13

The Harvard-Boston aviation meeting, under the auspices of the Harvard Aeronautical Society, proved to be one of the most successful meetings of its kind that has been held in this country. The management, the aviators and the visiting public are alike satisfied with the outcome. Many really fine performances were witnessed, and the participating aviators carried away with them prize money totalling in the neighborhood of $60,000. Of this sum, Grahame-White received $22,100 in prizes, his guarantee of $7,500, and an additional sum of about $2,000 earned in carrying passengers. The Wright operators, Brookins and Johnstone, received $9,250; Curtiss captured prizes amount to $2,000; and Clifford B. Harmon secured amateur prizes valued at about $7,500. Only one world's record was established at the meet—that for accuracy in landing going to Johnstone (Wright), the new record being 5 feet 4 inches. Grahame-White in winning the Boston Globe prize of $10,000 for the highest speed made in a double circuit between the field and Boston Light, a distance of 33 miles, maintained a speed that has never before been equalled in a contest in this country. The distance was covered by Mr. White in 34 minutes 1.2 seconds, or very nearly 60 m.p.h. average for the distance. This performance was made with the Blériot monoplane shown in the accompanying series of photographs. The Wright machines, with only the rearward horizontal surface for vertical control, proved very stable and handy, and captured all distance and duration prizes, events for which they are admirably suited because of their relatively great surface and low power. Curtiss and the Curtiss aviators succeeded chiefly in disappointing their friends, in so far as the winning of prizes and noteworthy performances were concerned. In the newer Curtiss machines, the biplane front control is displaced by a single surface, and the ailerons are double and trail the after edges of each of the main planes.

Scientific American, 24Sep'10: "...*The crowning event of the last day was a race for a $3,000 prize between (Grahame-)White and Curtiss. Just at sunset Mr. White brought out his Bleriot monoplane, and began circling the course at a 60-mile clip. Curtiss was soon in the air also, and a pretty race between the two types of aeroplanes was run off. The small Bleriot monoplane was an easy winner, although its power and weight were practically the same as the power and weight of the biplane. The times were 5 minutes 47 4/5 seconds and 6 minutes 4 3/5 seconds, respectively. These figures correspond to average speeds of 54.34 and 51.83 miles an hour (with no wind-shield). The diminutive, bird-like monoplane with its flat wings having only 120 square feet of supporting surface, readily bested the biplane on account of the greater head resistance of the latter, owing to its more numerous guys and struts. The outcome of this race makes America's chances in the Bennett trophy race on October 29th next seem slim, since France and England are sending over three monoplanes, each driven by skilled professional pilots, whereas America has none.*"

19Sep'10: Wilbur to Hoxsey: "*I sent a telegram to Mr. Johnstone last night giving instructions regarding the Detroit flight...I am very much in earnest when I say that I want no stunts and spectacular frills put on the flights there. If each of you can make a plain flight of ten or fifteen minutes each day keeping always within the inner fence well away from the grandstand and never more than three hundred feet high it will be just what we want...Anything beyond plain flying will be chalked up as a fault ...*"

...IATORS INCLUDING WRIGHT BROS. & BROOKINS

© 1910 E.J. GODSHALL

24Sep'10: *Scientific American*: "Glenn H. Curtiss has announced that he will soon withdraw from public flying."

26Sep'10: Captain *Washington Irving Chambers* is assigned responsibility for keeping in touch with aviation developments for the U. S. Navy.

22-30Oct'10: *The International Aviation Tournament* at the Belmont Park Race Track, Nassau County, New York.

Billed as America's answer to Reims, it was attended by 'everyone,' including Chicago's dapper *Harold McCormick* and nine-year-old *Henry Serrano Villard*.

Author's collection:

INTERNATIONAL AVIATION TOURNAMENT
BELMONT PARK
OCTOBER 22ND TO 30TH
1.30 P. M. DAILY
OFFICIAL PROGRAM 1910

It was only sanctioned by the Wrights after lengthy negotiations between the Aero Club's Bishop and their Andrew Freedman, who finally agreed that all exhibitors would recognize the Wright patents and legal position, and thus only Wright aeroplanes or those approved by them would compete.

The Wright brothers at the Belmont Meet, apparently after a contentious discussion:

It may have been agreed, but it didn't last long. Both Europeans and a stubborn American lot challenged the edict, stating flatly that unless the rules were eased they would not compete.

It was truly a time of "*flying in spite of the Wrights.*"

Finally the Wrights made a blanket agreement for 25 percent of the gate, subsequently amended to a flat $25,000 (well over $1 million today).

However, following the meet they obtained an injunction stopping the Aero Corporation from distributing the $198,000 gate receipts, demanding an additional $15,000.

Allen Ryan, chairman of the arrangements committee, branding the claim "*outrageous,*" said: "*it comes with ill grace from a company that has been treated...with the consideration and courtesy which has been extended...*"

This meet (attended by ten-year-old *Henry Serrano Villard*) had quite an international group of airmen competing for $74,800 in prizes ($3-1/2 million today), including English: Alec Olgivie (Wright), Ardle, James Radley (Bleriot) and Grahame-White (Farman and an intimidating *14-cylinder, 100-hp* Gnome-powered Bleriot).

The French were: Hubert Latham (100-hp Antoinette), Alfred le Blanc (Bleriot), Emile Aubrun (Bleriot), Count Jacques de Lesseps (Bleriot), Rene Barrier (Bleriot), Rene Simon (Bleriot), C. Audemars and Rolland Garros (Santos-Dumont's tiny Demoiselle).

Americans flying Curtiss aeroplanes were: Ely, Willard, McCurdy, Mars, and Hamilton (with a machine powered with *Walter Christie*'s 110-hp V8 engine).

And Tod Shriver (Curtiss's Reims mechanic) had a Curtiss-copy Dietz, which he immediately wrecked, Capt. Baldwin had his tubular-steel-framed "*Red Devil*" biplane, and John J. Frisbie had a Curtiss with a 2-cycle Elbridge engine.

WRIGHTS REFUSE TO MAKE CONCESSIONS

NEW YORK, March 23.—Foreign aviators are not all satisfied with the concession made by the Wrights to European competitors in the Gordon-Bennett aviation cup race. The Wrights consented to agree to waive legal rights so far as the patent situation is concerned in regard to foreigners who come to America to compete in the race. But they would not agree to lift their injunctive embargo if the foreigners took part in any other money-making exhibitions. This does not suit the foreigners at all, and they are shrieking vociferously per cable. Wilbur Wright has been in New York this week. He has been appealed to to allow foreigners to come over without any restrictions being put on their money-making activities, but so far he has refused to budge an inch.

Aero, 30Mar'10:

INTERNATIONAL MEET OF 'MEN-BIRDS' OCT. 22-30

Many Foreign Aviators, but Few Americans Scheduled for Tournament

NEW YORK, Oct. 15.—While it is believed that most of the world's records will go by the board at the International aviation tournament at Belmont Park, L. I., October 22-30, it it not so certain that all the speed prizes will go to the swiftest. Two air courses have been marked out on the racetrack, one five kilometers around and the other two and a half kilometers. Only the American elimination trials and the race for the international speed cup will be flown over the larger course. The rest of the speed events will take place on the two and a half kilometer circuit. This will give an advantage to the slower and more easily managed American biplane. It will be next to impossible, it is said, to make the small circle at sixty miles an hour. At the western end of the course the pylons form such a sharp angle that any attempt to drive a monoplane around the corner at anything approaching sixty miles an hour will end in disaster and possibly in a collision with the grandstand.

Mr. Herring, by the way, has just made it known that he was the designer of the fast machine in which Hamilton came to grief in Sacramento. This flyer, which is now in New York, has developed, it is said, 115-horse-power.

Members of the Aero Club of California are getting a little anxious over the makeup of the American team for the international aviation tournament. Although seven French, three English and a number of other foreign entries have been resting in the safe at the tournament headquarters for some days, so far not one American has officially signified his intention of taking part in the meet. The last day on which entries can be received for the elimination trials for the international speed trophy is October 15. Not only are the Americans needlessly slow over sending in their entries, but with one or two exceptions they are all without the necessary pilots' licenses. According to the rules of the International Aeronautic federation, every competitor at an officially sanctioned meet must hold a pilot's license. The Wright flyers and Charles K. Hamilton are among those who so far have not gone to the trouble of being O K'd by their national aero club. Glenn H. Curtiss, the present holder of the international speed trophy, has, of course, a license.

American aviators have always been inclined to ignore the rulings of the International Aeronautic federation and have, in fact, several times threatened to form a federation of their own. However, if they intend to take part in the big meet, the American aviators must get licenses. Such men as Brookins, Johnstone, Frank Coffyn, Hoxey, Hamilton and Willard would not be compelled to show their wings before being granted licenses.

And Tod Shriver (Curtiss's Reims mechanic) had a Curtiss-copy Dietz - which he immediately wrecked.

Capt. Baldwin had his tubular-steel framed "*Red Devil*" biplane, and John J. Frisbie a Curtiss with a 2-cycle Elbridge engine.

Flying Wrights were: Brookins, Christie, Coffyn, Hoxsey, Johnstone, Parmalee and Ovington, with a martinet-like Wilbur ruling "*his men with the sternness of a general...*(he) *values human life and limb somewhat more than prize money*...(deciding) *not to permit any of his men to enter the Statue of Liberty flight...*"

Other Americans were La-Chapelle, J. Armstrong Drexel (Bleriot), John Moisant (Bleriot), H. S. Harkness (Antoinette, and at North Island in 1911, <u>WALDO</u> pp. 52), and Clifford Harmon (Farman).

Baldwin then toured the Philippines, Japan, China and India with young pilots flying two *Red Devils* to tremendous "gates," coming home a rich man.

Hoxsey, Johnstone and Moisant died in 1910, and Frisbie in 1912, in Norton, Kansas..."*Having been driven to fly in unsuitable weather by the jeers of a hostile crowd.*"

Capt. Baldwin's novel biplane.

The rudder above the upper plane is worked by a fork fitting about the aviator's shoulders. It corrects the side-tipping of the aeroplane.

CAPT. BALDWIN'S BIPLANE.

One of our illustrations shows the new biplane of Capt. T. A. Baldwin, the dean of practical American aeronauts. This new biplane has a number of original features, chief of which is the method of preserving the transverse stability by means of a single vertical stability rudder placed above the upper plane. This rudder is turned about its vertical axis by means of a fork fitting around the aviator's shoulders, as in the Curtiss machine. When the aeroplane tips to one side or the other, by leaning to the high side the aviator sets the stabilizing rudder at an angle to the line of advance. This exerts sufficient force to bring the machine back to a level keel. The new stabilizing rudder is the outcome of experiments tried several years ago by the Aerial Experiment Association. It has been tried out by Mr. Curtiss, who claims that it worked satisfactorily upon his machine.

Scientific American, 19Mar'10: (This method of lateral control resulted in *Bell's 1913 patent No. 1,050,601.* But Baldwin's Shriver/"Red Devils" did not adopt it).

"The introduction by the Brothers Seguin of the Gnome rotary engine at...Reims...in August, 1909, completely revolutionised flying, for, whereas, before an aeroplane had to be fairly efficient to be lifted by the heavy engines then existing, the Gnome was so light itself that it was able to drag any clumsy old thing off the ground, so experimenters were enabled to go up in the air and experiment properly. Thereafter progress became very rapid, for, previously, designing aeroplanes had been rather like learning to swim before going into the water."

Charles G. Grey

Curtiss, trusting to his maxim of not competing if the competition was too tough, withdrew after seeing the Bleriot's powerful Gnome 14-cylinder, 100-hp engine. Therefore, the Americans selected to defend the *Gordon Bennett Cup* (first won by Curtiss at Reims) were Brookins, Drexel and Hamilton with a new Wright aeroplane.

The Wright *Baby Grand* had a short, 21-foot wingspan, was "headless," and was powered by a special 60-hp V8 engine (two standard 4-cylinder Wright engines in a V position on one crankshaft), which probably made it the meet's fastest.

On October 25, with Orville at the controls, it sped almost 70-mph. Unfortunately, engine failure caused a crash on takeoff from which pilot Brookins barely escaped alive.

Grahame-White, flying 61-mph with the Bleriot with the intimidating Gnome engine, won the Cup.

22Oct'10: Bishop Wright's diary: *"...Orville tried his eight-cylinder engine and it worked well. Weighs 100 lbs. more...77 or 78 miles an hour..."*

Orville in the new machine, the Model R *"Baby Grand"* or *"Baby Wright,"* chosen to defend the Cup.

"Headless" denotes no front controls, an innovation suggested by Bell to the A.E.A. in Oct'08: *"Should not the front control be at the rear instead of the front?...Would it not be better to use a horizontal tail at the rear? The natural action of the wind of advance upon the front control is to upset the whole machine upwards or downwards so as to make a complete somersault...Whereas the natural action upon a horizontal tail at the rear is to keep the longitudinal axis of the machine parallel to the line of advance and prevent any deviation up or down excepting by the will of the operator."*

The Wrights first tried it at Asbury Park in 1910, and then on the *Baby Grand*, above. In 1911, McCurdy, apparently, was the first of the old A.E.A. to fly a headless craft. Curtiss didn't use it until after Beachey's accidental discovery in 1912.

3Nov'10: Bishop Wright's diary: *"...Orville and Katharine came home at 9:am. They report eminent success. They got $20,000 for going,..$15,000 prizes. The Wright Company voted them $10,000, and declared a dividend of $80,000 (including their dividend share, about $3-1/2 million today). The New York papers lauded them highly."*

"The Wright brothers had peaked. There followed a succession of aircraft which were almost indistinguishable from the Model B..."   *Rubenstein & Goldman*

13Nov'10: The Bishop's diary: *"Orville started at 4:00, for...Berlin, to instruct them how to build better machines."*

THE PERFORMANCES AT BELMONT PARK

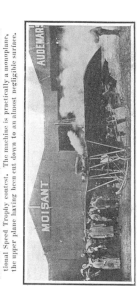

The small Wright racer undergoing an engine test. This remarkable little machine has a speed of about 68 miles an hour. The wing spread is about 20 feet; the engine horse-power about 60.

The new machine constructed by Curtiss for the Gordon-Bennett International Speed Trophy contest. The machine is practically a monoplane, the upper plane having been cut down to an almost negligible surface.

The Santos-Dumont "Demoiselle" which was piloted by Audemars. The machine proved very fast on the few occasions when it flew at the International Aviation Meeting.

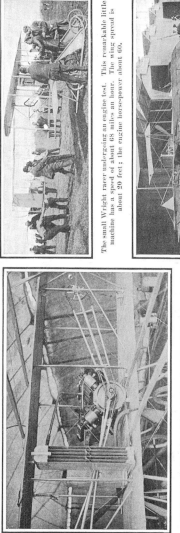

The V-motor of the small Wright biplane racer especially designed and constructed for the speed contests of the International Aviation Meeting. The motor is rated at 60 horse-power.

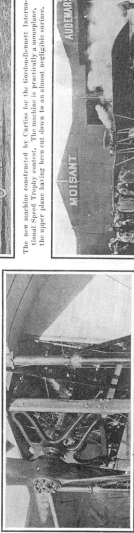

The 14-cylinder, 100 horse-power Gnome motor of Grahame-White's Bleriot monoplane, which won the Bennett cup race at 61.04 miles an hour.

Photograph by the Pictorial News Co.

When the propeller of a high-powered flying machine is started, several men are needed to hold the machine in leash, as it were. The machine which these six men are struggling to hold back is Grahame-White's 100-horse-power Bleriot monoplane in which he won the Gordon-Bennett International trophy.

SIX MEN AND ONE HUNDRED HORSE-POWER

14Nov'10: Hampton Roads, VA: Working with Capt. W. I. Chambers and assistants, Naval Constructors McEntree and Lt. N.H. Wright, Curtiss arranges for *Eugene Ely* (1886-1911) to make the *first flight from a ship*, the *USS Birmingham* - fitted with a sloping 28 x 83-foot wooden platform, Naval aviation's *first 'flight deck.'*

Initially, the New York *World* had arranged with Curtiss, McCurdy as pilot, to attempt this with the Hamburg-American Line.

However, by 12Nov, Bud Mars was planned to fly from the S.S. *Pennsylvania.* (with the S.S. *America* for a January attempt).

Captain Chambers, wanting to be first with the Navy, got the use of the Birmingham on 9Nov – but had no aeroplane.

McEntree suggested Wright, but a *"quick telephone conversation dashed any hope of cooperation"* from Orville Wright.

A broken propeller then aborted Mar's attempt, as Curtiss, responding to Chambers' plea, then gave the Navy his full cooperation.

Racing against the German line's second attempt, in two days Chambers and McEntee got everything ready and prepared.

But heavy weather, rain and impending fog almost canceled Ely's attempt in Curtiss's *Hudson Flier.*

Impatient, not even waiting for the ship to get underway to create a head wind, Ely took off - and virtually fell off the platform.

With its new 60-hp motor roaring, the struggling craft brushed the water, damaging its propeller.

Snatching off his spray-splashed goggles, Ely prudently headed for the nearest land, Willoughby Spit, where a landing near a row of beach cottages made the day a success.

MANBIRD FLIES 5 MILES FROM SHIP; AMAZES NAVY MEN

Ely Shows That Biplane Is a Factor That Must Be Reckoned with in War

NEW MARK SET FOR HISTORY

Aviator's Trip from Cruiser Birmingham Across Chesapeake Bay First of Kind

FORT MONROE, Va., Nov. 14.— Aerial navigation showed today that it is a factor which must be dealt with in the naval tactics of the future, if the successful flight made by Eugene B. Ely in a Curtiss biplane from the cruiser Birmingham can be taken as a criterion.

From Hampton Roads, the scene forty-five years ago of another epoch-making event in the history of warfare, when an ironclad proved its superiority over the former type of fighting vessel, the aviator today flew across the lower end of Chesapeake bay, landing on the shore opposite this fort.

In weather conditions unfavorable for flying, Ely shortly after 3 o'clock glided from the platform erected on the front of the cruiser, swooped down until he touched the water, then rose rapidly and was off in the direction of the Atlantic. Four minutes later he was lost on the eastern horizon, and an instant later had landed safely on Willoughby spit.

The impact with which the machine struck the water after its 37-foot drop from the cruiser split a small piece from a propeller blade.

SPEED NOT LESSENED

But the speed of the ship was not lessened, and it darted away with express train rapidity on its flight.

Intermittent rain throughout the day, several hail showers and a continuous fog almost compelled the aviator to postpone his attempt. But he was determined to prove, as he said after the flight that he could accomplish more than had been expected.

Furthermore, he did not wait for the Birmingham to get in motion, which would have added to his momentum, and thus have aided him, but seizing an opportune moment between showers he went off before those on the ship with him and on the other vessels stationed nearby to follow and assist him in case of need, were aware that he was ready.

Ely today said it would be an easy matter for an aeroplane to alight on a vessel, whether moving or standing still.

Naval experts who witnessed the flight expressed their belief that the navies of the future must take the aeroplane into consideration.

MAY BE USED FOR SCOUTING

Capt. Washington I. Chambers, who had been detailed by the navy department as chairman of a board for aeronautical investigation, declared the flight was more than he had anticipated, and is confident the time is near when all scout cruisers will be equipped with aeroplanes. They would not be of fighting use, he explained, but for scout duty.

The machine in which Ely flew was the one that Glenn Curtis used on his Albany-to-New York flight. It had seen two previous cross-water flights, one over Lake Erie from Euclid Beach to Cedar Point and back, a distance of seventy miles; the other by Curtiss himself over the Atlantic ocean, off Atlantic City, when it covered fifty miles.

The distance which Ely flew today was nearly five miles. It was 3:16 when he took to the air; five minutes later he was safe on Virginia soil, a few miles north of Norfolk.

Ely returned to Norfolk immediately after the flight. If weather conditions are favorable tomorrow he will attempt a flight over the city. It is understood Ely by his flight today won a $5000 prize, offered by John Barry Ryan for the first flight of a mile or more from any ship to land.

17Nov'10: Denver Air Show: Wright flyers Hoxsey, Brookins and Johnstone each flew their daring specialties. At 800 feet Johnstone began his famous spiral glide, but on the second circle went into an almost perpendicular dive. To the horror of spectators: *"Johnstone was seen to climb out of the seat and attempt to warp the wings by sheer strength."* He stuck the earth and died instantly, the first professional flier killed in America.

PLUNGES TO DEATH.

Aviator Johnstone Is Killed Instantly.

Biplane Drops Like Shot from Five Hundred Feet in the Air.

Nearly Every Bone in Body Broken — Famous Spiral Glide Fatal.

Denver Ghouls Fight for Gory Souvenirs Torn from Victim's Corpse.

[ASSOCIATED PRESS NIGHT REPORT.]

DENVER, Nov. 17.—With one wing of his machine crumpled like a piece of paper, Ralph Johnstone, the brilliant young aviator, holder of the world's altitude record, dropped like a plummet from a height of 500 feet into the inclosure at Overland Park aviation field and was instantly killed.

When the spectators crowded about the inclosure reached him, his body lay beneath the engine of the biplane with the white planes that had failed him in his time of need, wrapped about it like a shroud. Nearly every bone in his body was broken.

He had gambled with death once too often. But he played the game to the end, fighting coolly and grimly to the last second to regain control of his broken machine.

Fresh from his triumphs at Belmont Park, where he had broken the world's record for altitude with a flight of 9714 feet, Johnstone attempted to give the thousands of spectators who stood with craned necks to watch him, an extra thrill with his most daring feat, the spiral glide which had made the Wright aviator famous. The spectators got their thrill, but it cost Johnstone his life.

23Nov1910: Octave Chanute, 78, dies, in Chicago.

27Nov1910: Orville (Berlin) to Wilbur: "*...I have about made up my mind to let the European business go. I don't propose to be bothered with it all of my life and I see no prospect of it ever amounting to anything unless we send a representative here to stay to watch our interests...*"

There was an interesting exchange of letters:

30Nov1910: Wilbur to Curtiss: "*Your letter of November 23 received. The negotiation was initiated at your request and now seems to be similarly closed by you. As I stated in one of our conferences, any agreement, in order to be effective, must possess sufficient elements of advantage to each party to make both satisfied. If you do not consider that such advantages exist so far as you are concerned, it is well for both parties to revert to the established mode of settlement. We are compelled to push through a test case anyway against someone...*

"*Although I entered upon the negotiations without enthusiasm, I have endeavored in good faith to reach a mutually satisfactory basis of settlement and disarranged my plans to give you time to consider the matter carefully, without insisting upon anything definite from you. Now, however, I must consider the negotiations at an end unless you do something at once.*"

26Dec1910: Curtiss to Wilbur: "*I am afraid I deserve to be criticized for pressing the negotiations for a settlement with you, but when I first took it up I did not realize the intricacies of the case. I finally concluded that it would be necessary to go on with the trial, but I assure you that you can count on my co-operation in any matter in which we can get together to cut down the expense of the litigation, or to further the interests of the exhibition or manufacturing business.*"

The Wrights offered to drop litigation if he would take out a license and settle for past use. Curtiss demurred, holding the Wrights off until the courts finally decided against him on 13Jan1914.

29Nov'10: Prompted by Ely's success, and hoping to get the American military off dead center regarding aviation, Curtiss wrote Secretary of War Jacob Dickinson and Navy Secretary George Meyer, offering to teach one or more officers "*...in the developing the adaptability of the aeroplane to military purposes.*"

2Dec1910: Curtiss arrives in San Diego to set up his winter training/development camp on *North Island*, renting a cottage for him and Lena, a second for the men, both near the Hotel del Coronado: "*the largest all-year seaside resort hotel in the world.*"

Curtiss had a sharp sense of humor. When his mother, a chronic complainer, carried on about the sand fleas at Coronado, where he'd later built her a house, he said, "*After you've been there a year or so, you'll become distasteful to them.*"

23Dec'10: Naval Lt. *Theodore Gordon Ellyson* (1885-1928), Annapolis '05, ordered: "*...to establish a naval aviation camp at North Island at a place designated by Mr. Curtiss, who has offered the land...You are entrusted with the care and control of the Navy Curtiss machines, the Navy Wright machine being independently under the control of Lieutenant John Rodgers...*"

Other students during that first season (1910-11) were Army Lts. Paul W. Beck, George E.M. Kelly and John C. Walker; Civilians Hugh Robinson (to become his North Island right-hand man), Charles Witmer of Chicago, San Francisco's Robert (*Lucky Bob*) St. Henry, Greer, Purington, Shakelford - and Damon Merrill, chief mechanician.

Dec'10, Fresno, California newspaper interview:

CURTISS TALKS OF PLANS FOR OVER WATER TESTS

Government Accepts Offer to Have Naval Officer Fly During Trials

TO LAND ON WARSHIP

Likes Wet Weather For Flying; Tells of Devices For Safety

Glenn H. Curtiss, the most interesting figure in the world of aviation today, arrived in Fresno yesterday, and late in the afternoon, while he sat in the lobby of a local hotel, he talked about his airships, the weather, things and plans that are making world history and that will be cabled around the world for the nations to read, in a perfectly matter of fact and everyday manner.

He heard yesterday of the acceptance by the government of an offer he made to carry a naval officer with him through trials and tests to be conducted all winter long, principally in and about Los Angeles, and over the waters of the Pacific. In a statement on this he said:

"We have already assisted the government in aviation experiments on the Atlantic seaboard, notably in the matter of making a start from a warship in an aeroplane and reaching land without mishap. As we are to experiment for the rest of the winter in Los Angeles, I offered the government a short time ago to have an officer present throughout the trials, who will assist in handling the machines."

Then he launched out, quite as quietly and plainly, on a discussion of plans that promise to revolutionize the science of flying as it is now known to mankind—experiments for making flying across the water safe and certain.

FLYING OVER WATER

"Our experiments will be principally over the water," he said, "and we will try for the first time to land on a warship, beginning the flight on shore or upon another ship. We also expect to try flights in which we will land on the water, both as a maneuver for use in battle, and as a means of precaution against accident.

These latter trials are to be made with a machine that is at home in three elements, on the earth, in the air and on the water. It is fitted with pontoon arrangements for the aquatic stunts. Flying across large expanses of water is anything but certain work in the present status of the aviation business, because of the danger of the engine quitting or something going wrong that will prevent the aviator making land before being compelled to alight.

"No, it has not been decided where these trials down south will be made," said Curtiss. "It will, however, all be done at some port of Los Angeles, probably San Pedro. Arrangements have been interrupted by coming up here this week."

LIKES THINGS

Curtiss is, contrary to expectation, pleased with December weather in Fresno for flying purposes. He says that moisture in the air is a help in flying, as is also a heavy barometric pressure. "Machines that will not leave the ground at all in a climate like that of Arizona," he explained,

"will fly in damp air. The moisture aids quite a little. That is, anything short of actual rain."

The bird-man, who usually talks in a very quiet voice, and with slight signs of abstractions in his manner, enthused quite a bit when he launched onto the subject of the future of aviation, especially the things he himself is working out—though he doesn't put it just that way.

"Our new model machine," he observed, "has a new set of controllers; that is where it differs, generally speaking, from the older type. For instance, there are three elevators, one in front and two in the rear, and all arranged so that one or all can be used, and so that if one breaks it will become dormant and not interfere with the operation of the machine. That is a very important improvement. The same remark applies to the wing tips, as they will become dormant if broken or disabled in any way, and yet the machine, while flying, will maintain its stability without them, if no quick turns are tried. It takes some careful work, but the machine will not capsize.

"A great many lamentable accidents in aviation have been caused by the breaking of one of the controls; often we never know just what did happen to the machine of some man who has been dashed to the earth and death. It is a very important thing to make these controls as safe as possible, and harmless when they cannot be used."

He furnished a side-light on the nature of his so-called monoplane. Curtiss makes a distinction. It is not a monoplane, but a single-surface machine. Surface interferes with speed, so he has substituted one surface for the two usually used, he says. It is different from anything now called a monoplane.

The monoplane, proper, as it is known in Europe, is covered by the Wright patent, and may not be used generally in this country, if it includes the system of warping the wings to maintain stability.

However, this observation does not come from Curtiss. He just avoided the word "monoplane," and spoke instead of the "single surface."

Beckwith Havens (1890-1969), a handsome young automobile salesman, was hired as Curtiss's first salesman. Thinking he should know how to fly, he recalled: "*When I went to Hammondsport, Curtiss was still kind of a little country boy. He told me that he was going to start a school to teach people to fly.' It'll be five hundred dollars,' he said. 'If you have five hundred dollars, we'll teach you to fly. School hasn't opened yet.' I said, 'Mr. Curtiss, I'm already working for you. I'm on the payroll and have been for some time. So I think you ought to teach me how to fly for nothing.' 'No, I can't do that, I've got to charge you.' I was furious, and I went tearing back to New York and our business manager, Jerome Fanciulli, just laughed. 'Just sign a note for five hundred dollars,' he said, 'and I'll endorse it for you. I'm just inundated with telegrams and letters from all over the world. They want to see exhibition fliers, because people don't believe an airplane can fly. I'll put you right on, flying, and the first couple of days, you'll make the five hundred dollars.'*"

Havens learned to fly, and still had a valid pilot's license at his death in 1969.

> 9Dec'10: Wilbur to Orville (Berlin): "*...We must expect that in our absence the French and German companies will do many foolish things. We have a right to expect, however, an honest accounting...*
>
> "*I am having troubles enough at home. The Belmont swindlers are still trying to unload the results of their own incompetence on us....I refused to stand for this, and brought suit, and obtained a temporary injunction to prevent the payment of our money in settlement of other bills. Of course Ryan and Freedman are hot, but I intend to have the money collected.*
>
> "*...The Thompson and Curtiss negotiations have apparently fallen through...I had to go to Kansas City to Johnstone's funeral and could not force him to make up his own mind before leaving for California.*
>
> "*...The information from Denver is so conflicting that it seems to be impossible to determine the cause of Johnstone's accident...*"

In another letter, Wilbur wrote: "*...Orville and I have been wasting our time in business affairs and have had practically no time for experimental work or original investigations. But the world does not pay a cent for labor of the latter kinds or for inventions unless a man works himself to death in a business way also. We intend however to shake off business and get back to...other kind of work before a year is out...*"

"The Wright Brothers were bitter. All around them pilots were profiting hugely from an invention which they had perfected for the world; without their wing-warping system none of it would have happened, certainly not as quickly. They held patents...in all the leading aviation countries and they demanded royalties from any pilot using the system and flying for profit. If the pilot did not pay up, and many did not, they went to the courts. They made no exceptions - Paulhan, Grahame-White and others had writs served on them at air meets by Wright lawyers, and promoters of meets received demands for twenty per cent of the posted prize money and ten per cent of the gate receipts. But they reserved their harshest treatment for Glenn Curtiss who was selling aircraft in direct competition to them.

"Litigation began to dominate their lives, and Wilbur especially spent long periods in the courts giving expert evidence against Curtiss. But it was a hopeless task. There were too many people flying, and even when they were awarded judgment the battles continued; there was always another pilot or promoter to sue or an appeal to attend. They would not settle out of court. It's hard to fathom what it was that made them go on; it had to be something more than money.

"They were rich, they had sold aircraft to the Army as well as to professional pilots, and they received royalties from licensed manufacturers. In November 1910 the Wright company was incorporated with capital of $1 million, and the board was filled with Wall Street luminaries. The new company bought the patents from the Wrights for $100,000 (*almost $5 million today*) and Wilbur became president and went on battling in the courts."   *Ivan Rendall*

20Dec'10: Wilbur to Charles Chanute: "*During the last ten years of your father's life a very extensive correspondence was carried on between him and me...I refer especially to the series of tables of lifts and tangentials which was the foundation of our success. I do not know whether you have any intention of turning his papers over to a biographer soon, but I am writing to request that you do not permit any person interested in flying as a business to have access to these letters and talks at this time...*"

24Dec'10: Charles replied that, as the Octave Chanute estate owned the correspondence, he could give no assurances regarding its disposition. However, he did agree to prepare copies of all of their letters.

In 1911 a portion was reviewed by Albert Zahm - and in 1932, when he was Chief of the Library of Congress's Aeronautics Division, the library acquired Chanute's correspondence and other papers as a gift from his daughters, Elizabeth and Octavia.

29Dec'10: Orville came home from Europe.

31Dec'10: At the *second Dominguez Air Meet*, Hoxsey's Wright, spiraling to the ground after an altitude flight, crashes out-of-control and he is killed.

"The deaths of Johnstone and Hoxsey confirmed what had been hinted at Belmont - that high noon had come and gone in the careers of the Wright brothers. Much substantial flying still lay ahead for Wright pilots and airplanes, but the great moments were almost over. The French and German Wright companies were in trouble by the end of 1910 because of poor supervision. At home the brothers were embroiled in patent infringement suits with Glenn Curtiss and others. These took time and energy and slowed down the work of the two men in the design and production of new airplanes. The infringement cases had the further effect of committing the Wrights almost irrevocably to their basic wing-warping biplane design. After their dogged defense of the principles behind this design in the patent cases, they could not then discard them very easily and adopt some of the newer ideas."   *Sherwood Harris*

Demonstration of wing-warping, on a Florida beach - advertised thusly: "When anything happens to Machinery while in air, a great help in gliding to earth safely. Patented and controlled by Fathers of Aviation, Wright Bros. Not used on any other make of machine":

13Oct'10, *The Youth's Companion*:

FLYING.

DISINTERESTED spectators at the exhibition of heavier-than-air flying-machines during the recent months are inclined to agree with Mr. Wilbur Wright's view of their present uses. Mr. Wright is reported as saying that air-ships have no commercial value, but will be used for some time chiefly in sport and in war.

This opinion of a man who has done as much as any other person to demonstrate the possibility of travel through the air certainly deserves respect.

The air-ship is in an extremely primitive experimental stage. This was demonstrated at the Harvard-Boston exhibition in September, as well as at the various other less ambitious shows. It will probably be proved again at the meet at Belmont Park, New York, which begins a week from Saturday. The professional airmen have declined to exhibit their machines, or to compete for large money prizes, unless they receive from five to ten thousand dollars in addition to any prizes they may win. This has been partly because of the risk of ruining their machines and partly because of the risk of losing their lives.

Mr. Glenn Curtiss, at the Harvard-Boston meet, declined to compete for a ten-thousand-dollar prize, offered for a thirty-three-mile flight over water, for the reason that his motor did not work satisfactorily, and he was unwilling to take the chances of death. This, too, was after he had flown successfully from Albany to New York.

The price of the air-ships is so great and the chances of reaching a given point without accident are so small at the present time that, as Mr. Wright suggested, only the rich man will hazard the financial loss for the sake of the sport, and only the demands of national protection will justify the risk of life in case of war.

When some way of charting the air-currents is found, and some automatic method of preserving the equilibrium of the air-ships is devised, the experimental stage of air navigation will have approached more nearly to the practical.

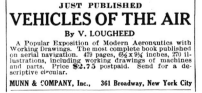
Scientific American, 6Aug'10: (Munn was also the publisher of *Scientific American*)

In 1910, *Victor Lougheed* (half-brother of Allan and Malcolm Lockhead, co-founders with Glenn Martin of Lockheed Martin), wrote in his 514-page Vehicles of The Air: "...*the Wrights levied upon every possible source of information and, frankly commencing with Chanute's help and a modification of the Chanute biplane glider, which they regarded as the most advanced construction existant...entered upon a deliberate, unremitting, and enthusiastic prosecution of an at first thankless task, which for sturdy perseverence in the face of obstacles and sensible disregard of ignorant opinions, has few parallels in the history of invention. Having from the onset more faith in experimental than analytical methods, the Wrights set themselves first to the task of confirming or correcting the various formulas of their predecessors concerning wind pressures, the sustaining effects of different inclined surfaces, etc. Progressing from these to the various possible methods of steering, and the maintaining of lateral and longitudinal balance, they tirelessly tested a constantly improving series of constructions by hundreds of kite and gliding experiments. Having thus secured an amount of practice that enable them to make reasonably safe gliding flights of considerable length in calms and moderate winds, they next undertook the application of a motor, naturally turning to an automobile mechanism as the most promising source...This resulted, on December 17, 1903, in four flights in calm air* (Not so! It was a virtual gale)...*On March 22, 1904, a United States patent was applied for on a wing-warping device, in combination with flat sustaining surfaces, indicating either a failure...to appreciate fully the absolute importance of definitely and correctly curved surfaces, or else, constituting a lack of the 'full disclosure' demanded by patent law. The construction described in the patent specifications being obviously inoperative, these were repeatedly objected to and rejected by the patent office examiners, and it was not until May 22, 1906, that the claims were allowed - even then on a basis of inoperative construction. Throughout 1904 the Wright experiments continued, surrounded by the utmost secrecy, but it was definitely attested by Chanute that during this year they increased the length of their longest flight to 1,377 feet. It was not until nearly the end of September, 1905, months after Montgomery's flights...and publication of his construction, and some time after his patent was applied for, that the Wrights commenced to be conspicuously successful - with parabolically-curved sustaining surfaces and a system of wing-warping closely resembling that of Montgomery's patent and not at all like that claimed in the Wright patent. Following these successes, which though well authenticated were kept out of the newspapers and well away from the general public, vigorous but quiet efforts were made during 1906 and 1907 to sell to European governments, not patent rights, but 'secrets' of construction Little success resulting, because of the terms and conditions that were stipulated, and European aviators having by this time progressed to the point of making long flights, this policy was abandoned late in 1908, and the Wrights came out into the open with their machines - Orville Wright in the United States and Wilbur Wright in France - with the result that they were quickly able to establish new distance and duration records, which stood for nearly a year. At the present time, however, the Wright machine does not hold a single distance, duration, speed, weight-carrying, cross-country, or altitude record in the world, and has borne out the numerous critics of its construction by being responsible for an undue proportion of the accidents that have occurred in the history of power-propelled heavier-than-air machines.*"

STARTING WRIGHT AEROPLANE MOST INTRICATE OPERATION; SUCH FUSSING AND TINKERING, THEN---SUCH A THRILL!

UPPER PICTURE.—PREPARING TO START MOTOR BY " TURNING OVER" PROPELLERS.

Special to The Record.

DAYTON, O., July 23.—You've seen a buzzard take wing from the ground? If you have you know how laboriously and awkwardly he runs and jumps and beats the air with his unwieldy pinions before he is able to get into the air.

But when he is once in the air and begins to climb the stairway of the skies, turning long loops on rigid wings, you forget how awkwardly and with what effort he began his flight.

It's much the same with a Wright aeroplane. When it is trundled from the aerodrome, you say to yourself that it is a commonplace looking contrivance. Nothing graceful about it, nothing bird-like. Just a four-cylinder engine set between two rectangular frames covered with unbleached cambric. It's anything but beautiful.

FIVE MEN NEEDED

Five men conduct the plane to the monorail track, one pulling at each wing tip, one at each of two detachable wheels like enormous casters, and one supporting the "tail." You say to yourself that it is absurd to have a machine that must needs be started from a track.

The plane is placed on the rail, which is just a board on edge, faced with strap iron. A flanged wheel on a cross-piece in front rests on this track. Another flanged wheel on a loose cross-piece that is pushed under the runners of the machine from behind rests on the track in the rear.

A man stands at the tip of one of the wings to keep the nicely balanced machine from tipping to one side or the other. Two other men go to the rear, one to each of the big propellers. A mechanician goes to the front of the machine, worming himself in between taut piano wires, and begins to test the motor.

AVIATOR ON THE JOB

Then someone else gets under the frame and makes the plane fast to the track by a wire that is anchored to the rail. This wire, which can be thrown by a trigger, is to hold the plane while the motor is working up to full speed.

Orville Wright comes up and looks the machine over. He tests wires and peers into oil cups and tries the control levers. Then he crawls in between the wires and pulls himself up into the little seat beside the motor.

The men at the rear reach up and grasp the outside blades of the propellers. The man at the wing tip grasps the end stay and braces himself like a sprinter preparing for a hundred-yard dash. You begin to take mild interest in the proceedings.

STARTING THE ENGINE

The men at the propellers begin to count in unison:

"One—two—three!"

At the word "three" they pull down on the propeller blades and "turn over" the motor. There is a cough and a splutter, and the big blades begin to whirl. The grass behind the machine bends before a perfect gale of wind.

Orville takes a last look at the motor. He nods to the man at the wing tip, whose duty it is to run with the machine to hold it level till it gains momentum. Last he reaches down and pulls the trigger which releases the wire that anchors the aeroplane.

The machine begins to slide down the track, slowly at first, but with ever increasing speed. Ten—twenty—thirty yards it glides, still clinging to the rail. The runner loosens his hold on the plane and drops behind.

Then the forward control planes are tilted upward a few inches.

As gracefully and sure as wild swan ever rose from the water, or as eagle ever took to air from his crag, the aeroplane rises from the track and climbs the air.

Chapter **8** *1911-1912*

Ford wins his patent fight. Curtiss begins instructing students, invents the seaplane, and co-founds Naval aviation. The Wright's troubles mount in their European and American business and infringement litigation. Wilbur dies. Curtiss invents the flying boat.

1Jan1911: Mr. & Mrs. Glenn Curtiss, honored guests in an electric Victoria, "*one of the most beautiful entries in the parade*" of the *Pasadena Rose Tournament and Carnival.*

9Jan1911: Henry Ford wins his Selden Patent fight against the "*Motor Trust.*" The appeals court found for him so strongly in dismissing Judge Hough's 1909 decision that the A.L.A.M. was disbanded, liberating the American auto industry from what some saw as an audacious and shameless conspiracy to limit its freedom.

This ruling, coming at a time when feelings were running high regarding the Wright's fight with Curtiss, strengthened the Curtiss faction's belief that the Wrights had lost their position as inventors by becoming J.P. Morgan/Wall Street-financed business-men attempting to monopolize aviation in America.

In 1909 another trust was born, the Motion Picture Patents Co., formed by Edison (likewise J.P. Morgan-backed) and nine associates to monopolize the new, rapidly grow-ing movie business. It would be broken up following the 1914 *Clayton Antitrust Act* and the establishment of the *Federal Trade Commission*, strengthening the 1890s *Sherman Antitrust Law* which had been enacted to deal with, among other things, the "*Whiskey Trust*" formed by 65 "*whiskey barons*" that "*became all powerful in fixing the price of whiskey - as well as mayors, governors and legislators.*"

Thus was government's response to the excesses of trusts, real (e.g., 1911's victory over Rockefeller's Standard Oil Trust) and attempted, as in Edison's motion pictures, Selden's automobile...and the Wright's aeroplane.

Scientific American, 17Nov'06:

In 1907 Ford's profits were a staggering 377% of net worth; following his adoption of the standardized Model T in 1908, they were 150% in 1914, finally lowering to 20% in 1924. In 1911-12 Ford sold an incredible 78,440 Model T's...by 1920 *half of the world's cars were Model T's* - which by 1923 sold for $260 ($7,750 today).

Curtiss, giving up competition flying, continued to develop aircraft. He was most interested in solving the problem of flying from and landing on the water, stating: *"Of course, one of the first developments in commercial aviation will be the use of flying boats and seaplanes for passengers and packages carrying between the largest seaports along the Atlantic coast and in the West Indies. I believe that we shall soon have transatlantic flights. The reason I believe that this will be true and the reason I believe marine flying will be developed quicker than land is because there are no new landing fields needed. In other words, terminal facilities are already provided...there is no limitation in the width of a plane because there is ample room for even our largest sea boats to maneuver. We know more about weather conditions on the sea...Another thing, the relative speed of boats is slow as compared with the speed of railway trains, so that aerial transportation at a speed of from 75 to 100 miles an hour is bound to cut down materially the time required to go from one seaport to another, thereby coming into early favor."*

Note: 28Oct*1990 The New York Times:* "A French group is encouraging...aerospace companies to develop a huge cargo seaplane to be called Hydro 2000...about 330 feet long, with a projected payload of 880,000 pounds (440 tons)...the Boeing Company's largest freighter, the B-747-200, is just 231 feet long, with a...payload of about 250,000 pounds (125 tons). The French Group...perceives the need for such a large, all-cargo aircraft to handle the continued growth in freight projected for the next century. Designed for sea-based operations...the plane would need no landing gear, and would...operate away from congested airports. Seaports already have the cargo infrastructure to handle large loads..."

18Jan'11: Related to his comment to Gen. Howe (31May'10), Curtiss wanted to explore the aeroplane as a military weapon. Ely, flying from the Selfridge aviation field (adjoining Tanforan racetrack in San Bruno, south of San Francisco), before a *"record breaking crowd of 120,000 people,"* in a new *D-IV* made the *first landing and takeoff from a ship,* the *USS Pennsylvania* (later renamed the *Pittsburgh*) in San Francisco Bay. The ship was fitted with a sloping, 125-foot by 30-foot wide temporary platform.

Ely's aeroplane was fitted with pontoons by the wheels, and three spring-actuated hooks, one behind the front wheel, one under the center, and one at the tail - a concept borrowed from Hugh Robinson's circus days.

Nearing the landing platform, Ely cut power and his machine settled. When the wheels struck, the hooks missed the first eleven of twenty-one ropes stretched half-a-foot above the deck between 50-pound sandbags, but caught the twelfth. After a *30-foot* landing the "tailhook" stopped the machine *two* feet short of the steel mesh safety barbette.

"Cheers greeted Ely...The airplane carrier had arrived!...Curtiss remarked, '*This amply demonstrates the value of aircraft to the Navy in time of need.*'...Chambers agreed."

Charles Fremont (Frog) Pond, the *Pennsylvania*'s skipper, "*I desire to place myself on record as positively assured of the importance of the aeroplane in future naval warfare. As a matter of fact, this feat which we are witnessing may revolutionize naval warfare even more than the first battle of the Merrimac and Monitor.*"

This was the *first use of an arresting gear* innovation, essentially the same as today's.

After a heart-thumping drop when leaving the flight deck, Ely flew back to Selfridge field. On 19Oct'11, when 25 years old, he was killed in an exhibition at Macon, Georgia

17Jan'11: Lt. Theodore G. Ellyson reported to the Glenn Curtiss Aviation Camp on North Island.

26Jan'11: The first 'official' flight (there were one or two earlier) of Curtiss's *Hydroaeroplane* (a Model D with floats) at North Island. This was the *first practical seaplane*, the result of approximately seventy attempts, countless calculations, sketches on anything handy, including the shop's whitewashed walls, and at least fifty combinations of float shape, size, location and angle of incidence.

Witmer and Curtiss:

Among those assisting Curtiss were "Spuds" Ellyson (who liked potatoes), Charles Witmer and George E. A. Hallett - with young *Waldo Waterman* an unpaid helper.

Curtiss wrote: *"We made flights nearly every day after this, taking the Army and Navy officers as passengers. I found the machine well adapted for passenger work and it became very popular. While experimenting we kept changing things from day to day, adding and taking off, lightening the machine, or adding more surface. We tried putting on an extra surface, making a triplane, and got remarkable lifting power. We changed the floats and finally made one long, flat-bottomed, scow-shaped float, twelve feet long, two feet wide, and twelve inches deep. It was made of wood, the bow being curved upward the full width of the boat and at the stern being curved downward in a similar manner. This single float was placed under the aeroplane so that the weight was slightly to the rear of the centre of the float, causing it to slant upward, giving it the necessary angle for hydoplaning on the surface of the water. I will confess that I got more pleasure out of flying the new machine over water than I ever got flying over land, and the danger, too, was greatly lessened."*

George van Deurs: "Though he was largely silent with the stunt men, Curtiss talked fluently when he had a companion who could understand his ideas. The inventor listened to all suggestions, explained his ideas as he worked, and displayed an amazing ingenuity with tools. Spuds soon believed the man could make anything."

Later, Ellyson, on working with him: "*You see, it was not Curtiss, the genius and inventor, whom we knew. It was 'G.H.,' a comrade and chum, who made us feel that we were all working together, and that our ideas and advice were really of some value. It was never a case of 'do this' or 'do that'...but always, 'What do you think of making this change?' He was always willing to listen to any argument but generally managed to convince you his plan was best. I could write volumes on Curtiss, the man.*"

AERO, 17Feb'12: "*...Whether the Oil Trust is responsible for the inability of the Navy aviators at San Diego to get high grade gasoline...is something they are seeking to find out. Lieut. Ellyson was told...that only the commercial grade of gasoline was sold on the coast and...high grade would have to be ordered from New York...*"

1Feb'11: Curtiss simplified the two float-design to a single float, standard into 1912.

But Ely's San Francisco flight hadn't yet convinced the Navy. What it wanted, Secretary Meyer wrote, was: "*...an aeroplane that can be picked up by a boat crane and dropped over the side to the water, so that the flyer can go off...and later return to the water alongside, get picked up by the crane and brought back to the deck...*"

Therefore, on 17Feb'11, in a hastily modified *Model D-III tractor* hydroaeroplane, Curtiss "flew to" (struggling for one 'photo' hop) the *USS Pennsylvania*, now in San Diego Bay. He was hoisted aboard, greeted by Captain Pond, and then lowered for the return "flight" in the badly out-of-balance machine (taxiing all the way). Thus he marginally demonstrated the Navy's desired capability.

The ship's log read: "*At 8:45 Aviator Glenn Curtiss came alongside in his hydroaeroplane and was hoisted aboard with the machine by crane. At 9:05 he was hoisted out and left the ship, the experiment being accomplished without incident.*"

The *San Diego Union*: "*It was just like any other day's work for Curtiss. He set about it with the same assurance with which he flew the now famous June Bug at Hammondsport, N.Y., and put a crimp in the plans of the Wright brothers for cornering the aviation business in the United States. The entire program required less than half an hour to carry out. There was no hitch and not the least difficulty...*

"'We know now,' Captain Pond said, 'that a machine can rise from the water, fly along-side and be picked up, then go over the side and sail away. Or the process may be re-versed as necessity requires.' Secretary of the Navy Meyer has been shown. Another page in aerial history has been written full by the hand that already has penned so many chapters. But that is nothing to the unassuming, almost bashful king of the birdmen. He had set about doing an ordinary day's work and inwardly hoped the boss of the Navy Department would be satisfied."

23Feb1911: The Curtiss *D-III Triad* (land, air and water), the *first amphibian* (a claim appropriated by Grover Loening in the 1920's) with its *"convertible running gear"* was flown at North Island. Taking Hugh Robinson's suggestion, Curtiss fitted the hydroaeroplane with a tricycle landing gear, which, with a simple lever, could be raised for water operation or lowered for landing or takeoff on the ground. It was originally equipped with a 50-hp motor, but soon after being delivered to the Navy as the *A-1* (see below) was equipped with a model *"M"* 75-hp motor.

25Feb1911: An interesting Saturday, <u>*The Associated Press*</u>: *"'Well, what shall we name the boat?' That was the point which most worried Glenn H. Curtiss, the daring American aviator, when he today landed at the Coronado Hotel...He rose from...San Diego bay, flew to the sand-spit connecting Coronado and North Island, came down to get a new grip on the tricky, fish-tailed (machine), (and) 25 mile-per-hour wind, then shot up from the land and alighted on the beach near the hotel just south of the pier. After luncheon (with his wife) he replaced his rubber boots, tucked a fresh newspaper between his waistcoat and coat, climbed into his 'what-you-may-call-it' and starting from the ground alighted on the water at the North Island hangar."*

And soon, Curtiss, *"agreeable to trying out all sorts of new ideas,"* tried Ellyson's dual-control concept, which became standard on all Navy training aeroplanes.

Ellyson also wrote: *"...I am more anxious than ever to remain with Mr. Curtiss as long as possible, because he made a suggestion after every flight which showed me just where I did the wrong thing, or how I could have done it better..."*

Curtiss and Ellyson:

30Jan'11: Competing for the *Havana Post*'s $5,000 prize ($245,000 today), Jack McCurdy, with a Curtiss, almost succeeds (but got the prize, anyway) in the longest over-water flight, flying 89 miles from Key West when forced down 10 mile shy of Havana. It was the *first* flight out of sight of land.

The US Navy positioned destroyers every 10 miles along the route, and one, the *USS Paulding*, rescued him before his feet were wet.

McCurdy recalled: *"I had quite a dashboard, an Ingersoll dollar watch and a 35-cent*

compass...I rose to one thousand feet and took the course. Ahead of me was a continuous mirage, the sea instead of being a horizontal plane below had the appearance of a huge vertical picture on which the funnel tops of the destroyers appeared like black spots..."

1911: The *Model D* was the most common Curtiss aeroplane. The Army purchased three, and later used 40-hp *Model D-III's*, designated *"D-E"'s*, at North Island.

7Mar'11: The *Model D-IV "military machine"* (capable of carrying a passenger) was demonstrated in Washington by McCurdy.　　*Curtiss with Ellyson at North Island:*

A French hydro-aeroplane that is being used for experimental purposes. It is a biplane with a barrel tail. mounted on a catamaran   A triplane of great lifting power which Curtiss used in his experiments but discarded. Note the central float and the buoys at the sides

BIRD-MAN AND DUCK-MAN

By GLENN H. CURTISS

IT IS my firm belief that the hydro-aeroplane represents one of the longest and most important strides in aviation since man first learned to fly. It opens up a new field of usefulness for the aeroplane, wondrous in its possibilities and undreamed-of by the most optimistic enthusiast a year ago. It robs aviation of half its dangers and adds to the pleasure of flying a hundredfold. As an engine of warfare it widens the scope of the aeroplane's utility beyond the bounds of the most vivid imagination and makes possible its adoption by the navies of the world.

The hydro-aeroplane can fly sixty miles an hour, skim the water at fifty miles, and run over the earth at thirty-five miles. It marks the conquest of three elements — air, water, and earth. Driven over the surface of the water, the new machine can pass the fastest motor-boat ever built, and will respond to its rudder more quickly than any water craft afloat. Its appeal will be as strong to the aquatic as to the aerial enthusiast.

Flying an aeroplane is thrilling sport, but flying a hydro-aeroplane is something to arouse the jaded senses of the most blasé. It fascinates, exhilarates, vivifies.

Fear, the one thing that has laid a restraining hand on the sleeve of many a man eager to fly, need no longer be a hindrance to the progress of the aeroplane's popularity. The timid may become successful aviators as well as the venturesome, the man of business as well as the practical mechanic.

Whether soaring above land or sea, the operator of a hydro-aeroplane may always feel sure of a safe landing. If there be no land suitable for alighting upon, there must be water. Either will do for the hydro-aeroplane.

The mobile character of this new craft of the air will make it the safest and most popular of all aeroplanes. It makes long, over-water flights possible — flights that may be stretched from time to time until even the broadest ocean will eventually be spanned and continents brought closer together.

These things the average man does not appreciate to-day; yet they are well within the range of possibility. As a people we are prone to accept, in this day of wonderful progress in invention, those things that add most to our comfort and pleasure without halting to wonder at them. The aeroplane, one of the greatest achievements of man, has thus been "adopted" without fuss or feathers and is fast being adapted to our everyday needs. The hydro-aeroplane, the latest development of aviation, is still so new to the world that it is a curiosity, but it, too, will quickly find its field of usefulness — more quickly, indeed, than did its predecessor. Its field will be broader because of its mobility, and I believe it will give fresh impetus to the art of aviation.

The idea of an aeroplane that could fly from the surface of the water and alight thereon with safety, was not a sudden inspiration with me. I had long had it in mind. In fact, I had made some experiments in that direction on Lake Keuka, N. Y., soon after I had succeeded in flying my first aeroplane, the *June Bug*, at Hammondsport. Lack of time, however, prevented my pursuing the problem to success until almost two years later.

The advantages of such a machine came forcibly home to me when I was making preparations for my flight from Albany to New York City for the New York *World's* $10,000 prize in May, 1910. On that flight I followed the Hudson River the entire distance because I thought it safer to fly over an even water surface than over a rough and dangerous series of hills and mountains. I reasoned that if I were obliged to make a sudden landing it would be less dangerous to drop into the water and be picked up after a wetting than to be deposited in a tree top or upon a mountain side. For this reason I equipped the *Hudson Flyer* with pontoons to sustain it in case it should fall into the water.

If pontoons could be carried that would hold an aeroplane safely on the surface of the water, why would it not be possible to devise a permanent float that would enable it to get up enough speed to rise from the water? With this idea firmly fixed, I only awaited the opportunity to prove the feasibility of it. That opportunity came during the past winter. I had invited the Government to send officers of the Army and Navy to San Diego, Cal., to be trained to operate an aeroplane, and I determined to work out the problem of a water machine at the same time.

The conditions at San Diego were as nearly ideal for such experiments as could be found. There was vast surface of smooth water, a genial climate, even in winter, and a minimum of wind. Instead of interfering with the work of training the officers who had been sent there by the Government, I believed the development of a machine capable of flying from and landing upon the water would greatly aid in the task. To take them up as passengers in a machine that could be flown over water entirely and at a very low altitude with perfect security, would be safer, than in one that must keep over land altogether.

January was well toward its closing days before the first machine was made ready for the initial test. It proved unsuccessful. This did not surprise me. The best I had hoped for was to gain some knowledge of the sort of float necessary to support the aeroplane and to study the action of the equipment when under the driving power of the propeller.

Day after day, for a period of almost two weeks, we dragged the aeroplane down to the water's edge and set it afloat on the placid surface of San Diego Bay. As often we drew it out of the water after unsuccessful attempts to make it rise from the surface into the air, and put it back in the hangar upon the beach. But each failure added to our knowledge and brought success nearer.

I say "we" because I was ably and enthusiastically assisted at every stage of the experiments by Lieut. Theodore G. Ellyson of the Navy, Lieutenants Paul W. Beck, John C. Walker, Jr., and G. E. M. Kelly, of the Army, all of whom had been detailed to learn to fly, and by Hugh A. Robinson and C. C. Witmer, of my camp.

Our experiments being on the water naturally took us into the water a good deal. There was no thought given to wet clothing or cold feet. Bathing suits were the rule with the men for hours each day. Notwithstanding the genial nature of "sun-kissed San Diego's clime" there were times when chilled bodies would have welcomed the garb of a less poetically celebrated but more northerly climate. But discomfort and delayed success did not discourage the men who daily waded or swam the waters of Spanish Bight or watched and worked upon the shore. On January 26th success finally came. On that day the first aeroplane in the brief but thrilling history of aviation rose from the water, flew in circles and, returning, alighted upon the water. My theory had thus been proved, but there were many things remaining to be solved. These were merely questions of time and labor.

In our experiments we had changed the equipment from day to day, adding something one day only to discard it the next; cutting down weight and surface here and building it up there. With each day's changes came improvement. There were scores of little things that cropped up to annoy and delay us. Perhaps it was the float that was too heavy, or else it sprung a leak and became waterlogged; or maybe it was the flying spray that chipped the whirling propeller. One day the aeroplane showed a tendency to dive when driven by the engine; perhaps the next day it would drop at the "tail."

All these faults were overcome, and when we hauled the float-equipped aeroplane out of the hangar on January 26th we felt that we would now get results. We got results, and rather unexpectedly, at that.

There were no crowds gathered around to witness the first successful flight — none other than the army and navy officers and members of my own staff. I had not expected to make a flight at that time and had so informed the newspaper men. For that reason there were none of these ever-curious gentlemen on hand to herald the news to the world.

I climbed into the aviator's seat on that day with the feeling that the aeroplane would certainly get up in the air when I wished, but that I would only try it out on the water to watch the action of the new float and the hydrosurfaces.

When Lieutenant Ellyson spun the propeller and set the engine going, I turned the machine and headed into the wind. It ploughed through the water rather deeply and heavily at first, but as the speed increased, higher and more lightly, until the float barely skimmed the surface of the bay. I tilted the control to watch the action, and instantly the machine leaped into the air like a frightened gull. So suddenly did it rise that I was taken somewhat by surprise.

I kept the machine up for perhaps half a mile, then dropped lightly down on the water, turned around, and headed for the starting point. The effect of that first flight on the men who had worked, waited, and watched for it, was magical. They were now running up and down the beach, throwing up their hats and shouting their enthusiasm.

Turning the machine to go with the wind I headed out into the bay toward the city of San Diego, and got up in the air more easily than the first time. I took it out perhaps half a mile then turned twice to see how it would act with the rather clumsy-looking float at-

tached beneath. Everything went smoothly. I was satisfied and came to a landing within a few yards of the shore where a few minutes before we had launched the amphibious craft.

The naval repair ship *Iris*, which lay about a mile off in the bay, caught sight of the hydro-aeroplane just as I was to alight on the water and set its siren screaming in one long, exultant blast. It was followed by the sirens of other craft in the bay until it seemed that all of San Diego had wakened to the new achievement in aviation.

There were flights almost daily thereafter. Some of these were for the purpose of trying

Hauling the machine down from the hangar	The start. Getting up speed on the surface of the water

Rising from the water	Keeping at a low level without danger

Dropping down to the surface again	Landing on the water with a landward rush

The finish. Slowing down, with the power off.	Ready to be hauled back to shelter. This is the *Triad;* note the wheels.

GLENN H. CURTISS IN A HYDRO-AEROPLANE FLIGHT ACROSS SAN DIEGO BAY — THE ACME OF EASE. COMFORT. SAFETY. AND EXHILARATION

Military students, top: Navy Lt. Ellyson, Army Lt. Beck, Curtiss, Army Lt. Kelly, Army Lt.Walker; bottom: John Walker, Hugh Robinson and George Kelly, March 1911:

Watching a student: Paul Beck, Robert St. Henry, Curtiss, Major Hill, Ted Ellyson:

Feb'11: Congress appropriates $125,000 (Approximately $5-1/2 million today) for Army aeronautics, and establishes training stations at North Island, College Park and Omaha.

Mar'11: The Hammondsport factory is auctioned by the trustee in bankruptcy of the *Herring-Curtiss Co.* Curtiss buys it back for $25,100 (about $1-1/4 million today)

Mar'11: The *Wright Company* offers to train a pilot if the Navy purchases an aeroplane, but due to Curtiss's unconditional offer, are forced to match his offer.

The Navy then orders Lt. *John (Jang) Rodgers* (1881-1926, Cal Rodgers' double-cousin) to Dayton for training, followed by Ensign *Victor Daniel Herbster* (ca. 1890-1946), with whom Waldo Waterman would fly - and crash - in 1912.

24Mar'11: Wilbur, in Paris, testifies in an infringement trial against twelve Frence aviators and manufacturers: Santos-Dumont's was dismissed because he built only for his own use; Bleriot tried to settle; but the other ten carried on the fight.

Delays, and the war, finally caused the Wrights to abandon the fight.

31Mar'11: Curtiss deems Ellyson a *"practical aviator."* He received *FAI Aero Club of America License No. 28* on 6Jul'11.

The Wright Army Biplane

ONE of our illustrations shows the Wright biplane which was recently loaned to the army by Mr. Robert F. Collier, in flight above the camp at San Antonio, Texas. Lieut. B. D. Foulois and Aviator Philip Parmalee have made some excellent scouting flights in Texas recently with this machine. The chief of these was made on March 3rd, when they flew from Laredo to Eagle Pass, an air line distance of 104½ miles, in 2 hours and 7 minutes. By following the Rio Grande they covered about 106 miles actual distance, their average speed being close to 50 miles an hour. On the return trip the machine met with an accident and landed in the river. It was transported back to camp, and, after repairs had been made, some more excellent scouting flights were accomplished. On March 18th they flew for several minutes in the pouring rain, thus demonstrating that the aeroplane could be used even under extremely adverse conditions. The Signal Corps acquired last week its first Curtiss biplane, and this has been taken to Texas for use at the maneuvers. The original Wright biplane which belonged to the Signal Corps has been returned to the factory for remodeling. It is probable that in addition to this the army will have several more Wright and Curtiss machines for use in the near future.

Scientific American 1Apr'11:

12Apr'11 Curtiss to Secretary Navy Meyer: "*I have the honor to report that Lieut. Ellison [sic] is now competent to care for and operate Curtis [sic] aeroplanes and instruct others in the operation of these machines...It is a pleasure for me to recommend Mr. Ellison as a man who will make a success in aviation.*"

He became *Naval Aviator No. 1,* followed by Wright-trained Rodgers 2; Curtiss-trained John Towers 3; and Wright-trained Herbster 4.

1911: Army Lt. G.E.M. Kelly, who had been partially taught at North Island, along with Lts. Paul Beck and John Walker was transferred to Ft. Sam Houston, Texas, where, with Lt. Benjamin Foulois, on *5Apr'11* the Army's *"Provisional Aero Company"* was organized.

Kelly was soon killed, in his qualification flight in the Army's new Curtiss *"Type IV, Military;"* a 50-hp machine far more powerful than Curtiss's North Island training aeroplanes - and, in Foulois's opinion, 'not well constructed.'

Ellyson, however, after carefully studying Beck's letter to Curtiss about Kelly's crash, felt that material failure did not cause his death.

Aviator Philip Parmalee and Lieut. B. D. Foulois flying above the army encampment at San Antonio, Texas, in the army Wright biplane.

31Mar'11: Wilbur (Le Mans) to Orville: "*I have been...over the CGNA accounts and I find that the trouble...has been more the result of bad management than rascality, though the latter may no be entirely lacking...There have been...times that we have regained the lead so far as the army is concerned, and each time have lost it again because the motors were no good. Even yet the officers prefer our machine...The offi-cers who ride Bleriots are all scared, and those who ride Farmans also when there is a little wind...The engineers prefer ours because they are more controllable, stronger, and have a higher dynamic efficiency..."*

31Mar'11-10Aug'11: Wilbur is obtaining patents and attending to business in France, Austria, Belgium, Germany, Great Britain, Hungary, Italy, Russia and Spain. But at times the problems seem overwhelming. One day he commented to his brother: *"Orv, in the days when we were making our aeroplane, and were as poor as church mice, it was all fun; but now, with the aeroplane finished and a lot of money in our pockets, it is all worry."*

14Apr'11: *Harold F. McCormick,* president of the Aero Club of Illinois, met with Orville to discuss the *"International Aviation Meet"* planned for August. Summariz-ing this discussion, where the Wrights demanded $10,000 to license the meet as well as financial guarantees for each Wright pilot, he wrote: *"He very openly stated there were three things he wanted: First, to prevent foreign aviators from coming to Amer-ica. Second, to get as much money out of the meet as possible. Third, to support his patents...He stated that he did not care whether aviation in America was helped or not...He stated he would sue every aviator they could afford to..."*

8Apr'11: *Charles Munn, Scientific American:*

THE presentation of the SCIENTIFIC AMERI-CAN Aviation Cup to Mr. Glenn H. Curtiss, as recorded elsewhere in this issue, gave the donors an opportunity to draw attention to the sportsmanlike spirit displayed by the winner in his persistent quest of this trophy. Although Curtiss is engaged in the manufacture and commercial exploi-tation of aeroplanes, and is therefore a professional, he has exemplified the best traditions of the amateur in his three-year quest of a trophy which brings no cash to the winner, and whose principal value lies in the distinction which it confers. The SCIENTIFIC AMERICAN has always deplored the fact that there was no competition for this trophy, and our regret was due, not so much to the consideration that we were its donors, as to the fact that the lack of interest in the cup proved that the spirit of commer-cialism was dominant among the ranks of the avia-tors, not one of whom, outside of Curtiss, cared to turn momentarily aside from the hunt for large money prizes and make an effort to win a cup which has the distinction of being the first trophy of any kind offered in America in connection with the new art of aviation.

Let it be understood that we have no prejudice whatever against the professional airman. When he hangs his life in mid-air, upon a flimsy fabric of wood, canvas and wire, for the special delectation of an assembled multitude, it is perfectly proper that they should pay adequately for witnessing his game of chance with Death. Moreover, aeroplane sport is costly, and not many among the airmen have the private means to enable them to last very long at the game. What we do regret, however, is that in the midst of all this money-getting, one looks almost in vain for the relieving contrast of a touch of the true old sporting spirit; the spirit which in other lines of sport is cherished and guarded so assidu-ously by various amateur associations throughout the world. Now there can be no question that the undoubted popularity of the winner of the SCIEN-TIFIC AMERICAN Trophy is largely due to the con-scious or unconscious recognition of the fact that he has in him, despite his professional standing, a strong dash of the true sporting instinct; and we commend his successful quest of this trophy to the consideration of the younger race of airmen, to whom we must look for the rescuing of the sport from the rank professionalism into which it has fallen.

joining the aviation course have all the practice required to fit them for aerial flight. Another aviation field has been established at Fort Leavenworth, and some at other places throughout the country for similar purposes.

"One of the features receiving close attention is the development of flying machines from the viewpoint of stability and safety. The government now has about $100,000 to spend for machines, and will put it into the different types. As more money is appropriated the field will be extended.

"It is the ultimate intention, I believe, to teach aviation to several thousand army men, who will be ready at any time to go aloft in their machines during the mobilization of troops, no matter for what purpose, and it is believed that they will be an extraordinary adjunct to the efficiency of the army as a whole.

"But it is of great importance to the public to know that while the aviation grounds of the government will be primarily for army men, they will be open to the general public as well, so that any person having a flying machine can use it in these places freely and also get the benefit of the instruction of experts in flying. Their opportunities will be as great as those afforded to army men in the matter of study and practice."

CURTISS'S CAREER AND EXPERIMENTS.

Glenn H. Curtiss, the man who has done so much toward the scientific advancement and the practical development of aviation, was born in Hammondsport, N. Y., on the shore of Lake Keuka, on May 21st, 1878. When a boy he delivered newspapers in his home town and worked later as a messenger boy for one of the telegraph companies in Rochester, N. Y. Returning home, he established a newspaper route, and while delivering papers to his scattered customers became interested in self-propelled vehicles. Before he was twenty, Curtiss had built a motorcycle to carry him over his route. This machine was developed into a commercial product, young Curtiss paying the expense of his experiments by doing bicycle repairing and electrical work. The embryo motorcycle manufacturer also took up the motorcycle sport, winning many contests, including the American championship. Aiming for the speed championship of the world, he built a special machine, and in 1907 at Ormond Beach, Florida, he is said to have covered a measured mile in 26.25 seconds, which, if correct, stands as the fastest mile ever traveled by man.

From motorcycles to aeroplanes proved a short step. The lack of a suitable motor had been the greatest obstacle in the way of air navigation. Curtiss developed his small engine for use in dirigible balloons with successful results, and was soon supplying the power plants of practically every successful dirigible in America, including the airship sold to the United States Army by Capt. Baldwin.

Invited by Dr. Alexander Graham Bell to become a member of the Aerial Experiment Association, Curtiss was made director of experiments, and in this capacity designed his first heavier-than-air machine, the "June Bug." With the "June Bug" Curtiss won the first aviation prize offered in America—the SCIENTIFIC AMERICAN Trophy—by flying a mile and a half on July 4th, 1908. He made a number of flights prior to this, using other machines built under his direction by the association.

While teaching members of the Aeronautical Society to fly in Mineola, L. I., in the spring of 1909, Curtiss was urged by the Aero Club of America to represent this country in the first international race. With an aeroplane that had never been assembled until after he arrived on the field at Rheims, France, he defeated Blériot and other leading foreign aviators, becoming the first international champion. After Rheims, Curtiss was numbered among the world's greatest aviators. At Brescia, Italy, he duplicated his success at Rheims, and since then his movements in America have been indelibly impressed upon the minds of the public.

His flight down the Hudson River from Albany, N. Y., to New York city on May 29th, 1910—150 miles in 152 minutes—will go down in history. By covering the first half of this distance—71½ miles—in 1 hour and 23 minutes, or at the rate of 51¼ miles an hour, Curtiss won the SCIENTIFIC AMERICAN Trophy for the third and last time, and secured final possession of the cup. This is but one of the many triumphs he has accomplished, almost any one of which would

Photo by Levick.

Glenn H. Curtiss at the wheel of his biplane.

Three-quarter rear view of the Curtiss military biplane.

Note balancing planes at rear of uprights and movable horizontal rudders at rear of tail.

Curtiss biplane mounted on a float and wheels.

This machine is shown emerging from the water and running up on the beach.

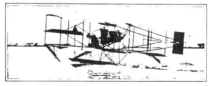

Skimming the surface before rising into the air.

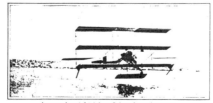

An experimental triplane flying above the water.

This picture shows very well the small size of float.

THE CURTISS MILITARY BIPLANE AND SOME OF HIS EXPERIMENTAL MACHINES

have been sufficient to win him enduring fame. Among the most notable of those following the Hudson flight might be mentioned his "Fifty miles over the sea" flight at Atlantic City, N. J., in July, 1910; his trip over Lake Erie from Euclid Beach to Cedar Point, Ohio—64 miles—and return the following September, and his more recent flights from the surface of the water in the new machine developed by him, which alights on and flies from land or water equally well.

Aviation for military purposes has been given its greatest impetus by the experiments made by Curtiss or conducted under his direction, such as bomb dropping, target shooting, sending wireless from an aeroplane in flight, as well as the flights of Eugene Ely from the decks of two of Uncle Sam's battleships, upon one of which he successfully alighted. In furtherance of the military idea, Curtiss has volunteered to instruct aviators for the army and navy, and has graduated three army and one navy officer from his school at San Diego, Cal., without a cent's cost to the government.

During the past winter Mr. Curtiss has been experimenting at San Diego, with a view to perfecting a suitable float for starting from and alighting upon the water. He had already tried experiments in this direction a number of years ago upon the lake at his home at Hammondsport, N. Y., and profiting by the experiments of M. Fabre in France, he was not long in making similar floats with which he was able, on February 1st, to rise from the water with his biplane. He afterward simplified the floats to a single long, narrow, scow-shaped pontoon, which worked better than the hydroplane floats used at first. He found experimenting on the water was preferable to experimenting on land, and he made numerous changes, such as placing the motor in front and the aviator's seat behind the main planes, and adding a third surface above the biplane, thus converting it into a triplane. One of the most interesting feats he is said to have performed was flying with but one aileron, or balancing plane, on his machine. In view of the patent litigation he has had with the Wright brothers, this should prove valuable in behalf of Mr. Curtiss's defense.

Finally, after all these other experiments, Curtiss early last month fitted wheels to his biplane in addition to the float, and rose from the water or from the land and alighted upon either at will. One of our photographs shows his machine coming out of the water and running up on the shore. Thus he succeeded in perfecting the machine so that it is now a true mechanical water fowl.

Only a couple of weeks ago, after having instructed four officers of the army and navy in flying at San Diego, Curtiss delivered to the War Department at Washington his first military biplane, a photograph of which is also reproduced on this page. This machine has several new points of interest, such as the placing of the ailerons at the rear of the machine instead of at the front, and the tail, the movable rear ends of the two triangular surfaces of which act in conjunction with the front rudder to steer the machine in a vertical plane. This biplane is very strongly built, and is capable of carrying two men and 300 pounds extra weight. It has a spread of 32 feet, an over-all length of 29 feet, and its total supporting surface is 320 square feet; the weight complete is 700 pounds. In making the acceptance flight Mr. McCurdy made two magnificent flights of 10 and 8 minutes' duration above the Potomac at Washington. The machine has been sent to San Antonio, Texas, where the officers will experiment with it. Mr. Curtiss himself will come East the middle of this month, and will conduct further experiments in the neighborhood of Annapolis. In all probability he will devote much of his time in the near future to perfecting the aeroplane for naval use.

Attended by Washington's Who's Who, many Bell's Wednesday Evening guests:

OFFICIAL PROGRAM
Washington Aviation Meet

UNDER THE PERSONAL DIRECTION OF

GLENN H CURTISS

AT THE

BENNING RACE TRACK
MAY 5, 6, 7, 1911

Special Committee of the Aero Club of Washington governing the contests for Trophies and Prizes.

GEO. OWEN SQUIRE, Chairman	GEO. OAKLEY TOTTEN, Jr., Vice Chairman
BUTLER AMES	EDWARD McLEAN
JOHN BARRETT	NELSON A. MILES
C. J. BELL	EDWARD A. MITCHELL
EMILE BERLINER	WILLIS A. MOORE
J. WESLEY BOVEE	LOGAN W. PAGE
H. C. FRANKENFIELD	THOMAS NELSON PAGE
GILBERT GROSVENOR	CUNO H. RUDOLPH
WM. F. GUDE	LAWRENCE TOWNSEND
F. ODEN HORSTMAN	HORACE H. WESTCOTT
C. L. MARLATT	A. F. ZAHM
ORMSBY McCAMMON	

Special Committee of the Aero Club of America governing the trials for Pilots' Licenses.

J. WESLEY BOVEE, Chairman

C. J. BELL   GEO. OAKLEY TOTTEN, Jr.   EMILE BERLINER   A. F. ZAHM

Motor Cycle Races

THOMAS WANSLEBEN, Fed. of A. M. C., Referee

RUDOLPH JOSE, Clerk of Course   THOS. M. MUDD, Chief Timer

C. S. FRENCH, Judge of Course

MODEL AEROPLANE COMPETITION

JUNIOR AERO CLUB OF WASHINGTON

8May'11: The Navy orders aeroplanes, two Curtiss and one Wright. One, the *A-1*, a Curtiss *Triad* (cost: $4,400, $200,000 today) had provision for a passenger and was equipped with (Ellyson's) dual control for instructor and student.

The *Navy's 1st aeroplane*; this date is often considered the birth of Naval aviation.

Holden Richardson and Jack Towers in the A-1, North Island, February, 1912:

This, the first order for the *Curtiss Aeroplane Company,* successor to *Herring-Curtiss Co.*

In 1914 several *Model E Triads* were delivered to Czarist Russia by Charles Witmer and George Hallett. Note: In 1911 the company, short on funds and unable to pay Witmer for an exhibition flight, gave him $500 in stock. Knowing that the company never paid dividends, he tried to sell it for $100 - but found no takers. Thus he had it with him on this trip when he received a cable telling him to come home, that he was a rich man – the value of his stock having increased to well over $100,000 ($4-1/2 million today).

7May'11: Bishop Wright's diary: *"Lieutenant Rodgers, of the Navy, and Lieuts. H. (Henry "Hap") H. Arnold (1886-1950) and T.D. Milling (1887-1960), of the Army, supped with us. They are here to learn to fly."*

28May'11: Orville to August Belmont: "...*The Wright Company is granting licenses to promoters of aeroplane meets on a basis of about 20% of the amount put up in prizes, where nothing is paid to the aviators as appearance money; and on a basis of 10% of the gross gate receipts and grandstand receipts, in cases where these two furnish the entire income for conducting the meet. In a few cases we are granting licenses for a lump sum, based on the estimated receipts as mentioned...*

"I have just received the opinion of the French court in our case against Bleriot, Farman, and nine other French infringers of our French patent. The decision...was so strong in our favor that the defendants are now negotiating with Wilbur for a

settlement for the one thousand machines already put out by the defendants and on the machines to be manufactured in the future. The French decision virtually clinches our case in the American courts."

30Jun'11: Wilbur (Berlin) to Orville: "...*If I could get free from business with the money we already have in hand I would rather do it than continue the business at a considerable profit. Only two things lead me to put up with responsibilities and annoyances for a moment. First, the obligations to people that put money into our business, and second, the reluctance a man normally feels to allow a lot of scoundrels and thieves to steal his patents, subject him to all kinds of troubles or even try to cheat him out of his patents entirely. So far as Europe is concerned I do not feel that we are in debt to either the French or German companies. We have not had a square deal from either of them. All the money we ever got from either of these companies will be fully paid for by future work and worries. But I hate to see the French infringers wreck our business and abuse us and go unscathed...For the good of the public and the protection of others we ought to do our share to discourage such people a little...*"

Berlin's Johannisthal aerodrome in 1912. Contrast the sophistication and variety of aircraft with the Wright Flyer, right:

8Jun'11: Curtiss granted *Aviator License No. 1* by the Aero Club of America under *Federation Aeronautique Internationale* (F.A.I.) authority, because of being *"the first person to publicly fly in the United States"* (4Jul1908 *June Bug* flight).

No.2 Frank P.Lahm (*Army Pilot No.1*); Paulhan No.3; Orville & Wilbur Nos. *4 & 5.*

Europe: Bleriot No. *1*, Curtiss No. *2*, Wrights Nos. *14 and 15.*

27Jun'11: Lt(jg) *John H. Towers* (1885-1955) detailed to Hammondsport for flying instruction.

As *"Handsome Jack"* at Annapolis '06, he *"was as introverted, serious, and abstentious as Ellyson was extroverted, carefree, and indulgent."*   George Wilson

Curtiss and Towers:

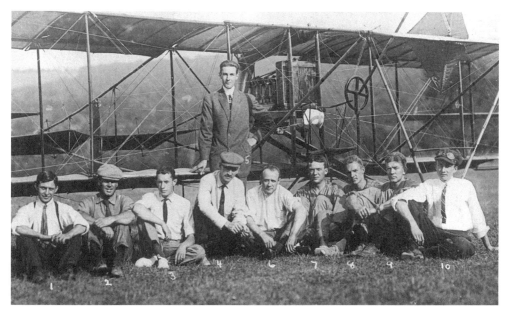

Godet, Russell, Doherty, Curtiss, Havens (standing), McClaskey, Beck, Towers, Ellyson and Dixon:

Spring 1911: The Curtiss flying school opens in Hammondsport. Among the students: Eugene Godet, R.B. Russell, W. Elwood (Gink) Doherty, Beckwith Havens, John Mc-Claskey/Marine, Towers and Ellyson/Navy, Beck/Army, and Seattle's Cromwell Dixon (in 1907, at 14, America's youngest airship pilot; killed at Spokane late in 1911).

27Jun'11: Lincoln Beachey, in a Curtiss, flew over Niagara Falls, down the Gorge and under the suspension Rainbow Bridge, while Harry Houdini slid across on a wire.

1Jul1911: Curtiss test-flies the Navy's newly-completed *A-1* on Lake Keuka. He then takes Ellyson as his passenger, and then Ellyson takes it alone for two flights – *marking the birthday of US Naval aviation.*

It was equipped with Curtiss' more powerful Model *"M"* 75-hp motor. Its two seats, control column, and foot rest bar were fastened on the forward diagonal struts connecting the main float and lower wing, and the engine throttle, similar to a car's accelerator, was at the pilot's left foot. The ignition switch was on the control wheel at the pilot's left thumb, where he could easily *"cut the switch."* Light, sturdy and well built, this machine, used the conventional Curtiss flight control system: directional control was by turning the wheel, like in an auto, connected to the rudder. Pitch control was by moving the control column forward or aft, operating the elevators; and banking was accomplished by Curtiss' unique shoulder yoke by which the pilot's instinctive leaning controlled the ailerons. And it had Ellyson's dual operation, yoked, throw-over wheel - making it easy to shift control between pilot and student (soon changed to two separate wheels). Its total weight, including two 175-pound men, was just under 1,600 pounds, which the 75-hp engine could handle with ease. Maximum speed was 60-mph; cruise was 45 to 50-mph.

*The new, the Curtiss hydroaeroplane, and the old, the Japanese training ship Taisei
Maru, San Diego Bay, 1911 (scouting for Japan's Baja California invasion? See 264):*

2Jul1911: Lt. Ellyson qualifies for his license, becoming the Navy's *first* aviator. He then flies the *A-1* twenty-two miles over Keuka Lake, successfully completing Naval aviation's *first* night flight.

On July 6th Captain Chambers took delivery of the *A-1*. It's flight history, beginning at Hammondsport that summer of 1911, shows it transferred in September to the *Greenbury Point Aviation Camp* near Annapolis, the Navy's *first*; in January, 1912, to North Island; and then, back to Greenbury Point in May.

On 10Oct1912 it had its last flight with Ellyson as "*operator*"..."*Machine wrecked last flight; Expended except motor. Not rebuilt.*" It'd flown a total of 54 hrs. and 47 min.

This differs slightly from that reported in the 11Nov 1911 issue of <u>*Fly*</u> magazine: "*Lieut. Theodore G. Ellyson and Lieut. J.H. Towers, the Navy's two accomplished aviators, made a remarkable flight on Wednesday, October 11th, in the Navy's Curtiss hydro-aeroplane. They started at the naval aviation station at Annapolis* (Greenbury), *at noon, and landed on the beach at Smith's Point, Va., at the mouth of the Potomac river, 65 miles south of Annapolis, an hour and a half later. The hydro-aeroplane used by Lieuts. Ellyson and Towers, is equipped with the dual control* (adapted from the French) *which allows for the shifting of the steering wheel to either man while in the air, without any effect whatever on the machine. The naval aviators were followed as closely as possible by the fast torpedo boat 'Bagley.'*"

America's *first* flight manual: Curtiss's 1911 *"Rules Governing The Use Of Aeronautical Apparatus."*

As to "the seniority...ascribed to the left seat (of a 2-pilot aircraft). It probably arose because Curtiss first carried passengers to his right."   *George van Deurs*

12-20Aug1911: The *Chicago International Aviation Meet* featured Lincoln Beachey, Ely, Coffyn, Parmalee, Mars, Ovington, Robinson, Brookins, T.O.M. Sopwith (1888-1990) - and beginner Calbraith P. Rodgers (1879-1912). Two were killed: St. Croix Johnstone, crashing into Lake Michigan, and William R. Badger, attempting to emulate Beachey's flying, as described by pioneer aviator *Guy Gilpatric:*

"*I have critically observed the work of some thousands of joystick virtuosi here and in Europe in the thirty years that have passed since Beachey's death, but for my money he remains what his twenty-four sheet posters proclaimed him to be: 'The Greatest of Them All.' Thirty years and two world wars have brought many improvements to airplanes, but when I say that Beachey's flying has never been surpassed, I say it without reservations of any kind. In his eighty-horsepower Curtiss pusher, designed by rule of thumb and built* like a bird cage, he did things which no other man has ever done in the latest products of wind tunnel, slide rule and million dollar factory. Beachey's forte was his ability to come close to things without hitting them. To do loops and flip-flops high in the air requires no great skill, but to fly between trees so close together that the machine must be banked sixty degrees to pass through, is flying of the most divine order.

"Another of Beachey's caprices was to fly around a half-mile race track and flick up the dust with a matter of half an inch; another half-inch would have tripped the plane and spattered Mr. Beachey all over the homestretch.

"For a couple of seasons, Beachey teamed up with Barney Oldfield in a racing stunt that was a corker. Oldfield would drive his Fiat Cyclone or his front-drive Christie Special and Beachey would stay no more than a foot above him all the way around the track. Call me a liar if you will, but these old eyes have seen Beachey rest his front wheel on Barney's head while both plane and car were doing better than sixty miles an hour. His flight down Michigan Boulevard, Chicago, eighteen inches above the fear-frozen traffic, will probably never be duplicated in the history of the world."

Barney Oldfield and Eddie Rickenbacker racing Beachey, Davenport, Iowa, 1914 (the author's father a spectator):

Beachey on spectators: *"They call me the Master Birdman, but they pay to see me die."*

316

*Ely and McCurdy at
the Chicago Meet:*

OFFICIAL PROGRAM

HARVARD-BOSTON AERO MEET
HARVARD AVIATION FIELD ATLANTIC MASS
AUG 26 · SEPT 4 1911

PRICE TEN CENTS

"...the Wrights developed a personal hatred of Curtiss that splashed over onto everyone remotely connected with him. At the Chicago meet, for example, they threatened to fire Frank Coffyn, one of their best pilots, because he gave Towers a ride in spite of the fact that he knew him to be a Curtiss student. This feeling restricted Rodgers and the other Navy fliers to casual contact at Chicago and led Chambers to operate the two types in separate camps until after Rodgers left aviation for ship duty in 1912."   *George van Deurs*

26Aug-4Sep'11: *Harvard-Boston Aero Meet.* Official Program (*author's collection*) is vivid testimony of the virulent bias of Wright partisans, apparently abundant in Boston: in its *"The Story of the Flying Machine"* there's <u>no</u> mention of Curtiss, his achievements and contributions to aviation; even his name is misspelled in aeroplane descriptions. Needless to say, he did not compete.

317

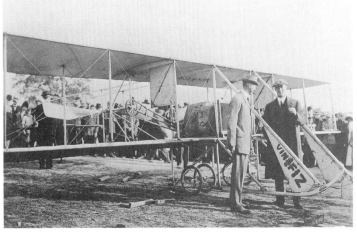

17Sep1911: *Calbraith Perry Rodgers*, in a *Wright EX Vin Fiz* (a new, grape soda pop) took off from Sheepshead Bay, N.Y. on a transcontinental flight, completed in Long Beach, CA 10Dec'11. Rodgers, 6'4" and 200 lbs., was a virtually deaf, difficult son of affluence. A daring and reckless pilot; when his flight was completed the Wright had crashed and been rebuilt so many times that only the rudder, engine drip pan, and a strut or two remained of the original plane.

Cousins John Rodgers, left, Cal, & Vin Fiz:

Scientific American, 18Nov'11:

The First Trans-continental Aeroplane Flight
Account of the Record-breaking Aerial Journey by Calbraith P. Rodgers on a Wright Biplane

BY his arrival at Pasadena, Cal., at 4:04 P. M. on the afternoon of November 5th, aviator Rodgers practically completed his great trans-continental flight, although the real finish did not occur until several days later, when he flew the 25 miles remaining, and landed on the shore of the Pacific Ocean. Rodgers' start was made from the Sheepshead Bay race track, near Coney Island, on September 17th last. He started with the intention of competing for the $50,000 prize offered by the proprietor of a New York newspaper. The time limit within which this prize could be won expired on October 10th, but Rodgers flew on just the same, despite many mishaps and breakdowns. His total time to Pasadena was 49 days. The distance covered was some 3,350 miles, and the time in the air 82 hours. This corresponds to an average speed of about 40 miles an hour.

Besides breaking all records, aviator Rodgers carried with him letters from Postmaster-General Hitchcock. Several of these were delivered in Chicago, and others, including one from Major-General Grant to the Department of the Pacific, and another from the commanding officer of the Atlantic fleet to Rear Admiral Thomas of the Pacific squadron, were carried the entire distance across the continent and delivered. We have followed the progress made by Rodgers from week to week in the columns of the SCIENTIFIC AMERICAN, and now that he has completed his flight, it will be interesting to summarize briefly and give the causes of his various delays. The two chief causes appear to have arisen from bad weather and breakdowns of the motor. He was forced to descend some eight or ten times on account of engine failures. Some of these were simple troubles, such as a wire coming loose or the fouling of a spark plug, but toward the end of his flight, at Imperial Junction, Cal., a connecting rod broke loose and punched a hole in the crank case, and Rodgers was obliged to replace the motor with a spare one which his special train carried. When starting from Middletown, N. Y., the second day, Rodgers fouled a tree and smashed his machine. This delayed him three days before he could effect repairs. At Hancock, N. Y., his next stop-

ping place, he descended on account of slight engine trouble and was delayed half a day because of a storm. After flying 50 miles farther to Canisteo, he again descended on account of engine trouble. He mistook a marsh for a solid field and damaged his machine in alighting. The next day, however, he flew 99 miles to Red House, where he alighted to change a spark plug. In restarting, he ran into a wire fence, smashing his machine and propellers, which caused a two days' delay. Engine trouble is of course blamed for this, as if he had not alighted at Red House, he would not have collided with the fence there. At one other point in Texas, in starting on a narrow road, Rodgers smashed his machine by colliding with a fence. Two days were spent resting and overhauling the machine at San Antonio and El Paso, Tex., respectively.

All told, some 13½ days were lost making repairs, and of these, 2½ days can be laid directly to engine trouble. The weather was responsible for the loss of 11 days, so that a total delay of 24½ days was occasioned from weather and repairs. Deducting this from the total time of 49 days, we have 14½ days as the actual time of making the flight, which shows the possibility of crossing the continent in a month's time by aeroplane, in case one does not meet with bad weather and serious mishaps. It should be remembered that Rodgers chose a roundabout way, going far south into Texas and then following the line of the Southern Pacific Railway. He broke the world's long-distance cross-country record on October 10th, when he reached Marshall, Mo., after a flight of 214 miles, as he beat by a few miles Atwood's record of 1,265 from St. Louis to New York, which flight was completed on August 25th.

One of the important events in the course of his flight was his meeting with Robert G. Fowler at Tucson, Ariz. Fowler, it will be remembered, previously tried to cross the Rockies in his Wright biplane, but failed. On October 20th he left Los Angeles, determined to make the flight across the continent by the southern route. Up to November 6th, he had covered 825 miles in 16 days' time.

A comparison of Rodgers' flight with the first tr[ans]continental automobile trip is interesting. The [first] attempt was made by Alexander Winton and Cha[rles] Shanks in 1901, but the Winton car was stuck in [the] sands of the great American desert. Two years la[ter], however, Dr. H. Nelson Jackson and S. W. Cro[cker] accomplished the feat of crossing from San Franc[isco] to New York in a Winton machine, having a dou[ble] opposed-cylinder engine, in 65 days. A sing'e-cyli[nder] Packard automobile, driven by Tom Fetch, acc[om]plished the journey in 62 days, including a four[days'] stop at Denver, and an Oldsmobile, driven by L. [L.] Whitman, made the journey in 72 days. All t[hese] trips were made in the summer of 1903. The follow[ing] year, Whitman and Harris crossed the continent f[rom] the Pacific to the Atlantic, a distance of 4,500 m[iles,] in 33 days, thereby beating by 28 days, the best pre[vi]ous record; and in 1906 a 6-cylinder 30-horse-po[wer] Franklin air-cooled automobile was driven 4,000 m[iles] across the continent in 15 days, 2 hours, and 12 m[in]utes. This cutting down of the time to one-quarte[r] but three years shows the rapid development of automobile from 1903 to 1906.

The aeroplane has developed so much more rap[idly] that two years ago the past summer, Olleslager[s] mained aloft more than five hours and covered a [dis]tance of 240 miles, while of late distances of betw[een] 700 and 800 miles have been covered in a day w[ith] only a few stops. With a reliable motor, and [the] development of an automatic stability device w[hich] will enable the aviator to fly in windy weather[, it] should be possible to cross the continent in ten d[ays'] time, and without doubt this will soon be done. [As] a great time saver the aeroplane is was demonstra[ted] time and again, especially in the far west, wh[ere] Rodgers frequently out-distanced his special trai[n] from one to two hours. Flying over mountains [and] canyons he found rather risky, but at the end of [his] journey he announced that Beachy's flight above [Ni]agara Falls and down the gorge last summer was[, in] his opinion, the greatest flight ever made. The Wr[ight] biplane had for the second time broken the c[ross] country touring record.

After Rodger's death (on 3Apr1912 he crashed in the surf off Long Beach, CA, in a *Wright B*) the *Vin Fiz* was exhibited until, in 1914, Rodgers's mother, Mrs. Maria Sweitzer (1855-1936), sent it to Dayton for restoration.

According to Orville, 29May1925: "*The plane used in the transcontinental flight was almost totally destroyed in an accident in California. The few remaining parts were shipped by Mrs. H. S. Sweitzer to Dayton in 1914, for...having it restored...for the Carnegie Institute. But when* (she) *learned the costs...she gave up the idea...The parts were still at the factory...and were later in 1916 destroyed.*"

In 1996, the Smithsonian, in a special national touring exhibit, featured the "original Vin Fiz." The author challenged its authenticity, to which, on 11Jan1996, Smithsonian curator *Peter Jakab* answered: "*As the Vin Fiz crossed the country it was rebuilt many times from replacement parts brought along the route...As a result, by journey's end, there were enough 'original' Vin Fiz parts to complete* <u>more</u> *than one airframe...All of these people claimed to have the Vin Fiz...They all did have the Vin Fiz. It is just that there in essence was 'more' than one Vin Fiz after the flight was over. In other words, there were more flown Wright EX parts than simply the airframe as it existed upon the completion of the flight...*"

1911: Robert J. Collier, publisher of <u>Collier's</u> magazine and an ardent Wright supporter, for $5,000 (around $235,000 today), is the first private person to purchase a Wright machine. He also loaned it to the Army (see page 306).

The Dec'11 issue of <u>Fly</u> magazine: "*On September 16th, O. G. Simmon, who is flying Robert Collier's Wright biplane, ascended at Wickatunk, NJ, to a height of 800 feet. At this altitude his engine quit, but Simmon made a spiral glide and a beautiful landing in the unromantic suburbs of a potato patch.*"

<u>Aero</u>, 7Oct1911: "20,000 SEE BEACHEY AT DUBUQUE. *Dubuque, Iowa...The Flight of Lincoln Beachey at Nutwood Park on September 28 and 29 was northeastern Iowa's introduction to air travel. It was witnessed by over 20,000 people, at least 19,500 of whom probably had never seen an aeroplane before...*"

14Oct1911: French aviator R. Level killed, the world's *100th* flying-machine fatality.

4Nov'11: Bishop Wright's diary: "*...The boys try a Curtiss machine, at Simms, and break it.*"
9Nov11: "*Wilbur went out to try the Curtiss machine. It is hard to fly with.*"

Nov'11: The Wrights withdraw from exhibition flying. *Of nine team flyers, five, Johnstone, Hoxsey, Welsh, Gill, and Parmalee had been killed.*

12Dec'11: Bishop Wright's diary: "*...The decision in the trial with Grahame-White resulted in his being enjoined, which stands good till reversed on appeal.*"

The Wrights sued Grahame-White, Britain's top aviator, claiming he had made $100,000 flying in the United States (he reputedly made an astonishing *$250,000*, over $11 million today). On 24Jan1912 they won a token $1,700, which served to discourage Wright-unlicensed foreign aviators from flying in America.

Orville Wright's Flights in a Glider at Kitty Hawk.— Upon his return home from his memorable flights without a motor at Kitty Hawk, N. C.—flights in which he remained aloft 7¼ and 9¾ minutes, respectively—Orville Wright said that these motorless flights were the most difficult he had ever undertaken, the conditions under which they were made being much more severe than those ever met with in a power-driven aeroplane. Measured with a Richard anemometer, the wind one day at the top of the hill had a velocity of from 17 to 25 meters per second (38 to 56 miles per hour), while 12 feet above the top of the hill the wind velocity was still greater. There was a difference of 5 meters per second in simultaneous observations made at heights of 6 and 12 feet, respectively. Mr. Wright believes his experience at Kitty Hawk will be of great assistance in designing new machines to meet severe weather conditions.

Orville Wright starting from the top of a sand dune with his new glider.

Scientific American, 4Nov'11:

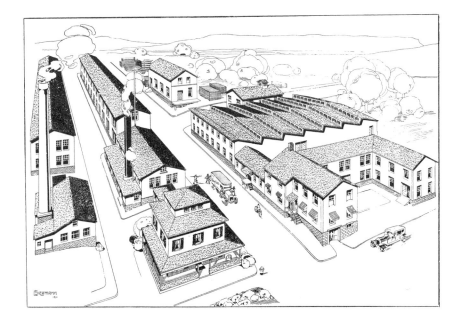

19Dec'11: The *Curtiss Motor Company, Inc.* is formed to control the *Curtiss Aeroplane Co.* and the *Curtiss Exhibition Co.*, capital stock $600,000 (over $25 million today), half retained by Curtiss. 1911 illustration, *above*, of Curtiss home and the "shop"/factory.

Hammondsport was becoming the *"unofficial" headquarters for naval aviation*, with a Navy Camp consisting of a tent for several naval officers and mechanics Dale Sigler, H.H. Weigand, Judson Scott and Percie Coffey.

The Navy ordered two *E's*, the *A-1* and *A-2* (delayed in manufacturing, no drawings – and the sketches on the shop walls had inadvertently been whitewashed over). The 75-hp *A-1* was fitted as a hydroaeroplane when piloted by Lts. Towers and *Holden Chester Richardson* (-1960) at North Island in Feb'12 (page 310), still with its forward elevator.

The *Model E (D-IV)*, "*The Weight-Carrying Curtiss Aeroplane*," with more wing/lifting surface, became the standard Curtiss. It was available with engines of 4-cylinder 40-hp; 8-cylinder 60-hp; or 8-cylinder 75-hp - and hydoaeroplane conversion kit ($500).

Scientific American, 2Dec1911:

THE first experimenter to succeed in making an aeroplane rise from the surface of the water was the French inventor, M. Fabre, who accomplished this feat with a monoplane of his own invention the last of March, 1910. About a year later Glenn Curtiss, at San Diego, fitted a float to his biplane and made it rise from the water and alight thereon with complete success during the course of his experiments. He flew out to the cruiser "Pennsylvania" anchored off the harbor and was lifted aboard with his machine. After paying a short visit to the ship, the aeroplane was lowered once more and Curtiss flew back to his starting point within the harbor. During the past summer the hydro-aeroplane has been experimented with by officers of the navy and two Curtiss hydro-aeroplanes have been purchased. These machines have found favor on account of their shift control, which consists of a movable wheel in front of the two aviators and mounted upon a vertical arm pivoted at its lower end so that it can be swung in front of either man. By this means it is extremely easy to shift the control wheel of the machine from one to the other pilot whenever it is desired to do so. In their long flight from Annapolis to Hampton Roads recently, Lieuts. Ellyson and Towers found this control of great benefit, as they were able to take turns in running the machine. Quite recently Mr.

Curtiss has received a large order for hydro-aeroplanes for the Russian navy, and he has sent one of his aviators to Russia to demonstrate these machines, while Capt. W. I. Chambers of our own navy believes that before long each battleship will have to carry one or more hydro-aeroplanes.

One of our illustrations shows Witmer skimming the surface of the waves in the Hudson River in one of the latest Curtiss machines. This biplane is mounted on a single float, the bottom of which is rounded upward at the front, while the top is rounded downward at the rear end. This float is made of wood and is 14 feet long by 2 feet wide by a foot in depth. It will sustain a weight of some

1,400 pounds without being submerged. The front horizontal rudder is mounted above the bow of the float, where it not only serves its purpose of steering the machine in a vertical plane, but also keeps the spray from striking the aviator. At each end of the lower plane there is an inclined air cylinder which acts as a buffer and buoys up the end in case the machine tips when skimming the surface of the water. Recently Hugh Robinson made a flight in one of these machines down the Mississippi River from Minneapolis, Minn., to St. Louis, Mo., for the purpose of demonstrating its use as a mail carrier. Some five thousand pieces of mail were carried, and mail pouches were taken on and put off at the various towns on the way.

Both the Wright and the Burgess-Wright companies brought out a hydro-aeroplane. A Burgess-Wright biplane, viewed from the rear, is shown skimming the surface of the water in one of our illustrations. Like the "Pelican," it is provided with double floats, but the skids instead of resting upon these floats, are rigidly attached to the aeroplane by means of suitable uprights. These floats are single-step, cedar wood hydroplanes 14 feet long by 2 feet wide, and having a 4-inch step placed about in the middle.

Curtiss V8 of 1908, held by (wire and) Hammondsport helicopter experimenter J. Newton Williams; a typewriter manufacturer of Derby, Connecticut:

AERO, 9Dec'11:

TOD SHRIVER KILLED IN PORTO RICO

New York, December 5.—According to advices received by his friends here, Tod Shriver, while flying a Baldwin biplane fitted with Hall-Scott motor, was killed at Ponce, near San Juan, Porto Rico, December 2. The biplane fell 200 feet into a cane field, while making a turn. He died on the way to the hospital.

Shriver left the Baldwin camp at Mineola three weeks ago with George Schmidt, aviator, and Peter McLaughlin, manager. They took with them two Baldwin biplanes for a South American tour. He was using crutches when he left New York.

Mrs. Shriver, who became the aviator's wife three years ago, is in Rochester. Thomas Scott Baldwin, designer and manufacturer of the machine, now in New York, is shocked and there is great grief among the many friends that Shriver had at the Long Island flying fields. "Tod was not foolhardy," said Baldwin. "He was as modest and unassuming an aviator as ever lived."

Shriver was born at Manchester, O., where the funeral will be, 38 years ago. He was a printer's boy until he joined Ringling Brothers' circus. Afterwards he was with Barnum, going around the world several years ago. Following this trip he joined Baldwin in the dirigible balloon business and assisted him at the trials of the U. S. Dirigible No. 1, being present at the Wright biplane trials which followed.

When Curtiss began manufacturing machines Shriver joined him and accompanied him to Rheims for the first international cup race, which Curtiss won. Last year he left Curtiss' employ as a mechanician, built a biplane and learned to fly in three weeks at Mineola.

On September 17, 1910, he obtained his pilot's certificate. He spent last winter in the Orient with Baldwin and Bud Mars and was decorated by the emperor of Japan.

He has had several accidents, twice breaking his leg. The first time was at Wilmington, Del., the last at Batavia, N. Y., six weeks ago.

TOD SHRIVER

1911: Curtiss awarded the *Aero Club of America Trophy*, soon known as the *Collier Trophy*, for his North Island hydroaeroplane development, the *first* presentation of this prized aviation award.

Few people knew more about Curtiss engines than *Waldo Waterman* when he wrote: *"The first 4 cyl water cooled Curtiss engine was installed in the Experimental Assn. plane - first to be sold by Curtiss and flown by Chas. F. Willard. It was 3 3/4" bore X 4" stroke. After this one engine, all Curtiss engines up to the summer of 1911 were 4" x 4". About this time Curtiss came out with a 4" bore X 5" stroke for both 4 and 8 cyl. (a few 6's). In 1916 he increased bore to 4 1/4" on the OXX-6 only (the "U" and "V" models had 5" bores)."*

25Jan1912: Wilbur to William F. de Hevesy: "...*During the past three months most of my time has been taken up with lawsuits and I have been away from home most of the time...It is much more pleasant to go to Kitty Hawk for experiments than to worry over lawsuits. We had hoped in 1906 to sell our invention to governments for enough money to satisfy our needs and then devote our time to science, but the jealousy of certain persons blocked this plan, and compelled us to rely on our patents and commercial exploitation...When we think of what we might have accomplished if we had been able to devote this time to experiments, we feel very sad, but it is always easier to deal with things than with men, and no one can direct his life entirely as he would choose...*"

The lawsuit required many hours of depositions by both the Wrights and Curtiss. Examples of their respective attitudes are shown in affidavits, first the Wrights:

"Mr. Curtiss's failure to perceive the real conditions cannot overcome the unchangeable laws of nature...The...affidavit of Mr. Curtiss is a most remarkable one and of itself constitutes an impeachment of his powers of correct observation and shows his incompetence to give expert testimony as to what actually occurs on his machine, and even seems to raise a direct question of veracity."

And Curtiss: "*The theories which they* (the Wrights) *have advanced are very misleading, and I know of my own knowledge from my numerous flights...that the actual facts which they assert as to the necessary operation of defendant's machine are erroneous...The actual facts are as I have set forth, and the actual facts are, I understand, the crux of the matter, and not the theories which may be advanced.*"

1912: Curtiss students at North Island and Hammondsport were "*of all classes and all nationalities. The list includes trades and professions, from horse trainers to bankers.*"

In addition to many Americans - Julia Clark of Denver, Al Mayo, W.H. Fisher, William Holt and Byron Pennington - there were English, French, Scotch, Irish, German, Russian, Spanish, Mexican – and Greek Army officer George Capitsini, several Japanese: C. Yamada, Motahisa Kondo (1885-1912, killed at Savona NY flying a Kirkham-built Curtiss-copy with an unfamiliar single stick operating both ailerons and the elevating rudder - the area's first aeroplane fatality), Lt. Kono Takeishi (killed in 1913) and C. Nakashima (commanding the Japanese Naval Aviation Service in 1929), and Puerto Rican Rafael Marti, Cuban Lt. Parla, and India's Mohan Singh.

Among first to qualify for licenses were Marine Lt. (retired) J.W. McClaskey (the US Marine's 1st pilot?), Chicago's S.C. Lewis, Harrisburg's J.B. McCalley, and Charles W. Shoemaker, Olean NY.

The Curtiss flying school certificate, which conformed to F.A.I. rules, became the most respected American proof of an aviator's ability.

Students, Curtiss Camp, North Island, 1912: L-R: M.M. Stark (Vancouver, BC), C.A. Berlin (Centralia, WA), R.E. McMillan (Perry, Iowa), ?, Spaulding, JLansingCallan, John G. Kaminski (Milwaukee, WI; only a year older than Waldo), KonoTakeishi (Japanese), *'Mascot'* Billy Maroney (on wing), Dad Maroney, FJ Terrill (Springfield, MA), Motahisa Kondo (sitting), Mohan Singh, Dunford (English), George Capitsini (Greek), Julia Clark and Davis:

The high percentage of Japanese students apparently was part of Japan's grand plans for Pacific dominance, noted by Billy Mitchell in 1924, particularly when one correlates these happenings with its (earlier noted) 1915 Baja California incursion.

17Jun'12: Julia Clark is American aviation's *first* woman fatality when she crashes into a tree during an exhibition in Springfield, IL.

LINCOLN BEACHEY AT BOSTON.

Aero And Hydro, *13Jul'12*:

1912: Both Curtiss models *D* and *E* are modified to headless, *removing the forward elevator* (demolishing his in an accident, Beachey continued flying, discovering better control).

Beckwith Havens: "*So I said to my head mechanic, 'Lou, here's a chance to take my front control off...Finally he gave in. 'All right, I'll do it on one condition, and that is I'll set the thing up the day before, and you come out and fly it before the crowd is here.' So I did, and it was like you'd been shackled all your life and you suddenly tore off your shackles. Oh, it could fly! It was a mistake having those two controls...in front...in back, because the two...were just fighting each other.*"

6Jan'12: *FLY* magazine: "*Jerome Fanciulli, vice-president and general manager of the Curtiss Exhibition Company, will sail on January 6th for St. Petersburg, Russia, accompanied by aviators Hugh Robinson and Eugene Godet, who are to demonstrate the hydroaeroplane before the Grand Duke Alexander Michaelovitch (a giant of a man), president of the Aerial League and a member of the Imperial Aero Club...Fanciulli will also take...a staff of expert mechanics. Before his return...not be for at least four months, Fanciulli expects to visit every important city in Europe.*"

AIRCRAFT

March, 191

ANOTHER VIEW OF THE FLYING BOAT WHICH GLENN H. CURTISS IS EXPERIMENTING WITH AT SAN DIEGO, CAL.

THE
TRADE

Jan'12: The first attempt at a *flying boat* (a modified Model D), at North Island was unsuccessful, primarily due to balance problems. In the photo (previous) McClaskey is stepping on the stern to hold it down.

1912: The Navy's *A-2* is changed, first to a hydroaeroplane, and then, with Holden Richardson (the Navy's *first* aircraft constructor/hull designer) following Captain Chambers' directives, it evolved as the *E-1* and *AX-1* into the *"OWL"* (over water and land), a transitional semi-flying boat with amphibious capabilities.

In May'12, it evolved into the *"first direct-drive flying boat,"* called the *Freak Boat:*

Feb'12: Hugh Robinson, demonstrating the Curtiss hydroaeroplane in Nice for representatives of several governments, makes the first water flights in Europe.

9Mar'12: McCurdy, working the winter on Bell's *Cygnet III*, a hybrid of tetrahedral cells with Curtiss-type undercarriage, front and rear control, tail, and a front elevator, made its final attempt at flight. It may have flown a foot or two, but was not judged a success, ending Bell's hopes for a tetrahedral-type flying machine.

Jan'12: The *Beachey-Curtiss Speed Tractor* - a high-performance, 75-mph machine developed for Beachey at North Island.

The Beachey Speed Tractor (next) racing past a marker in a time trial.
The young man in knickers is likely Waldo Waterman:

6Feb'12:
*Frank
Coffyn*
fits floats
to a
Wright in
New York,
Aircraft
Mar'12:

Frank T. Coffyn has been demonstrating lately that winter flying can be made just as popular as summer flying, on condition, of course, that the aviator is dressed warm enough. The above photograph shows him at the bow of his Wright machine, fitted with special rocker pontoons. As can be readily understood the effect of these pontoons is to skim along over the water easily and also over broken ice during the winter in case it is necessary to do so. Mr. Coffyn spent most of the month of February flying about the North and East rivers in juxtaposition to New York City. His flights were of the highly sensational order and were witnessed by hundreds of thousands of people.

1912: The Navy had difficulty justifying aeronautical expenditures of $25,000, returning much of it to the Treasury.

Feb'12: President Willian Howard Taft comments: "*I believe in the future of aviation, and I think that any encouragement or quasi-official recognition...is quite in order...We are in friendly rivalry with France in many things, and it is perhaps not pleasing to note that she is outstripping us in the number of her aviators.*"

The same could be said for the rest of Europe. Amounts appropriated by the countries of the world:

France: $7,400,000   Italy: $2,100,000   Russia: $5,000,000
Germany: $2,250,000   Japan: $600,000   England: $2,000,000
United States: *$140,000* (Army $115,000; Navy $25,000)

The United States ranked 14th in the world. <u>Chicago Tribune</u>, 2Mar'13:

Crash scene, Spanish Bight (now filled in), of Wright B-1 piloted by Ens. Herbster with passenger Waldo Waterman (standing, shirtless). W.B. Atwater, in Curtiss hydroaero-plane, and Glenn Curtiss, by boat, offered assistance; but Herbster refused to 'abandon ship.' See WALDO: Pioneer Aviator, *pp. 74-77:*

1Mar1912: The Navy's Wright hydroaeroplane crashes at North Island.

3Feb'12: Wilbur to Lieut. T. DeW. Milling: "*I have arranged for Lieutenant Foulois to come to Dayton...to testify in our patent suit. Would it be practicable for you to come...about the same time...? When you make the measurements of the power re-quired to move the ailerons on the Curtiss machine, and the power required to move the vertical tail, we would be glad if you could have one of the other officers present ...it is sometime desirable to provide a preponderance of testimony. Will you inquire among the other officers and find out whether any of them have ever noticed, in watching the Curtiss machine fly, that the tails move toward the high side when the lateral balance is being restored? I refer especially to the times when Captain Beck or other than yourself are flying...Do you think there is a possibility that Lieutenant Kennedy would testify all right in regard to the operation of the Curtiss machine?...*"

10Feb'12: Bishop Wright's diary: "*Lieut. Benj. D. Foulois' testimony in the Glenn Curtiss case was taken today. He stayed here.*"
    12Feb'12: "*Lieut. Thomas Milling's deposition is taken today, in the Curtiss in-fringement case. He sups with us...*"
    14Feb'12: "*Wilbur began his examination on the testimony in the Curtiss case. The amount of his intellectuality, in describing their invention, was marvelous. It must have greatly wearied him.*"

12Mar1912: Wilbur to Lt. Thomas Milling: "*...The Curtiss machine and its aviators seem to be having rather hard luck. I understand that a new two-man Curtiss was shipped to Augusta some 10 days ago...If there should be a prospect of having a* *machine in shape to fly, you would oblige us very much by sending a telegraphic notice as promptly as possible because it requires three or four days to give the necessary legal notice to the other people.*

"With pictures and newspapers, I am convinced that the Curtiss machine, used by Captain Beck at North Island in April 1911, had the black box (a still-current term, here for a device Curtiss used on a few machines, ostensibly to affect lateral balance without use of the rudder) *on it, but so far we have not been able to get any definite proof..."*

1912: The *Dayton-Wright* factory is in business. It will combine in 1916 with *Glenn L. Martin* (1886-1955, who began by building Curtiss-copies in Santa Ana, CA. With an unusually close attachment to his mother, Martin never married, much as with Wilbur and Orville) to form the *Wright-Martin Airplane Company* through a merger including the Simplex Automobile Co. In 1920 it would be dissolved with Martin and Wright Aeronautical becoming separate entities. The only name remaining today is *Lockheed Martin*.

These early aircraft manufactures had "little incentive before World War 1. There was popular prejudice among people who considered the airplane a dangerous toy of the rich which offered nothing to progress, and failed to see its potential. Second, although some builders tried to work together, patent suits and jealousy impeded their progress."   *Flight*

AERO, 2Dec'11: "A Milwaukee inventor has secured a patent that apparently covers everything the famous 'stability by manual means' clause misses, but we advise him to not attempt to enforce his claims. Judging from the history of the Selden patent case and similar efforts of justice, it will take about 40 years and 6,481 volumes of evidence before the thing is decided."

1912: The Wrights sue Aero Corporation, Ltd.

4May'12: Wilbur to Frederick Fish: *"Mr. Toulmin has shown me your letter in regard to postponing the hearing of the Herring-Curtiss case until next autumn. I fear Mr. Toulmin has not made it plain to you why it is so important that the case should be heard this spring. He looks at the matter from a lawyer's point of view, while I am compelled to consider our lawsuit nearly as a feature of our general business.*

"Unnecessary delays by stipulation of counsel have already destroyed fully three fourths of the value of our patent. The opportunities of the last two years will never return again. At the present moment almost innumerable competitors are entering the field, and for the first time are producing machines which will really fly. These machines are being put on the market at one half less than the price which we have been selling our machines for.

"...Up to the present time a decision in our favor would have given us a monopoly, but if we wait too long a favorable decision may have little value to us...I told Mr. Toulmin more than a year ago that under no conditions would I consent to further delays by stipulation of counsel..."

This was Wilbur's last letter.   Next: <u>Aero</u>, 30March1912:

The Only Safe Way to Judge an Aeronautical Motor Is by Its Accomplishments

THEIR EXISTENCE DENOTES STERLING WORTH AND SUPERIORITY—THEIR ABSENCE, WEAKNESS

CURTISS MOTORS

SCIENTIFIC AMERICAN TROPHY

Won the Scientific American Trophy, three years in succession

Won the Gordon-Bennett Cup

Won the Albany to New York, $10,000 prize, 180 miles, 150 minutes

Won the New York to Phildelphia race, 1911

Broke the World's Altitude Record at Chicago, 1911, 11,642 feet

Flew the greatest number of miles at International meet at Chicago, 1911

Won all speed events at International meet at Chicago, 1911

Won all speed events at Los Angeles, meet 1912

Have proven that they can stand the grind of exhibition work without fatigue

CAN YOU SAY AS MUCH FOR THE OTHER KIND?

IMMEDIATE DELIVERY COMPLETE POWER-PLANTS

Two Models   8 Cyl. 75 H. P.   4 Cyl. 40 H. P.

CATALOG Z IS ILLUSTRATED AND GIVES FULL DETAILS. IT'S FREE UPON REQUEST

THE CURTISS MOTOR COMPANY

HAMMONDSPORT, N. Y.

Printed for Aero Publication Company, 318 North 8th St., St. Louis, by Stewart Scott Printing Company

Copyright 1912 by Aero Publication Company

WILBUR WRIGHT

30May'12: Bishop Wright's diary: "*This morning at 3:15, Wilbur passed away, aged 45 years, 1 month and 14 days. A short life, full of consequence. An unfailing intellect, imperturbable temper, great self-reliance and as great modesty, seeing the right clearly, pursuing it steadily, he lived and died...*

(later, his father continued)...*In memory and intellect there was none like him. He systemized everything. His wit was quick and keen. He could say or write anything he wanted to. He was not very talkative. His temper could hardly be stirred. He wrote much. He could deliver a fine speech, but was modest.*"

"*The Conqueror of The Air,*" successful in grand achievement, fame and wealth, dies of typhoid fever (in TIME, 13Oct'24 the cause was "pneumonia." Also, it may have been food poisoning from a seafood meal in Boston.)

Flowers and telegrams, one from Curtiss, flooded the house on Hawthorn Street. The simple church service was attended by 25,000 people, and when the casket was laid to rest in Woodland Cemetery all Dayton was still for three minutes.

7Jun'12: Over College Park airfield, Captain Chandler, in a Wright C piloted by Lt. Milling, was *first* to successfully fire a machine gun from an aeroplane.

The air-cooled machine gun, a fearsome weapon, was invented by Col. Isaac Newton *Lewis*. When the War Department showed no interest he turned to Europe, founding the Armes Automatique Lewis Co. in Belgium in 1913. His gun played an important role in World War I, both on the ground and in the new, deadly game of aerial warfare.

11Jun'12: Arthur Welsh, taught by the Wrights at Montgomery in 1910, is killed, along with student pilot Lt. Leighton Hazelhurst, when an Army *Wright-C* goes out of control, nose-diving into the ground.

19Jun'12: Orville to William Kabitzke: "*...Poor Welsh met his death as a result of making a dive downwards at an angle of 45 degrees from a height of about 250 feet, and then attempting to make a very sharp turn upwards. It seems he made his dive in order to gain momentum to give him a quick start on an altitude test of the machine. He had done the same thing in a lesser degree in several previous flights. To do such a thing was so unlike Mr. Welsh, who had always displayed so much caution, that it was hard to realize that he did take such a chance...*"

1Jul'12: Orville to Army Lt. John C. Walker, Jr.: *"Your very good letter of March 27th...to Wilbur...he never had the pleasure of reading it. I wish to thank you for the information contained in it concerning the Curtiss machine used at North Island, and to say further that neither my brother nor I had any feeling against you on account of the newspaper clipping to which you refer* (In the 2Mar'11 <u>*San Diego Union*</u>, Walker, after having had his first flight in a Curtiss, was reported as having said that these flights proved the superiority of the Curtiss machine over the Wright machine for carrying passengers.).*..."*

15Jun'12 <u>*Scientific American:*</u>

Aeronautics

The Death of Parmalee.—On June 1st, Clifford O. Parmalee, one of the original Wright aviators, was killed at the Washington State Fair Grounds in the city of North Yakima, Washington, in the presence of his *finacée*. Parmalee was in the air only about four minutes when the accident occurred. His machine, which was identical with the one in which his partner Turpin fell upon the crowd in the grandstand two days before at Seattle, killing two spectators, was a two-propeller headless biplane, resembling the Wright, but with motor and propellers in front and aviator's seat at the rear. It was designed by Parmalee himself, who declared it to be the highest type of speed machine. A motor of nearly 100 horse-power drove two 6-foot tractors, the spread of the planes being 40 feet. Roy Knabenshue is authority for the statement that the machine was not properly balanced and that this fact, coupled with Parmalee's unfamiliarity with a tractor-and-motor-in-front aeroplane, was the reason for the accident.

A Glenn Curtiss Aeroplane Launcher.—A launching apparatus for aeroplanes has been patented (No. 1,027,-242) by Glenn H. Curtiss of Hammondsport, N. Y., in which an aeroplane supporting device in the form of swinging arms is mounted on a suitable mount and means are provided for imparting at a variable speed an angular throw to the supporting device.

Preservation of the First Wright Aeroplane.—A writer of a letter published in the London *Daily Mail* suggests that now is an opportune time for the British nation to obtain one of the original Wright biplanes at a comparatively moderate cost. He points out that at the South Kensington Museum may be found other interesting mechanical relics, such as George Stephenson's locomotive, the "Rocket." The suggestion is one that ought to be carried out in this country. Why does not the National Museum at Washington buy one of the early Wright machines, assuming that one is still to be had?

April-July'12: Following exhaustive testing of hull designs on Lake Keuka by Curtiss and the Navy's Richardson, Curtiss asked Kleckler: *"Why not put blocks on the bottom of the hull to make a step? Perhaps that way the suction aft on the hull could be broken up?"*

This was done; the flying boat, *to become the foundation of Curtiss's success,* broke free – successfully developing the *Curtiss Flying Boat Model E,* the *"No. 2 flying boat."*

Then, after an accident caused, he reasoned, by the pontoon having sprung a leak, he told Kleckler: *"By dividing all floats into several compartments, we can keep this fool trick from happening again."*

2Aug'12: Following up on Fanciulli's trip, Curtiss went to Europe to close hydroaeroplane contracts in England, France, Germany, Russia and Italy.

Concurrently, Charles Witmer, Hugh Robinson, and George Hallett went to Sevastopol to demonstrate hydroaeroplanes - with the result that by 1914 over half of Russian naval aircraft were Curtiss.

Next: July, 1912, A remarkable exhibition of stability: Curtiss, Post – and Ellyson aft:

3 Aug 1912 *Scientific American:*

The passenger lies well to the rear.

The new Curtiss hydroaeroplane in flight.

The Curtiss "Flying Boat"
A New Type of Hydro-aeroplane

SINCE he closed his camp and aviation school at San Diego last spring, Glenn Curtiss has been steadily at work at his home in Hammondsport, N. Y., making further improvements upon his hydro-aeroplane. The result of his recent experiments is shown in the photographs reproduced on this page, which give a good idea of his latest combined boat and biplane, known as the Curtiss "Flying Boat."

This boat is a single step hydroplane, 26 feet long, 3 feet wide, and having sides 3 feet high. It is surmounted by a regular Curtiss biplane, having planes of 30-foot spread by 5½-foot depth between the planes. The planes contain a total supporting surface of about 320 square feet, and support, when in flight, a total weight of about 1,000 pounds. As many as four people can be carried comfortably. One of our illustrations shows a man in a bathing suit lying on the deck of the boat behind the planes in addition to the pilot and passenger in front.

The power plant consists of an 80 horse-power Curtiss 8-cylinder, V-type engine and single propeller mounted high up between the main planes at the center. The motor is mounted sufficiently high to provide a liberal clearance between the end of the propeller blades and the boat, the propeller being just back of the main planes, as usual.

Above the tapered hull of the boat, at the rear, is a vertical fin terminating in a large vertical rudder. The tail is placed about half way between the boat and the top of this fin, and extends out on each side of it. The horizontal rudder consists of two hinged flaps at the rear of the two halves of the tail. No front elevator is provided, so that the pilot has a clear view in front over the spray hood that is fitted. The balancing planes are at the rear, half way between the main planes. Inclined cylindrical floats are fitted below the ends of the lower plane in case the machine tips in making a quick turn on the water.

This new flying boat of Curtiss's makes aviation perfectly safe, as one can travel 50 miles an hour on the surface of the water, or 60 or more miles an hour a few feet above the surface. It will open up to the motor boat enthusiast heretofore unnavigable streams. In fact all the unusued canals and shallow rivers of the country can be skimmed over always with complete safety by the yachtsman-aviator.

4 Oct'12: Curtiss to Captain Chambers: "*I have just returned from a very satisfactory trip abroad. Aviation in all its branches, and especially water-flying, is booming all over Europe, and there is a marked contrast when you reach America and find everyone sitting around and wondering what is going to be done.*"

Nov'12: Curtiss to Captain Chambers: "*In the first place, when the Wright Bros. made their application they found it necessary to confine their claims to just what was new in their machine, otherwise, the patent would not be allowed. The new things in their machine were a combination of the warping and the turning of the rudder to counteract*" *the turning effect caused by the warping. Their success in actual flying led them to try to make their patent cover things which it was not intended to cover, and their exploitation as the first to fly has been used in an effort to get the Court to enlarge the scope of their patent...The facts are, the honors bestowed upon the Wrights and the credit which is due them is not because of their patent, but because of their achievement. I hope their patent will be adjudicated and that the machines which operate as their machine does will be adjudged infringements, but all authorities agree that our machines operate on a diffe-rent principle, and I do not believe a disinterested patent attorney could be found who would allow that our machine infringes their patent. However, the litigation has cost us forty or fifty thousand dollars* (over $2 million today) *and the industry - or what there is of it in America - is entirely the result of our taking up this case...single-handed, and fighting it out. Had we not taken this stand, the Wright Co. would have been in position to enjoin all manufacturers and the whole industry would have been monopolized..."*

The evolving flying boat with Curtiss and Captain Chambers, Sep1912:

12Nov'12: Testing was done of the compressed-air catapult utilizing Captain Chambers' disposable cradle which *"went its way,"* first without an aeroplane at the Washington Navy Yard. It was then perfected by the Navy's Richardson and St. Clair Smith - and tested with the Curtiss *A-3* piloted by Ellyson in the *first successful catapult launch.*

Curtiss called it *"the greatest aviation advance since wheels replaced skids for aero-plane landing gear."*

The New York Times reported that the Navy planned to put catapults on battleship turrets - maybe one at each end so a plane could be started in either direction.

And at Hammondsport, on 7Sep'11, Curtiss and Ellyson tried an Ellyson-Towers idea using a taut cable for launching. It worked perfectly, but was deemed impractical for shipboard use.

Preparing for a catapult launch, Washington Navy Yard:

At this time Curtiss was advertising: *"We direct 80% of the successful aeroplane exhibits and contests in the United States...a striking testimonial to the efficiency and practicability of Curtiss aeroplanes."*

The Curtiss Exhibition Company carried out hundreds of flying dates; Curtiss considered its earnings important in paying the staggering costs of the Wright litigation and in keeping the Curtiss name in the public eye.

Many Curtiss aviators become wealthy very quickly flying for a small salary plus a percentage of the prize moneys, and, sometimes, a portion of gate receipts.

Airmen like the legendary Beachey, often flying on their own, made fortunes virtually overnight, regularly earning $1,000 (about $45,000 today) to $1,500, even $5,000 *per day* - but it was a risky, too often short-lived career.

By contrast, according to Frank Coffyn, the Wrights charged a fee of $1,000 per day for each of their pilots in exhibition, and paid them $20 per week plus $50 for every day they flew. Thus, in a six-day week of flying (no Sundays) the Wrights collected *$6,000 plus* the prize moneys - and paid their pilot *$320.*

Coffyn also said: *"We were taught by the Wrights that the Curtiss crowd was just no good at all. We turned up our noses at them. But we found out later on, by flying at the same meets, that they were a pretty nice bunch of fellows..."*

Beckwith Havens, one of the Curtiss *"fellows,"* recalled: *"The first year I was on the road was 1911. In the winter of 1911-1912 I was putting on an air show in Havana,*

Cuba, with Beachey and two other pilots, Charley Watts and Gene Godet. It was at Camp Columbia, which was way out in the country. We had to chase cows off the field before we could take off. And Gene Godet cracked up - poor fellow, he always did. Then they wanted us to fly over the city. Well, it's quite a flight from Camp Columbia to the city, and there was no place to land anywhere around there. We didn't want to do it. They went ahead and said in the paper we were going to do it. This boxed us in. If we had backed out, it would have looked terrible. So Beachey said all right, he'd do it. I said, 'All right, I'll do it.' So Charley Watts said he'd do it. He had his wife with him - his wife and children traveled with him - and she took a pair of pliers and stood right ahead of the machine and said, 'Charley, if you take off I'll throw these pliers right through your prop!' So he didn't take off. So Beachey and I had to do it. We flew across the town, around Morro Castle - me thinking all the time about all those sharks that are off Morro Castle - and out to the field. Oh, we got a terrific hand. It was the first flight over Havana."

Lincoln Beachey, Havana, Cuba, Jan1912:

Nov'12: *Air-to-ground wireless* demonstrated by the Army with a 2-man Wright.

Curtiss apparently began aeroplane wireless in Aug1908, with the military continuing development to its success in 1912.

16Nov'12: Orville to Army Capt. Charles Chandler: "...*There is only one explanation that I can give and that is the one that you suggest, that while trying to overcome this turning effect, Mr. Arnold may have allowed his machine to become 'stalled,' in which case it would have made a dive, and would have refused to respond to his horizontal rudder...I had tried to devise some way of overcoming this very feature which is present in all flying machines at the present time. The cause of the trouble is apparent, but I find it no easy matter to design a machine that will eliminate this ...without introducing some other undesirable features...I presume that you have noticed that a great many of the foreign military accidents have been described as ...similar to the experience of Mr. Arnold..."*

Note: In General Henry Arnold's memoir, <u>Global Mission</u>: *"In the fall of 1912 I had an interesting little experience...The plane spun completely around in a 360-degree circle. As we started to plunge down I looked back quickly, thinking one of the propeller chains had broken. It hadn't. Now in a whistling nose dive, I took in everything, as you do at such a time. Everything was all right, nothing broken, my hands doing all the right things on the controls. Nevertheless, we were diving straight down - without a chance. My observer didn't realize this and was taking photos. Somehow after every frantic yank and twist I could make, just a few feet over the ground I managed to pull the plane out of the dive. As soon as we had rolled to a stop I climbed down and said shakily, 'Come on, Sandy, let's walk over to the barracks.' 'Walk?' Lt. Sands said, 'Arn't we going to ----?' Then he must have seen my face for his own turned green..."*

Virtually identical to what Herbster and Waterman had experienced.

27Nov'12: The *Model F*, with an 80-hp Curtiss *Model O* V8 water-cooled engine, is the *first* flying boat delivered to the U.S. Army. The *SC-15* was used at the Army's North Island aviation school.

The *Model-F* continued evolving into 1913, as steps were also taken to get more power from the *Model O* motor. By 1913 the horsepower was 105-hp, and the model number changed to O plus (+). Mistaken as OX, the famous *Jenny OX-engine* was born.

1Dec'12: Curtiss delivered to the Navy the *C-1 (Model E)*, the *Navy's first flying boat* (later *AB-1*). Flown only on the East Coast, it ended its flying in Guantanamo, Cuba.
Note innovative beer keg carrier:

1912 had begun with the New York Automobile and Aeronautic Show with Curtiss featuring the "Flying Boat" (with Lansing Callan) which had failed at North Island:

But the end of 1912 saw it a resounding success: *The Flying Boat, piloted by Curtiss with passengers Post and Ellyson:*

Chapter  *1913 - 1914*

 he

phenomenal success of the Curtiss flying boat spurs production and innovation at a dizzying pace. Orville is confronted by the "Reign of Death." Henry Ford enters the Wright-Curtiss patent fight; the Langley aerodrome fuels the feud; and the legal battle reaches a climax.

Jan'13: The *Tadpole* - An experimental Curtiss flying boat with tilting lower wings designed to improve takeoffs and landings. They could also be differentially controlled as ailerons (similar to Lockheed's *S-1* sport-plane of 1919). Testing continued into 1914 with a second version.

21Feb'13: The *British Wright Company Ltd.* is organized with Orville as Chairman. He was also president of the *Wright Company*: "Rather than travel to the factory every day he found it more comfortable to transact most business from his office in the bicycle shop, where he was abetted in his habit of putting off the making of important decisions by Mabel Beck, the sharp-tongued secretary he had inherited from Wilbur."

Fred Howard

"During the day he stayed away from the Wright factory, holing up instead in an office two miles away. He talked interminably with his sister, Katharine, of his grudge against Curtiss, and he shared his feelings at times with his young friend, the Wright Company engineer Grover Loening.

"*As the months went by I learned that he was indeed a great genius but a troubled one,*' Loening observed. '*He brooded much on the injustice of the rising competition that was robbing him of the fruits of invention. On this subject he would talk for hours.*'

"Despite his concern about the competition, Orville did little to keep abreast of new developments...'*An interesting angle of his thinking was revealed one day,*' said Loening, '*when a discussion was held on the then-new vogue of the tractor types, with engine and propeller in front. Orville said, 'This type is really an invention of the French, and we should not be copying it just to keep up. There must be better reasons than that.' He picked up some foreign magazines and glanced at them. 'Since the chief use of airplanes for the military will be observation,' he continued, 'how can you justify putting the pilot behind so much engine-propeller interference, spoiling the view?' Having convinced himself, he threw the magazines down on the table.*' "

Curtis Prendergast

20Jun'13: "Ens. William D. Billingsley was in the air at the controls of a Navy-built Wright type hydroaeroplane carrying Towers as his passenger. A down-draft, a sudden squall, or some never-explained mechanical defect made the plane 'nose down.' Billingsley pitched forward, completely losing control and the plane capsized. Since there were, in those perilous days, not even the elementary safety belts, Billingsley fell instantly to his death. Towers, with an amazing coolness that may have been due, in part, to his being an expert gymnast, clung to the strut beside which he had been sitting. As the plane whirled and spun through its wild plunge, he held on, to fall some 1,600 feet into the water. He was picked up badly injured but undaunted, and after four months in the hospital back to the air he came." *Turnbull & Lord*

6May'13: Curtiss, along with *Gustave Eiffel* (builder of the *Eiffel Tower*), is awarded the *Langley Medal* (fashioned from a pound of gold).

Smithsonian Regent Bell, in a warm and cordial speech of his "*friend,*" said: "*By July 1912, he had developed that remarkable machine he calls 'the flying boat,' which represents the greatest advance yet made along these lines. It develops great speed upon the water and also in the air and is equally at home in either element. The world is now following Mr. Curtiss's lead in the development of flying machines of this kind.*"

12Jun'13: The *Model G Tractor Scout* - Army *SC-21*. This two-passenger (side-by-side), 80-hp, somewhat modern looking craft, had a geared 3-blade tractor propeller, tricycle landing gear, and a fabric-covered fuselage. Its top speed was 52-mph. Built to the Army's new design standards, *it was the forerunner of the Jenny.*

1913: Curtiss assisted *Elmer A. Sperry* (1860-1930), inventor of the gyrocompass, in applying it to aircraft. Assisting was Sperry's son, *Lawrence* (1892-1923), taught to fly by Francis "Doc" Wildman, who also assisted in the trials.

Sperry gyro "automatic pilot," Wildman. Square plate on radiator is air speed control:

30Aug'13: Sperry's gyro-scopic stabilizer is flight test-ed at Hammondsport in a Curtiss *C-2* flying boat by Navy Lt.jg. P.N.L. Bellinger (-1962).

Development continued that winter at North Island.

Curtiss is awarded the *Collier Trophy - for the second time –* for flying boat development:

Scientific American, 22Feb'13:

Curtiss Awarded Collier Trophy for 1912 and 1913.— Glenn H. Curtiss' flying motor boat, the last word in aviation, and the creation which is said to have made aviation a safer pastime than either automobiling or boating, has won him the distinction, for the second time, of receiving the Collier Trophy, awarded annually for the greatest contribution to the advance of aviation, which shall have been developed and demonstrated during the preceding year. The SCIENTIFIC AMERICAN Trophy was won by him in 1908 when at Hammondsport, N. Y., July 4th, he made the first public flight in America of more than one kilometer. He actually flew a distance in excess of a mile in the old "June Bug." In 1909, almost exactly one year later, Curtiss won the SCIENTIFIC AMERICAN Trophy for the second time at Hempstead Plains, he flew 24.7 miles, or nine-teen circuits of a circular course. His famous flight from Albany to New York, the longest flight of the year, won him the trophy in 1910, for the third con-secutive time, making him its holder in perpetuity. In 1911 the new trophy, to be awarded for the most signal advance in aviation each year, was offered by Robert J. Collier, then president of the Aero Club of America. It was awarded to Curtiss that year for the invention and demonstration of the single pontoon hydro-aeroplane, the first machine to successfully rise from and alight on the water. There is no record of a single serious accident to the operator of a hydro-aeroplane in America, though one machine and its operators were lost at sea in attempting to fly in a home-built hydro a distance of upward of 400 miles, from San Pedro to San Francisco, starting in a fog following a three days' storm. The hydro-aeroplane perfected by Curtiss has been adopted by almost every navy of the world's powers.

Apr-Jul'13: The *McCormick Flying Boats*: Two flying boats were built for Harold F. McCormick (*the "reaper king"'s son, John D. Rockefeller's son-in-law, and relative of ex-Smithsonian secretary, Robert McCormick Adams*).

HAROLD F. MCCORMICK, CHAIRMAN OF THE FINANCE COMMITTEE INTERNATIONAL AVIATION MEET ASSOCIATION.

The first was a unique four-passenger, 100-hp tractor craft with a "spoonbill" and double V bottom stepped hull (co-designed by the Navy's Richardson and William McEntee).

January 1913 *Cosmopolitan Magazine*

"A man whose name was of enough importance to demand the attention of the country, decided to be the world's first business-sportsman to commute with flying boat...That man was Harold F. McCormick of International Harvester fame. Mr. McCormick desired to fly from his suburban estate at Lake Forest (25 miles) to his office near the basin of the Chicago Yacht Club (His 1000 Lake Shore Drive home was "the most elegant barn on the Gold Coast." Fortune, Sep'1946). He visited Hammondsport, flew with Curtiss in the flying boat, and was quickly converted. Soon his frequent trips along the Chicago lake front attracted the attention of the newspapers and magazines of the country. Here was no scatter-brained youngster, but a man ranking high in the business and financial world. Mr. McCormick's lead brought other important names into the picture..."   *Lyman Seely*

Wealthy sportsmen emulating McCormick were fellow-Chicagoan Logan A. (Jack) Vilas, Philadelphia's Marshall E. Reid, Pittsburgh's William Thaw III, Detroit's William B. Scripps; and New Yorkers W. Stevenson MacGordon, G.M. Heckscher, J.B.R. Verplanck, Harry Harkness, George L. Peck (of the Pennsylvania Railroad), and George U. von Utassy (whose E-type flying boat "Babetta" was flown around Long Island Sound by pilot-instructor Jack McCurdy)...buying either hydroaeroplanes at $5000 each or flying boats for $7000 (about $350,000 today). And in the spring of 1912 Louis E. Stoddard, a former Yale football hero, organized the Hydroaeroplane Club of New Haven, soon copied in several cities.

The Curtiss Aeroplane Company was becoming commercially viable.

Frank J. Bersbach, Harold McCormick and "Jack" Vilas:

The *McCormick Spoonbill* was America's largest and fastest aeroplane in July, 1913 when delivered to Chicago by pilot Witmer and mechanican George Hallett (hired by McCormick after their return from Russia).

In the fall, a second flying boat of more conventional design (one of three "*English-type*" built during late 1913) was purchased by McCormick and named *"Edith," photo, left:*
Witmer and Hallett took her to Florida that winter, selling rides to help pay expenses. By spring (1914) salt corrosion necessitated a complete Hammondsport overhaul before a return to Chicago.

In 1915 McCormick sold it to Mr. B.R.J. Hassell, who, on his second flight, made a downwind landing and crashed: *"Hassell was picked up by a canoe about all in, and the boat is a total wreck except for the motor."*

1Jul'13: Jack Vilas, in his new forest green Curtiss Model E flying boat with its 70-hp OXX-6 engine, is *first* to fly across Lake Michigan. It was then flown to his summer place at Oswegatchie Point in the Thousand Islands of the St. Lawrence River where it ferried food, supplies and passengers around the resort. Later Vilas used it to propose marriage to Suzanne "Poppy" Wheeler – at 5,000 feet.

Vilas and Waldo Waterman were founding members of the *Early Birds of Aviation.*

Curtiss launched the new sport of aerial yachting with advertisements stating:

"ON the water, OVER the Country Faster than 60 miles an Hour!...For speed and pleasure, it puts motor boating out of the running. It's a revelation to the red-blooded sportsman"...and here was a *"flying machine in which it is practically impossible for the operator to suffer injury in case of accident. Even in the worst kind of accident, the most that can happen to the operator is an exhilarating plunge into fresh or salt water, as the case may be, with the beneficial effects of a good swim if so desired."*

Oct'13: The *Model F "English-type"* Flying Boat - Navy *C-2 (AB-2)* – Evolutionary, with a 90/100-hp V8. Its Elliott instrument panel included a clock, tachometer, air speed and barometer. It was to become the *standard* for Curtiss flying boats during World War I.

In 1913 Curtiss's flying boats increased business dramatically: Forty-four machines were sold; over a hundred men were employed at the Hammondsport factory.

"The new flying boats had mahogany hulls polished so brightly that a man could see to shave in them."

1913: Chancing upon Curtiss in the dining room of New York's Brevoort Hotel, Henry Ford said: *"Well, I see they have you with your back nearly to the wall, When they get you right up against it, come to see me."*

He thus encouraged Curtiss as Edison had encouraged him: Ford "is said to have walked in on Edison at his laboratory, unannounced, to seek his advice...Edison advised him to stay out of the automobile trade association and fight their licensing monopoly." *Matthew Josephson*

Ford had a keen interest in Curtiss's affairs, initially because of his patent problems and also, apparently, as a funding partner in the *"America"* project. But he was first-and-foremost an engine man, particularly interested in Curtiss's lightweight engines for possible use with his Model T. In the fall of 1913 *(next photo)* he visited Curtiss – and after discussions involving the on-going patent litigation, had him ship several engines to Detroit for testing. Though they were found too expensive for low-cost cars, his interest in flying grew. Later he got into aviation in a big way, building the famous *Ford-Stout* all-metal trimotors, the ill-fated *"Flivverplane,"* and even an airline.

And on 5Jan'14 he revolutionized American industry with *the $5.00 day*, almost doubling a worker's wage; the beginning of the creation of America's huge middle class with its discretionary income. Whether he did this to reduce his high labor turn-over rate; or to forestall a possible invasion of the International Workers of the World; or to share profits with his workers; or to create purchasing power for Model T's is still debated.

The photo, next, became a post-card; in 2001 the author acquired one of these with this written *by* Curtiss upon it, *see left:*

POST C

CORRESPONDENCE

Mr Henry Ford of Detroit the manufacturer of the Ford car paid us a visit. He wanted to go up but said, "My wife won't let me". The boat the old school boat has flown about 20,000 miles this year and is now relighted to the scrap heap

347

Glenn Curtiss and Henry Ford, Hammondsport, 1913:

Always interested in automobiles, Curtiss took one of his aviation motors and installed it in his large Keeton car, betting one and all that he could travel to Bath and back on one gallon of gasoline. The distance was 16 miles - and 10 miles-per-gallon was good then.

So certain of the preposterousness of Curtiss' wager, sportsman-pilot J.B.R. Verplanck bet first, putting up a hat and suit of clothes. Visiting correspondents, students and others immediately followed his example, betting various items of clothing.

The tank was drained, two gallons put in, and Curtiss and an observer started out.

Then, greatly excited upon their return, everyone was looking on as four quarts were drained from the tank. Curtiss glanced up, *"Anybody want to bet he wouldn't get another quart?"* No takers. One more quart was drawn. *"All right,"* he said, *"how about another pint?"* The few diehards who responded *"Sure, I'll see you"* whistled in amazement when another pint – and a few drops more - were drained.

He'd made 24-1/2-mpg!

It was years before he wore out the suit, shirts, collars and ties he'd won.

1913: Late in the year a new engine was developed: the Curtiss *Model V*, an 8-cylinder rated at 160-hp at 1400-rpm, followed by Model *V-2* of 220-hp, and a 12-cylinder Model *V-3* of 300-hp at 1500-rpm. The *V-2* was the most popular model.

Next four pages, 1914 Beachey Promotional Pamphlet (author's collection):

The Genius of Aviation

By LINCOLN BEACHEY

PRICE TEN CENTS | **PAY NO MORE**

America's own startling, amazing—BEACHEY

of space. have acquired the genius of aviation. It requires only practice, patience and courage to master an aeroplane. And be careful—that's all.

Withal, necessarily, be sober minded and temperate, as men should be who drive the fast locomotive, the racing motorcycle and the automobile. Surely at all times must they remember the Reaper who follows close at their heels.

It requires skill, perhaps, to become expert as a birdman and to acquire the proper knowledge of air currents, equilibrium, measurement of distance and space, engine and steering control, power requirements, as pertains to

And having once acquired the science of aviation through diligent practice and training. physical and mental, the knack of it "stays with you" the same as the art of swimming and the playing of golf and tennis and base ball.

Come along, come along, come with me aboard an aeroplane.

We will fly to a region where men who have courage will find an abundance of peace and good-will. We will fly through the clouds with their lining of gold and pure silver. We will fly to the skies where the birds through

From the Los Angeles Examiner, showing Barney Oldfield and Beachey starting second mile of race for "Championship of the Universe" at Ascot Park. Beachey frequently touched Oldfield's head with the wheel of his landing gear. The pair covered one mile in 46 3-5 seconds, just one-fifth of a second slower than Oldfield's world's record for circular tracks—not two feet separating them at the finish. Oldfield using his 300 h.p. Christie world's record car.

both engine and rudder as well as the wings of the aeroplane; of resistance force of the machine, as a whole, while flying under full power ahead, upwards or downwards and while driving with a straight drop or dive with power on or off. All this knowledge is necessary, with more, I assure you—but, withal and as complicated and difficult as it may appear, I may say the aeroplane, insofar as its construction and operation are concerned, presents itself to a novice in form more simple than does the automobile.

the ages have been welcomed and kissed by the glorious sunlight and where the moonbeams have caressed them and the cool winds and dew have rested and blessed them. It is there in the sky where men of all nations will some day learn the true meaning of brotherly love.

It seems not long ago that I stood on the crest of a mountain and gazed for miles over a magnificent stretch of valley land in Southern California. I was a mere lad then. Across the valley directly opposite me and on a level with my elevation was located the peak of another

From the San Francisco Chronicle.

Showing Beachey photographing himself while upside down 400 ft. in the air. The camera was strapped to the aeroplane and Beachey pressed the button at the proper moment.

Beachey on 90 degree "banque" just before turning over sidewise for upside down "Corkscrew Flop."

From San Diego (Cal.) Sun.

From San Francisco Examiner, January 4, 1914

The amazing photograph in the upper section of this picture was taken by E. Carl Wallen, who was aloft in flying boat. It shows Beachey at the apex of his ascent in his seventh loop with which he broke the world's record yesterday. He was about 600 feet in the air when the picture was taken, and Wallen was some 150 feet away. The word "Beachey" which is painted on top of the upper plane, indicates the perpendicularity of the aviator's ascent.

For Information Concerning Lincoln Beachey or Barney Oldfield Exhibitions Address Lincoln Beachey, Inc., Westminster Building, Chicago.

18Nov1913: Beachey first flew the *"Little Looper"* at North Island. The *Beachey Special Looper* - A 90/100-hp Curtiss *Model D* especially strengthened for looping: spars were double thickness; bracing was 3/32-inch Roebling wire, doubled near the engine; and seat-belt and shoulder-straps were installed, to compete with Frenchman *Adolphe Pegoud's* upcoming American looping tour.

On Thanksgiving evening Beachey wired Curtiss: *"Exhibition Polo Grounds today four thousand dollars* (about $200,000 today). *Flew upside down half mile, loop three times in succession; 800 feet first, 600 second, 500 third. Power on all the time, engine not missing. Leaving tonight for Washington. Invitation Secretary War and Navy to give my ideas aviation in connection with government."*

Though thought by many to have made the first loop, Pegoud was second to Russian *Petr Nesterov's* loop of 27Aug1913 over Kiev. Pegoud became France's *first* ace in World War 1 and was killed in 1915.

Called *"The Greatest of Them All"* by Orville, Beachey began his amazing flying career piloting Baldwin's airships. In 1910 he was taught aeroplane flying in San Francisco by Bud Mars, Baldwin's erstwhile associate then flying for Curtiss. About the same height as Curtiss at six-one, he stood out among the early aviators. His brother, Hillery, describes his flying: *"Lincoln's main stunt was to come down head first, to make a vertical dive from 5000 feet with his motor shut off and land exactly where he wanted to. I remember once in Dallas, Texas, he made two landings from this dive of his, and each time he came down within a foot of the other. He used to dive onto a race track, and he'd come to the starting wire and dive under it, and not hit the ground or the wire either."*

"The incomparable Beachey, considered the world's greatest stunt flier, who would scoop a handkerchief off the field with his wing tip. Before the word 'aviator' was used, the term 'birdman' was coined for men such as Beachey. Until 1908, the only fliers were the cautious builders and inventors who safely demonstrated their machines. Later, 'birdmen' appeared who lived excitingly a few months, testing planes for speed and endurance, then crashed. Always sensational...(Beachey) was drowned in San Francisco Bay (his hometown) in 1915, when his monoplane folded in air during World's Fair Exhibition. The 'Birdman Era' had come to an end."   *Flight*

22Nov1913: Orville to George Beatty: *"Replying to your telegram, 'What changes will be necessary in my Wright to enable me to loop?' I would not advise attempting to loop the loop with your present machine, on account of its low speed. Only high speed machines are suitable for the purpose. The four-cylinder B machine would lose practically all their velocity before reaching the top of the turn. The B machine has a velocity of only 40 to 42 miles...a high speed machine is desirable."*

Late in 1913: Bell's diary, comment on patents: *"But patents already granted give us complete control of the flying machine field exclusive of the Wright patents and everybody is using our inventions to avoid the Wrights' patents. So the Wright patents and the A.E.A. patents together control the whole field of aviation in America..."*

5Dec1913: Orville to Lt. Col. Samuel Reber (see pp. 369): "*I have your letter in regard to aeroplane accidents in the United States Army. These accidents are most distress-ing. I do not think, however, that the number in our army is out of proportion to the number in the French or German armies...*

"*These accidents are the more distressing because they can be avoided. I think I am well within bounds when I say that over ninety percent of them are due to one and the same cause - 'stalling'...When in this 'stalled' condition the machine will dive downward in spite every effort of the aviator to stop it...*

"*...I am preparing a diagram showing the quantity and direction of the forces act-ing on a stalled aeroplane descending at what appears...a perfectly safe angle. Every flyer knows the danger of stalling, yet he has but little idea of the causes that make it dangerous. The diagram, I think, will make this clear.*"

16Dec1913: The *Model H Tractor Scout - Army SC-22*. This more powerful (90/100 hp) evolution of the *"G"* was the sole survivor of Army trainers at North Island after Grover Loening's condemnation of the Wright training aeroplanes.

"Curtiss then worked simultaneously during 1913 on the Army tractor (to evolve into the *Jenny*), a tractor monoplane flying boat, a greatly improved biplane flying boat and on the...Wanamaker trans-Atlantic twin-motored flying boat (*"America"*). Before these un-dertakings were completed he was at work on the rehabilitation and final demonstrations of the original Langley machine from the Smithsonian...He added to this work personal supervision of his flying schools at Hammondsport and San Diego...It seems as though he must have had a faculty of working steadily with little rest or recreation. Certainly his preoccupation was remarkable. He seemed able while conversing with San Francisco or Washington, or dictating cablegrams, to engage his subconscious mind in checking blue prints or sketches of...various machines he was working on...Hammondsport was alive with newspapermen...All were anxious to make good on this important assignment... Some of them failed to realize that Curtiss was...far more interested in what he was try-ing to accomplish than in what other people thought or said about him, and they were grieved to find that the ordinary ritual employed in bluffing a politician into making state-ments he does not wish to make brought no statements from Curtiss..."   *Lyman Seely*

The immense flying boat success gained Curtiss international acclaim; this, combined with his patent problems, led to several lucrative inducements to establish manufacturing abroad, mainly in Russia and Germany. The Russian navy even selected a factory site near St. Petersburg where, in the fall of 1913, he sailed to investigate.

15Dec1913: Bishop Wright's diary: "*Col. Reber dined and supped with us. Also Mr. Loening supped with us. Reber is the son-in-law of Gen. Miles. He wants Orville to go to San Diego to teach aviators some of his theories...*"

31Dec1913: Waiting until the last day of the year, Orville demonstrates his patented version of an automatic stabilizer. Employing a pendulum and vane, it won 1913's *Collier Trophy*, but aircraft design progress and Sperry's autopilot destined it to oblivion.

Jan'14: The *Model M Flying Boat.* Built for Raymond Morris of New Haven, this handsome 90 hp craft was the *first monoplane flying boat.* It had a double V bottom hull similar to McCormick's, and was the fastest (over 100 mph) and smallest of Curtiss flying boats. Morris became Curtiss's California manager, where a 1915 photograph, *lower,* shows him in a flying boat (not the *Model M*) racing Curtiss's 90 hp, 51 mph speedboat in the Pacific off Coronado.

Curtiss in V8-powered speedboat in Spanish Bight, Coronado Polo Field in background:

Thrilling handicap race staged off the California coast between a seaplane and a motor boat. Although the latter developed a speed of over 51 miles an hour and had an additional large handicap allowance, the seaplane had the better of the argument and came in a decided winner.

26Apr'15 *Aerial Age Weekly*: *"While Vice-President and Mrs. Thomas R. Marshall, and Assistant Secretary of the Navy Franklin D. Roosevelt were being entertained by Admiral Thomas Benton Howard, commander in chief of the Pacific fleet, with a reception on board the flagship Colorado, Raymond V. Morris, the aviator, flew from North Island in his flying boat to pay his respects to the distinguished guests. Morris circled around the ship three times, and then came alongside the boom, where he was met by a launch which took him to the gangway.*

"After chatting with the vice-president and secretary for a while, and joining in the dancing on the quarterdeck, Morris boarded his craft and flew back to North Island. Vice-President Marshall is much interested in aviation, and particularly in the flying boats, and it was in a previous talk with Morris that he had asked for an opportunity to see the aviator handle his craft."

Note: During this visit to San Diego Franklin Roosevelt was the first federal official to cross on the new Laurel Street bridge into Balboa Park's Panama Canal Exposition.

Atlantic City, New Jersey, 1914. The flying boat is also popular on the other coast:

HYDROPLANE LEAVING FOR A FLIGHT.

HYDROPLANE RETURNED FROM A FLIGHT.

13Jan'14: U.S. Court of Appeals sustains Judge Hazel's 1910 opinion that the aileron infringed the Wright patent.

Curtiss, on business in Nice, France, cabled Orville: *"Congratulations. Curtiss."*

16Jan'14: Curtiss stated that he would take the case to the Supreme Court, and that none of the activities of the Curtiss companies *"would be affected by the decision."*

What *Mitchell Wilson* wrote of the Ford-Selden patent fight seems relevant: "Court records of patent trials are notoriously deceptive when it comes to giving a proper evaluation of a patent. It is the business of lawyers on either side to stress only the points which they feel are favorable to their clients, and to confuse and decry the points that count against them. Moreover, the decision of the court reflects the popular passions of the moment, the shrewdness of a lawyer capitalizing on the weakness or confusion of a given witness, and the judge's limited ability to understand the technical points involved."

19Jan1914: Orville to Andrew Freedman: "*The decision of the Court of Appeals sustained Judge Hazel in every particular. Claim 3, which was for warping wings or ailerons without a rudder, was sustained as I had hoped. This will give us an absolute monopoly* (certainly no mistaking the Wright's goals), *as there are no machines at the present time that do not infringe the claim...*

"*...Of course, we will make claim for damage done to our business and not a claim for the profits made by Curtiss. Curtiss will claim that there had been no profits. I presume that we will be able to at least recover the amount of his bond, which was $10,000. His other property, I understand, is not in his own name, so that it is probably nothing further can be recovered...*"

This appeared to be an opportunity for the Wright Company to exploit its position; but it did not for reasons commented upon by Loening: "*At any rate it did not happen because of one man - Orville Wright. With the winning of the suit, his revenge on Curtiss seemed satisfied, and all he wanted was tribute - royalties from everyone.*"

24Jan'14: Orville to Mortimer Delano: "*I have your letter informing me that the Governors of the Aero Club of America have awarded to me the Collier trophy for the year 1913 for the development and demonstration of an automatic stabilizer. Please extend...my appreciation of the honor.*"

31Jan'14: *Italian Model F Flying Boat.* Three were made for the Italian navy; each had a collapsible hood with transparent panels over a tandem-seated cockpit and *M*-type hull.

4Feb'14: Orville to Lt. Col. Samuel Reber: "*No doubt you have already read the decision of the Court of Appeals in the Curtiss case...The Court sustained our broad claims for warping, or ailerons alone, as well as when used in combination with the vertical rudder. This covers every machine that is being flown today, including the 'Dunne,' ' Etrich,' and the other so-called inherently stable machines. All of them have ailerons on the wingtips to be used in emergencies, and you will note that the court in the Curtiss case held that 'A machine that infringes part of the time is an infringement.'*

"*Some days ago I wrote the Secretary of War and the Secretary of the Navy ...notifying them that all of the Burgess-Curtiss machines delivered to them since the first of January 1913 were made and sold without license or authority from us and were infringements of our patents...We had a great deal of trouble with the Burgess Company and Curtiss...*" (Orville goes into considerable discussion, confusing and

"THE PASSING OF THE YACHT"

The Burgess Hydro-aeroplane is epoch making. It has brought flight into the field of yachting.

Wherever there is a small body of water, at the summer place, by the sea, on inland lakes and rivers, the Burgess Hydro-aeroplane meets the demand of the sportsman for safe flying.

In the 1912 models we offer no untried experimental devices, simply refinements in construction, additional strength and durability. Both the hydro-aeroplane and aeroplane may be started by the operator while in the machine.

The following aviators, when free to choose their own aeroplanes, selected a Burgess type:

C. Grahame-White	H. N. Atwood	C. K. Hamilton
Lieut. T. D. Milling	Clifford L. Webster	H. W. Gill
T. O. M. Sopwith	W. R. Brookins	U. S. Navy (hydroplane)
Phillips W. Page	U. S. Army.	

Training on Burgess Hydro-aeroplane equipped with duplicate control, under the instruction of licensed aviators only, may be secured during February and March at Daytona (aeroplane),Ormond (hydro-aeroplane), Fla., Los Angeles, Calif., or Marblehead, Mass. weather permitting.

BURGESS COMPANY & CURTIS

Dept. C   MARBLEHEAD, MASS.

really quite incredible since this firm was their *only* American licensee. The reader is led to believe that the 'Curtiss' is Glenn H. Curtiss, whereas *Greeley H. Curtis* was associated with Starling Burgess in the Burgess Company and Curtis, Inc.

Aircraft, March, 1912:

1914: The Army's *B.D. Foulois* wrote: "*On Februrary 9 Lieutenant Henry B. Post crashed in San Diego Bay during an attempt at a solo altitude record...Post had been flying old No.10 that had scared Hap Arnold so badly at Fort Riley in 1912...Post either fell or leaped from the machine at about 300 feet while in a steep dive. The official report cites the probable cause of the accident as 'due to pointing the machine down too steeply.' In view of the fact that Hap Arnold had almost been killed in an uncontrollable spin in the same machine, I think the same thing might have happened to Post.*

"*The plane that had caused Post's death was one of six Wright-C's purchased by the government; five of them had killed a total of six men. The sixth was lost in the Philippines when Lieut. Frank Lahm plunged into Manila Bay in September, 1913. Fortunately, Lahm was not injured.*

"*...I recommended that the Curtiss and Wright sections of the school be consolidated, and they were after Post's death. I also recommended discontinuance of the use of the Wright-B and Wright-C machines at San Diego, and that flying be limited to the single Curtiss and the four Burgess-Wright tractors assigned.*

"*...It was our job at San Diego to write the specifications which we hoped would get us a standard machine - one that had the same type of controls so that there wouldn't be any more 'Curtiss' and 'Wright' pilots. Standardization...was our most important problem and one that had to be solved if there was ever going to be a true military air force. The specifications we agreed upon for training planes prescribed a two-seater tractor biplane with dual controls, maximum speed at least 70 miles per hour...fuel for four hours...capable of assembly...in two hours...*

> *"...By the time of the competition twelve manufacturers had declared their intentions...But by October 20 only the Curtiss and Martin companies were ready...The competition was called off because there were so few qualified entries. However, we decided that Curtiss and Martin could demonstrate their machines...Only the Curtiss machine met every one of our requirements..."*

But, though Wright aircraft were probably most dangerous, all aeroplanes were hazardous. Curtiss commented: *"These accidents are dreadful. Every time a flyer dies in a crash, we not only lose a precious life, but public confidence as well. How can we ever sell the idea that flight can be a safe means of travel?"*

An interrelated perspective: Flyers were being killed in extraordinary numbers in Wright machines, a matter commented on by Charles G. Grey, editor of Britain's <u>The Aeroplane</u>...but most revealingly by Wright-disciple *Grover Loening*, who, *"...always watchful and suspicious of everything Curtiss did...(but with) a high appreciation of his qualities as a flyer and promoter, far outweighing, I have always felt, his talents as an engineer or scientist."*

In 1935 he wrote about *"The Reign of Death:*

> *"The series of deaths that took place in Wright planes was shocking. Cal Rodgers, Johnstone, Gill, Welsh, in civilian flying, and Lts. Hazelhurst, Kelly* (who'd trained with Curtiss), *Post, Ellington, Love, and many more* (likely including Selfridge, Philip Parmalee, Max Lillie, Heim in 1910, Lt. Lewis Rockwell and Cpl. Frank Scott in Sep'12, Lt. Loren Call on 8Jul'13, Lt. Billingsley on 20Jun'13, Lt. Moss Love on 4Sep'13, Lt. Percy Rich on 14Nov'13, Lt. Hugh Kelly and Eric Ellington on 24Nov'13, Hoxsey, Britain's Rolls, France's Lefebvre...and almost Hap Arnold, John Towers, Herbster, Waterman, Frank Lahm and Orville, himself) *had succeeded each other in a mounting list of tragedies.*
>
> *"What was happening, we now know, was just a plain case of stalling. But in those days even the word 'stall' was hardly used, and a 'spin' had never been heard of. All that happened was that the plane went into 'a deadly nose dive'. At most flying then was done at about five hundred feet, the results were almost always fatal. We all puzzled over these gruesome happenings, and finally, one day, Orville called me down to his office to show me some charts and curves he had studied out. They showed that in the high angle or stalled condition of the plane, if the controls were operated as usual the plane would stay in the stall even while falling...The early open pushers rarely spun. They just nosed down, stalled, in a sort of slow sinking and uncontrollable dive."*

Something had to be done to salvage the Wright reputation from the terrible wracking it was getting due to these crashes. *"The Army was desperate"*...condemning the Model C as *"dynamically unsuited for flying."*

14Jul1914: Loening was selected to transfer from Wright to Army employment, go to San Diego's North Island which, since May, 1913, was the Army's only pilot training facility (*where, in 1914 alone, already eight of the fourteen pilots licensed that year had been killed*), and take whatever steps necessary to correct the problem.

He wrote: "*It may have been somewhat disloyal to the Wright company, but after a thorough investigation and getting all possible dope on the accidents, I forthwith condemned all the Wright and Curtiss pusher planes in the army service as unsafe to fly, and the Lord knows they were. The pusher planes were not only easily stallable, but in a crash the engines generally fell on and crushed the pilots. In addition the Wright engines were none too good, and the installation of gas lines, throttles, etc., on the Curtiss pushers were the flimsiest mess..*"

He then undertook to make *"New Planes for Old:"*

"*The old Wright control on these planes operated the rudder by a little sideways-operated lever* ('split-handle lever') *on the end of the right-hand control stick, the elevator, and the ailerons* (?) *also, operated by a fore-and-aft movement of the individual levers. The result: none of the controls had the proper movement or sensitivity, and the large warping wings were so hooked up as to be ineffective on lateral control.*

"*Other faults were that the landing-gear skids had a tendency to drag a lot on take-off and to break on landing, the fore-and-aft stability was very poor, the whole tail shook ominously, and the high speed was only 58 miles per hour, which even at that date was considered a bit low.*

"*We decided to change the old-style warping wings to the more modern trailing edge aileron which was then a very much talked-of innovation on planes* (aileron/ balancing planes had been used by Curtiss for six years, since 1908)....

"*When the work was finished and the new Curtiss-type shoulder yoke control installed,* (we) *started the tests. It is difficult to conceive, at this distance in time, how so simple a piece of construction work could create such interest and excitement...*"

In effect, what Loening did was modify the Wright planes by incorporating features long-standard in Curtiss machines.

Feb1914: The Signal Corps issues specifications for a new Scout aeroplane which *Scientific American* observed "*are not nearly as rigid and difficult of fulfillment as they doubtless would be if the aeronautic industry in America had kept pace with that abroad.*"

21Feb1914: The Federal Court of Appeals - in a decision recognizing the Wright patent as entitled to very broad construction - grant a permanent injunction restraining Curtiss from the manufacture and sale of aeroplanes in which two ailerons functioned simultaneously to produce different angles on the right and left wing tips.

This meant survival or ruin for Curtiss, no appeal was possible.

At this time he was deeply involved in flying boat development, and resorted to the use of one aileron at a time (which promptly brought a new suit for infringement under Claim 1 of the Wright patent). He also began to look for some new '*evidence*' in the prior art that might scuttle the '*liberal interpretation*' of the courts.

28Feb'14: Captain Baldwin in <u>*The New York Times*</u>, a suspect interview because of several errors of fact, e.g., that he and Curtiss had been in Dayton for six months whereas it was but a week: "...*It is high time for all the rest of us to step up and admit that not a one of us ever would have got off the ground in flight if the Wrights had not unlocked the secret for us. I want to go on record as saying that the Wrights are fully entitled to the decision they have at last received...Mr. Curtiss is a friend of mine today, and I have served in his companies as a director. But it is due to the Wrights as a simple matter of justice to have the story of the actual genesis of flight fully established.*"

Curtiss made several attempts by wire and letter to arrange a meeting with Orville, all ignored or rebuffed.

8Mar'14: Confronted with Orville's obduracy, Curtiss resolved to fight. He wrote: "*In some New York daily papers there have been published during the past weeks certain statements attributed to Mr. Orville Wright, regarding his attitude in the aeroplane patent suit. Mixed in with these direct quotations were interpolated insinuations impugning my good faith in the patent litigation and carrying suggestions easily interpreted as such untruths as I cannot see how Mr. Wright or any other sane man ever made.*

"*The idea that any single line or part of any machine was either copied from the Wright machine, suggested by the Wrights or by their machine is absurd if not malicious. My first public flights, as a member of the Aerial Experiment Association, are a matter of record, and were made mostly before the Wrights exhibited their machine or made their first public flights.*

"*I have never had an item of information from either of the Wrights that helped me in designing or constructing my machines or that I ever consciously used. I believe today, as I always have believed, that the Curtiss control differs fundamentally from that employed by the Wrights, and that its superiority to that of the Wright system is demonstrated by the records of the two machines during the past five years.*

"*That I was unable to satisfactorily demonstrate this intricate technical point to the court I consider a misfortune largely due to the fact that our knowledge of aviation was vastly less when this case went to court several years ago, than it is today. I will continue to fight until the courts will eventually prove that I am correct.*"

Curtiss "believed sincerely in the aileron method of control - on which the United States Patent Office had granted a patent to the Aerial Experiment Association in December, 1911, but the Wright's interference action delayed its issuance until 1913 - differed completely from the Wright wing-warping system. He knew his cause was just, and he was determined not to be driven out of his native country (Germany, who did not recognize the Wright patent, offered Curtiss a most attractive proposition, and Canada, also not recognizing the patents, was considered a potential operations site) unless it was the only way to save his company."   *Scharff & Taylor*

The Wright Company announces that it would license the manufacture of aeroplanes under their patents for a payment of $1,000 ($45,000 today) a machine, plus a further royalty of 20 percent of the cost of all parts sold, including engines and propellers.

30Mar'14: Curtiss, Bell and Smithsonian Secretary Walcott, meeting at Bell's home, discuss the patent situation with A.E.A. trustee Charles Bell, McCurdy, and Sheldon Cameron, the A.E.A.'s patent attorney. They agree to pay Curtiss $2,000 to reconstruct and test the Langley flying machine, concluding with Bell's thought: *"It is the general impression that this* (A.E.A. aileron patent) *is a noninfringing device so far as the Wright patent is concerned...Mr. C. J. Bell concluded by saying the only practical means of raising capital to exploit aviation would be for the Wrights and Curtiss to get together in a new company which would control the situation without fear of litigation."*

CHARLES J. BELL, president of the American Security and Trust Co., of Washington, D. C., has been an exponent of flight from almost the earliest days. He was the treasurer of Graham Bell's Aerial Experiment Association in 1907–8, was treasurer of the Aero Club of Washington organized in 1909 and active in the raising of the $50,000 Washington-Baltimore fund to bring the 1910 Belmont Park meet to Washington.

Mr. Bell was born in Ireland in 1858 and became a citizen of the United States in '73.

After the invention of the telephone by his cousin, he became general manager of the National Telephone Co., and established exchanges in England. He organized Bell & Co., in Washington, and was its head till the Security company was formed. He has been president of this bank for thirty-two years.

He is a director of The International Bell Telephone Co. and many other Washington companies and societies.

When he returned from Europe, Curtiss found a letter waiting from Henry Ford stating that in his trying days fighting the Selden patent one man had *"saved the day for him."* He recommended that Curtiss meet with *W. Benton Crisp*, a New York patent attorney and former judge.

Curtiss took his advice. After a two-day conference in Detroit between Ford, Crisp, Monroe Wheeler and himself, a plan of action was laid out, with Crisp becoming Curtiss's chief counsel for the duration of the infringement suit, assisted by Wheeler.

Ford also insisted that *"my entire legal staff is at your disposal. Patents should be used to protect the inventor, not to hold back progress!"*

A glimpse into Orville's somewhat convoluted thinking, avoiding the mention of ailerons, is revealed in his talk at the Franklin Institute on 20May'14: *"...In order to secure greater dynamic efficiency and greater maneuvering ability, auxiliary surfaces mechanically operable* (ailerons) *are used in present flying machines instead of the practically fixed surfaces* (wing-warping) *of the inherently stable type. These machines possess the means of quickly recovering balance without changing the direction of travel and of maneuvering with greater dexterity when required..."*

In addition to the legal skirmishes planned by Crisp, in a meeting between him, Curtiss and Albert Zahm, it was suggested that if Langley's Aerodrome flew, its means of control, which preceded the Wrights, would be of material assistance in countering the Wright's patent claims. Thus, they set about to implement the long-held plans of the *"Friends of Langley,"* as noted below.

In Fred Kelly's *The Wright Brothers:* "A few days after the final court decision... Lincoln Beachey, a Curtiss stockholder, telegraphed Secretary Walcott, of the Smithsonian, asking permission to attempt a flight with the original Langley machine. That proposal was not accepted; but two months later, when Glenn H. Curtiss himself said he would like to test the Langley machine, his request was granted. The Smithsonian entered into a deal with Curtiss in which he was to receive a payment of $2,000, and was permitted to take the original Langley plane...to... Hammondsport..."

The Beachey, Curtiss and Smithsonian involvement smacked of collusion, on which *The New York Times* commented: "*People with minds naturally suspicious are likely to look for a connection between certain patent litigation and the announcement by Lincoln Beachey, the aviator* (who'd said 'you can fly a kitchen table if your motor is strong enough,' much as Victor Lougheed wrote in 1912: "*...flight by aeroplanes most outrageously ill-designed - rammed through the air with an engineering efficiency of a barn door in a cyclone.*"), *that he is going to prove that if Prof. Langley had been able to put a modern motor in his aeroplane it would have sailed the air as well as those since made.*"

A somewhat different aspect shows that, following a proposal made by Bell in 1904, *a decade earlier*, the *"Friends of Langley,"* believing the Great Aerodrome would fly if properly launched, formed the *"Langley Laboratory."* It was this group that spearheaded arrangements with the Smithsonian. Perspectives differ as to what happened after the Langley machine arrived at Hammondsport in April, 1914, with one writer summarizing the situation as "involving temptation for one side to exaggerate and distort favorably Langley's work, and for the other side to belittle and deny it."

Kelley states that Curtiss "made numerous vital changes in the machine, using knowledge of aerodynamics discovered by the Wrights but never possessed by Langley. No information is available to indicate that the Smithsonian offered any objection to these alterations being made. The Smithsonian's official observer...was Dr. A.F. Zahm (described by some 'as famous for distortions'), who had been technical witness for Curtiss in the recent lawsuits...No one officially representing any disinterested scientific body was present..."

The Smithsonian had Curtiss rebuild and attempt to fly the Langley machine *in two distinct phases*, each about a year apart (for the second, see 4Jun'15). The first phase was to duplicate *as closely as possible* the original craft.

The original Langley Aerodrome:

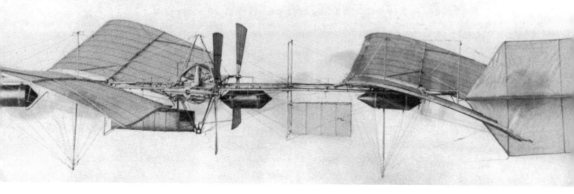

Charles Manly, Curtiss at the Langley's wheel, and Zahm, Hammondsport, 1914:

Curtiss had John Tarbox, his patent attorney and also an engineer, supervise the project, assisted by Manly - with Albert Zahm Smithsonian's observer.

Impossible to catapult-launch, adding pontoons made the *"Langley"* a hydroaeroplane. A two-edged sword: the pontoons added 350 pounds, but also provided strut bracing. At a later date, answering Casey Baldwin's query, Curtiss stated: "*It is true that it was flown without a single change that could have <u>improved its flying qualities</u>. The only changes were the replacements of the broken parts and the addition of the floats...The addition of the three floats and their supports added 350 pounds of weight to the machine, not to mention the head resistance.*"

Attaching the wings and floats (pontoons) to the Langley, Hammondsport, 1914:

28May'14: It was launched on Keuka Lake for a flight of approximately 150 feet, and on June 2nd for shorter flights, when photos were taken showing *"the craft in the air:"*

To Curtiss, telegram: *"Congratulations on your successful vindication of Langley's drome. This is really the crowning achievement of your career, at least so far. My best wishes for your continued success. Graham Bell."*

Based upon these demonstrations, the Smithsonian stated in its 1914 *Annual Report* that *"without modification"* the original Langley machine had at last flown.

Albert Zahm wrote: "*It has demonstrated that with its original structure and power, it is capable of flying with a pilot and several hundred pounds of useful load. It is the first aeroplane in the history of the world of which this can truthfully be said.*"

27Feb'14: Orville to *The New York Times:* In this interview Orville announced the Wright Company plans to collect a 20-percent royalty on all aircraft manufactured in the United States, and then went on at length relating how Curtiss had stolen the aeroplane from the Wright brothers over a period of years beginning with the Baldwin visit in 1906 ("*We told them all there was to tell*").

He also accused Curtiss of indirectly contributing to Wilbur's death in that Curtiss had "*worried Wilbur, first into a state of chronic nervousness, and then into physical fatigue, which made him an easy prey for the attack of typhoid which caused his death.*"

This caused Curtiss considerable anguish.

2Mar'14: Orville to Percy Noel, editor: "*...My reason for ordering the advertisements in Aero & Hydro discontinued was that I did not consider that we were treated fairly in the paper...What I object to is the suppression of news* (the Appeal Courts decision) *which does not entirely suit your own personal taste.*"

19Mar'14: Orville to Franklin Lane: "*...The interview published in The New York Times...was unusually good for a newspaper reporter. I stated that inventors were poorly protected by the law, and that unless they had large financial backing to maintain their claims through long-drawn-out litigation in the courts, patents were of no value to them...*"

Commenting on the original failure of the Langley machine, Orville stated: "*I. It was dynamically inefficient. II. It was structurally weak. III. It lacked adequate means for obtaining equilibrium. IV. It lacked practical means for launching. V. It lacked practical means for landing.*"

In the 1947 Smithsonian *National Aircraft Collection:* "The catapult launching was abandoned and floats substituted. This involved various changes from the original machine. The wings of 1903 were too damaged to permit their use; the new ones made by Curtiss were not of equal workmanship nor as large. The engine had suffered from the ravages of time and developed but 35 horsepower. Despite these handicaps, comprising less lifting area, less power, more resistance, and more weight than the original design called for, the aerodrome made several short flights. A second series of tests was made with modified power plant and controls."   *Paul Garber*

Hammondsport testing of the Langley continued: *Scientific American*, 10Oct'14:

Overloaded in front.

Clearing the water.

Further Flights with Langley's Aeroplane
By Our Staff Correspondent at Hammondsport

THE rehabilitation and first trials, at the Curtiss aerodrome on Lake Keuka, N. Y., of the great Langley monoplane of 1903 were described in the SCIENTIFIC AMERICAN last June. The tests showed that this scientifically designed pioneer flying machine was capable of flight with precisely its original propulsive plant, wings, and rudders, and with 40 per cent additional aggregate weight, due to floats and extra framing to attach them. Then the trials were temporarily halted in favor of the elaborate and feverish experiments with the "America," the Rodman Wanamaker transatlantic flyer. The Langley was unwinged and stored nearly three months in the hangar at the lake side.

Toward the middle of August Mr. Curtiss went to California, leaving further tests of the big monoplane in charge of his mechanicians. He had instructed them to mount one of his 90-horse O. K. motors with a direct-connected tractor screw on the fore part of the aeroplane frame, and to set aside for the present the original motor and twin propellers. As these had several times driven the machine in short flights, he saw no advantage in making them continue to bear a 40 per cent extra burden, especially as the ball-bearings of the propeller shafting never had been over strong for their normal work. In case of wreckage he would feel far less keenly the loss of a regular stock motor than the loss of that splendid pioneer engine, so much admired for its workmanship, and which truly may be called the first gasoline motor in history, adequate to carry a man in sustained mechanical flight. Moreover, he had from the beginning intended to use a Curtiss motor, but had not at first hit upon a simple way of mounting it and keeping the propeller free of the front stay wires.

As the chief designers and constructors at the factory were now very busy, the adjustment of the new motor and propeller, to the aeroplane, was left to a practical mechanic who worked at the job leisurely during his spare time. None of Prof. Langley's nice computations and preliminary studies were attempted. The machine was "balanced up" as a farmer balances hay on a wagon, by looking at it from different sides and applying horse sense. Presently the craft was placed on the water and moored, with a rope and spring-balance, to a stake on the shore. The propeller gave a static thrust of 410 pounds. Maybe that would do; if not, the screw could be quickly removed and one, two or three others, taken from stock, could be tried in turn. While the propeller was spinning, it sucked up water from the lake and blew a cold spray over the bystanders. Frank Klecker, the practical man in charge, put on his raincoat and finished the measurement. He now had the Langley ready for its wings and for its first run.

In the absence of Mr. Curtiss, his aviation instructor, "Doc." Wildman, piloted the aeroplane, with its new wings. Seated above the main frame, behind the front wings, he ran the craft cautiously over the lake, while some of the factory men and Dr. Zahm of the Smithsonian Institution accompanied it in a motorboat to observe its running balance. The pontoons were too far back, the weight too far forward, the rear wings set at too large an angle. The latter difficulty had been foreseen by Prof. Langley, who had provided notches for fixing the leading edges of the wings as high or low as seemed necessary. When the angle was lowered and the pilot and pontoons shifted along the frame, as a grocer slides weights along the beam of his scale, another run was made, resulting in several short flights. "Doc." Wildman was then called to California, and was succeeded by one of his pupils, Mr. Elwood Dougherty.

After some little "feeling out" of the machine, Mr. Dougherty notified the photographers of his intention to attempt a flight. Waiting till they were a thousand feet from shore in a motorboat, he started from the aeroplane to overtake them. The Langley, with its swollen wings gleaming bright yellow in the clear sun, and its floats skimming lightly with foaming heels, sped forward in graceful poise, cleared the water near the cameras, and soared half a thousand feet forward at an elevation of three or four yards. The flight was twice repeated, and the craft was then returned to shore for a longer voyage, as soon as a larger propeller could be added. A light breeze, not quite strong enough to raise white caps, was blowing during the trial.

Two days later some better results were achieved. The pilot had said the craft was in easy control, but mounted too readily and lacked thrust. Accordingly the front wings were lowered from an angle of 12 degrees to one of 10 degrees, and the 8.5-foot screw was exchanged for a 9-foot screw. The rear wings were left at about 10 degrees angle of incidence. When the photographers were again in place, the shining craft tripped lightly over the sunlit waves, and slid gracefully into the air in excellent poise and at a speed neighboring 35 miles an hour. Hovering within ten yards of the water, it ascended on a very easy grade, soared along 3,000 feet, declined to the wave tips and soared again 2,500 feet. Both on the water and in the air its movement was stable and majestic.

In all the foregoing experiments the aeroplane when fairly adjusted maintained a secure and steady poise, both in planing and in flying. By virtue of the dihedral angle between its wings it possessed good inherent lateral stability. No wing-warping or aileron attachment had been provided by Prof. Langley, and none was used either at present or last spring. True, Langley had placed well below the main frame a wind-vane (vertical) rudder, which could be made to exert a righting as well as a steering effect, but neither Curtiss nor his men ever employed this rudder since the first brief flight in June. It was, in fact, tied fast and remained inactive. In its stead the big tail was used to steer right and left. The big tail was used also as an elevator, as in Langley's day. The reason for steering with the tail instead of the wind vane rudder in Langley's scheme, was to secure a more powerful hold on the wind while the craft was running on the water. Once aloft, the little rudder could, if put to use, very well steer the machine, as Langley intended.

At the conclusion of the last trial, toward the closing hour on Saturday, September 19th, the Curtiss workmen volunteered their services for the morrow. They wished to see the aeroplane, after a slight shifting of the pilot's seat, fly several miles and cut figures in the air, before the rough autumnal winds should begin. But their superintendent, Mr. Kleckler, thought it best for them to rest on Sunday, and chance the weather following. Unfortunately the stormy weather came before the long flight could be attempted, and the scientific observations that were to attend it.

Culminating the experiments, in 1915 the *Langley*, incorporating several aeronautical refinements unknown in 1903 and a Curtiss 80-hp motor, was flown for almost 30 minutes and a ten-mile distance in a strong head wind.

The old "aerodrome" was then restored and, in 1918, exhibited at the Smithsonian with this plaque:

"Original Langley flying machine, 1903. The first man-carrying aeroplane in the history of the world capable of sustained free flight. Invented, built, and tested over the Potomac River by Samuel Pierpont Langley in 1903. Successfully flown at Hammondsport, N.Y., June 2, 1914."

Indignate with this implied slight, Orville complained to Secretary Wolcott, and a new, but still unsatisfactory label appeared:

"LANGLEY AERODROME OF 1903. RESTORED

"In the opinion of many competent to judge, this was the first heavier-than-air craft in the history of the world capable of sustained free flight, under its own power, carrying a man. This aircraft antedated the machine designed and built by Wilbur and Orville Wright, which, on December 17, 1903, was the first in the history of the world to accomplish free flight, under its own power, carrying a man."

Although far from fact, its *"imprimatur of the venerable Smithsonian,"* an institution

"FOR THE INCREASE AND DIFFUSION OF KNOWLEDGE AMONG MEN,"

gave it far-flung acceptance.

"The injustice of man is mitigated in effect by the understanding of its motives and compulsions, while the blows of fate appear as stark irrational cruelty. Thus the deeds of individuals almost become as pin pricks beside the pain inflicted by life without ascertainable reason, upon the personages of our narrative (Orville and Wilbur Wright)." *John McMahon*

24Apr'14: In competition for the new Signal Corps training machine, Curtiss builds the *Model J Tractor,* a tandem 2-seater designed by Douglas Thomas (late of Sopwith), powered with the 100-hp *OX* engine providing a speed range of 45 to 80-mph. It had turn-up ailerons on the top wings only, and a two-wheel landing gear augmented with a double skid forward and a tail skid. It was delivered to the Army *(SC-29, 30)* at North Island on July 28, 1914.

Development of this machine is an excellent example of Curtiss's thought process: When his first design of a tractor aircraft (the *Model G*) was unsuccessful, he reasoned he needed the best talent and hired Thomas, who began the design before leaving England.

8Oct'14: Captain H.K. Miller took the *Model J,* No. 30, up to 7,441 feet for a new American altitude record.

Curtiss, in Model N, explains controls to Col. Samuel Reber (see pp. 354), North Island:

10Oct'14 <u>*Scientific American*</u>**:** "*A new type of military aeroplane, designed by Glenn H. Curtiss, has been tried out at San Diego, Cal., and developed remarkable speed and climbing ability. The new machine has wings shaped like those used on the flying boat America, the under surfaces being almost flat while the upper surfaces are highly arched, with a wing spread of over forty feet. The official requirements were that a weight of 600 pounds of useful load should be carried at a speed between 45 and 70 miles an hour, and climb at least 3,000 feet in ten minutes. It must also be able to rise from long grass or harrowed ground. In the trials all of these requirements were* easily exceeded, although the engine was rated at only 90 horsepower, and a speed of 86 miles an hour is said to have been attained.*"*

In December, shortly after the Army's evaluation, the best features of the *J* and *N* (a re-worked *J*) were retained and the *Model J-30,* now a hybrid, became Model *JN-1.* Thus was born the *Jenny.*

AERIAL AGE WEEKLY, June 21, 1915   321

One of the new U. S. Army Curtiss Tractors at San Diego.

"British officers were sent to America to look into the possibilities of Curtiss production and engineering. They reported to Winston Churchill, then First Lord of the Admiralty. His answer was in effect, '*accept everything America can produce to these specifications.*' At first the British airmen look askance at the *Jenny*. The price of the machine, complete with engine, was said to have been less than British builders were charging their Government for machines without engines. To be sure their machines had a highly polished piano finish for the wooden parts, where the Curtiss machines were but substantially varnished. At first the British said: '*Just like the Ford automobile*'...after a little more than a year the *Jenny* with its Curtiss motor, was the most respected aeroplane, because of the distance flown and its general durability, in the British aeronautical training services."

Lyman Seely

British War Mission officers ordered 250 *JN's*, initiating Curtiss's move to Buffalo (where recent electrical development of Niagara Falls made virtually limitless power available), and the start of his tremendous wartime business.

By the end of 1915 Curtiss contracted for over $6 million in aircraft for the British, which showed a net profit of $2.5 million (over $110 million today) - and the 1916 contract was over $15 million (over $600 million today).

314   *AERIAL AGE WEEKLY, June 21, 1915*

CURTISS FACILITIES

This is the main factory of the Curtiss Aeroplane Co. at Buffalo where aeroplanes of tractor and pusher type for land and water are built under ideal conditions. The Curtiss Company is the largest and best equipped aeroplane manufacturing plant in the world.

INFORMATION ON REQUEST

THE CURTISS AEROPLANE CO.
BUFFALO, NEW YORK

View of the Wing Covering Department at the Busy Curtiss Plant at Buffalo

With both British and American aviators training in *Jennys*, by war's end over 6,000 had been produced (to glut the post-war American market). Approximately 95-percent of the almost 10,000 American WW1 pilots trained in or flew either Curtiss *JN*'s or *flying boats*.

The British make a settlement with the Wright Co., paying 15,000 pounds (about $3-1/2 million today) for prior use of the Wright patent.

Aero and Hydro, 14Nov'14: "*It is with a feeling akin to relief that one reads of the compromise just effected between the British government and the British-Wright Co., for it encourages one to believe that at last, after these years of weary waiting, the Wright Co. has finally awakened to the fact that business is business, and that it is better to take the market price for what they have to sell than to lock it up...*"

Charles G. Grey: "*After that meeting (Reims) flying went on quickly. The Wright Bros. alleged patents had been bought up by a group of financiers who tried to create a monopoly on absurd claims for a system of controls which could only be operated by jugglers. Bleriot, Curtiss, Farman and others fought them until war broke out in 1914...*"

August 1914: "France was the first to adopt the airplane as a military arm. When the World War broke France had 1,273 pilots, as against Great Britain's 750 and Germany's 680. France had 1,100 airplanes - Germany, 1,000 - Great Britain 450. Russia had 875 - Italy 600 - Austria 400 - and little Belgium 250...Uncle Sam at that time had but 100 planes and 252 pilots." *World in The Air*

"*Jane's All The World's Aircraft:* In March of 1914 the US Army had *1 Wright-B, 2 C, 2 D; 1 Curtiss-D, 2 E, 2 H; 1 Burgess-F, 4 H; 1 Wright, 1 Curtiss tractor and 1 Burgess tractor airplane* - at San Diego, Manila, Hawaii and San Antonio. The Navy had 10 seaplanes or flying boats, typically Curtiss, but also one or more Benoist, Burgess or Wright.

<u>AERIAL AGE WEEKLY</u>, 29Mar'15:

Wright Aeroplanes

FOR SPORT, EXHIBITION OR MILITARY USE, OVER LAND OR WATER now embody the improvements that have been suggested by the experiments, conducted during the past ten years

The New Wright Model "HS"
MILITARY FLYER

THE WRIGHT COMPANY
(The Wright Patents)

Dayton, Ohio   N. Y. Office, 11 Pine St.

"Grover Loening wrote Orville several times during the year he was with the Signal Corps, but Orville seldom answered his letters. Loening felt that Orville never forgave him for outlawing planes with pusher propellers. Tractor propellers would not appear on Wright... aircraft until the *Model K*, a seaplane...for the U.S. Navy at the end of 1915, when Orville was no longer president...The *Model K* was not only the first...to be equipped with such propellers but the first in which the outmoded wing-warping...was replaced with ailerons on the wings, the method of lateral control then in almost universal use."   *Fred Howard*

1915: The Wright *Model K* was the first tractor Wright, and the first to utilize ailerons instead of the wing warping on all Wrights since 1899.

But this is after what this advertisement shows:

Apr'14: The *Sperry F Flying Boat*: Built for Lawrence Sperry, it had a bulbous bow for the gyroscopic autopilot and was the *first* Curtiss *amphibious* flying boat.

18Jun'14: Sperry, competing for the French War Department's 50,000 franc prize, dramatically demonstrates his *gyrostabilizer* over the Seine at Bezons, near Paris - *beginning the era of the autopilot*. Later in 1914, the *Collier Trophy* was awarded his father, Elmer, for this invention.

STABILIZER ASTONISHES FRENCHMEN

PARIS, FRANCE, June 21.—At the *Concours de Securité pour Aéroplanes* on the Seine at Bezons, Lawrence Sperry, the young American pilot, has piloted a Curtiss flying-boat fitted with an automatic stabilizer invented by his father, Elmer A. Sperry, of New York.

During the flights over the Seine, Sperry's mechanic left his seat and climbed out on the wings while Sperry stood up with his hands above his head.

The aeroplane proved to be under complete automatic control and the correction of the angle of inclination was so accurate and immediate that the machine never appeared to dip dangerously. The aeroplane rose from the water and returned without control of the pilot.

This stabilizer is based on gyroscopic principles and the device weighs 21 *kilogrammes*. Four gyroscopes are grouped in two pairs to stabilize the machine both latitudinally and longitudinally, while the gyroscopes balance each other in turning.

These small gyroscopes rotate at a rate of 12,000 revolutions a minute and are propelled by a small electric motor driven by the aeroplane's engine. The gyroscopes control the various tail organs as well as the lateral stability planes and can be instantly cut in or out of operation at will. Sperry is continuing the demonstrations with considerable success.

Aero and Hydro, 4Jul'14:

French committee and Sperry's Curtiss flying boat:

1914: The Mentor Association:

URTISS FLYING BOAT AT LAKE KEUKA, NEW YORK, is the subject of one of the intaglio-gravure pictures illustrating "The Conquest of the Air."

THE HYDROAËROPLANE
Monograph Number Four in The Mentor Reading Course

ONE summer day, a short time ago, an aviation meet was being held in Chicago. One of the aviators, when flying over Lake Michigan, lost control of his machine and fell into the water. Three-quarters of a mile away was a hydroaëroplane circling around and occasionally skimming the surface of the water like a big seagull. The pilot of this strange water bird saw the aviator fall, and went to his rescue. Flying at a mile a minute, he reached the spot, landed on the water by the submerged aëroplane, and offered to take the aviator to land. This was the first public demonstration of the hydroaëroplane.

A little later another aviator took his hydroaëroplane to New York City and demonstrated that he could travel over the surface of the river, skate on the ice, or rise into the air—one as easily as the other.

The hydroaëroplane is operated in both the water and the air exactly like an aëroplane. The craft is driven by a propeller, traveling over the surface of the water until it has gained sufficient speed; then the elevating plane is tilted upward, and the machine rises gracefully out of the water. It is the safest and at the same time the most exciting phase of aviation. As a sport for amateurs it is already very popular. A hydroaëroplane is like a fast automobile with wings, and is as easy to operate as a motorboat. If anything goes wrong, the machine simply alights on the water, and no matter what happens it cannot sink.

The hydroaëroplane was an American invention. Glenn H. Curtiss may be called the real inventor of it. He made

one in 1911, which was very successful. Early in 1910 he was preparing to make a trip in an aëroplane from Albany to New York. He fitted his machine with pontoons so that in case he was forced to descend when over the river he would have the advantage of a non-sinking plane. After he had successfully made his flight he began to plan how to make it possible to rise from the water with a pontoon. He set to work, and succeeded a few months later.

The story of Curtiss' life reads like a romance. He was born at Hammondsport, New York, in 1878, and was left fatherless when only four years old. His schooling lasted only a few years; but even as a boy he showed himself wonderfully keen in mathematics. He always had a taste for going fast. In bicycle racing he won many trophies, and when he developed a motor-driven bicycle he worked to such good purpose that he won world's championships and established world's records. His mile in $26^1/_5$ seconds is the fastest ever traveled on the ground. Success in the development of light-weight motors led him into aëronautics and aviation, where his personal courage and mechanical ingenuity have made him a distinctive figure.

It is hoped that the hydroaëroplane will solve the problem of crossing the Atlantic Ocean. Lord Northcliffe has offered a $50,000 prize to the first person who shall make a transatlantic flight in a hydroaëroplane or flying boat in seventy-two consecutive hours between any point in the United States, Canada, or Newfoundland, and any point in Great Britain or Ireland, in either direction.

14Feb'14: *Rodman Wanamaker* to the Aero Club's Alan Hawley: "*In the cause of science and in the interest of world peace* (with World War in the offing, "*world peace*" was to become a somewhat bizarre crusade for Henry Ford, reputedly Wanamaker's partner in this endeavor), *I have the honor to announce...to make a purely scientific test of aeronautic powers by crossing the Atlantic by one flight...the operators and navigators may be from the Navy of the United States and of Great Britain... The transatlantic flyer to be used in the journey is now being constructed by Mr. Glenn H. Curtiss, from plans that we have been studying for a long time...*"

25Feb'14: Orville Wright to the press: "...(Curtiss would not be allowed to build an airplane unless he took out a Wright license and settled for all back business)...*The Curtiss machine can start from Canada, as Canada is the only civilized country in which our patents are not recognized. But I have not enough expectation that the craft will ever land near enough to any country where our patents are validated - that is, anywhere in Europe - to make it worth while to tell you what I would do in that case.*"

Curtiss was Bell's dinner guest during the flight's planning period. Bell's Diary: "...(I invited him to use Baddeck's laboratories, promising to) *give him every facility...we need not be surprised should* (Curtiss) *appear in the air there during the coming summer...I must write to Casey Baldwin...and recommend him to invite Curtiss to visit Beinn Breagh at the time of the yacht races...*"

23Jun'14: The *Wanamaker Model H Flying Boat "America."* Challenged by the London *Daily Mail*'s $50,000 ($2-1/2 million today) prize for flight across the Atlantic, department store owner Rodman Wanamaker ordered this giant flying boat for $25,000 (over a million today). [Note: Wanamaker pioneered the full-line department store in Philadelphia. In 1896 it opened in New York. Its last store, in Yonkers, closed in 1995. In 1914 Wanamaker was Ford's New York and Philadelphia dealer.]

The *America* was powered with two 100-hp Curtiss OX pusher engines (a third was temporarily added, making it the *first* American trimotor), and had a thirty-five foot hull with a fully enclosed cabin. It was designed by Douglas Thomas, assisted by several American naval officers, and built under the direction of Briton *John Cyril Porte*, to be its pilot, with George Hallett its copilot-mechanic. The route, in three stages: Newfoundland to the Azores to Spain to England.

"One of his (Porte's) ambitions was to fly the Atlantic, but until the *Curtiss Flying Boat* supplied the idea no reasonably safe way had offered. Porte met representatives of Mr. Wanamaker and convinced them his project was feasible. Then they hunted out Glenn Curtiss, who was in England...Curtiss at first demurred but finally agreed to design and build a flying boat according to Porte's ideas."   *Lyman Seely*

"Our preparations for in-flight maintenance may be of interest. I had a suit of 'overalls' made with pockets 18 inches deep, so nothing could blow out of them. In a pusher plane it is necessary to be very careful not to drop anything because it would certainly go into the propeller and possibly make serious trouble. Wearing a lineman's belt and having rings fastened in suitable places around the engines, I could hook on and have the use of both hands to work on anything within reach. One of the factory mechanics...made me a spring clip which I could push on to the end of an exhaust rocker arm to hold the exhaust valve off its seat to relieve compression in that cylinder so I could change a spark plug without stopping an engine. It was necessary to have a long socket wrench which fit quite tightly on the plug to hold it firmly until I could pull it loose and put it in my pocket. Of course I had to take some nasty shocks in disconnecting the spark plug wire and replacing it. It was easy to tell which cylinder was missing because there were no exhaust stacks or manifolds. I changed one plug in flight over Lake Keuka, to be sure that I could do so if necessary...In those days plugs often cracked, leaked or fouled with oil."

George Eustace Amyot Hallett
The America, Porte, left, and Hallett:

Noted by historian Peter M. Bowers in his definitive book, <u>Curtiss Aircraft 1907-1947</u>:
"Lt. Porte was recalled to duty in the United Kingdom and was able to persuade the Admiralty to purchase the America *and its sister ship. These were to become the prototypes of a long line of twin-engined biplane flying-boats that would serve Brtiain and the US Navy well into World War II. The original* America, *in fact, gave its name to the class, and later developments up to H-16 sold to Britain became known as Small Americas and Large Americas."*

Also of interest: "In 1914, another major patent suit was filed against Curtiss, this one by Albert S. Janin, who claimed that Curtiss's 1912 flying-boat infringed a patent applied for earlier by Janin. Janin had applied for a patent on a flying-boat design in 1911, but had never built one. Although Curtiss built a Janin hull in 1918 to prove the Janin claim unworkable, the Janin case dragged on and was not resolved in Curtiss's favour until 1921."

Peter M. Bowers

John Towers, Curtiss and Cyril Porte:

This project provides insight into the thinking between Curtiss and Orville, one thinking it possible, the other not so sure. The Springfield, Massachusetts, <u>Union</u>: "*Again we are confronted by the old problem 'Who shall decide when doctors disagree.' Orville Wright declares it is foolhardy...to attempt to cross the Atlantic with the comparatively weak engines now in use in aeroplanes, and with the present lack of staying powers characteristic of such light craft. He thinks it is most unwise to undertake a Trans-Atlantic flight when efforts to cover the same distance by land have failed. On the other hand, Glenn H. Curtiss has begun the construction of the curious new flying machine which he proposes to make the trip between continents, with funds provided by Rodman Wanamaker. Mr. Curtiss declares this machine will have both a special motor and the extra staying powers needed to attain the feat.*

"Possibly Mr. Curtiss and his associates know what they are about, but the opinion of Mr. Wright seems to an ordinary mind to be well weighed with common sense. If the proposed new flier seems theoretically equal to a Trans-Atlantic journey, it is quite the point of prudence to test it out on a land expedition of similar length before incurring the great hazard of a voyage across the ocean."

Later Curtiss commented: "*The Atlantic Ocean, one of these days, will be no more difficult to cross by air than a fish pond.*" Next, <u>*Aero and Hydro,*</u> 4Jul1914:

Vol. VIII
No. 14

AERO AND HYDRO

July 4,
1914

Edited by E. PERCY NOEL

AMERICA PASSES TESTS—PREPARED FOR VOYAGE

HAMMONDSPORT, N. Y., June 30.—The America rose from Lake Keuka today, carrying 1,850 pounds useful load. Lieut. Porte expects to leave for New York tomorrow night. The America will then be prepared for shipment.

HAMMONDSPORT, N. Y., June 29.—That the America, the giant Curtiss flying-boat built for the Rodman Wanamaker trans-Atlantic expedition, is a success no one here longer doubts. The final conviction came today when G. H. Curtiss, the constructor, admitted for the first time that the "big red whale" would carry the required 1,800-pound load. "Admitted" is the proper word, for since the trials commenced here a week ago, Mr. Curtiss has been the most conservative of any of the many observers and directly interested people.

There is no doubt now that the trans-Atlantic machine will carry fuel for at least 20 hours flying. She may carry more. She will not only carry it, but get off the water with that load aboard—a total weight of nearly 5,000 pounds. This she must do before Lieut. John Cyril Porte leaves here for New York, where he will sail Saturday for Halifax by the

Red Cross line. The machine, then, with George E. A. Hallett in charge, will follow July 13. The great aero-boat will be due in Halifax July 16. By July 18, if not earlier, she will be again ready for the water. After trial flights, Lieut. Porte will await the most propitious weather conditions, which he expects between July 18 and July 26.

This evening Lieut. Porte and Hallett went out for a hydroplane excursion in the America. There was no intention of trying to get off the water, as there were eight newspaper men aboard. But when the machine trotted along the water at a lively clip and climbed up nicely on her step, Lieut. Porte let her into the air for a short jump—about 100 feet. The total weight of the machine and load was 4,600 pounds and the head-resistance amounted to fully 10 miles reduction in speed on the water.

Sunday afternoon when the machine was about ready for the air, a storm in the form of a small tornado broke and it was with difficulty that the enormous machine was kept on the ground. No flying was attempted.

Saturday was the beginning of the end of experimenta-

THE AMERICA STARTING FOR A TEST ON LAKE KEUKA

AERIAL AGE WEEKLY, *June 21, 1915*   327

Drawings of the New Curtiss Flying Boat Patent

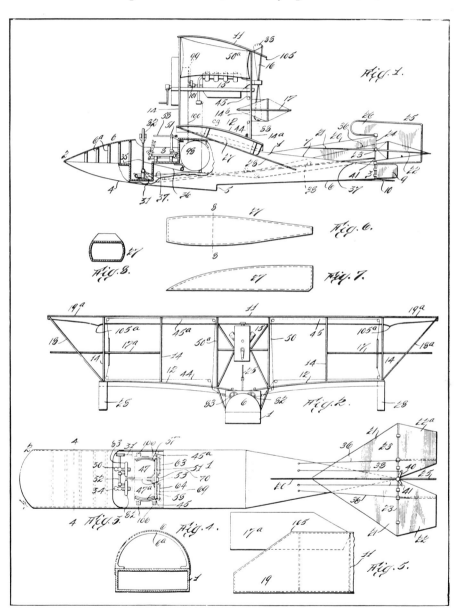

The Model F Flying Boat, Buffalo NY, 23Oct'16. More successful than Henry Ford's Model T (1908-1927), this model was still in worldwide use well into WW2:

The war dashed these plans.

In 1906 Germany began making *"Unterseeboots"* – "U-boats," little knowing how effective they'd become in the early years of WW1 in bringing England to its knees.

England was desperate; its lifeblood was draining away, as – with impunity – unseen U-boats sank countless ships. *Then a serendipitous event*: the Curtiss flying boat. The U-Boat's nemesis - with newly developed convoy tactics - *it helped save England.*

For anti-submarine patrol the British immediately purchased the *America (H-1)*, its backup, and *62* similar ones (8 built in England) known as *H-2* and *H-4* or *"Small America."* Up to September, 1915, the original *America* was credited for sinking three German U-boats (flying boats also shot down Zeppelins L.22, L.43 and L.62).

In 1916 Curtiss (whose staff included Chance Vought), working with Porte's British staff, produced *71 H-12 "Big America"* with an improved rough-water hull and powered with two 275-hp Rolls Royce *Eagles*. Then, in England, under Porte these evolved into the *Felixstowe F-2, F-2a (1917), F-3* - and as the war continued, the *F-5*; and finally into the *H-16*, with its tough *F-2a* hull and powered with 320-hp Rolls *Eagle-8* engines.

They were the only American-built aircraft to see combat in World War 1.

And in World War II history repeated itself when ConVair's I.M. "Mac" Laddon (once the author's neighbor) designed the *PBY* (Patrol Boat) *Catalin*a - which became *the first American aircraft to fight* - again helping Britain stave off the U-boat menace. It had evolved from 1928's *XPY-1 Commodores* – with which, in 1929, Ralph O'Neill's NYRBA Line *pioneered* air travel to South America. The *PBY* first flew in 1936 in San Diego (where Consolidated moved in 1935 - from Curtiss's ex-Buffalo factory where the British World War I flying boats were built). ConVair built 1,416 *PBYs*.

Curtiss H-12A Flying Boat, Felixstowe, upper; and an American H-12, lower:

Following the outbreak of World War I flying boats became the cornerstone for Curtiss's tremendous growth. The British, initially ordering *JN's*, were placing orders difficult to comprehend but a year earlier. When Curtiss needed working capital to carry out the first order he requested an advance of $75,000. The cable arrived minus the $ sign and the British forwarded 75,000 pounds (over $365,000), more than enough to get production underway. That order totaled approximately $14 million (over $600 million today), the largest ever for an American aircraft firm. By early 1915 Curtiss's backlog from Britain, Russia and Italy exceeded $20 million (approximately $900 million today).

A 1915 credit report on Curtiss rated him as *"a man of large means,"* with a worth estimated between $300,000 and $400,000 (around $15 million today), exclusive of his wife's *"substantial"* holdings. It summed up: *"If the European war continues another year and a half, Mr. Curtiss will be a multi-millionaire...Personally, he is highly regarded, spoken of as a man of good character and habits, is considered of high integrity, and authorities who are in a position to know him are of the opinion that he would not ask or contract beyond his ability to pay."*

But this wartime business was too much for little Hammondsport. In the fall of 1915 a special overnight train moved the entire Curtiss Aeroplane Company, its key employees, their families and household goods, initially to quarters in the abandoned Thomas Motor Car Co. factory in Buffalo (the company, now bankrupt, from which in 1902 Curtiss had ordered his first motor castings).

This move, in effect, was continued in 1935 when Reuben Fleet moved Consolidated from Buffalo by rail to San Diego.

Also, early in 1915, McCurdy, running the Curtiss School in Toronto (thus founding Canadian aviation with instructors Ted McCaulay, Bert Acosta and Guy Gilpatric. In 1915 and 1916 it had *"no fatalities or serious injuries"*), headed the new *Curtiss Aeroplane and Motor Company, Ltd.* to produce the Canadian *Canuck,* almost identical to the *Jenny* – but with a level motor bed, ailerons on both top and bottom wings, and a rounded rudder.

This facility enabled Curtiss to evade the Wright patent by building *JN's* in Buffalo to be fitted in England with ailerons made in Canada.

Engine production remained in Hammondsport, with *Charles Kirkham* in charge of the *Curtiss Motor Division*. Kirkham, who machined Curtiss's first motor, was responsible for the immense output of engines during the war. In 1916 he designed a 6-cylinder and a 400-hp V-12 liquid-cooled engine, the *Kirkham-6* – and the *K-12* with several important innovations, not least a design with minimum width/frontal area for reduced drag.

In 1918, after refinements by F. R. Porter, this 400-hp V12 engine evolved into the Curtiss Model 18-T: a powerful, compact engine for the newest fighter plane designs used in Curtiss racers and many Curtiss *Hawk* fighters.

In 1922, under Curtiss president C.M. Keys, Arthur Nutt, Curtiss' young chief motor engineer, *"undertook a complete redesign of the C-12 engine, which became the D-12. Curtiss now had a real winner. The D-12 was the finest inline liquid-cooled engine of the day; it set the pattern for subsequent development of the liquid-cooled engine. In the streamlined Curtiss racers, the D-12 Conqueror was unbeatable."* Eltscher & Young.

And this unprecedented wartime growth led to all sorts of new demands upon the Curtiss organization. It had to establish a secret developmental facility, and contend with considerable sabotage (one should understand that the United States' population was over sixty-percent German heritage; there were many strained allegiances). It was not uncommon to locate and remove enemy spies and workmen. Once a large bomb was found in the clothes of an employee, and several times struts, wires, and other parts were found to have been sawed nearly through and filled-in with sawdust and glue.

The Wright patent used the word *"simultaneously,"* prompting Crisp to have Curtiss and Douglas Thomas design a new interlocked *independent* aileron arrangement.
    This caused the Wright Co. to initiate a new suit, permitting Crisp to answer and thus defer the earlier injunction, while Curtiss manufacturing continued unabated.

And at this same time, Wright amends its licensing fees to $1000 per aeroplane per calendar year, plus $25 for each day that it was *"operated, used or exhibited for or in prospect of profit, prize, or reward."*

Curtiss rejected this *"liberalized license policy"* - and a new infringement suit began.

But the Wright Co. persisted, sending out the following notice: *"We are sending you this information in order that you may protect yourselves against making contracts for exhibition aeroplane flying, or other purposes, with persons using infringing machines without a license. This company intends to enforce its rights against all manufacturers and users of unlicensed machines, and we therefore wish to advise you that it would be unwise to engage or deal with anyone not using a licensed machine, and who cannot show proper authority and license from us. We shall hold all persons using or engaging others to use infringing machines strictly accountable for all damages and profits accruing therefrom."*

The result of this and other Wright Co. actions was an almost 100% support of Curtiss by the press - and concern and discussion in Congress and the Justice Department about putting an end to the *"air trust."* Orville, however, was considered somewhat removed from the actions of the company, and thus not personally accountable for its unpopular actions.
    19Nov1914: The *Model K Flying Boat* (enlarged and improved *F*). This three-passenger craft was powered by a Curtiss *VX* 160-hp engine, making it the largest and fastest single-engine flying boat. In mid-1915 over 50 were delivered to Russia (through Curtiss's agent, Mr. Ochs, briefly jailed as a suspected spy because he'd been in both Berlin and Vienna) and demonstrated in Sevastopol under most trying conditions by Walter Johnson, Witmer, and pilots Purington and Bennett. Dmitrii Petrovich Grigorovich produced over 300 of his version, the Shchetinin M-5, for the Czar's navy; many other variants were manufactured world-wide (e.g., Britian's *Walrus*), *many still in active service into WW2. Photo, next: Witmer, left, in cockpit beside Hallett, Mr. & Mrs. Ochs, right:*

6Dec1914: The *Model R Tractor* - a scaled-up *JN* fitted with a Curtiss 160-hp V8. It evolved into the *R-2* which was sold in quantity both to the U.S. Army and the British; and into a seaplane version, the *R-3* of 1915. The 200-hp *R-6* became the *first* American fighting plane to serve overseas *with* American forces: a squadron was based at Ponta Delgada in the Azores, where they flew anti-submarine patrols.

74 AERIAL AGE WEEKLY, *October 11, 1915*

MILITARY *Curtiss* TRACTOR

THE MODEL R
BUILT FOR SPEED
AND
WEIGHT CARRYING

POWERED WITH
CURTISS 160 H. P. MOTOR

SPECIFICATIONS ON REQUEST

THE CURTISS AEROPLANE CO.
BUFFALO, NEW YORK

After the war the 400-hp R-6L was the U.S. Navy's first successful torpedo-plane:

Chapter *10* *1915 - 1948*

*T*he

Great War and Britain's use of Curtiss flying boats cause unprecedented growth in Hammondsport, and the move to Buffalo where Curtiss rapidly becomes one of the world's greatest aircraft manufacturers. The Wright-Curtiss legal imbroglio ends with a war-time pooling of patents. Curtiss and the Navy team to make the first flight across the Atlantic. Curtiss becomes one of America's wealthiest men.

After the war, Bell dies; Orville becomes reclusive; and Curtiss is even more successful in Florida real estate development. The Curtiss companies continue aviation leadership; but, shortly after Orville ships the 1903 Flyer to Britain, Curtiss, in the prime of life, dies. Slowly, attitudes shift at the Smithsonian, and just after Orville's death - and the execution of a 'secret' <u>Agreement</u> – the Flyer is returned to America. The <u>Agreement</u>'s limited disclosure provided a hint of why Americans have been taught what they know of early aviation.

Then, a 1994 letter by the National Geographic's Gilbert M. Grosvenor reveals more, and much of the basis for Bell's misunderstood story.

25Jan'15: With Bell in New York, Watson in San Francisco, transcontinental telephone service is formally inaugurated with Bell saying: "*Mr. Watson, are you there?*" Watson, of course, was - and when Bell said: "*Hoy, hoy, Mr. Watson, come here, I want you,*" he replied that it would take him a week to get there!

1915: The *Model F Flying Boat* - Wartime exigencies cause standardization for the scores of flying boats built by Curtiss, including Deperdussin-type controls replacing the shoulder yoke, improved and stronger hulls, and trailing-edge ailerons on some British boats.

26   AERIAL AGE WEEKLY, March 29, 1915

Curtiss Flying Boat

February Class—Curtiss Aviation School
San Diego, California

THE Flying Boat in this picture has been in the air 500 hours, traveling 30,000 miles.   In this boat hundreds of passengers have been carried and dozens of persons have learned to fly.   There have been no accidents nor repairs. This machine is equipped with the newly developed and very efficient single-acting aileron system for lateral balance.

The Curtiss Flying Boat has made flying a safe sport.

Military Aeroplanes of both Tractor and Pusher types for land and water

Information on request

THE CURTISS AEROPLANE COMPANY
BUFFALO, NEW YORK

14Mar1915: "...after doing his standard fare in the Little Looper, he took off in the *Special* (an Eaton-built, 80-hp Gnome-powered monoplane). He flew out of sight across the bay, climbed to around 6,000 feet, and then reappeared, performing one loop and starting another. However, for some reason he stopped when only half through it, swooping in a long spiral to about 1,000 feet where he started banking for a turn. Then a wing failed - as the sleek craft fell faster and faster, the other one was seen to collapse. Lincoln Beachey and his wonderful new monoplane dove into the bay beside the city of his birth only 28 years earlier. He wasn't killed outright but drowned while frantically trying to disengage himself from the harness that held him in three places in that cramped cockpit."   *Waldo Waterman*

4Jun1915: *Lorin Wright* (Bath, NY) to Orville: *"Reached Buffalo...and came to Bath ...to Hammondsport arriving about one o'clock. I did not register at any of the hotels. Spent afternoon at hangars...They had the Langley machine about ready to try again and expected to try it this evening but the wind was too strong...They have changed the rear posts...to 1" steel tubing, probably the same as in the original, but the front one is same as before. The rudder or vane on the under side is hinged and connected up with the shoulder yoke. The big rudder at rear is hinged to swing to the right and*

left, the wire running...to the wheel. The old rear floats have been replaced by a boat which has a sheet-iron piece about two inches below the bottom...They had not made a trial at 6:30 when I left and came to Bath...I will go down at eight in the morning...

"The rear spar has a 1"x1 1/2" piece fastened below the ribs about halfway out. Langley propellers are not on but a regular Curtiss propeller, and Curtiss 90-100 H.P. motor. Took a number of pictures.

"Machine No. 1. The motor was off the school machine and there was no flying ...The ailerons are on the back uprights...I operated them and they drop as far down as the other goes up. It is a boat machine.

"Machine No. 2. This machine was in shed and has ailerons. It operates the ailerons upwards only and drops only to a neutral or a little below neutral...I did not get to see it very long but I operated the yoke and they both move at the same time ...Some visitors came and I was interrupted and have forgotten some of the details. It carries two men and has a 90-100 H.P. motor.

"Machine No. 3 is a boat with two cockpits. It has flap on rear upper surface. As it stood on the runway the left flap was below the chord of the upper surface...The other aileron was elevated. It had wires to front edge to keep it from dropping only so far...

"It seems everyone here is very loyal and I do not know what to do for confirmation of these points...I will get names and addresses of witnesses (of the Langley's trials) *anyhow whether they are friendly or unfriendly.*

"I came here as I was afraid to telegraph from Hammondsport...I am tired as a dog...I will make sketches...I cannot remember all the details. I will be known here and at H(ammondsport) *as W.L. Oren...."*

Industrial espionage ca. 1915.

5Jun1915: Memorandum by Lorin Wright: *"...The next morning, Saturday, June 5*[th]*... About 9:30 I saw they were making preparations to launch this machine...I watched the proceedings...through a pair of glasses* (binoculars)*...*

"About 10:00 o'clock Mr. Walter Johnson mounted the machine and started the motor. The machine gradually acquired speed and after running...about 1,000 ft. the rear wings broke about midway the length of the spars and folded upwards...When the machine stopped the outer edge dropped and dragged in the water.

"I immediately walked...over to the grounds. When I arrived at the hangars the machine had just been towed to shore and the workmen were trying to bring it up the runway. I took four pictures of the machine when some of the workmen noted the fact and notified Mr. Johnson. He demanded that I should give up the films. At first I refused and started to leave the grounds. Mr. Johnson and several others...came running up to me demanding the films, saying they could not allow any pictures of the wrecked machine to be made. I replied that the day before they had told me I could take all the pictures I wanted.

"At this juncture...Mr. Henry Weyman came up and apparently took charge of the situation. He insisted I should not leave the grounds until I had delivered up my pack of films. I asked him why. He replied that on account of 'legal complications' they wanted no pictures of the machine in its present condition to get out. I finally yielded

the film pack and he insisted on supplying me with another to replace it. I insisted that he should not but he sent a boy on a wheel uptown and in a few minutes the boy returned with a pack and Mr. Weyman insisted I should accept it. I refused and Mr. Weyman laid pack on my knee (I had gone over and sat down on edge of one of the runways) and walked away. I laid pack down on runway and left it there.

"In the meantime I had been walking around the other machines and watching the dismantling of the broken wings. Mr. Weyman followed me around most of the time, and upon my inquiry showed me the operation of the controls of the machine standing in the front doorway of the hangar. As he seemed very suspicious of me I did not question him much but observed several points about the machine which I failed to note the day before..."

These Hammondsport *Langley* trials were the *second* phase, noted earlier. Called by some *"propaganda pure and simple,"* in point of fact they were most likely adroit legal maneuverings of Benton Crisp. However, later Curtiss was known to feel that things had gotten a bit out of hand. He regretted what his eagerness to get the *Langley* to fly caused, but denied any intention of belittling the position of the Wrights. He felt that much of what had happened was due to *"The Friends of Langley"* - insisting that every repair and installation was done with the approval of Albert Zahm.

But to this day the *Langley* episode (coupled with Orville's lifelong, bitter intransigence regarding Curtiss) casts a dark cloud in the eyes of some historians incapable of accepting the circumstances and breadth of Curtiss's work.

11Jun1915: Curtiss to Orville: *"Through a letter to our Mr. Tarbox, from your attorneys some weeks ago, I learned of your willingness to talk over our differences with a view to a possible solution of the matter outside of courts. This seems to me a matter which should be handled between principals.*

"I believe you and I alone can make more progress than can be made by our representatives, and if you are willing to meet me halfway, I have confidence that we can arrive at a satisfactory arrangement of our mutual troubles.

"Unless I receive word from you not to come, I will be in Dayton on Tuesday morning next, to see you personally."

Orville to Curtiss: *"Your letter received. Will see you Tuesday morning in Dayton."*

Apparently a meeting took place, but not much of a thaw.

2Jul1915: Curtiss to Orville: *"Pursuant to our recent conversation, have you any proposals or suggestions...? Would it not be convenient for you to come to Buffalo?"*

And then, nothing.

15Sep'15: Curtiss tried again, and Orville replied: *"If you desire to have a conference in regard to settling the patent litigation, I would recommend that you see Messrs. Wing & Russell, 14 Wall Street, New York City."*

The 1910 Curtiss Flying Boat

Curtiss Granted New Flying Boat Patent

A patent, covering the most important invention in connection with water flying for which any patent has yet been granted, has just been issued by the United States Patent Office at Washington to Glenn H. Curtiss. It is listed officially as No. 1142754 and was granted at noon on June 8th.

The arrangement and construction of flying boats which enables them to readily fly from the water into the air is covered by this patent and the owner is given the exclusive rights of manufacture. Practically all flying boats as far as known and now used in this country or being built here embody this invention.

One of the principal features of the patent relates to the step or ridge formed in the bottom of flying boats.

In view of the widespread use of flying boats at the present time, the patent is considered of the greatest importance. The principal object of the invention is to provide a hydro-aero-machine having a relatively seaworthy and stable central body boat which may plane upon the surface of the water at high speed and readily break from the water into the air, and also readily alight upon the water.

The development of aviation during the last few years has been remarkable and great importance is attached to the construction of seaworthy flying boats made possible through the invention of Mr. Curtiss. Early experiments with flying boats were made by Mr. Curtiss in 1910 at Hammondsport, N. Y.

Continuing his experiments, Mr. Curtiss developed the now well-known flying boat as used by the United States Navy and during the summer and fall of 1914 built a huge machine for Mr. Rodman Wanamaker which was intended to fly across the Atlantic Ocean. The boat hull of this machine, which carried a covered cabin, was capable of withstanding severe weather and lifted an 1800 pound load in addition to its own weight. During its trials on Keuka Lake, it carried as many as twelve people at one time.

The following is a description of the invention as set forth in the patent. The full text of the claims will be published in the next issue of *Aerial Age.*

Description of Patent

To all whom it may concern:

Be it known that I, GLENN H. CURTISS, citizen of the United States, residing at Hammondsport, county of Steuben, and State of New York, have invented certain new and useful Improvements in Flying-Boats, of which the following is a clear, full, and exact description.

My invention relates to hydro-aero-machines, and more particularly to those adapted to rise from the water into the air when driven at speed upon the water.

The present application is a division of one previously filed by the same, inventor on September 6, 1912, Serial Number 718,840, and since patented as No. 1085575, January 27, 1914.

The principal object of my invention is to provide a hydro-aero-machine which may readily break from the water to rise into the air.

Another object of my invention is to provide a hydro-aero-machine of the above character having a relatively seaworthy and stable central body boat.

A further object of the invention is to provide a hydro-aero-machine of the above character which may plane upon the surface of the water at high speed and also readily alight upon the water without tipping over forward.

Further objects of my invention are to protect the aviator's body from head air currents and water spray, to give an unobstructed forward view to the aviator, and to so locate and arrange the aerial control and propelling means that they will be protected and will operate in an efficient manner.

The several advantages of the present improvement will more clearly appear from the following specification, while the scope of the invention will be pointed out in the appended claims.

In the specification and drawings I have shown and described the preferred embodiment of the invention, and in the drawings,—

Figure 1 is a side elevation of the entire machine; Fig. 2 is a front elevation of the same; Fig. 3 is a plan of the fuselage or boat portion with the supporting planes removed; Fig. 4 is a detail cross-section through said boat body along line 4—4 Fig. 3; Fig. 5 is a fragmentary plan of one end of the upper supporting plane; Fig. 6 is a plan of a wing tip pontoon; Fig. 7 a side elevation of said wing tip pontoon; and Fig. 8 a transverse section through line 8—8 of Fig. 6 of the wing-tip pontoon.

Referring more particularly to the drawings, there is shown a boat body 1 of sufficient buoyancy for supporting the entire machine upon the water and having mounted above the same one or more supporting planes 11 and 12 connected by the usual forward and rear struts 14, 14a forming an aeroplane. These supporting planes 11 and 12 are arranged in lifting relation to the boat

when floating on the water, and in the preferred form of the invention shown the planes are located with the center of gravity lying intermediate their forward and rear edges. The center of gravity of the machine, without the aviators aboard, is indicated by the dot *c, g,* somewhat forward of the step. Of course with the aviator or aviators aboard, the center of gravity is shifted somewhat forward and downward from the point *c, g.*

The machine is provided with suitable driving means consisting of engine 15 and air-propeller 16 of sufficient capacity to drive the machine at such speed as to enable the air planes to lift machine clear of the water in flight. The engine is preferably mounted between the air planes 11 and 12 and intermediate the forward and rear edges thereof with the aerial propeller mounted directly on the main shaft of the engine and located at the rear of the main planes. I prefer to use a single propeller located above the longitudinal axis of the boat where it will be substantially protected from flying spray by the body boat beneath the same. The bow of the boat as shown is free from aerial propelling means and stabilizing surfaces to give the aviator an unobstructed forward view and to protect such surfaces and propeller from flying spray and from damage when the boat is alighting on the water.

The boat body 1 is of seaworthy construction for travel on the water and contains therein, preferably at its forward part, the cock-pit 8 with the operator's seat and other controls more particularly described hereinafter, and extends as shown from the front to rear of the entire machine to serve as the fuselage therefor. To facilitate the breaking away of the boat from the water when the machine rises in flight, the bottom of the boat is flat as shown in Fig. 4, and is provided with a rearwardly facing step 5 (see Fig. 1) at a point approximately below its center of gravity. The bottom of the boat inclines from this step 5 upwardly toward the front at 4, and also upwardly at 6 toward the rear. The stern 3 of the boat looking from above is preferably pointed as shown in Fig. 3, while the bow 2 of the boat is broad with a scow-like prow.

It will be observed that the boat or floating means for the machine as illustrated in the present embodiment of the invention comprises forward and rear buoyant portions projecting respectively well forward and aft of the main planes, the machine being normally supported on both said buoyant portions to increase its longitudinal stability on the water. The rear portion is in the form of a long relatively light tail portion extending aft of the main air planes. In this embodiment of the invention the sides of the rear portion taper as stated to give a narrow tail.

The bottom of the forward portion of this boat is in the form of an effective hydroplaning surface extending from the nose of the scow bow downwardly and rearwardly to a point in advance of the main air plane surface, and thence rearwardly and more horizontally terminating at the rearwardly facing step approximately beneath the center of gravity of the machine and intermediate the forward and rear edges of the main air planes, from whence the bottom inclines upwardly as stated. This hydroplaning surface as shown in the drawings, extends the full width of the boat between the submerged sides of the boat extending along the length of this surface to get the maximum hydroplaning width for a given shaped boat, and the bottom of the boat extending along the tail portion is in the form of a reverse hydroplaning surface. By "reverse hydroplaning surface" I mean a surface which is inclined upwardly and rearwardly, permitting the stern to be tilted down (and thereby having just the opposite effect from a hydroplaning surface the function of which is to lift) and yet one that is not curved or rounded such as would produce suction at the tail to hold the tail of the boat in the water and interfere with the elevation of the tail or breaking of the tail from the water when the boat is planing at speed with a tendency to rock forward substantially about the rear extremity of its forward hydroplaning surface into a more horizontal position of less resistance to headway. In the present form of the invention as stated, this reverse hydroplane surface is flat. The forward broad and relatively sharply downwardly inclined hydroplaning surface beneath the bow gives substantial resistance to diving, should the boat take the water at too sharp an angle and helps to prevent the boat from tipping forward and tends to cause it to glide into a horizontal position.

When boats speed up on the water the tendency of the stern or tail of the boat is to suck or hog down in the water, and in hydroplanes it has been proposed to more or less prevent this by extending a deeply stepped bottom along the stern or tail of the boat, producing low water-resistant hydroplane surfaces tending to hold the stern up. In hydroaeroplanes, however, this is undesirable, since it is desirable at times for the tail of the boat to incline or rock downwardly about the rear extremity of the forward hydroplaning surface as well as to have the tail rocked upward about said extremity, and head resistant surfaces on the projecting tail portion extending down to or below the rear

(Continued on Page 331)

The "America," designed and built by Glenn H. Curtiss, the largest flying boat in the world. This machine was designed to fly across the Atlantic

Oct1915: For $500,000 (over $22 million today) in 1914 Orville bought out all the other Wright Co. shareholders (except for Robert J. Collier). He now sold out his interest in the company and patents (for between $675,000 and $1,500,000 - $30 to $65 million today) to a group of seven "*eastern* (New York) *capitalists*" headed by mining tycoon William B. Thompson, who, as he wrote: "*...went abroad and secured the Hispano-Suiza motor and began the manufacture of aeroplanes, and I was merely an engineer* (at $25,000 per year, over a million today) *and had no financial interest in the company.*"

Aerial Age Weekly, 21Jun'15: On the Wright *Model B* school machine at Dayton "*the original Wright lever control has been displaced by the new wheel control* (note, left), *which has elevator, warp and rudder all in the wheel and is simple and effective and not tiresome.*"

29Mar'15, *Aerial Age Weekly* & 11Oct'15: "*Miss Tiny Broadwick* (nee Georgia Anne Thompson) *of Los Angeles plunged headforemost from a military aeroplane from an altitude of 1,400 feet at the North Island aerodrome, San Diego, recently for the purpose of demonstrating to Brigadier General George P. Scriven...an aerial life preserver...invention of her father* (Charles Broadwick).
   "*Miss Broadwick's drop to the earth was perfect..from a Martin tractor No. 31...*"

Note: In 1974, as Waldo Waterman's guest at Boston's *Early Birds Meet,* the author met Miss Broadwick – and Jerome Hunsaker and Grover Loening.

5Nov'15: Lt.Cdr. *H.C. Mustin* (-1923) with Curtiss *F Boat No. AB-2* is catapulted from the *USS North Carolina* using Captain Chambers' compressed-air system, the *first ship catapult launch.*

1915: *Will Rogers* took his first airplane ride - in a Curtiss flying boat at Atlantic City.

1915: The A.E.A. patents are declared free of interference of the Wright's patents and early in 1917 sold to the Curtiss Company by the trustee for $5,899.49 in cash and $50,000 in stock. Later, in order to resolve the patent suits and expedite wartime aircraft production, the United States government bought both the Wright and Curtiss patents, noted later. Orville said that the litigation had cost them $152,000 while Curtiss estimated his at $175,000 (approximately $6 million and $7 million, respectively, today).

Winter, 1915: Preparing for war, the Navy's Captain Mark Bristol sends Lt. Cdr. Mustin "on a tour of the factories, then rumored to be crowded with foreign orders...(Mustin reported)...*'the Wright factories to be without any foreign orders and, at the moment, in... reorganization after purchase by a New York syndicate.*

"'Curtiss had delivered to Europe 125 JN tractor planes with the OX motors, and 40 America-type flying boats. He had on hand 200 of the JN type with OX motors, 100 RT tractor planes with V-2 motors, and 50 America-type boats. His capacity was five planes, five OX motors and five V-2 motors a day, all of excellent workmanship. His research department under Dr. A. F. Zahm was active and progressive.

"'A third firm, Thomas Brothers, had completed 24 planes of their T-2 type but these were still disassembled and without motors; its ultimate capacity would be two planes a week and it had no foreign orders on hand.

"'Fourth, the Burgess Company had supplied 36 of the Type Q pusher planes, equipped with Sturtevant motors, to Great Britain, and although it had no foreign orders in hand, it was negotiating for a large Russian order

"...it was clear that there were ample facilities to begin production for the United States Navy. However, only 29 planes had been ordered by the end of 1915, and (*USN Captain*) Bristol promptly insisted that more orders must follow because *'it would be a grave error in preparedness' to neglect them.*"

Turnbull & Lord

13Jan'16: Absorbing the aeroplane and motor companies, the *Curtiss Aeroplane and Motor Corporation* is formed by a New York syndicate. With $6 million in preferred stock and $750,000 in common stock, Curtiss received $4.5 million (approximately $185 million today), plus 50-percent of the common stock, with the prosperity extending handsomely to most of the old Curtiss employees and stockholders (except those that had supported Herring).

But events soon saw this organization having difficulties managing wartime growth. Curtiss's friend, *Clement Mellville Keys*, a Canadian-born investment counselor (who'd advised Curtiss with his new-found wealth), former college professor and *Wall Street Journal* editor, restructured and refinanced the company. But briefly successful - in 1917, needing more help, Curtiss again went to Detroit for meetings with Ford. But Keys vetoed any suggestions of Ford's involvement, preferring to keep "*auto*" money out of the business ('auto money,' typically not beholden to J.P. Morgan's 'Eastern Money Establishment,' was discriminated against by it).

But the immense and growing strength of the auto interests, coupled with the fact that Curtiss was aviation's major player, forced a combination shortly after America's entry into the war: In June, 1917, *John North Willys* (1873-1935) became president of Curtiss (with plans to merge it with Willys-Overland Co., America's second-largest auto manufacturer, 1912-1918, after Ford) as Curtiss and Keys assumed lessened roles.

But at heart a Yankee tinkerer longing for his "*shop*," Curtiss was never cut out to be an industrial titan. He commented: "*Right at the beginning we learned an invaluable truth. We learned that so long as we were experimenting we never grew tired. Experimenting is never work - it is plain fun. Most of my time I have been able to put in eighteen hours a day when occasion required without feeling any special fatigue, because I never worked more than half the time. The other half was devoted to experimenting in some form or other. That was not tiring but rejuvenating. The man who works himself down can work himself back up if he will develop a turn for experimenting.*"

CURTISS SCHOOL°fAVIATION

Buffalo, N. Y.
Newport News, Va.
Miami, Fla.
Hammondsport, N. Y.
San Diego, Cal.

Under Aviation Section, United States Army, Supervision

1916: Preparations for war saw Tom Baldwin managing the large Curtiss Flying School at Newport News, VA, where Billy Mitchell learned to fly winter of 1915-16. Other Curtiss schools were at Atlantic City and Miami, where, in January, 1912, "*instructor-in-charge*" Charles Witmer introduced aviation to south Florida with a North Island-type school.

1916: The Wright Company..."changed into ...the *Wright-Martin Company*...to take over the Wright Company, and the Glenn L. Martin Co....the Wright-Martin Co. owned the Wright Co., and it continued...operation of it until the spring of 1917."

Wright-Martin Aircraft took over the Wright Co., the Martin Co., Simplex Automobile Co. and the General Aeronautic Co. of America.

During 1916 and the early part of 1917, Orville was occupied with building and testing the wind tunnel at his laboratory at 15 N. Broadway, Dayton, where he carried out wartime experiments in aerodynamics. One of the few records made during this period seems to be, in part, an analysis of slipstream and propeller action applicable to wind tunnel operation, and, in part, an attempt to collate the propeller data of earlier work.

1917: Orville: "*...in the early months of 1917...we started a* (civilian) *school at what is now known as the McCook Field...*"

April 1917: *The Dayton-Wright Company* was formed, with Orville an incorporator ("*The Wright name was purely advertising. Orville Wright was a consultant to the company, but he had very little to do with its affairs.*" John B. Rae). It would produce *Liberty* engines, Curtiss *Jennys,* and British *DH-4*s, delivering more than 3500 airplanes in 1918 alone. This company was eventually absorbed by General Motors, and ceased aviation activities in June, 1923, when its aeronautical designs were sold to Reuben Fleet's new Consolidated Aircraft Corporation (occupying Curtiss's old wartime Buffalo plant).

The Curtiss "Autoplane, an Aerial Limosine." A flying auto shown at the First Pan American Aeronautic Show, New York, Feb'17. The wings and tail could be removed as a unit to permit the car component to operate as an auto. It made only a few short straight-ahead hops before development was abandoned upon entry into the war. See pp. 477-79.

19May1917: Orville to Glenn Martin: "*I was glad to receive your letter asking for some particulars of the Dayton-Wright Airplane Company.*

"*The company was organized by Messrs.* (Edward A.) *Deeds and* (Charles) *Kettering* (of General Motors fame) *and H.E. Talbott, Senior and Junior. These men are extraordinary good businessmen with lots of financial backing. They are going to carry out some of my ideas in creating a sport in aeronautics. Since the war has started, they are considering undertaking the building of a number of school planes for the government* (on land owned by and sold to the company by Deeds)...

Note: In 1913 Deeds back-stabbed Thomas J. Watson, forcing his departure from John Patterson's National Cash Register Company, with Deeds later becoming its president. "*The man dad hated was Deeds, for setting him up.*" Thomas J. Watson Jr.
"In August 1917 he [Deeds] was commissioned a colonel and made Chief of the Equipment Division of the Signal Corps under General Squier. After divesting himself of his Dayton-Wright holdings, he was in a position to divert a sizable amount of business to the companies run by his friends in Dayton."   *Fred Howard*
The U. S. Attorney General would later find Deeds '*guilty of censurable conduct*' but weak statutes prevented his criminal prosecution.

Orville continues: "*...I have viewed with much regret the troubles of the Wright-Martin Company...It would seem to me that they have lost at least several millions in the past year. I think I could have saved them some of this loss, but all new people taking hold of the business are inclined to think that they know a good deal more about it than those who have had experience...*"

"In April 1917, when the United States formally declared war, the Aviation Section of the Signal Corps, at the time representing the bulk of the nation's air strength, possessed only fifty-five airplanes in dependable flying condition. Most of these were antiquated and unarmed trainers, little better than powered box kites by European standards. The most advanced American plane at this critical juncture was the Curtiss *JN-4 Jenny* - well constructed machines with wide wings and reliable Curtiss engines of ninety horsepower. By the end of the World War I some 5500...would be manufactured as primary trainers, but they sorely lacked the smart performance of contemporary fighters abroad. Top speed of the *Jennys* approximated seventy-five miles an hour...the *Spad S-13*...better than 115 miles an hour...The gap between America and Europe in aviation technology, as events would later prove, had become too great ever to be closed in the nineteen months that remained of World War I...The situation was such, asserted General Pershing upon his appointment as commander in chief of the A. E. F., '*that every American ought to feel mortified to hear it mentioned.*'"

Aaron Norman

"...progress in America had become so retarded that by 1917 it fell to England and France to provide necessary 'know-how' to enable that great country to participate in the air war..."

Francis Mason

24Jul'17: The original American War Program, based on an army of a million men, made the air service a relatively insignificant portion of military forces. However, after the arrival of a British and French aviation mission, the General Staff revised their views and concurred with the recommendations of the Aircraft Production Board, calling for the construction of *22,500* airplanes, and twice as many engines. Congress thus appropriated the unheard of sum of *$640 million* (about *$25 billion* today) to build, within eighteen months, a military aeronautics establishment - from an industry which had produced *fewer than five hundred* aircraft in the *thirteen* years since the Wright's first flight.

17Aug'17: Acting on the *National Advisory Committee for Aeronautics* (NACA) recommendations, the *Manufacturers Aircraft Association* was organized to implement a cross-licensing agreement (prepared by Benton Crisp) of all aeronautical patents, thus allowing government contracts to be fulfilled without hindrance. Aeronautical firms pooled their patents, and a fee program was established that eventually saw the Curtiss company receive approximately $2 million, the Wright company about $3 million for their patents.

The situation *before* this agreement: "But the American industry was in bad shape. There were then about one hundred and thirty airplane patents actually issued. Others were pending. Of those already issued some were basic and without which no real plane could be built. There were others, say half the total number, which were of doubtful value. But each patent could cause a lawsuit. When a builder turned out a flying machine he invariably was threatened with court action for infringement on an airplane patent.

"He might even pay royalties to one or two patent owners and still be confronted with claims from several others. Thus all the constructors, designers and experimenters were snarling and yipping at one another, some of them jealous of the prior claims advanced by competitors, others defiant and prepared to fight for what they believed to be their rights to use any patent. Had there been no war, those conditions might have continued and repeated the history of other industries."

Howard Mingos

But the most important aspect was that it spelled the end to the fighting between Wright and Curtiss. The dam, so long holding back American aviation, burst, progress was now at hand.

Curtiss's first interview after the declaration of war (a prediction of WW2's air war): *"If the German line is to be rolled up before too many American lives pay the cost of an offensive, the German positions must be turned by fleets of aeroplanes so many and so powerful that they can sweep the German flyers from the skies, blind the enemy gunners and cut their supplies of food and munitions a hundred miles back of the fighting line."*

Curtiss Aeroplane Plant, Buffalo, N. Y.

As noted, the Curtiss organization went through tremendous change, e.g., in July, 1917, in Buffalo (for its labor supply, good transportation, and industrial power), on a seventy-two acre site, a $4 million ($160 million today) modern glass, steel and concrete facility - *seventy-one acres under roof* - was constructed in ninety days, and the payroll went from less than a thousand to over *forty-thousand* (with 3,500 women).

This huge organization was unwieldy at best and rarely ran smoothly. There were problems with labor organizations, spying and sabotage - and constant change due to the war and growing aeronautical knowledge. Topping this, the country suffered 1918's deadly flu epidemic - and the Willys organization's efforts were hampered by its knowing little of airplane manufacturing, and by an indecisive government's learning about aviation.

Regardless, a great quantity of aircraft was produced: by early 1918 Curtiss was manufacturing 50 airplanes a week, at war's end almost 115.

Wartime Curtiss produced some eleven thousand airplanes and flying boats and fifteen thousand engines. And largely unheralded, Curtiss trained as many as 1,400 pilots a year in a cooperative enterprise with the government.

At war's end *Curtiss was America's largest aircraft manufacturer – and arguably the second-largest in the world.*

This was the second of four decades in which Curtiss, described as *"the colossus of aviation,"* garnered more *"firsts"* than any other firm in the history of aviation.

"In May, 1917, we had one elementary training school for flyers, at North Island, San Diego, and in the whole Army just one small, poorly equipped flying squadron, with about fifty-five airplanes, and only thirty-five men who could fly. On the signing of the Armistice we had actually at the Front forty-five squadrons, 767 pilots, 481 observers and 740 airplanes. But this represents only a fraction of the real advance we made during that time. At the close of the war there were perhaps fifteen thousand men who could take a plane into the air, and the poorest of them could do infinitely more with it than the best of our flyers in 1917."   *Warren Jefferson Davis*

13May'18: Orville made his last flight as a pilot, flying a 1911 *Wright Flyer* beside the first American-built *DeHavilland DH-4* (produced by Dayton-Wright)

2Aug'18: *Liberty*-powered *DH-4*'s (regarded as "flying coffins") were the only American-made *and* flown aircraft *over* enemy land in World War I.

Aerial Age Weekly, 8Mar'20: *"July 24, 1917, Congress appropriated $640,000,000 to...the aircraft program...A further appropriation of $884,304,758...found necessary... and with this record of failure, Col. Deeds, Director of Aircraft, who has been removed and...recommended for court-martial by Justice Hughes, was banqueted...by Chief Signal Officer Squier and others for the kind of record he had made...The whole country was becoming discouraged with Squier, Deeds, et al., and no relief ever in sight...Vice President Keys, of the Curtiss Co., sets forth some of the contradictory orders received... while 789 changes were made under orders of the War Department in the attempted production of the discarded Bristol...The Curtiss firm received an order for 3,000 fighting 'Spads' on Sep. 19,1917. (it) was canceled November 7, 1917. But this one factory could have produced 30,000 fighting planes a year, according to Keys, if given a free hand..."*

With the U. S. entry into the war Bell revived his earlier hydrofoil boat developments. He and Casey built the *HD-4 (previous photo)*. With its streamlined 60-foot hull, fore-and-aft reefing hydrofoils, and two 250-hp Renault aircraft engines driving propellers on wing-like appendages, it sped 54-mph. In 1919, with more powerful 350-hp Liberty engines, they upped that to 71-mph, unmatched for ten years. But the Navy didn't want to pursue it and in 1921 it was dismantled. Apparently after some persuasion, on 28Mar'22, a patent was granted Bell and Baldwin for hydofoil-related innovations, it was Bell's *final* patent.

Early in 1918, "because of their common use of wood-frame bodies and petrol engines, aeroplanes and cars were considered by the planners...to be so similar that established motor manufacturing and management techniques could easily be applied to aircraft production. This assumption proved to be one of the greatest fallacies of all time. The aircraft industry...was much more closely related to small boat business, with its high percentage of hand work...small production run (s), and individuality of finished product...

"...the new (Willys) management...began to run the Curtiss factories like big car plants, to the chagrin of the original Curtiss personnel. These, with their limited educational and managerial backgrounds, plus their 'cut-and-try' developmental procedures, were a serious handicap to the new order. (Thus) an entirely new...experimental plant was set up, far removed from Buffalo and the efficient production operation that was expected...there. This was the *Curtiss Engineering Corp. (photo below)*, with Glenn Curtiss in charge...(beside) the Army's Hazelhurst Field in Garden City on Long Island. Here Curtiss and...other old timers (Kirkham, Manly, Tarbox, Kleckler, Zahm and Frank Russell [formerly Burgess's president - and the Wright Co.'s first manager] as manager), aided by qualified engineers and up-to-date research facilities (including America's largest wind tunnel), were able to concentrate on new designs while the motor experts took care of mass production in Buffalo." *Peter Bowers*

Curtiss bought a large home in Garden City, where he lived with his wife and young son, Glenn Jr. Later he built another home and laboratory in Coral Gables, Florida, but kept the home "*on the hill*" in Hammondsport (site of a brick school today).

7Nov'18: Orville to Dr. Wallace Sabine (Harvard): "*...We are all rejoiced today to learn of the armistice just signed with Germany, which, no doubt, means the war is entirely at an end. The aeroplane has made war so terrible that I do not believe any country will again care to start a war...*"

Comment: *"While the investigations of the wartime aircraft program made much of the fact that not a combat-worthy aeroplane of American design and manufacture reached the front, and this statement is widely accepted as gospel 50 years later, it should be pointed out that this referred to Army aviation. Little publicity has been given to the fact that single and twin-engined flying-boats built by Curtiss and its licensees were operated from US Navy bases in France, the United Kingdom and Italy and that JN trainers were delivered to AEF training bases in France."*   Peter M. Bowers

31Mar'19, *Aerial Age Weekly:* "*Train service in the air may be expected at no distant date , according to Dr. Alexander Graham Bell, inventor of the telephone...He declared a lighter than air machine is best adapted to for commercial purposes, and there is no reason why a fleet of such dirigible cars might not be run, drawn by one machine...And repeating his 1896 thought: He predicted that before long it would be possible to have one's breakfast here and supper in Ireland.*"

7Apr'19, *Aerial Age Weekly: Another commentary involving Bell - and Octave Chanute:*

On the Chanute and Bell Airway in 1922—*Courtesy N. Y. Globe*

18Sep1919: In the new, high-speed Curtiss *WASP S3 Speed Scout* triplane, powered with Curtiss' latest engine, the innovative (low frontal area) 400-hp *Kirkham K-12*, Roland Rohlfs, chief test pilot for Curtiss, establishes a new world altitude record of 34,910 feet. Here (*next photo*) he shows Curtiss the barograph of that flight:

Late in 1917, Curtiss and RAdm. David W. Taylor, Cdr. G. Conrad Westervelt, *"Superintending Constructor of Aircraft, U. S. Navy"* (Boeing's first design-partner) and *Jerome Hunsaker*, worked out a plan for flying European-bound flying boats (already proven effective against U-boats) rather than using critical shipping to cross the Atlantic. This called for an entirely new design; a very large, very rugged flying boat with great range.

Its final design (*remarkably similar to Loughead's 10-passenger Model F-1, which Hunsaker et al had earlier carefully studied at North Island*) was the work of the Navy's Westervelt, Hunsaker, Richardson and William McEntee, working with MIT's Charles McCarthy, Curtiss, and Bill Gilmore.

Accommodating a crew of six, the huge machine, *the largest ever built in America*, had a length of just over 67 feet and a wingspan of 126 feet. The unique, strong, short hull was 45 feet 9 inches long, divided into six watertight compartments. Its weight was 28,000 pounds (14 tons); and four of the new 400-hp *Liberty* engines, three tractor and one pusher, provided power. Also, an aluminum gasoline system, box section beams, and a box tail designed to be high above the waves were major innovations. Crewmen were strapped in by the *"Curtiss belt,"* standard equipment since Towers' 1913 fall in Billingsley's out-of-control Wright (apparently the first American seat belt was made by Lt. Benjamin Foulois from trunk strapping for his Wright in 1910 [as the author did for his 1951 Singer sports car]. Californian Leslie Irvin, earlier with Curtiss in Buffalo, co-perfected the modern parachute, jumping on 28Apr'19. He then formed the Irving Air Chute Co.).

4Oct'18: *Holden Richardson*, the *NC* (*N*avy *C*urtiss)'s hull designer, was pilot for the first flight of *NC-1*. Testing was then done at the nearby Rockaway Point Naval Air Station. On one occasion a world record of 51 men (50 plus a stowaway) were carried aloft.

On 7Nov1918 Richardson piloted a shakedown flight to the Washington Navy Yard and inspection by the navy's top brass. But only the *NC-1* was completed when, on 11Nov1918, the Armistice ended WWI. Then, following Towers' proposal, on 17Feb 1919, Admiral Taylor ordered the program continued until four *NC*s were completed. Yacht builders Lawley of Neponset, MA and Herreschoff of Bristol, RI, subcontracting to Curtiss, built three of the hulls.

16May'19: Under Towers' command, the *NC* flying boats take off to cross the Atlantic, following the route planned for the *America* five years earlier. Three craft, *NC-1, 3* and *4* made the attempt (the *NC-2* damaged earlier), and one, the *NC-4*, commanded by *Albert Read* (1887-1967), successfully completed the flight from Trepassey Bay, Newfoundland, to the Azores, flying approximately 1200 nautical miles in 15 hours and 13 minutes flying time. On May 27 *NC-4* flew to Lisbon, Portugal, and on May 31 to Plymouth, England.

Forced down by fog, the *NC-1* was lost under tow. The *NC-3* made it to the Azores, flying most of the way, but taxiing through heavy seas for several hours to reach safe harbor at Ponta Delgada.

No lives were lost in this epic crossing of the Atlantic. The Navy had done it, and Curtiss's dream had come true. The NC-4 is now the proud centerpiece of the National Museum of Naval Aviation, Pensacola, Florida.

The success of the NC saga marked the apex of Glenn Curtiss' life in aviation.

19May'19, *Aerial AgeWeekly* (next page):

GLENN H. CURTISS ON THE TRANS-ATLANTIC FLIGHT

THE American N-C Planes will gain nine (9) hours from favorable winds if the average weather conditions for May prevail during the coming week. Such is the statement of Glenn H. Curtiss, inventor of the flying boat, and joint designer and producer with the U. S. Navy, of the Navy-Curtiss flying boats which are now at Newfoundland ready for the trans-Atlantic take-off. "The conditions governing the trans-oceanic flight," said Mr. Curtiss, "are partly created by the weather and the route chosen, and partly by the flying craft themselves. The Navy has obviously given a long and careful study to both. In my opinion Naval flyers have chosen the best route and are employing a type of seaplane which gives them the largest possible factor of safety.

Advantages of the Azores Route

"There has been a difference of opinion as to whether the Newfoundland-Ireland or the Newfoundland-Azores-Portugal route is the better. The former is more direct. As one who has been interested in trans-Atlantic flight since 1914, however, I can see five distinct advantages to the southern course. They may be listed as follows:

1. It requires a maximum flight without landing of almost seven hundred miles less than does the northern route. The distance to Flores, the first Azores Island, is only 1200 nautical miles as against 1890 to the Scilly Islands, the nearest point off the Irish coast.

2. It avoids the dangerous fog belt which lies to the east and northeast of Newfoundland.

3. It is attended by more favorable weather generally,—warmer, clearer, and freer from atmospheric disturbances.

4. It is in the path of steamer traffic, and hence offers a greater element of safety in case it is necessary to make a descent in mid-ocean.

5. It is in the path of winds which, under normal circumstances, will increase by 40% the speed of the aeroplanes.

"The N-C planes could doubtless have gone by the northern route. It is shorter than the southern. If the trans-Atlantic voyage were to be admitted a hazard, better indeed to get it over with in the

(Continued from page 485)

wind three miles an hour, flying 222 miles at the end of the first three hours. The next three hour period would find them with a wind directly on their tails, going at a speed of 70.5 miles, raised to 100 miles an hour by the wind. The sixth hour would thus find them 522 miles out. From that point on the winds would be favorable. Making from 99 to 95 miles an hour, the aeroplanes would swing slightly to the southeast for the first nine hours, and would then change to an almost due east course to take advantage of changing winds, swinging again to the southeast at the fifteenth hour of flight. Flying this course they would arrive at the Azores."

It would be possible, Mr. Curtiss pointed out, for the flyers to steer directly for the Azores, allowing for drift. This would not be as economical a procedure as the one just described, but

quickest possible time, like a cold shower. But the Navy, I believe, wishes to prove that for the right type of plane the Atlantic trip is not a hazard. The present flight is to be the demonstration of how others like it can be made regularly."

The Problem of Weather

Mr. Curtiss then discussed the question of wind and other atmospheric elements. The weather conditions for any part of the ocean during a given month are, he pointed out, in the large constant. Over the water lying between Trepassey Bay and the Azores the average winds blow from the northwest. This produces an exceptionally favorable condition, as the flying boats will be blown away from the fog belt (once they are through a small wind zone just off Cape Race) and almost directly toward the Azores. The velocity of these winds, rising so far as can be computed, to 30 miles per hour at 1500 feet elevation, is such that a course plotted to take full advantage of them will bring the aircraft to the Azores in about twenty hours, while if there were dead air the trip would take thirty.

Whether average weather conditions will prevail is a question. British flyers at St. Johns have been waiting over a month for the usual easterly winds, which they expected to find. It is not probable that the Navy boats will wait for ideal conditions, even though ideal conditions may be said to be the norm. They will be satisfied with conditions not distinctly unfavorable.

Other Factors Governing Speed

"But wind," said the flying boat designer, "is not the only matter to be considered. It will be interesting to more to know that the speed at which an aeroplane flies is determined by a number of considerations. The N-C boats will not fly as fast as they can, for to fly at top speed would not be economical under the circumstances. Top speed uses up more fuel in proportion to distance covered than certain lower speeds, and in a trip like this gasoline and oil must be carefully conserved. In other words, an economy of energy is necessary for the purpose in view. The flying boats are in a sense like a runner. To start for the Azores at top speed would be somewhat like beginning a mile run with a 100 yard dash. They might draw on their fuel supply to a dangerous point. In

might be preferred on account of its simplicity. If there were no winds at all, or contrary winds, the trip to the Azores would be one of thirty hours or more, as the speed of from 71 to 61 miles an hour would require that length of time for the flight.

Margin of Safety

As the Azores route follows for a considerable distance the course of trans-Atlantic steamers going from the United States to Europe, or from Europe to the United States, these will join with the Government destroyers on duty in eliminating any chances of disaster to the flying crews. It is not probable, however, that these vessels will have an opportunity to practice life-saving. The N-C boats, if forced to descend, can ride a fairly high sea. Repairs made, they can ascend again. But even the possibility of their descending is remote. Of the four

any trip, therefore, where a saving of gasoline is desired, the motor is run at what is called *the economic speed*. This is the speed at which the greatest ratio of miles per hour to gasoline consumed may be obtained.

For instance, going at 75 miles an hour might demand a larger consumption of gasoline in proportion to speed than going at 70 miles an hour.

But the economic speed also varies with the amount of load carried. For instance, at the beginning of the present trip a speed of 71 miles an hour (regardless of wind) ought to be most efficient. This speed is higher than it would be if 28,500 lbs. did not have to be supported. Consequently as this weight is reduced by the consumption of oil and gas the economic speed lessens, less power being required to support less weight, and less power resulting in slower forward progress.

Thus if a flight of 30 hours were to be made, the economic speed would have decreased at the end of the voyage from 71 to 61 miles per hour. This would have followed a decrease in load of 11,000 lbs., the consumption for that period of oil and gasoline. The reduction would have been marked by the shutting off of one of the three motors with which the flying boat had been propelled after its take-off, it being possible to support the aeroplane with two motors after about 6,500 lbs. of gasoline and oil had been consumed, leaving a reserve of two motors during the remainder of the trip.

Prediction Possible Under Certain Conditions

If the speed of the flying boat were determined by wings and motor alone, we could thus estimate scientifically, knowing the load of 28,500 lbs., the position of our aircraft at any stage of the journey. Since the weather is an additional factor, however, we can only guess. With average wind velocity and direction, it should take just 21 hours for the N-C's to reach San Miguel, the Azores island at which they plan to stop unless it is advisable to descend at Flores.

If normal wind conditions should prevail, the boats would have, at the beginning, a flight for three hours against a cross wind. They would fly at 71 miles per hour in order to sustain their load of 28,500 lbs., and would gain from the

(Continued on page 510)

motors which each "ship" mounts, one will always be in reserve, and after the first fourteen hours, two will be in reserve. It is scarcely probable that with the quality of engines used and the expert care given them any difficulty necessitating descent will arise.

Gasoline, another important element, had in Mr. Curtiss's opinion been adequately provided for.

"For a twenty-hour flight such as that described above, about 8,000 lbs. of gas would be required. A thirty-hour flight, with consumption lessening as the motor power required is less, would need 11,000 lbs. This, I should estimate, will be the capacity of the N-C planes, and in case unfavorable winds prevail, a stop will be made at Flores instead of at San Miguel, and a saving made of almost five hundred miles. In any case the supply of gasoline will be ample."

The New York Times, Mid-Week Pictorial, 5Jun'19, three pages:

MID-WEEK PICTORIAL

American Aviators First to Cross the Atlantic and

The NC-4 alighting on the water at Ponta Delgada in the Azores after her flight from Horta. The distance was 150 nautical miles and the trip was made in 1 hour and 44 minutes. A United States naval launch is here seen speeding to the plane to assist her in anchoring. Ponta Delgada is in the background.
(© International Film Service.)

CREW OF THE NC-4 BEING RECEIVED AT HEADQUARTERS OF U. S. ADMIRAL JACKSON AT PONTA DELGADA.

Horta was the point in the Azores where the NC-4 made her first landing after her flight from Trepassey Bay. From there, on May 20, she flew to Ponta Delgada, also in the Azores, a distance of 150 nautical miles, which she accomplished in 1 hour and 44 minutes. The crew met with a great reception there and were officially received and welcomed by U. S. Admiral Jackson, who was in charge of the naval arrangements at that place. From left to right are seen Lieutenant Elmer F. Stone, Chief Mechanic E. S. Rhodes, Lieutenant Walter Hinton, Pilot; Ensign H. C. Rodd, Radio Officer; Lieutenant James L. Breese, Engineer, and Lieut. Commander Albert C. Read in command. Admiral Jackson is addressing them. The crew were extremely fit, despite the strain they had undergone.
(© International Film Service.)

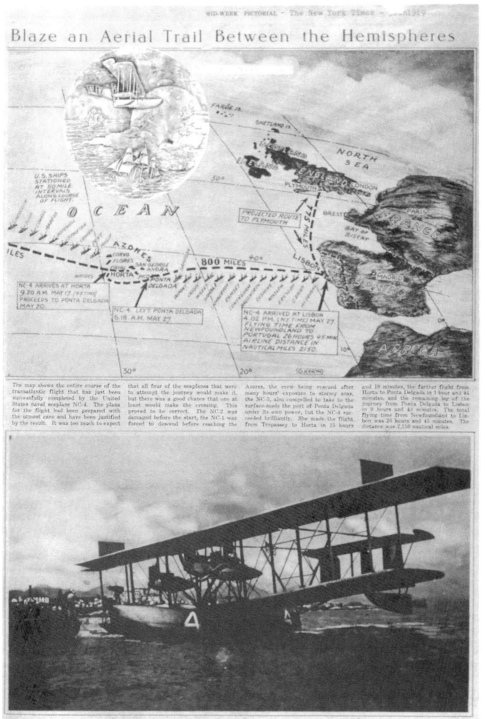

The map shows the entire course of the transatlantic flight that has just been successfully completed by the United States naval seaplane NC-4. The plans for the flight had been prepared with the utmost care and have been justified by the result. It was too much to expect that all four of the seaplanes that were to attempt the journey would make it, but there was a good chance that one at least would make the crossing. This proved to be correct. The NC-2 was damaged before the start, the NC-1 was forced to descend before reaching the Azores, the crew being rescued after many hours' exposure to stormy seas, the NC-3, also compelled to take to the surface, made the port of Ponta Delgada under its own power, but the NC-4 succeeded brilliantly. She made the flight from Trepassey to Horta in 15 hours and 18 minutes, the further flight from Horta to Ponta Delgada in 1 hour and 44 minutes, and the remaining leg of the journey from Ponta Delgada to Lisbon in 9 hours and 43 minutes. The total flying time from Newfoundland to Lisbon was 26 hours and 45 minutes. The distance was 2,150 nautical miles.

CLOSE-UP VIEW OF THE U. S. NAVAL SEAPLANE, THE PIONEER IN AERIAL TRANSATLANTIC FLIGHT, ARRIVING AT HER ANCHORAGE AT PONTA DELGADA AFTER HER JOURNEY FROM HORTA.

Non=Stop Seaplane Flight From America to Europe

American naval seaplane NC-4, first ship of the air to fly the Atlantic, lying in the harbor of Lisbon, Portugal, after accomplishing a record-breaking flight. Her course was from New York to Halifax, from Halifax to Trespassey Bay, Newfoundland, thence to the Azores, and from there to Lisbon.

Start of the three NC boats from New York on the first leg of the transatlantic flight. From left to right they are: NC-4, NC-3, NC-1. The huge seaplanes headed for Halifax, a distance of 540 miles. Thence they voyaged to Trespassey Bay, Newfoundland, where the actual "hop off" on the transatlantic journey was to take place.

American seaplane NC-4 taxiing to her moorings in the Harbor of Ponta del Garda, the Azores, with her full crew aboard shortly before she left on her successful trip to Lisbon, the last lap of the transatlantic flight. The total distance covered to Lisbon was about 3,000 miles. The total flying time from Newfoundland to Lisbon was 26 hours 45 minutes.

431

As the decade dawned, Curtiss found himself less and less involved with the company. He'd served as "*Chairman of The Board*" but relinquished that title early in 1920 when the postwar recession forced Keys to again reorganize the company, ousting the Willys interests and installing Frank Russell.

Russell persuaded Curtiss to remain as "*Chief of Engineering*," but he soon found himself spending more and more time in Florida. He was then reputed to have "*amassed a fortune estimated at some $32,000,000*" (over a billion today).

However, in his engineering capacity he supervised debugging several of the company's newest airplanes.

One, the *Eagle*, an "*aerial limousine*" that "*luxuriously*" carried eight to ten passengers (including one or two pilots). Hoping to emulate European developments, it was an attempt to penetrate a virtually non-existent commercial market. It was powered by either three *K-6* or two *K-12* engines, cruised at over 100-mph and had a range of 750 miles – and was *America's first airliner* (a claim challenged by Alfred Lawson's "*26-passenger Air Liner*" of 1919).

Curtiss's interest in Florida led him into a new and different enterprise: real estate development. In 1917, searching for a new training airfield, he met jockey-sized cattleman *James H. Bright* and became interested in ranchland near Miami, then a city of only 30,000 population.

In 1918 Curtiss bought out Bright's brother and became Bright's partner in what became ownership of over 120,000 acres.

In 1921 they began to develop *Hialeah*, a new town, where, in addition to countless homes, land was set aside for the Miami Jockey Club's luxurious race track, Hialeah

Park, long "*the showplace of American horse racing*;" for the Miami Kennel Club; and for a Jai Alai Fronton Palace, a sport just imported from Cuba.

Hialeah's tremendous success prompted *Curtiss-Bright Industries* to begin their second town, originally called Country Club Estates, now known as *Miami Springs*. There he built homes for himself, his mother, sister, and half-brother, G. Carl Adams (1897-) - and many others from Hammondsport who came to escape the cold.

In 1925 they began a third town, originally called by its Indian name "*Opatishawa-kalocka*," a mouthful soon shortened to *Opa-locka*. But it was too late in the cycle of Florida development to realize its fanciful Arabian Nights design (inspired by Douglas Fairbank's 1924 epic, *The Thief of Baghdad*). Today, in addition to an airport Curtiss founded in 1927 (one of the world's busiest in general aviation), Opa-locka is a somewhat forlorn city with, arguably, America's most interesting city hall (also see page 422).

The Florida real estate boom's crash in 1925 - followed by the terrific destruction of Miami's 1926 hurricane (registering winds of 132 mph before the gauge blew away) - ended Curtiss's development activities. But even after spending huge sums helping victims and in reconstruction, their success left them very wealthy men.

Curtiss once said: "*I made more money in five years in Florida than I did in all my days of aviation*;" while James Bright said of him: "*No man could have asked for a better partner or a better friend.*"

"But money, though he had come from poverty to great wealth, had never been a primary concern of Glenn Curtiss. Conceiving an idea, and the challenge of making it a reality, had always been his greatest pleasure." *Frank FitzGerald-Bush*

Today, Hialaeh, Florida's fifth-largest city, is Miami's industrial center, and *well over three hundred thousand* people live in the cities Bright and Curtiss founded.

Curtiss donated the WW1 training field to the Navy; it became the *birthplace of the Marine Air Corps*. He also donated Miami's original airport, making him the *father of municipal aviation in Miami*. When he was asked about giving up flying, the profession he loved, he said: "*Aviation has just passed me by. It's now big business...for engineers, financiers and the like - not for a simple bicycle mechanic from Hammondsport.*"

"Mr. C. R. Fairey in 1923-24 had the courage to import Curtiss designs and Curtiss aero-motors to this country and thereby revolutionised English ideas and design."

Charles G. Grey, 1938

1920: The *Pulitzer Trophy Race*, in memory of publisher Joseph Pulitzer by his three sons, was inaugurated to promote American aviation and stimulate lagging aircraft development. "It set the stage in American aviation history for a racing craze that swept military and civilian alike. Nothing like it had ever manifested itself before and, except for the early years of space exploration and the first landing on the moon, nothing like it has occurred since. And, in this brief period in the pageant of flight, it was Curtiss that dominated the racing scene."

Rubenstein & Goldman

The Army's 156-mph Verville-Packard racer won the first event, followed in successive years by Curtiss-built Navy and Army planes.

Bert Acosta won this at a speed of 176 mph:

In 1925, for the *Schneider Cup International Seaplane Race* – with foreign contestants - held at Bay Shore Park, Baltimore, Maryland, Curtiss took its Pulitzer Race winning R3C-1 and substituted regulation Navy pontoons for wheels – which Jimmy Doolittle then masterfully flew to victory, as noted on the next page.

The Curtiss R3C-2, with a 610-hp Curtiss D-12/V-1400 engine, was flown 232-mph by Jimmy Doolittle to win the international Schneider race in 1925:

1Aug1922: Alexander Graham Bell, 75, died at Beinn Bhreagh. His chosen epitaph: *"Died a Citizen of the USA."* As his body was placed in its tomb every telephone in North America observed a minute's silence. Edison said: *"My late friend Alexander Graham Bell, whose world-famed invention annihilated time and space, and brought the human family in closer touch."*

3Jan1923: Mabel Hubbard Bell, *"Who made Possible the Aerial Experiment Association,"* dies. Two days before her death she wrote Bert Grosvenor: *"You must see that the biography does not picture Father as a perfect man. He was a very clever man and a good man, but he had his faults, just like every other human being. And I loved him for his faults..."* She is buried beside him.

13Oct'24, <u>TIME</u> Magazine: Under *Aeronautics*, an article about *"Dayton's fifth international air meet"* held at Wilbur Wright Field with the..."*program of events dedicated to both the pioneering Wright brothers. Orville Wright, on the scene, mused: 'As I stand ...where our earlier experiments were conducted and see how the principles of flight we used 21 years ago are still being used, I am extremely proud.' Nearby stood the first airplane hangar erected in the U.S.; and in it the machine, a biplane with a 12-horse motor and antique arm controls, in which the Wrights effected the first heavier-than-air flight at Kittyhawk, N.C., in 1903...* Next, author's collection:

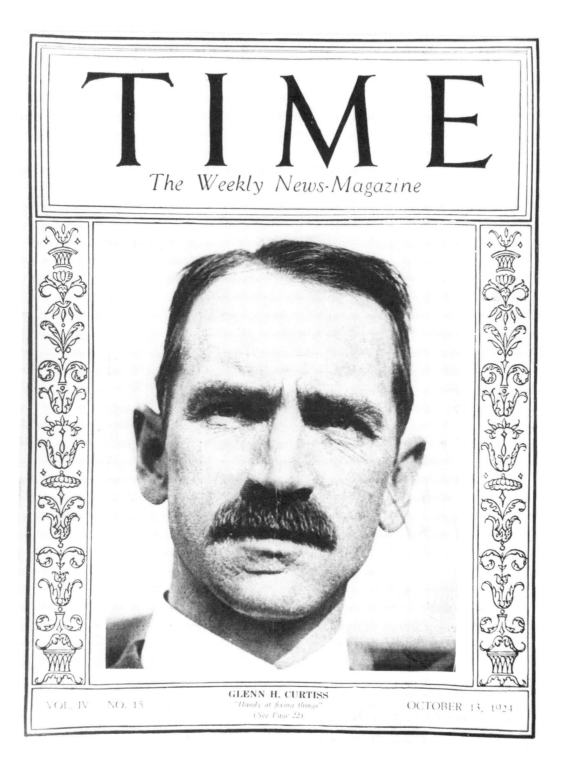

TIME

The Weekly News-Magazine

VOL. IV   NO. 15

GLENN H. CURTISS
"Handy at fixing things"
(See Page 22)

OCTOBER 13, 1924

"*Absentee. Though his works were everywhere present, his name on every man's lip, the face and figure of Glenn Hammond Curtiss were not in evidence in Dayton. At least every other plane of those assembled bore a Curtiss motor. Not one plane but bore some evidence to the contributions he has made to mankind's knowledge of the air and his agility in it...In 1905 it was...Curtiss who designed the motor of U.S. Dirigible No. 1...He is active today as head of the Curtiss Corporation at Garden City...*

"*In Hammondsport...they used to call him 'handy at fixing things.' Also, they would say: 'I knew he could do it.' Ingenuity, mechanical skill, persistence, enterprise, daring - these were Glenn Curtiss' qualities as early as the days when his bicycle was the speediest...Now 46, he still ponders engine construction, streamline, weight reduction in hopes of letting man move faster.*"

During the Twenties, *barnstormers*, the result of thousands of young men taught to fly, bargains in war surplus airplanes (typically Curtiss Jennys), and a postwar economy scarce of jobs, transfixed America. It was a brief, wild, exciting time..."The unique juxtaposition of the Jenny and hundreds of itching aviators looking for something 'after they'd seen Paree' created a part of 'that crazy age,' luminescent though brief. We'll never see anything like it again."

Waldo Waterman

Barnstormers Merle Fogg and George Sparks, ca. 1925, were trained to fly like this:

But they often flew like this; <u>The New York Times Pictorial</u>, 1922:

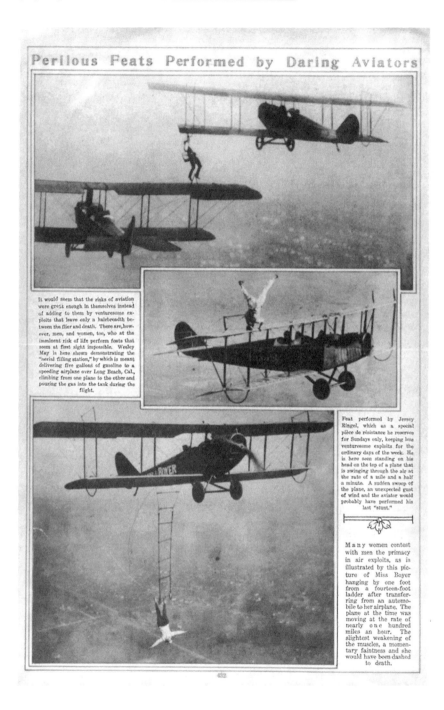

One shouldn't forget that, more than anything else, Curtiss was an engine-man. From 1916, when Charles Kirkham conceived the innovative 400 hp *K-12* – to F.R. Porter's refining it into *Model 18-T/C-12* – and then to its complete redesign in 1922 by Arthur Nutt. With its high power, small frontal area, light weight, compactness and reliability it was "the finest in-line liquid-cooled engine of the day" - and in streamlined Curtiss racers was unbeatable.

"One of the finest aircraft engines ever designed...purchased by England, France, Italy and Czecho-Slovakia..."

In 1922, under C.M. Keys, *Arthur Nutt*, Curtiss' young chief motor engineer, *"undertook a complete redesign of the C-12 engine, which became the D-12. Curtiss now had a real winner. The D-12 was the finest in-line liquid-cooled engine of the day; it set the pattern for subsequent development of the liquid-cooled engine. In the streamlined Curtiss racers, the D-12 was unbeatable...In 1928 the company unveiled the Conqueror, a more refined and more powerful engine...600 hp and increased the maximum speed of the P-1 by 20 mph over the same airplane powered by the older D-12 engine."* Eltscher & Young

The D-12 was the world's best in-line aircraft engine, powering the Schneider Trophy and Pulitzer winners, Germany's huge DoX, and was the foundation for the famed engines built by Rolls-Royce during WW2...

...as recounted in Arthur Nutt's autobiography: "In 1923 the Fairy Aviation Company of England obtained a license to build the D-12 engine. Several engines were delivered to Fairy and an installation was made in a Fairy Fox Military Airplane. It was a beautiful sleek streamlined airplane. Some of these engines went to Rolls-Royce for test and inspection. However the British wanted a British engine and they were encouraged apparently by their government to develop the Rolls-Royce *Kestral* engine. They obtained some Curtiss *Conqueror* engines at a later date. As a result there are ear-marks of the D-12 and *Conqueror* designs in their *Kestral* and *Merlin* engines. Rolls did not use the D-12 valve gear but opted to use rocker arms in their valve gear thereby resulting in a more bulky design with increased frontal area."

17Nov'22: Orville to George Spratt: "*I am writing to inquire whether you have the letters written by Wilbur and myself in our correspondence of twenty years ago... whether you would be willing to let me have copies...?...You and Chanute were our most intimate associates in those early years...*"

27Nov'22: Spratt to Orville, paraphrased: Spratt declined to exchange letters, stating that "*history writes itself*" and whatever Orville might write would make little difference. And he stated his grievances concerning certain measurements he'd volunteered in 1901...and that, through secretiveness and obstructionism, the Wrights had sacrificed much of the credit and compensation that might have come to them... that aviation deserved a leadership of greater vision and generosity than they, in his view, seemed capable of.

21May'27: *Charles A. Lindbergh* (1902-1974) flies nonstop, New York to Paris.

22May1927, *The New York Times: No one watched the progress of Captain Charles Lindbergh's flight from New York to Paris with more eagerness than did Orville Wright, who was doubtful of its success. Mr. Wright...a man of few words on any subject...tonight...broke all his conversational records in praise of Lindbergh...'The flight is beyond all expectation,' he said. 'It just goes to show that everything that has usefulness can be done and is worth working for. Back in 1911 we had it all figured out...how they might cross the Atlantic. But it couldn't be done in those days and we hardly dared dream that some day it might be accomplished. What I was most afraid of was that Lindbergh might lose his way. Fog is the bane of all flyers, and until we are able to navigate better...such flights as this one will not become common. Lindbergh took great chances. What did he possess that brought him through? Grit, you say? Yes, but more than that. Good judgment, for one thing. I do not know Lindbergh but I cannot help but feel that he is an unusual boy.'"*

Lindbergh, N.Y.-Paris, 21May1927; Richard Byrd, N.Y.-France, 1Jul (thanks to Bernt Balchen's heroic piloting); and Clarence Chamberlin & Charles Levine (right, above), N.Y.-Germany, 6Jun (flight sponsor Levine was the First Trans-Atlantic Air Passenger):
Soon after his flight, Lindbergh arrived at the office of Frank Russell, the Curtiss company's president, then meeting with *Ralph O'Neill* (founder of the *New York, Rio and Buenos Aires Airline,* Pan Am's predecessor to South America), who witnessed an interesting dialogue: "*...Well, then,' Frank said, 'though I am sincerely honored by your visit I'm wondering why you wanted to see me.' Lindbergh's reply struck me as a hesitant admission of a childish dream, unbelievably naive and self effacing. He shyly related that it had been his life's ambition to work for the great Curtiss Airplane Company and requested this appointment simply to apply for a job in person!...Russell's reply was absolutely incredible...that because Lindbergh was not an aeronautical engineer...the best he could offer...*(was a) *job on a drafting board, so that he could learn about aviation 'from the ground up'!...With dignity he* (Lindbergh) *rose, shook hands, and backed himself out of the office...*"

CURTISS ENGINEERING

The development of modern aircraft is a highly specialized science, requiring in the proper co-ordination of its phases the finest of scientific equipment and the highest types of engineering skill.

In these respects, the resources of the Curtiss Company are unequalled. The Curtiss wind tunnel, for instance, is the only one in the United States that is owned and operated by an aircraft manufacturer, and recent additions to its equipment have made it one of the most modern in the world. In this tunnel, the performance and flying characteristics of all Curtiss aircraft, are definitely determined by trained engineers, in advance of the actual construction of the full-size aircraft.

The Curtiss Aeroplane & Motor Co., Inc.
Offices: Garden City, N. Y.
Factories: Garden City & Buffalo, N. Y.

Curtiss

Aviation, 12Dec'27:

29May'25: Orville to James Magee (Carnegie Institute): "*...I regret as much as anyone the condition in our country which led me to offer our machine to a foreign museum...The National Museum* (Smithsonian) *was the only one in this country having such an exhibit. But it did not want our machine* (as it had turned down Curtiss' *June Bug* offer).

Note: In 1916 the original Wright Flyer (apparently after a *complete* restoration – for, if one recalls, in 1905 Wilbur wrote that *"...we did not try to preserve them..."*) was exhibited at an MIT building dedication, which Bell, the Guest of Honor, then tried to get for the Smithsonian; in 1917 and 1919 it was exhibited in New York City; in Dayton in 1918, and again, for legal suit purposes, in 1921. Its last American exhibit before going to England was at the 1924 Dayton National Air Races, noted in 13Oct'24 <u>TIME</u> article.

"I have held the machine for years at great risk in the hope that conditions in the Smithsonian might improve, but they seem to be going from bad to worse. I therefore finally offered the machine to the South Kensington Museum (England)*...I did reserve the right...of bringing it back to America, if I found a suitable home for it here. However, the likelihood of this seemed so remote that I did not expect its return...*(this letter also related the fate of the *Vin Fiz*, noted earlier)"

FLIGHT, John W.R. Taylor, 1956:

Germany's Dornier Do-X needed twelve engines to lift it off the water. Powered initially by 550-h.p. Siemens radials, it was later re-engined with 615-h.p. Curtiss Conquerors, which gave it a top speed of 130 m.p.h. The Do-X weighed 55 tons and could carry 169 passengers. During a visit to England in 1930 it was piloted for 10 minutes by the Prince of Wales. Later, it flew to New York and back.

In another letter, Orville wrote: *"I believe that my course in sending our Kitty Hawk machine to a foreign museum is the only way of correcting the history of the flying machine, which by false and misleading statements has been perverted by the Smithsonian Institution. In its campaign to discredit others in the flying art, the Smithsonian has issued scores of these false and misleading statements. They can be proved to be false and misleading from documents. But the people of today do not take the trouble to examine the evidence.*

"With this machine in any American museum the national pride would be satisfied; nothing further would be done and the Smithsonian would continue its propaganda. In a foreign museum this machine will be a constant reminder of the reasons for its being there, and after the people and petty jealousies of this day are gone, the historians of the future may examine the evidence impartially and make history accord with it. Your regret that this old machine must leave the country can hardly be so great as my own."

There is the question why the Wrights, once they had proven the airplane's practicability, allowed others to race ahead in what had become a rapidly advancing technology. The answer appears to have been their overriding focus on and protection of what they'd already achieved; in effect, *to rest on their oars.* They were uninterested in further achievement; only in benefiting from and being recognized for what they'd accomplished prior to 1906.

Curtiss, Ellyson and Mrs. Curtiss, Nitcheroy, Bahia de Guarnahora, Cuba, ca. 1926. Ellyson was killed 27Feb'28:

20Nov1926: Katharine Wright, 52, after a secret engagement, marries 1890's Oberlin College classmate Henry J. Haskell, editor and part owner of *The Kansas City Star*. Upon the engagement, Orville's mood alternates between furious and inconsolable; he all but reads her out of the family, relenting only at her deathbed three years later.

"When Secretary *(Charles Greeley) Abbot* supplanted Secretary Wolcott in 1926 as director of the Smithsonian...the olive branch was at last extended to Orville. Not only did Secretary Abbot publish an article in the <u>U.S.Air Services</u> magazine expressing regret for the act of the past which permitted a business antagonist of the Wrights to handle the restoration of the Langley aerodrome, but he declared that a new label would be attached to the Langley machine which would give the brothers full credit for their discovery."   *Chelsea Fraser*

But it's too late.

March 1928: Orville's Memorandum: "*I sent our original 1903 machine to the British National Museum because of the hostile and unfair attitude shown towards us by the officials of the Smithsonian Institution.*

"*...Following the controversy on this* (Langley) *subject three years ago the old label was removed and a new one still containing false and misleading statements was put in its stead...*"

The original 1903 Wright Flyer in the Science Museum, London:

ORIGINAL WRIGHT AEROPLANE.

This was the first power-driven, man-carrying aeroplane to make a free controlled and sustained flight. It was designed and built by Wilbur and Orville Wright and flown by them on December 17th. 1903. The aeroplane has been lent by Mr. Orville Wright.
The Science Museum. London.   No. 108

The Secretary of the Smithsonian found himself anguishing with a conundrum, possibly the most vexing psychological and historical riddle in the institution's history; attempting to meld historical fact, public perceptions, and an unparalleled legal riddle with an individual's all-consuming embitterment: How could they recognize and balance the greatness of one man's achievement with the obsessive, vindictive intransigence - *and* achievement - of another?

But, overriding all: *how could they get the 1903 Flyer returned to America?*

16Dec1928, *The New York Times:*

PLANE THE WRIGHTS FLEW

IF you go to the Smithsonian Institution in Washington you will see many strange types of aircraft and some modern ones, too; but you will not see there the first man-carrying airplane to fly under its own power. To see the plane which the Wright brothers made and first flew at Kitty Hawk twenty-five years ago tomorrow, you will have to go to London, to the Science Museum of South Kensington, to which this most famous of all airplanes has been lent.

Strangely enough, in the Smithsonian you will find a machine called the Langley Aerodrome, a label affixed to it reading:

"Langley Aerodrome—The original Langley flying machine of 1903 restored. In the opinion of many competent to judge, this was the first heavier-than-air craft in the history of the world, capable of free, sustained flight under its own power, carrying a man. This aircraft slightly antedated the machine designed and built by Wilbur and Orville Wright, which, on Dec. 17, 1903, was the first in the history of the world to accomplish sustained, free flight under its own power, carrying a man."

Behind this label lies a story no less dramatic in its own way than the story of the first flight. Samuel Pierpont Langley, the inventor of the Langley Aerodrome, was the first man to conduct scientific investigations into the principles of physics governing the science of aerodynamics. He has been described as a "reticent, self-effacing, lonely thinker, given to nocturnal wanderings through the streets of Washington." He staked his reputation as an astrophysicist and as secretary of the Smithsonian Institution on the solution of the problems of flying, and he died a disappointed and embittered man—"the butt of a nation's ridicule."

Nevertheless, he had made positive contributions to our knowledge of aerodynamics and some of his discoveries still stand good, but many of them do not, and it is to Wilbur and Orville Wright that we must look for the principles of correct aerofoil design and control. Basically, these still hold good, although many refinements of detail have improved

It Is Now in London, While a Dispute Rages Here

upon the plane surfaces and control mechanism which the two brothers employed in their first historic airplane.

Langley knew nothing of the effect of cambered aerofoil surfaces; the Wrights discovered them through intensive experimentation in a wind-tunnel. Now we all know that two-thirds of the lift is exercised by suction on the top of the plane surface; without camber, sustained flight in heavier-than-air craft is not practically possible. They discovered, too, that in order to prevent sideslipping, some sort of control over the wing surfaces was necessary. Professor Langley knew very little of this.

The Wrights solved the problem by introducing what was called torsional control—the warping of the wing-tips in order to increase or decrease the angle of incidence at which the wing plane meets the wind stream, thereby exerting a greater or lesser air pressure on the wings. Later, the same effect was obtained by the introduction of the aileron. Now we all know that practical flight would not be possible without lateral control of an aircraft. These were the great contributions of the Wrights to the science of aerodynamics, and they owe nothing to anybody for their success.

It was on Sept. 7, 1903, that Langley first tested his aerodrome. It was mounted on top of a houseboat on tracks. It had two sets of wings with flat surfaces, one in front of the other, each with pronounced dihedral. In relation to its size, it had adequate keel surface to prevent it from slipping easily out of the line of flight. It was, in short, of the type of model with which Professor Langley had successfully experimented. But on this occasion it ran along the tracks and, instead of leaping into the air, leaped into the Potomac. Subsequent examination showed that a guy-post supporting the front set of wings had broken, thereby making flight impossible. Repairs were made and a second

test attempted on Dec. 8, 1903. As in the first attempt the machine dived into the Potomac, this time tail first. It was then alleged that the machine had not been properly launched, but further experiments were cut short by the triumphant flight of the Wrights at Kitty Hawk and the death in 1906 of Langley, who was convinced that he had the secret of successful mechanical flight well within his grasp.

One look at the Langley machine will convince most of us that even if it were capable of flight back in 1903, it was not a practical flying machine. Examine the Wright biplane and it will be found, the necessary exceptions being made, that it is aerodynamically more efficient than are some of the planes which fly today. That is saying a great deal.

The Wright airplane was a biplane, the two wings being connected by struts and wires about five feet apart. The aspect ratio was about six to one, that is the span was six times greater than the chord or width. The operator had to lie on his face on the lower plane beside the engine, from which point he controlled the machine. Out in front were long booms holding the horizontal rudders, which are now called elevators, and in between them were two moon-shaped fins. Behind, two spars ran back to support the vertical rudder.

The mechanism required to operate the warping of the wing tips also operated the rudder, both being necessary to a turn and to avoid sideslipping. The wings were thin with a cambered upper surface. The machine was very strongly built and was supported on the ground by skids instead of the now familiar undercarriage on wheels. The engine, built by themselves, gave considerably more than the eight horsepower expected, and this enabled the inventors to add some 150 pounds of weight in strengthening the wings and other parts. The motor drove two airscrews, also designed by the brothers, on an indirect drive. This is the father of the modern airplane and the machine in which the Wrights made the dramatic first flight.

C. M.

29Sep'28: Publication of Charles Abbot's *"The Relations Between the Smithsonian and the Wright Brothers."* A review and qualified apology: *"I acknowledge with regret that the summary of the proceedings given at an earlier page of the <u>Smithsonian Annual Report</u> for 1910 (pp. 22-23) is misleading...I concede to Mr. Wright that it lacked of consideration to put the tests of the Langley plane into the hands of his opponent, Mr. Curtiss ...(it was not improper to make the tests)...But I feel that it was a pity that Manly, Doctor Langley's colleague, could not have been the man chosen to make them* (but Manly was a participant; see pp. 364)*...Finally, as a further gesture of goodwill, I...have directed that the labels on the Langley Aerodrome shall be so modified as to tell nothing but facts, without additions of opinion as to the accomplishments of Langley."* Thus, Label Number IV, the fourth within a decade:

"LANGLEY AERODROME
THE ORIGINAL SAMUEL PIERPONT LANGLEY
FLYING MACHINE OF 1903, RESTORED
DEPOSITED BY
THE SMITHSONIAN INSTITUTION"

Orville did not respond.

16Dec'28, *The New York Times*: "At a dinner to Orville Wright in celebration of the twenty-fifth anniversary of the first flight the speakers included several young aviators from the Wright Field...Orville Wright, as usual, smiled, bowed and said nothing. The first of all men to fly has the further distinction of never having made a public speech. He sits silent at banquets commemorating the greatest creative achievement of this century..."
Anne O'Hare McCormick

Jan1929, *Popular Science:* "Man flew for the first time on December 17, 1903, when Wilbur and Orville Wright, Americans, launched themselves in the air...They discovered the secret of flight...They are the immortal pioneers who lifted man from the earth...These are facts accepted by a minority of informed persons. For the public at large the Wright's title is under a cloud. Indeed many intelligent folk believe that Professor Langley of the Smithsonian Institution and a lot of clever Frenchmen collaborated to secure the conquest of the air. Langley's attempt at a flying vehicle is now on view in the Smithsonian...with a noncommittal label that credits it as the ancestor of aerial navigation. Because of that label Orville Wright, last year, declined to exhibit the real pioneer machine in our national museum at Washington and instead sent it to the friendly exile of the Science Museum in London. The English have been more hospitable to the Wrights than their own people..." *John McMahon*

3Mar1929: Katharine, married less than three years, dies of pneumonia.

Orville is now alone, his activities limited. Among them, following the 1926 Air Commerce Act he signs pilot's licenses (many with a rubber-stamped signature).
    A quiet, bland man, he tended to exhibit a self-righteous disdain for compromise

(surely unassuaged by Curtiss's half-foot height advantage; see photos pp. 185 of Orville and Post and pp. 423 of Post and Curtiss) that bedeviled many that tried to deal with him.

A lifelong problem solver, Curtiss was always the inventor. One of his last was the "*Aerocar*," a sophisticated predecessor of today's travel-trailer. *Fortune, March, 1934:*

RIDE *through* Sales Resistance
With CURTISS AEROCAR

AEROCAR IS A SUPER SALESMAN FOR FOSTORIA

Fostoria Glass Company — Fostoria — Moundsville, W.Va. U.S.A.

VICTOR RADIO WENT AEROCAR 3 YEARS AGO

NORGE GOES DIRECT TO THE FINER HOMES

J. E. BURKE COMPANY HAS TRAVELING DISPLAY

ONE OF THE FLORIDA YEAR ROUND CLUBS AEROCAR FLEET

WARM SPRINGS INVALIDS KNOW AEROCAR COMFORT

GENERAL ELECTRIC ADOPTS UNIQUE BODY DESIGN

open new outlets .. rouse drowsy markets

FLEXIBLE . . . in its thousand and one adaptations to merchandising . . . attention compelling, by virtue of its striking appearance . . . practical in its extreme roominess, smoothness, high speed, economical operation, lightness and great load capacity (double that of the average truck per pound of dead weight) . . . Curtiss Aerocar has won an important place in the merchandising programs of many of the country's greatest manufacturing and selling institutions.

THE PERSONAL AEROCAR

Long recognized as a revolutionary mode of passenger and light freight transportation, it is now generally accepted as a powerful medium of advertising and sales stimulus.

Rolling demonstrations and mobile showrooms . . . presenting the "line" in spectacular fashion to remote markets as well as to thickly populated areas . . . have proved their value in creating new consumer inter-est, helping established dealers speed up sales and opening new outlets, (note photos of Fostoria traveling display, Victor Caravan, etc.)

Curtiss Aerocar combines all of the virtues of the conventional truck, bus or trailer for these purposes with the added **exclusive** advantages of almost negligible weight, immense strength, easy handling and extremely low upkeep.

Any standard coupe or roadster serves as motive power for the Aerocar. Costs little more to operate than the power unit alone. Because of the lightness of its airplane type construction, minimum of unsprung weight, three-point suspension and patented pneumatic coupler which provides an air-cushioned universal joint absorbing thrusts from every direction, it has no tendency to side-sway and is unbelievably quiet and smooth even when traveling at high speed.

CURTISS AEROCAR CO. INC.
CORAL GABLES . . . MIAMI FLORIDA

"A DRAWING ROOM ON WHEELS"   NEW YORK OFFICE . . . . 535 FIFTH AVENUE

Old friends Augustus Post and Glenn Curtiss, ca. 1928:

The years in Florida were possibly his busiest in business ventures, experiments and out-door recreations (he excelled at archery). He organized eighteen Florida corporations, including a bank to help finance home builders, and along with his Miami Springs friend, W.K. Kellogg, played a part in introducing avocados, mangoes and papaya to the United States, believing them healthful fruits that ought to be popularized.

An avid outdoorsman and excellent archer, in 1917 Curtiss developed a folding tent-type trailer. In 1919 it evolved into a streamlined, lightweight 5th-wheel trailer to become known as the Aero-Car. Its aircraft-type *"stick and wire"* construction (it weighed 1,200 pounds) had a spruce frame covered with thin plywood and canvas; and it was pneumatically hitched with a flat rubber donut in a steel box which cushioned shock forward, back, up, down or sidewise. The first models were built in Garden City, and then at Hammondsport's Keuka Industries, managed by Carl Adams, Curtiss' half-brother. The *Curtiss Aerocar Co.* – with Hugh Robinson its president, existed into WW2.

For demonstration, in Aug1928 he pulled one from Miami to New York in 39 hours!

26Jun1929: *The Curtiss-Wright Corporation*, essentially combining an aircraft manufacturer (Curtiss) with an engine manufacturer (Wright), was an amalgamation of the Curtiss-Keys Group and the Hoyt Group (*Richard Hoyt*, another Wall Streeter, was Chairman of Wright Aeronautical). Eighteen affiliated companies and twenty-nine subsidiaries made up *North American Aviation*, a new holding company with pooled assets of $70 million and a paper stock value of $220 million (about $6 billion today). Clement M. Keys was its first president, succeeded a few years later by Ralph S. Damon.

North American controlled Transcontinental Air Transport, TAT, which, on 7Jul1929, with Ford-Stout tri-motors initiated the famed *"Lindbergh Line"* and its coast-to-coast air-rail service. In Oct1930, money-losing TAT merged with Western Air Express, eventually becoming Transcontinental & Western Air, and then known as TWA.

Clement Mellville Keys: *"The son of a minister, he grew up in a small town near Toronto and attended the University of Toronto. He taught classics at a small Canadian college for several years and in 1901 left for New York City to seek his fortune. He worked as a journalist, first at the* Wall Street Journal *and then a monthly journal* World's Work, *where he soon became the financial editor.*

"He left in 1911 to set up his own investment bank, underwriting securities and advising wealthy clients on investments. Glenn Curtiss sought Keys' investment advice soon after selling his company (1916) and then asked Keys to join the Curtiss Aeroplane and Motor Corporation as vice president for finance."

Eltscher & Young

Clement Mellville Keys:

Keys then guided post-WW1 Curtiss, sustaining the company during the difficult 1920s, and is today known as *"The Father of American Commercial Aviation."*

14Oct1929: Curtiss wrote Orville, suggesting a meeting and talk. It was unanswered.

<u>Fortune</u>, Apr1930: *"...Planes which are not safe to fly have been put on the market ...made their contribution to the record of crashes. This is more true of the small companies than of established and well-backed companies. A distinct exception is the Curtiss Aeroplane & Motor Company, Inc., which now has two hundred engineers on its pay roll and which is pressing, not so much toward current earnings, as toward an investment ...which will pay returns four or five years hence.*

"From Curtiss, too, has come another contribution to the equipment problem, this time...to safety. While all aviation publicity men make much of the thought that it is not more safety which is needed, but public acceptance of existing safety, yet aviation engineers admit that there is much to be done in technical design...the Guggenheim Fund...offered a prize...The Curtiss Tanager won the competition...the engineers...are... studying...to apply its principles to planes built for commercial safety."

31May'30: *"Curtiss Celebrates 20th Anniversary of His Historic Albany-New York Flight."*

In his last public appearance, piloting (briefly) America's newest airliner, a Curtiss *Condor*, he reflew the 1910 Hudson River route:

Mr. & Mrs. Glenn H. Curtiss deplaning after the Albany-New York flight:

Condor in a 1934 photograph:

1930: <u>The New York Times</u> asked him for an article: *"The outlook for aviation is, in my opinion, about the same as the outlook for the automobile industry thirty years ago. There were some who thought the automobile a rich man's toy, others foresaw a great industry; but so far as I can recall, no one predicted the immense development which has taken place.*

"The expansion of the automobile industry depended largely on the construction of good roads, where the future of aviation depends largely upon...flying fields...

"Saving time is the equivalent of increasing the duration of life. To business men and executives, time used in traveling from point to point is largely wasted. This is where the airplane comes in."

DOWN THE HUDSON IN A BOX-KITE PLANE

Glenn H. Curtiss, Who Made the Epochal Flight From Albany to New York Just Twenty Years Ago, Describes the Difficulties of the Journey and Compares It With Accomplishments Today

Twenty Years Ago: The Glenn Curtiss Plane in Flight.

Photographs at Top From Keystone.

The following article by Glenn H. Curtiss describes what was an epochal event twenty years ago—his flight from Albany to New York—and compares this accomplishment with flying today. As a reward for his flight, Mr. Curtiss received the prize of $10,000 offered by The New York World.

By GLENN H. CURTISS.

TWENTY years ago, when I flew the 150 miles from Albany to New York in 2 hours and 46 minutes, aviation was still in its swaddling clothes. Today an airplane can cover the same distance in less than an hour and the event is a commonplace. Then, it was the record long distance flight in America.

For in those days men gaped at the idea of a heavier-than-air machine flying at all. It was news if an airplane engine continued to run, once it was started. Today, with our endurance fliers staying up for more than 400 hours at a stretch, it is news when an airplane engine stops. Instead of sitting on the front of a plane exposed to all the elements, as I did in the Albany-to-New York flight, air travelers now ride in luxurious cabins. And instead of depending on the flutter of one's coat sleeve as a speed indicator, guessing at your altitude, and gauging balance by comparing the airplane level with the level of the horizon, we now have exact instruments for all these requirements.

Twenty years ago the air, from a flier's point of view, was completely unexplored. Now it has been flown between Albany and New York under every conceivable circumstance—day and night, in sunlight and in storm. We have weather reports from meteorological stations before we start and data on the peculiar air conditions that may be encountered along the way. But at the time of the Albany flight, the knowledge was so scant that I did not know why the plane dropped and dipped suddenly when I passed Storm King Mountain. Now we know a good deal about rising and falling air currents.

The machine in which I flew from Albany to New York twenty years ago looked very much like a box kite. It was a biplane, thirty feet long and thirty feet wide. The elevator was set in front of the pilot's seat; which was completely open. The wings were arched, but rigid. Instead of warping the wings to balance, I had ailerons on either side of the machine.

It was, of course, a home-made machine. The fittings were sheet iron. The wire was twisted cable and the turnbuckles were made of bicycle spokes. The outriggers were made of bamboo and the covering for the wings was rubberized cloth, which got slack in wet weather and tightened under the sun.

The machine was the smallest that had ever attempted a distance flight and skeptics of its ability to carry me through safely were not wanting. Nevertheless, on the morning of May 29, 1910, I decided to make the flight. There was a slight head wind blowing from the south, but weather reports obtained from Poughkeepsie by telephone were favorable. I did not know

then, of course, of the anxious minutes I was going to have in that air when the currents above the Highlands nearly ended the flight in a catastrophe.

The mud flats of Rensselaer's Island had been selected for the field for the start. At 7:03 o'clock in the morning I got into the pilot's seat — it was scarcely more than a plank placed on the edge of the lower wing—and "gave her the gun." I set my course, straight down the Hudson to Poughkeepsie, flying at an altitude of about 700 feet.

The river below me looked particularly uninviting. But, as there were no landing places along most of the course, I had made preparations to land in the water if it became necessary—or probable. Two pontoons were fastened to the lower part of the plane just above the wheels and, in addition, a planing boat was down the centre. That was really the first amphibian plane, and the seaplane and the flying boat were its lineal descendants.

Besides these precautions, my mechanician at the last moment had insisted upon strapping a set of cork life preservers to my waist. I wore long wading boots that came up to my chest, too—but these were not to use in case I landed in the Hudson. They were to keep warm. I had found them the best sort of a flying suit then available.

As I flew along toward Poughkeepsie I did not notice the ground below me much, except to look at the smoke from chimneys to see which way the wind was blowing. From time to time I caught sight of the special train chartered by THE NEW YORK TIMES, which was

following the flight. It was running on the time of the Twentieth Century, and early in the flight I outdistanced it. I remember that was considered a remarkable thing in those days. I was making between fifty and sixty miles an hour. I reached Poughkeepsie sooner than I had expected, after about

days, as today, particularly on an unsuitable field. It would be easy to misjudge the distance and crash. There was only one spot in the field free from trees and ditches. But the machine came down without mishap. I jumped out and went over the engine. It was all right. A wire that had worked loose and given me some trouble in the air was quickly fixed.

The supply of gasoline and oil I had ordered by telegraph from Albany, however, had not showed up. So I borrowed some from a motorist and got ready to take off again. First we had to cut down a few small trees, but that did not take long. And once in the air again I returned to the river course.

Now the perilous part of the trip began. Flying over the Highlands I ran into some air currents that I knew something about from experience and from the stories of sailing captains, who told me of the treacherous winds they had encountered on the river there. But the reality was worse than the expectation. And the machine barely weathered the invisible storm that tossed it about.

Just as I got past Storm King the worst of the air currents struck the plane. The first thing I knew, the machine plunged forward on its nose and sideways at the same time. I very nearly dropped out, and I didn't know what was going to happen next. A few seconds later it began to toss and eddy about almost beyond control. My heart was in my month. I thought it was all over.

By pushing the controls forward I managed to gain control, steady the plane and right it. Perhaps, I

thought, it would be calmer near the surface of the water. So I dropped to a point about forty feet above the level of the river. The way was smoother going there, so I held to that level. After I had passed Peekskill the river widened out. The battle with the air currents was over.

But now I had something else to worry about. The supply of lubricating oil was running low again. My motor was lubricated by pumping oil into it by hand. About once in every ten minutes I had to push on the lever of the pump and I must have been too enthusiastic about using that pump handle, because I used up the oil much too fast. I was bent on getting within the city limits of New York before I stopped again, but I did not know whether I was going to make it without more oil. I was approaching the city limits. Far ahead I could already see the tower of the Metropolitan Life, then one of the city's outstanding landmarks. So I decided to keep on. And, with the oil tank practically empty, I crossed the line.

* * *

NOW the problem of finding a place to land arose. I had planned to go on to Governors Island, where there was a landing field ready made in the parade ground, but that was impossible without more oil. So I began to cast about for a suitable field within the city limits.

Flying fairly low, I saw a green space just beyond the Harlem River that I thought might do. I swung around toward the Jersey shore and made a complete circle, reconnoitring. The greener space was a field of grass which turned out to be a hillside, and I decided to bring the machine down on it. There was more slope to the ground than I had expected and the machine came quickly to a stop and started rolling backward. I jumped out and held it. Then two young men came running up and I got them to hold it while I went down to telephone that I had arrived within the city limits, complying with the requirement for the prize.

By the time I got back quite a crowd of people had gathered around the machine. They were all exclaiming and asking questions at once. It was pleasant to find such friendly interest, but I wanted to get under way again. And, first of all, I wanted some oil. A gentleman who owned a boat works nearby very kindly got me some oil and I filled the tank. The next problem was to get back into the air, and in this, the third take-off of the day, I very nearly had an accident. As I have said, the field sloped toward the river and, as I had to get up a speed of 45 miles an hour to take the air, that required quite a run. But, by running the machine up to the edge of the plateau-like formation there, I managed, after a drop of several feet, to clear the ground and head for Governors Island.

Flying down the Hudson once more I encountered air currents that tipped the machine and made it jump about once or twice, but the rest of the flight was uneventful and just at noon I landed at Governors Island.

Glenn H. Curtiss as He Is Today.

Photograph from Matlack Studio.

an hour's flying. There was not a single real landing field along the whole course. But at Camelot, near Poughkeepsie, I had made arrangements beforehand to land and replenish my oil and gasoline in a side-hill pasture. The superintendent of the insane asylum at Poughkeepsie had, it is true, invited me to use the asylum grounds. He said that almost all flying machine inventors landed there in the end, anyway. But I did not accept his invitation.

Landing was the risk in those

23Jul1930: Glenn Hammond Curtiss, 52 years old, dies of a heart attack brought on by appendicitis (and possibly the still-ongoing Herring litigation), in Buffalo, N.Y.

At the time of his funeral, attended by friends and dignitaries, including representative of Navy and Army, planes were dropping flowers over his grave-site in Pleasant Valley Cemetery, flags at half-staff and every business closed in Hammondsport - and Miami, now a city of 110, 000, observed an hour of mourning.

Miami's mayor, *C.H. Reeder,* who attended the funeral said: "*This is the greatest loss the state has sustained. He was so modest and retiring that few people actually knew what he had done for the state.*"

Captain Chambers: "*I understand better than any other person in the Navy how much we owe to him for progress in naval aviation through his generous and kindly cooperation with us in the pioneer development of that which is destined to be one of the greatest factors in national defense and future peace.*

"*But it was his personal characteristics, his personality and understanding more than his remarkable foresight and skill, that endeared him to me in a bond of friendship that is one of the most cherished memories of my life.*"

In time Lena Curtiss remarried - to H. Sayre Wheeler, Monroe Wheeler's son - and her financial adviser – and lived until her death in 1949 in Curtiss' last Florida home.

In 1969 a once-obese Glenn, Jr. of 8585 Cutler Road, Coral Gables, courted comely, young Jeanne Weldon to be his third wife. He died on 7Nov1969, age 57 "after a lengthy illness."

The legacy of Curtiss' achievements and wealth has tended more towards the vacuity, excesses, and idle comforts of the rich rather than to progress and enlightenment.

1929: John McMahon in *Popular Science:* "*I met Orville Wright for the first time years ago in the lobby of a New York hotel. He was a small figure, neatly dressed, wearing a derby hat. One noted that his feet and hands were small. He limped a trifle in result of the one air crash in his career* (which killed Tom Selfridge). *His voice was low, his words pleasant but few, his manner oddly constrained...his eyes were cast down and his fingers twisted and twiddled a button on the front of his coat!"*

1930: *The New Yorker* "*Profile*" on Orville Wright: "*...a gray man now, dressed in gray clothes. Not only have his hair and his moustache taken on that tone, but his curiously flat face...a timid man whose misery at meeting you is obviously so keen that, in common decency, you leave as soon as you can.*"

1934: Tom Watson, having lived a most interesting and comfortable life, dies at 80.

15Mar'35: Orville to Secretary Abbot: "*Instead of a paper such as you have proposed may I offer the following suggestion: That the Smithsonian publish a paper presenting a list of specifications in parallel columns of those features of the Langley machine of 1903 and the Hammondsport machine of 1914, in which there were differences, with an introduction stating that the Smithsonian now finds that it was misled by the Zahm report of 1914; that through the Zahm paper the Institution was led to believe that the aeroplane tested at Hammondsport was 'as nearly as possible in its original condition'; that as a result of this misinformation the Smithsonian had published erroneous statements from time to time alleging that the original Langley machine, without modification, or with only such modifications as were necessary for the addition of floats, had been successfully flown at Hammondsport in 1914; that it ask its readers to disregard all of its former statements and expressions of opinion regarding the flights at Hammondsport in 1914, because these were based on misinformation as the list to follow will show. The list and specifications are to be agreed upon by the Smithsonian, Colonel Lindbergh and myself.*"

Secretary Abbot did not respond.

In 1939 Lindbergh noted in his diary: The fault lay "*primarily with the Smithsonian people. But Orville Wright is not an easy man to deal with in the matter. I don't blame him much, though, when I think of the way he was treated for a period of years. He has encountered the narrow-mindedness of science and the dishonesty of commerce.*"

26Jun'37: Henry Ford restores the original Wright cycle shop, moving it to the Ford Museum at Greenfield Village, Dearborn, Michigan. To accomplish this he sent a man to California to locate Charles Taylor: he wanted him "found and retrieved so he could direct the reconstruction of the Wright home and bicycle shop in his Greenfield Village museum. Taylor was uniquely qualified. Wilbur was dead, Orville couldn't be bothered and no one else on earth knew as much about the Wright's bicycle shop and airplane workshop, circa 1903, as Charles Taylor." *Mark Bernstein*

Cecil R. Roseberry wrote: "As secretary of the Smithsonian, Dr. Charles G. Abbot could not rest while Orville Wright maintained his grudge and the original Kitty Hawk machine was in a foreign land. In 1937, he sent Wright another feeler: *'I desire not to die before*

Orville Wright, Charles Taylor and Henry Ford:

clearing our situation if possible.' There was no reaction from Dayton. Dr. Abbot enlisted the efforts of Colonel Charles A. Lindbergh as a mediator, again to no avail.

"When Great Britain went to war in 1939, facing the certainty of bombing by the Luftwaffe (first trained by the Wrights), the Kitty Hawk was stored for safety in a sub-terranean shelter in the west of England, with many other museum and art treasures.

"Abbot finally reopened a channel of communication with Wright in 1940, offering to publish a fresh statement of the case if Orville would specify in writing precisely what were his terms for patching up the quarrel. Wright demanded nothing less than a public apology with inclusion of these words in the statement: '*I sincerely regret that the Institution employed to make the tests of 1914 Glenn H. Curtiss, who had just been adjudged an infringer of the Wright patent by the U. S. Court.*'

"The renewed negotiation almost foundered on this obstacle, as Abbot replied: '*You, no doubt, see bad motives where I do not...Apparently our present stumbling block is your insistence on a particular form of mention of the Wright-Curtiss litigation. To me this litigation appears wholly extraneous to all issues between the Smithsonian and the Wrights, except that it seems an indelicacy to have employed Curtiss as the Institution's agent when a successful flight of the Langley machine would have meant so much to the Wrights. For me now to use your language about the court decision pronouncing Curtiss an infringer of your patent in this important proposed paper would seem to me to be setting up the Smithsonian Institution as an historical authority pronouncing the last word about a litigation in which it has no concern, whereas it is my understanding that further litigation was begun but was discontinued under an agreement between the parties.'*

"A compromise was reached when Abbot bent the knee to this extent: *'I sincerely regret that the Institution employed to make the tests of 1914 an agent who had been an unsuccessful defendant in patent litigation brought against him by the Wrights...I sincerely regret that statements were repeatedly made by officers of the Institution that the Langley machine was flown in 1914 with 'certain changes of the machines necessary to use pontoons,' without mentioning the other changes included in Dr. Wright's list.'*

"Abbot acceded to Wright's insistence on verbatim publication of the lengthy enumeration of all the changes which had been made in the *Langley* during its stay in Hammondsport, as he and Brewer had worked them out in their collaboration in Dayton. In doing so, however, he attributed this to Orille Wright, not to the Smithsonian itself. (Zahm called Brewer's listing of the changes made on the *Langley* "*multitudinous, minute, inconsequential, they read like a laundry list...the objection of a book-keeper rather than an engineer.*")

"When Dr. Abbot's new pamphlet was published in 1942, it mollified Orville Wright, and shortly afterward he wrote to the director of the British Science Museum: *'I have decided to have the Kitty Hawk returned to America when transport hazards are less than at present.'* He also made a change in his will to that effect. Abbot's paper was widely interpreted as an *'apology'* by the Smithsonian Institution. Many years later, Dr. Abbot privately told the present author (Roseberry) that he did not intend it as an apology, but that; *'I wanted to do anything within reason to settle the controversy. I didn't want Orville Wright to die without making peace between him and the Smithsonian.'"*

In 1972, when "Tip" Roseberry (whom the author knew) wrote the above, the *"Agreement"* of 23Nov1948 between the Estate of Orville Wright and the Smithsonian Institution was unknown to him, or for that matter, to all but a select few within that institution. It was not until 1976 that it was *"publicly"* disclosed through the efforts of William J. O'Dwyer, champion of Gustave Whitehead, coupled with the clout of U.S. Senator *Lowell P. Weicker Jr.*, but even today it has been given limited view and most are unaware of it, *as if its disclosure occurred in an anechoic chamber, its reverberations stilled.*

In 1989 *Peter Jakab* of the N.A.S.M. answered the author's request made to Secretary Robert McCormick Adams that the Smithsonian abrogate the *Agreement*: "*...this document was created primarily to deal with a potential inheritance tax problem for the Wrights heirs, and was only secondarily intended to address the question of priority of invention...If it could be shown that Whitehead, or anyone else, made a true flight before the Wrights, we would never consider disregarding or ignoring such a finding for fear of breaking this agreement...*" (Note: See Library of Congress' 1993 <u>Flight Before Wright</u> calendar).

The *Agreement*'s provisions appear to be 'the final nail in the coffin' of efforts initiated by Secretary Abbot to meet the demands of Orville Wright.

With his primacy established, his fight with Curtiss won, Orville could rest in peace.

Or could he?

The *Agreement* – though possibly not as pivotal in this story as the author first thought - merits study and is included in the appendix. Arguably its most revealing section is 2(d): *"Neither the Smithsonian Institution or its successors nor any museum, or other agency, bureau or facilities, administered for the United States of America by the Smithsonian Institution or its successors, shall publish or permit to be displayed a statement or label in connection with or in respect of any aircraft model or design of earlier date than the Wright Aeroplane of 1903, claiming in effect that such aircraft was capable of carrying a man under its own power in controlled flight."*

28Jan1942: Just prior to Abbot's paper, in a letter to John Victory of the National Advisory Committee for Aeronautics, Orville wrote a letter opposing the naming of NACA's new Cleveland engine laboratory after *Charles Manly*: *"...I think it is about time the Committee (NACA) entirely disregard the constant importunities of the Smithsonian to use the Committee as a cat's-paw in its controversies."* (See Appendix page on Manly)

Another (purported) incident may help illuminate Orville's mind-set. When writing Pendulum the author was told by one very credible man - and confirmed by another (both having been told it firsthand) – that during WW2 a young Army pilot in Dayton was passing an office signed "ORVILLE WRIGHT." The door was open; he spied Orville at his desk. Venturing in he was cordially greeted – and soon Orville inquired as to his duty. *"I'm flying a Curtiss P-40..."* was all he'd blurted out before, very agitated, Orville jumped to his feet, exclaiming he'd hear nothing more of it!

Seeking confirmation, I located the 'pilot,' an "engineering officer and test pilot" – who confirmed the meeting but denied the above scenario – possibly confirming how an event may be altered by 'political correctness.'

But by 1943 things were thawing out.

16Nov'43: Orville to *President Franklin Roosevelt: "I think your suggestion of having the announcement of the future return of the Kitty Hawk plane made at the dinner on December 17th a good one. I had intended that the announcement be made as soon as the Smithsonian Report appeared, but I now shall have it withheld for the dinner. If you personally were to make the announcement it would be particularly pleasing to me."*

"The *Collier Trophy* for 1943 was to be awarded to the U.S. Army Air Forces ..accepted...by General Hap Arnold, who had learned to fly at...Simms Station...

"Orville disliked formal dinners, but accepted the invitation because the President himself was to make the announcement about the return of the Flyer. The President, however, had recently returned from conferences at Teheran...and (*weary and close to death*) was unable to attend...

"Orville became upset when he learned that Secretary of Commerce Jesse Jones, who was standing in for the President, had arranged for Orville to present the Collier Trophy to General Arnold while newsreel cameras recorded the event...broadcast on a national radio network. Before the dinner Orville reminded Jones that he had agreed to attend only on condition that he would not be required to take an active part in the program, but after Jones had made the announcement about the return of the 1903 Flyer and the awarding of the Collier Trophy, he read aloud the concluding words of the President's message: '*In closing I can think of only one additional tribute to General Arnold. Will you please ask Orville Wright, the greater teacher, to act for me in handing the Collier Trophy to General Arnold, the pupil.*'

"Confronted with a microphone, Orville remained adamantly tight-lipped. There was absolute silence on the air until the radio announcer filled in by saying that Orville was now presenting the trophy to General Arnold. Arnold rose to the occasion gracefully. There was no one, he said, from whose hands he would rather receive the trophy than Orville Wright."   *Fred Howard*

Penuriousness was legend in the Wright household, Orville always frugal:

24Jan1948: Orville to the *General Electric Company: "I have a 10-H.P. General Electric motor that I would like to sell. This motor was purchased in 1917 for use in my laboratory on a wind tunnel. I would estimate it had about 200 hours of running...Would you be interested in purchasing it...?"*

This, his last letter, from a millionaire wanting to sell a motor he'd used for *31* years.

30Jan1948: Orville Wright, 76, dies of a heart attack.

On February 2nd, the day of the funeral, with flags at half mast Dayton's city and county offices closed, school was let out at noon, and at 2:30 P.M. a minute of silence was observed as Orville joined his mother, father, Wilbur and Katharine in Woodland Cemetery.

He left an estate of more than a million dollars (about $30 million today), his largest bequest, $300,000, to Katharine's alma mater, Oberlin College, smaller ones to a half-dozen others.

Charles Taylor, left $800 per year, in 1948 said: "*Some of the personal feeling of the old days when there were just the three of us, was gone."* (In 1911 he'd left the Wrights to join Cal Rodgers and his *Vin Fiz* transcontinental flight.)

There was a farcical, somewhat melancholy sequence of events as the heirs attempted to get access to Orville's papers (mainly relevant to the disposition of the *1903 Flyer*). Mabel Beck, his indomitable secretary for over 35 years, refused to turn them over until an executor had been appointed. She then refused to work for the family unless she received a raise over the modest wage Orville had paid her. *She was fired.*

Photograph (author's collection): 19Nov'48, Inscribed reverse: "The 'Kitty Hawk' arriving back in the U.S. after 20 years in England. The Navy gave me the honor of meeting it at Bayonne N.J., escorting it to Washington and assisting in its assembly at the Smithsonian." The writer was *Paul Garber*, whom the author knew:

As earlier noted, on 22Dec'05 Wilbur wrote Zahm: *"...The machines themselves were not constructed as to be transported from Kitty Hawk so we did not try to preserve them..."*

The 1903 Wright Flyer was then prominently exhibited in the Smithsonian:

It's unclear, but apparently the flyer's remains, virtually abandoned for five years, were shipped to Dayton in 1908. A 1916 exhibition first showed its weathered and 1913 flood-ravaged remnants restored, questioning much of its authenticity.

Of interest, the truest example of an early Wright may today hang in Munich's Deutsches Museum (viewed by the author in 1991).

"The Wright's principle of simultaneous control of attitude in the three axes or dimensions of space was the key to the riddle of flight which had completely escaped the nineteenth-century experimenters...The Wright's disclosure of simple means to control yaw, pitch and roll was easily comprehended and promptly adopted by others. It is a mystery...that this now obvious solution did not occur to someone in the previous century." *Jerome Hunsaker*

In 1986 the *Miami Herald,* in "*the ten people and the ten events that had the most impact on the* (Dade) *county's history,*" listed Curtiss, the "*developer and promoter of the area's aviation potential,*" along with Henry Flagler, who "*brought the Florida East Coast Railway to Miami.*"

The firm that Glenn Curtiss founded was the world's second-largest aircraft manufacturer in World War I and America's second-largest defense contractor in World War II, attainments unrivaled by any other American company.

"Unlike 'lone wolf' Wright brothers, Curtiss always worked as a member of a team, albeit usually the head." Many extraordinary men worked with him: Bell, Selfridge, Baldwin, Beachey, McCurdy (lieutenant governor of Nova Scotia, 1947), Post, Ellyson, Kirkham, Chambers, Manly, Richardson, Robinson, Towers, Thomas, Hunsaker, Verville, Keys... with loyalty and steadfast friendship - and Henry Ford was his partisan supporter.

Augustus Post:..here was "*a boy who worked his way up from the making of bicycles to the making of history.*"

Captain Washington I. Chambers: "*I believe that the progress made by the United States Navy in developing aviation during its early and critical period is due to Mr. Curtiss more than to anyone else.*"

RAdm. John H. Towers, U.S.N., when Chief of the Bureau of Aeronautics, wrote: "*The story of Glenn Curtiss does not follow the usual pattern of that of the traditional American who 'made good.' What his boyish ideals may have been I never discovered, but I know they were not riches, position or power. He seemed always to be trying to find means of doing things in a better way and thereby helping his fellow-men. He was modest and diffident to a degree which was really embarrassing to those who did not know him well, yet behind it all was a cold courage and a determination which ever drove him on-ward, and enabled him to hurdle obstacles which would have stopped most others.*"

"Mr. Curtiss was a silent, almost taciturn man. Courteous and kind he always was, but conversation to him was a waste of time unless it was for a purpose of transmitting ideas ...(he) eschewed the use of tobacco and alcohol, but for reasons of health rather than re-ligious principles. He gave generously to churches of every denomination, and felt churches a required part of the communities he built...My father said of him, '*I never knew a more honorable man than Glenn, or a more moral man. If he had any religious convictions, he never spoke of them to me...despite his reticence on the matter - I think it must have been just a firm faith in honesty, decency and goodness.*'"

Frank FitzGerald-Bush

Jerome Hunsaker reminisced in <u>American Heritage</u>: "Glenn Curtiss was a very modest man. Some of his success perhaps came from his modesty, because people always wanted to help him. He wasn't quite sure what he ought to do, and people pitched in to help. I had a very pleasant experience whenever I went up to Curtiss's on my Naval inspection jobs. We'd never heard about payola then, and the danger of having a meal with a contractor. When I went to Hammondsport, I usually stayed in the spare guest-room of Curtiss's house, and Mrs. Curtiss looked after me. I had a very pleasant time, stretching my visit a little longer than necessary in the autumn because Curtiss loved to shoot pheasant. Curtiss liked a glass of wine; he liked to hunt pheasant with a good dog. Part of the reason he de-cided to retire to Florida and to experiment with farming was that he would have plenty of opportunity to shoot. He withdrew, again as a modest man, feeling he'd done about as much as he could in his art and feeling that the industry was getting beyond his compre-hension. He wasn't an engineer; he didn't understand what some of the improvements were. He didn't understand Wall Street and public participation in corporations. I think his withdrawal was a realization that he was no longer a leader in the art, and the time had come for him to step aside."

"It seems probable that no one ever had more co-operation in gathering material for a book than I have received from the family and former associates of Glenn Curtiss. He had the ability to inspire such loyalty and devotion in all who knew him, that, even so long after his death, they blazed with enthusiasm at the mention of his name and labored for days ransacking their files and searching their memories for every scrap of information which might help me to describe him more fully. This, I realize, was in order that I might do justice to a very great American..."   *Alden Hatch*

Tip Roseberry quotes from Curtiss papers: "...Glenn H. Curtiss was in reality one of the most prolific of inventors, with at least 500 inventions to his credit, any one of which may have been patentable. The main difference between him and most other inventors was that he knew little of patents and took no interest in them, until the Wright suit compelled him to learn something of patent law. He was wholly absorbed in his work and *'generous to a fault with his ideas as well as his purse.'* Even then, he patented only what he conceived to be his few most significant developments. He never made a move toward patenting any of the motorcycle innovations, obviously in a class by themselves.

"He permitted anyone who willed to use the principles used in the inventions he had made, and the aeronautical industry shall forever be in debt to him for his magnanimity. Scores of experimenters and struggling investors would, during the infancy of the art, have been prevented from securing any foothold whatever had Mr. Curtiss insisted upon enforcing his rights. His value was proved by the universality of adoption of his principles.

"The 'Big Five' of Curtiss inventions, the 'backbone' of the early aeronautical industry: 1. *The Curtiss airplane,* as such. 2. *The Curtiss motor.* 3. *The Curtiss control system.* 4. *The hydroplane,* including the amphibian. 5. *The flying boat.*

"The aileron itself, a joint development, was covered in the A.E.A. patent. Curtiss did obtain patents on the hydroplane, amphibian, and flying boat; on his shoulder-yoke control; and on the device for the training dual control. Among specific examples of consequential but unpatented Curtiss inventions, which he allowed to enter the public domain...sectional wings, which could be *'knocked down'* for compact stowage; interplane engine mounting; improved wing dope; and the high-pressure, forced-feed lubricating system, along with efficient crankcase drainage, making possible motors of large size and high-speed operation."

In 1912 Curtiss wrote Capt. Chambers concerning flying boat duplicators: "...*I am beginning to think...that the best plan is to let the patents go, and go after the business.*"

Grover Loening, in his memoirs, wrote that the Wright brothers: "...*turned the hand of almost every man in aviation against them...that Orville sued Curtiss for revenge and prestige...*"

A summary of Curtiss aircraft manufacturing during the years from 1920-on (much of which Curtiss was not directly involved with) shows: Between 1923 and 1936 the *Hawk* family of fighters was developed; one of the early 1924 *PW-8* models crossed the United States in 21 hours 48 minutes, capturing the world speed record and winning the *Schneider Trophy*. Using a descendant of Curtiss' famed *D-12* engine, the Curtiss *R3C* was the fastest of all. The *D-12* eventually developed into the *Conqueror* (and several Rolls Royce engines, including the *Merlin* of *Spitfire* and American P-51 *Mustang* fame) used in many fighters and bombers. In parallel with Army and Navy Hawk fighters, Curtiss built many versions of the *Falcon* two-seat observation aircraft, several after the 1929 merger which resulted in the giant Curtiss-Wright Corporation. In addition to *Condors, Helldivers, Falcons, Sparrowhawks, Shrikes, and Seagulls,* in 1935 Curtiss-Wright built the first monoplane Hawk 75. It went into production for the French and others, and as the *P-36* for the U.S. Army; later development included the *P-40 (which "held the line" in World War II until newer fighters were available, see below).* Other wartime aircraft were the *SB2C/A-25 Helldiver* and the *C-46 Commando (on 30Oct1945 the author hitched a ride "in General Beach's C-46 to Austin, TX").* Despite the development of the *SC-1 Seahawk,* several piston and piston/jet fighters, and the *XF-87* four-jet night fighter, Curtiss-Wright failed in post-war aircraft sales. In 1947 it closed its airplane division.

In 1998 Twayne/Simon & Schuster Macmillan published CURTISS-WRIGHT: Greatness and Decline, Louis R. Eltscher and Edward M. Young: a history of a very successful aircraft company and how it took itself out of the business. It spans the time period from 1945-1953.

It is an excellent book: thorough. scholarly and objective, concisely detailing the history of Curtiss, Wright, and Curtiss-Wright - which I highly commend it to anyone wanting a brief history of this great organization, which, unfortunately, fell upon poor management following WW2 and is today but a mere shadow of its former self.

"Curtiss-Wright did five billion dollars worth of business in WW2 and never recovered."

From its Introduction: *"The opinions expressed in this book are essentially those of the vital generation of men who created Curtiss-Wright industry and made it the war-winning weapon it was in World War II. They were unhappy about what happened to their company with its adequate funds in the postwar years.*

The Curtiss-Wright Corporation owed some of its troubles in WWII to its own success. In 1934 it had begun preparing for the coming of World War II and had a successful line of fighters which it was selling at home and abroad. With sales to the United States forces limited, the latter was especially important. However, the Neutrality Acts and the attitude of both the people and the government made it very difficult for American firms to get their equipment combat-tested. As a result, Curtiss fighters were not as up-to-date as their European counterparts..."

AVG Headquarters, 27Mar'42. First to fight: Claire Chennault's "Flying Tigers" American Volunteer Group, with 90 Curtiss P-40 "Flying Sharks" began supporting the Chinese against Japan months before December 7, 1941. The most successful of American fighters, they accounted for 296 enemy aircraft while losing but four pilots:

C-46 Curtiss Commando (previous photo): This largest of twin-engine transports (larger than a 4-engine B-17 Flying Fortress) became a legend flying the *"Hump"* from India into China in a WW2 operation in which over a thousand men and 600 aircraft were lost, *more* than in combat with the Japanese. (In 1940 its CW-20 prototype was flown by Boeing's *Eddie Allen* at the Curtiss-St. Louis Division. Allen, America's best test pilot, also tested Douglas' DC-1 in 1933. See <u>WALDO Pioneer Aviator</u>: pp. 335)

"Glenn Hammond Curtiss...whose name is almost as synonymous with aviation as that of the Wrights. Curtiss was one of the most spectacular pilots of his time, but more than that he was a motor and plane designer - a prize-winning demonstrator of his own equipment."
Harry Bruno

"When Orville Wright, in a letter to Curtiss dated July 20, 1908, fired the opening gun with a charge of patent infringement, Bell, greatly disturbed, was at pains to make clear that his suggestion regarding movable wing tips had been submitted without prior knowledge of the Wright invention. Technically almost anyone who built a workable aeroplane was guilty of infringement; for the Wright patent to a considerable degree covered the whole range of flying machines. But the Wright-Curtiss battle was particularly venomous and protracted. The case was not settled until January 1914, when the court ruled that wing warping and aileron action were essentially similar. Ironically the Wright system of control was to be abandoned within a decade; the Aerial Experiment Association's principle of the aileron, patented on December 5, 1911, came to be universally adopted."
Henry S. Villard (who the author knew)

"Comparing Curtiss with Wright, one might say that the Wright brothers, to whom belongs the credit for the fundamental developments that made flight possible, having made their contribution, then settled back in to take their ease and to enjoy the financial fruits of their initial accomplishment. Little or no advance in aeroplane design or construction came from them after 1910, and as a result the name of Curtiss became synonymous with progress in aviation in the United States from 1908 to 1919. It has often been said that the Wrights and Curtiss were the physicians responsible for the life of aviation in the United States. The brothers from Dayton brought the flying machine into the world, but it was Curtiss who doctored and cared for it through its infancy.

Curtiss' contributions to aviation were numerous. Anyone of them - flying boat, hydro-aeroplane, amphibian aeroplane, dual controls, tricycle landing gear - was important enough to land him in Aviation's Hall of Fame. But his most outstanding achievement was that of keeping American aviation alive - through his flights, aeroplane designs, and court actions - when the Wrights wanted to keep it for themselves. The history of the world could have been different, for instance, if Curtiss had decided to abandon his Wright patent fight and move his concern to Germany. This would have left the United States without a major aircraft-producing company at a time when it was needed most...

Perhaps nobody has done more for the progress of aviation than Glenn Hammond Curtiss."
Scharff and Taylor

In 1981, *Louis S. Casey*, former Curator of Aircraft at the Smithsonian's National Air and Space Museum, wrote:

"In the field of aeronautics no name is better known, or has had greater influence, than the name of Glenn H. Curtiss. The name brings visions of a pioneer, a giant industrial complex, an era of aviation and many other things to many people. Curtiss is all of these and second only to the Wright brothers in the annals of aviation.

Curtiss, the man and the company, moved with the vanguard of aviation. From the birth of the airplane at the turn of the century, to the mid-century, the Curtiss name was synonymous with aircraft of quality and quantity.

The record of the development of the Curtiss airplane is, in fact, a tracing of the evolution of the airplane as we know it. On Dec. 17, 1903 the Wright brothers, Orville and Wilbur, had succeeded in doing what man has dreamed of doing down through the centuries: they had successfully flown. More specifically, they had designed, constructed and flown the first heavier-than-air machine to carry a man in powered, controlled flight. Of related interest was the fact that they had patented the general configuration of this machine and, most important, their system of control.

From their eminent position the Wrights made it clear that if any flying was to be done, it would be done under license from them. The result was years of guerrilla warfare between the Wrights and other aircraft designers. This conflict continued until WW1, when military necessity demanded a solution to the multitude of legal skirmishes that were sapping the physical and financial resources of the embryonic aviation industry.

Many persons entered the legal arena with the Wright brothers, but none were as active and as ingenious in evading legal restrictions as Curtiss. The Wright's excessive licensing fees, said to be over $1000 per day (a dollar then over *45*-times-as-much today), stimulated Curtiss and others to evade the patent laws and continually search for ways to accomplish controlled flight without infringing upon the Wright patents. Throughout the early development of Curtiss aircraft there is ample evidence that Curtiss had one eye on the air and the other on the Wright patents."

16May1994: When preparing <u>PENDULUMII</u>'s preface, the author wrote the Secretary of the Smithsonian, President of the National Geographic Society, and Managing Editor of Time-Life Books, requesting their comment The following letter was received from Gilbert M. Grosvenor of the National Geographic Society (and Bell's great grandson):

GILBERT M. GROSVENOR
1145 SEVENTEENTH STREET, N. W.
WASHINGTON, D. C. 20036

July 7, 1994

Mr. G.J. Carpenter
Arsdalen, Bosch & Co.
22762 Tolana Drive
Laguna Niguel, CA 92677

Dear Mr. Carpenter:

I am responding to your letter concerning the role of Alexander Graham Bell in early aviation. Clearly Baddeck, Nova Scotia dominated his choice of location. He sought out brilliant young Canadians and Americans to work together in aerial experimentation. Have you ever visited the Bell Museum in Baddeck, Nova Scotia? I think not. The museum curator (Jack Stevens) has no knowledge of such a visit. To produce a book on Bell's aviation activities without studying the voluminous museum material is inexcusable. Original Bell material in Baddeck (along with volumes of handwritten notebooks) are crucial to understanding Bell's interests.

Your theory of the family trying "to deify our Canadian heritage" is also flawed if you haven't visited that environment. Do you realize Bell chose to be buried in Baddeck? Do you realize that almost <u>all</u> of Bell's post-telephone experiments (other than some summer aerial experiments in the United States) were undertaken in Canada? The family <u>donated</u> (no tax write-off!) all of Bell's memorabilia to Canada because the government built this museum devoted to Canadian inspired inventions. Further, you are ignoring 50 years of continuous research by two pioneering Canadians: Douglas McCurdy and Casey Baldwin. They played vital roles in aviation and marine propulsion. Indeed Bell himself has written that it was McCurdy and Baldwin who were the impetuous behind his early aviation work. The Silver Dart was purely Canadian: Douglas McCurdy designed, helped construct and flew it. Flights at HammondsPort are incidental; the first flight in the British empire in Baddeck is history. You choose to ignore the whole point of the <u>Silver Dart</u>.

Your bashing of the not-for-profit National Geographic Society did not escape me. You should know that the National Geographic Society has pumped more than $75,000,000 in the last six years into resurrecting geography education into the school systems of the United States. Indeed when you combine geography education, public service, scientific research, and exploration grants that are awarded to college professors you will find that in the last six years the National Geographic Society has contributed more than $125,000,000 (-- some three times the percentage of a Foundation's portfolio that must be spent to fulfill its core mission).

Your comment about the Grosvenor "largess" telephone money is amusing. To put this in perspective, when my Grandmother died (a Bell daughter) her total estate was less than 10 percent of what Michael Eisner made in <u>one</u> <u>year</u> as CEO of Disney. Bell had great skills, but financial management was not one of them. Money interested Alexander Graham Bell only to the extent that it allowed him to tinker with his endless inventions (the iron lung, x-ray, fiber optics, aviation, hydro-foils, experiments in aeronautical engineering with kites, propellers, etc.). Accumulation of AT&T stock never interested Bell. My grandparent's estate had a greater value in Eastman Kodak stock than in telephone stock!

For me to convince you that you really have not done your homework on Bell is fruitless for two basic reasons: one, unless you create "fresh new revealing information" you have no book; secondly, failure to visit the Bell Museum housing almost all of Bell's memorabilia flaws your effort.

Best regards,

Gilbert M Grosvenor

The author replied:

"12Jul94

Dear Mr. Grosvenor:

Your letter of 7Jul94 is reckless, presumptive, offensive and insulting. But I thank you for providing insight and confirmation of my concept of your mind-set.

I think it best to respond sequentially, much as I do in my writing, laying things out chronologically:

1. "*...he sought out brilliant young Canadians and Americans to work together ...*' This is almost a non sequitur. Curtiss and Selfridge were brilliant, but John or Jack (the names *he* preferred) McCurdy and Casey Baldwin, though solid performers, were not in their league. As I'm sure you are aware, McCurdy's principal contributions to aeronautics were either as a partner of or as an employee of Glenn Curtiss. Baldwin, though an able partner in the group's endeavors, contributed little in later years as he relished his affluent life in Baddeck.

2. '*Have you ever visited the Bell Museum...? I think not.*' Such as puzzling question and statement. Responding to Tony Doherty's letter of 8Oct92, I wrote Jack Stephens on 19Oct92 (copies enclosed), noting an earlier *un*answered letter while commenting about my earlier visit. I also sent him copy No. 198 of *Pendulum*, for which I also received *no* acknowledgment. I wonder what he advised you.

3. '*To produce a book...without studying the voluminous museum material is inexcusable...*' More to the point, Mr. Grosvenor, it is inexcusable to accuse one without knowing the facts. I *have* visited Baddeck. I *have* visited the Library of Congress, where I studied certain Bell materials, including *his* personal photograph collection. I *have* visited the Curtiss Museum - *and* the Smithsonian NASM. Anyone perusing my bibliographies will recognize extensive research (I will forward a copy of the in-process bibliography for *Bell & Curtiss* if desired). I have never felt it necessary to reinvent the wheel, to re-plow ground by using *only* original research. I feel the work of competent, objective authors one of the best foundations from which to build a new work.

4. '*...Bell chose to be buried in Baddeck?*' He also chose as his epitaph, carved on his tomb: '*...Citizen of the United States...*' Earlier, after gaining his prized American citizenship, he stated: '*I am not one of those hyphenated Americans who claim allegiance to two countries.*' I fear that the '*flaw*' exists in your comprehension of what Bell wanted. Your apparent desecration of his wishes is unfortunate and reprehensible.

5. '*...other than some summer aerial experiments in the United States...*' Such an inaccurate, biased statement! The greatest year in the early development of American aviation was 1908. It was also the year of greatest triumph to Bell and his partners, Curtiss, Selfridge, McCurdy and Baldwin. In January of that year Bell wires Curtiss (in Hammondsport NY): '*Start building. The boys will be down next week.*' By mid-March they have completed AEA Drome No. 1, Selfridge's *Red Wing*, and by mid-May were ready, with Bell present, to try out Drome No. 2, Baldwin's *White Wing*. Yes! It was (finally) summer when, on 21Jun'08, Drome No. 3, Curtiss' *June Bug*, was ready for flight. Its flight on the 4th of July, winning the Scientific American Trophy for the first time (he won it two more times for its permanent possession), was 'The First Official Flight in the

Werstern Hemisphere.' It was also the first publicly-observed flight in America. The AEA's experiments continued in Hammondsport (interrupted by Curtiss's work with Tom Baldwin and Selfridge's death while attempting flight with Orville Wright) until, on 6Dec'08 Drome No. 4, McCurdy's *Silver Dart*, an evolution from the *June Bug*, made its first flight - in Hammondsport. As I see it, virtually everything occurring that year (the only significant year for the AEA) took place, *not* solely in the summer, and *not ever* in Canada.

6. '*...the family donated (no tax write off!) all of Bell's memorabilia to Canada...*' Gosh! But I've always felt that there never was a philanthropist that couldn't afford to be one. However, knowing of Bell's love for the United States, *and* the fact that his home was in Washington DC (Baddeck was his summer place), wouldn't *he* have felt it more appropriate to have gifted these items to the Smithsonian or the Library of Congress?

7. '*...ignoring 50 years of continuous research...by two pioneering Canadians...McCurdy and...Baldwin...*' I believe facts speak otherwise. Most of McCurdy's work was either in partnership *with* or working *for* Glenn Curtiss, and most of Baldwin's limited successes were as Bell's understudy while living a somewhat indolent life in Baddeck.

8. '*The Silver Dart was purely Canadian...*' Balderdash! The only point I ignore is one of bias. The *Silver Dart* was a continuum. Its only Canadian significance was that it was flown there, establishing some sort of **British empire** record. You, as an American citizen (which I presume you to be) *should* celebrate what Bell and Curtiss and Selfridge and McCurdy and Baldwin accomplished on the 4th of July in Hammondsport, **USA!**

9. '*...bashing of the not-for-profit National Geographic Society...*' I have an MBA (Stanford) and can read a financial statement. Might you send me those summarizing the Society's finances for the past 6 years so that I can then determine how relevant '*$75,000,000*' is as a percentage of Society revenues? Also, might you provide me information as to what you and members of your family received in direct *and* indirect compensation during that same period?

10. '*...her total estate was less than 10 percent of what Michael Eisner* (or maybe Michael Milken?) *made in one year...*' Ridiculous! What Eisner made is obscene, certainly nothing for comparison except by ones envious of his excesses. As to what Elsie Bell Grosvenor left as an estate in 1963, it was in the millions (the '*10%*' would be over $20 million, something like $50 million today) - and this after leading a very comfortable, affluent life supported largely by Society revenues. Of course, during her life she probably gifted considerable sums to her offspring.

Incidentally, you may have noticed if you read *Pendulum* that I have routinely converted contemporary dollars to present-day figures in order to give the reader a better understanding. Apparently this is somewhat unique. I recently wrote Alan Greenspan about it. Donald Kohn, Director, Division of Monetary Affairs, Federal Reserve System, replied: '*...I certainly agree with your point...You basic approach...is correct...*' Hence, as you will note, the many references made in 'authorized' biographies of Bell (e.g: Robert Bruce's) have been amended so that there is reader comprehension of *all* money amounts, including such as how wealthy the Bell/Grosvenor clan/et al was - and probably still is.

Again, Mr. Grosvenor, thank you for providing me with so succinct an example of why I am writing *Bell & Curtiss*. As I noted in *Pendulum*'s preface, just as I was '*led to suspect problems with the Smithsonian Institution's National Air and Space Museum, and thus to carefully review inputs from it in my work*,' you have confirmed why I consider the National Geographic Society's story of Bell '*flawed*.' Would-be gunslingers shooting from the hip, as you have done, usually died young, shot between the eyes.

Possibly your reappraisal and quiet contemplation of these materials will lead to redress of your comments about me and my work while correcting and enhancing the memory of your great grandfather - and of his life as learned by our children. And I hope that you may see how important was the partnership of Alexander Graham Bell and Glenn Hammond Curtiss in the founding of the aviation industry of the United States of America.

Sincerely,

G.J. (Jack) Carpenter"

Note: The "Bell & Curtiss" mentioned became this PENDULUM2 manuscript.

The author studying Bell's personal photograph collection, Library of Congress, March, 1991:

446

Charles G. Grey, summarizing flight's early history: *"Although none of these things really flew they all showed trends in the right direction. And they show how ridiculous is the claim that the Wrights 'INVENTED the aeroplane.' The Wright type biplane with the small leading plane and a method of control which hardly anybody other than the Wrights could manage, killed most of its pilots and was obsolete...by 1912 when many other designs were flying strongly and developing fast. It was...simply a 'dead end' design ...In 1908 Cody and Roe had flown...in England; Bleriot, Farman, the Voisin Brothers and others...in France; the Wright Brothers were flying properly in the USA, and so was Glenn Curtiss, who as history shows, was the greatest of all American airmen, because his work developed so that it is still with us."*

*Bell and Curtiss were truly figures to restore one's
faith in the American dream and the measure
of what an individual can accomplish.
The greatness of a man is as his role
model is for those who follow.*

The End

APPENDIX

Though principally a 20th-century American story - one involving two of the great innovators of the 19th century: Bell and Edison – we should also give a bow other individuals and events tangential to this story.

As Charles Grey wrote in 1916: *"Giving full credit to Daedalus, Icarus. Leonardo daVinci, Sir George Cayley and his coachman, and the early gliding experiments of Lilienthal, Chanute, Pilcher and the others, we arrive at the fact that the first person to fly on a machine heavier than air and driven by its own power was Orville* (Wilbur!) *Wright."*

In 1804 English baronet *George Cayley* (1773-1857), to be known as *"The Father of Aerial Navigation,"* stated that a powered plane could use air resistance to support weight. In 1810 he built a glider; while in 1811 in Ulm (Einstein's birthplace) *Albrecht Berblinger* (1770-1829) flew his glider. Another Briton, *William S. Henson* (1812-1888), conceived an *"aerial steam carriage"* - and with triplane designer *James Stringfellow* (1799-1883) worked on steam-powered models, which Stringfellow then flew in 1848.

In 1890 Frenchman *Clement Ader* claimed flight in his *Eole*, driven by a 20-hp steam engine - the *first* aircraft to leave the ground under its own power – which crashed after an unwitnessed jump of 185 feet. In 1871 *Alphonse Penaud*, invented the rubber-band-powered model - and *Jean Marie Le Bris* and *Mouillard* were experimenting with large gliders after mid-century, about when *Felix Du Temple* flew his small powered model.

Power came from *Nicholas Otto*'s *"four stroke"* engine (1877), perfected by *Eugen Langen, Carl Benz, Gottlieb Daimler* and *Wilhem Maybach* (1893), with *Robert Bosch*'s low-tension magneto – first proven in 1896 on a *deDion-Bouton* engine (arguably the model for Curtiss' first engines).

Preston Watson of Blairgowrie, Scotland (another claimant for "*first flight*"), apparently used this popular engine in 1902 to power his novel aircraft – as also, it appears, did Denmark's J.C.H. Ellehammer for his jump of 12Sep1906 (preceding Santos-Dumont).

In 1883-84 Californian *John Montgomery* designed hang-gliders – and balloon-lofted tandem-winged manned gliders in the early 20th century. Though his contributions remain speculative, he is often called *"The Father of Gliding."*

Others, such as Briton *Percy Pilcher* (1867-1899) followed Lilienthal and the Chanute-Herring glider innovations.

Chanute's well-known work was largely based upon Englishman *Francis Herbert Wenham*'s 1866 patent of the biplane, the box-kite designs of Australian *Lawrence Hargrave* (1850-1915), and the airfoil determinations of Briton *Horatio Phillips* (1845-1924). Wenham also found a long, narrow (high aspect ratio) wing more efficient than a short, broad one – and in 1871 built the world's *first* wind tunnel. All added to later by the work of "*The Father of Aerodynamics*," German *Ludwig Prandtle* (1875-1953).

And Hargrave's opinion that *"a patentee is nothing but a legal robber"* is the basis for the Smithsonian *Paul Garber's* comment: *"It was his generous custom to give unrestricted publication to his work"* - an attitude dramatically changed by the Wrights and the advent of the 20th century.

The story of *Gustave Whitehead/Weisskopf* (1874-1927) is of interest. A student of Lilienthal before coming to America, from 1897 to 1901 he experimented with powered flight in Boston, New York, Baltimore, Johnstown, Pittsburgh and Bridgeport, CT.

By combining an evolution of Lilienthal's hang-gliders with contemporary technology in lightweight steam engines, he constructed an aircraft, similar to today's ultralights, but *lacking* 3-axis control (see photo, next) – and on *14Aug1901* reportedly flew his *"Model 21 Airship at Bridgeport."*

The claims for Whitehead, ridiculed by Orville Wright, arguably should be judged in the light of his time (when *Scientific American's* Frederick Beach gave him considerable support) and in the logic of what he actually did. Whether or not there are in-flight photographs shouldn't dissuade a reasonable conclusion that his work was sensible, substantial – and possible (nor for the earlier efforts of another German-American, *Jacob Brodbeck,* who, in 1865 in Fredericksburg, Texas, purportedly flew his sophisticated clock spring-powered "Airship" – or several others noted by the Library of Congress, below).

In 1976, long after the events of our story, then-U.S. Senator *Lowell P. Weicker, Jr.* of Connecticut prevailed upon the Smithsonian to divulge the 1948 *Agreement* between it and the Wright Estate. This interesting document may provide an insight of what transpired as to its being - and of its effect - upon Smithsonian attitudes as to Curtiss and the Wrights. It is the author's belief that it added to the biases of the Smithsonian and National Geographic's telling of America's early aviation history and of its pioneers. It follows.

FLIGHT BEFORE WRIGHT

1993 CALENDAR   THE LIBRARY OF CONGRESS

In 1993 the Library of Congress published its "FLIGHT BEFORE WRIGHT" calendar, *left,* Susan Sharp, editor: *"...History also shows that, alas, pivotal accomplishments are not always immediately recognized or appreciated. For the Wright brothers, it took more than four years – from late 1903 to early 1908 – for the world to become fully aware that they had achieved sustained mechanical flight. Thus Flight before Wright in a practical sense encompasses the continuing experimentation that took place through the years leading up to 1908..."* with an interesting assemblage of photographs and drawings, one reproduced next page:

January: *"R. J. Spaulding's Flying Machine, Patented March 5, 1889;"* February: *"Israel Ludlow's 'New Aeroplane,' July 15, 1905;"* March: *"Gustave Whitehead's Triplane, September 19, 1903;"* April: *"Henri Giffard Balloon Ascension, 1878;"* May: *"Otto Lilienthal (1848-1896) In His Plane No. 14, 1895;"* June: *"Wright Brothers' Glider, Wrecked by wind, 1900;"* July: *"G. Curtis Gillespie's Aeroplane, June 24, 1905;"* August: *"Frederick R. Merritt's Airship, Patented December 6, 1898,"* and *"Edwin Pynchon's 'Albatross,' Patented November 14, 1893;"* September: *"Plane No. 22 in which Gustave Whitehead made a circle above Long Island Sound, Jan. 17, 1902. Whitehead and daughter beside plane;"* October: *"'Aerostat,' October 8, 1883,"* and *"Zeppelin 'LZ-1,' July 2, 1900;"* November: *"Octave Chanute's Glider, c. 1896;"* December: *"A. H. Herring's Soaring Aeroplane, 1894."*

September, 1993: *"Plane No. 22 in which Gustave Whitehead made a circle above Long Island Sound, Jan. 17, 1902. Whitehead and daughter beside plane,"* next page:

A G R E E M E N T

THIS AGREEMENT made by and between HAROLD S. MILLER and HAROLD W. STEEPER as Executors of the Last Will and Testament of Orville Wright, deceased, hereinafter called the Vendors, Parties of the First Part, and THE UNITED STATES OF AMERICA, hereinafter called the Vendee, Party of the Second Part, W I T N E S S E T H:

WHEREAS there is included in the residuary estate of Orville Wright the Wright Aeroplane of 1903, invented and built by Wilbur and Orville Wright and flown by them at Kitty Hawk, North Carolina on December 17, 1903, and

WHEREAS it is in the public interest that said plane be preserved for all time and made available as a public exhibit in an appropriate place and under proper auspices, and

WHEREAS the Probate Court of Montgomery County, Ohio, having jurisdiction over the administration of said estate, after full hearing in a proceeding to which all persons and institutions having any interest under the will of Orville Wright were parties and had submitted themselves to the jurisdiction of the Court, has officially found that the known wishes of Orville Wright will be carried out and the highest and best interest of the estate will be served by recognizing the public interest and has accordingly authorized and directed the Vendors to enter into this Agreement,

NOW, THEREFORE, THIS AGREEMENT WITNESSETH:

1. For the consideration hereinafter set forth the Vendors agree to sell and do hereby sell to the United States of America, and agree to deliver to the United States National Museum, Washington, D.C., within the current fiscal year ending June 30, 1949, and subject to the terms of this Agreement, the original Wright Aeroplane of 1903.

2. In consideration thereof the Vendee agrees to pay to the Vendors the sum of One ($1.00) Dollar in cash and to comply with the following requirements: 451

"The first flight lasted only twelve seconds, a flight very modest compared with that of birds, but it was nevertheless the first in the history of the world in which a machine carrying a man had raised itself by its own power into the air in free flight, had sailed forward on a level course without reduction of speed, and had finally landed without being wrecked. The second and third flights were a little longer, and the fourth lasted 59 seconds covering a distance of 852 feet over the ground against a 20 mile wind."

Wilbur and Orville Wright
(From Century Magazine, Vol. 76, September 1908, p. 649.)

(d) Neither the Smithsonian Institution or its successors nor any museum or other agency, bureau or facilities, administered for the United States of America by the Smithsonian Institution or its successors, shall publish or permit to be displayed a statement or label in connection with or in respect of any aircraft model or design of earlier date than the Wright Aeroplane of 1903, claiming in effect that such aircraft was capable of carrying a man under its own power in controlled flight.

3. The title and right of possession to be transferred by the Vendors hereunder shall remain vested in the United States of America only so long as there shall be no deviation by the Vendee from the requirements in the foregoing paragraph, and only so long as neither the Estate of Orville Wright nor any person having an interest therein is required to pay and does bear without indemnity an estate or inheritance tax, assessed by the State of Ohio, the United States or any other taxing authority, based upon a valuation of property of the Estate which includes said aeroplane at a value in excess of One ($1.00) Dollar.

4. Upon the failure of the Vendee to remedy any deviation from the requirements set forth in paragraph 2, within twelve months after written specification thereof shall have been given to the Smithsonian Institution on behalf of the United States or upon (a) the final assessment of any state or federal inheritance, succession or estate tax whereby the Estate of Orville Wright or any person or persons having an interest therein shall be required to pay a higher tax by reason of a valuation of

452

(a) Said aeroplane is to be displayed as a public museum
exhibit in the Metropolitan Area of the United States
National Capital only, and except as hereinafter provided in paragraph (b) is to be housed directly facing
the Main Entrance in the fore part of the North Hall
of the Arts and Industries Building of the United States
National Museum. It shall never be removed from such
public exhibition except as may be required temporarily
for maintenance or protection.

(b) If the proper authorities of the Smithsonian Institution
or its successors (acting for the United States of America)
at any time in the future desire to remove said aeroplane
to any other building in the Metropolitan Area of the
national capital, such removal shall be permitted on the
following conditions:

1. That the substituted building shall have equal
   or better facilities for the protection, maintenance and exhibition of the aeroplane.

2. That the Wright Aeroplane of 1903 be given a
   place of special honor and not intermingled
   with other aeroplanes of later design.

3. That such building be not a military museum but
   be devoted to memorializing the development of
   aviation.

(c) There shall at all times be prominently displayed
said aeroplane a label in the following form and la.

The Original Wright Brothers' Aeroplane

The World's First Power-Driven Heavier-than-Air Machine

in Which Man Made Free, Controlled, and

Sustained Flight

Invented and Built by Wilbur and Orville Wright

Flown by Them at Kitty Hawk, North Carolina

December 17, 1903

By Original Scientific Research the Wright Brothers Discover

the Principles of Human Flight

As Inventors, Builders and Flyers They Further Developed the Aeroplane

Taught Man to Fly and Opened the Era of Aviation

Deposited by the Estate of Orville Wright.

453

said aeroplane for tax purposes in excess of One ($1.00) Dollar, and (b) the omission of the United States or others on behalf of the United States within twelve months of written notice of the final assessment by the person assessed to provide for the payment thereof by appropriations or otherwise, title to and right of possession of said aeroplane shall automatically revert to the Vendors, their successors and assigns.

5. In the event of a termination of title in the United States by reason of an omission on the part of the United States to provide for the payment a tax assessment as aforesai be United States shall have an option to repurchase the plane at any time within five years of the tax payment by reimbursing the taxpayer in the amount paid with interest thereon at six per cent from the date of payment. Upon the exercise of such option, this Agreement, in all of its terms, shall automatically again become of full force and effect.

WITNESS the due execution hereof in duplicate this ___23rd___ day of ___November,___ 1948.

Harold S. Miller (SEAL)

Harold S. Steeper (SEAL)
Executors of the Estate of
Orville Wright, deceased

UNITED STATES OF AMERICA

BY _A. Wetmore_
Secretary of the Smithsonian Institution

Highlights of the career of Glenn Curtiss:

He was one of the *first motorcycle manufacturers* in the United States.

He was the *world's motorcycle speed champion;* the *fastest man in the world.*

He manufactured *America's fastest motorcycles and best lightweight engines.*

He was *Bell's senior partner* in the Aerial Experiment Association.

He was the *first* person to *publicly* fly an aeroplane in the United States.

He was *first* person to win the *Scientific American Trophy* for a flight of a kilometer. He then won it for the next two years, and its *permanent* possession.

Curtiss and Bell *first used ailerons in America,* and an aircraft control system essentially unchanged today.

He was the *champion* at the world's *first* air meet.

He was awarded the *first* aviator's license in the United States, Europe's *second.*

He was a principal flyer at America's *first* international air meet.

A Curtiss aeroplane made the *first* takeoff from a ship.

A Curtiss aeroplane made the *first* landing and takeoff from a ship, using an arresting gear *("tailhook")* designed by Curtiss - basically the *same* as used by aircraft carriers today.

The *first U.S. Naval aviator* was trained by Curtiss.

Curtiss invented the *first practical seaplane,* and was the *first* person awarded the *Collier Trophy,* "America's most respected aviation award."

Curtiss *invented the flying boat,* and was awarded the *Collier Trophy* a *second* time.

Curtiss was *awarded* the Smithsonian Institution's *Langley Medal* (as were the Wright brothers and Charles Lindbergh).

Curtiss, assisted by *Henry Ford,* fought the Wright patent interests and *stopped the monopoly of American aviation.*

Wright aircraft, before falling into total disuse, *adopted* ailerons and Curtiss-type control systems.

Curtiss was the *second-largest (largest in America) aircraft manufacturer* in World War I.

Curtiss-built NC aircraft *first flew the Atlantic Ocean* to Europe.

Curtiss *Jennys* were America's favorite aircraft in the 1920's.

Curtiss co-developed three cities in Florida, home for 400,000 people today, and is regarded as *one of ten most important historical personages* in the development of Dade (Miami) County.

The Curtiss company merged with the Wright company to form the Curtiss-Wright Corporation, America's *second-largest* (after General Motors) WW2 defense Contractor.

"*Inventions of Curtiss:* (*patented)

*Aileron, *Hydroplane step, Tricycle Landing Gear, Hydroaeroplane, Amphibian Aeroplane, Flying Boat, Method of joining wood parts in aeroplane construction, Machine for forming laminated wood ribs, Laminated-wood propeller and forming machine, Aerodynamically balanced rudder, Enclosed cockpit for aeroplanes, Biplane elevator control system for dirigibles, Caster wheel chassis, aeroplane, Streamlined tank mounting, All steel propeller, Crankcase reduction gear for propeller drive, Steering landing gear, Combined skid and wheel landing gear, Wheel brake for aeroplanes, Electrically operated throttle control, Retractable landing gear (with Hugh Robinson), System of compression bracing for wings, Double-surface wings, Watertight double-surface wings, Interplane drift trussing for wing, *Hydroaeroplane pontoon, Pontoon frame construction, *Compartmented pontoon, Propeller-tip reinforcement, Submerged hydroplanes, *Longitudinally continuous pontoon, Friction throttle control, *Dual controls, Dual foot control, Control wheel, Control column, Aileron control, *Vent tubes to hydroplane step, Cable launching device, Wing beam construction, System of aeroplane anchorage, Folding hood, Automatic aileron control, *Automatic operation of all controls (with Sperry), V-bottom flying boat hull, Multiengine flying boat, Life preserver, Adjusting & locking mechanism for retractable landing gear, Detachable wings for aeroplane, Flexible tail skid, Aeroplane drag brake, Folding operating brace for control surfaces, Tank suspension for upper wing, Streamlined radiator, Streamlined landing gear, Wind tunnel, Unit engine section wing construction.

"This is a partial list of Curtiss' aircraft inventions. It does not include his numerous inventions for motors, motorcycles, automobiles, trailers (Aerocar hitch), speedboats, etc."   *Alden Hatch*

On 16July2001 Joe Bray wrote the following; see page 79: "Amos I. Root, an eccentric polymath...ran a bee-keeping supply manufacturing business in Medina, Ohio. In conjunction with his bee business, Root published Gleanings in Bee Culture, a periodical catering to the interests of beekeepers. In the Jan. 1, 1905 issue of Gleanings (pp.36-39), under Root's 'Our Homes' byline there appeared a wonderful detailed account of the Wrights' successful flights at Huffman Prairie, made in the fall of 1904. This description...which also includes the first account of a successful circular flight, is the first accurate printed description of the pioneering flights undertaken by the Wrights at Huffman Prairie near Dayton (and) was highly significant, as it was there that the Wrights mastered controlled flight and perfected the Wright Flyer. The earlier and more famous flight experiments near Kitty Hawk, North Carolina, which had culminated in the first powered sustained flight in an airplane, were undertaken in isolation and secrecy. Before Root's eyewitness account...the only published descriptions of Wright flights came through the wildly inaccurate coverage provided by a few newspapers. At least one authority has asserted that the Wrights fully intended for Root to be a spectator, as they knew him to be a trustworthy vehicle for recording their flights accurately and in an obscure publication not likely to encourage curiosity seekers. The Wrights were notoriously secretive about their flight experiments and were probably wary of their impending fame. That the Wrights trusted Root to print this historic eyewitness account speaks for the latter's integrity..."

Chronological Table:

	A. Graham Bell	Wright Bros.	Glenn H. Curtiss	Others
1832				**Chanute** *born, Paris*
1847	*Born, Edinburgh*			**Edison** *born, Ohio*
1863				**Ford** *born, Michigan*
1867		**Wilbur** *born, Indiana*		**Herring** *born, Georgia*
1870	*Emigrates to Canada*			
1871	*Moves to Boston*	**Orville** *born, Ohio*		
1874	*Tom **Watson** assist.*			
1875	*Perfects telephone*			
1876	Patents telephone			
1877	Marries Mabel			
1878	*NewEngElecTelCo*		**Curtiss** *born, NY*	
1881	*VoltaPrize/Lab.*			
1882	*U.S. Citizenship*		*Father dies*	
1885				Daimler-Maybach 2-wheel "Einspur"
1886				**Benz** *Motorwagen*
1887				**Bosch** *magneto*
1888	*NatGeoSocFounded*			
1889				**deDion-Bouton** *engine*
1891	**Langley** *friendship*	*Buys 'safety' bike*		
1892	*Patent vindication. Build Beinn Bhreagh in Baddeck, Canada*		*Works at **Eastman** Dry Plate and Film Co., Rochester NY*	
1893		*Wright Cycle Co.*		**Duryea's** *runabout*
1895			*Buys first bicycle*	
1896	Langley's models	*Chanute-Herring perfect glider, Indiana*	*Champion bike racer, Lower Lakes Region, N.Y.*	**Lilienthal** *killed;* Ford's 1st engine and "Quadricycle"
1898			*Marries **Lena***	Herring jumps?
1899	*Tetrahedral kites* **GHGrosvenor** *joins NatGeographicSoc.*	*Wilbur writes Smithsonian for aero. information*		*England's Percy **Pilcher** killed*
1900		*To Kitty Hawk*	*Opens bike shop*	
1901		*Glider No. 2; build wind tunnel*	*Expands bike business*	*Barney **Oldfield** races Ford's 4-vert.*

			Builds 1st motor-bike	cyl. "Arrow' and "999"
1902		*Glider No. 3*	*Stores in Bath and Corning; Sells 2nd motor-bike. Mfgrs. Hercules motorcycles; Races at Queens. Becomes an "automobilist"* **GHCurtiss Mfg. Co.** *formed*	**Whitehead** *flies?*
1903	*Langley "great aerodrome" failure,* **Manly** *pilot 17Oct, and 8Dec. Potomac D.C.*	*Build motor & Flyer No. 1; 14Dec Kitty Hawk NC: 1st trial Wilbur; 17Dec:* 2nd *trial Orville (photo of jump)* 3rd *trial, Wilbur.* 4th *trial, Orville.* 5th *trial,* **59 second FLIGHT! Wilbur.**		*FordMotorCo. formed.*
1904		*Flyer No. 2, Ohio. Improve flyer. 20Sep04, first circular (practical) flight*	*New Curtiss logo. Ormond Beach trials 7-year WorldRecord. Meets Tom* **Baldwin,** *California Arrow. Builds Wind Wagon*	New Ford logo
1905	*Becomes an "automobilist"*	*Make offers to Britain, USA and France. French contract. Flyer No. 3, Ohio.*	**G.H. Curtiss Manufacturing Co.** *incorporated.*	*Incorporation of Ford Mfg.Co., Ford controls 51%* **Montgomery** *glider flights inCalifornia;* **Maloney** *killed.*
1906	*Meets Curtiss. Langley dies.* *Orders 2nd Curtiss motor*	*European travel and negotiations; Offers to Britain, Germany; French forfeit. Associate with* **JPMorgan** *and* **Flint.**	*Meets Bell. Develops 18-hp V4. Tom Baldwin moves from SF to Hammondsport. Writes Wrights, no response. Meets Wrights at*	*Alberto* **Santos-Dumont** *flight, Paris (many believed `first to fly').*

1907	*Visits Hammondsport* **Aerial Experiment Association** *(AEA) formed: Bell, Curtiss,* **Tom Selfridge, Casey Baldwin** *and* **John McCurdy.**	*European travel; German/French/ English negotiations. Signal Corps issues Flying Machine Specifications.*	*Dayton Fair.* *With new 40-hp V8 races 136-mph at Florida Speed Carnival, Ormond Beach. Flies California Arrow Visits Baddeck Joins AEA.*	*Ford Model T* **Sequin** *rotary engine introduced.*
1908	*Makes several AEA visits to Hammondsport*	*Signal Corps contract. French contract. Return to Kitty Hawk.* *1st passenger flight. Wilbur to France. Orville writes Curtiss re patent infringement. Wilbur flies France. Orville flies in D.C. Orville crashes,* **Selfridge killed.** *Wilbur w/passenger.*	**AEA** *Hammondsport Glider;* **Selfridge-Wright** *letter and reply. Tom Baldwin Signal Corps contract.* **AEA** *Red Wing flies* **AEA** *White Wing flies* **Selfridge 1st US military pilot.** **Curtiss flies.** **AEA June Bug** *W/40 hp ac V8. Wins 1/3* **Scientific American Trophy.** *Herring to Hammondsport. Baldwin-Curtiss demonstrate SC-1airship.* **AEA** *Silver Dart flies.*	*Ford Model T on sale* **Farman** *flies in France* **Christmas** *flies USA Farman flies USA Herring Signal Corps failure.*
1909	*AEA disbands.* **McCurdy/Silver** *Dart fly in Canada. Canadian Aero Co. Discussions w/Curtiss re Wright suits.*	*Wilbur flies at Pau Sue Herring-Curtiss & Curtiss. Orville flies Ft Myer, sell Miss Columbia. Orville to Berlin. Wilbur flies NY. Wright Co. formed.*	*19Mar* **Herring-Curtiss Aeroplane Co.** *formed (Apr1910 bankrupt; dissolved 1926) Aero Society plane: 1st airplane sale in America. Marvel Motor CycleCo Wins 2/3 SATrophy. Reims Meet, Curtiss wins* **Gordon**	**Bleriot** *flies English Channel.* **Selden**/*ALAM suits*

			Bennett International Cup	
1910		Enforce license, Herring-Curtiss injunction. Charles Rolls killed. Belmont Meet.	Dominguez Meet H-C bankruptcy Albany-NY flight. Blanche **Scott** flies Sep: **TheCurtiss ExhibitionCo.** formed. Ely 1st ship flight San Diego Aviation Camp 3Dec: **CurtissAeroplane Co.** formed 19Dec: **Curtiss Motor Co.** formed	**Paulhan** injunction **Rolls** flies Channel. **Lougheed** opinion. **Chanute** dies.
1911		Wilbur in England, Germany, France, Russia, Italy, Austria, Belgium, Spain & Hungary. **Collier** buys plane Wrights exit exhibition flying - five of nine team killed: **Johnstone, Hoxsey, Welsh, Gill** and **Parmalee.**	PasadenaRose Parade. Ely ship landing. **Perfects seaplane. Invents amphibian.** EllysonNavalAvatr1. Wins 3/3 SATrophy. **Navy Orders A-1 (birthday of U.S. Naval aviation). Curtiss License #1. Curtiss Exhibition Co.** 19Dec**Curtiss Motor Co.**(controlled Curtiss Aeroplane Co. and Curtiss Exhibition Co.) Collier Trophy.	Ford beats Selden. McCurdy flies to Havana. **Beachey** flies. **Rodgers** Vin Fiz transcontinental Wright flight.
1912		Curtiss litigation Dayton-Wright Co. Wilbur dies. **Herbster**-Waldo **Waterman** crash Hap **Arnold** crash Rodgers killed.	Wright litigation. **Invents flying boat. Chambers** catapult. Collier Trophy.	
1913	Assists Curtiss in Wright litigation.	British Wright Co. **Billingsley** killed. Collier Trophy	Langley Medal. Ford-Curtiss talks. Beachey Lil Looper.	**Sperry** Gyro Compass. **McCormick** plane.

		Orville's "How We Made The First Flight" crediting himself for "first flight," Flying		
1914	*Litigation planning*	*Curtiss litigation* **Post** *killed.* **8 of 14** *new Wright pilots killed at San Diego/NorthIsland. Wrights' injunction. Orville's "How I learned To Fly," Boys' Life.*	*Wright litigation Langley aerodrome testing controversy.* **Thomas** *designs JN* **"Jenny."** Wanamaker-Porte *"America."* Britain orders JN Jennies & flying boats.	**Loening** *"Reign of Death" report.* Ford assists Curtiss Collier Trophy for Sperry
1915	*Assists Curtiss in litigation. Trans-continental telephone service.*	*Litigate & license. Orville sells out. Patent settlement.* **Last Wright plane.**	*Litigation. Buffalo Factory* **CurtissAeroplane& MotorCoLtdCanada** McCurdy runs Toronto School. Model K flying-boat worldwide sales. Patent settlement	*Ford assists Curtiss Beachey killed.*
1916		*Wright-Martin Co. formed.*	**Kirkham** *K-12 engine* *13Jan:* **Curtiss Aeroplane & Motor Co. formed.**	
1917			*Largest US manufactr.*	
1918		*Orville last flight*	**Curtiss Engrng Co.** K12 becomes 18T.	
1919	*Hydofoil boat*		**NC-4 Atlantic Flight.**	
1920s	*1922: Bell dies 1923: Mabel dies*	*1928: 1903 Flyer to England 1929: Orville's revealing article on Wilbur in Encyclopedia Britannica. Curtiss-Wright Corp.*	Model 18T evolves to C-12 engine; which in 1922 Arthur Nutt evolves to the D-12 Conqueror, winner of the **Schneider** Trophy. Florida developer. **Curtiss-Wright Corp.**	1926: Herring dies **Lindbergh** Paris 27

1930-on	1994: Gilbert Grosvenor's letter to Jack Carpenter reveals for the first time the incorrect story told by the Grosvenors/National Geographic of Bell, Curtiss and the AEA.	1943: Orville's "Our life in Camp," <u>US Air Services</u> (the story of first flight <u>not</u> included). 1948: Orville dies 1948: 1903 Flyer return to USA. 1949: Wright papers to Library of Congress. 1953: <u>The Papers of Wilbur and Orville Wright</u> published by LOC (the full story is now known)	1930: Curtiss dies	1947: Ford dies

North American P-51B *"Mustang"* by Dan Witkoff

Of interest: In 1939, Britain, desperately in need of fighter planes and unable to await new designs, decided that the Curtiss P-40 was the best then available. However, Curtiss, at full capacity and unable to accept new orders, recommended they contact their affiliate company: North American Aviation (NAA), James H. *"Dutch"* Kindelberger, president. (Note: *"The culmination of Keys activities during the year* (1928) *was the formation of North American Aviation, Inc. North American evolved into a holding company and management vehicle through which Keys could invest funds and coordinate the activities of his rapidly diversifying group..."* Eltscher & Young.)

Kindelberger advised them that it'd take four months - and when OK'd by the British, Lee Atwood, NAA's vice-president, obtained the Curtiss XP-46 (Curtiss built two prototypes 1940-41) design and wind tunnel data, inter-company purchased for $56,000.

Edgar Schmued was then charged with refining the XP-46's design, assisted, principally, by Ed Horkey, Raymond Rice, Larry Waite and Art Chester - and after 102 days and 78,000 man-hours - the prototype, NA-73X, sans engine, was rolled out.

Its Allison V-1710-39 engine was installed 18 days later, and on 26 October 1940, Vance Breese (an old friend of Waldo Waterman's...who also knew Kindelberger well) took NX19998 up for its first flight test.

On 9Dec 1940 the British advised NAA that the NA-73 had been given the official designation: *"Mustang."*

Americans designated it the P-51.

As the war progressed - *and both greater range and higher altitude became a necessity* - the (13-1400 hp) Rolls-Royce/Packard V-1650 *"Merlin"* - which had *"descended from the Curtiss D-12,"* was chosen as the *Mustang* P-51D's final engine selection, as noted below:

In 1918 *Arthur Nutt,* Curtiss' brilliant engine designer, improved upon *Charles Kirkham*'s innovative K-12 of 1916, creating the 400-hp D-12/V-1150 c.i. (see pp. 414) which was first used in 1922.

In 1924, the British purchased this D-12 engine *"for their high performance development,"* which, by further refinement led to Rolls-Royce's *Falcon* and finally, in the mid-thirties, to the 1650 c.i. PV.12 *Merlin* of approximately 12-1300-hp (its horsepower would raise, dramatically, to 1,760-hp, during WW2 when used on the *Spitfire* - and to as much as 3,600-hp for a *full-race* model today)...

Noting this may be challenged (even by Jane's), its source is Briton *Charles Grey* (1875-1953. Founder and editor, *The Aeroplane*, 1911-1939; editor, *Jane's All The World's Aircraft*, 1916-1941), arguably the world's most knowledgeable person on flight's early days, who, in 1953, shortly before his death wrote:

"Strange thing isn't it that the U.S.A. has never recognized Glenn Curtiss as by far the greatest man America has ever produced in Aviation? ...And the D-12 engines, from which the Rolls Falcon*, & ultimately the* Merlin *are descended...So far as I know there is nobody in the World who has claim to have influenced aircraft design & production as he did, or had done..."*

...while Curtiss improved its D-12 to over 500-hp - and in 1928 to its famed 600-hp *"Conqueror"* V-1570 c.i. The D-12 powered many winners of Pulitzer and Schneider Trophy races in the mid-twenties...and in 1930, the Germans, their engines lacking, used twelve *Conquerors* to power their huge Do-X flying boat.

And much as with Rolls' experience, the *Conqueror*'s power was raised to 675-hp - and by the mid-thirties was superceded by more powerful designs.

As such, both the *Mustang*'s design roots, airframe *and* engine, were Curtiss.

AIRCRAFT June, 1910, next two pages, (see 30Jan'10):

horizontal surface in the rear; and as, when tilted, horizontal surfaces develop vertical resistances, the assertion that a "tail" exercises a certain effect, as regards lateral balance, seems a fairly plausible one.

The Wright brothers, however, would probably meet any such flank movement on their positions with the statement that they adapted a tail to the machine they sold to the Army recently and saw no reason to modify their manœuvres to obtain lateral control, in consequence of the change.

Whether the Wrights themselves realize just what the forces are which they have to contend with when changing the equilibrium or course of their flyer, was another point brought up, although its relevancy was not very clear.

It is to be hoped a decision in the matter will not be deemed necessary: aeronautical experts are agreed on the broad lines of the question, but their testimony on the finer points raised would be liable to differ as much as that of their confrères in handwriting; the debate over tilt, drift, and side-slip, center of pressure, inertia, and centrifugal force would wax heated indeed and the difficulty of deducting absolute facts from a maze of learned hypotheses would be the only obvious point in the controversy.

When all is said and done it would seem as if the views of Wilbur and Orville Wright were at present being sustained; Curtiss and Paulhan have obtained rehearings, however, and the fight will, no doubt, continue from Court to Court for many months to come.

Whether the Wrights will ultimately gain their point, it is at this time hard to say, but if it is for a moment admitted that they will do so, there is still room for ample discussion on what might variously be called the social, moral, and sentimental aspect of the case: whether their attitude and action would not retard the progress of their country in the new art, and, if so, whether they would be justified in bringing about such a state of affairs.

This side of the question is just as open to debate as its legal aspects—which is saying anything but little—but it would be beyond the scope of an article which merely aims at opposing, in the simplest manner compatible with the complexity of the questions at issue, the claims made on either side in what promises to be as "Célèbre" a "Cause" in the annals of Aeronautics, as the Bell and Selden lawsuits were in those of two other of the greatest inventions of modern times.

THE WRIGHTS' CONTENTIONS GROUNDLESS

By Louis Paulhan

IT is naturally with a good deal of surprise and annoyance that I learned on setting foot on American soil, that efforts would be made by the Wright Brothers to prevent me from flying on the ground that my machines were an infringement of theirs.

I had removed the usual devices for warping the wings which form part of the Blériot XI of the standard type before taking possession of my Blériots at Pau last December. I have never flown in an aeroplane with warping wings and prefer machines in which lateral control is otherwise secured.

The Blériots I have cannot, therefore, be in question at all. As to the Farmans, I cannot for the life of me see how they can be considered infringements of the Wright Brothers' patent of 1906. In the Wright aeroplane, when one side is warped down to reëstablish equilibrium, the brake effect is so pronounced on that side that the rear rudder has to be used to prevent the machine turning around the warped side. Why they should think aeroplanes using "ailerons" or flaps, such as mine, should do the same thing, I don't know. When I pull down an aileron to secure a lift on that side I obtain the lift and *no retarding effect* is produced to warrant my using my rear rudder.

I never use this rudder for this purpose in straightaway flight, never having occasion to do so.

One of my counsel holds that the reason this occasion never arises is that as the ailerons fly normally perfectly freely in the line of the wind, their lifting effect commences directly they are made to make any angle with it, and a very small angle is all that is needed to secure a lift; in the small angles the lifting effect is immensely greater than the brake effect, the latter being wholly negligible in fact.

If the ailerons were normally at an angle of several degrees and no lifting effect was available until they had been further lowered, the brake or retarding effect would be very noticeable indeed, for its proportion to the lifting power would be much greater and I might have to use my rudder just as the Wrights use theirs.

This may well be the scientific explanation, but whatever it is, I do not use my rudder in conjunction with my ailerons to reëstablish my equilibrium, when for any reason it is affected in straightaway flight.

Neither is there necessity in the Farman for the simultaneous use of these controls in turning.

I can make quite wide turns by lifting up one side through the use of the aileron, and once the turn is started, letting the aileron go, but I usually make turns through the use of the rear rudder alone, like a ship does, and it is only if I want to make a very sharp turn that I may make use of an aileron as well as the rudder, the aileron being used to secure a greater tilt.

What I *do* consider necessary, however, is to lower the forward horizontal rudder or stabilisator when about to make a turn. I invariably do this and make the turn as the biplane dips.

That is one reason it is a good idea to fly high; another is that the air-currents are much more steady than on the surface, as the natural or artificial asperities of the earth's surface cause the sudden and dangerous gusts and whirlpools in the air.

I am glad that I am being given a further opportunity of showing America what can be done in the line of flying with high-class aeroplanes and aeronautic motors.

The machine I have is built by Henry Farman, whose competency in aviation matters is certainly equal to that of any man living. If anything is disposed in a certain way on the machine it is for some special purpose; the special disposition of the ailerons and their being allowed to fly behind like flags when not in use, is no exception to this rule.

The motor is one of the famous Gnôme revolving motors designed by the Brothers Seguin; in the nine or ten months I have been flying I have never used any other on my biplanes.

The impressions I have had of my American trip have naturally been affected by the efforts made to stop my flights, but I still hope that ere I return to France the removal of these restrictions will have enabled me to leave with a pleasant impression of my journey across the Atlantic.

LETTERS FROM SIR HIRAM MAXIM, BLERIOT AND ESNAULT-PELTERIE

E recently wrote to Sir Hiram S. Maxim, the famous inventor, to M. Louis Blériot, the well-known French aviator and builder of monoplanes, (which were recently declared to be infringements of the Wright patent) and to Mr. Robert Esnault-Pelterie, President of the Syndicate of the aeronautical constructors of France, for their points of view on the Wright question, and have received in reply the following letters:

SIR HIRAM MAXIM'S LETTER

Dear Sir:

I have read with a great deal of interest the correspondence and editorials which have appeared in AIRCRAFT relating to the Wright patents in America.

To make the front edge of an aeroplane rigid and the rear edge thin and flexible and to keep the machine on an even keel, by flexing the thin edge, is certainly not new.

Lord Kelvin took a keen interest in my work at Baldwyn's Park: he visited my place on many occasions and brought some very distinguished scientists with him. He spoke very highly of my work but he had his own ideas and in time these ideas may be proved to be right. He thought it would be possible to make a machine in which the aeroplanes, although very large, could still be revolved at a low speed, the machine moving forward through the air the same as at present. I thought the matter over and it appeared to me to be quite plausible and I ultimately applied for a patent on a flying machine having eight aeroplanes mounted on two shafts. These were to be placed at a very low angle, to rotate slowly to get their lifting effect principally from being driven forward onto undisturbed air.

The machine took the form of both a helicopter and an aeroplane. This patent is referred to in my book "Artificial and Natural Flight." It can be seen that it is claimed as an aeroplane as well as a helicopter and the flexing of the outer and rear edge of the aeroplanes is certainly shown and described and is used for keeping the machine on an even keel. In fact the flexing aeroplanes represent the pith of the whole patent.

The law relating to patents is not by any means a fixed quantity. There are many factors in the equation and the strongest factor in the Wrights' favor, in the United States, is, without doubt, the factor of patriotic bias.

Everyone who has anything to do in the decision will naturally have a strong bias; they will even strain a point to give the credit of the invention of a flying machine to an American: I have no doubt, however, that a determined effort on the part of American aviators, if supported by money, would be quite able to greatly curtail the preposterous claims made by the Wrights.

I was present at the Rheims meet last year and I noted what people had to say; it generally amounted to this: "The Wright machine has had its day; it is now a back number." Whether this be true or not the Wrights are certainly entitled to very great credit for the part they have played in the history of aviation.

With the money that they have at their disposal they may be quite able to greatly retard the progress of aviation in the United States, but in Europe I do not anticipate that they will be able to give aviators any trouble whatsoever unless these aviators use the *specific* device of the Wrights, as described in their patent.

Yours sincerely,

Hiram S. Maxim

BLERIOT'S LETTER

Dear Sir:

Concerning the Wright patents my opinion is that the warping of the wings, taken in itself, is public property, and I think this can easily be shown: the vertical rudder is itself public property and it is only the combining of these two effects—balancing and steering—in a single lever of control which can with some show of reason be claimed by the Wright brothers.

I have personal reason to regret that they did not confine their claim to this single lever, for it is an interesting improvement and one concerning which we could have established with the Wrights an understanding, which would have been of profit to all aviators.

In all my present French machines the warping of the monoplane surface is brought about by the left hand, while the steering is dependent on foot control. These two effects are completely independent and in no way necessarily corrective, as called for in the Wright patents; on the contrary experience shows that the major part of the time their effects should be added one to the other instead of corrective of each other. This independence of control necessitates a somewhat more delicate and longer apprenticeship, but one which the present uncompromising attitude of the Wrights forces me to maintain.

I have gone further; in view of their threats I have tried to completely do away with warping, using only for balancing purposes a somewhat larger vertical keel. The result was entirely satisfactory; I was in this manner able to fly without warping, in winds as strong as those faced by the Wrights.

I delivered to Paulhan two such machines for his American trip and, in his trials at Pau, prior to leaving France, he flew perfectly without any warping device. He made as sharp turns as previously and merely had to use a greater tilt, when doing so.

To sum up, this question of warping, about which so much fuss has been made, and which seemed to be a *sine quâ non* condition of lateral equilibrium, proves to be of far less importance than this. If warping renders signal service in keelless machines of wide wing area, such as the Wright machines, it becomes a far less necessary improvement in machines of small breadth of wing, provided with keels, and is entirely needless in machines with vertical partitions, such as the Voisin biplanes.

As aeroplanes will tend more and more toward increasing speed and diminution of breadth of wing, the question of warping will more and more lose its importance.

I merely wish to say that it was regrettable to see at the dawn of a science, (to encourage which all should have united in their efforts) inventors make the unjustifiable claim of monopolizing an idea, and, instead of bringing their help to their collaborators, prevent them, for no reason, from profiting by some ideas which they should have been happy to see generalized.

ESNAULT-PELTERIE'S LETTER

Dear Sirs:

I duly received your letter of the 18th inst., and sincerely thank you for the impartiality which you are good enough to show in the question of the Wright patent.

I can only repeat what I have already said, that I consider the judgment rendered against Paulhan unjustified. As regards the practical result of the action of the Wright brothers, it has been that we have joined together on the continent and taken measures to eventually have justice rendered to us in our country. We will also try to reach this result in America. It is true that the precedent of the Selden affair is unfortunate and tends to make one doubtful of success, but we are decided that, if we do not succeed on judicial territory, we will take up the conflict on other lines.

I remain, yours very truly,

When writing to advertisers, please mention AERO, the first weekly.

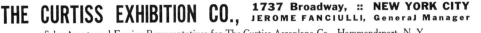

The Curtiss Three-Passenger ORIOLE

Aerial Carriers de Luxe

Air travel at from 75 to 100 miles per hour is now luxurious, safe and efficient.

These machines will be included in Curtiss Exhibits at the Chicago Aeronautical Show, January 8th to 15th, and at the New York Aeronautical Show, Seventy-first Regiment Armory, March 6th to 13th.

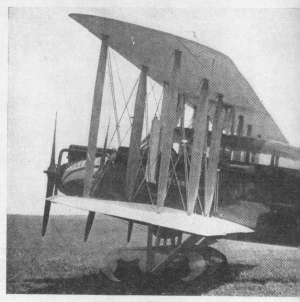

The Curtiss Eight-Passenger

The Curtiss Aeropl

Sales Office, Room 1456, 52

Factories—Garden City, L. I.; Buffalo, N. Y., and M.
—Garden City; Atlantic City, N. J.; Newport News, Va
all parts of the United States. Special Representatives in

The Curtiss Three-Passenger SEAGULL—Flying Boat

—An Aerial Superlimousine

Motor Corporation

ilt Avenue, New York City

ss. Flying Fields, Training Schools, and Service Stations
.; Buffalo and Marblehead. Dealers and distributors in
a, the Philippines and the Far East.

The Science back of the NC-4

The Science back of the NC-4, first to cross the Atlantic, and the Curtiss Wasp, altitude r e c o r d maker, has been applied to these new passenger a n d merchandise aeroplanes by the organization which has long been the dominating center of aeronautical activity in America.

Member Manufacturers'
Aircraft Association

160

OFFICIAL SOUVENIR BOOK & DAILY PROGRAM, *Glenn H. Curtiss Aviation Meets,
April 1911 (author's collection):*

The first public flight in America, Glenn Curtiss in the "June Bug"—and at the wheel.

THE STORY OF THE AEROPLANE

SO successful and so unlooked-for has been the realization of man's desire to fly that it seems impossible that thinkers the world over have for centuries worked on the problem of mechanical flight. Punctuated with achievements of importance and scarred with many fatalities, the progress of aerial flight has been slow. The exciting story of aviation shows that the aeroplane is a product of centuries of devotion to experimentation and study and is not an invention in any sense of the word.

Beginning with the story of Icarus, who, according to Greek mythology, flew in a pigeon with wings of wax until the sun melted them and he fell into the Icarian sea, we have interesting accounts of man's ambition to emulate the birds.

It is said of two English inventors in 1810 that they contrived a machine with which they succeeded in making a number of gliding flights from hills in calm weather, but they were ridiculed and discredited, and their work

is almost forgotten. Similar experiments were conducted nearly twenty years ago by Otto Lillienthal, a German, who might be called the pioneer of the present day school of aviation, since it is from his work that scientists have gained much of their practical knowledge of the principles of flight. Lillienthal made upwards of one thousand glides, only to fall and break his neck after he had developed the principle of the curved wing surface and had planned a double surface machine, or biplane.

A little later, Prof. Samuel P. Langley, of the Smithsonian Institution, was busily engaged in developing his tandem plane machine for the government after having delved deeper into the science of mechanical flight than any of his predecessors. Large-sized models built by Prof. Langley, one driven by steam and another by gasoline, made remarkable flights over the Potomac, but an unfortunate accident to his launching device put an end to his experiments by wrecking his man-carrying machine at the start of what was to have been its

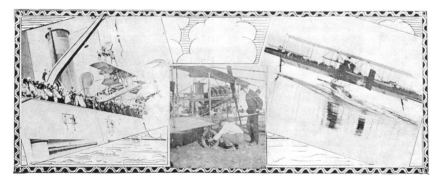

Hoisting Curtiss in his Hydroaeroplane aboard U. S. S. Pennsylvania, San Diego, Cal.—Curtiss and Robinson inspecting machine—Curtiss speeding up Hydroaeroplane for flight.

2

initial flight. Discouraged by public ridicule, Langley gave up his work.

Sir Hiram Maxim, also in the last decade of the nineteenth century, carried on a series of experiments somewhat similar to Langley's, and built a gigantic machine which was propelled by two immense, steam-driven propellers. This aeroplane, which developed a lifting power of more than two tons, was wrecked in a preliminary test. The builder has since declared, however, that had his aeroplane proved otherwise successful, it would not have been capable of flights of more than three minutes' duration because the water capacity of his boiler was limited.

Octave Chanute, the late Chicago engineer who has often been called "Father of Aviation," because of the valuable experiments conducted under his direction, had long been a student of the problem, and developed several new principles, most important of which was probably the bridge trussed system of building the biplane of to-day. With Mouillard he developed a method of balance by means of warping wings and then, considering himself too old to go on with the work himself, freely lent his assistance to younger men who had taken up the problem.

Called upon by the Wright Brothers for assistance, Chanute became their chief advisor. They took up his two-plane glider, which they developed into their present aeroplane, putting power into the machine only after conducting a long series of gliding flights during which they took and developed the principle of wing warping for balance.

While these experiments were being conducted, Glenn H. Curtiss was busily engaged in building motors for dirigible balloons. It was this development of light motors which brought the young motorcycle manufacturer into the field of aviation.

Dr. Alexander Graham Bell, who as a friend of Prof. Langley had become interested in the subject and was then working on the tetrahedral principle of construction, invited Curtiss to become a member of the Aerial Experiment Association, which made him director of experiments. From the first the association tried out on its aeroplanes the principle of the movable wing tip for maintaining lateral stability, and successful flights were accomplished immediately.

When the association disbanded at the expiration of the time limit for which it was organized, Curtiss took this system and developed the aileron system of keeping equilibrium which is used on all his machines. From the time he made the first public flight ever made before Aero Club officials on July 4, 1908, aviation developed rapidly. European designers followed closely on the heels of the Americans, and when Curtiss finally consented to enter the international races at Rheims in 1909, it was to face a field of a score of machines, the flyers of which were already famous.

Government encouragement abroad, together with Congressional apathy in America, for a time threatened to wrest the leadership in aviation from this continent, but it has remained for Curtiss, the American, to take the world leadership in nearly every step that has been made toward making the flying machine commercially practical.

The aeroplane has come upon us suddenly after all the years of striving for it. Now that it is here, it is being put to new uses almost every day.

Ely leaving U. S. S. Pennsylvania, San Francisco, Cal.—Ely at the wheel—Ely in flight—Ely and McCurdy "talking it over"—McCurdy and Indian Princess starting flight.

3

Flying Machine Patent, 5Dec1911:

FORTUNE, April, 1930:

Four Major Aviation Groups

AVIATION CORP.
Air Line Subsidiaries controlled through newly formed American Airways, Inc. (Partial list):

COLONIAL AIRWAYS CORP.—(Colonial Air Transport, New York-Boston; Colonial Western Airways, Albany-Cleveland, Buffalo-Toronto; Canadian Colonial Airways, New York-Montreal; Colonial Flying Service)

CUBAN AVIATION CORP.—(Servicio Cubano de Aviacion)

EMBRY-RIDDLE AVIATION CORP.—(Embry-Riddle Co., Chicago-Cincinnati)

INTERSTATE AIRLINES—(Chicago-Atlanta, St. Louis-Evansville)

SOUTHERN AIR TRANSPORT—(Gulf Air Lines, Atlanta-New Orleans-Houston; Texas Air Transport, Dallas-Galveston and Dallas-Brownsville; T.A.T. Flying Service, Dallas-El Paso, Dallas-Brownsville, and Dallas-Houston; T.A.T. Flying Schools; Southern Aeromotive Service; Dixie Motor Coach Corp.)

UNIVERSAL AVIATION CORP.—(Robertson Aircraft Corp., Chicago-St. Louis and St. Louis-Kansas City-Omaha; Continental Air Lines, Cleveland-Louisville; Northern Air Lines, Cleveland-Chicago-Kansas City-Garden City; Braniff Air Lines, Tulsa-Oklahoma City-Dallas; Central Airlines Co., Kansas City-Wichita and Wichita-Tulsa; Robertson Flying Services; Mid-Plane Sales & Transit Co.; Egyptian Airways Co.)

· · ·

FAIRCHILD AVIATION CORP.—(Fairchild Airplane Mfg. Corp.; Kreider-Reisner Aircraft Co.; Fairchild Aerial Camera Corp.; Fairchild Aerial Survey; Fairchild Aircraft; Fairchild Engine Corp.)

AVIATION SHARES CORP.—(Aviation Patent & Research Corp.; New York Aviation Corp.)

ROOSEVELT FIELD, Inc.

CURTISS-WRIGHT CORP.
Subsidiaries (partial list):

CURTISS AEROPLANE & MOTOR CO.	CURTISS-WRIGHT FLYING SERVICE
CURTISS AEROPLANE EXPORT CORP.	CURTISS-CAPRONI CORP.
CURTISS-ROBERTSON AIRPLANE MFG. CO.	REEP PROPELLER COMPANY
CURTISS AIRPORTS CORP.	KEYSTONE-LOENING
WRIGHT AERONAUTICAL CORP.	AERONAUTICAL CORP.
MOTH AIRCRAFT CORP.	NEW YORK AIR TERMINALS
TRAVEL AIR CO.	NEW YORK and SUBURBAN AIRLINES

Affiliates:

CURTISS REID AIRCRAFT CO.	AVIATION CREDIT CORPORATION
CURTISS ASSETS CORP.	
AVIATION EXPLORATION	AVIATION CORP. OF CALIFORNIA
COMPANIA NACIONAL CUBANA DE AVIACION CURTISS	

NORTH AMERICAN AVIATION—(Eastern Air Transport Inc.; Miami-New York mail route; Sperry Gyroscope Co.; Ford Instrument Company)

NATIONAL AVIATION CORP.—(Aeronautical Industries, Inc.)

TRANSCONTINENTAL AIR TRANSPORT-MADDUX (across continent by air and rail; Los Angeles-San Francisco, Los Angeles-Phoenix, and Southern California)

NATIONAL AIR TRANSPORT—(Dallas-Chicago and Chicago-New York)

UNITED AIRCRAFT & TRANSPORT CORP.
Subsidiaries:

PRATT & WHITNEY AIRCRAFT CORP.	STANDARD STEEL PROPELLER CORP.
BOEING AIRPLANE CO.	STEARMAN AIRCRAFT CO.
BOEING AIR TRANSPORT	SIKORSKY AVIATION CORP.
PACIFIC AIR TRANSPORT	STOUT AIR SERVICES
CHANCE VOUGHT CORP.	NORTHROP AIRCRAFT CORP.
UNITED AIRCRAFT EXPORTS.	

DETROIT AIRCRAFT CORP.
Subsidiaries:

AIRCRAFT DEVELOPMENT CORP.	BLACKBURN AIRCRAFT CORP.
RYAN AIRCRAFT CORP.	EASTMAN AIRCRAFT CO.
AIRCRAFT PARTS CO.	LOCKHEED AIRCRAFT CO.
GROSSE ILE AIRPORT	PARKS AIR COLLEGE
MARINE AIRCRAFT CORP.	GLIDERS, INC.
DETROIT AIRCRAFT EXPORT CORP.	

A supplementary list is printed on page 144.

strength of inspiration than with a clear eye to the industry's needs. Planes which are not safe to fly have been put on the market, have made their contribution to the record of crashes. This is more true of the small companies than of established and well-backed companies. A distinct exception is the Curtiss Aeroplane & Motor Company, Inc., which now has two hundred engineers on its pay roll and which is pressing, not so much toward current earnings, as toward an investment (in the form of new designs) which will pay returns four or five years hence.

From Curtiss, too, has come another contribution to the equipment problem, this time in relation to safety. While all aviation publicity men make much of the thought that *it is not more safety which is needed, but public acceptance of existing safety*, yet aviation engineers admit that there is much to be done in technical design. So vital did the Guggenheim Fund think this technical work that it offered a prize of $100,000 for the plane which showed the greatest advance in adoption of safety devices. The Curtiss *Tanager* won the competition, with somewhat too much ease. And the engineers who planned it are now studying how to apply its principles (floating ailerons, wing slots, flaps, etc.) to planes built for commercial safety.

The Railroads

When Mr. John Maddux became president, last January, of T.A.T., the new régime was inaugurated by the dismissal of half a dozen high subordinates and their replacement by operating men from the Pennsylvania Railroad. The significance of this move escaped no director of his company and no railroader. It suggested that not only might aviation turn to the railroads for counsel, but that by a gradual process of acquisition and substitution the country's airplane service might become an integral part of the railroads. Blunt Daniel M. Sheaffer, then Pennsylvania's able vice president in charge of traffic, had foreshadowed the upheaval with a pregnant forecast for 1930. "Pennsylvania management," observed Mr. Sheaffer, "is keenly enthusiastic on the future of commercial aviation. Foundations have now been laid, and 1930 should be a year of substantial progress and traffic building. Great distances between boundaries of the United States . . . assure broad market for *well-planned and competently managed flying service. It will continue to develop as it has been initiated; primarily as auxiliary and supplementary service to that of the railroads.*"

This picture, however reassuring for the companies which have been losing money, is scarcely recognizable as the picture of 1927 or even of 1928. In place of a goggle-eyed, enthusiastic World-in-the-Air, we have a carefully selected portion of the world, using the air for a restricted and computed part of the time. The particular portion and the allotted time being under the control of another form of transport.

Such a complete recasting of the future of aviation is probably too radical for the industry to embrace. While the arms of the railroads offer what seems like warmth and safety, the price of entering them is too heavy to be paid all at once. Too many men must lose their jobs and their reputations; too many planes must be scrapped. Yet if the Pennsylvania succeeds with its rebuilding of T.A.T.-Maddux, if the New York Central makes Universal into a useful and integral part of its mighty system, if one or two others take over ailing lines and restore their health, a great impetus and a continuing temptation will face the industry. If aviation cannot make itself transport, why should the railroads not try? Profits and peace are, in the long run, more satisfying than the elusive World-in-the-Air.

The JOURNAL of The Society of Automotive Engineers, November, 1927:

Vol. XXI	November, 1927	No. 5

CHARLES MATTHEWS MANLY

IN the passing of Charles Matthews Manly the Society and the industry have suffered great and irreparable loss. A man of great native ability and thoroughly devoted to good principles, he was a master of friendship; a master of fair dealing; a master of courage; a master of work.

A pioneer in aviation, a wholehearted disciple of science and scientific methods, he had amazingly comprehensive knowledge of the almost unlimited number of phases of automotive engineering. The Society never had a better, more intelligent, more effective, or more helpful friend. He was a tireless worker, exerting tremendous long-sustained energy in analyzing problems and in formulating elucidations and deductions relating to them.

He served the Society in a surprising number of capacities. The S.A.E., so frequently in his thoughts, was very dear to him and was a major interest in his life. He always advocated straightforward approach and getting things done, regardless of precedent when necessary. He was President of the Society in 1919. The Society never had no more earnest or capable President. He divined and set forth clearly its functions and the methods it should pursue.

During his presidency, he laid the groundwork for the present Operation and Maintenance movement of the Society. In his 1919 presidential address he said on the subject of the need for engineering in operation:

The work of the automotive engineer is not finished, but merely begun, when the machines are designed and built, whether they be motor-trucks, tractors, aircraft or other vehicles. There is more need today for real engineering work in connection with the planning and organization of the operating end of automotive vehicles and machines than there is in connection with the design and construction of them, just as there are more engineers engaged in the operating and maintenance end of railroads than are engaged in the design and construction of locomotives and railroad cars.

In the subdivision of automotive engineering work having to do with motor-trucks, the real work of the engineer has hardly as yet been begun. True it is that motor-trucks are being sold and are daily hauling thousands of tons of merchandise and general freight, but the careful study and collection of data for accurately predetermining the best operating equipment, organization and personnel to meet given conditions at a definitely predetermined cost has hardly been started. This single phase of automotive engineering presents more problems for the engineer to solve than would be needed if all our records and data in railroad transportation engineering were suddenly swept away and it became necessary to reestablish such data immediately for the determination of proper freight rates.

In this same address, he said of standardization, of which he was a most aggressive proponent: "The S.A.E. has done more to show the importance and economic value of standardization, both to the producer and the consumer, than any other single organization in the world."

Mr. Manly was a pillar in the standardization work of the Society. During many years he was a member of various divisions of the Standards Committee, as well as its Vice-Chairman. He presided at many meetings of the Standards Committee. During the World War he represented the Society in aeronautic standardization activities both in this Country and abroad. His work on the Patents Committee and on the Standardization Policy Committee was of great value. He was well informed on patent matters, as well as on engineering; and was an excellent logician. It has been said of him as an engineering expert witness that he was "in a class by himself." He had been one of the representatives and the principal spokesman of the Society on the American Engineering Standards Committee since the inauguration of that Committee. In his discussions of complicated phases of national and international standardization and cooperation he showed a very high order of understanding and ability. He was without a peer in this field of work.

Mr. Manly was born at Staunton, Va., in 1876. He was graduated at Furman University as master of mathematics and mathematical physics; and at Cornell University as mechanical engineer. He was engineer in charge of aviation research work for the United States Government under Prof. Samuel P. Langley at the Smithsonian Institution, City of Washington, from June, 1898, to April, 1905. He designed and built the Langley flying-machine and the gasoline engine therefor. This engine was of great significance, in view of its light weight and general characteristics, as a forerunner of developments thereafter. In 1901 the development of the internal-combustion engine was still so slight that it did not admit of the construction by any European maker of an engine weighing less than 12 lb. per hp. The five-cylinder radial-type engine built by Mr. Manly was characterized by design and workmanship which showed a remarkable advance in construction. At 950 r.p.m. it developed 52.4 hp., weighing only 2.4 lb. per hp., a weight per horsepower record not equalled until the building of the 400-hp. Liberty engine. In addition to its other achievements the engine pointed the way to the development of other than the vertical-type engine. In building this engine Mr. Manly showed not only his inventive genius but an ability to cope with the lack of manufacturing methods and facilities. Later he was engaged in automobile engineering, especially relative to transmissions of the hydraulic type, for which he held patents. During the World War he was consulting engineer, chief inspection engineer and assistant general manager of the Curtiss Aeroplane & Motor Co. Another war activity was his work with the British War Office. Mr. Manly designed the first multi-engine airplane bomber which not only met but surpassed the specifications laid down. The bomber was known as The Canada and had a total power of 500 hp.

He was the editor of the Langley Memoir on Mechanical Flight, which was published in Vol. 27 of Smithsonian Contributions to Knowledge. He had the greatest admiration for Dr. Langley and devoted a great deal of time to making clear what credit Dr. Langley was entitled to in the solution of problems of flight of heavier-than-air craft. He believed thoroughly that the Langley machine was capable of flight. Undoubtedly, Mr. Manly was one of a half-dozen early pioneers who did most to develop heavier-than-air craft before it was generally understood that flight of such craft is possible. In recognition of his work in this field he was elected an honorary member of the National Aeronautic Association.

Mr. Manly died last month at Kew Gardens, Long Island, of acute indigestion. He is survived by, in addition to his mother, two sons, two brothers and four sisters.

He was a keenly interested attendant at Society and Metropolitan Section meetings for many years. At the first meeting of the Society held subsequent to his death, the Aeronautic Meeting last month, the following resolution was passed:

WHEREAS, the members of the Society of Automotive Engineers are deeply conscious of the irreparable loss they have suffered in the passing of Charles Matthews Manly, and

WHEREAS, the services of Mr. Manly to the aeronautical art can never be overestimated and should never be forgotten, therefore,

Be It Resolved, that the members of the Society in Aeronautical Meeting assembled desire to make expression of their own grief and of their sympathy with the family of Mr. Manly.

Mr. Manly was very near and dear to many, including the office staff of the Society, whom he was always most generous in assisting. These will long remember this noble man.

Aero Club of America
12 East Forty-second Street
New York

ALFRED W. LAWSON,

      EDITOR FLY:

It has been decided by the Aero Club of America to erect a memorial in honor of the late 1st Lieut. THOMAS E. SELFRIDGE, 1st Field Artillery U. S. Army, who met his death at Ft Myer, Virginia, on September 17, 1908, in falling with the Wright aeroplane.

First, as Secretary of the Aerial Experiment Association, and afterward in the Aeronautical Division of the Signal Corps of the Army, Lieut. SELFRIDGE had devoted himself exclusively to aeronautics since the summer of 1907, and was the first in this country to give up his life in the advancement of the new science.

Contributions have already been received unsolicited, from abroad as well as from America, and due to the widespread interest in this project, opportunity is given to all of Lieut. SELFRIDGE'S friends, in the Aero Club and out of it, who desire to share in honoring his memory.

The memorial will be placed in Arlington Cemetery where Lieut. SELFRIDGE is buried, or at Ft. Myer, Virginia, where he met his death.

Kindly make checks payable to Charles J. Edwards, Treasurer Aero Club of America, 12 E. 42d St., New York City.

      Very truly yours,

          THE COMMITTEE,
             Alexander Graham Bell
             Glen H. Curtiss
             Frank P. Lahm, Chairman.

THE CURTISS AUTOPLANE

SO UNUSUAL IN DESIGN AND SO EPOCH MAKING IS THIS NEW CURTISS CRAFT THAT STORIES AND PHOTOGRAPHS OF IT WERE PRINTED IN HUNDREDS OF NEWSPAPERS ALL OVER THE UNITED STATES AND ABROAD.

THE CURTISS AUTOPLANE.

"One of the greatest attractions of the Pan-American Aeronautic Exposition last week was the 'Autoplane' exhibited by the CURTISS COMPANY. Great secrecy surrounded the exhibit prior to the opening of the show, when it was formally 'unveiled' before Governor Whitman and a party of distinguished visitors at 8.10 P.M., February 8th.

"The machine is really a 'limousine of the air' and compares favorably with the appearance and furnishing of the modern sedan or limousine. Upholstery and tapestries have been given much thought, and except perhaps for slight reduction in size, the car leaves nothing to be desired in appointment.

"In performance there is every reason to believe the machine to be quite practical, in spite of its bulkiness and the consequent rather high dead head resistance which it possesses. The body has been partially streamlined to reduce resistance, an advance over ordinary limousine design.

"Apart from its unique appearance special interest is attached to the machine because it is the first modern triplane that the average aero-enthusiast has had an opportunity of inspecting.

"Above the front wheels is a small plane, extending from either side of the motor hood, carrying out the idea of mud guards.

GENERAL DIMENSIONS.

Span, upper two planes	40 ft.	6 in.
Span, bottom plane	23 ft.	4 in.
Chord, upper two planes		48 in.
Chord, bottom plane		42 in.
Gap between planes		39 in.
Stagger		11 in.
Height overall	10 ft.	0 in.
Length	27 ft.	0 in.
Motor, Curtiss "OXX"		100 H.P.
Speed range		65-45 m.p.h.
Useful load		710 lbs.

PLANES.

"Wing curve is the 'F-2,' planes at an incident angle of 4 degrees, and the lower plane with a 3 degree dihedral. Wing area, 420 sq. ft.

"Struts are built up K-shape. Ailerons on upper and center plane.

"Sections of the top plane are joined at the center of the machine. Center sections attach at the top of the body and lower plane sections are attached to the body about six inches above the floor of the car.

BODY.

"Forty-two inches in its greatest width. The body is of aluminum; windows of celluloid. The motor is situated in the forward part of the body as in automobile practice, with a shaft extending to the rear of the body, and power transmitted to the propeller located at the top. Seats are provided for a pilot 'chauffeur' and for two passengers. Standard single Dep control is installed, arranged to steer the forward wheels at the same time as the rudder is moved. The four wheels are sprung on concealed rubber shock absorbers.

TAIL PLANE.

"Two outriggers carry the stabilizing plane, elevators, fin and rudder, braced to outer struts of main plane by heavy cable. The outriggers are spaced 9 ft. 0 in. apart, allowing just enough clearance for the propeller. They are attached just above the central main plane.

MOTOR GROUP.

"The motor is a Curtiss 'OXX,' 100 H. P. motor, turning at 1,400 r.p.m., and driving an 8 ft. 8 in. four-bladed pusher type propeller with a 5 ft. 6 in. pitch at a reduced speed of 1,100 r.p.m. The propeller revolves clockwise.

"A circular radiator, placed as in automobile practice, provides cooling for the water.

"The fuel tank is located at the center of gravity. It has a capacity of 30 gallons. The motor consumes 10 gallons per hour. Four gallons of oil are carried in the crankcase of the motor. Tanks are located in the space above the passengers' seats and just forward of the propeller."

—Aerial Age, Feb. 19, 1917.

PROGRESS IN AVIATION IMPRESSED UPON VISITORS.

"Another interesting and novel exhibit in the Aeronautical Show is the CURTISS 'Autoplane,' a unique combination of an automobile and an aeroplane, a real aerial limousine. The main body of this craft bears a marked resemblance to an automobile, but it is fitted with three planes attached just back of the side doors. These vary in size, the largest being at the top and the smallest at the bottom. The machine rests on four wheels, the two front ones being capable of being turned in the same manner as those on a motor car."

N. Y. Evening Mail, February 9, 1917.

AUTOPLANE A HIT OF AERO EXHIBITION.

Prospective elopers get cue on how to escape from irate parents.

"No longer is it the really smart or swagger thing to elope in a 90 H. P. decollete racer, burning up the dust while irate parent hums along in the family limousine two miles to the rear. From this day hence the only proper way to do it will be for the stalwart hopeful to swoop down in his autoplane, swing the waiting beauty to the upholstered seat beside him, and then waft away to some mountain fastness where the irate parent cannot follow in his landlubber's car.

"It really is a great boost that this very latest of plain and fancy aircrafts has given to romance and at the far end of the Grand Central Palace, where the Aero Exposition is being held, there is a continuous bevy of new and almost new debutantes who clutter around the device, speculating what a wonderful honeymoon trip it would furnish. Altogether it is quite a relief from the serious business of war and the score that more other machines seem to exemplify. Dainty, graceful, and exquisitely finished, with its triple sets of

478

T H E   C U R T I S S   "A U T O P L A N E "   "A N   A E R I A L   L I M O U S I N E "

wings extending from each side of the enclosed limousine body, set on four wheels, it is strangely yet properly out of place.

COMBINATION AIRPLANE AND TOURING CAR.

"Among the many interesting and new things shown at the first Pan-American Aeronautic Exposition held in the Grand Central Palace, New York City, is this flyer, a Curtiss combination airplane and touring car. In it one can move comfortably along roads as well as through the gales of the upper world. It shows that one need not take to the air on a seat below something that looks like a sausage or part of a box, but may loll on upholstered seats in a car as graceful as any town car. The women in particular were interested in this conveyance."

Boston, (Mass.) Transcript,
Feb. 12, 1917.

AUTOPLANE DESIGNED TO RUN ON GROUND AND FLY IN THE AIR.

"One of the most interesting exhibits seen at the Aeronautic Show in New York City is the Curtiss Autoplane, a unique combination of an aeroplane and an automobile—a veritable 'aerial limousine,' which will not only run over the ground, but at approximately 45 miles per hour, will leave the surface of the ground and fly away like the magic chariots of old. Entirely different in its construction from any aeroplane heretofore produced, this latest creation of Glenn H. Curtiss's brain is decidedly a step in advance."

San Diego (Cal.) Herald,
Feb. 15, 1917.

CURTISS AUTOPLANE TO BE TESTED HERE.

Latest Creation in Flying Machines Now on Exhibition in New York.

"Captain Thos. S. Baldwin, head of the Atlantic Coast Aeronautical Station, announced upon his return yesterday from New York that the new Curtiss 'Autoplane' will be brought here soon and given its initial test.

"The new Curtiss machine has a limousine body that vies with that of the most pretentious automobile and will run equally well on land or in the air.

"Captain Baldwin said that the machine would make a speed of 85 miles an hour. It is of the pusher type and is built like a tri-plane flying boat.

"The machine is the first of its kind ever constructed and is designed for the use of people who want the comforts of a flying machine and automobile combined. It was the feature of the aeroplane show and is the talk of all who have seen it."

Newport News Press, Feb. 16, 1917.

LAND AND AIR MACHINE.

"This particular machine has just been fashioned at the CURTISS factory and is the first attempt ever made to combine a land car with an air machine purely for fashionable use. The 'Autoplane' has three seats and the interior resembles a modern sedan. It is a triplane model and is equipped with an eight-cylinder, 100 horse power motor. Until a speed of 45 miles per hour is reached the machine runs on the ground. At greater speed it takes to the air and is capable of attaining 65 miles per hour."

N. Y. Sun, February 10, 1917.

SHOPPING OR SHEEP HERDING.

"A machine adapted to the purpose of Fifth Avenue shopping and sheep herding was what appeared from under the veil that covered the Curtiss mystery until 9 o'clock last night. It is an air limousine capable of traveling in air or on land with several passengers, making a speed of sixty miles on land, according to Curtiss representatives, and sixty-five miles in air.

"The rather trim looking limousine body gives the present day machine an unusual aspect, suggesting that subway travelers will presently ride to business on interborough air line expresses. Its luxurious accommodations are such as appeal to J. Stanley Smith of Martinsdale, a wealthy young sheep owner, who has announced that he will soar over the hills of Montana in search of his little black sheep. Smith has an idea that he can keep his herds and herders better located by the use of an air machine than an automobile. His idea is that he can cover five times as much territory in an air machine and watch the drift of his livestock much better and locate his strays with much less trouble than with an auto. A machine that combines land running ability with flying is just the sort that appeals to the modern young sheep owner."

N. Y. Evening Sun, Feb. 9, 1917.

THE CURTISS AUTOPLANE, THE AIR AND LAND NOVELTY SHOWN AT THE PAN-AMERICAN AERONAUTIC EXPOSITION, GRAND CENTRAL PALACE, NEW YORK.

"It is a touring car or airplane at pleasure, traveling on land or in the air with equal facility."

N. Y. Times.

Dead Men Tell No Tales......*or do they?*

This is the true story of two days in the life of Wilbur Wright, his story...*history*; of two moments, one very brief, but (approximately) 12 seconds, the other considerably longer, 59 seconds ...and infinitely more important.

In 1899 Wilbur first wrote the Smithsonian for information on flight. From then, until late in 1903, he worked at perfecting how to attain it - with Orville, his younger brother, his helpmate in constructing the gliders, photographing their glider flights, etc. Finally, by December, 1903, after copying an automobile motor and designing two pro- pellers, they *"tossed for first whack"* at attempting to fly their new machine.

Now things get interesting.

There appear to be two vastly different scenarios of what happened next, and since the Wrights, faithful to their heritage (their mother, Susan Katharine, was the daughter of German-born Johann Gottlieb Koerner), punctiliously recorded almost everything, there is today a wealth of writings (summarized in THE PAPERS OF WILBUR AND ORVILLE WRIGHT, Including the Chanute-Wright Letters. Library of Congress, 1953...**except for those many personal papers, etc. burned on 19Feb1948*, per Orville's orders, following his death):

Here's what was written *at the time* of the first of those moments:

14Dec03: The Papers of Wilbur and Orville Wright (1903/1953): *"Flyer No. 1 - whopper flying machine"* is ready. Due to little wind, they set their launching rail on a slight downward slope, and *"after tossing for first whack,"* Wilbur is first to try: *"We gave machine first trial today with only partial success..."* He's aloft for 3-1/2 seconds, attain- ing a height of approximately 15 feet and a distance of 105 feet before grounding. Wilbur then wired his father: *"Misjudgment at start reduced flight one hundred twelve power and control ample rudder only injured success assured keep quiet."*

17Dec1903: The Papers of Wilbur and Orville Wright (1903/1953): 10:35 am, winds *very* strong, a 22 to 27-mph gale as they set their launching rail on a flat near their camp. Camera ready, Orville piloted the flyer in a *virtually identical trial* to Wilbur's - crunching down *"about a 100 feet from the end of the tracks. Time about 12 seconds (not known exactly as watch was not properly stopped)... "*

*But there was that photo...*arguably the basis for the strange story that Orville would write ten years later.

These were two of five trials, all detailed below.

But I believe that the reader should understand several things. First, that knowing Orville's mind-set, *where he was coming from*, is crucial - for he's central in this story. Though many believe (or would want you to believe) that the brothers were almost twins; they were, in fact, quite different. Wilbur was over four years older, about three inches taller, arguably brighter...the author of *virtually everything important* in the 1899-1903 developmental period, and the spokesperson. And of possibly greater importance, in 1912, at the height of their acclaim - and problems - he died, and a `Cain and Abel'-nu- anced scenario ensued.

Orville was now thrust upon a center stage he was ill prepared for; increasingly he becomes morose, withdrawn, and as questions grew that his contributions during the brothers' creative years (and thereafter) were of little consequence, virtually silent.

Further, this was exacerbated by the public's growing mistrust of Wright aircraft (they were becoming known as "killers" and a `dead-end' design) while Curtiss (his arch-enemy) was dramatically rising in dominance.

The glory years - 1908-09 - had been brief; the Wright aeroplane was beginning its free-fall when Wilbur died - *and after 1916 was but a has-been.*

Further, one should know that *after* Wilbur's death their private writings (notes, and letters to such as Octave Chanute) were *accessible only to Orville.* The 1968 publication of WILBUR & ORVILLE WRIGHT, A Bibliography (Library of Congress, Arthur G. Renstrom) reveals that Wilbur wrote virtually everything prior to his death (all but two minor pieces by Orville: one in Country Life, January, 1909, the second in Figaro illustre, February, 1909. However, in Century Magazine, September, 1908, there was "The Wright Brothers Aeroplane" article listing "Wilbur and Orville Wright" as authors. This was untrue, for it was written by Orville, alone, as noted in (1) the above referenced WILBUR & ORVILLE WRIGHT, A Bibliography, page 9, which states *"...the article was entirely the work of Orville Wright."* - and (2) WILBUR & ORVILLE WRIGHT, A Chronology, Library of Congress, 1975, page 31, which again states *"Though it appears under joint authorship, the article was entirely the work of Orville."*).

But with Wilbur dead, Orville blossomed (though briefly) as a writer.

In FLYING magazine, December, 1913, he wrote what Renstrom describes as the "First extensive authentic account of the Kitty Hawk flights of December 17, 1903," including this statement: *"...A sudden dart when a little over a hundred feet from the end of the track, or a little over a 120 feet from the point at which it rose into the air, ended the flight. As the velocity of the wind was over 35 feet per second and the speed of the machine over the ground against this wind ten feet per second, the speed of the machine relative to the air was over 45 feet per second, and the length of the flight was equivalent to a flight of 540 feet made in calm air...the first time in the history of the world in which a machine carrying a man had raised itself by its own power* (what of the gale?) *into the air in full flight, had sailed forward without reduction of speed, and had finally landed at a point as high as that from which it started."* Thus, by tortuous logic (underlining, above) he laid claim to having flown *over 300 feet* and to being the *first to fly...*

> Note: One should understand that when Orville wrote this he was most certainly aware of what Wilbur wrote to Octave Chanute* on November 2, 1906: *"...From our knowledge of the subject we estimate that it is possible to jump about 250 ft., with a machine that has not made the first steps toward controllability and which is quite unable to maintain the motive force necessary for flight...You have possibly forgotten that we stayed in the air 59 seconds in a wind of twenty miles' velocity in the year preceding 1904...When someone goes over three hundred feet and lands safely in a wind of seven or eight miles it will then be important for us to do something. So far we see no indication that it will be done for several years yet. There is all the difference in the world between jumping and flying..."* (note the specific reference to *59 seconds* and *three hundred feet*).

...which, with their private writings unavailable, *four generations* of Americans swallowed - *hook, line and sinker.* There was no reason to challenge it; there wasn't any other story *that they knew of* (even today, with the facts easily available, most Americans are ignorant of them - still believing Orville's myth of being the first to fly).

The next year Orville buttressed the <u>FLYING</u> story by telling Leslie Quirk, writing for <u>Boys' Life</u> magazine, about his Ft. Myer accident (which had killed Tom Self-ridge; ironically the partner of Bell and Curtiss) and establishing *his version* of this tragedy in its August, 1914 issue - and next, "How I Learned To Fly" in September's <u>Boys' Life</u> (see below), and repeated in its October, 1953 issue.

Then, to confuse things further, fifteen years later, in 1929, there was an article by Orville about Wilbur signed *"O.W."* in <u>The Encyclopaedia Britannica</u> which read: *"...Tested at Kitty Hawk, N. C., on Dec. 17, 1903, the machine carrying a man made four sustained free flights. The longest of these had a duration of 59 seconds and a speed of 30 m. an hour. This machine is now exhibited in the Science museum at South Kensington, London."* Note *no* specific reference to the 12-second trial; only to the 59-second one piloted by Wilbur. Please, read it (http://www.glennhcurtiss.com/id50.htm) and judge for yourself "what actually happened" on that cold, windy day in 1903.

Orville wrote a few other writings, but nothing about their history until "Our Life in Camp at Kitty Hawk" in the December, 1943, <u>U.S. Air Services</u> magazine which is *"Made up entirely of excerpts from letters at Kitty Hawk by Wilbur and me to our sister Katharine... The story of the first flight is not included.*

The last comment caught my eye: *why?*

Things are now dormant...until Orville's death in 1948.

In 1949 their papers were donated to the Library of Congress, which began its review and, in 1953, published <u>THE PAPERS OF WILBUR AND ORVILLE WRIGHT</u>, noted earlier.

At long last - *after a half-century* (1903-1953) - the public *could* know *"what actually happened."* It's a revealing read...but one for which few, apparently, have `connected the dots'* (or if so, like good partisans, they've kept it to themselves).

OK, so Orville concocted a false story - one which, around 1915, he may have thought better of; one for which he'd be `outed' when the papers were made available; but the deed was done, the Genie was out of the bottle.

He could stop writing...what to do?

He may have thought, `Burn the papers** (like Richard Burton's wife did in 1890), but no! too many people knew of them, especially Mabel Beck, the redoubtable secretary he'd inherited from Wilbur (arguably Orville's only life-long confident). Better to `hunker down,' say nothing, write nothing, certainly never an autobiography; he'd be dead when the public discovered his perfidy (and he wasn't alone, anyway, in cobbling a self-serving story, human nature being what it is; in the then-popular field of discovery there'd been several). `No, I'll just ignore it; if it won't go away at least I'll be gone when it happens.'

Compare the following, both versions *written by Orville Wright*:

14Dec03: <u>The Papers of Wilbur and Orville Wright</u> (1903/1953): *"Flyer No. 1 – whopper flying machine"* is ready. Due to little wind, they set their launching rail on a slight downward slope, and *"after tossing for first whack,"* Wilbur is first to try: *"We gave machine first trial today with only partial success..."* He's aloft for 3-1/2 seconds, attaining a height of approximately 15 feet and a distance of 105 feet before grounding. Wilbur then wired his father: *"Misjudgment at start reduced flight one hundred twelve power and control ample rudder only injured success assured keep quiet."*

Boys' Life (1914/1953): *"The initial attempt was not a success. The machine fluttered for about a 100 feet down the side of the hill, pretty much as gliders had done. Then it settled with a thud, snapping off the propeller shaft, and thus effectually ending experiments for the time being."*

17Dec1903: The Papers of Wilbur and Orville Wright (1903/1953): 10:35 am, winds *very* strong, a 22 to 27-mph gale as they set their launching rail on a flat near their camp. Camera ready, Orville piloted the flyer in a *virtually identical attempt* to Wilbur's - crunching down *"about a 100 feet from the end of the tracks. Time about 12 seconds (not known exactly as watch was not properly stopped)..."*

Boys' Life (1914/1953): *"My brother climbed into the machine. The motor was started. With a short dash down the runway, the machine lifted into the air and was flying. It was only a flight of twelve seconds, and it was an uncertain, wavy, creeping sort of a flight at best; but it was a real flight at last and not a glide."*

The Papers of Wilbur and Orville Wright (1903/1953): At 11:20 am *"Wil made the second trial. The course was about like mine, up and down but a little longer over the ground but the same in time. Dist. Not measured but about 175 feet..."*

Boys' Life (1914/1953): *"Then it was my turn. I had learned a little from watching my brother, but I found the machine pointing upward and downward in jerky undulations. The erratic course was due in part to my utter lack of experience in controlling a flying machine...but I flew for about the same time my brother had."*

The Papers of Wilbur and Orville Wright (1903/1953): At 11:40 am Orville made the next attempt *"When out about the same distance as Will's, I met with a strong gust from the left which raised the left wing and I sidled the machine off to the right in a lively manner..."* - a little over 200 feet in 15 seconds.

Boys' Life (1914/1953): *"He tried it again, the minute the men had carried it back to the runway, and added perhaps three or four seconds to the records we had just made."*

The Papers of Wilbur and Orville Wright (1903/1953): At 12 o'clock *"Will started on the fourth and last trip. The machine started off with its ups and downs as it had before, but by the time he had gone over three or four hundred feet he had it under much better control, and was traveling on a fairly even course. It proceeded in this manner till it reached a small hummock out about 800 feet from the starting ways, when it began its pitching again and suddenly darted into the ground...the distance over the ground was 852 feet in 59 seconds..."*

Boys' Life (1914/1953): *"Then, after a few secondary adjustments, I took my seat* (actually, he was prone) *for the second time. By now I had learned something about the controls, and about how a machine acted during a sustained flight, and I managed to keep in the air for fifty-seven seconds. I couldn't turn, of course - the hills wouldn't permit that - but I had no great difficulty in handling it. When I came down I was eager to have another turn...And then, quite without warning, a puff of wind caught the forward part of the machine and began to tip it...When the machine had been pinned down at last, it was almost a complete wreck, necessitating...days and days of rebuilding...we could do no more experimenting that year."*

There you have it, what was written at the time: four "trials" or "jumps," one successful flight - and what, *after the fact*, Orville wrote: *different as night and day*.

The result: for almost 90 years Americans have believed that Orville Wright was `first to fly' - while it was his brother's honor.

Think about it.

*Years later, long after Octave Chanute's death, Orville asked his estate for copies of the letters between Chanute and Wilbur. He was rebuffed...for before his death Chanute had broken with the Wrights (and allied with Curtiss) - and sometime later his daughters deposited them with the Library of Congress, where they properly became part of the public record.

**"Wright Flyer," Joe Gertler, pp. 52, <u>FLIGHT Journal</u>, Dec2002.

How I Learned to Fly

Fifty years ago man first left the earth under power. Here is the original story as told to Leslie Quirk • By ORVILLE WRIGHT

I SUPPOSE MY BROTHER and I always wanted to fly. Every youngster wants to, doesn't he? But it was not till we were out of school that the ambition took definite form.

We had read a good deal on the subject, and we had reverently studied Otto Lilienthal's tables of figures. He was the greatest aeronautical engineer in Europe. Then one day, as it were, we said to each other: "Why not? Here are scientific calculations, based upon actual tests, to show us the sustaining powers of planes. We can spare a few weeks each year. Suppose, instead of going off somewhere to loaf, we put in our vacations building and flying gliders." I don't believe we dared think beyond gliders at that time—not aloud, at least.

That year—it was 1900—we went down to North Carolina, near Kitty Hawk. There were hills there in plenty, and not too many people about to scoff. Building that first glider was the best fun we'd ever had, too, despite the fact that we put it together as accurately as a watchmaker assembles and adjusts his finest timepiece. You see, we knew how to work because Lilienthal had made his tables years before, and men like Chanute, for example, had verified them.

To our great disappointment, however, the glider was not the success we had expected. It didn't behave as the figures on which it was constructed vouched that it should. Something was wrong. We looked at each other silently, and at the machine, and at the mass of figures compiled by Lilienthal. Then we proved up on them to see if we had slipped

Originally published in BOYS' LIFE, September, 1914.

somewhere. If we had, we couldn't find the error; so we packed up and went home. We were agreed that we hadn't built our glider according to the scientific specifications. But there was another year coming and we weren't discouraged. We had just begun.

We wrote to Chanute, who was an engineer in Chicago at the time. We told him about our glider; we drew sketches of it for him; we set down long rows of figures. And then we wound up our letter by begging him to explain why the tables of Lilienthal, which he had verified by experiments of his own, could not be proved by our machine.

Chanute didn't know. He wrote back it might be due to a different curve or pitch of surfaces on the planes, or something like that. But he was interested just the same, and when we went down to Kitty Hawk in 1901 we invited him to visit our camp.

Chanute came. Just before he left Chicago, I recall his telling us, he had read and O. K.'d the proofs of an article on aeronautics which he had prepared for the Encyclopedia Britannica, and in which he again told us of verifying Lilienthal's tables.

Well, he came to Kitty Hawk for a visit, and after he looked our glider over care-

Recently the author acquired a most historic copy of the <u>Annual Report of The Board of Regents of THE SMITHSONIAN INSTITUTION for the year ending June 30, 1908</u>. Charles D. Walcott, Secretary, Alexander Graham Bell was one of fourteen regents.

On page 8 under *"Aerial Navigation"* Secretary Walcott wrote: *"Within the past year there has been a renewed interest in experiments in aerial navigation, to which this Institution, through my predecessor, Mr. Langley, made notable contributions. Toward the end of the year the demand for literature on the subject so entirely exhausted the supply of papers on hand, that a special edition of some of Mr. Langley's more popular memoirs was issued. It is gratifying to me to be able to say that his pioneer work in heavier-than-air machines, resulting as it did in the actual demonstration of the possibility of mechanical flight, has now received universal recognition.*

"Besides numerous popular papers, Mr. Langley wrote two technical works relating to the general subject of aerodynamics, which form parts of an incomplete volume of the Smithsonian Contributions to Knowledge. The record of his experiments from 1893 to 1905 was kept by him partly in manuscript form and largely in the shape of voluminous notes and wastebooks. These have been turned over to his principal assistant in this work, Mr. Charles M. Manly, who has been for some time engaged in preparing them for publication and adding such necessary information, especially on the engineering side, as comes within the immediate purview of Mr. Manly's work. It is a source of regret that the memoir has not yet been completed for publication, but I hope that during this year it will be possible for the Institution to issue the volume, thus bringing to a conclusion a record of Mr. Langley's original and epoch-making contributions to a science and an art which bid fair to engage the attention of mankind for many years to come."

On pages 117-144 Major George Q. Squier wrote of *"The Present Status of Military Aeronautics, with 23 Plates"* (photographs). Following a discussion of French, German and English dirigible/blimps, he discusses the August, 1908, flights of Signal Corps Dirigible No. 1, when Curtiss assisted Baldwin (its motor America's *first* military aircraft engine, see pp. 181-182). *Plate 9, below, shows Curtiss bending over its motor:*

Appendix

Maj. Squier continues with a discussion of *"The Wright Brothers Aeroplane"* with *ten* plates (and with but this passing reference to its crash which killed Selfridge: "...*a few days before the accident which wrecked the machine,*"), *"The Herring Aeroplane"* which "...*embodies new features for automatic control and contains an engine of remarkable lightness...,"* *"The Farman Aeroplane,"* *"The Bleriot Aeroplane,"* and only *a half*-plate of *"The June Bug...With this machine, Mr. G. H. Curtiss, on July 4, 1908, won the Scientific American trophy..."* From this discourse – so heavily weighted in the Wright's favor – is a hint of the Smithsonian to come.

To the author's knowledge, the first side-by-side of the Wright Flier and the "June Bug":

Smithsonian Report, 1908.—Squier. **PLATE 22.** Smithsonian Report, 1908.—Squier. **PLATE 23.**

WRIGHT BROTHERS' AEROPLANE, FORT MYER, VA., SEPTEMBER 12, 1908.
Orville Wright and passenger. Time, 9 minutes 6 seconds.

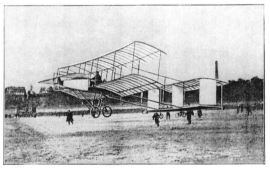

FIG. 1.—FARMAN AEROPLANE.

FIG. 2.—"JUNE BUG" AEROPLANE, HAMMONDSPORT, N. Y.
Aerial Experiment Association.

Appendix

ACKNOWLEDGEMENTS

Due to the nature of this work - its premise controversial and against conventional wisdom - and the author's credentials including no degrees in history nor related memberships - those that have given assistance are special.

Therefore, my heartfelt appreciation to Bill Immenschuh, George G. Spratt, Hugh Sidey, Dan Witkoff, Cheryl Hogue, Tony & Dianne DeWitte, John Wysong, Stuart Klaskin, Tom Gonzales, Dale & Darcy Hall, Howard Rettberg, Philip Jarrett, Lindsley Dunn, Tony Doherty, Henry Serrano Villard, Chuck Haberlein, Leonard Bruno, Peter Murphy, Nancy Stickley, Bill Oswald, Beth King, Mario Michetti, Bill Hardy, Pat Purcell, Art & Mollie Charbonneau, Michael Harrison, Jack & Carolyn Fleming, Philip Welsh, Burke Hintz, Peter Hahn, John & Josie Trujillo, Bob Hilton, Jim Corbett, Peter Wood, Roger Long, Ray Kingsley, John Haynes, Peter Selinger, Terry Rook, Chuck Harlow...

PHOTOGRAPH CREDITS

Glenn Curtiss Museum, Hammondsport: 106, 108, 111, 114, 117, 118, 122, 129, 148, 152, 153, 154, 159, 160, 165, 166, 168, 196, 197-top, 155-top, 222, 230, 258, 259, 263, 322-top, 339, 344-top, 345, 348, 364, 365, 376, 377, 380, 381, 395, 407, 409, 423

US Naval Historical Center, Washington: 297, 299, 300, 301-bottom, 304, 305, 310, 313, 324, 326, 329, 335, 336, 337, 339-bottom, 384, 418

Library of Congress, Washington: 134, 135, 183, 185, 219-bottom, 290, 311, 316, 373

Note: The fascinating illustration, page 487, was by Anita Hamo, Sarajevo, 1986:

From the first edition: The author thought the reader may be interested in PENDULUM's first chapter's preface, 1992:

"We begin at one of the most dynamic periods in American history. The passion, plunder, destruction and death of the Civil War are now bitter memories for virtually every American. The man that would become out most prolific inventor, Thomas Alva Edison, is about to receive his first patent. A young Scot immigrant, Alexander Graham Bell, is working on sending sound by wire, for which he will receive his telephone patent in 1876. The railroad, connecting East with West, is to unleash westward migration and the settlement of America's mid-continent on a grand scale, while the craftsmen and mills of New England are disgorging vast quantities of mechanical marvels and manufactured goods from a maturing industrial revolution. On every hand is undreamed of change, innovation, progress and growth, with a glimmer of man's greatest conquest, flight, and of other marvels to come – and three men are born of destiny."

Remembering… In 1941, when I was 15, I began a '5-year diary.' Below are a few select-ed entries on my family's involvement in WW2. My brother, Win (Winecke) was first to enlist; he became an Army Air Corp bomber pilot in 1943. My sister, Alice, after earning her BA at MacMurray College, enlisted as a WAVE. Then at 17, I enlisted in the Navy to fly – and was sent to the University of Notre Dame for training…

This mid-1945 photograph shows me, left, still in training at Notre Dame; my brother Bob, too young to serve; then Alice, a Link-Trainer operator at Pensacola; and Win, just home from Stalag Luft 3 (note how thin he is).

December 7-8, 1941:

May 24, 1944:

June 6, 1944:

489

June 7, 1944: "1944 Wed. – worked in orchard all day till 3:30, went to J'ville – WIN'S PRISONER! (Germans) Cleaned up, phone

June 8, 1945: 1945 – Friday – classes – letters from folks & Pat – Win is home!!!!!!! Econ, chow, speech, cut two classes, got special leave from Lt. Cmdr. Olney, left N.O. 1500 – train home, hitched from Springfield – saw Win arou 19 12:30 A.M. – !! – bed.

June 30, 1945: When photo was taken in Jacksonville, IL; last time we were all together:
1945 Sat. – up little late – Alice, Win, & I cleaned house – ran some errands with Win – got photos (snaps) – O.K. – fooled around home, rain – drove around with

September 1, 1945: 1945 Sat. – letter from Mom & Pat – Win in Louisville. Money & BK – wired Win & Mom – Bus. Laws – cleaned up for review etc. Review of articulation at 1100 – Middlin & R.O. – hitched with Bill Jones

September 2, 1945: 19 part way – went to Louisville, finally found Win at Bowman field.

September 3, 1945: 1945 – Sunday – up pretty early – chow at Officers' Club – went to "line", etc. Finally Win & I flew in BT-13 (9582) to Scott Field (St. Louis) – over orchard, & home to J'ville

December 14, 1945: 1945 – Friday – arrived N.O. at 9:30 A.M. – stopped by U.S.O. – went out to Navy airfield – sweated out ride all 19 afternoon – weather = no ride! – hitched to Mobile – rain! Bus to Pensacola – Alice had passed away at 5:45 P.M.

She who loved life is gone, but do not grieve.
No need to rack your heart, only believe.
Never will she grow old, as we grow old.
Forever young she lives, buoyant and bold.
She races with the wind, through starry space …
and laughs with boundless joy to know God's face.
Then will you wish her back, who loved life so?
Better trust God, and let her go.
Rev. Harris Pankhurst 1945

BIBLIOGRAPHY

The publisher is grateful to quote from the following asterisk-noted works:

The Illustrated History of the Centennial Exposition, 1876/1975, James D. McCabe, National Publishing Co., Philadelphia.

The Telephone: an account of the Phenomena of Electricity, Magnetism, and Sound, as involved in its Action. With Directions for Making a Speaking Telephone, 1877, A.E. Dolbear, Lee & Shepard, Boston.

Visitor's Guide to the Smithsonian Institution and National Museum at Washington, D.C., ca.1889-90, William J. Rhees, author's collection.

My Air Ships, 1904, A. Santos-Dumont, Century Co., NY.

Annual Report of The Board of Regents of THE SMITHSONIAN INSTITUTION, 1908, Government Printing Office, 1909, author's collection. An 801-page 'time capsule,' *(Plates 22 and 23 show the Wright's and the "June Bug's" first public flights.)*

Vehicles of The Air, Second Edition, 1910, **Victor Lougheed**, Reilly&Britton, Chicago.

Hammondsport An Aeroplane Laboratory, August, 1910, A. Kruckman, *The Outing Magazine*, NY.

The Boy's Book of Model Airplanes, 1910, Francis A. Collins, The Century Co., NY.

The Curtiss Aviation Book, 1912, **Glenn H. Curtiss** and **Augustus Post**, FAStokes, NY. The author's copy was *Post's personal copy*. Its dedication:
"To Mrs. Mabel G. Bell - Who Made Possible The Aerial Experiment Association – This Book Is Dedicated By The Authors."

Aeroplane Designing For Amateurs, 1912, Victor Lougheed, *"Founder Member of the Society of Automobile Engineers,"* The Reilly & Britton Co., Chicago. Courtesy of Daniel Witkoff.

The Mentor, Great American Inventors, 1Sep'13, H. Addington Bruce, NY.

Annual Report of The Board of Regents of THE SMITHSONIAN INSTITUTION, 1914, Government Printing Office, 1915, author's collection. Two interesting articles: "Stability of Aeroplanes" by Orville Wright and A. F. Zahm's account of the Langley Aerodrome tests as carried out at Hammondsport by Curtiss.

Janes All The World's Historical Aircraft, 1917, **Charles G. Grey**, Sampson Low, Marston & Co. Ltd., London/Doubleday & Co NY, 1973.

Military Aeroplanes, 1917, **Grover Loening**, Boston.

Janes Fighting Aircraft of World War 1, 1919, **C.G. Grey**, editor, Jane's Publishing Co., London/Military Press, Crown Publishers, NY, 1990.

The World's Wings, 1927, **Warren Jefferson Davis**, Simmons-Boardman, NY.

Alexander Graham Bell, 1928, **Catherine Mackenzie**, Houghton Mifflin, Boston.

Historic Airships, 1928, Rupert Sargent Holland, Grosset & Dunlap, New York.

The Wright Brothers, Fathers of Flight, 1928, **JohnR. McMahon**, Little, Brown, Boston.

The Conquest of The Air, 1928, **Anne O'Hare McCormick**, The New York Times.

The Real Fathers of Flight, 1929, **John R. McMahon**, Popular Science, NY.

The World's Aeroplanes and Airships, 1929, G. Gibbard Jackson, J.B. Lippincott Co., Philadelphia.

Flying Pioneers at Hammondsport, New York, 1929, **LymanJ.Seely**,Fenton,AuburnNY.

Curtiss Special Ground School Course, 22 Lectures, 1929, W.F.Gerhardt, CFS,Detroit.

The Birth of an Industry, 1930, **Howard Mingos**, private, NY.

The World In The Air, Volume II, 1930, **Francis T. Miller**, G.P. Putnam's Sons, NY.

The Historical Air Mail Catalogue, 1930, K. Lissiuk Philatelic Co., Atlantic Press, NY.

Our Wings Grow Faster, 1935, **Grover Loening**, Doubleday, Doran, Garden City, NY.

The World Was My Garden, 1938, **David Fairchild**, Charles Scribner's Sons, NY.

Famous American Flyers, 1941, **Chelsea Fraser**, Thomas Y. Crowell Co., NY.

Glenn Curtiss, Pioneer of Naval Aviation, 1942, **Alden Hatch**, Julian Messner, NY.

The Flying Tigers, 1942, Russell Whelan, The Viking Press, New York.

The Wright Brothers, 1943, **Fred C. Kelly**, Harcourt, Brace & Co., New York.

Wings Over America - The Story of American Aviation, 1944, **Harry Bruno**, Halcyon.

Man's Fight To Fly, 1944, John P.V. Heinmuller, Funk & Wagnalls Company, NY.

National Aircraft Collection, 1947, **Paul Edward Garber**, Smithsonian.

The Legend of Henry Ford, 1948, **Keith Sward**, Rinehart & Company, Inc., NY.

History of United States Naval Aviation, 1949, Archibald **Turnbull** & Clifford **Lord**, Yale Press.

The Wright Brothers As Aeronautical Engineers, 1951, **M. P. Baker**, Smithsonian.

The Road Is Yours: The Story of The Automobile and The Men Behind It, 1951, Reginald M. Cleveland & S. T. Williamson, Greystone Press, New York.

The Flying Years, 1953, Lamont Buchanan, G.P. Putnam's Sons, New York.

How We Invented The Airplane, 1953, Orville Wright, edited by Fred C. Kelly, 1988, Dover, NY.

Flight - A Pictorial History of Aviation, 1953/55, Year Inc., Los Angeles. Possibly the *best* overall book on flight that I have seen, very objective, with little bias evident. I highly recommend this to anyone who desires a fair picture of what happened.

The Papers of Wilbur and Orville Wright, 1953, **Marvin McFarland**, Editor, McGraw-Hill, NY. Source for most of the Wright quotes.

American Science And Invention, 1954, **Mitchell Wilson**, Simon and Schuster, NY.

Flight – A picture History, 1956, John W. R. Taylor, Pitman Publishing Co., London.

Great American Automobiles, 1957, John Bentley, Prentice-Hall, NY.

The Silver Dart, The Authentic Story of Hon. J.A.D. McCurdy, 1959, H. Gordon Green, Brunswick Press, New Brunswick.

American Automobile Manufacturers, The First Forty Years, 1959, John B. Rae, Chilton Co. Book Division, Philadelphia & New York.

American Heritage, Edison: Last Days of The Wizard, 1959, **Matthew Josephson**.

Smithsonian Treasury Of Science, Volume III, 1960, **Webster P. True**, Editor, Simon and Schuster, Inc. in co-operation with The Smithsonian Institution.

The Chord of Steel: The Story of the Invention of the Telephone, 1960, **Thomas B. Costain**, Doubleday & Co., Inc., Garden City, NY.

Make a Joyful Sound: The Romance of Mabel Hubbard and Alexander Graham Bell, 1961, **Helen Elmira Waite**, Macrae Smith Co., Philadelphia.

Historical Society of Southern California Quarterly 1961, J. Wesley Neal, LA.

The American Heritage History of Flight, 1962, American Heritage Publishing.

The Heritage of Kitty Hawk, 1962, Walter T. Bonney, W.W. Norton, New York.

The Picture History of Inventions, 1963, Umberto **Eco** & G B **Zorzoli**, Macmillan, NY.

Bell And Baldwin, 1964, J. H. Parkin, University of Toronto Press. *Master of minutiae-thorough, thoroughly biased, the forest unseen (but excellent research/reference!).*

James Means and the Problem of Manflight, 1964, **James Howard Means**, Smithsonian.

Aircraft, Aircraft, 1967,70, John W. R. Taylor, Hamlyn, London. Excellent collection of photographs – but highly biased by Charles Gibbs-Smith's 'research.'

Keuka Lake Memories; The Champagne Country, 1967, W.R.Gordon, Rochester NY.

The Billy Mitchell Affair, 1967, **Burke Davis**, Random House, New York.

Jackrabbits to Jets, 1967, Elretta Sudsbury, Neyenesch Printers, San Diego.

*_Canada's Aviation Industry_, 1968, **Lorne Manchester**, McGraw-Hill, Toronto.

Conquerors Of The Air; The Evolution of Aircraft 1903-1945, 1968, Heiner Emde & Carlo Demand, Bonanza Books, NY.

*_Contact: The Story of The Early Birds_, 1968, **Henry Serrano Villard**, ThomasY. Crow-ell, NY. The author's copy is inscribed: "*To Jack Carpenter, with respect and admiration, Henry Serrano Villard, 29 August 1994.*"

*_The Great Air War_, 1968, **Aaron Norman**, Macmillan, N.Y.

*_Over Land And Sea_ - A Biography of Glenn Curtiss, 1968, Robert **Scharff &** Walter S. **Taylor**, David McKay, NY.

WILBUR & ORVILLE WRIGHT, A Bibliography, 1968, Arthur G. Renstrom, Library of Congress.

*_From The Wright Brothers To The Astronauts_, 1968, Benjamin D. **Foulois** with C.V. **Glines**, McGraw-Hill Book Co., NY.

*_Climb To Greatness: The American Aircraft Industry, 1920-1960._ 1968, **John B. Rae**, The MIT Press, Massachusetts Institute of Technology, Cambridge MA.

*_See Them Flying,_ **Houston Peterson's** *Air-Age Scrapbook, 1909-1910,* 1969, Richard Baron, NY. *Source for many of the contemporary clippings in the manuscript.*

Pioneers of Flight, 1969, Henry T. Wallhauser, Hammond, Inc., Maplewood NJ.

*_First To Fly The Atlantic_, June, 1969, **Bernard Weisberger**, American Heritage, NY.

United States Naval Aviation 1910-1970, 1970, courtesy of Lee M. Pearson, CNO(Air) & NASC, Washington DC.

*_The First To Fly - Aviation's Pioneer Days_, 1970, **Sherwood Harris**, Simon and Schuster, NY.

*_A Dream of Araby - The Story of Opa-locka_, 1970, **Frank S. FitzGerald-Bush**, Private edition, Opa-locka, Florida.

Looking Forward: Life in the Twentieth Century as Predicted in American Magazines 1895-1905, 1970, Ray Brosseau and Ralph Andrist, American Heritage Press, NY.

Those Inventive Americans, 1971, **Robert Breeden**, National Geographic Society.

The American Car Since 1775, 1971/76, Automobile Quarterly, L. Scott Bailey, NY.

Atlantic Fever, 1972, **Edward Jablonski**, Macmillan, NY.

*_Glenn Curtiss - Pioneer of Flight_, 1972, **Cecil R. Roseberry**, Doubleday & Co., Garden City NY. The definitive Curtiss biography. The author's copy is inscribed: *"To Jack Carpenter - a fellow admirer of Glenn Curtiss - with regards - C.R.(Tip) Roseberry."*

*_FIRST ACROSS! The U.S. Navy's Transatlantic Flight of 1919_, 1973, **Richard K. Smith**, Naval Institute Press, Annapolis.

*_Bell - Alexander Graham Bell and the Conquest of Solitude_, 1973, **Robert Bruce**, Little, Brown & Co., Boston.

*_A Dream of Eagles_, 1973, **Ralph A. O'Neill** with Joseph Hood, Houghton Mifflin, Boston. *The book that prompted my writing; I corresponded with O'Neill.*

*_The First Air Race, The International Competition at Reims_, 1909, 1974, **Owen S. Lie-**

berg, Doubleday, Garden City, NY.

To Join With The Eagles - Curtiss-Wright Aircraft 1903-1965, 1974, Murray **Rubenstein** & Richard **Goldman**, Doubleday, NY.

WILBUR & ORVILLE WRIGHT, A Chronology, 1975, Arthur G. Renstrom, Library of Congress.

THE INTREPID MR. CURTISS, One of Aviation's founding fathers, Stephen W. Sears, American Heritage, April, 1975. An excellent mini-biography!

One Day at Kitty Hawk, 1975, **John E. Walsh**, Thomas Y. Crowell Co., New York. Note: Though unappreciated at first, I now rate this work *most highly!*

Pioneers of Aviation, A Photo Biography, 1976, **D. D. Hatfield**, Northrop LA.

The Water Jump, The Story of Transatlantic Flight, 1976, **David Beaty**, Harper & Row.

The Flying Machine, 1977, **Allen Andrews**, G.P. Putnam's Sons, New York.

The International Encyclopedia of AVIATION, 1977, David Mondey, editor, Crown, NY.

Anchors In The Sky, Spuds Ellyson, the First Naval Aviator, 1978, **George van Deurs**, Presido Press, San Rafael CA.

Flight With Power, The First Ten Years, 1978, **David W. Wragg**, St. Martin's, NY.

History By Contract - The Story of Gustave Whitehead, 1978, William J. **O'Dwyer &** Stella **Randolph**, Fritz Majer & Sohn, Leutershausen, Germany

Curtiss Aircraft 1907-1947, 1979/1987, **Peter M. Bowers**, Naval Institute Press, Annapolis, MD. A 'must' book for any serious Curtiss researcher!

Kill Devil Hill - Discovering the Secret of the Wright Brothers, 1979, **Harry Combs**, Houghton Mifflin, Boston.

Conquest Of The Skies, 1979, **Carl Solberg**, Little, Brown and Company, Boston.

A Streak of Luck: The Life and Legend of Thomas Alva Edison, 1979, **Robert Conot**, Seaview Books, NY.

The Compact History of The United States Air Force, 1980, **Carroll V. Glines, Jr.,** Arno Press, NY.

The First Aviators, 1980, **Curtis Prendergast**, Time-Life Books, Alexandria, VA.

The Pathfinders, 1980, **David Nevin**, Time0Life Books, Alexandria, VA.

The Road To Kitty Hawk, 1980, **Valerie Moolman**, Time-Life, Alexandria, VA.

Curtiss: The Hammondsport Era, 1981, **Louis Casey**, Crown Publishers, NY

Tesla, Man Out of Time, 1981, Margaret Cheney, Prentice Hall, NY.

Air Mail - An Illustrated History, 1981, **Donald B. Holmes**, Clarkson N. Potter, NY.

World Encyclopedia of Civil Aircraft - From Leonardo daVinci to The Present, 1981, **Enzo Angelucci**, Crown, NY. *Highly recommended - objective, thorough, fair.*

High Frontier: A History of Aeronautics in Pennsylvania, 1982, William F. Trimble, University of Pennsylvania Press.

Great Exploration Hoaxes 1982, **David Roberts**, The Sierra Club, San Francisco.

The Timetable of Technology, 1982, **Ayensu, Marshall & Whitfield**, Hearst, NY.

Genius At Work, Images of Alexander Graham Bell, 1982, **Dorothy Harley Eber**, The Viking Press, NY.

The Montgolfier Brothers and the Invention of Aviation, 1783-1784, 1983, **Charles Coulston Gillispie**, Princeton University Press, New Jersey.

Wind and Sand - The Wright Brothers at Kitty Hawk, 1983, Lyanne **Wescott** & Paula **Degen**, Harry Abrams Inc., New York.

Flight of the Vin Fiz, 1985, **E.P. Stein**, Arbor House, New York. *Excellent.*

Ford - The Men and The Machine, 1986, **Robert Lacey**, Little, Brown and Co., Boston.

The Launching of Modern American Science 1946-1876, 1987, **Robert V. Bruce**, Alfred A. Knopf, New York

*Wilbur And Orville, 1987, **Fred Howard**, Alfred A. Knopf, New York. The definitive Wright brothers biography.

*Another Icarus, Percy Pilcher and the Quest for Flight, 1987, **Philip Jarrett**, Smithsonian Press, Washington & London. *Inscribed to this author by its author.*

Never The Twain Shall Meet, Bell, Gallaudet, and the Communications Debate, 1987, Richard Winefield, Gallaudet University Press, Washington.

*Waldo - Pioneer Aviator, 1988, **Waldo Dean Waterman** with Jack Carpenter, Arsdalen, Bosch & Co., Carlisle MA (now Box 1, San Juan Capistrano, CA 92693).

*Reaching for the Skies, 1988, **Ivan Rendall**, BBC Books, London, England.

Landmarks of Science, From The Collections of The Library of Congress, 1989, **Leonard C. Bruno**, Facts on File, Inc. New York.

Aviation On Long Island, 1989, George **Dade** & Frank **Strnad**, Dover, Mineola, NY.

From L'Eole to Hermes, 100 Years of Engines in The Sky, 1990, **Alfred Bodemer**, Musee national des techniques, Conservatoire national des Arts et Metiers, Paris.

Barons of The Sky - The Story of the American Aerospace Industry, 1991, **Wayne Biddle**, Simon & Schuster; 1993, Henry Holt, NY. (good – but flawed on the Curtiss years).

*China Clipper - The Age of the Great Flying Boats, 1991, **Robert L. Gandt**, Naval Institute Press, Annapolis. Its first photo is Glenn Curtiss, *"father of the flying boat."*

Le Temps Des Helices, 1991, Andre Domine & Jean Salis, Jean-Baptiste Salis, Aerodrome de Cerny, France.

Hundert Jahre Deutsche Luftfahrt, 1991, Museum Verkehr & Technik, Berlin.

Flying the Edge, The Making of Navy Test Pilots, 1992, **George C. Wilson**, Naval Institute Press, Annapolis. Inscribed *"To Jack Carpenter. Keep shining your light into the dark corners of aviation. All the best..."*

*Pendulum, The Story of America's Three Aviation Pioneers, 1992, **Jack Carpenter**, Arsdalen, Bosch & Co., Carlisle MA. (the 1st edition of this book).

Flight Before Wright, 1993 Calendar, 1992, **Susan Sharp**, Library of Congress, DC.

The Timetables of Technology, 1993, Bryan **Bunch** & Alexander **Hellemans**, Simon & Schuster, NY.

ROBERT BOSCH, His Life and Achievements, 1994, Theodor Heuss, Henry Holt, NY.

NAWCC Bulletin, The Fax About Bain, Morse and Kennedy, June, 1994, Iain Cleator, National Association of Watch & Clock Collectors, Columbia PA.

*The Third Wright Brother, Charles Taylor...*by **Mark Bernstein**, September, 1996, Ohio Magazine.

CURTISS-WRIGHT: Greatness and Decline, 1998, Louis R. Eltscher & Edward M. Young, Twayne Publishers/Simon & Schuster Macmillan, N.Y.

INDEX

Jack Carpenter and Dan Witkoff, Pauma Valley, 2002:

of the Curtiss

23. A view on the assembly floor at one of the Buffalo plants.
24. Another one of the Buffalo assembly floors.
25. A panoramic photograph of the general assembly floor at one of the six Curtiss Buffalo plants.
26. The motor assembly at Hammondsport.
27. A Curtiss F. boat.
28. The Curtiss H. S. Flying boat.
29. A few of the thousands of women employed in Curtiss plants.

30. Two Curtiss Triplanes.
31. Assembly floor—Fuselages.
32. A skeleton of the Curtiss J. N. showing construction.
33. The Curtiss R. 4 Mailplane.
34. An aeroplane photo of the Buffalo North Elmwood plant just before completion.
35. Girls sewing wing panels.
36. The new Curtiss M. F. flying boat.
37. The fastest aeroplane in the world. The Curtiss type 18, credited in government reports with 160

miles per hour, with full military load of 1100 pounds.
38. The most efficient Hydro in the world.
39. The first hull of the FSL flying boat.
40. The Curtiss J. N. 4 D.
41. The Curtiss H. 12 flying boat.
42–45. Various departments in the Buffalo plants of the Curtiss.
46. A general view of one of the Curtiss metalworking shops.

See our exhibit at Aeronautical Exposition at Madison Square Garden, New York City, March 1st to 15th.

Sales Office: 52 Vanderbilt Avenue, New York City
CURTISS ENGINEERING CORP., Garden City, L. I.   **THE BURGESS CO.**, Marblehead, Mass.